D0560939

Dartmouth Bookstall, Inc.
265 Dartmouth St., Boston

THE BEST PLAYS OF 1930-31

EDITED BY

BURNS MANTLE

THE BEST PLAYS OF 1919-20
THE BEST PLAYS OF 1920-21
THE BEST PLAYS OF 1921-22
THE BEST PLAYS OF 1922-23
THE BEST PLAYS OF 1923-24
THE BEST PLAYS OF 1924-25
THE BEST PLAYS OF 1925-26
THE BEST PLAYS OF 1926-27
THE BEST PLAYS OF 1927-28
THE BEST PLAYS OF 1928-29
THE BEST PLAYS OF 1929-30
THE BEST PLAYS OF 1930-31

"Elizabeth the Queen," copyright, 1930, by Maxwell Anderson.
Copyright and published, 1930, by Longmans, Green & Co., London, New York and Toronto.

"Tomorrow and Tomorrow," copyright, 1930, by Philip Barry.
Copyright and published, 1930, by Samuel French, New York, Los Angeles and London.

"Once in a Lifetime," copyright, 1930, by Moss Hart and George S. Kaufman.
Copyright and published, 1930, by Farrar and Rinehart, New York.

"Green Grow the Lilacs," copyright, 1930, by Lynn Riggs.
Copyright and published, 1931, by Samuel French, New York, Los Angeles and London.

"As Husbands Go," copyright, 1931, by Rachel Crothers.
Copyright and published, 1931, by Samuel French, New York, Los Angeles and London.

"Alison's House," copyright, 1930, by Susan Glaspell.
Copyright and published, 1931, by Samuel French, New York, Los Angeles and London.

"Five Star Final," copyright, 1930, 1931, by Louis Weitzenkorn.
Copyright, 1931, by Samuel French, New York, Los Angeles and London.

"Overture," copyright, 1930, 1931, by Sybil Bolitho Ryall.
Copyright and published, 1931, by Simon & Schuster, New York.

"The Barretts of Wimpole Street," copyright, 1930, by Rudolf Besier.
Copyright and published, 1930, by Little, Brown & Co., Boston.

"Grand Hotel," copyright, 1930, by Vicki Baum.
American adaptation, copyright, 1930, by W. A. Drake.

Copyright, 1931,
By DODD, MEAD AND COMPANY, Inc.

PRINTED IN THE U. S. A. BY
Quinn & Boden Company, Inc.
BOOK MANUFACTURERS
RAHWAY, NEW JERSEY

808.82
B

THE
BEST PLAYS OF 1930-31

AND THE

YEAR BOOK OF THE DRAMA
IN AMERICA

Edited by
BURNS MANTLE

With Illustrations

98 32

DODD, MEAD AND COMPANY
NEW YORK - - - 1931

Metcalf
withdrawn 3/94

Photo by Maurice Goldberg, New York.

"ALISON'S HOUSE"

Elsa, in Alison Stanhope's room, has taken two silver candlesticks from the mantel and lighted them. She pauses at Alison's desk before she places the candles on the table and, by their light, opens the portfolio her Aunt Agatha gave her.

(*Eva Le Gallienne*)

INTRODUCTION

WELL, as the clowns of the circus were wont to shout in the old, old days, here we are again!

The sun shines, the government at Washington still lives and the living theatre has not been crushed, either by the economic depression or the threat of cheaper entertainment.

The season of which this volume of the "Best Plays" series is a record has been a slightly skeletonized season. In New York there have been something like fifty fewer plays produced than were produced last year, and probably sixty below the average number produced the last five years.

But again standards have not been lowered nor the percentage of successes and failures noticeably changed.

Significance of a kind attaches also to the fact that there has been greater activity in the direction of restoring the road to something of its old-time importance this year, and particularly this last spring, than has been noted in the last ten years. Reports from the touring territory are almost excitingly optimistic.

Civic bodies in many of the minor centers that have been held rather rigidly to a talking picture and silent movie diet the last dozen years are taking action. In many instances they have induced the lessee of the leading motion picture theatre to permit a flesh and blood dramatic attraction to be booked into his theatre at least one night each week.

Various commercially-minded organizations, working in the interest of one manager or more, have inaugurated subscription audience campaigns in many small cities adjacent to the larger and more active theatrical centers. It is the hope of these organizations to provide an audience of guaranteed proportions with which they can barter for touring attractions of guaranteed merit. Thus the hope is to secure legitimate theatrical entertainment for interested playgoers and at the same time do away effectively with the old-time methods of cheating showmen.

The New York Theatre Guild has expanded its own subscription audience lists to include twelve key cities. The Messrs. Shubert have met this competition by organizing second groups of organized playgoers in practically the same centers. The Erlanger interests have entered into agreements with many cities under the terms of which outstanding attractions are to be booked in civic auditoriums and other halls made available by the town authorities.

All these activities, whether purely experimental or soundly practical, are working toward a definite revival of interest in the spoken drama such as has not been noticeable for many years.

The ten plays selected to represent the season of 1930-31 indicate no particularly new trends in drama. They seem somewhat more varied in character than usual, and a shade more serious. Curiously, as has before been pointed out, periods of depression produce few comedies to lighten a people's burden. And these are not generously patronized when they are produced. A half-dozen musical revues seem to provide all needed relief for the worried business men, and their sentimental mates flock to the heavier drama.

"Elizabeth the Queen," after a considerable experience touring and experimenting with new titles and new twists in action, came to the home theatre of the Theatre Guild to score the most pronounced success of that organization's six subscription offerings. It has the advantage, as written by Maxwell Anderson and impressively played by Lynn Fontanne and Alfred Lunt, of being at once as true as historical drama need be and more entertaining than most historical dramas succeed in being.

Philip Barry's "Tomorrow and Tomorrow," outstanding among the serious domestic dramas, translates an Old Testament miracle into terms of modern life with skill and feeling. It is a play that is sensitively fine in writing and emotionally stirring in story. There is neither waste in it, nor padding. If its ethical or moral conclusions are disturbing they are also provocative of interesting argument.

The Moss Hart-George Kaufman "Once in a Lifetime" is the light comedy success of the season. Its amiably exaggerated satire is keenly revealing of those Hollywood conditions about which legends have been built up the last several years. Produced in Los Angeles it was laughingly approved by its most obvious targets.

"Green Grow the Lilacs," while no more than a subscription audience success with the Guild's local public, found understanding audiences on tour. It is distinctly a western creation, invades territory and reveals typical American characters unfamiliar to the Eastern playgoer. It also serves to introduce in Lynn Riggs a new writer of promise in the field of native drama. I found its humor bold, its characters true and its story interesting in revealing a new division of the American scene.

Rachel Crothers' "As Husbands Go" is a typical Crothers comedy in that it is light in weight yet weighty in purpose. The story is the fairly trivial adventure of two ladies from Dubuque who find themselves staggered by their re-discovery of romance in Paris. The insistent proposals of a pair of what might be classified as super-gigolos (that they boldly assert their individual right to cling to the new romance) disturbs them greatly. Returning to this crude America they are rather sanely set back in their rightful domestic jobs without doing violence to the logic or proper sentimental values of their experience.

"Alison's House," when it was awarded the Pulitzer prize as the original American play produced last year that best represented the educational value and power of the stage came in for a great deal of discussion and criticism. A majority of the professional play reviewers were opposed to the award, but their objections in general were, to me, based largely on their disappointment in the drama as entertainment.

This was, I feel, unfair to Susan Glaspell, who wrote "Alison's House," as well as to the play, which had been cast and produced by Eva Le Gallienne and her Civic Repertory company, and was necessarily subject to the usual stock company handicaps.

As for the play, I found it interesting in story and sound in drama, with such added attraction as biographical drama offers to those interested in its subject. Emily Dickinson, who had been dead some eighteen years before she was recognized as one of the greater American poets, is a fascinating personality in the history of American literature and Miss Glaspell's sensitively written and honestly sympathetic use of her story in this drama must find a public strong in loyalty if limited in numbers.

"Five Star Final" is a crusading melodrama. It deals with that phase of so-called "yellow journalism" which is of vital interest to many American newspaper readers. It is written, and was staged, with such skill as to arouse its audiences to a pitch of honest resentment as well as tolerant smiles of disbelief when the author, Louis Weitzenkorn, permits his prejudices to override his judgment. For these reasons I included it in this list as representative of American melodrama inspired by honest indignation.

Critical disagreement and a failure to achieve popular approval can also be charged against the late William Bolitho's "Overture." Dealing with the rise and fall of a citizens' revolution in a small town in Germany after the war, nobly led to ignoble defeat by a pitifully sincere idealist, the play awakened unpleasant memories and inspired unhappy fears for the future, which was enough to deny it general support. But it remains, to me, a thoughtful, provocative and generally important contribution to the season's drama.

Rudolf Besier's sentimentally moving recital of the Elizabeth Barrett-Robert Browning romance, "The Barretts of Wimpole Street," is one of the better type biographical dramas. Such liberties as the author may have taken with the character of Elizabeth Barrett's father, Edward Moulton-Barrett, have been subject for discussion and controversy, particularly in England, between the Barrett heirs and those literary historians of psycho-analytical leanings. In America, whatever the seeming exaggeration, it did not throw the play out of plumb, nor materially affect its value as drama. Its production and performance established Katharine Cornell as an actress-manageress of brilliant promise.

"Grand Hotel" I have previously spoken of as a great adventure in the theatre rather than a great play, despite the fact that from the day of its production till well into the summer it remained at the top of the list of dramas most in demand in New York.

This play, written by Vicki Baum, represents a definite playwriting trend at the moment, being an adaptation of that cinema technique which cuts a play into many short scenes. This is as important a development in play building, I feel, as was the first introduction of the flashback in "On Trial" fifteen years ago. In story "Grand Hotel" skillfully weaves together one day's adventure in the lives of six or eight guests temporarily resident in such a Grand Hotel as may be found in any European city.

Plays I find named on various tentative lists prepared during the season include Benn W. Levy's "Mrs. Moonlight," Frank Craven's "That's Gratitude," Robert E. Sherwood's "This Is New York," Noel Coward's "Private Lives" and Francis Goodrich and Albert Hackett's "Up Pops the Devil."

"Mrs. Moonlight" was a great popular success, outrunning "Overture," for instance, 321 performances to 41. Still I found it a play that falls between two technical forms. As fantasy it was decidedly shaky in its foundations and as believable drama it was wildly improbable.

"That's Gratitude" is a well written comedy, plausible in story and character, but also frankly light in theme. "Private Lives" is a deft and amusing farce, but largely dependent upon the personalities and skillful playing of its actors.

"This Is New York" was, to me, an especially well thought out comedy that brought into interesting contrast American character types from west and east. It was, I feel, somewhat overwritten and its appeal was local to New York. Failing of local support there was no excuse for substituting it for any of the plays selected.

"Up Pops the Devil" was a sanely motivated and brightly written story of life among the free young souls of Greenwich Village, also local in theme and appeal. A cut above the run-of-the-village plays, it did not develop sufficient strength of itself to overcome its molded conventionalities.

Otherwise this volume of "The Best Plays," being the twelfth, goes to you with all its previously acquired features intact and such added information as the season's record has developed.

B. M.

Forest Hills, L. I., June 15, 1931.

CONTENTS

	PAGE
INTRODUCTION	v
THE SEASON IN NEW YORK	3
THE SEASON IN CHICAGO	18
THE SEASON IN SAN FRANCISCO	23
THE SEASON IN SOUTHERN CALIFORNIA	26
ELIZABETH THE QUEEN, BY MAXWELL ANDERSON	29
TOMORROW AND TOMORROW, BY PHILIP BARRY	74
ONCE IN A LIFETIME, BY MOSS HART AND GEORGE S. KAUFMAN	110
GREEN GROW THE LILACS, BY LYNN RIGGS	147
AS HUSBANDS GO, BY RACHEL CROTHERS	186
ALISON'S HOUSE, BY SUSAN GLASPELL	222
FIVE STAR FINAL, BY LOUIS WEITZENKORN	254
OVERTURE, BY WILLIAM BOLITHO	286
THE BARRETTS OF WIMPOLE STREET, BY RUDOLF BESIER	317
"GRAND HOTEL," BY VICKI BAUM	355
THE PLAYS AND THEIR AUTHORS	392
PLAYS PRODUCED IN NEW YORK, 1930-31	398
LONG PLAY TOURNAMENT	524
STATISTICAL SUMMARY	536
LONG RUNS ON BROADWAY	537
PULITZER PRIZE WINNERS	538
PREVIOUS VOLUMES OF BEST PLAYS	539
NECROLOGY	554
INDEX OF AUTHORS	561
INDEX OF PLAYS AND CASTS	566

ILLUSTRATIONS

Alison's House . . . . *Frontispiece*

FACING PAGE

Elizabeth the Queen 34

Tomorrow and Tomorrow 82

Once in a Lifetime 114

Green Grow the Lilacs 162

As Husbands Go 194

Five Star Final 258

Overture 290

The Barretts of Wimpole Street 322

Grand Hotel 370

THE BEST PLAYS OF 1930-31

THE BEST PLAYS OF 1930-31

THE SEASON IN NEW YORK

THE theatre season of 1930-31, of which record is about to be made, started excitingly with a war to end war with the ticket speculators.

Three of the theatre's conscientious producers, the Messrs. Arthur Hopkins, Brock Pemberton and Gilbert Miller, variously backed by their brothers in business, finally brought about the organization of the League of New York Theatres.

The purpose of the League was to control the sale of theatre tickets. Its membership was to, and at one time did, include sixteen accredited ticket brokers as well as practically all local theatre lessees and owners.

A certain allotment of seats was to be turned over to the accredited brokers, who were bound by their signed agreement to charge no more than the legal 75 cents advance over the price of the ticket for such services as they might render.

The manager-members of the League for their part agreed to keep a percentage of their best as well as their worst seats on sale at their respective box offices and to abandon their former practice of selling blocks of seats to the brokers whenever their plays happened to be in demand.

Everybody connected with the theatre, in other words, was to work for the best interests of the theatre and for the protection of the theatre going public which supported the theatres.

A manager for the League (Mr. Harlow D. Savage) was engaged at the excellent hard-times salary of $25,000 a year. Offices were set up and the League began to function. At least the League began to begin to function.

Unfortunately it did not function long. Soon the broker-members were again at war with the manager-members, and the outlaw brokers, who had been denied admission to the League, were at war with both brokers and managers, going so far as to sue out an injunction denying the right of the League to operate in restraint of what they jokingly called a legitimate trade in tickets.

Producers who had been offered a six- or eight-week "buy," or pre-sale, of a certain number of tickets for each performance of a play they were about to produce, protested their right to protect themselves to this extent. Brokers who refrained from secretly violating the agreement not to buy blocks of seats complained that less scrupulous associates were cheating them as well as the public.

For months the fight waged and the fate of the League hung in the balance. Finally the accredited brokers withdrew in a body and it looked as though everything was over. But at this psychological moment in stepped the Postal Telegraph company with a proposal that each of its hundred and sixty odd branch offices be made a branch theatre ticket office as well, selling tickets by phone and by telegraph, delivering them by messenger and charging no more than 50 cents above the price of the ticket for this service.

The League hailed the offer with joy, a huge central office practically lined with telephones and clerks was set up, and a new era in theatre ticket control was inaugurated.

This Postal Telegraph service, having been taken over to some extent by the late Joseph Leblang's brokerage concern, is still functioning with a degree of success. But the older speculators are also back in the Broadway saddle, buying what they will when they will in the way of blocks of seats.

The last seen of the Regular Playgoer who was to be protected, he was running aimlessly up and down Broadway with a bag in his hand.

The League of New York theatres is also still in existence, under the executive direction of Dr. Henry Moskowitz. By binding together the interests of dramatists and actors with those of producers and theatre owners, the League has been able to do good work in such matters as quashing vicious censorship legislation at the state capitol. Through the efforts of the League a conference board representing the theatres, the actors, the playwrights, the district attorney and the local constabulary has been organized to take action whenever a play or a musical comedy shall offend the public sense of what is lawful and decent.

Otherwise the theatre season was neither very exciting nor in any notable way unusual. It was an anxious season for producers, an active season for courageous angels (with both theatres and actors to be hired at bargain rates), a season of job-hunting for the players and a season of average compensations for playgoers.

The Theatre Guild, holding its own as the American theatre's most important producing unit, brought out six plays and scored but a single outstanding hit, that of "Elizabeth the Queen."

Eva Le Gallienne's Civic Repertory Theatre, also an important if minor producing unit, held steadfastly to its repertory program, adding five new productions to its established list. The five included Susan Glaspell's "Alison's House," which was awarded the year's Pulitzer prize, and a revival of "Camille," which, a little to everybody's surprise, proved the hit of the Le Gallienne season.

As an indication of the scarcity of new plays I may tell you that there were no less than twenty old plays revived, and seven brought back for return engagements. Nor did we get many importations of foreign troupes. Maria Cotopouli a favorite of Athens, gave performances of the Elektra and Iphigenia in Greek, a company of Hindus performed a native drama, "Sita," briefly, and a French company gave a week to Marcel Pagnol's "Topaze," a hit of last season.

The summer season proceeded with complete normalcy, after we left it on June 15, 1930. George M. Cohan, turning back from a tour to the coast with the melodrama "Gambling," came home and revived "The Song and Dance Man" for two weeks. George had thought to go through to the moving picture country and try again at making screen dramas. But his experiences on the way to Chicago convinced him that he was still stage struck and that he wanted to continue exclusively in the living theatre.

In many towns he was fêted, in all of them he was received with acclaim. Later he revived "The Tavern" and took that on a small-town tour. Again he was received with cheers, but the "Tavern" satire was a bit too subtle for those publics that had been trained for the last ten years on screen drama. Business was nothing to brag about.

The first day of July Earl Carroll brought his 1930 "Vanities" into the New Amsterdam Theatre, this being the first time he, as a producer, had been permitted to enter the sacred portals of this particular theatre. The New Amsterdam has been devoted since its erection to the attractions of the House of Erlanger and their chief lieutenants, Florenz Ziegfeld and Charles B. Dillingham.

Mr. Carroll's summer show was talked about for its limits in nudity and a perfected tank exhibit in which, by an arrangement of mirrors, several ladies and one gent were exposed swimming lazily in pursuit of each other at the bottom of the ocean.

At the moment the gent caught the leader of the mermaids the curtains were drawn.

The "Vanities" were halted briefly by the police who objected, as I recall it, to the size or shape or manipulation of a fan held by a shapely chorister named Faith Bacon. Miss Bacon had nothing else with which to protect her person from the glare of the footlights and the courts thought the fan was not enough. There was also objection to certain of Mr. Carroll's coarser sketches. The sketches were modified, the fan enlarged, or made more opaque, and the "Vanities" went on prosperously for 215 performances.

A crowd of Lambs' club actors attempted a coöperative revue assembled largely by Joseph Santley and called "Who Cares?" but it lasted only four weeks. At the end of the month the Shuberts offered Walter Woolf and Violet Heming in a comedy called "Ladies All" which was spicily seasoned and fairly amusing. It ran for twenty weeks.

As had been his custom for some years, the late David Belasco brought a comedy to his own theatre the first week in August to take the place of "It's a Wise Child," which had run through the better part of the previous year. The new one was called "Dancing Partner" and its cast was headed by Lynne Overman and Irene Purcell. During the evening Mr. Overman sought to win a wager by proving that any woman in love is easy prey for a properly accoutered male, but Miss Purcell withstood his advances, even in an airplane, and thereby won his respect, his hand and his uncle's fortune. "Dancing Partner" did nicely for a while, but it was not the hit Mr. Belasco had hoped for and after fifteen weeks he replaced it with "Tonight or Never," of which more later.

August was the first month to indicate that this was indeed to be one of the seasons in which the great slump figured. There were but seven productions in all, as opposed to the usual list of twice that number. And only one half-hit among these. Arthur Hopkins' production of "Torch Song," which also started well, ran eighty odd performances and then faded out of the picture. In it Mayo Methot played a Salvation Army lassie who loved a traveling salesman better than she did her religion, and was led into a backsliding adventure that seared her soul but strengthened her resolution and put her finally back in the army. An Owen Davis mystery, "The Ninth Guest," did fairly well and a colored revue called "Hot Rhythm" retained its heat for eight weeks.

The season went normal in September. Lee Shubert started it with one of those real life comedies set in Greenwich Village called "Up Pops the Devil." Written by Frances Goodrich and Albert Hackett, it detailed rather convincingly the adventure of two free souls who lived together a year and then had a time of it deciding whether or not they should get married. They did—and went temporarily on the rocks because the wife insisted her husband should stay home and write while she earned the living as a dancer. The husband rebelled finally, the two split and were later brought together in better understanding.

There was a "Second Little Show" on the 2nd that failed to duplicate the success of the first "Little Show" of the year before. John Golden scored an early season hit for his theatre with Frank Craven's "That's Gratitude," which ran happily along for forty-five weeks with and without Craven in the cast. An amusing and observing study of character, this one, in which a middle-aged traveling salesman, suffering a sudden attack of acute indigestion, is so overwhelmed with gratitude when a fellow guest saves his life with a drink or two of whisky that he insists on taking his life-saver home. The accidental samaritan accepts the invitation and stays on indefinitely, to the irritation of his host and the explosive joy of the audience.

George Cohan started his season with a drama he had written with Dr. Louis Anspacher called "The Rhapsody." It held on only two weeks. The Shuberts introduced the first musical comedy hit of the new season in "Nina Rosa" and Ivor Novello, the English screen and stage star, offered a comedy of his own writing called "Symphony in Two Flats." The Novello comedy had novelty of setting, with two dramas being played in adjoining apartments, but it lacked popular values and went out after six weeks.

Now came three hits in a row and everybody was greatly cheered. On the 23rd the widely-popular Joe Cook moved into Erlanger's Theatre with "Fine and Dandy" and didn't move out again until he had made an engaging fool of himself for 255 performances. On the 24th "Once in a Lifetime" started a riot of laughter at the Music Box and, though it has changed over to the Plymouth Theatre for the summer, this Moss Hart-George Kaufman satirical slam at Hollywood is still going. On the 25th William Harris, Jr., grinned as he raised the curtain on Zoe Akins' "The Greeks Had a Word for It," which proved the last word in sophisticated cleverness and stayed on for 253 showings.

There was still another success to September's credit. On the

29th Charles Hopkins offered a Benn Levy comedy built along A. A. Milne and J. M. Barrie lines called "Mrs. Moonlight." It did not jump into its success immediately, as other Hopkins productions of similar character had done, but its sentimental sweetness slowly attracted the large public that revels in the cleaner drama and it ended by playing through the season.

Two regretted and unexpected failures occurred about this time. One was "Mr. Gilhooley," with which Jed Harris had made a return to production, and in which the Irish actor, Arthur Sinclair, and the American actress, Helen Hayes, were co-starred. Despite a generally favorable press "Mr. Gilhooley" lasted but four weeks. The other was "Stepdaughters of War," a fairly dramatic story of the lady ambulance drivers in France with which Chester Erskin hoped to establish a new production policy at the Empire. "Stepdaughters" was taken off after its third week.

The musical comedy success of the year was a piece called "Girl Crazy," which Aarons and Freedley did at the Alvin Theatre. It had a George Gershwin score, which helped considerably, and a Guy Bolton-John McGowan book with more sanity than most, which also helped. Seeing the hits were coming in groups, the night following the appearance of "Girl Crazy" Max Gordon produced a revue called "Three's a Crowd" at the Selwyn, with Fred Allen, Libby Holman and Clifton Webb starred. This, too, struck the fancy of the crowd and ran the season through.

It was in the midst of such competition that Jane Cowl brought her season's production of Shakespeare's "Twelfth Night" to the Maxine Elliott Theatre, and to the surprise of those who do not think much of Shakespeare these days did surprisingly well with it. The production, an idea of Miss Cowl's, was novel. A facsimile book of the play of heroic size was set up on the stage and the play began when Feste, the fool, danced out and opened it to the title page, announcing the revels. Then he motioned to the musicians in a stage box and as the overture was played, turned the second page to a scene illustrating a room in Orsino's palace. So on through the play. Miss Cowl later produced Benn Levy's comedy, "Art and Mrs. Bottle," dividing a season of 115 performances between them.

It was this same week that "Princess Charming" was offered. One of the cleaner romantic operas, much was hoped for it. The book had been revamped by the late Jack Donahue and there was a cast headed by Evelyn Herbert and Robert Halliday that included Victor Moore and the Jeanne Aubert who was later to achieve local popularity. But it was also an operetta that followed an outworn operatic form and this, added to the expense of carrying it, proved too much. Seven weeks and it was gone.

Lenore Ulric, who had been fairly inactive for some time, came to town in October with a drama that sought to duplicate the situation in "Rain." It was titled "Pagan Lady," and in it Miss Ulric played a loose one who sought to lure a young theological student into those sex adventures of which he had practically no knowledge. The boy learned a lot from Lenore, but she was forced to give him back to the church in the end. Which is probably just as well.

An English gangster melodrama, written by the Edgar Wallace who is the Crime Club authority and called "On the Spot," was imported in October. It proved so exciting, with Crane Wilbur playing its leading rôle, an Englishman's idea of Chicago's own Al Capone, that it continued the better part of the winter. Afterward, when it was taken to Chicago, the locale was changed and local references to Cicero and Wabash Avenue were cut out. They could not fool the Chicagoans, however. The play failed.

November was also spotted with several successes. The Guild, as previously mentioned, followed "Roar China" with "Elizabeth the Queen" and thereupon went into the success column for the first time. Two weeks later Herman Shumlin, in association with an underwear magnate of Cleveland, Harry Moses, produced a melodrama that had figured as a Reinhardt production in Berlin. "Grand Hotel," as Mr. Shumlin called the American version, was an overnight sensation, though it may be a little difficult to discover the reason for that from the account of it contained in other pages of this book. "Grand Hotel" is an exciting adventure in the theatre, jumping from one scene to another with the same effect of sustained variety that is gained from the motion picture drama. It continued the most popular of the dramatic successes through the season and also through the summer.

Fanny Brice's husband, Billy Rose by name, having acquired confidence in his judgment as a producer through a variety of experiences as a song writer and vaudeville accompanist, decided to stage a revue for Miss Brice and several professional playmates. These latter included George Jessel and James Barton. The name selected for the revue was "Sweet and Low," with greater dependence placed upon the low features than upon the sweet. The revue ran long enough and well enough to justify a second edition, which Mr. Rose wanted to call "Sweeter and

Lower." He was induced to change his mind, however, and settled on "Crazy Quilt."

Mr. Belasco, having been disappointed in "Dancing Partner," took it off in November and substituted Helen Gahagan in a comedy with song called "Tonight or Never." Miss Gahagan, after achieving success as a dramatic actress, had gone to Europe to study voice and make a successful début in opera. She was ideally suited to the rôle of the heroine, an opera singer with a manager who insists that until she has a love affair she will never sing her best. Miss Gahagan played and sang the "Tonight or Never" part to a complete success, and finished by marrying her leading man, Melvyn Douglas. It was, as it happened, the last production Mr. Belasco ever made. He was taken ill with pneumonia while the piece was on its try-out tour and kept to his bed for several months following. When the comedy was brought to New York it was the first of his first-nights that he had missed in fifty years. He saw the play later, when he was up and about in February. A heart attack carried him away in the spring while he was preparing another comedy for his regular August opening.

A comedy brought to the Playhouse by Dwight Deere Wiman, who continues to put Deere plow money into show business with such good judgment that it returns handsome dividends, was called "The Vinegar Tree," and written by Paul Osborn. Mary Boland played it with great success and it, too, ran through the season. Mary was a lady whose marital romance had gone cold. She thereupon tried to dramatize a romantic incident of her past when she had spent a purple afternoon with an eager young genius. The genius is an invited guest at her house and she seeks to recall to him the happy affair, only to find that she has her geniuses mixed. He is not the same one at all.

Sam Harris did a rowdy farce entitled "Oh, Promise Me" which kept a rowdy patronage laughing for 144 performances, and Arthur Hopkins failed with a legitimate and worthy comedy of city life written by Robert E. Sherwood and called "This Is New York." Lois Moran from the cinema was an attractive ingénue heroine in this play, which had to do with the adventure of a booming U. S. Senator from the West who seeks to stop his daughter from marrying a Broadway playboy and becomes involved in a racketeer scandal which bothers him considerably. "This Is New York" got fifty-nine performances. It was one of the failures hardest to understand.

Ethel Barrymore, courageously sticking to her determination

to play a blackface rôle in "Scarlet Sister Mary" whether her personal following approved or not, brought her dramatization of Julia Peterkin's prize-winning novel to New York at Thanksgiving time. She declared her right to add to her repertory such characters as she thought within the scope of her art, but her fair-comedy friends would not rally. At least it took no more than three weeks for the more loyal of them to see "Scarlet Sister Mary," after which it was withdrawn. In the cast was Ethel Barrymore Colt, making her début under her mother's wing. Following the New York withdrawal Miss Barrymore resumed her touring and had a fine success on the road with "The Love Duel." It was during this tour that another young Barrymore, John Drew Colt, made his first stage appearance. His uncle sent him a red apple from the Pacific Coast, which is a Barrymore-Drew family tradition.

It was about this time, which was early December, that Eva Le Gallienne produced Susan Glaspell's "Alison's House" at her Civic Repertory Theatre in Fourteenth Street. It was a fairly busy week in the theatre and not a great deal of newspaper attention was paid to Miss Glaspell's drama. Neither did it achieve wide popularity with the Le Gallienne following. But none the less it was chosen four months later as the American play worthiest the annual Pulitzer prize. Miss Le Gallienne, being tired, had announced the close of her season and her own retirement from the theatre for a year. She now agreed to play an extra week, however, that the prize-winning drama might be given a good start on Broadway, whither Lee Shubert had moved it. The play lasted but a fortnight uptown.

By December interest in the season had begun to wilt. The papers were full of the depression and the streets were full of bread lines. The more successful productions, however, continued as before to attract large audiences. It was the in-betweens that were falling here, there, and practically everywhere.

There were also several moving picture temples that were not doing at all well. There was plenty of room to drill a company of ushers in the best of them. One such house was the Broadway, built by B. S. Moss for motion picture uses but with a large and convertible stage. This was now turned over to Ray Goetz who announced that he would offer therein the largest revue to be found on Broadway and at the lowest admission. He could do this, he said, because the theatre seated something like 1,000 persons on its lower floor and as many more in its balcony. "The New Yorkers" was organized with a spectacular cast headed by those night-club favorites, Clayton, Jackson and Durante. Both Frances Williams of Broadway, and Hope Williams of Park avenue, were leading women. Charles King was a singing juvenile and those veterans of another day, Richard Carle and Marie Cahill, were at least names in the lights. "The New Yorkers" started with a noisy performance and an equally noisy reception. Mr. Goetz forgot the lower price scale the first few weeks. The takings were over $50,000 every eight performances. Then the demand began to ease off and the popular scale was tried. With its help, and later with the coöperation of the principals, who took a cut in salary, "The New Yorkers" played 165 performances. But the Broadway Theatre remained closed afterward.

Helen Hayes, her pride bruised a bit by the failure of "Mr. Gilhooley," found compensation in "Petticoat Influence," which Gilbert Miller brought over from London and offered at the Empire. She played the heroine in what was practically an all-English cast, and gracefully overcame such handicap as being unmistakably American presented.

Christmas week Arthur Hammerstein, who had suffered a pretty severe defeat with "Luana," a musicalization of "The Bird of Paradise," staked his other shirt on "Ballyhoo," a musical comedy with W. C. Fields. It was a good try, but it was not a Hammerstein year. "Ballyhoo" went down by the head in two weeks, the expense of it and the lack of immediate response serving to further distress the Hammerstein credit. Fields and the cast took over the property and continued the run coöperatively for another four weeks. And Arthur embraced bankruptcy.

Another holiday present was a return visit by Fritz Leiber and the Chicago Civic Shakespeare society. They stayed four weeks and did moderately well. Ivor Novello, having failed with "Symphony in Two Flats," was still in town and eager to try again. Lee Shubert gave him a chance with another Novello piece, "The Truth Game." With Billie Burke and Beerbohm Tree's rangy daughter, Viola, in the cast the comedy did very well for fourteen weeks.

Theatrically the year went out in a flare of enthusiasm with the production of "Five Star Final" and "Meet My Sister" on the night of December 31. "Five Star Final" is Louis Weitzenkorn's savage attack on the coarser tabloids, excerpts from which you will find farther on. It was played with spirit and staged with skill. It ran on successfully until spring. "Meet My Sister" was two acts of pleasantly simple operatic romance and a middle act of rough farce. With Bettina Hall and Leo Slezak's son, Walter, in the chief rôles it got 165 performances, without a chorus.

The mid-winter lull threatened to continue indefinitely. For two weeks in January the season was apparently over. Nothing produced, nothing promised. Depression, unemployment, cheaper talkies, and all the better playwrights lured away to Hollywood.

But the theatre, as usual, just refused to die. On the 12th it started back with George Kelly's "Philip Goes Forth." On the 13th it scored its biggest recent success with Philip Barry's "Tomorrow and Tomorrow." On the 19th a popular vaudeville revue, "You Said It," cheered the Broadway boys a lot. On the 26th the Guild came in with Lynn Riggs' freshly atmospheric "Green Grow the Lilacs." On the 26th Eva Le Gallienne revived "Camille" at the Civic and scored the success of her season. On the 27th Noel Coward and Gertrude Lawrence romped through Mr. Coward's "Private Lives" to the roars of those who could afford seats, and on the 28th Judith Anderson scored a hit with the thoughtful by making the mysterious Pirandello's mysterious "As You Desire Me" a little more mysterious.

Now the legitimates had taken heart and all was as well as well could be with the better liked attractions. The weaker sisters were still failing without loss of time and practically no regrets.

Early in February Katharine Cornell, who had decided to become an actress-manager, produced Besier's "The Barretts of Wimpole Street" at the Empire and again the drama-lovers were ready to stand in their places and cheer. Miss Cornell's career as a manageress was thus successfully launched, with the aid of her husband, Guthrie McClintic, who staged the play for her. "The Barretts" was played to a succession of sold-out houses through the spring and summer and probably could stay until next holiday time if Miss Cornell chooses to run it that long.

A new musical comedy, "America's Sweetheart," spoofing Hollywood again, came in with more promise than results justified, but the speculators, just out of the woods in their fight with the Theatre League, overloaded their racks with tickets and thus helped out the producers.

Came then a series of cheaply-priced revivals and return engagements of former successes. "Death Takes a Holiday" was brought back from the road. "Topaze" was played by a French company. "Gods of the Lightning" was tried again in Greenwich Village. "An American Tragedy" was revived at such prices as attracted audiences for another 125 performances. Again the end of the producing season was announced. Nothing more could be expected in the way of original plays.

But again the wiser prophets were a little fooled. It was in March that Charles Hopkins brought out another sentimental piece by A. A. Milne called "Give Me Yesterday." It had been previously played in England as "Success," and went to show that a man might rise to envied heights in politics or business and still regret the loss of a first love and an easy conscience. The Hopkins public rallied smartly to it.

Rachel Crothers, taking advantage of John Golden's absence in Florida, presented him with a hit in "As Husbands Go." George C. Tyler revived Barrie's "The Admirable Crichton" with Walter Hampden and Fay Bainter heading an impressive cast. Crosby Gaige produced Channing Pollock's newest sermon play, "The House Beautiful," which disappointed the Pollock critics by proving to be both well written and well staged and much to the liking of a considerable public.

Of course there were the usual failures, too. The Guild suffered two of them this late in its season—"The Miracle at Verdun" and a revival of Shaw's "Getting Married." The best either could do was to fill out the subscription period of six weeks.

Al Jolson came back in an imported novelty, "The Wonder Bar," for which the Shuberts rebuilt the stage of the roof theatre, the Bayes, to look as much like a continental night club as possible. It did, though probably there is nothing quite like it on the continent. The Shuberts also scored a late success with "The Silent Witness," an English mystery play which Harry Wagstaffe Gribble skillfully rearranged as to scene, and Lionel Atwill played impressively.

The lease of a theatre is assessed against what used to be the nine sure months of the theatre year from September to June. It therefore behooves lessees to keep their houses occupied during these paying months. This year of depression found some playhouses vacant all season and others as early as March. April added more to the number. You could, being so minded, rent a theatre for practically nothing at all by the week or month, and without more guarantee than the first week's rent.

As a result there were many plays produced in April and May that never should have been produced. Most of them were quick failures. But scattered here and there were good plays, too. Jed Harris tried again with a well-written but over-sophisticated comedy called "The Wiser They Are." Completing the phrase—"the harder they fall"—tells the history of this one. Constance Collier and Lee Shubert revived "Peter Ibbetson," with Dennis King in the name part which John Barrymore played originally, and Jessie Royce Landis playing opposite as the countess. It got five weeks, but not very encouragingly.

Down in the village a courageous group of young producers staged a play called "Precedent," which I. J. Golden, a former St. Louis attorney, had built up around the Mooney-Billings case. The reviewers, having nothing else to write about, drifted south for the first performance and were delighted to find a stirring melodrama splendidly acted. "Precedent" prospered and was brought uptown, where it continued through the spring and into the summer.

A Bernstein melodrama, he being the author of "The Thief," made what the aviators call a three-point landing with Edna Best, Basil Rathbone and Earle Larimore. It was a pretty artificial plot, but it offered good acting opportunities, Miss Best being married to Mr. Larimore and finding herself desperately in love with his best friend, Mr. Rathbone. She tried artfully to poison Mr. Larimore, but failed, and sadly threw herself into the Seine. The men were saddened, but managed to pick up their friendship years later.

Alice Brady, who had been none too fortunate the last several plays she had tried to save, took on another job with "Brass Ankle," written by the Du Bose Heyward who was co-author with his wife of the successful "Porgy" of some years back. It proved a sound little drama telling of a Tennessee wife who discovers with the birth of her second child that she is of colored blood. To save her husband and her first child, who has been accepted as white, she goads her husband into killing her and the baby by swearing that she has a black lover. Miscegenation is not a popular theme, either north or south. "Brass Ankle" could not be forced past six weeks.

Milton Aborn, who deserves a plaque or a scroll or something for his steadfast loyalty in the revival of the older and better musical comedies and operettas, found himself a new job this spring by staging a Gilbert and Sullivan season at popular prices. He started with "The Mikado" at a $2 top and packed Erlanger's Theatre. He followed with "Pinafore" and did it again, Fay Templeton coming over from Pittsburgh for a farewell farewell as the bumboat woman, fat Little Buttercup. The season was still flourishing as we started for the presses.

Walter Hartwig was forced to abandon his annual Little Theatre contest. The distant groups found it too expensive to travel and the home groups too hard to sell seats. He did stage a second Long Play contest, however. This was won by a Lincoln drama, "If Booth Had Missed," written by Arthur Goodman and played by the Morningside players of Columbia University. William A. Brady is reported to have bought it for regular production this fall. The story carries the Lincoln career through to a second tragedy. His adventures are largely those that befell his successor, Andrew Johnson. He is impeached on the charge of having violated the Tenure of Office Act in seeking to force the resignation of Seward, and though he is acquitted by a single vote, he is shot as he rises in the senate to give thanks. Samuel French gave a $1,000 prize to the winner.

Lew Leslie, who had had considerable experience with colored revues, being the producer of the "Blackbird" entertainments, decided to ring a change on this form of show. He did so with a sort of concert-vaudeville, "Rhapsody in Black." In this one a robed choir takes the place of the familiar jiggling chorus, and though there are the usual character song and tap dancing interludes there are few of the old time colored comedy features.

Arthur Sinclair and his wife, Maire O'Neill, once of the Abbey players in Dublin, were induced to play a light Irish comedy, "Old Man Murphy," and succeeded in bringing it a measure of popular success. The Shuberts tried another thin but exciting sex affair called "A Modern Virgin," written by the Elmer Harris who had been successful with "Young Sinners." An interesting new ingénue, Margaret Sullavan, helped it to eight weeks of profits.

The Players' Club elected to try a revival of Congreve's "The Way of the World" for its annual all-star celebration. It proved a poor choice, being rather dully played by Walter Hampden, Fay Bainter, Ernest Cossart, Alice Fischer, Selena Royle, the Lockharts, Kathleen and Eugene; Eliot Cabot, Cora Witherspoon and a lot of others. The public did not rise to Congreve and the Players were glad to get a $5,000 profit out of it, which is the least they have made since first they started resurrecting classics.

Early June saw the summer show business started with two outstanding hits. "The Third Little Show" was no sooner bowling along on the crest of an adjectival tidal wave than "The Band Wagon" came in to top that success with another even greater. "The Third Little Show" had Beatrice Lillie as its chief comedy exhibit, with Ernest Truex and Walter O'Keeffe to assist. "The Band Wagon" had Fred and Adele Astaire, Frank Morgan, Helen

Broderick and Tilly Losch, the German dancer, effectively spotted.

It looked like a lively summer from this point, with Mr. Ziegfeld's first "Follies" in four years and Mr. Carroll's "Vanities" to follow later. At any rate it was a lively finish to a season from which practically nothing had been expected.

There were 190 odd new shows produced during the year, as compared with recent annual averages of 240 odd. However, 190 is enough.

THE SEASON IN CHICAGO

By Charles Collins
Dramatic Critic of the *Chicago Tribune*

A SUPERFICIAL observer of the theatre in Chicago during the summer and early fall of 1930 would have had grounds for the conclusion that the stage was a dying institution. A city of metropolitan stature with a tradition as a "summer show town" could offer for the amusement of its inhabitants and visitors only one play—a smutty, fourth-rate comedy, in itself symptomatic of an art in economic and spiritual decadence.

Labor Day, the customary date for the beginning of the new season, failed to bring the usual blooming of premières. The summer doldrums prolonged their emptiness into the fall. Not until October was there any definite stirring of new life in the playhouses. Then, however, the silent panic ended, and the Chicago stage started on a determined and fairly successful up-hill march out of the valley of the shadow of general business depression.

At the end of the nine months' campaign, for which Memorial Day serves as a convenient date, a survey of those theatrical activities which fall under the technical label of "legitimate" reveals the fact that Chicago has given a decidedly creditable account of itself. The playbills that have passed into the files of the dramatic critics number 84—only ten or a dozen less than those of the preceding year. Of this number, 72 represent the field of drama. Operettas and musical comedies contribute 9 titles, and revues, 3. This low percentage of lyric entertainments is, of course, another indication of the economic drift of the era. There was a time when song-and-dance shows were as frequent as dramatic productions on the Chicago stage; but the risks attendant upon the staging of these costly affairs and the obsolescence of "the road" have changed all that.

In drama, the back-bone of the year was formed by the programs of the Theatre Guild and the Dramatic League of Chicago; and the subscription audiences of these organizations have good reason to rise up and call them blessed. It becomes increasingly apparent that the new forces in the national theatrical structure—

the trend toward the organization of audiences that are hospitable toward the treatment of the drama as a fine art—are leading the stage, so far as Chicago is concerned, out of the wilderness.

These new forces were also represented by the Chicago Civic Shakespeare Society, which enabled Fritz Leiber's company to give its second season of classic repertory, eight weeks in length; and the Goodman Theatre's Repertory Company. The latter group had the best season since its foundation five years ago, but ended with the discouraging announcement that this was its swan-song. The background of this abandonment will be discussed later.

The Theatre Guild's program was intermittent. Three productions were offered in the Blackstone at the opening of the season, and three in the Illinois at its close. This broken schedule caused some worrying and fretting among the subscribers, but in good time they learned that the Guild's word was as binding as its bond. Its contributions to the Chicago stage year, each for three weeks, were: "The Apple Cart," by Shaw; "The Garrick Gayeties," a revue given outside the subscription; "A Month in the Country," by Turgenev; "Elizabeth the Queen," by Maxwell Anderson; "Green Grow the Lilacs," by Lynn Riggs; and "He," by Alfred Savoir.

The engagement of "Elizabeth the Queen," with Alfred Lunt and Lynne Fontanne in the leading rôles, was the most notable affair of the season. The public demand for this brilliant achievement in historical drama was so great that the play could have remained for months. The staging of "He" marked the fulfillment of the Guild's promise to give Chicago an occasional chance to anticipate New York opinion. "He," a comedy of Gallic wit and light irony which deals with the idea of God, is a likely candidate for next year's lists of the Ten Best Plays, as discovered in New York.

The Dramatic League of Chicago, a link in a chain of organized audiences to which a pool of old-line Broadway managers (captained by Lee Shubert) submits plays of superior quality, made a definite advance. It offered six first-class productions, for engagements of four weeks each, and also two supplementary plays. Its pledges to its subscribers were fulfilled to their complete satisfaction; its program was well balanced; and its casts were admirable. In the preceding year, "The First Mrs. Fraser" emerged from the League's Chicago season to become a New York hit; and in the season of 1930-31 that achievement was repeated with "As You Desire Me."

The plays that the Dramatic League presented in Chicago, with their leading personalities, were: "Topaze," with Frank Morgan; "Death Takes a Holiday," with Philip Merivale; "Michael and Mary," with Madge Kennedy; "As You Desire Me," with Judith Anderson; "Scarlet Sister Mary," with Ethel Barrymore; "Art and Mrs. Bottle" and "Twelfth Night," with Jane Cowl; "The Man in Possession," with Leslie Banks and Isabel Jeans; and "The First Mrs. Fraser" (return engagement) with Grace George.

The dramatists represented by these titles, taken in order, were: Marcel Pagnol, Alberto Cassella, A. A. Milne, Luigi Pirandello, Julia Peterkin, Benn W. Levy, Shakespeare, H. M. Harwood and St. John Ervine. This roll-call has a cosmopolitan tone which ends the life of the wisecrack of the preceding year about the League's "London season."

Fritz Leiber's company found that Chicago had no ravenous appetite for Shakespeare in bread-and-butter form, but drove vigorously through the eight weeks of its schedule, giving "Hamlet," "The Merchant of Venice," "As You Like It," "King Lear," "Twelfth Night," "Macbeth," "Julius Cæsar" and "Richard III." Mary Hone's Viola and Cordelia had distinction and charm. The Chicago Civic Shakespeare Society—in other words, Harley L. Clarke, its head and body—plans to strengthen the company for next season.

The abandonment of the Goodman Repertory Company, at the end of its best year, came as a shock to its subscribers and followers. There had been marked artistic progress under the new directorate of Hubert Osborne, and attendance had been growing rapidly. The board of directors of the Art Institute cited "lack of public support" as the reason for their decision to abolish professional activities on the Goodman's stage.

They would have come closer to the facts in the case if they had frankly admitted that they were tired of meeting deficits out of their personal pocket-books, and also weary of the exasperations attendant upon theatrical management. They seem to have come to the conclusion that an art museum and an art theatre are incompatible activities. They now have a vacant shrine of drama on their hands. They have closed their acting company, but continued their school of acting—which, when one stops to think it over, is a bit of a paradox.

The Goodman's plays for the season were: "The Firebrand," by Edwin Justus Mayer; "Hotel Universe," by Philip Barry; "The Sea Gull," by Anton Tchekhoff; "Rebound," by Donald Ogden Stewart; "Lazzaro," by Luigi Pirandello (American première); "The Adding Machine," by Elmer Rice; and "The Sacred Flame," by W. Somerset Maugham.

The old slogan, "Chicago as a producing center," was again heard when the stream of plays from New York began to dwindle. Tracy C. Drake, owner of the Blackstone Theatre, assumed its direction after the withdrawal of his tenants in mid-season; and surprised old-school impresarios with his resourcefulness and luck. He took up Mrs. Fiske when her management deserted her, sponsored the re-staging of "Torch Song" and "Stepping Sisters," and secured a prize booking in "That's Gratitude." Altogether, box-office traffic at the Blackstone since Mr. Drake seized the helm has surprised the Erlangers.

George E. Wintz, jocularly known as "the king of the one-night stands," decided that Chicago was an excellent spot in which to pitch his tent. He prospered with "Jonesy" and "Apron Strings," but lost with "When Father Smiles," a farce in which De Wolf Hopper tried to escape from the comic operas. Ralph T. Kettering was another Chicago producer of the season, with "Lady in Pawn," starring Guy Bates Post. He failed, but remained undiscouraged.

Several theatres that are familiar landmarks on the Chicago Rialto went practically out of commission. The Princess lapsed into disuse when the Dramatic League transferred its second play to the Harris. The Garrick and the Studebaker found only a few bookings. The Cort was in darkness most of the year. The Majestic, built for old-style vaudeville and regarded as a derelict, was reopened for "Lysistrata," but after that run it sank back into oblivion. Most of the other theatres had occasional dark spells between bookings. The Great Northern, which specializes in operettas, had the best luck. It sheltered "Three Little Girls" from late in September until the middle of May—the banner engagement of the year, and the only one which extended more than twenty weeks.

Nevertheless there were periods when, through coincidental groupings of New York hits, the Chicago stage had an air of veritable brilliance. Walter Prichard Eaton, veteran dramatic critic and member of the Pulitzer prize play committee, happened to visit the city during one of these "highs" on the season's graph, and was much impressed. In a letter dated Oct. 19, 1930, he wrote:

"After looking over the list of plays now being acted or soon to be acted in Chicago, it is amusing to hear people say that the 'legitimate' theatre is dead. . . . Here is a musical piece, 'Strike Up the Band,' with lyrics of Gilbertian pungency; here is a play by George Bernard Shaw; in the offing are two American plays of quite different style, but each characterized by distinguished merit—'The Last Mile' and 'Hotel Universe.' Coming is 'Death Takes a Holiday,' a romantic drama from Europe of unusual quality.

"From ancient Greece comes a modernistic revival of the 'Lysistrata' of Aristophanes, and from Elizabethan England comes a whole repertory of Shakespearean drama. From Russia comes 'Uncle Vanya,' by the greatest of all the naturalists, in a distinguished adaptation. Presently will come, also from Russia, 'A Month in the Country,' with scenery reproducing some of the finest sets ever made in Moscow.

"I haven't at hand the London or Paris papers, but I will wager that in neither capital this autumn is any such variety of dramatic fare offered, or offered, on the whole, so effectively. You would have to go to Berlin to match it."

Other notable engagements, in addition to those which have been mentioned, were: Katharine Cornell in "Dishonored Lady," "Subway Express," George M. Cohan in "The Tavern," Mrs. Fiske in "Ladies of the Jury" and "Becky Sharp," "Berkeley Square," with Leslie Howard and Margalo Gillmore, Otis Skinner in "Marius," "Up Pops the Devil," and Helen Hayes in "Petticoat Influence." The most effective musical shows were "Sweet Adeline," Fred Stone and daughters in "Ripples," "Sons-O'-Guns," "Three Little Girls," Joe Cook in "Fine and Dandy," and "Meet My Sister." Two so-called "smash hits" from Broadway had their verdicts reversed into failure: "The Greeks Had a Word for It" and Lenore Ulric in "Pagan Lady."

The year's catalogue contained several flagrant examples of licentious vulgarity written and staged to cater to sexual curiosity alone. It was demonstrated, however, that plays of this sort do not thrive when they are bluntly defined by candid critics as abominations that deserve to be kicked into the lake.

To conclude: the history of the Chicago stage for the year of 1930-31 is not the story of a débâcle. The theatre has borne up bravely and stanchly through a full season of economic storm. The play-going population of the city has manifested an insistent demand for the "legitimate" in spite of the prevalence of the talkies. Although offered the cake of the cinema palaces on every hand, the public has continued to ask for the nourishing bread of the living stage.

The moral of the story seems to be: The stage may be down, even for a long count, but it is never out.

THE SEASON IN SAN FRANCISCO

BY GEORGE C. WARREN

Drama Editor of *The San Francisco Chronicle*

THE year from June 1, 1930, to May 31, 1931, was quiet in the San Francisco legitimate theatres; quiet and spotty. There were weeks when only one of the six playhouses was open, and other weeks when all were in operation.

Notable features of the year were the comeback of Henry Duffy and the continuing brilliance of the productions made by Edward Belasco and Homer Curran. This firm has presented many of the New York season's successes, given them fine casts, and productions that had beauty and character.

The Pacific Coast has become almost completely autonomous in its drama. Only three companies of importance have come from the East, all other productions having been made locally for San Francisco and Los Angeles. The three companies that braved the long and almost unbroken trip from the Mississippi River were Brock Pemberton's "Strictly Dishonorable" with Margaret Perry; David Belasco's "It's a Wise Child" and Katharine Cornell in "Dishonored Lady," Miss Cornell making her début in California in this play. Incidental to the presentation of "Strictly Dishonorable," Flobelle Fairbanks, a niece of the renowned Douglas, made her stage début during the run of the comedy. Later she succeeded Miss Perry in the part of the Southern girl, that young actress having been called to New York to head the cast on the defection of Muriel Kirkland.

But the lack of traveling companies did not cloud the brilliance of the season, which began with a production of Donald Ogden Stewart's "Rebound" with Ina Claire in the chief rôle. Clark Gable and Edward Woods, both since important on the screen, played the two principal rôles in John Wexley's "The Last Mile," and Sil-Vara's "Caprice" was acted by a cast headed by Fay Bainter, Reginald Owen and Lily Cahill. These at the Geary and Curran theatres.

"Subway Express" had a brief run at the Columbia Theatre, where also "Fata Morgana" was revived with Elsie Ferguson as Mathilde and Tom Douglas as the boy. "Candle Light" was done at the Geary Theatre with Eugenie Leontovich, who since has conquered New York in "Grand Hotel"; Alan Mowbray and Reginald Owen, and "The Crimson Hour," which was acted in New York as "Scarlet Pages" with Elsie Ferguson, was produced and had a fine run with Pauline Frederick as the woman lawyer at the Curran.

Edward Rowland revived "Little Orchid Annie" with Betty Bronson, the screen actress, in the title rôle, and Dorothy Mackaye made her return to the stage in a comedy by Lynn Starling called "A Cup of Sugar." Neither of these pieces is important. Ralph Pincus, of the Columbia, induced Mrs. Patrick Campbell to play Mrs. Alving in Ibsen's "Ghosts," with Tom Douglas as Oswald, and also presented Leon Errol and a good cast in "The Lost Sheep."

George Bernard Shaw's "The Apple Cart," produced by the Hollywood Repertory Players, had a good run at the Geary with Alan Mowbray as King Magnus and Doris Lloyd as Orinthia. Bert Lytell and Grace Menken, with two or three others of the New York cast, played "Brothers" for several weeks at the President Theatre for Henry Duffy, who also presented Kenyon Nicholson's "Torch Song" at the Alcazar with Mayo Methot and John Junior of the New York cast, and Robert Keith.

The Hollywood Repertory Players sent "Peter Pan" and "Porgy" to San Francisco. The former had Marion Clayton for its Peter, and the all-negro cast of "Porgy" was headed by Clarence Muse and Evelyn Preer, both formerly with the Lafayette Players in New York.

Belasco and Curran made productions of "Up Pops the Devil," "Young Sinners" and "Topaze" in the latter having Alan Mowbray, Mary Duncan and Henry Kolker for their leads.

Sid Grauman did Hart and Kaufman's "Once in a Lifetime" with Aline Macmahon, Moss Hart and Marie Nordstrom, and Grauman also produced "Street Scene" with sixteen of the New York cast. Pauline Frederick was chosen by Belasco and Curran to play the title rôle in Maxwell Anderson's "Elizabeth the Queen," with Ian Keith as Essex.

William Thornton, a youthful and ambitious seeker for laurels in the classic field, came to the Columbia Theatre, after a tour of the South and Middle-West, and gave respectable performances of "Hamlet," "The Taming of the Shrew" and "The Merchant of Venice." At the same house the year closed with Walker Whiteside, Florence Reed and Guy Bates Post in a revival of Melchior Lengyel's "The Typhoon," Whiteside and Miss Reed acting the rôles they played when the drama was first done in America.

The same trio has in prospect a production of Frank Harvey's "Cape Forlorn," to be done under the title "Three Men and a Woman." This piece will have its American première June 22.

There was a considerable lack of new plays during the year, and of those presented none was of importance, excepting Emmerich Kalman's "Paris in Spring," an operetta splendidly produced by Lillian Albertson and Louis Owen Macloon. Leo Carillo tried out a play called "Kebec" by Cyril Wood, at the Dufwin Theatre, Oakland, and at the same house "Two-Gun Grandman" was produced with Florence Roberts in the title rôle. This play is by Ann Lovell, who is Mrs. Carlton Miles.

A play called "Quits" by Cyrus Wood and Leonard Ide had several performances at the San Francisco University, and the Players' Guild offered an interesting play by Marianne King, called "The Prodigals." The Reginald Travers Repertory Players produced "Love Apples" by Katherine Brocklebank, and Harry Green presented at the Geary Theatre a play called "The Shyster" by the Spewacks, Bella and Sam. It flopped.

An amateur production of "Lysistrata" ran several weeks at the tiny Travers Theatre in the Fairmont Hotel, and at the same place Henry B. Lister's classic "Tiresias" was produced. The Little Theatre of the University of California produced two new plays, "The Twelfth Disciple" by Mary Kouse Sachs of St. Louis, a study of Judas Iscariot, and a new translation of Maxim Gorki's "The Lower Depths," the adaptation made by Professors Alexander Kaun and George Noyes of the Slavic Department of the university. The Little Theatre transferred its productions from Wheeler Hall, which has only a platform stage, to the auditorium of the International House, a gift to the university from John D. Rockefeller, Jr.

Stanford University kept up its production schedule, offering "Big Game Gaieties" and "Junior Opera," purely local affairs, and a fine production of "Wings Over Europe." The Playmakers of Berkeley presented four groups of one-act plays written, directed and acted by its members, and Theatre Arts, Inc., presented both one-act programs and full length plays.

The San Francisco Players' Guild, besides its production of "The Prodigals" presented Lonsdale's "On Approval" and Oscar Wilde's "Salome," a really fine staging of this classic with Virginia Phillips a beautiful and splendid daughter of Herodias, and Cameron Prud'homme a fine Herod.

Promises for the immediate future are Billie Burke in "The Vinegar Tree"; Ethel Barrymore in "The School for Scandal" and "Hedda Gabler"; Jane Cowl in "Camille" and Lionel Atwill and Anna May Wong in "On the Spot."

THE SEASON IN SOUTHERN CALIFORNIA

By Monroe Lathrop

Drama Editor of the *Los Angeles Express*

TRYING times, the past twelve months have been for the custodians of the legitimate theatre in Southern California. With the public's purse-strings tightened here, as elsewhere, owing to the world's economic maladies, there has been a recession from the boom days of a couple of years back when as many as sixteen playhouses were more or less active in and around Los Angeles.

And yet, with half as many pennants flying, there has been the anomaly of one of the best theatrical years (drawing the line through the month of June for convenience, since there is no defined "season" here) on record. As against about 125 presentations formerly, the number dropped to a few less than 100. But the loss has been more in figures than in quality.

The situation has forced a keener selection, and the result has been a sifting of chaff all to the good from the audience' standpoint. An epitome of the year is found in the fact that of about a score of the New York season's definite hits, twelve promptly made their appearance here or are in preparation as this is written.

Of Mr. Mantle's "Ten Best," chosen for this volume, four have been seen, one is about to come in, and two are unavailable without the original New York casts. Twenty-six premières (with the customary small percentage of hopeful projects) maintained the standing of this area as the second most important production center in the country.

Of classics and semi-classics there was the small leaven of five to tone up the lump, and two musicals stood out as conspicuous exceptions to the almost wholly dramatic fare, probably owing to cost risks.

The year took its toll in the break-up of Henry Duffy's chain of high-grade legitimate theatres on the coast, the retirement of Edward Everett Horton as a producer, and the collapse of the Civic Repertory movement in its third season, under the economic pressure.

But such gaps as these left were promptly filled by the entry of

Sid Grauman and Dickson Morgan into the field, the concentration of Duffy's activities in Hollywood, and the entry in a limited way of the Erlanger interests. In the main we have relied, and not in vain, upon Belasco and Curran, Duffy and Grauman, who carried on bravely with some of the most beautiful and expensive presentations in years.

To Belasco and Curran we are indebted for such new things as "Elizabeth the Queen," with Pauline Frederick and Ian Keith; "Berkeley Square," with Leslie Howard and Margalo Gillmore; "It's a Wise Child," with the New York cast; "Rebound," with Ina Claire; "Topaze," with Alan Mowbray; "Tomorrow and Tomorrow," and "Up Pops the Devil."

Grauman set a high standard upon his entry with "Once in a Lifetime" and "Street Scene" with the original casts; Mrs. Fiske in a revival of "Mrs. Bumpstead-Leigh," and "The Man in Possession," with Douglas Fairbanks, Jr., and Nora Gregor from the Vienna stage.

Duffy brought us "Michael and Mary," "Torch Song," Frank Craven in "That's Gratitude," "Whispering Friends" and a beautiful revival of "Irene," among his numerous offerings.

At the Erlanger houses we got Rachel Crothers' latest, "As Husbands Go," "Lost Sheep," with Leon Errol; Shaw's "The Philanderer"; "The Dishonored Lady," with Katharine Cornell; "Caprice" and "Death Takes a Holiday."

The Civic Repertory group started bravely with splendid productions of Shaw's "The Apple Cart," "The Infinite Shoeblack," "Porgy," "The Champion," with Grant Mitchell, and a revival of "Peter Pan" before adversity overtook the enterprise. Following them to the same stage Dickson Morgan brought Mrs. Leslie Carter back to the footlights in a revival of "The Shanghai Gesture" and made the first local production of "Waterloo Bridge."

The Pasadena Community Playhouse gave its always fine staging to "Othello," the semi-classic "Richelieu," Jules Romain's "Doctor Knock," the première of Martin Flavin's "Dancing Days"; a revival of "What Every Woman Knows," with Frances Starr; the first presentation in America of "The Watched Pot," by H. H. Munro (Saki); "Spring Song," by Bella Spewack (a première); Monckton Hoffe's "Many Waters"; "The Man Saul" (première), with Paul Muni; "No More Frontier," by Talbot Jennings (première), and "Green Fire" (première), by Glenn Hughes and John Taine.

Revivals on this stage also included "Death Takes a Holiday" and Elmer Rice and Philip Barry's collaboration, "Cock Robin."

Other notable revivals of the season include Ibsen's "Ghosts," with Mrs. Pat Campbell; "Fata Morgana," with Elsie Ferguson; "The Bad Man," with Leo Carrillo; "Elmer the Great," with Joe E. Brown; "Parlor, Bedroom and Bath," with Charlotte Greenwood; "The Poor Nut," with Elliott Nugent; "To the Ladies," with Glenn Hunter; "Bird in Hand" and "Tea for Three."

Excepting those mentioned at Pasadena, most of the new play ventures came by way of the minor experimental and "little" playhouses. Most active was the Theatre Mart where, under various auspices, there were tried out "Balloon," by Padraic Colum; "Thought," by the Russian Andreyeff (first time in English)—these by the Potboilers group; "The Devil's Sideshow," by Henry Gordon; "Easy Living," by Madeline Blackmore; "Barren Trees," by Arthur Gregor; "The Mountains Come to the Goldsteins," by William A. Jefferis; "Napoleon Had It Too," by Sada Cowan and Madeline Blackmore; "O. Henry in Prison," by Upton Sinclair; "Round Heels," by Paul Fix; "The Ostrich," by Olga Printzlau; "Decency," by Arthur Gregor.

New ventures on other stages included "The Ambulance Chaser," by Bella Spewack, with Harry Green; "Here Comes the Hero," by Ann Murray; "Under the Virginia Moon," by Kenneth Cole; "The Glory Declared," by Ralph Culver Bennett; "El Dorado," by John Steven McGroarty; "Between Covers," by William A. Jefferis; "Last Night," by Richard Spencer and Frederick Russell.

Few of these rose above mediocrity or carried any novelty or significance, but "Green Fire," "The Ambulance Chaser," "The Watched Pot," "Spring Song," "Napoleon Had It Too," "Last Night" and "The Devil's Sideshow" gave some promise of value to the commercial theatre.

Traveling by caravan over the coast highways much as Edwin Booth and Lawrence Barrett did half a century ago, William Thornton, an ambitious young actor with a troupe and scenic equipment, put a picturesque note into the year's classic division. His "Shakespeare Guild of America" carried a repertory of the Bard's plays to hamlets as well as cities.

"Lysistrata," by one of the little theatre groups; "Othello," at Pasadena; "Medea," at the University of Southern California, and "The Merchant of Venice," with Maurice Moscovitch, under Civic Repertory auspices, were other classics which gave "tone" to the dramatic panorama of a year both prolific and of high average quality despite the unusual hazards of adverse financial conditions.

ELIZABETH THE QUEEN

A Drama in Three Acts

By Maxwell Anderson

THE THEATRE GUILD began its thirteenth subscription season in New York with the production in September of a melodrama from the Russian Soviets entitled "Roar China." It consisted principally of a magnificent battleship built into the stage of the Martin Beck Theatre, and a colorful text expounding with a certain impressive frankness propaganda seeking to expose galling injustices put upon the poor coolies by the overpoweringly arrogant white race in China. The play had a moderate success but did not last beyond its subscription season, its apparent bias arousing some little resentment.

The second production of the season was that of Maxwell Anderson's historical drama, once called "Elizabeth and Essex" but later changed to "Elizabeth the Queen" to avoid threatened conflict with a similarly titled biographical work by Lytton Strachy.

Mr. Anderson's drama, because its text was forthright and eloquent, its slightly romanticized historical interludes steadily interesting and the performance of its chief characters by Lynn Fontanne and Alfred Lunt unusually impressive, was promptly set among the more notable of the Guild successes. Miss Fontanne's nightly receptions as the queen grew to the proportions of minor ovations and the play ran well past its subscription period, being played to a succession of large audiences until the first week in March, when it was sent touring. No historical drama of recent times has earned so definite a triumph.

The scene of the play's opening is the gray, grim and more than a little forbidding "entrance hall before a council chamber in the palace at Whitehall. The entrance to the council room is closed and four guards with halberds stand at either side."

It is early morning, and though the guards "stand immobile," they find pleasure in doing their share of Elizabethan gossiping. The talk runs mostly to the queen and her moods; how she is ever out of sorts "once the earl's gone"; how her temper is unconsciously assimilated by her maids, causing a serious lack of sociability below stairs, so to speak; how the queen must be aging, even though she doesn't show it—as—

"They say the queen's getting to be an old woman," remarks Guard No. 4, "but I swear she looks younger than my wife, whom I married, a young thing, six years come Easter."

"It would age a girl fast, just the look of you," suggests Guard No. 3.

"As for the queen, powder and paint accounts for some of it," adds Guard No. 1. "To say nothing of the earl. A young love will do much for a lady's face."

Sir Walter Raleigh is an early caller. He is gayly set out in shining silver armor and he is looking for the Earl of Essex. Essex has not arrived, but Raleigh is confident he is momentarily expected. The fact that Penelope Gray, an alert and attractive lady-in-waiting to Her Majesty, passes quickly through the room to get to the window is evidence to Sir Walter that she is really anticipating the arrival of Essex.

Penelope, however, denies the charge with some briskness, despite Raleigh's repeated conviction that on those days when the earl returns every petticoat in the palace is hung with an eye to pleasing him. Still Penelope is firm.

RALEIGH—I relinquish you, lady. Run to the window! He will be here and you will miss him!

PENELOPE—Is there a lady would run from Sir Walter in his silver suiting? Since the sun is up . . . I have no errand.

RALEIGH—Is there no limit to a woman's deception, wench? Would you go so far as to appear pleased if I kissed you?

PENELOPE—And no deception. (*He kisses her.*) I call the Gods to witness . . . did I not blush prettily?

RALEIGH—And meant it not at all. Tell me, did the queen send you to look out the casement for news of her Essex, or did you come at the prompting of your heart?

PENELOPE—Shall I tell you the truth?

RALEIGH—Verily.

PENELOPE—The truth is I cannot answer.

RALEIGH—Both, then?

PENELOPE—Both or one or neither.

RALEIGH—Fie on the baggage.

PENELOPE—Is it not a virtue to be close-mouthed in the queen's service?

RALEIGH—If you kept the rest of your person as close as your mouth what a paragon of virtue you would be!

PENELOPE—Indeed, my lord, I am.

RALEIGH—Indeed, my lady? Have there not been certain deeds on dark nights?

PENELOPE—Sh! Under the rose.

RALEIGH—Meaning under covers . . .

PENELOPE—Fie on my lord, to make me out a strumpet!

RALEIGH—It is my manner of wooing, fair maid! I woo by suggestion of images . . .

PENELOPE—Like small boys on the closet wall . . .

RALEIGH—Like a soldier . . .

PENELOPE—Aye, a veteran . . . of encounters . . .

RALEIGH—I will have you yet, my love; I will take lessons from this earl . . .

PENELOPE—Take this lesson from me, my lord: You must learn to desire what you would have. Much wanting makes many a maid a wanton. You want me not . . . nor I you. You wear your silver for a queen.

It is true that the Earl of Essex has arrived and craves an audience with his queen. A captain brings the news and Sir Robert Cecil shortly confirms it. There is something like a sneer in Raleigh's voice as he accepts the situation.

"So: The heavenly boy, clad in the regalia of the sun, even now extracts his gallant foot from his golden stirrup and makes shift to descend from his heaving charger. Acclamation lifts in every voice, tears well to every eye . . . with the exception of mine, perhaps, and yours, I hope . . ."

"I am at a pass to welcome him, myself," agrees Cecil. "This Elizabeth of ours can be difficult on her good days . . . and there have been no good ones lately."

Two men at arms arrive, each bearing a suit of silver armor. To Sir Walter's consternation the armor is an exact duplicate of his own. Shortly two other men at arms have arrived, and they also carry duplicate sets of silver armor, by which time Raleigh's rage is mounting past control. The Earl of Essex, tall, handsome, in his early thirties and evidently enthused by the nature of the jest he is about to launch, briskly enters the hall. Now he stands before Raleigh and speaks with a show of passion.

ESSEX

Felicitations on your effulgence, sir!
You're more splendid than I had imagined! News came of
your silver

Even in my retreat! I was ill and I swear it cured me!
You should have heard the compliments I've heard
Passed on you! Sir Walter's in silver! The world's outdone
They said—the moon out-mooned. He gleams down every corridor
And every head's turned after him. The queen
Herself has admired it—the design—the workmanship!
There's nothing like it this side of Heaven's streets.
And I said to myself—the great man—this is what we have needed—
More silver everywhere—oceans of silver!
Sir Walter has set the style, the world will follow.
So I sent for the silver-smiths, and by their sweat
Here's for you, lads, tailored to every man's measure—
Shall Raleigh wear silver alone? Why, no,
The whole court shall go argent!

RALEIGH

Take care, my lord.
I bear insults badly.

ESSEX

And where are you insulted?
For the queen's service you buy you a silver armor.
In the queen's service I buy you a dozen more.
A gift, my friends, each man to own his own,
As you own yours. What insult?

RALEIGH

Have your laugh,
Let the queen and court laugh with you! Since you are envious
You may have my suit. I had not thought even Essex
Bore so petty a mind.

ESSEX

I misunderstood you
Perhaps, Sir Walter. I had supposed you donned
Silver for our queen, but I was mistaken . . .
Keep these all for yourself. The men shall have others . . .
Some duller color.

RALEIGH

I have borne much from you
Out of regard for the queen, my lord of Essex.

ESSEX

And I from you
By God . . .

CECIL

You have forgotten, Sir Walter,
A certain appointment . . .

RALEIGH
And you will bear more, by Heaven! . . .

CECIL
He is going to the queen,
Remember. And we have an errand.

ESSEX
You presume to protect me,
Master Secretary?

CECIL
I protect you both, and our mistress.
There can be no quarreling here.

RALEIGH
That's very true. Let us go. (CECIL *and* RALEIGH *go out right.*)

Sir Francis Bacon, having arrived for the council and been witness to the meeting of Raleigh and Essex, is eager that Essex should take more heed of his actions. It were not enough for Essex to quarrel with the queen, protests Bacon, but he must now quarrel with Raleigh.

Essex cannot, however, "quarrel on order or avoid a quarrel at will." He had quarreled with the queen because she fights a silly, womanish war with Spain.

None the less, Essex is riding straight to a fall in the estimation of Sir Francis, and it were well that he pause long enough to ask himself one question honestly: Whether he would retain the favor of the queen, remain her favorite, and keep all that goes with that position, or set himself against the queen and trust himself to popular favor?

Essex is not prepared to answer such a question, and Bacon, rebuffed, would let the matter drop.

ESSEX
Forgive me, dear friend, forgive me.
I have been ill, and this silly jackanapes
Of a Raleigh angers me with his silver mountings
Till I forget who's my friend. You know my answer
In regard to the queen. I must keep her favor.
Only it makes me mad to see all this . . .
This utter mismanagement, when a man's hand and brain
Are needed and cannot be used.

BACON

Let me answer for you;
You are not forthright with yourself. The queen
Fights wars with tergiversation and ambiguities . . .
You wish to complete your record as general,
Crush Spain, subdue Ireland, make a name like Cæsar's,
Climb to the pinnacle of fame. Take care.
You are too popular already. You have
Won at Cadiz, caught the people's hearts,
Caught their voices till the streets ring your name
Whenever you pass. You are loved better than
The queen. That is your danger. She will not suffer
A subject to eclipse her; she cannot suffer it.
Make no mistake. She will not.

ESSEX

And I must wait,
Bite my nails in a corner, let her lose to Spain,
Keep myself back for policy?

BACON

Even so.

ESSEX

I come of better blood than Elizabeth.
My name was among the earls around King John
Under the oak. What the nobles have taught a king
A noble may teach a queen.

BACON

You talk treason and death.
The old Order is dead, and you and your house will die
With it if you cannot learn.

ESSEX

So said King John
Under the oak, or wherever he was standing,
And little he got by it, as you may recall.
What the devil's a king but a man, or a queen but a woman?

BACON

King John is dead; this is Elizabeth,
Queen in her own right, daughter of a haughty line.
There is one man in all her kingdom she fears
And that man's yourself, and she has good reason to fear you.
You're a man not easily governed, a natural rebel,
Moreover a general, popular and acclaimed,
And, last, she loves you, which makes you the more to be feared,
Whether you love her or not.

Photo by Vandamm Studio, New York.

"ELIZABETH THE QUEEN"

Elizabeth: Whoever makes you angry has won already.
Essex: They have planned this. . . . If this pet rat, Lord Cecil, wishes to know my mind about him, and it seems he does, he shall have it!

(*At the left, Alfred Lunt; on the throne, Lynn Fontanne*)

ESSEX
I do love her! I do!
BACON
My lord, a man as young as you—
ESSEX
If she were my mother's kitchen hag,
Toothless and wooden-legged, she'd make all others
Colorless.
BACON
You play dangerously there, my lord.
ESSEX
I've never yet loved or hated
For policy nor a purpose. I tell you she's a witch—
And has a witch's brain. I love her, I fear her,
I hate her, I adore her—
BACON
That side of it you must know
For yourself.
ESSEX
I will walk softly—here is my hand.
Distress yourself no more—I can carry myself.
BACON
Only count not too much on the loves of queens.

With a promise to remember that injunction Essex is gone, but not without another fling at Raleigh, who is standing with Lord Cecil in a doorway with a change of armor now decorating his noble lines. He carries his silver suit in his arms.

"Sir Walter, take care of your health," admonishes Essex.

"My health, sir?"

"Wearing no silver, in this chilly weather!"

In anger Raleigh casts his silver armor with the others and instructs the guards to melt the pile of them down and sell the silver.

Shortly Sir Francis has also left and Raleigh and Cecil are at liberty to put their heads together. The time has come, apparently, when something must be done to curb the popularity of Essex. The queen, Raleigh is convinced, if put to the test, loves her kingdom far more than she loves her earl. "She loves her kingdom more than all men, and always will," insists Raleigh.

If Essex "could be made to look like a rebel, which he is close to being," Raleigh argues, "and she could be made to believe it, which is harder, you'd be first man in the Council."

"And you would be?" queries Cecil.

"Wherever I turn he's stood square in my way," admits Raleigh, "My life long here at court he's snatched honor and favor from before my eyes . . . till his voice and walk and aspect make me writhe . . . There's a fatality in it!"

"If he could be sent from England . . . we might have a chance to come between them."

"Would she let him go?"

CECIL
No . . . but if he could be teased
And stung about his generalship till he was
Too angry to reflect . . . Suppose you were proposed
As general for the next Spanish raid?

RALEIGH
He would see it,
And so would she.

CECIL
Then if you were named
For the expedition to Ireland?

RALEIGH
No, I thank you.
He'd let me go, and I'd be sunk in a bog
This next three hundred years. I've seen enough
Good men try to conquer Ireland.

CECIL
Then how would this be?
We name three men for Ireland of his own supporters;
He will oppose them, not wishing his party weakened
At the court. Then we ask what he suggests
And hint at his name for leader . . .

RALEIGH
Good so far.

CECIL
He will be angry and hint at your name; you will offer
To go if he will.

RALEIGH
No. Not to Ireland.

CECIL
Yes!
Do you think he'd let you go with him and share
The military glory? It will go hard,
Having once brought up his name, if we do not manage

To ship him alone to Dublin.

RALEIGH

We can try it, then,
Always remembering that no matter what
Is said . . . no matter what I say or you . . .
I do not go. You must get me out of that,
By Christ, for I know Ireland.

CECIL

I will. Be easy.

RALEIGH

When is the council?

CECIL

At nine.

RALEIGH

You'll make these suggestions?

CECIL

If you'll play up to them.

RALEIGH

Count on me. I must look after
These silver soldiers.

CECIL

At nine then.

RALEIGH

Count on me.
(*They go out in opposite directions. The curtain falls.*)

ACT I

The queen's study, which adjoins her bedchamber and the council hall, "is a severe little room with chairs, a desk and a few books, huge and leather-bound." Essex is there now, awaiting an audience. Penelope Gray is also there, and worried.

Quite frankly Penelope would know whether or not Lord Essex loves the queen. And being assured that he does, does he love her very dearly? If so, as it is so, Penelope could wish that Essex had loved someone who loved him better, for the love of this queen is uncertain, and Penelope is afraid for Essex.

"I have heard her when she thought she was alone," confesses Penelope, "walk up and down her room soundlessly, night long, cursing you . . . cursing you because she must love you and could not help herself . . . swearing to be even with you for this love she scorns to bear you. My lord, you anger her too much."

Essex is not worried. Such scenes and conclusions are common to lovers. Still Essex promises to beware his queen.

A moment later Elizabeth, drawn majestically to her full height, looking her years no more than necessary, signing imperiously to her maid that she is no longer needed, sweeps into the study. That she is angered there is no doubt. She had thought never to see her Lord of Essex again. Had vowed, in fact, that their last parting should be forever. And the fact that she has but now passed her Penelope in the door "with eyes and lips that looked the softer for kissing," adds a little to her irritation. Penelope, to Essex, is just a crazy child. And children, counters Elizabeth, have their little ways with each other.

ESSEX

Must we begin
With charges and counter charges, when you know . . .

ELIZABETH

Do I indeed? . . .
You have been gone a week, at this Wanstock of yours . . .
And a week's a long time at court. You forget that I
Must live and draw breath whether I see you or not . . .
And there are other men and women, oh, yes, all fully
Equipped for loving and being loved! Penelope . . .
You find Penelope charming. And as for me
There's always Mountjoy . . . or Sir Walter . . . the handsome,
Sir Walter, the silver-plated . . .

ESSEX

He'll wear no more
Silver at your door.

ELIZABETH

What have you done . . . come, tell me.
I knew this silver would draw fire. What happened?

ESSEX

Nothing . . . But the fashion's gone out.

ELIZABETH

No, but tell me!

ESSEX

He happened to be in the way
When the upstairs pot was emptied.
He's gone to change his clothes.

ELIZABETH

You shall not be allowed

To do this to him . . .

ESSEX

(*moving toward her*)—You shall not be allowed
To mock me, my queen. (*He kisses her.*)

ELIZABETH

Isn't it strange how one man's kiss can grow
To be like any other's . . . or a woman's
To be like any woman's?

ESSEX

Not yours for me,
No, and not mine for you, you lying villain,
You villain and queen, you double-tongued seductress
You bitch of brass!

ELIZABETH

Silver, my dear. Let me be
A bitch of silver. It reminds me of Raleigh.

ESSEX

Damn you!

ELIZABETH

Damn you and double damn you for a damner!
Come some day when I'm in the mood. What day's this? . . .
Thursday? Try next Wednesday . . . or any Wednesday
Later on in the summer . . . any summer
Will do. Why are you still here?

ESSEX

Oh, God, if I could walk out that door
And stay away!

ELIZABETH

It's not locked.

ESSEX

But I'd come back.
Where do you think I've been this last week? Trying,
Trying not to be here! But you see, I am here.

ELIZABETH

Yes, I see.

ESSEX

Why did you plague me without a word?

ELIZABETH

Why did you not come?

ESSEX

You are a queen, my queen. You had proscribed me,
Sent formal word I'd not be admitted if I came.

ELIZABETH

I may have meant it at the time.

ESSEX

I think I have a demon, and you are it!

ELIZABETH

If ever a mocking devil tortured a woman
You're my devil and torture me! Let us part and quickly,
Or there'll be worse to come. Go.

ESSEX

I tell you I will not.

ELIZABETH

Come to me, my Essex. Let us be kind
For a moment. I will be kind. You need not be.
You are young and strangely winning and strangely sweet.
My heart goes out to you wherever you are.
And something in me has drawn you. But this same thing
That draws us together hurts and blinds us until
We strike at one another. This has gone on
A long while. It grows worse with the years. It will end badly.
Go, my dear, and do not see me again.

ESSEX

All this
Is what I said when last I went away.
Yet here I am.

ELIZABETH

Love someone else, my dear.
I will forgive you.

ESSEX

You mean you would try to forgive me.

ELIZABETH

Aye, but I would.

ESSEX

What would you have to forgive?
I have tried to love others. It's empty as ashes.

Elizabeth would know what others Essex means. What others has he tried to love? And what does he care for the misery he causes her? And so they must quarrel again, then grow gentle again, and agree to keep their silence when they are tempted to speak. Which would be completely satisfying to Essex if only Elizabeth would agree that even her lover might be right—sometimes, "instead of flying instantly into opposition as soon as I propose a shift in policy!"

But Essex *is* wrong, Elizabeth insists. Or was wrong, to urge another campaign in Spain, and to strike at Flanders at the same moment. Let him consider the risk, and the drain on the treasury, and the lack of troops and money—

Why lack money when England is rich, demands Essex. "It's the same ancient, unprofitable niggardliness that pinches pennies and wastes a world of treasure! You could have all Spain, and Spain's dominions in the new world, an empire of untold wealth . . . and you forgo them because you fear to lay new taxes!"

"I have tried that," answers Elizabeth; "and never yet has a war-like expedition brought me back what it cost!"

But, insists Essex, it is only half measures that she has tried. His plea is that she should be bold just once and give the gods a chance to be kind.

Elizabeth will not have it. She has kept the peace, has kept her people happy and prosperous. And at no cowardly price. "It requires more courage not to fight than to fight when one is surrounded by hasty hotheads," she warns him.

"They will set you down in history as the weasel queen who fought and ran away, who struck one stroke, preferably in the back, and then turned and ran . . ."

"Is it my fame you think of, or your own, my lord?" demands the queen.

Has he not had his chance at Cadiz? Is it not true that he is even now the hero of the common people, the one they cheer when he and his queen ride in the streets together? Can he not be satisfied with this?

"Is it for fear of me and this hollow cheering you hold me back from Spain?" demands Essex.

"It is because I believe in peace and have no faith in wars or what wars win," answers Elizabeth.

And yet she is free to confess that there is a fear she has of him, knowing that he feels he could govern England better than she; that he trusts her no more than he would trust any other woman to be in power.

Which is true, his lordship admits. But that does not mean either that he does not love her, or that because of his love he cannot see the mistakes she has made and would make again. "A woman cannot act and think like a man," Essex charges.

"Act and think like a man," counters the queen. "Why should I think like a man when a woman's thinking's wiser?"

But now a tenderer mood has again swept over Elizabeth. If it be true that he tires of her a little; if it be true that sometimes she may seem a little old to him, let him promise that he will tell her first; let him promise that in all kindness and in memory of a great love. Yet she knows he will not.

"It is not in a man to be kind that way, nor in a woman to take it kindly. I think I'd kill you in a first blind rage."

"Kill me when I can say it."

ELIZABETH
Love, will you let me
Say one more thing that will hurt you?
ESSEX
Anything.
ELIZABETH
Your blood's on fire to lead a new command
Now that you've won so handsomely in Spain,
And when I need a general anywhere
You'll ask to go. Don't ask it . . . and don't go.
You're better here in London.
ESSEX
Was this all you wanted? (*Stepping back.*)
To make me promise this?
ELIZABETH
(*softly*)—Not for myself,
I swear it, not because I think you reckless
With men and money, though I do think that,
Not because you might return in too much triumph
And take my kingdom from me, which I can imagine,
And not because I want to keep you here
And hate to risk you, though that's also true . . .
But rather . . . and for this you must forgive me . . .
Because you're more a poet than a general . . .
And I fear you might fail, and lose what you have gained,
If you went again.
ESSEX
God's death! Whom would you send?
ELIZABETH
I asked you not to be angry.
ESSEX
Not to be angry!
How do you judge a leader except by whether
He wins or loses? Was it by chance, do you think,

That I took Cadiz?

ELIZABETH

Very well. You shall go.
Go if you will. Only I love you, and I say
What would be wiser.

ESSEX

You choose the one thing I must have
And ask me not to ask it! No. Forgive me.

ELIZABETH

I'll not say it again.

ESSEX

But if I'm more poet than
General, why poets make better generals
Than generals do, on occasion.

ELIZABETH

You've proved it so
On more than one occasion. (*A clock strikes. She rises.*)
There's the chime
The council's waiting, and we shall hear about Ireland,
If Cecil has his way. One thing remember,
You must not go to Ireland.

ESSEX

No. That's a war
I'm content to miss.

ELIZABETH

Thank God for that much then. I've been afraid
Ireland might tempt you. And one more thing remember . . .
I'll have to oppose you in the council on
The Spanish hostages . . . You'll have your way . . .
But I'll have to oppose you, lest they think it's your kingdom.
Will you understand . . . ?

ESSEX

I'll play my part perfectly. (*He kisses her hand, then her lips.*)

ELIZABETH

Now what can come between us, out of heaven or hell, or Spain or England?

ESSEX

Nothing . . . never again.

Now the doors of the council chamber have been thrown back. The queen sits in her chair of state and beneath it, at a table, her councilors are gathered. They include Raleigh, Cecil, Essex,

Burghley and Howard. At the queen's feet her Jester sits cross-legged.

The council, as Lord Burghley points out, stands in disagreement with Lord Essex in the matter of the war on Spain. Essex would "throw a challenge down, raid the Escurial and sack the empire," rather than continue to fight Spain annually in chronic fashion.

There is also the matter of the Spanish ransoms. Essex' soldiers, having been promised prize money for the prisoners they have taken, are clamoring for their rewards. Heretofore it has been the custom to so reward them, but Elizabeth is against the policy. The queen has been told that the war would be paid for in booty. Now they purpose to give that booty to the men. To that she is unalterably opposed. Even though Lord Essex may have made such a promise to his soldiers in her name the throne is not bound, nor shall be.

The throne, Lord Essex agrees, can repudiate what it likes, but not without breaking faith. Reluctantly Elizabeth admits as much and finally agrees, in this instance, to withdraw her order. But in future all prisoners shall be held in the name of the state, and whatever price is on their heads shall belong to the crown.

There is one other matter that now must be brought before the council—the perpetual subject of Tyrone's rebellion in Ulster and what's to be done about Ireland.

"We must conquer Ireland finally now," warns Lord Cecil, "or give over what we have won."

Furthermore, it is Lord Cecil's conviction that what is most needed is a Lord Protector of Ireland "who can carry sword and fire from one end of the bogs to the other, and have English law or Irish rebels until there are no rebels."

For this assignment Cecil would select a proved and able general such as Lord Howard, Lord Essex, Sir Walter Raleigh, Knollys or Mountjoy. But which of these, demands Elizabeth.

Sir Walter suggests that two might be sent together, one to Dublin, one to Ulster, to work toward a meeting halfway. But there are no two who could work together upon whom the council can agree.

If Sir Walter were to go, suggests Lord Cecil, Lord Essex should go with him. They should have coeval power but Raleigh should be named as Lord Protector. It is a suggestion that Essex wrathfully resents. Here is a planned insult, and one which he is quick to check.

"Whoever makes you angry has won already, Essex," warns Elizabeth.

"They have planned this," repeats the infuriated Essex.

CECIL
I say no more.
Raleigh will go to Ireland as Lord Protector
And go alone, if the queen asks it of him,
And since you will not go.

ESSEX
I have not said
I would not go. But if I were to go I would go
Alone, as Lord Protector!

ELIZABETH
That you will not.
I have some word in this.

ESSEX
If this pet rat
Lord Cecil wishes to know my mind about him,
And it seems he does, he shall have it! How he first crept
Into favor here I know not, but the palace is riddled
With his spying and burrowing and crawling underground!
He has filled the court with his rat friends, very gentle,
White, squeaking, courteous folk, who show their teeth
Only when cornered; who smile at you, speak you fair
And spend their nights gnawing the floors and chairs
Out from under us all!

ELIZABETH
My lord!

ESSEX
I am
Not the gnawing kind, nor will I speak fair
To those who don't mean me well . . . no, nor to those
To whom I mean no good! I say frankly here,
Yes, to their faces, that Cecil and Walter Raleigh
Have made themselves my enemies because
They cannot brook greatness or power in any but
Themselves! And I say this to them . . . and to the world . . .
I, too, have been ambitious, as all men are
Who bear a noble mind, but if I rise
It will be by my own effort, and not by dragging
Better men down through intrigue! I admit
Sir Walter Raleigh's skill as a general

And Cecil's statecraft! I could work with them freely
And cheerfully, but every time I turn
My back they draw their knives! When Cecil left England
I guarded his interests as I would my own
Because he asked me to . . . but when I left,
And left my affairs in his hands . . . on my return
I found my plans and my friends out in the rain
Along with the London beggars!

CECIL

I did my best . . .

ESSEX

Aye . . . the best for yourself! For the good of the state!

RALEIGH

If Lord Essex wishes
To say he is my enemy, very well . . .
He is my enemy.

ESSEX

But you were mine first.
And I call the gods to witness you would be my friend
Still, if I'd had my way! I take it hard
That here, in the queen's council, where there should be
Magnanimous minds if anywhere, there is still
No trust or friendship!

ELIZABETH

I take it hard that you
Should quarrel before me.

ESSEX

Would you have us quarrel
Behind your back? It suits them all too well
To quarrel in secret and knife men down in the dark!

BURGHLEY

This is fantastic, my lord. There has been no knifing.
Let us come to a decision. We were discussing
The Irish protectorate.

Craftily now Lord Cecil is willing to leave the question of who shall go to Ireland up to Lord Essex, unless, seeing it is a difficult and dangerous post, he had rather refuse to risk his fame there.

There is no fear in Lord Essex, but he will not go as second in command. Nor will Raleigh go unless Essex go with him. Which brings a sneer from Essex.

"Why, what is this that hangs over Ireland," he demands, "is it haunted, this Ireland? Is it a kind of hell where men are damned if they set foot on it? I've never seen the place, but if it's a country like other countries, with people like other people in it, it's nothing to be afraid of, more than France or Wales or Flanders or anywhere else."

"We hear you say so," Lord Cecil smiles.

"If I am challenged to go to Ireland then, Christ, I'll go!" cries Essex. "Give me what men and horses I need, and put me in absolute charge, and if I fail to bring this Tyrone's head back with me, and put the rebellion to sleep forever, take my sword from me and break it . . . I'll never use it again!"

And to Elizabeth, now powerless to stop him, though she cautions that he reflect a little, Essex says:

"My queen, I can see that Raleigh and Cecil have set themselves to bait me into Ireland! They know and I know that Ireland has been deadly to any captain who risked his fortunes there; moreover, once I'm gone they think to strip me here at home, ruin me both ways! And I say to them 'Try it!' There are men who are greater than Ireland or their chicane. Since this is a challenge I go, and go alone, and return victorious, and, by God, more of a problem to Cecils and Raleighs than when I went!"

Thus the matter is settled to the distress of the friends of Essex and the exultation of his enemies. Even the queen's fool would plead with his lordship not to undertake the mission.

"I come from Ireland," says the fool. "All the best fools come from Ireland but only a very great fool will go there."

Essex pushes the fool aside and is content. The council files from the room as Elizabeth rises from her chair.

The queen is anxious, and a little sad, when she and Essex are alone. She had tried hard to warn him as she saw them drawing him into their trap. There is still time for him to withdraw, if he will.

But Essex will not withdraw, nor let her countermand the order. They shall not have the laugh on him. He will win in Ireland, and have the laugh on them. Let her mistrust all her forebodings.

"Remember this when I'm back and all turns out well," he cries with feverish enthusiasm; "that you felt all would turn out badly."

ELIZABETH

Oh, my love,
Come touch me, tell me all will happen well.

ESSEX
And so it will.

ELIZABETH
Do you want to go?

ESSEX
Why, yes . . .
And no. I've said I would and I will.

ELIZABETH
It's not yet
Too late. There are no announcements made, no orders
Given. If you win, that will divide us . . .
And if you lose, that will divide us too.

ESSEX
I'll win, and it will not divide us. Is it so hard
To believe in me?

ELIZABETH
No, I'll believe in you . . .
And even forgive you if you need it. Here.
My father gave me this ring . . . and told me if ever
He lost his temper with me, to bring it to him
And he'd forgive me. And so it saved my life . . .
Long after, when he'd forgotten, long after, when
One time he was angry.

ESSEX
Darling, if ever
You're angry rings won't help.

ELIZABETH
Yes, but it would.
I'd think of you as you are now, and it would.
Take it.

ESSEX
I have no pledge from you. I'll take it
To remember you in absence.

ELIZABETH
Take it for a better reason. Take it because
The years are long, and full of sharp, wearing days
That wear out what we are and what we have been
And change us into people we do not know,
Living among strangers. Lest you and I who love
Should wake some morning strangers and enemies
In an alien world, far off; take my ring, my lover.

ESSEX
You fear

You will not always love me?

Elizabeth

No, that you
Will not love me, and will not let me love you.

(*She puts the ring on his finger as the curtain falls.*)

ACT II

In the queen's study, some months later, the Court fool is seeking to interest the Lady Penelope in his raillery. The fool loves Penelope, it may be; or it may be that, knowing her heart to be elsewhere, the fool is only sorry for Penelope. In either case neither is happy. Lord Essex is in Ireland and his friends are uneasy.

Robert Cecil shortly meets Sir Walter Raleigh in the study. Lord Bacon, they know, is expected by the queen and they plan to intercept him. When he joins them Cecil would know from Bacon certain things concerning his correspondence with Lord Essex, and impart to Bacon the information that the queen is even now in possession of news that Essex has allied himself with the Irish rebels and is leading his army back to England to usurp Elizabeth's throne.

Lord Bacon is not convinced. If it be so he would credit it to their own schemes. He does not accuse them of treason, but is frank to say that "if the queen were aware of certain matters she would herself accuse you of treason."

Cecil—Look to yourself, Master Bacon. If you intend to accuse any man of the suppression of letters written by Essex to the queen, or the suppression of letters sent by the queen to Essex, you will be unable to prove these assertions and you will argue yourself very neatly into the Tower.

Bacon—My lord . . . I had no such business in mind.

Raleigh—Then what? . . .

Bacon—I hope I can keep my own counsel. The truth is, my lords, you are desperate men. You have overreached yourselves, and if wind of it gets to the royal ears you are done.

Raleigh—We shall drag a few down with us if we are done, though, and you the first.

Cecil—You have but a poor estimate of me, Master Bacon. If you go in to the queen and reveal to her that her letters to Essex have not reached him . . . as you mean to do . . . the queen will then send for me, and I will send for Lord Essex' last letter to you, containing a plan for the capture of the City of London. It will interest you to know that I have read that letter and you are learned enough in the law to realize in what light you will stand as a witness should the queen see it.

BACON—I think it is true, though, that if I go down I shall also drag a few with me, including those here present.

CECIL—I am not so sure of that, either. I am not unready for that contingency. But to be frank with you, it would be easier for both you and us if you were on our side.

BACON—You must expect a man to side with his friends.

CECIL—A man's friends . . . who are they? Those who can help him to what he wants.

BACON—Not always.

CECIL—When he is wise. You have served Lord Essex well and I believe he has made you promises. But the moment Essex enters England in rebellion, he is doomed, and his friends with him.

BACON—One word from the queen to him . . . one word from him to the queen . . . one word from me, revealing that their letters have been intercepted, and there can be no talk of rebellion. There has been some underhand traffic with the couriers between here and Ireland. Their letters have been lost, you have induced the queen to promulgate arbitrary orders . . . and since they are both proud, you have bred distrust in her and defiance in him. Your machinations have been so direct, so childish, so simple . . . and so simply exposed . . . that I wonder at you!

CECIL—My friend, a child could trip him. Not so simple as your own. I have news this morning that Lord Essex has already landed in England and set up his standard here. He is a rebel, and when a man is once a rebel, do you think there will be any careful inquiry into how he happened to become one?

BACON—Essex in England!

CECIL—In England.

RALEIGH—And has neglected to disband his army.

CECIL—You speak of explanations between the queen and Essex. Unless you betray us there will be no explanations. They are at war and will never meet again.

BACON—That is, if your plan succeed.

CECIL (*standing aside*)—Very well, then. Go in. You have chosen your master. I have done with you.

BACON (*not moving*)—And if I say nothing?

CECIL—Then . . . whatever you have been promised, whatever

you have desired, that you shall have. There is no place in the courts you could not fill. You shall have your choice. If you need excuse, no one should know better than you that this Essex is a danger to the state, a danger to the queen, a danger to liberty.

BACON—If I need excuse I shall find one for myself.

Queen Elizabeth finds them there. Her greeting of Cecil and Raleigh is curt. She dismisses them with a word and turns to Bacon with but little more show of friendliness. She would know where he stands. Is he still with his friend, Lord Essex? Or is he prepared to change that allegiance?

Lord Bacon has been the friend of Essex many years and has no cause now to desert him. Nor will desert him without stronger proof than rumor of his alleged rebellion against the queen.

That Elizabeth has proof she believes. She has at least enough proof to impel her to suggest that if Lord Bacon would escape the Tower, as one accused with Lord Essex as a rebel, he would better make his choice immediately. Still Bacon will not change.

"I neither believe our Essex a rebel nor that you believe so," he says. "If you intended to place me in the Tower . . . I would be in the Tower . . . and no talk about it."

"You are shrewd indeed."

"I am Essex' friend."

"If that were true . . . if I could speak to you . . . if there were only the sound of one honest voice! . . . I must rule England, and they say he is rebel to me . . . and day and night, waking, sleeping, in council, there is always one thing crying out in me over and again . . . Waking and sleeping I hear it crying: He cannot, cannot fail me! But I have written him my love and he has not answered. What you know of this answer me truly, truly . . . bitter or not, and you shall not lose!"

It is Lord Essex' silence that worries Bacon. If he could understand that he could explain a great deal. Has Elizabeth angered Essex?

She has, Elizabeth admits, ordered Essex to disband his forces and return to England. And she has cut off his revenue and supplies. But has she not had great cause? She has written Lord Essex lovingly, and he has ignored her letters. That she cannot forgive.

"He has written you, but not me," charges the queen. "Or are you traitor to him also? . . . I think you are! I think you lie to me! I am encompassed by lies! I think you, too, betray him . . . but subtly, with infinite craft, making me believe first you would not wrong him! No, no . . . I'm gone mad pacing my room, pacing the room of my mind. They say a woman's mind is an airless room, sunless and airless, where she must walk alone saying he loves me, loves me, loves me not, and has never loved me. The world goes by, all shadows, and there are voices, all echoes till he speaks . . . and there's no light till his presence makes a light there in that room. But I am a queen. Where I walk is a hall of torture, where the curious gods bring all their racks and gyves, and stretch me out there to writhe till I cry out. They watch me with eyes of iron waiting to hear what I cry! I am crying now . . . Listen, you gods of iron! He never loved me . . . He wanted my kingdom only . . . Loose me and let me go! I am yet a queen . . . That I have! That he will not take from me! I shall be queen and walk his room no more. He thought to break me down by not answering . . . Break me until I'd say, I'm all yours . . . what I am and have, all yours! That I will never, never, never say. I'm not broken yet."

Bacon is sympathetic. He is the queen's friend. If she wills that he shall see Essex no more he will agree. But though she assures him that he has her trust Lord Bacon is no more than out of the room before Elizabeth has summoned her guard and ordered that he be followed and that a watch be put upon his house and his correspondence.

Furthermore the queen instructs the guard, Captain Armin, to heed no other orders but her own; that if Lord Essex shall appear, even though it be reported that he heads a rebellious army, he shall not be denied access to her presence. She will risk whatever danger there may be to her person. Her one command is that Captain Armin shall be ready for danger and, if need be, for death.

Now the fool, grown playful with the ladies of the court, having filched a garment from one of them which they all try to take from him, romps into the room, followed by several shrilly protesting females. It is boisterous play and they do not see the queen until she turns and leaves the room. Then they are anxious lest they be whipped for their fooling.

The scene shifts to the interior of Lord Essex' tent on the coast of England. His lordship is reading dispatches by the light of the candle when Marvel, his towering orderly, announces a courier from the queen.

It is word that Essex has long been waiting, and he is suspicious of its delayed delivery. He may want to test this messenger's honesty by threat of torture or death. If so Marvel shall stand by.

The courier is quick to explain that he has, in fact, been delayed by robbers. They had taken from his party their horses and their money but had returned the letter he bears untouched, seal unbroken.

Essex will not believe the story. This courier is a liar, he loudly insists, as were the two others who preceded him. And this one shall pay for being the third.

"Take his weapons from him, lieutenant," Essex orders. "Set him against the post there. Not so gently. He shall lose his ears first and then his lying tongue."

Pitifully the courier pleads his innocence, nor can he give the names of any accomplices, for there have been none. Even as they approach him to tear out his tongue the unhappy man continues to protest not only his innocence, but his refusal to believe that so noble and well-loved a leader as Essex would torture innocent men.

"If my Lord Essex is as I have believed him, he will not hurt me," declares the courier, calmly. "If he will hurt me, then he is not as I and many thousands believe him, who have loved him, and I shall not mind much dying."

The courier is, on Essex' order, unbound. He has convinced his general that he has spoken the truth and held nothing back. The message, the courier repeats, was handed to him by the queen herself and there was no other message.

A moment later Lord Essex has issued orders that his command shall break camp the following day and proceed to London, though not under orders. The dispatch from the queen reads:

"Lord Essex is required to disperse his men and return to the capitol straightway on his own recognizance, to give himself up."

ESSEX

Give out the necessary orders, we shall
Move at daybreak.

MARVEL

Yes, my lord.

ESSEX

And it is
As well it falls out this way! By right of name
And power and popular voice this is my kingdom . . .
This England under my feet, more mine than hers,
As she shall learn. It is quite as well.

MARVEL

There is no man
But will think so. There is victory in your path,
My lord. The London citizens will rise
At the first breath of your name.

ESSEX

Yes . . . that I'm sure of.

MARVEL

And with London in your hands . . . well . . . it's your world then.
As far as you like.

ESSEX

And I am glad for England.
She has lain fallow in fear too long! Her hills
Shall have a spring of victory. Good night.

MARVEL

Good night.

ESSEX

And for this order, I received it not. (*He tears the paper.*)

The council hall has been cleared for court assembly. Already many are gathered—the fool, Penelope, Ellen, Mary, Tressa, and many other ladies-in-waiting. Sir Francis Bacon is there. Lords Burghley and Cecil are talking earnestly at one side.

The talk is desultory. Mostly, so far as Cecil and Burghley dominate it, the subject is that of certain players who have had the audacity to repeat the tragedy of "Richard II" in public, a play in which, as Cecil points out, a king is deposed. The play, therefore, is treasonous in that it teaches treason.

The others are less concerned, the fool least concerned of all. He would have the players repeat the play. Burghley is convinced it was the Essex faction that had sent money to the actors to pay for their performance of Richard. Which, argues Cecil, would make the actors accessory to the treasonous intent of the Essex party—a purpose proved by the fact of Lord Essex having led his army into London.

Lord Bacon can see no proof in this. Essex' men live in London. The order to disperse his army on landing may not have been received. Such things have happened.

Now the conversation is general and airy. Elizabethan puns fall here and there, being tossed about by the fool and the courtiers who would match wit with him. Occasionally there is mention of Essex' approach and its possible consequences. Burghley and Cecil continue to be disturbed because Her Majesty has refused to show a proper fear nor made a move toward the defense of the city.

"Essex draws near with his army and we swing the gates as usual," protests Cecil.

"Is that a symptom of danger . . . that an English general should return with his army to the English capital?" asks Bacon.

"Are you aware that Essex' house in the Strand is a camp brimming full of armed nobles coming and going?"

"It is much more likely to be brimming with drunken nobles coming and going brim full," chortles the fool.

Now Her Majesty has entered, quietly, followed by two of her ladies. She is looking for Lord Burghley and it is in regard to the players that she would speak to him. On what ground did he forbid the performance of "Richard II" without asking her advice?

The play is treasonous, insists Burghley. For that reason he forbade it. Its performance was procured by rebels. What rebels? To discover that he has sent for the players.

THE QUEEN—They will laugh at you, dear Burghley.

BURGHLEY—Others have laughed at me, Majesty.

THE QUEEN—They will laugh at you, sir, and you will deserve it. Is my kingdom so shaky that we dare not listen to a true history? Are my people so easily led that the sight of a king deposed in play will send them running thither to pull the queen out of her chair? Have we not passion plays in every little town showing the murder of our Lord? You are nervous, Lord Burghley. Let these children play their plays.

CECIL—Your Majesty, I very much fear they are not all children, and that they mean to do harm.

THE QUEEN—Then let them. Let them do all the harm they can. Are we too stupid to see that to prohibit a rebellious play is to proclaim our fear of rebellion? Who is there here who fears a rebellion against me? I do not.

CECIL—It is dangerous to let these mutterings grow, dear queen.

ELIZABETH—It is dangerous to touch them. Let them mutter, if they will. Let them cry out . . . let them run the streets, these children! When they have worn themselves weary running and crying "Up with Essex!" "Down with Elizabeth!" and got themselves drunk on mutual pledges, they will go to bed and sleep soundly and wake up wiser. Let me speak to these players. Bring them to me.

BURGHLEY—Here, madame?

ELIZABETH—Here.

CECIL—Majestas, adsunt legati de curia Galliæ. Placetne eos recipere antequam . . .

THE QUEEN—Cras illos recipiam.

CECIL—Sed maxime præstat . . .

THE QUEEN—Si bene mihi videbitur, crasredituros recipiam! Nay, I can bang you in Latin too.

Cecil has gone, and Elizabeth turns to her fool to change her mood. This fool, she has heard, has fallen in love and should be whipped for it. If so, counters the fool, his queen should buy more than one whip so there would be several with which she might whip herself.

But he has not fallen in love, pleads the fool. A pretty little strumpet has fallen in love with him and he has promised to marry her.

"What," demands Elizabeth in solemn protest, "are there strumpets at court?"

"Oh, they are all strumpets here at court," answers the fool. "Some are here because they are strumpets and some are strumpets because they are here, but strumpets they are all."

It is Tressa the fool would marry. Or Ellen. Or Mary. He cannot remember positively.

"I feel sure it was one of them, Majesty . . . but it was dark at the time . . . and in truth I gave her my word of honor in the dark that I would make an honest woman of her by daylight. It is thus that most marriages are made."

"How, fool?"

"In the dark, my lady. Quite in the dark."

For his sins the queen would have the fool put in the dark for three days, with very little bread and water. And let them take Penelope Gray with him, though they are not to see each other. Let them be whipped first—

"Your Majesty, what is this?" protests the surprised Penelope.

"I am weary to death of you," Elizabeth answers her. "I am weary of all men and women, but more of you than any! You have written. You have had letters! I say, take her out of my sight! (*The soldiers start to take out* PENELOPE *and the fool.*) Whip them first, whip them both! (*The two are taken to the door.*) Nay, leave them here, leave them, knaves . . . leave them. Damn you, do you hear me! You are too quick to obey orders! You like this whipping too well, sirrah! You have an itch for laying on! You beef-witted bastards! And now let us have entertainment, gentle lords! Let us be merry! The players are here! Let us have a play!"

And now a herald interrupts the court, entering without ceremony. He is breathless with excitement and come to report that there is a rising in London; that crowds of people are thronging through Fleet Street, sacking groceries and wineshops and shouting, "Up with Essex!" "Down with Elizabeth!" But the queen is not troubled.

"What else would they be crying?" she demands. " 'Up with Essex!' Viva! 'Down with Elizabeth!' A bas! The queen is dead, long live the king! If I were there I would cry it myself. It has a marvelous ring. 'Up with Essex!' 'Down with Elizabeth!' "

Such a rising, Elizabeth decides, to the consternation of Burghley and Cecil, is the Lord Mayor's business and none of hers. Let the Lord Mayor look to his own people. And if the revolution should spread to the Palace, what of it? The queen would be amused to see it. "They are children, Burghley, drunken children," she answers them. "Would you fire on children?" Let them forget the revolution and bring in the players. A moment later Richard Burbage and John Hemmings stand before her.

ELIZABETH—Ah, yes, bold Burbage and handsome Hemmings. Well, my masters, I understand that you have come to me to have your noses slit and your thumbs branded? Is it so?

BURBAGE—Only if unavoidable, Your Majesty.

ELIZABETH—You have put on a play, I believe?

BURBAGE—Many, Your Majesty.

ELIZABETH—You have revived the old play of "Richard II," including in it the deposition scene which was censored on its first presentation, and you have done this to foster treasonous projects.

BURBAGE—No, Your Majesty, I swear it.

ELIZABETH—You have not played this play?

BURBAGE—But not to foster treason, that I swear.

ELIZABETH—If you played Richard with that pot belly it was treason indeed. Then for what purpose?

BURBAGE—To make money.

ELIZABETH—On an old play?

BURBAGE—We were paid in advance . . .

ELIZABETH—By whom?

BURBAGE—By Lord Southampton.

BURGHLEY—You see? A friend of Essex.

ELIZABETH—You have much too handsome a nose for slitting, Master Hemmings, yet you say nothing.

HEMMINGS—There is only this to say, Your Majesty . . . that we knew nothing of any traitorous intent in the matter . . . and that, if we had known of such intent, we would not have given the performance.

ELIZABETH—I think you are all traitorous knaves and rascals, as a matter of fact, in league with Essex and Southampton and the smoothest liars in Christendom. Is there something in this?

HEMMINGS—No, madam.

ELIZABETH—You know Essex and Southampton?

HEMMINGS—We know Lord Southampton.

ELIZABETH—How much were you paid for the revival of "Richard?"

HEMMINGS—Three pounds, Your Majesty.

ELIZABETH—No more?

HEMMINGS—No more.

ELIZABETH—Play it again this afternoon, masters, play it at my request this afternoon, and you shall have ten pounds for it. Lord Cecil, pay Master Burbage ten pounds from the royal exchequer for one performance of "Richard." And let it stand in the record.

CECIL—Yes, madam.

ELIZABETH (*to* HEMMINGS)—And tell Lord Southampton when you see him that I paid ten to his three. Will you tell him?

HEMMINGS—Yes, Your Majesty.

ELIZABETH—And when you have all this treason out of your systems be ready to play Sir John Falstaff for me at the end of the week. I should like to see your Falstaff again, sir.

BURBAGE—Yes, Your Majesty.

ELIZABETH—You may go.

The queen, insists Lord Cecil, is quite mad. Rebellion flares at her very door and she takes no heed of it. Half the town is in uprising and she will do nothing. Lord Essex has been seen with an armed force in the city—

At that news the queen is more attentive. If one might guess Essex is probably even then on his way to the palace? Good. The queen will be glad to see him. How long do they think the revolution will last once she has looked on it.

A door is suddenly thrown open, and from the hall a chorus of angry voices breaks. Rising above the tumult is the voice of Lord Essex. "I say the queen will see me! Stand back!" There is a clank of armor and Essex strides defiantly into the room.

"You come with a file of soldiers at your back, my Lord Essex," greets the queen.

"Do I need them, Your Majesty?"

"No."

"Then be off with you," Essex commands the officers at his back. "Follow my orders." His troops fall back.

"They told me you would not see me," explains Essex.

"They were wrong," the queen replies. "I will see you. It seems you are in rebellion, my good Lord. Enter and state your grievance, if you have a grievance. For myself, I have a great affection for rebels, being one myself much of the time."

He is no rebel, Essex explains. He has but recently come from Ireland with news of Her Majesty's subjects there. He did not disband his army at the coast, as ordered, because he thought it unwise. An army turned loose becomes a mob. He had himself paid his men, which, though it may have increased their devotion to him, as she charges, also made them as devotedly hers as was their leader.

What of Ireland? Essex should have conquered Ireland, with time and proper support, he insists. As it is he left it worse than it was before. But the fault, if any, lay with Elizabeth for failing in that support. It is true, as she intimates, that he had had conferences with the rebel Tyrone, but these were part of his plan.

And why did he not write her of these plans?

He did write, fully many times, and received no answer to what he wrote.

This is news indeed to Her Majesty. "Before God if the couriers were tampered with there shall be some necks stretched here," she promises, as she turns to Cecil and Burghley. "My lords, I wish to speak with Lord Essex here alone. Leave us."

They are loath to go, but withdraw with the others. As soon as she and Essex are alone Elizabeth returns to the subject of the letters. "What did you write me?" she asks anxiously.

ESSEX

I wrote you of my love—for I thought you loved me then—
And then I pled with you not to bring me home
In the midst of my mission—and then at last angrily—

For I had not heard—but always to say I loved you—
Always.

ELIZABETH
But is this true?

ESSEX
Would I lie?

ELIZABETH
Someone
Has lied and will pay with his life if this is true!—
Before God and hell—someone will pay for this.

ESSEX
What did you write me?

ELIZABETH
I wrote—my love—
God keep you safe—I know not—and then, not hearing,
I wrote God knows what madness—as to a rebel—
Thinking you no longer mine—faithless!
Thinking—

ESSEX
I would I had known—I was in torment—
I—forgive me—

ELIZABETH
You should never have gone away.
God, how I've hated you!—

ESSEX
No!

ELIZABETH
Planned to put you to torture!

ESSEX
I have been in torture. (*He steps toward her.*)

ELIZABETH
Not yet—I can't breathe yet—I can't breathe—
Or think or believe—

ESSEX
Nor I.

ELIZABETH
Can we ever—
Believe again? Can it be as it used to be?

ESSEX
We can make it so.

ELIZABETH
Come, kill me if you will. Put your arms round me—
If you love me. Do you still love me?

ESSEX
Yes.
ELIZABETH
Yes, yes—
If this were false then, then truly—then I should die.
I thought because I was older—you see—someone else—
ESSEX
No one—never a breath—
ELIZABETH
Is it all—all as before?
ESSEX
We have not changed.
ELIZABETH
No. Yes, a little, perhaps.
They have changed us a little.
ESSEX
Not I. I have not changed.
ELIZABETH
Can I trust you now?
ESSEX
Sweet, think back, all those months,
All those hideous months! No word, no love.
And when word did come, it was to make me prisoner!
Christ, I have pride!
And though I came here in defiance, I came truly to find you
Who have been lost from me.
ELIZABETH
Do you ask forgiveness?
It is all forgiven.
ESSEX
Then, why then, hell's vanished—
And here's heaven risen out of it, a heaven of years
In the midst of desolate centuries.
ELIZABETH
We have so few years.
Let us make them doubly sweet, these years we have,
Be gracious with each other, sway a little
To left or right if we must stay together—
Never distrust each other—nay, distrust
All others, when they whisper. Let us make this our pact
Now, for the fates are desperate to part us
And the very gods envy this happiness
We pluck out of loss and death.

Essex

If two stand shoulder to shoulder against the gods,
Happy together, the gods themselves are helpless
Against them, while they stand so.

Even in the ecstasy of this reunion personal ambition issues a threatening call. Elizabeth would give all to her Essex now. "You shall stand back of my chair and together we shall build an England to make the world wonder and the new world worship."

But Essex, seeking to be entirely honest, questions whether such a union as Elizabeth proposes would work to a desirable end. After all has he not an army at his back that would make him king? Being equal in love should they not be also equal in power?

"Am I not—and I say this, too, in all love—as worthy to be king as you to be queen? Must you be sovereign alone?"

"You are young in policy, my Essex, if you do not see that if I should grant high place to you now it would show ill to the kingdom. It would be believed that you had forced this on me, would be called a revolution. It would undermine all confidence. What is built up for years in people's minds blows away like thistledown when such things get abroad."

Frankly Elizabeth further admits that she would not trust Lord Essex as king. Nor would not willingly give up her prerogatives. She may, as he intimates, be his prisoner even now, with the palace and the city practically in his hands, and England his for the taking—if so she is grievously disappointed. Is this his friendship? Is this his love?

"As water finds its level, so power goes to him who can use it, and soon or late the name of king follows where power is," Essex answers.

And so, Elizabeth discovers, because she had purposely taken no action in her own defense; had let Essex and his army come bravely home from Ireland unopposed that there might still appear to be a semblance of peace between them, she is now his prisoner!

And what does he purpose to do with her? Send her to the Tower? The block?

"You could hardly take a queen prisoner and have no thought of her destiny," declares Elizabeth. "I am my mother's daughter. I, too, can walk the path my mother walked."

"These are heroics," Essex insists. "You know you are free as air."

"If I do as you ask."

"Is it so hard to share your power with your love? I could have all and I offer to share with you."

ELIZABETH
Let's have no more pretending.
I'd have given all—but you came with an army, demanding—
In short, you don't love—nor trust me—no—nor want me—

ESSEX
God knows I have wanted you. I have wanted power—
Believed myself fitted to hold it—but not without you.

ELIZABETH
If you had wanted me would you rise and strike
At me with an army? Never, never! You'd have come
To me quietly, and we'd have talked of it together
As lovers should—and we'd both have our way—
And no one the wiser. But now, to take the palace,
Hold me prisoner—no—what you wanted you've taken—
And that is all you shall have. This is your kingdom—
But I—I am not yours.

ESSEX
But I am yours
And have been.

ELIZABETH
Who will believe that? Not the world,
No, and not I. I'd rather go to the Tower
Than share my place on terms like these. Put me where I
Will do least harm.

ESSEX
I cannot, could not, will not.

ELIZABETH
If I could have given freely—
But not now. Not surrendering. Not to a victor.

ESSEX
I am no victor if I lose you. The only gift
That I could take from you, is that we are equals.

ELIZABETH
Yes, but not now.

ESSEX
I ask one word from you.
Give me this word—this one word—and these soldiers

Shall leave, and you shall be free.

ELIZABETH

I'll believe that
When it happens.

ESSEX

I'll believe you when you promise.

ELIZABETH

Then you have my promise.
You shall share the realm with me. As I am queen,
I promise it.

ESSEX

Then this is my answer. (*He kisses her then calls.*)
Marvel! Marvel! (MARVEL *enters.*)
Carry out the order of release. Dismiss my guard—
Return the palace into the queen's hands.
Retire with all our forces to the Strand.
Release all prisoners. Release the queen's guard
And send them to their stations. (MARVEL *goes out.*)
The palace will be
Returned as quickly as taken. This is our last quarrel.

ELIZABETH

Yes—our last.

MARVEL'S VOICE (*off-stage*)

Form for retire!

ANOTHER VOICE

Form for retire!

A MORE DISTANT VOICE

Form for retire!

A VOICE (*in the distance*)

Ready to march!

ANOTHER VOICE

Ready to march!

ANOTHER

All ready!

ANOTHER

Ready, captain! (MARVEL *enters.*)

MARVEL

The order is obeyed, my lord.

ESSEX

Follow your men.

MARVEL

Yes, my lord. (*He goes out.*)

ESSEX
It is as I planned. They are leaving the palace.
Now let us talk no more of this tonight—
Let us forget this matter of thrones and kingdoms
And be but you and me for a while.

ELIZABETH (*immobile*)
Yes—yes—
Let us forget. Have you kept your word indeed?

ESSEX
I have kept my word.

ELIZABETH
If I clapped my hands
Would my guard come now—or yours?

ESSEX
Yours only. Shall I call them?

ELIZABETH
No—I'll call them. (*She claps her hands four times.* CAPTAIN ARMIN *appears in the entrance followed by four beef-eaters with halberds. They stand at attention in the entrance.*)
To be sure I have a guard
Once more. (*To the* CAPTAIN.)
The palace has been returned? It is in our hands?

CAPTAIN
Yes, Majesty.

ELIZABETH
I have ruled England a long time, my Essex,
And I have found that he who would rule must be
Quite friendless, without mercy, without love.
Arrest Lord Essex!
Arrest Lord Essex! Take him to the Tower
And keep him safe.

ESSEX
Is this a jest?

ELIZABETH
I never
Jest when I play for kingdoms, my lord Essex.

ESSEX
I trusted you.

ELIZABETH
I trusted you,
And learned from you that no one can be trusted.
I will remember that.

ESSEX

Lest that should be all
You ever have to remember, Your Majesty,
Take care what you do.

ELIZABETH

I shall take care. (ESSEX *unsheathes his sword, breaks it across his knee, flings it at the foot of the throne, turns and walks out between the two files of guards. The curtain falls.*)

ACT III

It is dawn of the day set for Lord Essex' execution. In the queen's apartments in the Tower, "a square and heavy room, long and with a raised stone platform, at one end of which stands a regal chair, the fool, who has been trying to sleep wrapped in the draperies of the queen's chair, is aroused by the weeping of Ellen, who has but now come from Her Majesty's chamber after having been slapped by the queen and curtly dismissed."

Ellen's reading aloud had worn upon the patience of a nerve-taut sovereign.

The Lady Penelope is also close to tears. Nor can her grief be lightened by the anxious fool, who still is certain Her Majesty will not let Essex die, even though it is now five o'clock and the execution set for six.

Yet the queen has sent many messages, Penelope reports, and Essex has answered none of them. "He's as silent as if he wanted to die," or so it seems to Penelope. And the queen would have her proud prisoner beg her pardon.

"She says she gave him a ring once," says Penelope. "If he ever wanted forgiveness he was to send the ring. And he sits there stubbornly with the ring on his finger. Oh, God, will nothing happen?"

Now Elizabeth has come from her chamber, restless and heavy-eyed from nights of wakefulness. All but Penelope she sends from her. There is now a bond of sympathy between these two. Penelope has also loved Essex, yet knew his heart was given to his queen.

"He said 'I love her dearly,' " confesses Penelope to Elizabeth, "I wanted him for myself and I warned him against you. He laughed at me. He said, 'I love her very dearly.' "

"You tell me this because you want to save him."

"No, dear queen, it's true."

"This is the end of me, dear," sighs Elizabeth, "this is the end.

It comes late. I've been a long while learning, but I've learned it now. Life is bitter. Nobody dies happy, queen or no. Will he speak, think you? Will he send to me?"

"No, not now."

"You see, this is the end of me. Oh, I shall live, I shall walk about and give orders . . . a horrible while . . . a horrible old hag."

"You must send for him," urges Penelope. "He's proud as you are, and you have the upper hand. He'll say nothing. You must send for him, bring him here."

Chimes ring the quarter hour. Querulously Elizabeth demands that the players, who have been sent for, be brought forth. She calls, too, for her fool. But he is not a merry fool. A weeping fool, rather, and is sent away again.

When the actors arrive, costumed for Falstaff, they are urged by their queen to hurry into their scene, the comedy scene beginning with Falstaff's speech: "I call thee coward? I'll see thee damned ere I call thee coward!"

They play it heavily through to the end, the queen hearing little of it, pacing the floor in torment and finally dismissing the players as vile actors performing in a vile play.

Now the clock has chimed the half hour and still there is no word. Cecil has come, and there is a momentary hope that he has brought word from Essex, but he has come only to report the gathering of a protesting mob in the courtyard and to ask that the queen send her guard to disperse it.

The sneer in Elizabeth's voice is but thinly veiled as she answers him.

"It is your day, Cecil," she says. "I daresay you know that. The snake-in-the-grass endures, and those who are noble, free of soul, valiant and admirable . . . they go down in the prime, always they go down."

"Madam, the guard is needed at once."

"Aye . . . the snake mind is best . . . One by one you outlast them. To the end of time it will be so . . . the rats inherit the earth. Take my guard. Take it. I thought you brought word from . . . Go, call Lord Essex for me from his cell . . . and bring him thither! I'll wait no longer."

"Lord Essex is prepared for execution. The priest has been sent to him."

"Bring him here, I say, and now, at once!"

Elizabeth is seated in the royal chair to receive Essex, dressed in black and very pale.

Having been summoned he has come, Essex announces. But it would have been kinder, he thinks, had he been left with his thoughts until the ax came down and ended them.

"Are you so set on dying?" demands the queen.

"I can't say I care for it," answers Essex. "This blood that beats in us has a way of wanting to keep right on. But if one is to die it's well to go straight toward it."

"You must have known I never meant you to die."

"I am under sentence from Your Majesty's courts. There's no appeal that I know of. I am found guilty of treason on good evidence, and cannot deny it. This treason, I believe, is punishable with death."

Even though the prompting is apparent Essex refuses to take advantage of this opportunity further to plead his cause, nor yet to talk as a lover might for fear by doing so he would seem to be trying to save his head.

ELIZABETH

It's true that you never
Loved me, isn't it? You were ambitious, and I
Loved you, and it was the nearest way to power,
And you took the nearest way? No, no . . . one moment . . .
This is an hour for truth, if there's ever truth . . .
I'm older than you . . . but a queen; it was natural
You'd flatter me, speak me fair, and I believed you.
I'm sorry I believed you. Sorry for you
More than for me.

ESSEX

Why, yes . . . that's true enough.
Now may I go? This dying sticks in my mind,
And makes me poor company, I fear.

ELIZABETH

It was true?
It was true, then?

ESSEX

If you wish to make me tell you.
What you well know, how much I used to love you,
How much I have longed for you, very well, I will say it.
That's a small victory to win over me now,
But take it with the rest.

ELIZABETH

You did love me?

ESSEX
Yes.
ELIZABETH
And love me still?
ESSEX
Yes. You should know that, I think.
ELIZABETH
You kept my ring. You never sent my ring.
I've been waiting for it.
ESSEX
You may have it back
If you have use for it . . . I had thought to wear it
As far as my grave, but, take it.
ELIZABETH
I'd have forgiven
All that had passed, at any hour, day or night,
Since I last saw you. I have waited late at night
Thinking, tonight the ring will come, he will never
Hold out against me so long, but the nights went by
Somehow, like the days, and it never came,
Till the last day came, and here it is the last morning
And the chimes beating out the hours.
ESSEX
Dear, if I'd known . . .
But I could not have sent it.

If he had sent the ring, if he had claimed that promise of Elizabeth and she could not have kept it, explains Essex, it would have been much harder for him to die than it now will be.

But it is not too late, even now, insists the queen. If he will but offer the ring her forgiveness will be complete. Essex shall be pardoned, set free, and his estates returned to him. All will be as it was.

But that could never be, insists Essex, unless Elizabeth would also lose her throne. If he were free he would surely take it from her.

"Again?" protests the unhappy Elizabeth. "You'd play that game again?"

ESSEX
The games one plays
Are not the games one chooses always. I
Am still a popular idol of a sort.

There are mutterings over my imprisonment,
Even as it is . . . and if you should set me free
And confess your weakness by overlooking treason
And setting me up in power once more, the storm
That broke last time would be nothing to the storm
That would break over you then. As for myself,
I played for power and lost, but if I had
Another chance I think I'd play and win.

ELIZABETH

Why do you say this?

ESSEX

I say it because it's true.
I have loved you, love you now, but I know myself.
If I were to win you over and take my place
As it used to be, it would gall me. I have a weakness
For being first wherever I am. I refuse
To take pardon from you without warning you
Of this. And when you know it pardon becomes
Impossible.

ELIZABETH

You do this for me?

ESSEX

Why, yes,
But not altogether. Partly for England, too.
I've lost conceit of myself a little. A life
In prison's very quiet. It leads to thinking.
You govern England better than I should.
I'd lead her into wars, make a great name,
Perhaps, like Henry Fifth and leave a legacy
Of debts and bloodshed after me. You will leave
Peace, happiness, something secure. A woman governs
Better than a man, being a natural coward.
A coward rules best.

ELIZABETH

Still bitter.

ESSEX

Perhaps a little.
It's a bitter belief to swallow, but I believe it.
You were right all the time. (*The chimes ring three-quarters.*)
And now, if you'll pardon me,
I have an appointment near-by with a headsman.
He comes sharp on the hour.

ELIZABETH
You have an hour yet.
It's but struck five.

ESSEX
It struck five some time since.

ELIZABETH
It cannot go this way!

ESSEX
Aye, but it has.
It has and will. There's no way out. I've thought of it
Every way. Speak frankly. Could you forgive me
And keep your throne?

ELIZABETH
No.

ESSEX
Are you ready to give
Your crown up to me?

ELIZABETH
No. It's all I have. (*She rises.*)
Why, who am I
To stand here paltering with a rebel noble!
I am Elizabeth, daughter of a king,
The Queen of England, and you are my subject!
What does this mean, you standing here eye to eye
With me, your liege? You whom I made, and gave
All that you have, you, an upstart, defying
Me to grant pardon, lest you should sweep me from power
And take my place from me? I tell you if Christ his blood
Ran streaming from the heavens for a sign
That I should hold my hand you'd die for this,
You pretender to a throne upon which you have
No claim, you pretender to a heart, who have been
Hollow and heartless and faithless to the end!

ESSEX
If we'd met some other how we might have been happy . . .
But there's been an empire between us! I am to die . . .
Let us say that . . . let us begin with that . . .
For then I can tell you that if there'd been no empire
We could have been great lovers. If even now
You were not queen and I were not pretender,
That god who searches heaven and earth and hell
For two who are perfect lovers, could end his search
With you and me. Remember . . . I am to die . . .

And so I can tell you truly, out of all the earth
That I'm to leave, there's nothing I'm very loathe
To leave save you. Yet if I live I'll be
Your death or you'll be mine.

ELIZABETH

Give me the ring.

ESSEX

No.

ELIZABETH

Give me the ring. I'd rather you'd kill me
Than I killed you.

ESSEX

It's better for me as it is
Than that I should live and batten my fame and fortune
On the woman I love. I've thought of it all. It's better
To die young and unblemished than to live long and rule
And rule not well.

ELIZABETH

Aye, I should know that.

ESSEX

Is it not?

ELIZABETH

Yes.

ESSEX

Good-by, then.

ELIZABETH

Oh, then I'm old, I'm old!
I could be young with you, but now I'm old.
I know how it will be without you. The sun
Will be empty and circle around an empty earth . . .
And I will be queen of emptiness and death . . .
Why could you not have loved me enough to give me
Your love and let me keep as I was?

ESSEX

I know not.
I only know I could not. I must go.

ELIZABETH (*frozen*)

Yes.
(*He goes to the door.*)
Lord Essex.
(*He turns.*)
Take my kingdom. It is yours!

(ESSEX, *as if not hearing, bows and goes on.* PENELOPE *runs in, meeting him.*)

PENELOPE

My lord! She has forgiven you?

ESSEX

Good-by, my dear.

(*He kisses her.*)

PENELOPE

No, no! She loves you! Go to her.

(ESSEX *goes out.*)

Run to her! She waits you still! See if you turn

She waits you still! Dear queen, would you let him go?

He goes to his death! Send, send after him!

(*The queen lifts her face and shows a face so stricken that* PENELOPE, *who has gone to her, says no more. The clock strikes six.* ELIZABETH *bows her head on* PENELOPE'S *knees, her hands over her ears.*)

CURTAIN

TOMORROW AND TOMORROW

A Drama in Three Acts

BY PHILIP BARRY

THE early theatre season of 1930-31 in New York had been fairly barren of impressive drama, which may have had something to do with the immediate and unmistakable success of Philip Barry's "Tomorrow and Tomorrow," presented in mid-January at the Henry Miller Theatre.

Stanch adherents of the play, however, would be quick to resent the suggestion. This play's success, they insist, and I happen to agree with them, is due primarily to the power and appeal engendered by its writing, which is expert. It is a physically compact and psychologically sound drama. Few plays are written with as little waste and few with as strong a human appeal as this one.

The framework of "Tomorrow and Tomorrow" (which originally was called "Hail and Farewell") is found in the Old Testament, beginning with the eighth verse of the fourth chapter of II Kings. It is the story of the prophet Elisha, his servant, Gehazi, and the Shunammite woman, in which the miracle of the birth of a son to the woman who thought herself barren is biologically modernized and dramatically romanticized.

It is a play so sensitively and delicately wrought in both character and situation that it demands intelligent casting and direction. These, fortunately, it received at the hands of Gilbert Miller in the New York production.

The scene of "Tomorrow and Tomorrow" is the living room of Gail and Eve Redman's house in Redmanton, Ind. "It is a spacious, high-ceilinged, rectangular room in a house that was the town's and Gail's grandfather's pride when he built it in 1870."

Of this room Mr. Barry also says: "It has been lived in long enough to have lost a portion of the forbidding dignity that was its original chief characteristic. Now it presents itself as a fairly comfortable, agreeable enough old room, for brighter, newer things have been added, such as lamps and sofa-cushions and vases full of flowers, deftly placed. Chairs and sofa are covered for the summer with slip-covers."

It is 1 o'clock in the morning of an early summer day, "several years ago." A dim light has been left in the hall and a reading lamp is lighted in the living room. Otherwise the house is dark.

Gail Redman, "thirty, tall, well-built, likeable-looking," lets himself in through the hall. He carries a suitcase and a light overcoat. He apparently is stiff and tired from a long ride. He would put out the lights and go to bed, but at the moment he spies a plate of sandwiches and a thermos bottle of milk on a side table. They interest him, despite his weariness.

Eve Redman has heard Gail come in. She calls from the top of the stairs and a moment later comes down to join him. It has been ten days since Gail left for the reunion of his college class and it seems something more than an age to both of them.

Now we have Gail's first fragmentary reports of the reunion and the fun of it. The fun and the disappointments. Reunions do make a fellow feel aged, if not infirm. And yet at the moment Gail, to Eve, seems terribly young—younger even than she had remembered his being.

There are also Eve's casual reports of the ten days that have passed slowly at home. Things have happened at the works and at the college. The works have received a big order for harrows from Brazil or somewhere and President Adee of the college—Redman college—has announced a summer course that is to be for women as well as men.

The idea of the college his grandfather founded going co-educational, even to this extent, without so much as consulting him, a member of the board, is not altogether pleasing to Gail. But Eve loves it. She even plans to attend the summer classes.

There is a certain nervous excitement in Eve's enthusiasm that startles Gail. She is, he notices, awfully jumpy. Why?

Eve knows no particular reason. She is restless. She must, she feels, find something to do; something more than she has been doing. . . . She is talking rapidly now and has become suddenly conscious of a worrisome thought. She hurries on with her report.

"I gave two hundred dollars to the Infants' Summer Hospital —was that all right?"

"I guess so."

"The roof above the storeroom leaks. I've ordered it mended. The horses are fine. O'Brien says Eli's foot is coming along nicely.—The Science Department's got hold of a man called Hay, from Montreal—isn't that where McGill is?—Dr. Nicholas Hay, I think his name is—to start things with a four weeks' lecture-course, beginning Monday. The Adees say he's really fine. They heard him at Ohio State last winter. He's on a kind of tour. I told them he could stay with us."

Gail is a little disturbed at the idea of taking the visitor in. He will probably have whiskers and be very cranky. But, Eve is quite definitely pleased. It will be pleasant to have someone to do for. She hopes Dr. Hay is so old and absent-minded that he will not be able to do one thing for himself. It has been a long time since Eve has had anyone to look out for. Gail is one of the independent kind. He does everything for himself.

"You still love me, don't you, dear?" Gail asks, a shade of anxious doubt in his voice.

"—I love, Gail. So it must be you I love," Eve answers, simply.

That, thinks Gail, is a queer way to put it. It is another convincing note that Eve seems changed, someway . . . Now he knows . . . She has been on another of her reading jags! She talks like a book.

That much Eve is willing to admit. She has been fairly devouring books, one after another.

"What makes me do it?" she wonders.

"Oh, you just get lonely, that's all," answers Gail. "I don't see that it's a very harmful vice."

They are silent for a moment. His long drive home from the reunion is beginning to tell on Gail. He is noticeably sleepy.

"The Jessups had their baby Tuesday," reports Eve.

"Good—what was it?" drones Gail. He is very sleepy now.

Eve—A girl. A very small one. (*She looks away again.*) I should have a strapping boy, with a broad, high forehead and a mass of curly hair. That's the kind of baby *I* should have—

Gail—Will have, some day.

Eve—When?

Gail—You never can tell. Soon, maybe.

Eve—I hope it will be soon. (*There is a silence.* Gail *is breathing with the regularity of impending sleep.*)—Because I'm getting scared, Gail.

Gail—What's that? (*He half-rouses himself, and sinks back again.*) There's no cause to be. No cause at all.

Eve—We've been married almost six years, now.

Gail—That's nothing. Lots of people wait a dozen.

ST. PAUL ACADEMY

EVE—I'm tired of waiting. (*Another silence.*) I'm really frightened now, Gail. (*She seats herself near him.*)

GAIL—Foolish to be.

EVE—But I'm—I was an only child, you know. So was my mother. Maybe there's something wrong with me.

GAIL (*from far away*)—Don't you believe it.

EVE—Maybe I ought to find out if there is—but I dread to know it. (*Another silence.*) I can't sleep for thinking of it. I don't know why I shouldn't have one. I'm quite strong. I've never had anything really the matter with me. And I love children, I do love them. If loving children made you have them, I'd have a houseful. And besides, I would so love the actual having of one. I shouldn't mind any kind of pain at all. I'd welcome it. I'd know then that I was living—making—and not slowly dying, a little more each day like this. (*Again* GAIL'S *chin has sunk upon his breast.* EVE'S *eyes are straight ahead, her voice low. A silence.*) They must be even sweeter when they're all your own. There's nothing about them I don't like. Even if it should be a girl—but of course it wouldn't be, not the first one. (*Another silence. Her voice becomes lower still.*) Heaven shine on me, rain on me. Bring something out of me to hold in my arms, send me some small thing to care for. I'll love it tenderly. Only I shall look after it, ever. I shall become wise. I shall know what is good for him. I shall find out everything there is to know. Don't keep me empty this way any longer. I have room. I'm strong. I'm well. (*A longer silence. Then:*) Listen to me, Gail: I'm speaking honestly: I must have a child, or in a while I shan't be good for anything at all. Help me to life, Gail. Hold fast to it with your strong hands and bring me to it—(*Blindly, she reaches her hand out to him. He does not take it. Slowly, she turns and looks at him. He is asleep. A silence. She drops her hand lifelessly into her lap. Then she speaks in another voice.*) Gail— (*And again:*) Gail.

(*He raises his head slowly, then opens his eyes and looks at her, dully. At last he laughs, and rises from the sofa.*)

GAIL—Lord! I guess I must have dropped right off—

EVE—Yes.

GAIL—What time is it, anyhow? (*He turns and looks at the clock.*) Ouch! Work tomorrow, darling.

EVE—Yes.

GAIL—What is it you were saying?—I'm still in a fog.

EVE—It will keep. (*She rises.*)

9832

GAIL—Oh, yes!—Now look here, Eve; don't you worry about that another bit.

EVE—All right, Gail.

GAIL—Because worrying doesn't help, and I'm perfectly sure that sooner or later, if we're only patient, we'll—

EVE—It's all right, Gail. (*He moves toward the doorway.*)

GAIL—Just a matter of a little patience, that's all— (*He stops and turns.*) Oh—the lights—

EVE—You go ahead. I'll put them out. (*He precedes her into the hall, and mounts the stairs. She puts out the lamps, then goes into the hall and turns out the light there. A faint glow lights her way up the stairs from above. Then it, too, goes out and the darkness is complete.*)

At 5 o'clock the next afternoon the living room is brightened somewhat by the presence of flowers in the vases, but it still is far from a cheerful room. This has been a dull, gray day, with a light rain falling since morning.

Ella, the Redman maid, lets Nicholas Hay and Samuel Gillespie in at the front door. "Hay is thirty-four, fine-looking, strong-looking." Gillespie, who carries two large suitcases and a brief case "is a year or two younger, small, slight and unsmiling."

Dr. Hay's room, Ella indicates, is next the library, but he may wait for Mrs. Redman if he likes. She is in the garden. Ella evidently is puzzled by the presence of Gillespie, until Dr. Hay explains that Gillespie is his secretary.

Neither Dr. Hay nor Gillespie seems at all pleased with the altered plan that has put them in the home of the Redmans rather than in a hotel. They would have preferred the hotel. Dr. Hay is fearfully tired. He wanted to be alone. He feels that he has lost the art of talking to people, if he ever had it. Gillespie will have to get him out of this situation—

"Lord, how I hate money," mutters the doctor. "God, how I hate the need of it. How was it I didn't save some in eight years of general practice?"

"You didn't have me then, sir," cheerfully suggests Gillespie.

"That day I sat there realizing there aren't half a dozen drugs you can count on in the whole pharmacopœia, realizing what a great hoax the whole thing really is, that all I cared for in this world is human emotion and the whys and wherefores—Lord, Gillespie, was I crazy?"

"I don't think so."

The general atmosphere of gloom in the Redman home adds to

Dr. Hay's depression. And the people! What does Gillespie imagine they will be like?

"They may be a nice old couple who go to bed right after dinner," ventures Gillespie. And adds, on reflection: "And, of course, they may be perfect bastards."

In any case there ought to be some way of getting out gracefully, insists Hay. "I feel like a swine, but all I want is a hotel room, and to be left alone."

"Of course we'll have to stay a day or two," he adds; "but—(*after a moment's reflection*) Look here: I think if it's arranged straight off—this afternoon—it will be all right. You find a chance to say, 'Oh—Dr. Hay—about Monday—' and I'll tell them as graciously as I can that I've had to make a rule never to stay more than a day or so in a private house—that I—that I cannot take my responsibilities as a guest lightly enough to give my work the attention it demands. Does it sound too pompous for words?"

"No, it sounds pretty good . . . 'Oh, Dr. Hay—about Monday—' "

There are other reasons why they should be somewhat cheered, Gillespie points out. They are, after all, nearing the end of a ten weeks' lecture tour; they will soon be on the boat, Europe-bound. Might be a good thing for them to try to line up a publisher while they are in New York.

But Dr. Hay is too tired to think kindly of any such suggestion. Whoever would want to buy anything he might write? He's stale. The whole world's stale.

"If I didn't realize that I've got hold of something that's going to change the whole system of education, of literature and art as well—if I didn't believe that the future of my findings may be the future of the human race—"

"What would you do, sir? Go fishing?"

"—That's just what I would do."

Now Eve hurries through the French windows from the garden. "She is wearing a hat and a light raincoat, both wet with rain." For a moment she does not see Dr. Hay and Gillespie. When she does her greetings are friendly and informal.

"Have you been here long?" she asks.

"Just a few moments," Dr. Hay assures her. "The maid said your mother would be in directly. She said that she was in the—"

He realizes his mistake, stares a little confusedly at her, and they both laugh.

"I thought you'd be much older, too," she says.

Mr. Gillespie, Eve explains to Ella, is to have the room at the top of the stairs. Dr. Hay will be next the library, which has been cleared out a little to make a sort of study for him. Gillespie carries the doctor's bags in there.

"Your room is away from the rest, so you'll be able to come and go as you like," Eve continues. "There's just my husband and me. It's not precisely a cheerful house, but the sun comes in everywhere, when there is sun."

"It's a pretty town."

EVE—The country is flat. Plains, and more plains. There should have been a hill or two. But I'm afraid it's too late to do anything about it. (HAY *laughs.*)

HAY—Oh, I don't know!

EVE—Can you make mountains out of mole-hills?

HAY—It's part of my profession to.

EVE—Do your first one under the College, please. I've always thought it should stand upon a hill.

HAY—"Redman" it's called—is it named for your husband?

EVE—For his grandfather. He built it. It was his one tame oat, sowed very late. I hope you'll like it. I do. I'm going to your lectures.

HAY—That isn't fair.

EVE—I shall sit very still.

HAY——And sleep peacefully.

EVE—Oh, no! I shall be all ears. And when you say, "Are there any questions?"—Do you say, "Are there any questions?"

HAY—I'm afraid I do.

EVE—Well, I shall ask the most stupid ones you have ever heard.

HAY—I doubt that.

EVE—You will see. You've probably never met a more uneducated person. It was nice of you, thinking I was my daughter. Tell me what you expected.

HAY—Tell me what you did.

EVE—For some ridiculous reason—though I know no one has them any more— (HAY *indicates a beard. His gesture says, "Was that it?" She nods. He laughs.*)

HAY—No—I can never rise to that.

EVE—And what was I?

HAY—Quite large—a little flushed, and slightly out of breath. And I believe you sang, when urged. (EVE *laughs.*)

EVE—I think we're quits, don't you?

HAY—So soon?

EVE—I mean as far as preconceptions go.

HAY—Oh—preconceptions— (*They look at each other, smiling. The silence becomes a little too long, and* EVE *goes on, hastily:*)

EVE—Perhaps I ought to warn you: it's a—ours is pretty much of a haphazard household. It more or less runs itself. My father hated punctuality, so I fell into bad ways early. You'll ring for breakfast when you want it, won't you? And at any other meal-time that you don't feel quite like sitting down in a stiff chair—they *are* so stiff—you can have a tray. We'll understand. Heavens! How well *I'll* understand! (*She rubs the small of her back reminiscently, then rises and looks in surprise at her hand.*) Why, I'm wet. I'm soaking wet. (*He is watching her, fascinated. She laughs, slips off the raincoat, and stands forth in a bright summer dress.*) I hope the state I'm in is what they call "a pretty confusion." Otherwise—

HAY—You're lovely.

EVE (*startled*)—What?

HAY—I say you're lovely. (*A moment. Then:*)

EVE—But how nice of you to think that.

The incident of their meeting, and their surprise, is still on Eve's mind. She recalls the speech she had prepared to say to Dr. Hay. "We are very honored and very happy to have you here, Dr. Hay, and sincerely trust your stay with us will be as—will be as— (*She stops and throws out her hands.*) I remember the words, but I forget the gestures."

"Miss Redman will please see me after class," prompts Dr. Hay.

Now Gail has come, been formally presented, and has assured the doctor that the Redmans are delighted to have him as a guest.

A moment later Gillespie returns and there is something of which he would like to remind Dr. Hay—"about Monday!" But Dr. Hay has quite forgotten about Monday.

Gail and Eve leave their guests until dinner. A fairly thick silence falls upon Dr. Hay and Gillespie as the Redmans disappear. Then Dr. Hay drops a cube of ice in a glass and pours himself a drink. Gillespie has lighted a cigarette and is watching Hay's back quizzically, without a word.

"Shut up, Gillespie," commands Hay, as the lights fade.

Three weeks later, on a bright Sunday morning, Gillespie is waiting in the Redman living room to hear from Dr. Hay. The secretary is accepting life quite as calmly as usual, but the doctor has taken on a new energy. The hot weather, he concludes, agrees wonderfully with him.

As Hay emerges now from the library he reports that he has been spending the morning working in bed on his next Tuesday's lecture, the twelfth of the series, and he thinks he will entirely rewrite all the others. The old cases appall him.

The Redmans have not appeared. Gail, Gillespie suspects, is with his four-footed friends. And Mrs. Redman has probably gone to church. There is a plan, Dr. Hay believes, to have a picnic lunch up the river, but Gillespie prefers the beer in Railroad Avenue, if there is no objection.

There is news from the French line about their reservations. Their steamer will be sailing in two weeks, and because Dr. Hay's lectures have been creating something of a stir in the east he is to be accorded special privileges as a traveler.

Dr. Hay is not eager to leave Redmanton. He has come to like the little town, and the people.

"They have such fresh, free, open minds," he reminds Gillespie. "They're so fine and simple." He is silent for a moment, and then he adds: "Gillespie, what am I to do for a woman like Mrs. Redman? I mean to repay her—"

"She won't want repaying."

HAY—I know, but when I came here three weeks ago I was in pieces. I wondered when they'd come to sweep me up.

GILLESPIE—It wasn't that bad.

HAY—It was bad enough. But just to have been in the same house with her, to have heard that quiet voice, never insisting, never insisting anything. To have walked with her over that lovely lawn, through those lovely meadows—

GILLESPIE—I know.—A very pleasant set-up on the whole.

HAY—It's made a new man of me, that's all.

GILLESPIE—I haven't heard you singing in your bath, yet. (HAY *laughs.*)

HAY—A man, I said. I leave that happy practice to boys like Redman.

GILLESPIE—I think his voice is changing.

HAY—Still, they seem to be pretty well suited to each other, don't they?

GILLESPIE—Well enough, I guess.

Photo by Vandamm Studio, New York.

"TOMORROW AND TOMORROW"

Gail: "O'Brien said he never in his life saw him ride better. He made a perfect jump, O'Brien said—and came back at a dead trot and—and then—just fell off in his arms. He went out like a light—and, oh, Eve—what are we going to do?"

(*Zita Johann, Drew Price and Harvey Stephens*)

HAY—He's a fine, good fellow. It seems a fine life for her. Yet underneath one feels some kind of lack, some kind of longing, I can't make out what it is she wants. There's never a complaint, of course—not she! She wears her rue with a difference.

GILLESPIE—Got awfully small bones, hasn't she?

HAY—What's that got to do with it? (GILLESPIE *does not reply. He begins to sketch with a pencil upon the back of* HAY'S *lecture notes.*) It's queer about her; we've talked for hours on end and still I don't feel I know her one bit better than the day I came.

GILLESPIE—No?

HAY—Maybe I'm not quite the bright fellow I thought I was.

GILLESPIE—Or maybe it's all there is to know.

HAY—Don't you believe it.

GILLESPIE—Reads a lot, doesn't she?

HAY—Book after book. Why? (GILLESPIE *shrugs.*)

GILLESPIE—Don't ask me.

HAY—That's what you always say when you think you know something. (*Another silent shrug.*) What? Some sort of creative impulse gone wrong? (*He rises abruptly.*) An artist without an art—is that it?

GILLESPIE—Or a woman without love.

HAY—There's her husband, isn't there?

GILLESPIE—I mean love.

HAY—It's not that simple. But it's something—and if I can't dig it out, I'm not much on— But I'm going to dig it out. I'll tell you by evening what it is. I'll— (GILLESPIE *cocks his head admiringly at the sketch.*) What's that?

GILLESPIE—A cenator.

HAY—A what?

GILLESPIE—A cenator. Half man, half horse. (HAY *laughs.*)

HAY—Gillespie, you're a joy to me. I believe I'll have you stuffed.

Eve is home from church. Gillespie has gathered his papers together and gone to his room. Dr. Hay has lingered. He is interested in Eve's reactions to the sermon she has heard, but Eve found it difficult to keep her mind on the sermon. She was thinking, she admits, too steadily of yesterday's lecture.

She is standing near the window now, framed in a picture with the garden flowers beyond. Dr. Hay would have her hold the pose for a minute, that he may remember her long afterwards as she looks at that moment. It is Eve's confession that she thinks she shall also miss him a great deal—afterwards.

They drift into an exchange of intimacies concerned with the people they were before they met. Dr. Hay, born in Montreal, had, as she suspects, been compelled to fight rather steadily uphill. His none too happy childhood he prefers not to discuss. In fact he is much more interested learning about her than telling about himself.

Eve's life, to Eve, has been fairly uneventful. A professor's daughter, a professor of Romance languages, she had lived simply, caring for a father who was very dear and very learned but rather frail.

There is the river—the Willing River—on the banks of which they are to picnic for the first time today—that has meant a good deal in Eve's life.

"It's why I married Gail, I think," she says, "it's so like him. In summer I swim down it. Perhaps we shall swim today. In winter I skate up it all the way to O'Fallon's Falls—though of course I never dare quite go there—"

"Why not?"

EVE—Well, if I did—I'd have done it!—You see? It's something to skate up the Willing all the way from Redmanton to O'Fallon's Falls. But I'm a very good skater. You should see me do an inside edge. Fresh, new black ice, ready to be written on. Oh, it's the finest sort of river! You'll see! Of course, after this morning I shan't be able to go there for a while, so—

HAY—Not able? What's to prevent you? (*She smiles and lays her finger to her lips.*)

EVE—Sh!—the laurel. There's a bank covered with it. It's ready to bloom, now. It blooms for twenty days. (HAY *frowns.*)

HAY—I'm even stupider than I supposed. Does laurel—? (*She laughs.*)

EVE—Give me hay-fever? No—it's just an idea of mine. When I was fifteen, my first summer here, there was one very bright night, and I went walking by myself. All at once I came upon the bank of laurel. It was— I can't tell you. I've never known beauty like it, before or since. I think it was the first time I ever felt myself alive. But when I could, I ran from it. I haven't been back there since—not at that time of year. (*He is watching her intently. She reseats herself.*)

HAY—No, of course not.

EVE—You see, I shouldn't dare. I want it as it was then. It may have changed—or I may.

HAY—Or possibly it was too real for you. Possibly you are afraid it will be too real again. (*She looks at him, startled.*)

EVE—Too—? (*And averts her head again:*) You don't see what I mean.

HAY—I see precisely what you mean. (*He rises.*) What are you going to do with your life here? (*She smiles.*)

EVE—Why—very much what I've always done, I think.

HAY—That's all you ask, is it?

EVE—It's a pleasant place. I'm fond of the people here, and they of me. I should be very happy, don't you think?

HAY—Some women might. Not you.

EVE—But I'm not unusual in any way.

HAY—Except that you're a different order of being entirely.

EVE—I? How?

HAY—How often have you made your little world here over?

EVE—Why, I don't know.

HAY—Countless times, haven't you? And now there's nothing left to work on—it's all worn thin—won't take the paint— (EVE *smiles.*)

EVE—I'm not following very well, Dr. Hay.

HAY—Did you ever hear of an artist without an art?

EVE—No. What are they like?

HAY—Miserable, usually. Probably the most wretched people in the world.

EVE—I'm afraid I still don't—

HAY—Because they aren't like other people. They must do something about life, with it, to it,—or else—

EVE—What?

HAY—The sooner they die the better for them.

EVE—Oh.

HAY—There are artists outside the arts, you know—that's where most of them are. All I'm trying to say is that somewhere, for part of the time at least, you might find—material you can work with.

Dr. Hay thinks Eve should come East in the winter for a month or two months. There she would find new faces, new interests, plays, music, exhibitions. Even better still, let her come to Paris in April! Tremendous things are happening in Paris—a new music, a new literature—and she does need something so very much. Eve admits that. What else is there that could lift her away from the humdrum routine of her everyday life? Why not a houseful of children? That idea enthuses Dr. Hay.

"Let's see, now," he runs on; "the first son in just about a year. There's creation! There's art for you!"

"You must not make fun of me," Eve protests.

HAY—But I'm not! I'm doing nothing of the sort! I'm simply convinced you're what I say you are. (*She rises and moves away. He is silent a moment, watching her closely. Then he goes on.*) Yes, it's quite plain, now. I see him with your eyes, your brow and Gail's deep chest and fine long back—

EVE (*a murmur*)—It would be good.

HAY—He'll be very grave and solemn for a while, until things have grown familiar. Then he'll laugh out loud. He'll laugh a great deal, first sons do, you know.

EVE—I hope—

HAY—And you'll sing him to sleep of nights— (*He sings.*) "Frèr-e Jacq-ues, Frèr-e Jacq-ues—"

EVE (*continuing the song*)—"Dormez-vous. Sonnez les matin-es—"

HAY—It's true: I believe he might be the answer for you.

EVE—I should set great store by him. (HAY *advances.*)

HAY—Then I tell you to have one—have one quickly. I shall be happier about you, then. (*He senses an embarrassment in her, turns away again to relieve it, and continues more lightly.*) Let's see now: we must find a name for him. "Gail" is good but he must have one of his own. Names are important. Redman is a fine name—he must have one as fine, to go with it. "Peter"—"David"—no, those are too romantic, now. "Adam"—no, that's affected, and there would be dismal jokes about "Eve and Adam." It's a good name, though—a good, plain name. Of course it must be a plain one. (*A moment. Then, suddenly:*) I know! "Christian!" He shall be Christian Redman!

EVE—"Christian Redman."

HAY—And no one must call him "Chris"—or "Christy." You must insist on that. (*She does not answer. Her head is bowed upon her breast. A moment, then he goes to her and gently turns her about, facing him. Her eyes are filled with tears.*) Tell me—what is it?

EVE—All that you've said—it would be very fine. Yes—now you are the wise man I thought you. (*She moves away from him and begins to range about the room again touching things here and there.*) Did Gail show you this medal? It was presented to his grandfather by Lincoln and his Cabinet.

HAY—You must tell me, Eve—

EVE—Mrs. William A. Plant herself insists upon giving a reception in your honor the night before you leave.

HAY (*in appeal*)—Eve—

EVE—I wonder what can be keeping Gail so long. He said he wouldn't be a moment.

HAY—Eve—my dear— (*She turns and meets his eyes.*)

EVE—You see—it seems I cannot have one. (*A silence. Then:*)

HAY—Forgive me, please. I'm sorrier than I can possibly tell you, to have spoken so.

EVE—It's all right.

HAY—Will you let me ask you one thing?

EVE—Ask what you like—

HAY—Are you sure you're not afraid to have one? (*She draws herself up.*)

EVE—Afraid!—I—?

HAY—I don't mean in that way. I mean for some reason that even you yourself—

EVE—I am not afraid for any reason on this earth. (*A moment. Then:*)

HAY—Eve—

EVE—What is it?

HAY—Adopt one. (*A silence. She turns away.*) I beg you to do that. I know it's right for you. You'd love it, as much, I know. I believe you'd soon love anything you had to care for.

EVE—But Gail—things must be Gail's own.

HAY—Ask him! Insist! You must have *something*—

EVE—Oh, I know, don't I know!

HAY—Do as I tell you, Eve.

Gillespie has brought in the typewritten copy of Dr. Hay's notes for the doctor's approval. A moment later Gail Redman has come from the barn to report with great excitement his belief that he can buy a hackney stallion for twelve hundred dollars that he is convinced would produce a breed of animals on the Redman place that would take prizes right away from Eastern stables.

"There are only three things in this world my husband really loves," explains Eve, affectionately; "horses, corn soup and me."

"Reverse the order and you may be right," laughs Gail.

The Redmans have gone to complete arrangements for the

picnic. Dr. Hay is in his room in search of a coat. His voice can be heard gayly raised in song. Gillespie listens, with something like mock anxiety.

"Shall I draw you a bath, sir?" he calls, smiling broadly, as the curtain falls.

ACT II

It is near midnight, ten days later. The Redman living room is dimly lighted. A small table near its center is set for supper. There are four places, wine glasses, a plate of sandwiches, a jar of cheese, etc. Ella completes the arrangements by adding a bottle of wine and a rack of toast to the supplies.

It is the last night of Dr. Hay's stay. His arrangements for leaving on the 8:45 train next morning have been made, and are again warningly confirmed by the anxious Gillespie.

The supper has been arranged by Dr. Hay for Mr. and Mrs. Redman, Gillespie and himself. But now Eve reports that Gail will not be able to make it, having been detained out of town on a business errand, and Gillespie, still full of Mrs. William A. Plant's excellent chicken salad and cocoa, begs to be excused.

Dr. Hay and Eve sit down alone . . . Now they have drunk their formal toasts—he "To my host—and to my hostess, who has cared for me with all this care"; she "To our most welcome guest."

There are subjects which Eve would avoid in the conversation, but for which Dr. Hay demands answers. Why, for one thing, did she deliberately run away the last three days of his stay?

Because, insists Eve, a little unconvincingly, because Gail was to be away; because she had not seen her aunt in a long, long time, and this seemed as good a time as any—

But she is not speaking the truth, Dr. Hay insists. Was it not because she had to run again from what was real? Isn't the laurel in bloom again?

This is not questioning that Eve enjoys. Her protest is firm. Yet, when Dr. Hay would ask her pardon and moves away from the table she is quick to call him back.

"Nicholas—please— Please come back, Nicholas. This is your last night with us. Please let me remember it as I would. I have been at such pains with this little supper—"

"That there should be just enough of everything?"

"That there should be just enough."

Gillespie has finished putting the last things in their bags in

Dr. Hay's room. He comes now to say his good nights and leave them.

Again an embarrassing silence.

"You'll be sorry to hear it's as I thought," reports Eve; "Gail doesn't want to adopt a child."

"You must persuade him."

"I shall keep trying," Eve says, as her head sinks for a moment. "How I shall try."

Dr. Hay has moved away from the table again. The very bright moonlight is too strong for his eyes. As he returns he stops beside Eve's chair, the spell too strong for him. His hand falls upon her shoulder. "Her whole frame stiffens as from a shock, then she relaxes and for a moment rests her cheek upon his hand."

"I want to tell you something— Look at me," he says.

"I can hear you as I am," Eve answers, in a small voice.

"I try to be an honorable man, Eve."

"I think you are a great and honorable man," she answers.

"And such a wise one!" There is bitterness in his voice, now. "Didn't I tell three hundred people only Wednesday precisely what love is made of?" He is laughing. "Oh, God; oh, God!"

"Don't, Nicholas. . . ."

She has held out her hand to him, palm upward, across the table.

"Take my hand in yours—" she commands.

"It's so small—"

"It holds my heart's thanks."

"For what?" he cries in pain. "What for?"

Eve—For giving me, for a little while, the illusion of being alive. (Hay's *bitterness returns.*)

Hay—Illusion—you're right there! That's all you've had. That's all you're ever likely to.

Eve—It may be that I ask less than other people. (*She rises, he with her, her hand still in his.*) Good night, Nicholas. (*He draws her to him, takes her shoulders in his hands and stands gazing into her eyes. Finally she smiles and speaks:*) Yes, yes. Of course. With my whole heart. You must know that.

Hay—But what are we to do?

Eve—What is there to do, but to remember—

Hay—We need more.

Eve—No. We have it truly now, forever as it is.

Hay—You think that it might change—

EVE—Things change.

HAY—Come with me, Eve—

EVE—No, that I can't.

HAY—I want you. You want me.

EVE—Still, I cannot.

HAY—You love him, too.

EVE—Yes, I love Gail.

HAY—But this has nothing to do with him.

EVE—My love for you has not. My going with you would. (*A moment.*)

HAY—It's hail and farewell for us, then, is it— (*Her head lowers. He waits a moment. Then:*) If you ever send for me—whenever—whatever your reason, I shall come. Remember that.

EVE—I shall remember.

HAY—But when you do, you'll be ready to go with me. Remember that, as well.

EVE (*in a lower voice*)—I shall remember.

HAY—Oh, Eve—this is cowardly. We want each other. We must have each other. (*She turns away.*)

EVE—No, no—

HAY—But we must! It's the only real thing in this world, Eve! (*She shakes her head.*)

EVE—Not for me. So fare you well, Nicholas. Till the morning my dear one, when I shall tell you fare-you-well all over, with perhaps a brighter face.

HAY (*not knowing what*)—Oh, something to take with me! Something real— (*She looks at him for a moment, then moves to his arms and lifts her face to his. They kiss. She strains against him, then buries her face in her hands, upon his breast.*)

EVE—It's true. It's the same sense that the laurel gave me. (*She leaves his arms.*) I can't stand it. Be sad for me.

HAY (*wiser—aware that it is too late for them now*)—For us both, now. Now I am in your heart. I shall remain there. You will have no peace—nor I.

EVE—I have no peace, anyway. (*She turns and moves towards the doorway.*)

HAY (*deferring to her*)—Look then— (*She stops and turns. He takes up one of the candle-lamps.*) You—and me— (*Reluctantly, he raises it to extinguish it, but she cries:*)

EVE—No! (*Comes to him swiftly, takes it from him and replaces it on the table.*) Oh—how could you!

HAY—Eve—my darling— (*A brief silence. Then she looks up at him and murmurs:*)

EVE—Yes. (*She moves to the French windows and opens them to the moonlight. Then she turns and holds out her hand to him.*) Come—I should like you to see the laurel. I think there is nothing will ever change it. (*He goes to her and takes the hand outstretched to him. She leads him through the windows, across the porch. The stage is darkened, except for the two candles, which still burn.*)

It is 8:30 the following morning. The maids are clearing the supper table, on which the candle-lamps are still burning lowly. In the dining room Gail Redman is finishing his breakfast. Mrs. Redman has not come down yet, Ella reports. Dr. Hay had a cup of coffee in his bedroom at 7 and has gone for a little walk.

Time grows short. Gillespie has the bags down. The clock has struck the half hour when Dr. Hay comes from the garden. He is followed by Jane, her arms full of laurel.

Still Eve does not appear.

The taxi is at the door. Gillespie and the bags are in. Gail has said his formal farewells. Suddenly he remembers that Eve had told him to tell Dr. Hay that she had made her farewells the night before and knew he would not mind her not coming down.

"You have been so kind to me here. I can't even attempt to thank you," Dr. Hay assures Gail.

"Not me—" protests Gail. "I've done nothing. It's all been Eve."

"She is a great woman."

"Eve? Oh, yes—you bet your life—a great girl, Eve."

Gail is a little embarrassed. There is something he would like to ask Dr. Hay before he goes, but the words are difficult. Finally he manages it.

"Do you think Eve is happy?" he asks.

"I'm not sure," answers Hay. "But I believe she can be."

"That's fine," hastily adds Gail, "because you see I'm fairly dumb in a lot of ways, and inclined to take things for granted, I'm afraid. But Eve's everything to me, and I've sort of bothered lately about—"

"If I were you I should do anything and whatever she asks you out of her real feelings . . . Mistrust her reason if you like, but trust her emotions always, and in everything."

Jane has put the laurel blossoms on the table. Hay pauses to call attention to them.

"I came on this out walking just now," he explains to Gail. "I thought that she would like it. Will you say that I gathered it for her?"

"Why, yes—of course. That's awfully nice. She'll be so pleased."

"I wish I might lay it at her feet."

"I'll tell her."

The klaxon has sounded imperiously. Dr. Hay has gone. Gail has followed him through the hall. Eve comes quietly down the stairs. She is standing at the French windows as the taxi drives away.

"Good-by! Good-by, Nicholas!" she calls softly. "Good-by, my love. Remember—"

There is the sound of the taxi's wheels on the gravel roadway. Eve is sitting in a chair staring straight before her when Gail comes in. Too bad, he thinks, that Eve just missed Hay. But he (Gail) had explained. He was a queer sort, wasn't he?

"He's a great man," says Eve, quietly.

"It's a mutual admiration society, all right," laughs Gail. "He thinks you're a great woman."

He tells her about the laurel, and what Hay had said about wishing he might lay it at her feet. That was sweet of him, agrees Eve.

There is still something Gail wants to say. It is about adopting a child. She may be right about that. Anyway, he is prepared to make certain preliminary investigations.

Eve is happy at the suggestion.

Now it is 8:45 and Gail must be getting along. He will expect her to call for him at 5. Being hot, they might drive out somewhere and cool off before dinner. The lights fade.

It is October. The days are noticeably shorter and there is a chill in the air. Coming from the works Gail Redman has started a fire in the library grate and told Ella a fire in the living room would also be a help. Mrs. Redman will probably want one when she comes in. He goes back to the library.

Eve has been home some time. She comes now from upstairs, followed by Dr. Walter Burke, "a short, bald, round, genial" person of fifty-five. Eve's face looks a trifle white and drawn.

The doctor is not worried. He has left some rhubarb and soda powders. They sometimes do some good. And they can't do any harm in any event. Might as well be honest about it. Why not?

"These little upsets are like the common cold," says Dr. Burke. "Once I asked Sturgis at P and S—'Doctor,' I said, 'what is your treatment for the common cold?' 'Doctor,' he said, 'two dozen soft linen handkerchiefs.' "

The doctor enjoys his own jokes as well as anyone. Eve, he repeats, is all right. Nothing to worry about. But she might, if she will, stop in at the office when she is in town. Why? Dr. Burke chuckles, but refuses to satisfy her curiosity.

Eve is standing in front of the sofa, "her apprehension growing in her eyes," when Ella finds her. She is so white that Ella is worried. But Eve is sure there is nothing the matter with her. Where is Mr. Redman?

Ella opens the library door and the click of a typewriter is heard. Gail is rapping out a few letters. One is to the Indianapolis Infants' Home:

"They asked more fool questions," he calls through the door. "You'd think we'd picked one out already. They practically wanted to know if my aunt's stepmother ever had prickly-heat, and was she kind to animals—"

Eve has made her way around the sofa and stands, swaying slightly.

"Here is what I wrote—" calls Gail—

"My wife and I, having no children of our own, wish to legally adopt an infant from three to six months of age, provided we can obtain a suitable infant, of unquestionably good parentage."—That's only fair. (EVE *begins to hum "Frère Jacques" lowly, and with difficulty makes her way to the hall doorway.*) Then I go on to say that either party, they or us, are at liberty to reconsider the adoption within a six months' period, and give a list of names for reference: the Adees, the Proctors— (EVE's *humming becomes louder. She grasps at the heavy curtains to steady herself.*) Say! Are you listening?—Dr. Burke, Mrs. William A. Plant, the James Russells in Indianapolis, and so on. (EVE's *grasp upon the curtain has given way and she has slumped silently to the floor.*) Do you think that's all right, dear? (*There is no answer. A moment.*) All right with you, Eve? (*Again no answer. He calls:*) Oh, Eve! (*Silence. He waits a moment, then goes on typing.* ELLA *comes down the hall with a glass of sherry and a few crackers upon a tray. She does not see* EVE *until she is nearly upon her. She screams involuntarily and puts down the tray. The typing abruptly stops.*) What's that?

ELLA—Oh, Mr. Redman! Quick! (*She bends over* EVE. GAIL *hurries in from the library, in boots and riding breeches and goes to* EVE.)

GAIL—Bring the whiskey— (ELLA *goes to the library and returns with a small glass of whiskey which she gives him.*) Go turn her bed down and call Burke. (ELLA *hurries out.* GAIL *rubs* EVE'S *wrists, murmuring gently:*) Eve—Eve dear—it's Gail, darling. It's all right, dear. Poor lamb—come on, Sweet—it's all right. Eve—Eve— (*A moment, then she lifts her hand to her head and tries to sit up.*)

EVE—I—I—

GAIL—Take it easy, darling. It's all right. Here—drink this— (*He holds the whiskey to her lips.*)

EVE—I can't—

GAIL—Try—just a swallow— (*She takes a swallow.*) One more— (*She takes another, then pushes it away.*) That'll fix you. That'll do the trick.

EVE—How foolish. I—I must have—

GAIL—Lord, Angel, behave, will you?

EVE—I'm so sorry.

GAIL (*agonized*)—Shut up, will you? Do you want to break my heart?

EVE—Poor Gail—

GAIL—Poor Gail, my eye. Poor you. Do you think you can make the stairs now?

EVE—Of course.

GAIL—Take it easy. (*He helps her to her feet.*) Doctor Burke's coming. You've simply got to see him, dear.

EVE—I've seen him.

GAIL—You've—what did he say?

EVE—He just said— (*She stops, then turns to him.*) Gail—

GAIL—What, Sweet?

EVE—The letter about the baby—don't send it.

GAIL—There now—don't you worry about letters— (*Then, suddenly:*) Eve! Why not? What *is* this?

EVE—I've got one of my own, Gail.

GAIL (*increduously*)—You've—? (*Then, with enormous joy:*) Oh, Eve! *Darling!*

(*Exultantly, he draws her into his embrace. Her eyes close. She stands rigid in his arms. The curtain falls.*)

ACT III

It is December of the current year. There have been changes in the Redman living room. It is fresher and brighter. Most of the old furniture has been replaced and the decorations changed. A handsome but plain radio is one of the new pieces.

Gail and Eve Redman are in the dining room. Their voices can be heard as Gail relates an adventure of the day. Their conversation has died away to a murmur when a boy of seven steals in from the library. He is Christian Redman, "a pale, sweet-faced, bright-looking child," dressed in boots and riding breeches and carrying his coat and riding crop. He is sitting on the sofa binding the buckles of his boots when he overhears his father say: "Just what I told my boy, Christian. I said: 'You can lead a horse to water but you can't make him *jump*.'"

Christian stiffens at this. His body is trembling as he gets awkwardly into his coat.

"I'll show him—" he mutters. "I'll show him—"

He tiptoes quietly out through the French windows, though he hears his mother's voice calling his name.

Gail and Eve come from the dining room. Gail has not changed perceptibly. "One senses rather than sees the difference in him." Eve is older and more beautiful. "The look of anxiety and defeat has departed from her face, leaving a fine serenity in possession."

They had left Christian sleeping. They believe he is still sleeping. Eve goes to listen at his door and reports her son as quiet as a mouse.

Gail has taken advantage of Eve's absence to tune the radio in on a certain station. There is something on at 2 o'clock, he explains to Ella, that he does not want to miss.

The discussion with Eve turns on Christian and his recent illness. There has not been any fever now for two days. Still Eve is anxious. She does not think she will move Christian back to his own room just yet, even though his father is eager to have his son near him. They have a lot of fun in the morning when Gail goes in to waken Christian and stirs him into veritable paroxysms of laughter by pretending to be some kind of animal. Eve appears a bit doubtful of this game, but lets it pass.

"Dr. Burke says the bandages can come off tomorrow," she reports.

"It's about time."

EVE—I went over the photographs again with him. There's not a sign of a fracture.

GAIL—I never thought there would be. Wasn't I right behind him the whole time? He just got timid at the water-jump and pulled up. You know it takes three good falls to make a horseman. Let him have them young, and get them over with. I had mine by the time I was six. He's slow.

EVE—I didn't tell you: Burke finally admitted that if the fever had gone on another day, we— (*She stops.*)

GAIL—We what?

EVE—We might not have him now.

GAIL—He doesn't know what he's talking about.

EVE—He seems to, usually. This time I wasn't sure. I hope I was right to let the nurse go.

GAIL—Now listen, dear—

EVE—Anyhow, I'm going to keep him absolutely quiet for a while. He'll have to have Christmas in bed, poor lamb.

GAIL—But he's all right again now—he's all *right,* Eve! Haven't you just said—?

EVE—I'm not going to risk that fever again.

GAIL—Darling, you certainly take motherhood hard. You came within an ace of dying when you had him, and now, every time he has the slightest upset, you think *he's* going to die.

EVE—It was more than a slight upset.

GAIL—It's just as I've always said: you're with him too much. Nurse, governess, mother, sister—

EVE—I love him. I love to be with him. (*She seats herself beside him.*) Tell me, Gail—what's the surprise you said you had for me?

GAIL—It isn't 2 o'clock yet.

EVE—But why just two?

GAIL—You'll see!

EVE—I shall wait patiently.

With elaborate casualness Gail brings the name of Dr. Nicholas Hay into the conversation. He wonders what has become of their erstwhile guest.

Eve doesn't know. Evidently Hay has become quite a celebrated person, Gail agrees. There are articles in the newspapers and magazines both by him and about him. Yes, Eve recalls, Dr. Hay did write a few times, just after he left them. He wrote as long as she did. Then she stopped writing. She did not want him to feel that he was obligated.

"I don't suppose he even knows that we've got Christian," Gail ventures.

"No. I don't see how he would," Eve answers. "I'd stopped writing him by then—"

"It'd be funny if the door should open and he should walk in right this minute," suggests Gail.

The idea is startling to Eve. She can't understand whatever put it in Gail's head. Nor does Gail undertake to explain, save to say that anything can happen in an Age of Wonders.

Again the question of Christian's recovery and immediate activities interests them. It is Gail's idea that the first day the boy is able he should climb right back on a horse again. He does not want his son to lose his confidence.

But Eve is quickly and sharply opposed to any such experiment. She does not believe, as Gail does, that the first thing to do after a fall is to get up and ride. Neither does she believe that Christian loves horses as Gail does. She fears that her son is as she was for so many years—painfully, agonizingly anxious to be what people wanted her to be. She wants Christian to be himself—"to the furthest reaches of himself—but himself first, last and always. That isn't easy for a son of mine to learn."

"Maybe not," Gail counters. "But it is easy for a son of mine to take to horses."

"I'm sorry to tell you, but I think he has a deathly fear of them," she says.

The idea, to Gail, is the bunk. Furthermore, he would like to say, and does say, that he has felt for a long time that Eve is off on the wrong foot with Christian and always has been. In the first place, the boy should be in school, however much his mother believes she can teach him by keeping him at home.

EVE—Don't you think I know as much as the teachers there? I worked awfully hard for my degree at Redman. (EVE *smiles.*)

GAIL—I'm not thinking only of him. I'm thinking of you, too. You never see your old friends any more—

EVE—I have a more attractive young friend, now.

GAIL—But hang it, Eve—he can't even read or write yet!

EVE—It does seem late, I'll admit. But they'll come so easily, when they come. So far, he's been so occupied with real things.

GAIL—Oh? What for instance? Tell me three things he knows— (EVE *looks away.*)

EVE—Well, he knows how he came about. He knows anatomy.

GAIL (*ironically*)—Fine. What else?

EVE—He has a sense of the strangeness of the world, of himself in it.

GAIL—I'm talking about practical things.

EVE (*finding them*)—Well, he knows where the trout lie—how to make a telephone—what to do for a mother-sheep at lambing-time. Every stick of furniture in his room he made himself. He can grow things out of the rocks, it seems to me. I've seen him let a swarm of bees settle on his bare arm, and bring them to a new hive.

GAIL—Very valuable in after life.

EVE—He knows that Jesus lived, and was a hero. He can lead you to a spring in any patch of the woods you take him to—he can *smell* water. (*Then, in a rush:*) He knows how to—the difference between—he can tell you why—oh, what a lot he knows! And all of it his—his own—a part of him!

GAIL—Hang it, you don't *want* to see what I mean!

EVE—Yes, I do. Tell me, Gail. (*He turns away.*)

GAIL—What's the good?

EVE—Darling, let's not be ridiculous. Christian is our one and only. But all the same, children are my specialty. I'm wiser about them than you'd believe. I've made myself wise. I don't spoil him, truly. I'm harder with him than you could ever be, but in another way. I don't try to tell you how to school horses. Please trust in my way with Christian.

GAIL—Now you're making me self-conscious about him.

EVE—No, no! I don't want to do that!

GAIL—Well, I've always done as you said about him so far, haven't I? But when I see a boy turn yellow as he did— (EVE *turns upon him.*)

EVE—Yellow! What are you talking about?

GAIL—He was yellow at that jump, Eve, and that's all there is to it. There, now you've got it. (*A moment, then:*)

EVE—Yes.

GAIL—And don't think I like to say a thing like that about my own kid, either. But when—

EVE—I've got it, Gail.

Eve moves toward the hall as though she would leave the room, but changes her mind and comes back to the radio. Perhaps if she were to get a little music—she turns the radio on. A low, clear voice is heard—

"But the fact is," the voice is saying, "the human race was born with its emotions. Reason it acquired later, slowly, painfully. Possibly that is why it puts so high a premium upon it."

The voice is that of Dr. Hay. That was Gail's surprise. He had read in the radio news of the doctor's scheduled broadcast from Chicago.

Eve is sitting on the sofa staring straight ahead. Gail is near the radio. Ella passes through the hall to the front door. Hay's voice continues—

"Emotion, whether of joy or fear, of love or hate, of hope or of despair, is strengthened by indulgence, weakened by denial. That is the part that reason plays in the scheme of life. That is why the game is worth the candle, why the fight to be and realize ourselves, is worth the effort."

Ella has come from the door. She is plainly frightened. She tries to attract Gail's attention, to tell him that O'Brien is at the door and wants to see him. Gail does not want to be disturbed. But Ella is insistent, and Gail goes to the door.

Eve continues oblivious to what is happening. Again Nicholas Hay's voice can be heard—

"For me, I believe the highest point a human being can reach is that at which he knows he has earned the right to depend upon emotion to prompt action. It is a right hard to earn, almost impossible to earn, but the true heroes of this world have earned it. Who does not know the power of small things to recapture lost emotions? The sight of a green lawn curving beneath chestnut-trees—the rush of water running past—the smell of certain flowers—"

"Nicholas, Nicholas—" mutters Eve.

"Lost, did I say?" continues the voice. "But they are never lost."

Gail appears in the doorway. He is holding Christian, limp in his arms. He calls Eve, but she does not hear—

"Emotion is the only real thing in our lives," Hay's voice drones on; "it is the person, it is the soul."

Now Eve hears Gail calling to her, and a moan from Christian strikes sharply upon her ears. She has rushed to them. The touch of her hand on the boy's brow confirms her worst fear. The fever has returned. "He's burning up," she murmurs.

"O'Brien said he never in his life saw him ride better," Gail reports, excitedly. "He made a perfect jump, O'Brien said—and came back at a dead trot and—and then—just fell off in his arms. He went out like a light—and oh, Eve—what are we going to do?"

Gail carries the boy into his room. Eve stops in the door. Gail's agonized query: "Eve, what are we going to do!" is still ringing in her ears. Dr. Hay's voice is continuing on the radio—

"He'll know!" Eve mutters. "*He* will know!"

She is at the telephone now, excitedly calling Long Distance.

"Emotion we were created with," declares the doctor's voice. "Reason came after. Reason is our own invention."

EVE—Long Distance? I want to talk with Chicago. Dr. Nicholas Hay. N-i-c-h-o-l-a-s H-a-y— Just a moment, I'll find it. No, I don't know the number. Oh, please wait a moment! It's important! It's—

HAY'S VOICE—So if we earn the right, we may trust emotion over it, confident that in it we have, somehow, the whole experience of the human race to draw upon. It has its physical instruments surely—nerves, brain, the endocrines. But they are only instruments. It is the difference between the voice and the wires which carry it, the poem and the handful of pied type one may compose to set it down. (*A silence.*)

EVE—Oh—please wait! (*Then once more in a controlled, precise voice:*) Main 856—Mrs. Gail Redman. Yes, I want to speak to him himself—no—no—*Hay*—H-a-y— The address? One moment, I'll give it to you— (*She listens intently to the announcer's voice, which has already begun:*)

ANNOUNCER'S VOICE—You have been listening to Dr. Nicholas Hay, the eminent educator and man of science, now lecturing at the University of Chicago, in his first talk for this station on "The Science of Emotions." The second of Dr. Hay's interesting talks will be given at the same hour—2 o'clock P.M. Central Standard Time, next Sunday, December the twenty-eighth. This is station WMAQ, Chicago, Columbia Broadcasting Company, 410 North Michigan Avenue, Chicago.

EVE—Columbia Broadcasting Company, 410 North Michigan Avenue—Please hurry it. It's most urgent! No—I'll hold on— (*She turns toward the library and calls:*) Gail!—Is he all right?

GAIL—Not yet—

ANNOUNCER—And now we shall have the pleasure of hearing Luke McAllister and his Lazy Blue Lads, in a few selections from the current dance hits. Station WMAQ, Chicago, Earle Walker announcing.

ANOTHER VOICE—Good afternoon, friends and playmates. You look well—how do you feel? What would you like to hear? Yes?—I guessed it! Leave it to Luke. (*A popular dance tune begins.* EVE *waits. The music continues. She makes a move-*

ment toward the radio, to stop it, but just then a voice is heard on the telephone.)

EVE—Hello? Hello—yes, yes—that's right— (*A moment.*) Nicholas! This is Eve—Eve Redman. Oh. Who is it?—Oh—This is Mrs. Redman, Gillespie. I must speak to Dr. Hay at once. Quickly—quickly! (*A pause. The music continues.*) Nicholas? —Yes—This is Eve. Yes—I know. Yes, yes! But, Nicholas, you must come here at once. (*His voice is heard, an indistinct murmur, through the music.* EVE *speaks from a dry throat, with a desperate control:*) My child is ill—so desperately ill. My child, Nicholas. We don't know what it is, or what to do. (*Again his voice is heard in reply. She waits, agonized, her face contorted with suffering. Then:*) You see, about three weeks ago—Thanksgiving Day it was—he was thrown from his horse. (*At last her control breaks.*) And ever since, Nicholas—ever since then, he's— (*Her voice, and the music, and the lights have faded out. The stage is silent and dark.*)

Three days later, early in the morning, while the lamps in the living room are still burning, Dr. Burke and Samuel Gillespie are finishing out a visit. The years have changed Gillespie but little. Dr. Burke is a little balder and a little ruddier, but he still likes his stories, and Gillespie is a fairly patient listener. As for Christian's condition, Dr. Burke is frankly puzzled. He has not given up hope, but he is puzzled. Christian has lain in a complete stupor for three days. Even Dr. Hay, as Gillespie admits, has not been able to "get through to him."

Dr. Hay is puzzled, too. He admits as much when he comes from the library a moment later. The report of the nurse, and a thermometer reading that puts the boy's temperature at 94-point-2 are further cause for anxiety.

"He won't rouse," Dr. Hay reports. "He just stares at you. His eyes are like blue glass. I thought I'd got his attention once half an hour ago, but it was like trying to hold on to water."

"What have you been using to get at him with?" inquires Gillespie.

"Anything I could think of—old toys, reading baby stories—nothing's any use."

"Maybe Mrs. Redman has ideas."

"I've had so little chance to talk to her. I want to talk to her now. She said she'd come in a moment. (*A pause. He thinks.*) I wish I knew whether he's their own child or whether they adopted him."

Gillespie obviously seeks to conceal his surprise at the doctor's suggestion.

A moment later Gail Redman has come into the room. His anxiety has told on him. His nerves are none too sure and he is inclined to resent Dr. Hay's request that he should keep out of Christian's room as much as possible. Gail should try to get some sleep insists Hay.

There is no sleep for Gail. And, as Christian's father, he feels that he should know exactly how matters stand with his son. Isn't there someone they should call?

Dr. Hay has already talked with Sprague in Chicago and Macomber in New York.

"There aren't two better men anywhere," he reports. "Both of them agree with Burke: that it's probably some sort of infection that existed before the fall, that the fall was a mere coincidence."

Dr. Hay, it happens, does not agree with this diagnosis. "I don't believe the condition has any physical basis," he tells Gail. "I believe it's all in his mind—or heart—"

Gail doesn't understand that. And he is sure Christian has not been under any unusual strain. He is a terribly happy kid and always has been.

HAY—If I can get his attention I think he'll tell me what's troubling him. I've worked with children for a long time, now. I'm supposed to be able to win their confidence and to think with them in their own terms. I've no doubt we'll find the trouble so simple it will break your heart. Then it will be up to his mother and you to straighten it out for him. My part will be to try to tell you how to go about it. It may take a little time, but don't think there's any mystery to it—there isn't—there's none whatever.

GAIL—But if he can't even— Doctor, what *is* it? What's doing it?

HAY (*after a moment's consideration*)—I believe it's a wall of childish reasoning he has built between you and his emotions. The real problem is to find a way to him through it, before he starves behind it. I hope we'll be successful. I think we will.—Go on now, will you?—Put on your coat and get some air.

GAIL—Oh, Christ, Doctor—you don't know what it's like. You wait for years for a kid, and then you get one, and then all of a sudden—

HAY—Stop it!

GAIL—But I've got the—(*his voice sinks*)—the most terrible feeling that he's—

HAY—Then get rid of it! (*He gestures toward the hall.*) Go on, please—do as I say. (GAIL *goes to the hall and out. It is now light outside.* HAY *sighs and covers his eyes with his hand.*) Put out those damn lamps, will you? They're like ghosts. (GILLESPIE *extinguishes the lamps.*) And kick up the fire. God, it's a tomb. (*A moment.*) Well, we've got him out of that room. Now the point is to keep him out. I don't like the way the boy keeps looking at him.

GILLESPIE (*at the fireplace*)—"And then you get one," he said.

HAY—I heard him.

GILLESPIE—That probably means he's their own.

HAY—Probably. I'm still not sure.

GILLESPIE—Why didn't you ask him point-blank?

HAY—Somehow I couldn't. (*He rises, and turns to put out his cigarette.*) Make out an adrenalin prescription, will you? And go for it yourself. Three or four ampules. We'll give him five minims at a time.

GILLESPIE—Right.

Dr. Hay is alone when Eve comes from the sick room. She moves quite naturally into his arms and rests her head upon his breast. She, too, has come to him for the truth. Will Christian get well?

There is a brief pause before Dr. Hay answers, and then his answer is a firm "Yes." He knows, though he cannot tell her how he knows. His confidence brightens Eve a little. She remembers that it was in that very room that she and Nicholas first talked of Christian. It was there that he had named him "Christian." And told her what to sing to him.

HAY—He's such a dear child—

EVE—Why not? Why shouldn't he be? Oh, why not, why— (*Her voice breaks. She buries her face in her hands.*)—It was you who gave him to me—give him back! (*He looks at her uncertainly, not comprehending.*)

HAY—Hush, dear—he'll be all right, I promise you. (*She looks up at him.*)

EVE—Do you, Nicholas?

HAY—I promise.

EVE—But he doesn't even listen. He doesn't even hear us.

HAY (*still gazing, puzzled*)—He will.

EVE—He just looks at Gail.

HAY—It's Gail that he's really afraid of, isn't it?

EVE—Yes. I think so. Does that make a difference?

HAY—A very great one. (*A moment. Then:*) Eve—did you adopt him, darling? (*In a swift gesture she covers his hand with hers, then shakes her head slowly, silently, unable to speak.*) He's all your own, then. (*Her hand closes more tightly over his.*)

EVE—Nicholas—

HAY—Yes, dear—

EVE——And yours.

HAY—And—? (*She nods dumbly. He bends and kisses her hand.*) Oh, my dear—my dear one.

EVE—I couldn't tell you. You had so much to do. I was afraid it would interfere. Forgive me—

HAY—My love, I love you.

EVE—And Gail—it meant so much to Gail to have him—

HAY—Of course, of course.

EVE—Just now—in there—the most horrible thing came over me: It's I who've done it—no one else—

HAY—Done what?

EVE—Knowing he was yours—not his—always I have been trying to keep him from him, keep him yours. He's been pulled this way, that way—never knowing why, by what—every which way, until at last he—oh, poor child, poor child—

HAY—Eve, listen—

EVE—No, it's true. It could be that—*couldn't* it. (*He does not answer.*) Tell me! (*Again no answer.*) Yes. (*She averts her head.*) So go to him. Do what you can. Give him to Gail, or take him for yourself. Only don't—unless you must—don't let him know what I did to him. (HAY *rises.*)

HAY—I must tell you one thing: I knew with the first word you spoke the other night that it had not changed for us—that it was only the time between that made it seem so distant. So when he's well again, you both come with me. That's all, Eve.

EVE—I—if— (*The front door is heard to open. She glances toward it and starts to rise.*)

HAY—No, you stay here. (GAIL *comes in, his collar turned up, his hair blown, staring vacantly.*) Think of some way through to him. Only you can find it. You must find it. Think—*think*—

Dr. Hay has gone back to Christian. Gail finds Eve on the sofa and tries to comfort her. They are doing everything that can be done for Christian; he is a strong, normal boy; only the fever has weakened him, and he will conquer that—she'll see—

But soon the strain has proven too much for Gail. He is sobbing now and clinging to Eve, demanding brokenly that she will tell him Christian will live, yet fearing the truth if she should speak it.

"You love him so much, don't you?" Eve's voice is uncertain.

"*Love* him?" Gail answers, hysterically. "Love Christian? Oh, Eve!—God, he's my—oh, love him! Do I love him! Love Christian, that sweet kid—why, if I'd ever thought I'd ever love a—

EVE—Hush, dear. He will get well.

GAIL—He must. He simply must. Or I'll— (EVE *rises abruptly.*)

EVE—Wait! (*She listens. From the bedroom beyond the library,* CHRISTIAN *is heard calling in a small young voice:*)

CHRISTIAN—Mummy! (EVE *stands rigid. Again he calls:*) Mummy—! (GAIL *grasps* EVE's *arm fearfully.*)

GAIL—Oh, Eve—his voice—it's like it was when he was two. He's slipping back—he's slipping over—

EVE (*to herself*)—When he was two. When he was— (*Swiftly, she goes out into the library.* GILLESPIE *comes in, in hat and overcoat, a small paper package in his hand.* GAIL *is following* EVE *into the library.*)

GILLESPIE—Redman! (GAIL *turns.* GILLESPIE *murmurs.*) Don't go in there. (*They listen intently as* EVE *is heard singing softly:*)

EVE—"Frèr-e Jacq-ues, Frèr-e Jacq-ues, dormez-vous, dormez-vous. Sonn-ez les matin-es, sonn-ez les matin-es—" (*It is* CHRISTIAN's *voice which concludes:*)

CHRISTIAN—"Ding, dang, dong—" (*Then stronger, more clearly.*) "Ding, dang, dong!"

EVE (*joyfully*)—Christian.

(GAIL *looks wonderingly to* GILLESPIE, *who glances down at the bottle in his hand, smiles confidently and tosses it away upon the sofa. The stage is darkened.*)

A week later Ella and a second maid, are denuding the Redman living room of its Christmas greens and wreaths. There is quite a basket of them when the girls have finished. The tree, by Mrs. Redman's orders, is to be left standing in the library because Christian will want to have one more look at it lighted.

Eve, coming in from the hall, does not at first see Dr. Hay. He has been standing at the French windows looking into the yard. He turns as he hears Eve's voice and now, for a long moment, they stand looking at each other.

For hours Eve has been walking the grounds and searching for the momentous decision. She is convinced now that she cannot make it alone. Nicholas will have to help her.

HAY—What have you been telling yourself?

EVE—First—and always—that I love you as no one ever was loved before— (*He smiles and covers her hand with his.*)

HAY—It sounds final. What else?

EVE—That in some way I have learned to get on without you. (*A sudden cry:*) Oh, Nicholas—help me! *Tell* me what to do! (*He shakes his head.*) But when I know that whatever you decide for us must be right— (*Again he shakes his head.*)

HAY—What else have you told yourself? (*A moment. Then:*)

EVE—That Christian and I are really yours—

HAY—Yes.

EVE—And if we are to go with you it must be truly with you—now—this afternoon.

HAY—Ten minutes.

EVE (*distraught*)—Short—so terribly short, for a lifetime. (*Again she begins to range about the room.*) If I go, it will break Gail's heart. And if I take Christian—it will be the end of him. It's one thing, believing that love overtook us suddenly, in a day or two, just now. It's another to know that day after day for years, one has been— Oh, but I never felt the deception—I promise you I didn't! It hasn't been at all what you'd call "living a lie." If you knew how happy and proud he's been—how satisfied with life, how—to think he had a son of his own!—It gave him such a feeling of—

HAY—I know that feeling, Eve. (*She looks at him.*)

EVE—But now to as much as say to him: "Look, you, *you've* got no child—you never had. This is another man's. And the wife you thought was yours—she's his, too." It would destroy him. (*Again she looks at him, reads his question.*) No. Heaven's own judgment could not destroy you, Nicholas.

HAY—Well, Eve?

EVE—You are the wise one! *You* say!

HAY (*at last*)—The truth is the truth. For years we have loved each other, and Christian is our child. That is the truth.

EVE—No—those are the facts. It may be that the truth is simply that I'm Gail's wife, and my place is here, because he needs me.

HAY—Do you need no one? (*She is silent. Involuntarily,*

she seems to gain stature.) No—not any more, do you? You have yourself now.

EVE—That, too, you've given me. (*Then her head lowers again. She murmurs:*) Should I ever again be able to hold my head up?

HAY—There is a finer pride than you have now, Eve. (*She looks at him and looks away.*)

EVE—Oh, but I love you, my sweet, my great—I love you, love you—

HAY—Then— (*She goes to him.*)

EVE—Say that you love me, too—

HAY—I love you, too, my sweet, my great—

EVE—It—somehow, just as it is, it's so complete. Still—then I look at you—and think of you not here like this— (*Blindly her hand travels up to his arm, across his face, over his head.*) And I don't know. (*A moment.*) Leave me alone a moment. Let me try once again, without you. (*He picks up her hand, kisses it. She holds his for a moment against her cheek, then drops it. The library door opens and* BURKE *comes in.*)

Dr. Burke is happy to report that Christian's as fine as silk, and Eve is as happy to receive the news. Dr. Burke is also prepared to say his formal good-bys to Dr. Hay. Quite a bright fellow, Hay, Burke agrees, though, of course, Christian would have got well, anyway. Hay had also better take care of himself, Burke suggests; he has been going too hard; he needs rest, and perhaps a little iodine.

The doctors have both left Eve when Gail comes. His old buoyancy has returned. He has brought Christian an iceboat model and is happy about that. So happy, in fact, that he finds it difficult to take Eve seriously when she wants to talk with him about what he would do if anything were ever to happen to her.

Gail cannot conceive of a life without Eve. He would, he guesses, just curl up and die. Still, as Eve reminds him, there would still be Christian. But Gail would not even know what to do with Christian without Eve. He is, if she insists upon it, willing to promise, solemnly, that he will let the boy's education be finished in Eve's way, by one she shall appoint. And then, grateful for the interruption of Gillespie, Gail is off to make Christian's eyes dance with the iceboat.

Eve has taken up her hat and coat and started for the hall when Christian's shout of joy over the boat, and Gail's answering ejaculations of satisfaction come to her from the library. Her coat drops in her hands. She turns to Gillespie. He shakes his head and murmurs, significantly:

"Not possible!"

Lifelessly, Eve has thrown her hat and coat on the sofa when Dr. Hay comes from the hall. Her decision has been made.

Nicholas must promise, she says, that he will take care of himself; let him heed Burke's warning; let him give up everything that is not important; let him—

"You're talking about me without you, Eve," he says.

"Yes." She nods her head slowly.

"You've decided?"

"Yes."

"You were never not decided."

"I think that's true," Eve admits. "I want to think so. Because now I see that even if there weren't Christian— Oh, if I didn't love *us*—you and me—! (*She concludes, simply:*) And I couldn't, then—I simply couldn't. (HAY *takes her in his arms, kisses her tenderly.*)

"Eve!"

"Oh, my Nicholas—thanks—thanks!" There is a note of triumph in Eve's voice as they draw reluctantly apart.

Now they are talking of irrelevant things; of Nicholas' watch and the excellent time it has kept through many, too many, years; of how Nicholas lives when he is traveling; of the seasons of the year and their preferences—

EVE (*quickly*)—Which do you like best? Spring, summer, autumn, winter?

HAY—Winter.

EVE—It's not *true!*

HAY—It's gospel.

EVE—Of course, we're fools to, you know that.

HAY—All right.

EVE—All *right.* (HAY *looks at his watch again, then at her, then turns reluctantly toward the library. She takes a quick step after him, speaking hurriedly.*) Do you get up early mornings?

HAY—Yes, like an idiot.

EVE—Then what do you do?

HAY—Eat breakfast.

EVE—Then what?

HAY—Mail.

EVE—Then what?

HAY—Work.

EVE—*Then* what?

HAY—Work.

EVE—Finally what?

HAY—Sleep.

EVE—Do you sleep well?

HAY—No.

EVE—Sleep well, darling.

HAY—Thank you, darling.

EVE—Pleasant dreams, darling.

HAY—And to you, my dear. (*A long silence. Then again he taps the watch and replaces it in his pocket.*) I'll say good-by to Christian. (*He goes to the library door and out.* GILLESPIE *comes in from the hall wearing his overcoat and carrying his hat.*)

GILLESPIE (*to* EVE)—The car's here.

EVE—Good.

GILLESPIE—Are you coming to see us off?

EVE—No.

GILLESPIE—Good-by, Mrs. Redman. (*She turns to him.*)

EVE—Good-by, Gillespie—look after him.

GILLESPIE—I will.

EVE—Now and then—write me about him.

GILLESPIE—Yes.

EVE—Be my friend, Gillespie.

GILLESPIE—God—Mrs. Redman—you two are all I love. (*She holds out her hand to him. He takes it.*)

EVE—That's good to know. Thanks. (ELLA *passes through the hall with* HAY'S *small bag.* HAY *follows her. He pauses for a moment in the first doorway.* GILLESPIE *sees him.* EVE *does not.* GILLESPIE *goes into the hall and out.* HAY *gazes silently at* EVE *for a moment. She turns. They look at each other for a long moment, without a word. Then he passes from view. Then for an instant he is seen through the other doorway, taking up his hat and coat, but* EVE'S *eyes remain where he was. He goes out down the hall. The front door closes after him. A motor is heard starting. Then, at last,* EVE *turns, face bright, no tears.*)

EVE (*to herself*)—Not changed. Complete— (*Then suddenly, swiftly, she goes to the French windows, opens them and flings her arm up: hail and farewell. The motor is heard departing, more distant, still more distant—*)

THE CURTAIN FALLS

ONCE IN A LIFETIME

A Comedy in Three Acts

BY MOSS HART AND GEORGE S. KAUFMAN

NOTHING was exactly normal around the Broadway district at the opening of the 1930-31 theatre season. David Belasco had started bravely with a comedy farce called "Dancing Partner" in early August, and had been credited with a hit of sorts. The Shuberts had scored another promising success with a Greenwich Village study in gin and the newer domesticity entitled "Up Pops the Devil." And Frank Craven had registered a definite Craven success with "That's Gratitude."

But it was not until the Moss Hart-George Kaufman satirical comedy, "Once in a Lifetime," came in on September 24 that the first "smash" hit of the season was achieved. This one was received with cheering and there was great rejoicing. George Kaufman, the collaborating author, played the rôle of Lawrence Vail, playwright, and made a curtain speech in which he insisted that Mr. Hart was responsible for at least two-thirds of the play. With little, if any, cessation in interest "Once in a Lifetime" ran the season through.

As the play begins the small-time vaudeville trio of Hyland, Daniels and Lewis is at liberty in New York. At the moment of the curtain's rise one of its male members, George Lewis, is resting in a furnished room in the West Forties, "a replica of the countless other furnished rooms in the neighborhood—cheerless and utterly uninviting."

"George is about twenty-eight, a clean-cut, nice-looking young fellow with the most disarmingly naïve countenance it is possible to imagine." He is also "the sort of person insurance men and book agents instinctively head for and, in the case of George, it might be noted, usually succeed in selling."

George is contentedly munching Indian nuts and reading *Variety*. Nor is he more than momentarily disturbed when May Daniels, the lady member of the sketch, enters from her room across the hall. Miss Daniels is a good deal of a person. A tall, good-looking, well-poised blonde. "There is a sharp, biting incisiveness about everything she says and does—a quick mind and a hearty, earthy sense of humor."

May is troubled. May has been troubled for the last four weeks. Jerry, who manages the act, has been trying between first-nights to get bookings and with no success. The bank roll at the moment has dwindled to $128, and three people cannot hope to live long on that, particularly if one of them continues to haunt the theatre as a diversion and another spends most of his allowance for Indian nuts and ball games. Something will have to be done and done quick. May is thoroughly fed up with living at the Automat. "We do everything but sleep there," she declares, "and we'd be doing that if they could get beds into them slots."

George sees nothing much to worry about. After all, $128 is $128 and something always turns up. At least something always has turned up. George is not what might be termed an ambitious type.

But now the picture changes. Jerry Hyland barges suddenly and a little explosively into the room, "looking like one of those slick men's clothing advertisements in *Vanity Fair.*" Dynamic and likable, "Jerry is in his early thirties, and the major part of his late twenties has been spent in concocting one scheme or another to get them out of vaudeville and into the Big Money."

Jerry is excited. He has just seen history made. He has heard the Vitaphone's first talking picture, with sound, and is completely sold on the idea that the new invention will revolutionize amusement business within six months. And they're leaving for Los Angeles in the morning! That's the big news!

"Are you out of your mind?" demands May, not at all convinced that this new excitement of Jerry's is anything but one more wild dream. But Jerry refuses to be depressed.

"Don't you understand, May?" he counters. "For the next six months they won't know which way to turn! All the old standbys are going to find themselves out in the cold, and somebody with brains and sense enough to use them is going to get into the big dough! The movies are back where they were when the De Milles and the Laskys first saw what they were going to amount to. Can't you see what it would mean to get in now?"

MAY—What do you mean get in, Jerry? What would we do there—act, or what?

JERRY—No, no! Acting is small potatoes from now on! You

can't tell what we'll do—direct, give orders, tell 'em how to do things! There's no limit to where we can go.

MAY (*vaguely groping*)—Yah, but what do we know about—

JERRY—Good Lord, May! We've been doing nothing but playing the act in all the small-time houses in the country. Suppose we do cut loose and go out there? What have we got to lose?

GEORGE—A hundred and twenty-eight dollars.

MAY—Shut up, George! I don't know, Jerry—

JERRY—We gotta get out there, May! Before this Broadway bunch climbs on the bandwagon. There's going to be a gold rush, May. There's going to be a trek out to Hollywood that'll make the '49'ers look sick.

MAY—Y' mean thar's gold in them hills, Jerry?

JERRY—Gold and a black marble swimming pool, with the Jap chauffeur waiting outside the iron-grilled gate—all that and more, May, if we can work it right and get in now! They're panic-stricken out there! They'll fall on the neck of the first guy that seems to know what it's all about! And that's why we gotta get there quick!

MAY—Yah, but give me time to think, Jerry. (*A hand to her head.*) Suppose we don't catch on right away—how are we going to live? You heard what the boy wonder said—a hundred and twenty-eight dollars.

JERRY (*exploding the bombshell*)—I've got five hundred more!

MAY—What?

JERRY—I've got five hundred more! Right here!

MAY—Where'd you get it?

JERRY—Now don't yell, May! I sold the act!

MAY—You did what?

JERRY—I sold the act! I took one look at that picture and sold the act outright to Eddie Garvey and the Sherman Sisters for five hundred cash. Now don't get sore, May! It was the only thing to do!

MAY (*slowly*)—No, I'm not getting sore, Jerry, but—

GEORGE (*coming to life*)—You sold the act to the Sherman Sisters?

JERRY—My God, if people once took a mule and a covered wagon, just because they heard of some mud that looked yellow, and endured hardships and went all the way across the country with their families—fought Indians, even—think what it'll mean, May, if we win out! No more traveling all over the country—living in one place instead of—

MAY (*catching some of his excitement*)—Okay, Jerry— I'm with you! You had some helluva nerve, but count me in!

JERRY—Good for you! How about you, George?

GEORGE—What?

JERRY—Are you willing to take a chance with us—leave all this behind and cut loose for Hollywood?

GEORGE—Well, but look—if you sold the act—

JERRY—Sure I sold the act! We're going out and try this new game! Now what do you say?

MAY—Come on, George!

JERRY—It's the chance of a lifetime!

GEORGE—But what'll we do there?

JERRY—We can talk that over on the train! The important thing is to get out there and to get there fast!

GEORGE—But if you've sold the act— (JERRY *gives up;* MAY *leaps into the breach. They are working in relays now.*)

MAY (*as to a child of ten*)—George, listen. We're giving up the act. We're not going to do the act any more. Don't you understand that?

GEORGE—Yah, but he sold the act— (*It seems that they sold the act.*)

MAY—I understand that he sold the act. Look, George. There is a new invention called talking pictures. In these pictures the actors will not only be seen, but will also talk. For the first time in the history of pictures they will use their voices. (*And in that moment a notion comes to her. Slowly she turns to* JERRY.) I've got an idea.

JERRY—What?

MAY—I think I know what we're going to do out there.

It's May's idea that practically all the motion picture actors in the world will now be wanting to know how to talk. Few of them have had any experience in speaking in public and they will be frightened stiff. Why not open a school of elocution and voice culture!

Jerry is a little stunned. It's a swell idea, all right, but what do they know about elocution? George, for one, never heard of it. But May is confident. Once she had attended a school of elocution and she knows the patter. With twenty-five dollars' worth of books and four days on the train she will know more about voice culture than the inventor. Right now she knows enough to practice on George. Let him repeat after her: "California, here I come!" George does so and it sounds pretty flat.

But with his stomach in, his chest out and his vision fixed firmly on an old covered wagon moving slowly across the plains in the general direction of a marble swimming pool, George is able to put a lot of feeling into the lines:

"California, here I come!"

"It works, Jerry—it works!" gleefully shouts May.

"And if it works on George it will work on anybody," agrees Jerry, as the curtain falls.

A few days later George, Jerry and May are on board a Pullman car, Los Angeles bound. They have reached the desert country of the southwest and the state of their nerves is none too good. "Jerry is in the middle of his hundredth cross-word puzzle, George is busy with *Variety* and the inevitable Indian nuts, while May gazes straight ahead, a troubled expression in her eyes."

May's principal trouble is listening to George crack nuts. Another day of that and she will be raving. How can she concentrate on elocution when the cracking of nuts is beginning to sound like cannons going off! The only place she can find any relief is in the ladies' smoker, whither she is now going. She does pick up a good dirty story there occasionally.

Jerry is worried about May. He and George will have to do something to keep her spirits up. They've got to put up a million-dollar front or they're sunk. Jerry knows that.

But May, darting back, has found something more cheering than anything Jerry could have thought of. In the ladies' smoker she has come practically face to face with none other than Helen Hobart! And Helen Hobart is probably the most widely read moving picture critic in America. Everybody knows her—even George reads her stuff. And May used to troupe with her.

"Say," explodes Jerry, as the full significance of May's discovery breaks upon him. "If she ever sponsored us we'd have all Hollywood begging to get in. She's a powerful, important lady, and don't you forget it."

Convinced that at the worst they have nothing to lose, they send the porter to tell Miss Hobart that May Daniels is on the train and would like to see her.

In meeting Miss Hobart it is May's idea that they should be very careful. "If you ever let her know we're just a small-time vaudeville act you'll get the prettiest freeze-out you ever saw. Unless she thinks you're somebody she won't even notice you."

Photo by White Studio, New York.

"ONCE IN A LIFETIME"

"It is the last day of shooting on Susan Walker's picture, 'Gingham and Orchids.' 'Set against a background of church wall and stained glass windows are pews, altar and all the other paraphernalia that go to make up the filming of a movie wedding.' "

(The bishop, Granville Bates; the director, at the extreme right, Hugh O'Connell)

It is May's idea that George and Jerry should let her do all the leading. She knows how to impress the Hobart type.

And then Helen Hobart appears. A woman of early middle life, "she positively glitters. Jewels stud her person from the smart diamond arrow in her hat to the buckles of her shoes, and her entire ensemble is the Hollywood idea of next year's style à la Metro-Goldwyn."

Miss Hobart is delighted, positively delighted, to find her old friend on the train. And May does what she can to convince her that the excitement is mutual. Mr. Hyland, May explains by way of the introductions, is her business manager, and Dr. Lewis is her technical advisor. They have been in England for eight years, which naturally explains their almost complete ignorance of the fact that Miss Hobart is probably the most widely circulated newspaper syndicate feature in the United States, as Helen admits she is.

"If you don't know, my dear, I can't quite tell you all," Miss Hobart protests. "But I think I can say in all modesty that I am one of the most important figures in the industry. You know, it was I who gave America Gary Cooper and Rex the Wonder Horse. Yes, I've done very well for myself. You know I always could write, May, but I never expected to be *the* Helen Hobart! Oh, I can't tell you *everything,* one—two—three, but movie-goers all over the country take my word as law. Of course, I earn a perfectly fabulous salary—but I'm hardly allowed to *buy anything*—I'm simply deluged with gifts. At Christmas, my dear—well, you'll hardly believe it, but just before I came East they presented me with a home in Beverly Hills!"

"No kidding!" ejaculates May, in spite of herself.

HELEN—They said I deserved it—that I simply *lived* in the studios. I always take an interest in new pictures in production, you know, and suggest things to them—and they said I ought to have a home I could go to and get away from the studios for a while. Wasn't that marvelous?

MAY—Marvelous!

HELEN—I call it Parwarmet. I have a penchant for titles.

MAY—You call it *what?*

HELEN—Parwarmet. You see, I always call my gifts after the people who give them to me—rather a nice thought, you know. And I didn't want to offend anybody in this case, so I called it after the three of them—Paramount, Warner, Metro-Goldwyn—the first syllable of each. Parwarmet.

GEORGE—Won't Fox be sore?

HELEN—Oh, no, Doctor. Because the Fox studios gave me a wonderful kennel, and I have twelve magnificent dogs, all named after Fox executives. But listen to me rattling on and not asking a word about *you!* Tell me what you've been doing. And what in the world took you abroad for eight years? The last I heard of you—

MAY (*quickly*)—Yes, I know. Well, of course, I never expected to stay in the theatre—that is, not as an actress. I always felt that I was better equipped to teach.

HELEN—Teach?

MAY—Voice culture. I began with a few private pupils, and then when I was abroad Lady Tree persuaded me to take her on for a while, and from that I drifted into opening a school, and it's been very successful. Of course, I accept only the very best people. Mr. Hyland and Dr. Lewis are both associated with me, as I told you—

HELEN—And now you're going to open a school in Hollywood!

MAY—What? Why, no—we hadn't expected—

JERRY—Hollywood? We hadn't thought about it.

HELEN—Wait till I tell you! Of course, you don't know, but something is happening at the present time that is simply going to revolutionize the entire industry. They've finally perfected *talking pictures!*

MAY—No!

HELEN—Yes! And you can't imagine what it's going to mean! But here's the point! Every actor and actress in the industry will have to learn to talk, understand? And if *we* were to open the first school—my dear!

MAY—But, Helen, we couldn't *think* of such a thing!

JERRY—Oh, no, Miss Hobart!

GEORGE—Sure! That's why we— (JERRY *silences him.*)

HELEN—I simply won't take no for an answer!

MAY—But what about our school in London?

JERRY—We've got a good deal of money tied up in London, Miss Hobart.

HELEN—May—America needs you. You're still, I hope, a loyal American?

MAY—Oh, yes, yes. But—

HELEN—Then it's settled. This is Fate, May—our meeting—and in the industry Fate is the only thing we bow to.

MAY—But—

HELEN—Now, please—not another word! Oh, but this is

marvelous—right at this time! Of course, it'll take a certain amount of money to get started, but I know just the man we'll take it to—Herman Glogauer! You know—the Glogauer Studios!

It appears, as Helen rattles on, that Herman Glogauer is probably the very most important figure in the fourth greatest industry, and a man open to any important suggestion affecting the future of pictures. Having been one of the first to turn down the Vitaphone, Mr. Glogauer, at the moment, is buying up everything anyone suggests, and a school of voice culture, Helen is ever so convinced, is simply crammed with possibilities. "I should say my half interest alone would bring me in—I just don't know how much," Miss Hobart ventures, tentatively declaring herself in, as it were.

Now Helen has been discovered by a fan. Little Susan Walker, who is also traveling westward to put her services at the call of the movies, is eager to have a chat with Miss Hobart and to get the benefit of her advice. "Susan, to give you the idea immediately, is the female counterpart of George, very young, very pretty, very charming, and, as you must have guessed by this time, very dumb." Susan and George are quite taken with each other. Which helps Miss Hobart a little in getting rid of Susan when George offers to take her back to her car—and her mother, who is traveling with her.

Now they find a moment to talk figures.

"How much would it cost, May, to start things going?"

"Fifty thousand," ventures Jerry.

"A hundred thousand," insists May.

"Oh, that's more like it," agrees Helen Hobart. "Now we get to Hollywood Tuesday. On Wednesday everybody gathers at the Stilton—"

She is going right on but the lowered curtain cuts her off.

The following Wednesday we are in the gold room of the Hotel Stilton in Los Angeles. The room is "early De Mille. Gold-encrusted walls, heavy, diamond-cut chandelier, gold brocade hangings, and simply impossible settees and chairs." And yet— "This particular room, for all its gaudiness, is little more than a passage to the room where Hollywood really congregates—so you can imagine what THAT is like. The evening's function is approaching its height, and through the room, as the curtain rises, there pass various gorgeous couples—one woman more magnificently dressed than another, all swathed in ermine and so hung with orchids that it's sometimes a little difficult to see the girl. The women, of course, are all stunningly beautiful."

In the distance an orchestra is playing "Sonny Boy" with determined persistence. "Weaving through the guests is a cigarette girl—but not just an ordinary cigarette girl. Like every other girl in Hollywood, she is beautiful enough to take your breath away. Moreover, she looks like Greta Garbo, and knows it. Hers is not a mere invitation to buy her wares: on the contrary, her 'Cigars, Cigarettes!' is charged with emotion. You never can tell, of course, when a director is going to come along."

Now the cigarette girl has met the coat check girl and they are talking shop. The coat check girl has just told the cigarette girl that there is a call out for talking prostitutes for Wednesday when a procession enters the room and sets them right back in their places.

The procession "is headed by Phyllis Fontaine and Floribel Leigh, two of filmdom's brightest and most gorgeous lights—or at least they were until yesterday, when Sound hit the industry. They are dressed to the hilt and beyond it—ermines, orchids, jewels. Behind each of them walks a maid, and the maids are hardly less beautiful than their mistresses. Next comes a pair of chauffeurs—tall, handsome men, who were clearly cut out to be great lovers, and who will be just as soon as the right director comes along. Each of the chauffeurs leads a Russian wolfhound—smartly jacketed animals who are doing their respective bits to celebrate the fame of their mistresses. For on one jacket is lettered: 'Phyllis Fontaine in "Diamond Dust and Rouge"' and on the other 'Florabel Leigh in "Naked Souls!"'" All in all, it is an imposing procession. Led by its haughty stars it advances and prepares for the Grand Entrance.

Now Miss Leigh's chauffeur makes sure that the stairway is clear, and with the final powdering touches attended to, and their respective wolfhounds on leash, the girls sweep grandly toward their triumph. As they disappear the beautiful Florabel Leigh's voice, a bit harsh when raised in warning, floats back from her bower of orchids:

"If they put us at that back table I'm going to raise an awful stink," she is saying.

"Yes, God damn it," agrees Phyllis Fontaine acidly, "they ought to know by this time . . ."

The help returns to the shop. A bellboy is in to announce that the French Revolution they were making at Universal, and which was later changed to a college picture on account of the sound, has just been changed back to a French Revolution picture in the men's room. This means that they will be playing the guillotine all the way through it, the bellboy is informed, which lets at least one of the maids out because she doesn't know one note from another.

Susan Walker and her mother are in. Susan is having the hardest time containing herself, so great is the excitement, and Mrs. Walker has already seen at least a half dozen John Gilberts. It is still early, Ernest, the head waiter, tells them. (ERNEST *was one of the John Gilberts before he spoke.*) "Of course, no one of any consequence gets here before ten," he says. "You get a smattering of Pathé and First National, but you don't get United Artists until ten-fifteen."

When George Lewis arrives on the scene he is also considerably bewildered by what is going on, but able to keep going. Susan Walker finds him a little excited over the fact that probably right in that very room they will later meet Herman Glogauer himself. That is practically enough to floor Susan, though she accepts the announcement gleefully. George has been hearing Susan recite Kipling's "Boots" and other poems and has been visibly impressed with her talking picture possibilities. His is an enthusiasm, however, that neither May Daniels nor Jerry Hyland share with him. Nor do they like the idea of George trying to speak to Mr. Glogauer about anything.

"George, when Mr. Glogauer gets here and you're introduced to him just say 'Hello.' See" is May's first warning. "In a pinch, 'Hello, Mr. Glogauer.' Then, from that time on—nothing."

"But suppose I have an idea?"

"That's when I sing 'Aïda'!"

The excitement grows with the entrance of Helen Hobart, and Helen is responsible for her part of it. Just everybody, Helen reports, is talking about sound and nobody is at all sure where he is at. The Schlepkin Brothers—and there are twelve of those—have just decided to scrap a silent super-super, "The Old Testament," and devote all their attention to talkies. And this, mind you, on the advice of the oldest Schlepkin, who is really the brains of the business and who made his start when he had the cloak room privilege in all the West Coast theatres.

Outside there is the whirr of an expensive car. Inside there is a marshaling of forces. Mr. Glogauer is arriving. And Mr.

Glogauer, Miss Hobart would have you remember, is the man who, just because he was lacking in vision, turned down Vitaphone and has been buying everything else offered to him ever since.

There is some little trouble getting Mr. Glogauer into the place, even with the police holding the mob in check. Literally everybody seems to want just a minute of his time. But the nervous little man is obdurate. He will only do business with them at his office. The police and bellboys finally get the crowd out and the doors shut. Then after Mr. Glogauer has assured the bellboys that he is not, at the moment, in the market for a great trio, Helen Hobart is able to get his attention. It is pretty hard on Mr. Glogauer, this series of assaults by the artistic unemployed.

"It's terrible," Mr. Glogauer admits. "Terrible! Everywhere I go they act at me! If I only go to have my shoes shined, I look down and someone is having a love scene with my pants."

"That's the penalty of being so big a man," ventures Helen, coyly.

GLOGAUER—All over the hotel they come at me. Ordinarily I would say, "Let's go out to my house," where we got some peace. But Mrs. Glogauer is having new fountains put in the entrance hall.

HELEN—It's the most gorgeous house, May. You remember—we saw it from the train.

MAY—Oh, yes. With the illuminated dome.

HELEN—And the turrets.

GLOGAUER—In gold leaf.

HELEN—But the *inside,* May! I want you to see his bathroom!

MAY—I can hardly wait.

HELEN—It's the show place of Hollywood! But they can see it some other time—can't they, Mr. Glogauer?

GLOGAUER—Any Wednesday. There is a guide there from two to five. I tell you what you do. Phone my secretary—I send my car for you.

MAY—Why, that'll be wonderful.

HELEN—Yes, and what a car it is! It's a Rolls-Royce!

MAY—You don't say?

GEORGE—What year? (*It is, to say the least, an awkward moment.*)

JERRY (*coming to the rescue*)—Well, Mr. Glogauer, we understand that you're in the midst of quite a revolution out here.

HELEN—I should say he is!

GLOGAUER—Is it a revolution? And who have we got to thank for it? The Schlepkin Brothers. What did they have to go and make pictures talk for? Things were going along fine. You couldn't stop making money—even if you turned out a *good* picture you made money.

JERRY—There is no doubt about it—the entire motion picture is on the verge of a new era.

HELEN—Mr. Glogauer, I tell you the talkies are here to stay.

GEORGE (*who knows a cue when he hears one*)—The legitimate stage had better—

MAY—All right, George.

GLOGAUER—Sure, sure! It's colossal! A fellow sings a couple of songs at 'em and everybody goes crazy. Those lucky bums!

HELEN—He means the Schlepkin Brothers.

GLOGAUER—Four times already they were on their last legs and every time they got new ones. Everything comes to those Schlepkin Brothers. This fellow Lou Jackson—sings those mammies or whatever it is—he comes all the way across the country and goes right to the Schlepkin Brothers. (*The* BELLBOY *enters.*)

BELLBOY—I beg your pardon, Mr. Glogauer.

GLOGAUER—Yes, yes? What is it?

BELLBOY—The twelve Schlepkin Brothers would like to talk to you. They're downstairs.

GLOGAUER—Tell 'em later on. I come down later.

BELLBOY—Yes, sir. (*Goes.*)

GLOGAUER—Schlepkin Brothers. I know what they want! They're sitting on top of the world now—with their Lou Jackson—so they try to gobble up everybody! All my life they been trying to get me! Way back in the fur business already, when I had nickelodeons and they only had pennylodeons! And because there's twelve of them they want odds yet!

That is the moment for Jerry to step forward and suggest to Mr. Glogauer that he let his own people learn how to talk. The time, too, for May to suggest that "abdominal respiration is the keynote of elocutionary training."

"We'll not only teach your people to talk, Mr. Glogauer, but we'll have them talking as well as you do," promises Jerry.

"Well," protests Mr. Glogauer, whose accent is typical, "I don't ask miracles."

Mr. Glogauer is, however, greatly interested in the proposition being presented to him. If Phyllis Fontaine, for instance, who was worth her $7,500 a week every time she undressed in a silent picture, can be taught to talk so she can be heard, "the most beautiful legs in America" will again have commercial value.

"They're beautiful girls, but unspeakable," laments Mr. Glogauer.

Presently Florabel and Phyllis have been brought from the supper room and presented to Miss Daniels and to Mr. Hyland, voice specialists from England. And after May has listened to them breathe, and explained to them that if they can learn to breathe rhythmically, as she believes they can, she assures them they can surely learn to talk correctly.

Mr. Glogauer is practically overjoyed. As May lifts her ear from Florabel's chest he demands, eagerly:

"We got something?"

"Absolutely," replies May, with quiet confidence.

HELEN—Isn't that wonderful?

PHYLLIS—We can do it?

GLOGAUER—Keep still, girls! We got something, huh? We ain't licked yet? What's next? What do they do now?

MAY—For the present they should just keep breathing.

GLOGAUER—Hear that, girls? Wait around—don't go home. Now I tell you how we handle this! I give you rooms right in the studio and as fast as you turn 'em out we put 'em right to work! We got to work fast, remember!

JERRY—Right!

MAY—Right!

GLOGAUER—You teach these people to talk and it's worth all the money in the world!

JERRY—We'll teach 'em!

GLOGAUER—You people came just at the right time! We'll show 'em—with their Lou Jackson! This is a life-saver! To hell with the Schlepkin Brothers. (GEORGE, *breathless, runs back into the room, dragging* SUSAN *after him. You begin to understand what he went out for.*)

GEORGE (*indicating* GLOGAUER)—There he is, Susan! Right there!

SUSAN (*rushing right up to him and starting in*)—"Boots," by Rudyard Kipling.

GLOGAUER—What?

SUSAN (*making the most of her opportunity*)—"Boots, boots, boots, boots—"

GLOGAUER—What? What? I don't want any boots!

SUSAN—"Marchin' up and down again . . ."

BELLBOY—The Schlepkin Brothers! (*As* SUSAN *continues her recitation the Schlepkin Brothers march in. And when the Schlepkin Brothers march in they march in. There are twelve of them—all shapes and sizes.—Two abreast, they head for* GLOGAUER.)

MOE SCHLEPKIN (*at the head of the line*)—Listen, Herman, we're flying back to New York tonight—

GLOGAUER—No, sir! I wouldn't merge! I got something better! I wouldn't merge!

SUSAN—"Five, seven, nine, eleven, four and twenty miles today—"

THE CURTAIN IS DOWN

ACT II

The reception room at the Glogauer studio is "ultra-modernistic in its décor." It is "meant to impress visitors and seldom falls short of its purpose. The walls are draped in heavy gray plush, the lighting fixtures are fantastic and the furniture is nobody's business."

Seated at the reception secretary's desk—"modernistic as hell, but a desk," is the secretary herself. "She wears a flowing black evening gown, although it is morning, fondles a long string of pearls and behaves very much like Elinor Glyn."

"Also present is Lawrence Vail—a nervous young man who is waiting, none too comfortably, in one of the modernistic chairs. He wears the hunted look of a man who has been waiting for days and days, and is still waiting."

It is a busy reception room. Things are happening every minute, and often at a rate of two a minute. There are many telephone calls. At periodic intervals a page "wearing a simply incredible costume," appears with an illuminated sign of which he is careful to see everyone in the room makes note. The one he is holding at the moment reads: "Mr. Glogauer is on Number Four."

"Miss Leighton at this end," intones Miss Leighton, picking up the receiver of the telephone. "Who? . . . Oh, yes. Yes, he knows you're waiting. . . . How many days? . . . Well, I'm afraid you'll just have to wait. . . . What? . . . Oh, no, you couldn't possibly see Mr. Glogauer. . . . No, I can't make an appointment for you. . . . Oh, no, you can't see Mr. Weisskopf. . . . You can only see Mr. Weisskopf through Mr. Meterstein. . . . Oh, no, no one *ever* sees Mr. Meterstein."

A second page, with a second sign, draws himself up, clicks his heels military fashion, and from his sign we learn that "Mr. Weisskopf is on Number Eight!"

From Miss Leighton's answers, to page or phone, it is learned that Miss Daniels is busy with her 10 o'clock voice class. From Mr. Weisskopf and Mr. Meterstein, who are volubly explosive as they walk through the room, it is discovered that retakes are most important in their business. Mr. Sullivan and Mr. Moulton, also passing through, recall parts of the story of a super-special in which the kid sister of the heroine is convinced she is being double-crossed. And so it goes.

Finally Miss Leighton is moved to notice Mr. Vail. Mr. Vail, having been noticed before, does not accept the experience as being exactly in the nature of a novelty, but he is glad to repeat his name, to add that he is still waiting to see Mr. Glogauer, and that he is a playwright, just as he was yesterday, the day before and the day before that.

Miss Leighton will see what can be done about informing Mr. Weisskopf. But Mr. Weisskopf, according to the placard another page has just brought in, "Is on Number Six."

"Thank you so much," says Mr. Vail.

"You're welcome, sir," replies the page, clicking his heels a second time.

"Now," continues Mr. Vail, "I'll give you a piece of news. I'm going to the men's room and if anybody wants me I'll be in Number Three."

Phyllis Fontaine and Florabel Leigh come from their lesson with Miss Daniels. Phyllis has practically conquered the "She sells seashells by the seashore" speech and Florabel is doing right well with "Sixty simple, supple sirens, slick and smiling, svelt and suave."

"Ain't it wonderful, Miss Leighton? We can talk now," sings Phyllis.

"Really?"

"Yes, and a damn sight better than most of them," chips in Florabel.

Miss Leighton—I think your progression has been just marvelous. I can't see why they keep bringing people from New York.

FLORABEL—Yeh—people from the "legitimate" stage, whatever that is.

PHYLLIS—Yes, Miss Leighton, we've been wondering about that. What the hell is the legitimate stage, anyway?

MISS LEIGHTON—It's what Al Jolson used to be on before he got famous in pictures. He worked for some real estate people—the Shuberts.

FLORABEL—Do you know what someone told me at a party the other day? They said John Barrymore used to be on the legitimate stage.

PHYLLIS—I heard the same thing and I don't believe it.

MISS LEIGHTON—My, you'd never know it from his acting, would you?

FLORABEL—And that ain't all. I've heard that since *he's* made good some sister of his is trying to get out here.

MISS LEIGHTON—Yes, Elsie Barrymore. . . . It must have been kind of interesting, the legitimate stage. Of course, it was before my time, but my grandfather used to go to it. He was in the Civil War, too.

PHYLLIS—The Civil War—didn't D. W. Griffith make that?

May Daniels comes from her classrooms, eager for a vote of confidence from someone. Florabel and Phyllis assure her that they are doing fine and Miss Leighton is eager to add her endorsement. Miss Leighton would also like to recite Kipling's "Boots" for Miss Daniels when opportunity offers.

"I've been having some trouble with the sibilant sounds," reports Miss Leighton, "but my vowels are open all right."

Which is fine, May admits, so long as there isn't any fever. She is about to return to the classroom to straighten out a mix-up in which the nasal throat toners have gone in with the abdominal breathers when Jerry breezes in.

Jerry has been more than busy the last few weeks. No time for May, he admits. No time for anyone. A fellow has to be on the jump and very particular about keeping in with the right people if the school is to continue prospering.

May is worried. No report has come from Glogauer since he has heard Phyllis' and Florabel's tests. That looks bad to May, but Jerry isn't worried. Neither is George. At least George isn't worried about the school. Only about Susan Walker. Susan is a wonderful girl; George is convinced of that. And since he has heard her recite the one beginning, "Yes, I'm a tramp—what of it? Folk say we ain't no good—" George is interested in Susan and Susan has admitted she likes George. But Susan has also announced that she wouldn't think of getting married until she has carved out her career. That takes a load off May's mind. May doesn't want George to think seriously of marriage until he's sure—sure of a lot of things. . . .

Now Lawrence Vail is back in his old chair, waiting. May notices him. She has noticed him before.

"Isn't there some disease you get from sitting?" she asks him.

"If there is, I've got it," agrees the playwright.

"What do you do about your meals? Have them sent in?"

"What's the record for these chairs—do you happen to know?" counters Vail, passing the query.

"I'm not sure—I think it was a man named Wentworth. He sat all through Coolidge's administration," reports May.

Vail is not the only one in trouble. Rudolph Kammerling, German director, takes over the reception room as being a good place in which to express a mood. Mr. Kammerling is about ready to return to Germany and UFA on the next boat unless he can get something resembling satisfaction in Hollywood. What right have they to send him the somewhat notorious Dorothy Dodd to play the country heroine of his new picture and thereby threaten the ruin of his American career? Mr. Kammerling simply will not stand for it.

Again Miss Leighton becomes conscious of Lawrence Vail. She almost remembers his name, but she certainly has forgotten his face. Which is naturally a little disappointing to Mr. Vail. He had so hoped that Miss Leighton would come to know him in time.

VAIL (*ready to commit murder*)—Say it ain't true, Duchess—say you remember?

MISS LEIGHTON—Oh, yes. An appointment, wasn't it?

VAIL—That's it—an appointment. I got it through a speculator. Listen, maybe this will help you. I work here. I have an office—a room with my name on the door. It's a big room, see? In that long hall where the authors work? The people that write. Authors! It's a room—a room with my name in gold letters on the door.

MISS LEIGHTON (*visibly frightened by all this*)—What was the name again?

VAIL—Lawrence Vail.

MISS LEIGHTON—Oh, you're Lawrence *Vail*. Well, I'll tell Mr. Weisskopf—

VAIL (*stopping her*)—No, no! Nothing would come of it.

Just let the whole thing drop. Life will go on. Only tell me something—they make talking pictures here, is that right?

MISS LEIGHTON—What?

VAIL—This is a picture studio? They make pictures here—pictures that talk? They do *some*thing here, don't they?

MISS LEIGHTON (*edging away*)—I'll tell Mr. Weisskopf—

VAIL—Don't be afraid of me, little girl. I'll not harm you. It's just that I've been in that room—my office—the place with my name on the door—for months and months—nobody ever noticed me—alone in there—the strain of it—it's been too much. And so I came out. I don't expect to see Mr. Glogauer any more—I just want to go in and wander around. Because tomorrow I'm going home, and I want to tell them I saw 'em made. Who knows—maybe I'll run into Mr. Glogauer—I'd love to know what God looks like before I die. (*He goes.*)

Miss Leighton is shaking with apprehension as Mr. Vail storms out. Nothing could convince her that Mr. Vail is not drunk. And the next moment Helen Hobart has come to inquire if the Glogauer studios know anything about a playwright named Lawrence Vail. Her New York newspaper is inquiring. Vail, they say, is supposed to have come to Hollywood a long time ago and nothing has been heard from him.

No, Miss Leighton doesn't think there is anyone around there by that name. Perhaps Paramount— But Miss Hobart has tried Paramount. Paramount has lost six playwrights of its own the last six months, but none of them was named Vail. And then, surprise after surprises, Miss Leighton does find Lawrence Vail's name right there in the playwrights' book. "Lawrence Vail, playwright, dark hair, brown eyes." He had come out with a shipment of sixteen playwrights from New York in October. He must be somewhere around. Probably in the playwrights' room. Miss Leighton will look in there, though she really hates to do it. The playwrights' room always frightens her, with its padded walls and barred windows! . . .

Helen Hobart is quite snippy with May Daniels when they meet a moment later. Suddenly there seems to be a complete lack of interest on Helen's part, not only in the voice school, but in May herself and all her activities. It is an ominous change.

"Then you *have* heard something, haven't you, Helen?" demands May. "Who from—Glogauer?"

"Why, of course not, May—whatever gave you such an idea? Of course you never can tell about things out here—sometimes something will just happen to catch on, and then again—well!"

"Thanks, Helen. I'm very grateful." May's fears have been confirmed. But even if they had not been the arrival of Mr. Flick, with his kit of tools, would have settled matters.

Flick is the man who puts names on and takes names off the office doors. He is looking now for the offices of Miss May Daniels, Mr. Jerry Hyland and Dr. George Lewis. He has to take their names off. Quite a common experience for Flick.

"I do more door work than anybody else in Hollywood," he explains to May, cheerfully. "Out at Fox the other day I went right through the studio—every door. Why, some of the people didn't even know they were out till they saw me taking their names off."

Jerry can't believe that it has happened when May passes the sad news on to him, using the nursery parable form.

"Did you ever hear the story of the Three Bears?" she asks Jerry.

"Huh?" Evidently Jerry never had.

May—There was the Papa Bear, and the Mamma Bear, and the Camembert. They came out to Hollywood to start a voice school—remember? A couple of them were engaged to be married or something—that's right, they were engaged—whatever happened to that?

Jerry—Wha-at?

May—Well, anyway, they *did* start a voice school—what do you think of that? They started a voice school and had a big office, and everything was lovely, and then suddenly they came to work one morning, and where their office had been there was a beautiful fountain instead. And the Mamma Bear said to the Papa Bear, What the hell do you know about that?

Jerry—May, stop clowning! What is it?

May—And this came as a great big surprise to the Papa Bear, because *he* thought that everything that glittered just *had* to be gold.

Jerry—Say, if you're going to talk in circles—

May—All right—I'll stop talking in circles. We're washed up, Jerry.

Jerry—What are you talking about?

May—I said we're washed up. Through, finished and out!

Jerry—What do you mean we're out? Why—who said we're out?

May—I knew it myself when we didn't hear about those tests—

I felt it. And then ten minutes ago Helen Hobart walked in here.

JERRY—What did she say?

MAY—She handed the school right back to us—it seems she had nothing to do with it. That tells the story!

JERRY—That doesn't mean anything! You can't tell from what she says!

MAY—Oh, you can't, eh? Then I'll show you something that does mean something, and see if you can answer this one! (*She starts for the door through which* MR. FLICK *has vanished. The arrival of* GEORGE *stops her.*)

GEORGE—May! May, something terrible has happened!

MAY—I know it!

GEORGE—You can't! It's Mr. Walker! Susan has to go back home—they're leaving tomorrow!

JERRY—May, what were you starting to tell me?

GEORGE—Did you hear what I said, May? Susan has got to go back home!

JERRY—Shut up, George! (*To* MAY.) What were you going to tell me?

MAY (*breaking in*)—For God's sake, stop a minute! George, we've got more important things!

GEORGE—There couldn't be more important things!

JERRY—Oh, for the love of—

MAY—Well, there are! We're fired, George—we haven't got jobs any more!

GEORGE—What?

JERRY—How do you know, May? How do you know we're fired?

MAY—I'll show you how I know! (*She goes to the door and opens it. In a trance, they follow her and look off.*)

JERRY (*in a hushed tone*)—Gosh!

GEORGE—You mean the window washer?

JERRY (*stunned*)—Why—why, I was talking to Glogauer only yesterday.

MAY—Well, there you are, Jerry. So you see it's true.

GEORGE—You mean—you mean there isn't any school any more?

MAY—That's the idea, George.

GEORGE—But—but—why? Then—what about Susan?

MAY—Oh, let up on Susan! Besides, I thought you said she was going home.

GEORGE—Yah, but if we could get her a job right away. (MR.

FLICK *returns with scraper and tool-kit in hand. Crosses cheerfully, with a nod to all.*)

MAY—Well, that was quick work.

FLICK—Oh, it don't take long. You see, I never use permanent paint on those doors. (*A pause after his departure.*)

MAY—Well, I suppose we might as well get our things together. (*She looks at the disconsolate figure of* JERRY.) Don't take it so hard, Jerry. We've been up against it before.

JERRY—But everything was so—I don't know which way to turn, May. It's kind of knocked me all of a heap.

MAY—Don't let it lick you, Jerry—we'll pull out of it some way. We always have.

JERRY—Yah, but—not this. A thing like this sort of—what are we going to do?

MAY—What do you say we go to Hollywood? I hear they're panic-stricken out there. They'll fall on the necks of the first people—

May and Jerry have gone. George is still considerably dazed, but he manages to forget his own troubles when Susan Walker bounces in with hers. Susan is terribly unhappy, even in George's arms. Her career apparently is blasted even before she had a chance to start carving. When she had pleaded with her father to let her wait for Technicolor he had rudely advised her "to stop being a goddam fool and come on home."

There is no hope of changing father's mind. Susan is convinced of that. He is the sort of man who, "when the first talking picture came to Columbus, stood right up and talked right back to it."

But George is not discouraged. He will do something. He will see Mr. Glogauer personally. He asks Miss Leighton where he can find Mr. Glogauer. Miss Leighton cannot tell him. She has trouble enough. She is looking for a playwright and there is a drunken man following her around. So George asks Lawrence Vail. Vail doesn't know, either. He has put in a lot of time looking for Mr. Glogauer himself, and he is beginning to doubt if there is any such man, really. Mr. Vail, in fact, is pretty low. A sympathetic ear appeals to him. When George asks what he is doing, the story of Lawrence Vail just naturally comes out.

VAIL (*sadly*)—Don't ask me that. I don't know. I don't know anything about it. I didn't want to come out to this Godforsaken country. I have a beautiful apartment in New York—and friends. But they hounded me, and belabored me, and hammered at me, till you would have thought if I didn't get out here by the fifteenth of October every camera in Hollywood would stop clicking.

GEORGE—You don't say?

VAIL—And so I came. In a moment of weakness I came. That was six months ago. I have an office, and a secretary, and I draw my check every week, but so far no one has taken the slightest notice of me. I haven't received an assignment, I haven't met anybody outside the girl in the auditor's office who hands me my check, and in short, Dr. Lewis, I haven't done a single thing.

GEORGE—Why do you suppose they were so anxious to have you come out, then?

VAIL—Who knows? Why do you suppose they have the pages dressed the way they are, and those signs, and that woman at the desk, or this room, or a thousand other things?

GEORGE—Don't you like it out here?

VAIL—Dr. Lewis, I think Hollywood and this darling industry of yours is the most God-awful thing I've ever run into. Everybody behaving in the most fantastic fashion—nobody acting like a human being. I'm brought out here, like a hundred others, paid a fat salary—nobody notices me. Not that I might be any good—it's just an indication. Thousands of dollars thrown away every day. Why do they do that, do you know?

GEORGE—No, sir!

VAIL—There you are. Plenty of good minds have come out here. Why aren't they used? Why must everything be dressed up in this goddam hokum—waiting in a room like this, and having those morons thrust a placard under your nose every minute? Why is that?

GEORGE—I don't know.

VAIL—Me neither. The whole business is in the hands of incompetents, that's all. But I don't have to stay here, and I'm not going to. I've tried to see Mr. Glogauer—God knows I've tried to see him. But it can't be done. So just tell him for me that he can take his contract and put it where it will do the most good. I'm going home, and thank you very much for listening to me.

GEORGE—There's a lot in what you say, Mr. Vail. I've been having a good deal of trouble myself.

VAIL—You bet there's a lot in what I say. Only somebody ought to tell it to Glogauer.

GEORGE—That's right. Well, look—why don't you make an appointment with Mr. Glogauer and tell him?

This is too much for Lawrence Vail and he passes disconsolately from the room. A moment later George's great opportunity arrives. Herman Glogauer himself, in person, enters the reception room. He is in the midst of a hot argument with Kammerling, the German. It is mostly about Dorothy Dodd. She simply will not do, insists Mr. Kammerling. What he wants is a simple country girl, and Dorothy Dodd knows men. Dorothy Dodd, as a matter of common report, asserts Mr. Kammerling, "has lived with a dozen men—and looks it." Mr. Kammerling, not being God, cannot hope to make her over. They will simply have to get somebody else. Maybe they could borrow somebody—somebody like Janet Gaynor. But that doesn't sound reasonable to Mr. Glogauer.

Now George has an idea. George knows just the person. Her name is Susan Walker. True, Susan has never done anything. Nor has she a name. But why do they have to have a name? Let Mr. Glogauer tell George that. Why?

"Because Susan Walker as a name wouldn't draw flies—that's why. Not flies," explodes Mr. Glogauer.

"But she could play the part," persists George.

GLOGAUER—So what? Who would come to see her? Why do you argue on such a foolish subject? Everybody knows you can't do a picture without a name. What are you talking about?

GEORGE (*his big moment*)—Mr. Glogauer, there's something you ought to know.

GLOGAUER—What?

GEORGE—This darling industry of yours is the most God-awful thing I've ever run into.

GLOGAUER—Huh! (*Stares at him.*)

GEORGE—Why don't people act human, anyhow? Why are you so fantastic? Why do you go and bring all these people out here, whoever they are, and give them all this money, and then you don't do anything about it? Thousands of dollars—right under your nose. Why is that?

GLOGAUER—Huh?

GEORGE—Can you tell me why in the world you can't make pictures without having the stars playing parts they don't fit, just because she's got a good name or something? How about a girl that hasn't got a good name? And how about all these signs, and this room, and that girl, and everything? And everything else? It's the most God-awful—all kinds of people have come out here—why don't you do something about it? Why don't you do something about a person like Miss Walker, and give her a chance? Why, she'd be wonderful. The whole business is in the hands of incompetents, that's what's the trouble! Afraid to give anybody a chance! And you turned the Vitaphone down! (GLOGAUER *gives him a startled look.*) Yes, you did. They're all afraid to tell it to you! That's what's the matter with this business. It's in the hands of—you turned the Vitaphone down!

GLOGAUER (*stunned; slowly thinking it over*)—By God, he's right!

GEORGE (*not expecting this*)—Huh?

GLOGAUER—He's right! And to stand up there and tell me that—that's colossal!

GEORGE—You mean what I said?

GLOGAUER—That's what we need in this business—a man who can come into it, and when he sees mistakes being made, talk out about them. Yes, sir, it's colossal.

GEORGE (*if it's as easy as that*)—Why, it's the most God-awful thing—

KAMMERLING—Who is this man? Where did he come from?

GLOGAUER—Yes, who are you? Didn't I sign you up or something?

GEORGE—I'm Dr. Lewis.

GLOGAUER—Who?

GEORGE—You know—the school.

GLOGAUER—You are with the school? But that school isn't any good.

GEORGE (*moved to accidental assertiveness*)—It *is* good!

GLOGAUER—Is it?

GEORGE (*with a sudden realization that an emphatic manner can carry the day*)—Why, of course it is. You people go around here turning things down—doing this and that—

GLOGAUER (*to* KAMMERLING)—He's right! Look—I pretty near fired him! I did fire him.

GEORGE—You see? And here's Susan Walker—just made for the talkies.

GLOGAUER—Say, who is this girl?

KAMMERLING—Where is she?

GLOGAUER—Tell us about her.

GEORGE—Well—Mr. Kammerling knows her—I introduced her.

GLOGAUER—She's here in Hollywood?

GEORGE—Oh, sure! She just went—

KAMMERLING—I remember! She might be able to do it! She is dumb enough.

GEORGE—Shall I bring her in?

GLOGAUER—Yes, yes—let's see her!

GEORGE—She's right out here. (*Rushing out.*)

GLOGAUER—Fine, fine! There is a big man, Kammerling! I can tell! Suddenly it comes out—that's the way it always is!

KAMMERLING—In Germany, too.

GLOGAUER—Turned the Vitaphone down—no one ever dared say that to me! I got to hang on to this fellow—take options.

Another ten minutes and Susan has been brought in, found to look the part perfectly, proved that she can repeat "I love you" and "I hate you" after Mr. Kammerling with really astounding results and Susan is hired. More than that, Mr. Glogauer has ideas. He tells them to Meterstein. He wants the office to drop everything and concentrate on the discovery of Miss Walker. She will be an English actress recently arrived in New York. There will be a reception for her at the Savoy-Plaza and she will be photographed with Mayor Walker.

"I want national publicity on this," shouts Mr. Glogauer; "outdoor advertising, twenty-four sheets, everything. Meterstein, arrange a conference for me with the whole publicity department this afternoon! That's all!"

This attended to Mr. Glogauer is ready to turn again to George. "Now then, Doctor, tear up your old contract!" he instructs the still slightly befuddled Lewis.

"I haven't got one!"

GLOGAUER—You are in charge of this whole thing—understand? What you say goes!

GEORGE—Yes, sir.

SUSAN—George, does that mean—

GLOGAUER—When I have faith in a man the sky's the limit! You know what I do with you, Doctor? I make you the supervisor in full charge—over all productions of the Glogauer Studio!

SUSAN—George—!

GEORGE (*very matter-of-factly*)—All right. (MAY *and* JERRY *enter*—JERRY *carrying a brief case,* MAY *with her hat on, both obviously ready to leave.*) May! Jerry! What do you think! I've just been made supervisor!

SUSAN—Yes!

JERRY—Huh!

MAY—What!

GEORGE—I told him about the Vitaphone!

MAY—You did what?

GLOGAUER—The one man! (*To* GEORGE.) Tomorrow morning you get your office—with a full staff!

GEORGE (*to* MAY *and* JERRY)—You hear that?

GLOGAUER—That's the way we do things out here—no time wasted on thinking! I give you all the people you need—anybody you want! All you got to do is say so!

GEORGE—I know who I want, Mr. Glogauer!

GLOGAUER—Already he knows—see, Kammerling?

KAMMERLING—Wonderful!

GLOGAUER—All right! Name 'em—name 'em.

GEORGE—I want Miss Daniels and Mr. Hyland!

JERRY—What is this?

GLOGAUER—What? Those people? (*A deprecatory wave of the hand.*) You don't want them! They're fired!

GEORGE—Mr. Glogauer, I know who I want!

GLOGAUER—But you could have Weisskopf, Meterstein—

GEORGE—No, sir. I have to have Miss Daniels and Mr. Hyland or I can't do anything. If I can't have them (*in a very small voice*) I walk right out.

SUSAN—George, you mustn't!

MAY—California, here we go! (*But it doesn't seem to be true.* GLOGAUER *fairly throws his arms around* GEORGE, *pleading with him to stay.*)

GLOGAUER—No! No! . . . Miss Daniels! Mr. Hyland!

MISS LEIGHTON (*entering, followed by two pages bearing an enormous silver coffee service*)—Here you are, Mr. Glogauer. (*The phone rings.*) Miss Leighton at this end.

THE CURTAIN IS DOWN

ACT III

There is "tremendous but rather vague activity on the Glogauer lot. It is the last day of shooting on Susan Walker's picture, "Gingham and Orchids." "Set against a background of church wall and stained glass windows are pews, altar, wedding bell and all the other paraphernalia that go to make up the filming of a movie wedding."

The players, costumed to represent bridesmaids and ushers, mill about a good deal. Bits of gossip break through the drone of conversation. The Bishop himself dozes peacefully in one of the pews. When he is awakened by a page boy calling Mr. Meterstein the Bishop recalls that he has not seen the Racing Form for which he has been waiting. He must check up on what the ponies are doing at Caliente.

Orders are shouted by and to sound men, camera men, light men and helpers. Mrs. Walker arrives with the exciting news that Mr. Walker has agreed to come on for Susan's wedding.

Now there is considerable added excitement because Mr. Kammerling has decided to take the scenes on the church step and Susan cannot remember whether Miss Daniels has rehearsed her in that one or not. They did rehearse a scene outside the church, as May reminds her, but Susan never thought of that as being the scene on the steps. Yet it is. "In practically all the churches they now put steps on the outside," explains May, and this serves to clarify Susan's mind.

Jerry Hyland has also come to the set for this last day's shooting. Jerry is very happy to report that Mr. Glogauer is tickled pink, which, May agrees, should be a becoming color. For the first time in the history of the Glogauer studios, Jerry reports, a picture has been finished exactly on schedule and it is going to be a knockout.

May is not that enthusiastic. After all there is no use kidding yourself. There are, in this "Gingham and Orchids," many scenes so dark no one can see anything. George, it seems, had forgotten to turn on the lights and the director thought he meant it that way. Furthermore, asks May, has Jerry noticed the knocking that has gone on whenever parts of the picture have been shown? Yes, Jerry has noticed the knocking and the sound engineers are even now working on some plan to eliminate it. But what caused the knocking? "That was George cracking his goddam Indian nuts," May explains.

Even as she is explaining the great Dr. Lewis is announced and in comes George, "preceded by a pair of pages bearing a silver coffee service and the inevitable box of Indian nuts."

George is kept pretty busy these days making decisions. He has decisions to make, in fact, at practically every hour of the day. Just now he decides that Mr. Kammerling can go ahead with the scene of the wedding ceremony where it had been left, and that helps everybody. They will, of course, use the pigeons. When the bride says "I do" the Bishop must remember to pull the ribbon that releases the pigeons and they will fly out. They will fly out, and the Bishop hopes they will not also fly down upon him.

"Those pigeons know what to do," George reassures him. "They were with Cecil De Mille for two years."

And then George suddenly remembers that there aren't any pigeons. Feeling sorry for them, all cooped up the way they were, he had sent them home. So they will have to shoot the scene without shooting the pigeons.

Now the cry goes up and up: "Mr. Glogauer is coming!" "Mr. Glogauer is coming!" . . . "He arrives all bustle and importance. He is followed by one page who carries a portable desk and a telephone, by a second page who brings a small folding chair, and by the ubiquitous Miss Chasen and her notebook. Immediately the page puts together the desk and plugs in the telephone; Miss Chasen settles herself, and in the twinkling of an eye the place is open for business."

Mr. Glogauer is beaming. He has come, it appears, to offer his sincerest congratulation to Dr. Lewis on his amazing record in finishing "Gingham and Orchids" exactly on schedule. Never before since Mr. Glogauer started to make Glogauer Super-Jewels has such a thing been known. And as a slight token of his regard he takes great pleasure in presenting Dr. Lewis with a solid gold dinner set with his initials in diamonds on everyone of the 106 pieces.

George is all but overcome. Seeing that it is the first dinner set he ever received he hardly knows what to say and, to be consistent, doesn't say it. They go on with the filming of the scene.

But now there is real trouble. Mr. Glogauer does not recognize the picture. That cannot be the end of it—that simple embrace and fadeout. Where is the backstage scene? Where is the scene in which the heroine, even though her mother is dying, has to act anyhow because the show must go on? Mr. Glogauer had twelve playwrights working on that scene, and naturally wants to see it. But that scene, George assures him, was not in the picture.

GLOGAUER (*dangerously calm*)—This is a picture about a little country girl?

GEORGE—Yes, sir.

GLOGAUER—Who gets a job in a Broadway cabaret?

GEORGE—There isn't any Broadway cabaret.

GLOGAUER—No Broadway cabaret?

GEORGE—She doesn't come to New York in this.

GLOGAUER—Doesn't come—you mean the cabaret owner doesn't make her go out with this bootlegger?

GEORGE—Why, no, Mr. Glogauer.

GLOGAUER—Well, what happens to her? What *does* she do?

GEORGE—Why, this rich woman stops off at the farmhouse and she takes her to Florida and dresses her all up.

GLOGAUER—And there is no backstage scene? Any place?

GEORGE—No. She goes out swimming and gets too far out and then Cyril Fonsdale—

GLOGAUER—Let me see that script, please.

GEORGE—It's all there, Mr. Glogauer. (GLOGAUER *looks through the script.*) See? There's where she goes swimming.

GLOGAUER (*closing the script with a bang*)—Do you know what you have done, Dr. Lewis? You have made the wrong picture! (*Consternation, of course.*)

GEORGE—Huh?

KAMMERLING—What is that?

GLOGAUER—That is all you have done! Made the wrong picture!

GEORGE—But—but—

JERRY—Are you sure, Mr. Glogauer?

GLOGAUER (*looking at the thing in his hand*)—Where did you get such a script?

GEORGE—Why, it's the one you gave me.

GLOGAUER—I never gave you such a script. She goes swimming! Swimming! Do you know who made this picture? Biograph, in 1910! Florence Lawrence and Maurice Costello—and even then it was no good!

JERRY—But look, Mr. Glogauer—

GLOGAUER—Sixty thousand dollars I paid for a scenario, and where is it? In swimming!

GEORGE—Well, everybody was here while we were making it.

GLOGAUER—Everybody was here! Where were their minds? Kammerling! Kammerling!

KAMMERLING—It's not my fault. Dr. Lewis gave us the script.

GLOGAUER—I had to bring you all the way from Germany for this. Miss Newton! You held the script in your hands! Where were your eyes?

MISS NEWTON—I got it from Dr. Lewis—right in his office. I'm sure I couldn't—

GLOGAUER—So, Doctor! On Wednesday night we open and we have *got* to open. And after that it goes to four hundred exhibitors and we got signed contracts! So tell me what to do, please!

GEORGE—Well, couldn't we release it as a super-special?

GLOGAUER—Never in my life have I known such a thing! After this I make a ruling—every scenario we produce, somebody has got to read it!

JERRY—Yes, Mr. Glogauer.

GLOGAUER—You know what this does to *you,* Miss Walker! You are through! Swimming! This kills your career! And you know who you got to thank for it? Dr. Lewis! (SUSAN *meets the situation by bursting into tears.*) A fine supervisor! The business is in the hands of incompetents, he says! So what do I do? I give him everything the way he wants it—his own star—his own staff— (*It is a new thought. He fixes* MAY *and* JERRY *with a malignant eye.*) Oh, yes. And where were *you people* while all this was going on?

JERRY—Mr. Glogauer, I was on the cost end. I didn't have anything to do with the script. Dr. Lewis was the—

GLOGAUER—But Miss Daniels was here—all the time! Right with Dr. Lewis! What about *that?*

MAY (*not frightened*)—Yes. I was here.

GLOGAUER—Well! Where was your mind?

MAY—To tell you the truth, Mr. Glogauer, I thought it was just another Super-Jewel.

GLOGAUER—Oh, you did?

MAY—I couldn't see any difference.

GLOGAUER—You couldn't, huh?

MAY—And while we're on the subject, Mr. Glogauer, just why is it Dr. Lewis' fault?

GLOGAUER—Why is it his fault? Who did this thing? Who else is to blame?

MAY—Well, if I'm not too inquisitive, what do *you* do with yourself all the time? Play marbles?

GLOGAUER—What's that?

MAY—Where were you while all this was going on? Out to lunch?

GLOGAUER (*drawing himself up with dignity*)—I go to my office. That will be all.

Kammerling dismisses the company. Susan Walker is in tears and refuses to be comforted. May is angry with Jerry because he had not stuck up for George. Jerry's gone Hollywood, that's what happened to him, and, so far as May is concerned, that's that.

As for George, nothing is quite so serious with him as Susan's refusal to listen to him. Nor can he understand why everything has happened as it has or why it is so terribly serious if it has.

GEORGE—Susan ought to know I didn't do it on purpose. I tried to tell her. Look, May, do you think the picture's so bad?

MAY—Bad as what, George?

GEORGE—Bad as he thinks it is?

MAY—Well, I think it's got a good chance.

GEORGE—Chance of what, May?

MAY—Of being as bad as he thinks it is.

GEORGE—Oh!

MAY—By the way, George—just to keep the record straight—how'd you come to *make* the wrong picture? Or don't you know?

GEORGE—Well, I've been trying to think. You know that thing in my office where we keep the new scenarios—well, if you're in a hurry it looks exactly like the wastebasket—and so I reached into it, only it was the wastebasket—

MAY—And thus endeth the first lesson.

GEORGE—But look, if I go to him and tell him how it happened—

MISS CHASEN (*in the distance*)—Paging Dr. Lewis! Miss Daniels!

MAY—Ah, here we are! Right in here. I thought it was taking a long time. (MISS CHASEN *enters.*) You're late.

MISS CHASEN (*giving her two envelopes*)—Executive office! No answer! (*Turns to go.*)

MAY—Wait a minute. Who else have you got? (*Examining remaining envelopes.*) Kammerling, Weisskopf, Meterstein—Ah, yes. (MISS CHASEN *goes.* MAY *turns back to* GEORGE.) Do you want yours?

GEORGE—Do you mean we're—fired, May?

MAY—Good and fired!

GEORGE (*in a daze, opening his letter*)—Yah.

MAY (*looking at hers*)—Me too. Well, George— We've got a solid gold dinner set, anyway. A hundred and six pieces, and every piece marked with your initials in diamonds. That's not bad for two months' work. (*Two pages enter and carry off the dinner set.*) No, George—you *haven't* got a gold dinner set.

(*The curtain falls.*)

In the same Pullman car in which Jerry, May and George had traveled to California weeks before May Daniels now sits by herself. The train is headed east. It is nearing Needle's Point. There is a sanitarium there. The porter would be pleased to get her anything she wants at the station.

May can think of nothing she would like, unless it is Thursday's Los Angeles papers. And if they are not Thursday's she doesn't want them . . .

A passenger climbs aboard at Needle's Point. He turns out to be Lawrence Vail, the playwright. He, too, is heading East, and feeling fine after a few weeks at the sanitarium. It is a grand place to rest. Started by a playwright who went mad his eighth month in Hollywood. Run exclusively for playwrights. Great place.

"First three days they put you in a room without a chair in it. Then they have a big art gallery—life-size portraits of all the studio executives. You see, for an hour every day you go in there and say whatever you want to any picture."

Vail is surprised to find Miss Daniels and to hear the story of *her* Hollywood experiences. She recalls the incident of Dr. Lewis' telling Mr. Glogauer boldly about his having turned Vitaphone down. She reminds him of the sudden elevation of Susan Walker. And then—

MAY—With that to start with, the Doctor cinched things by working from the wrong scenario. Some little thing from 1910. The picture opened Wednesday. And how is *your* uncle, Mr. Vail?

VAIL—My recollection of the 1910 pictures is that they weren't so bad.

MAY—They didn't have the Doctor in those days. Most of it you can't see because the Doctor forgot to tell them to turn the lights on; Miss Walker has a set of gestures that would do credit to a traveling derrick—and did you ever happen to hear about the Doctor's bright particular weakness?

VAIL—There's something else?

MAY—It's called Indian nuts. (*A glance around.*) There must be one around here somewhere. Anyhow, he eats them. With sound. He kept cracking them right through the picture, and they recorded swell.

VAIL—That, I take it, decided you?

MAY—That, and—other things.

VAIL—Funny—I should think there would be a great field out there for a man who could turn out the wrong picture.

MAY—Yes, if he could do it regularly. But sooner or later Dr. Lewis would make the right one.

VAIL—Not the Doctor.

MAY—Well, maybe you're right.

The porter has brought in the papers. Vail helps May find the notices. It isn't difficult. They are pretty generously displayed—"Gingham and Orchids—an all-talking, all-singing—" all-lousy picture. That is what May expected to read. But—

Wonder of wonders! They can't believe their eyes! "Never in the history of Hollywood has so tumultuous an ovation been accorded to any picture—" Vail reads. "Herman Glogauer's 'Gingham and Orchids' is a welcome relief from the avalanche of backstage pictures. It marks a turning point in the motion picture industry—a return to the sweet simplicity and tender wistfulness of yesteryear.

"A new star twinkled across the cinema heavens last night and the audience took her at once to its heart. Here at last is an actress who is not afraid to appear awkward and ungraceful."

Everything is praised. The fact that at last there is a wedding without pigeons; the originality of the lighting, with the climaxes played in the dark.

"The whole thing couldn't be a typographical error, could it?" quietly queries Vail.

And as for the cracking nuts! "In the opening sequences," May reads, "the audience was puzzled by a constant knocking, and it seemed to many of us that something might be wrong with the sound apparatus. Then suddenly we realized that what was being done was what Eugene O'Neill did with the constant beating of the tom-tom in the 'Emperor Jones.' It was the beat of the hail on the roof. (*She looks up at* VAIL, *who nods.*) It is another of the masterly touches brought to the picture by that new genius of the films, Dr. George Lewis."

They have not much time to be flabbergasted. The porter is in with a telegram for Miss Daniels. It is from the new genius of the films. She reads it aloud: "The picture is colossal. It has put the movies back where they were ten years ago. I am the Wonder Man of the Talkies. They keep coming at me to decide things. Please take next train back—Jerry is gone and I am all alone here. They made me an Elk and Susan is an Eastern Star.

Please take next train back—I need you. Where is Jerry? I am also a Shriner."

VAIL—Well, what are you going to do about that?

MAY (*looking at the telegram*)—"Jerry is gone and I am all alone here." (*Letting the telegram slowly fall.*) Well, it looks as if I'm going back.

VAIL—I think you have to.

MAY—Because if George is alone out there (*she breaks off*)— And then there's another thing. As long as George owns Hollywood now, there are two or three reforms that I would like to put in effect. Do you know what I'm going to do?

VAIL—What?

MAY—I'm going to get all those page boys together and take their signs away from them—then nobody will know where anybody is. I'm going to pack up the Schlepkins and send 'em back to Brooklyn, and then I'm going to bring their mother out here. I'm going to take Miss Leighton out of that reception room—

VAIL—Put cushions on those chairs—

MAY—And make her ask for an appointment to get back in!

VAIL—Great.

MAY—And when I get that done, I'm going out to Mr. Glogauer's house, put the illuminated dome where the bathroom is, and then I'm going to take the bathroom and drop it into the Pacific Ocean.

Back in Hollywood the decorative scheme of Mr. Glogauer's reception room is somewhat altered. Over every door now there is a life-size bust picture of Dr. George Lewis, and things have been so arranged that whenever a door is opened the picture above it lights up.

The Doctor himself is present and fairly busy. An artist is sketching his portrait. Miss Newton is trying to get decisions on an armful of scripts. Two or three newspapermen are there for interviews. There is a man who wants an endorsement for a patent necktie and another who would like to publish the Doctor's autobiography.

The Doctor is pacing the floor "and handling all comers." His message, so far as the outside world is concerned, is simple and direct. The coming year, the Doctor is convinced, will be a Glogauer year. "The legitimate stage had better look to its laurels."

George has just sent word by his secretary to the Knights of Columbus waiting downstairs that he will join later, and has got as far in his biography as the momentous hour in Medallion when, as an usher, he was put in charge of the last two rows of the mezzanine, when in breaks Susan Walker a little more aflutter than usual. The picture is wonderful. Seeing her name in lights is wonderful. Everything is just wonderful.

George has another surprise for Susan, too. He has an aeroplane for her! A man had given it to him because he had bought quite a few aeroplanes for Mr. Glogauer.

There is only one thing that is worrying George at the moment. If Jerry and May would only come back. It is the first time they have not been together and George does not feel right about it.

A moment later George has many more things to worry about. Mr. Glogauer has just barged in and is very angry. Outside the lot is simply jammed with aeroplanes. They are arriving in lots of fifty and more are expected. The order, according to Miss Leighton, is for two thousand of them! Mr. Glogauer is beside himself with rage. Still, George cannot understand why. All he has done is to buy a few aeroplanes— He follows Mr. Glogauer away to explain.

Then May Daniels arrives. She is looking for Mr. Hyland. Miss Leighton does not know what has become of Mr. Hyland. She understood after he left the company he started almost immediately for the East.

When George comes back he is overjoyed to find May, but he knows no more about Jerry than Miss Leighton. Jerry, says George, had gone to find May. He said, reports George, that nothing else mattered.

A moment later the trio is again complete. Jerry, too, has come back. May is pretty cross about the way Jerry has acted—but they are all together again. That's something. That's something that a lady might be permitted to shed a tear or two about if she were left to herself. It makes May feel "like a second act climax." It seemed so long when they were separated.

"From now on it's the army with banners, no matter what happens," says May, a little exultantly. "George is the biggest man in Hollywood and we're riding the high wave!"

George is not so sure. Mr. Glogauer is awful mad at the moment. All because of those 2,000 aeroplanes. Yes, George admits, he had bought 2,000 of them—and got one for nothing.

JERRY—What! In God's name, George, what did you do it for?

GEORGE—Can't we do something with them? There ought to be some way to use 2,000 aeroplanes.

MAY—Sure—make applesauce!

JERRY—Well, you can't lick that! It's all over but the shouting, May. For God's sake, George, how could you do such a thing?

MAY—Well, there you are, Jerry, and what are you going to do about it?

JERRY—Why did you do it, George?

GEORGE—Well, if somebody offered you an aeroplane— (*And back comes* MR. GLOGAUER, *followed by* SUSAN *and about half the studio force.*)

GLOGAUER (*who seems to be beaming*)—Well, Doctor, we have done it again! Isn't it wonderful?

SUSAN—George!

GEORGE—Huh!

GLOGAUER—We've done it again! What a man you are, Doctor—what a man you are!

JERRY—What's this?

GLOGAUER—Miss Daniels! Mr. Hyland. Did you hear what the Doctor did? He went out and bought 2,000 aeroplanes! Wasn't that wonderful?

MAY (*trying to get her bearings*)—Wonderful!

JERRY—Wonderful.

GLOGAUER—The trend is changing, Miss Daniels—they just been telephoning me! Everybody wants to make aeroplane pictures, but they can't make 'em because the Doctor bought up all the aeroplanes! Every company is phoning me—offering me any amount!

GEORGE—Yes, I thought they would.

SUSAN—Isn't it wonderful?

GLOGAUER—So, Doctor, you saw the trend coming! You saw the trend.

MAY—Saw it? He *is* the trend!

JERRY—You don't realize the kind of a man you've got here!

GLOGAUER—Yes, I do! Doctor—this is the way you work—always you make believe you are doing the wrong thing—and *then*. Doctor, I bow to you!

SUSAN—Oh, George!

MAY—George, you don't need us. You just go ahead and be yourself.

GEORGE—Mr. Glogauer, there's something we've got to take up.

GLOGAUER (*anxiously*)—What?

GEORGE (*pointing to the door through which* GLOGAUER *has just entered*)—One of my pictures doesn't light up!

GLOGAUER—What! Meterstein! Weisskopf! (METERSTEIN *and* WEISSKOPF *hurry off, to rectify the error.*) Doctor, you're not angry! Tell me you're not angry!

MISS LEIGHTON (*entering*)—Mr. Glogauer—

GLOGAUER—Yes?

MISS LEIGHTON—Do you know the studio's being torn down?

GLOGAUER—What?

MISS LEIGHTON—There's a lot of workmen downstairs. They have orders to tear down the studio!

GLOGAUER—Tear down the studio!

MISS LEIGHTON—Yes, sir!

GLOGAUER (*looks slowly to* GEORGE *to see if he is the man who gave the order.* GEORGE *wears a broad grin of perfect confidence. He nods.* GLOGAUER *turns back to* MISS LEIGHTON)—Tell 'em to go ahead! I don't know what it is, but it'll turn out all right! (METERSTEIN *and* WEISSKOPF *dash in, indicating the relit picture.*)

METERSTEIN—O.K. now, Mr. Glogauer!

GEORGE—We're putting up a bigger one, Mr. Glogauer.

JERRY—Say, that's a good idea!

GLOGAUER—Wonderful! There's another trend coming, eh, Doctor?

GEORGE—Sure, sure!

SUSAN—Isn't he wonderful, May?

MISS LEIGHTON (*at phone*)—Construction department, please.

THE CURTAIN IS DOWN

GREEN GROW THE LILACS

A Comedy in Three Acts

By Lynn Riggs

THE fourth production of the Theatre Guild season brought an American folk play to the stage. This was Lynn Riggs' "Green Grow the Lilacs," which tells, with interludes of cowboy songs, a romance of the prairie country the time Indian Territory was still outside the union and before the now proud state of Oklahoma was more than a politicians' dream.

Mr. Riggs, who hymns with poetic fervor the open country, the friendly neighbors and the gorgeousness of nature, had had two of his plays previously produced in New York, but neither was successful.

One was a serious drama of youth caught in the meshes of physical passion, called "Big Lake," which was given a semi-professional production by the Laboratory Theatre in 1927. The other a roistering open country comedy entitled "Roadside," which Arthur Hopkins produced this season but decided to withdraw two weeks after its first performance.

Neither the reviewers nor any considerable number of playgoers approved "Roadside," though Mr. Hopkins, one of the most astute of judges among the producing managers, thought, and still thinks, of it as "the first American dramatic classic."

The Guild bought "Green Grow the Lilacs" a year or so back, and held it against the time it could be fitted advantageously into its repertoire. The play was produced in January, Herbert Biberman directing. Originally it did not have the song interludes arranged as they were worked out by the Guild, nor do they appear in the Samuel French printed version of the play, approved and expanded by Mr. Riggs. They proved an important and attractive feature of the stage production, however.

Mr. Riggs sets the mood of "Green Grow the Lilacs" with his first scene, which shows the front room of a farmhouse set in a wheat field in what was the Indian Territory on a day in June. The room is three-sided, the fourth wall removed, and occupies the center of the stage as a single unit of scenery. The audience sees all around it. Across the yard stands a smoke-house with two windows exposed.

"It is a radiant summer morning several years ago," writes the author; "the kind of a morning which, enveloping the shapes of earth—men; cattle in a meadow; blades of the young corn; streams—makes them seem to exist now for the first time, their images giving off a visible golden emanation that is partly true and partly a trick of imagination focusing to keep alive a loveliness that may pass away."

It is also a typical territorial front room in that "it rests upon and glorifies scrubbed floors of oak, bright rag rugs, rough, hide-bottomed hairy chairs, a rock fireplace, a settee, an old organ magnificently mirrored, ancestral enlargements in their gilt and oval frames."

Back of the house containing the front room, and to be seen around the corner of the building, is a stretch of fence. Behind the fence is a row of cowboy farmers, leaning on their elbows mostly and listening to the baritone voice of another of their number who has not yet put in an appearance. The song floats in:

As I was a-ridin' one morning for pleasure
I met a bold cowboy a-lopin' along.
His hat was shoved back an' his spurs was a-jinglin'
As he come a-near me a-singin' this song.
Huppy Hy, yi, yo! Git along, little dogies,
It's yore misfortune and none of my own.
Huppy Hy, yi, yo! Git along little dogies
For you know Montana will be your new home!

The singer is Curly McLain, "a tall, waggish, curly-headed young cowboy in a checked shirt and a ten-gallon hat. The boys are inclined to ride Curly. He is not one who loves work. He does, it may be gathered, a lot better singin' than he does workin'.

The sound of someone approaching in the house sends the young farmers scurrying. Curly McLain drops quickly on all fours beneath the window, hiding.

Aunt Eller Murphy, "a buxom, hearty woman about fifty," carries in a tall, wooden, brass-banded churn and sets it down preparatory to continuing her work after she has discovered what the racket outside is about.

Knowing the voice to have been that of young McLain, Aunt Eller is not altogether mystified. Just a casual glance out the window is revealing. No need of Curly's trying to hide himself with feet like his, even if his head isn't showing.

Curly is quick to admit his identity and his business. He had come to sing to Aunt Eller and was getting along fine when the hired hands interrupted. Aunt Eller would, she allows, be much pleased if he would finish the song. Curly certainly does sing purty.

"If I wasn't an old womern," confesses Aunt Eller, shaking a threatening finger at Curly, "and if you wasn't so young and smart-alecky—why, I'd marry you, and git you to sit around at night—and sing to me."

"No, you wouldn't neither. If I was to marry—anyone—I wouldn't set around at night a-singin'. They ain't no tellin' *what* I'd do! But I wouldn't marry you ner none of yer kinfolks, if I could he'p it."

"Uh, uh!" protests Aunt Eller, wisely, "none of my kinfolks neither, huh?"

"No, an' you can tell them that, all of 'em, includin' that niece of yourn, Miss Laurey Williams, if she's about anywhurs."

Now Curly has climbed through the window and is in the front room. He isn't askin' anything but he would kinda like to know where Aunt Eller would say Laurey Williams is at if she were to say. He's even willing to sing another song as a bribe, except he can't sing unless he's lonesome.

"Out in the saddle where it ain't so sunny, or on a dark night close to a fa'r, when you feel so lonesome to God you could die—that's the only time a man can sing."

"Lonesome?" echoes Aunt Eller; "then if I was you I'd be a-singin' and a-singin' then. A long song, with forty 'leven verses and a chorus 'tween every verse. Fer as fur as I c'n make out, Laurey ain't payin' you no heed a-tall. You might jist as well be ridin' the rails as a-ridin' that range of yourn. So sing yer head off, you lonesome dogie, 'cause you shore have got into a lonesome sidepocket, 'thout no grass, you dehorned maverick, you!"

"What'd I keer about that?"

Curly would be nonchalant, even though he may be worried. He rolls himself a cigarette.

AUNT ELLER—She goes around with her head some'eres else, don't she?

CURLY—How'd I know? Ain't looked at her nary a time since Christmas.

AUNT ELLER—'Twasn't yore fault though, if you didn't. (*Jeering good-naturedly.*) She don' see *you,* does she, Mr. Adam's Off Ox! You've got onto the wrong side of the wagon tongue!

CURLY—Go on, you mean old womern! *Brand* a steer, till you turn a hole in his hide!

AUNT ELLER—*Mr.* Cowboy! A-ridin' high, wide and handsome, his spurs a-jinglin', and the Bull Durham tag a-whippin' outa his pocket! Oh, *Mr.* Cow Puncher! 'thout no home—ner no wife—ner no one to muss up his curly hair—er keep him warm on a winter's night! (*Roar ha! ha!*)

CURLY (*swelling up, defensively*)—So she don't take to me much, huh? Whur'd you git sich a uppity niece 'at wouldn't pay no heed to *me?* (*Rises.*) Who's the best bronc buster in this yere state?

AUNT ELLER—You, I bet.

CURLY—An' the best bull-dogger in seventeen counties? Me, that's who! And looky here, I'm handsome, ain't it?

AUNT ELLER—Purty as a pitcher.

CURLY—Curly-headed, ain't I? And bow-legged from the saddle for God knows how long, ain't I?

AUNT ELLER (*agreeing*)—Couldn't stop a pig in the road.

CURLY—Well, whut more does she want then, the damned she-mule?

AUNT ELLER—I don' know. But I'm shore sartin, it ain't *you.*

CURLY (*sitting*)—Ah-h! Quit it, you'll have me a-cryin'!

AUNT ELLER—You better sing me a song then, like I told you to in the first place.

CURLY—Ain't you a bother though—keep on a-pesterin'! You go and tell Laurey to drop a stitch, and see what Sandy Claus brung her.

AUNT ELLER (*rises and crosses to him*)—Meanin' you, I guess. Whut'd you want with her, Curly, nohow? I'm her aunt, so you better tell me first, and see if I likes the looks of it.

CURLY—You're jist nosey. Well—if you have to know my business—ole man Peck over acrost Dog Crick's givin' a play-party and I come to ast if Laurey ud go with me.

AUNT ELLER—An' me, too, huh?

CURLY—Yeow, you too. If you'll go an' knock on the door there an' bring Laurey out where a man can git a look at her.

Laurey Williams is not one to be called out of her room if she doesn't want to come. At the moment coming out apparently is far from either her thought or her intention. She is full of questions and indifference as Aunt Eller calls through the door to her about the play-party and the caller who has come to see her.

Finally when she does put in her seemingly reluctant appearance Laurey is far from pleasant. "She is a fair, spoiled, lovely young girl about eighteen, in a long white dress with many ruffles. Her hair is in a pompadour."

Laurey sees Curly McLain, but the sight of him stirs no receptive emotions. She thought perhaps there was someone there who meant something. She had heard someone "a-talkin' rumbly" with Aunt Eller, and she had heard someone "a-singin' like a bull-frog in a pond." But she didn't know who it was. All men sound alike to Laurey.

"You knowed it uz me, so you set in there—a-thinkin' up somethin' mean to say," ventures Curly doggedly. "I'm a good mind not to tell you nuthin' about the play-party now. You c'n jist stay at home, fer yer tongue. Don't *you* tell her where it is, Aunt Eller. Me 'n' you'll go and leave her at home."

"If you *did* ask me, I wouldn't go with you," snaps Laurey. "Besides, how'd you take me? You ain't bought a new buggy with red wheels onto it, have you?"

"No, I ain't."

"And a spankin' team with their bridles all jinglin'?"

"No."

" 'Spect me to ride on behind ole Dun, I guess. You better ast that ole Cummins girl you've tuck sich a shine to, over acrost the river."

"If I was to ast you—they'd be a way to take you, Miss Laurey— Smarty."

"Oh, they would?"

Now Curly has fashioned himself a surrey from a couple of high-backed chairs, with Aunt Eller's apron as a top. He is ridin' high, he shouts, and anybody ridin' with him is sure to feel like a queen with a crown on her head with diamonds in it as big as goose eggs. It's a yeller rig, with a lot of fringe on it, and isinglass windows and a "red and green lamp set on the dashboard, winkin' like a lightnin' bug."

Laurey has to laugh at that exhibition. Where could Curly McLain get a rig like that, less he hired it over at Claremore, thinking she would go with him? Well, she won't. And if he made it all up out of his head, he'd better be gettin' out of there before she takes a stove iron to him!

She is after him now, in a burst of peevishness. He is dodging her and taunting her with the fine ride she might have a-goin' to the play-party, to do a hoe-down till morning if she had a mind to, and ride home again, " 'ith the sun a-peekin' at you over the ridge, purty and fine."

"I ain't wantin' to do no hoe-down till mornin'," says Laurey, with deliberation; "an' what would I want to see the sun come up fur, a-peekin' purty and fine, alongside of you?"

"Whyn't you jist grab her and kiss her when she acts that-a-way, Curly?" interposes Aunt Eller, standing, an amused observer, at the edge of the rumpus. "She's jist achin' fur you to, I bet."

"Oh! I won't even speak to him, let alone 'low him to kiss me," furiously shouts Laurey; "the braggin', saddle-awk'ard, wish-'t-he-had-a-sweetheart bum!"

Laurey has flounced herself out of the room and Curly, dazed and amazed, is pulling himself slowly together. Only Aunt Eller is able to retain a sense of perspective.

"She likes you—quite a little," she says, slowly, to Curly.

"Whew! 'F she liked me quite a *lot,* she'd sic the dogs onto me, or shoot me full of buckshot!" says Curly.

Aunt Eller holds to her conviction. She knows women and she knows Laurey Williams. She has been father and mother to Laurey ever since the girl's parents died. She knows it's Curly that Laurey's caring about more than any of the others. There aren't any others, really.

"From the way she flew at you, jist now, I got my mind all made up," concludes Aunt Eller. " 'F she don't git *you,* Curly, she'll waste away to the shadder of a pin point. Yes, sir. Be put in a sateen coffin dead of a broken heart."

"I wouldn' want her to do *that,*" Curly allows, ironically, "I'd consider lettin' her have me, 'f that ud keep her from dyin'."

AUNT ELLER (*wisely*)—She's a young girl—and don't know her mind. She don't know her feelin's. You c'n help her, Curly —and they's few that can.

CURLY—They must be plenty of men a-tryin' to spark her. And she shorely leans to one of 'em, now don't she?

AUNT ELLER—Ain't no one a-sparkin' her. Well, there *is* that ole widder man at Claremore, makes out he's a doctor er a Vet'-nary. And that fine farmer, Jace Hutchins, jist this side of Lone Ellum—

CURLY (*crosses, picks up his hat*)—That's whut I thought!

AUNT ELLER—Not to say nuthin' about someone nearer home that's got her on his mind so much he don't know a plow from a thrashin' machine—

CURLY—Who'd you mean by that?

AUNT ELLER—Jeeter. (JEETER *drops to the ground.*)

CURLY—Jeeter who?

AUNT ELLER—Don' you know Jeeter Fry, our h'ard hand?

CURLY—What! That bullet-colored growly man 'th bushy eyebrows that's always around orderin' the other hands how to work the mowin' machines or sump'n! (JEETER *crawls below window. Crosses to porch, picks up wood out of sight.*)

AUNT ELLER—Now you don't need to go and say nuthin' agin him. He's a big help aroun' hyur. Jist about runs the farm by hisself. Well, two women couldn't do it, you orter know that. (LAUREY *heard humming.*)

CURLY—Laurey'd take up 'th a man like that?

AUNT ELLER—I ain't said she's tuck up with him.

CURLY—Well, he's around all the time, ain't he? Eats his meals with you like one of the fambly, don't he? Sleeps around here some'eres, don't he?

AUNT ELLER—Out in the smoke house.

CURLY—Laurey sees him all the time, then, don't she? Whyn't you say so in the first place? (*Crosses to window, turns and faces* AUNT ELLER.) Whur is this Jeeter, till I git a look at him and mebbe black his eyes fer him?

AUNT ELLER (*slyly*)—Thought you'd moved yer camp some-'eres else?

CURLY (*with exaggerated bravado*)—My camp's right here till I git ready to break it. And moreover,—whoever puts his foot in it's liable to get shot for a stinkin' skunk er a sneakin' wildcat!

The front door bangs open. Jeeter Fry, "the bullet-colored, growly man, with an armful of wood for the fireplace, comes in." He throws the wood in the woodbox, pauses at Laurey's door on his way out, listens to the girl humming to herself and, with a surly grunt, passes out without a word, banging the door behind him.

Curly looks wonderingly after Jeeter. The sight of the hired man who lives in the smokehouse helps him to make up his mind.

Laurey sticks her head through the door of her room. She won't have time to help Aunt Eller with the churning, she announces, because she will have to get herself fixed up for the party. She's goin' to Ol' Man Peck's with Jeeter. He'd asked her a week ago. She looks at Curly with a kind of defiant helplessness as she slams her door to and disappears.

Curly stands very still, staring at Laurey's door. Through the smokehouse window Jeeter can be seen puttering around the drawer to a table. Presently he takes out two guns, cocks them and sights them, and lays them down. Then he produces a package of thumbed postal cards and becomes absorbed in them.

Curly has moved over to the organ. "Now, wouldn't that jist make you bawl!" he mutters, ruefully, as he soberly strikes a chord or two. He sinks into a chair and soon he begins to sing, satirically at first, though soon the song has absorbed him and his voice becomes plaintively sentimental—"his head back, his eyes focused beyond the room, beyond himself, upon the young man having his sad say, the young man who'll go into the army, by God, and put an end to his distemper, his unrequited fervor:

"I used to have a sweetheart, but now I've got none,
Since she's gone and left me, I care not for one,
Since she's gone and left me, contented I'll be,
For she loves another one better than me.

"I wrote my love a letter in red rosy lines,
She sent me an answer all twisted in twines,
Saying 'keep your love letters and I'll keep mine,
Just write to your sweetheart and I'll write to mine.'

"Green grow the lilacs, all sparkling with dew,
I'm lonely, my darling, since parting with you,
And by the next meeting I hope to prove true,
To change the green lilacs to the red, white and blue."

Aunt Eller is standing above Curly, seriously considering his state of mind.

"Now, don't you be discouraged none, Curly," she warns, sympathetically. "Laurey's good. She's got sense. She don't let you know too much—keeps you guessin'. An' you shore got her wonderin', too! You're a pair—full of life—made for each other! Got to have each other, got to, shore as fate! Thought I'd die when you made up all that about the rig and told her—"

"Well, we got a date together, you and me," says Curly. He is grinning now, and whistling softly.

Aunt Eller—We have?

Curly (*putting his arm through hers*)—We shore have. We're goin' to that party we've heard so much about.

Aunt Eller—How we goin', Curly? In that rig you made up? (*She chuckles.*) I'll ride a-straddle of them lights a-winkin' like lightnin' bugs, myself!

Curly (*pointing to it*)—That there rig ain't no made-up rig, you hear me? I h'ard it over to Claremore.

AUNT ELLER—Lands, you did!

CURLY—And when I come callin' fer you right after supper, see that you got yer beauty spots fastened on to you proper so you won't lose 'em off, you hear? Now then. (*Gets hat. He rises, and goes round to the back of the settee, grinning mischievously, enigmatically.*) I think I'll go out here to the smoke house for a while.

AUNT ELLER—Whur Jeeter's at?

CURLY—Yeow, whur Jeeter's at. Thought mebbe I'd play a game of pitch with him, 'fore I mosey on home. You reckon he'd like that? (*He starts singing, and opens the door onto the porch.*)

I passed my lover's window, both early and late
The look that she gave me, it made my heart ache.

(*He stops and looks off toward* LAUREY'S *bedroom, and then turns to face the smoke house, still singing. As he turns to go to the smoke house, he sings defiantly*)

The look that she gave me was harmful to see,
For she loves another one better than me.

The cowboys are gathering for the play-party, awaiting the arrival of the girls. While they wait they sing, lustily, freely, bravely, after the manner of cowboys with a play-party in the offing:

"As I was walkin' one mornin' for pleasure
I saw a young cowboy a-ridin' along
His hat was throwed back and his spurs was a-jinglin'
As he approached me a-singin' this song:

"Huppy Hy, yi, yo'. Git along, little dogies,
It's yore misfortune and none of my own.
Huppy Hy, yi, yo'! Git along little dogies
For you know Montana will be your new home."

Now the girls, starched, curled and frilled, come trooping in. They, too, are singing—also freely, melodiously, perhaps a little shrilly, but with unaffected enthusiasm:

"The next bigga river I'm bound to cross
The next bigga river I'm bound to cross
The next bigga river I'm bound to cross
O ladies, fare you well."

The cowboys have selected their partners and are turning them around for inspection:

"How old are you, my pretty little miss?
How old are you, my honey?
She answered me with a tee ha ha,
I'll be sixteen next Sunday.

(*Sung by girls alone:*)
"The next bigga river I'm bound to cross
The next bigga river I'm bound to cross
The next bigga river I'm bound to cross
O ladies, fare you well.

"Sugar grows on a white oak tree,
The branches flow in brandy,
This world is full of five dollar bills,
The girls are sweeter than candy."

Now the lights are dimming and the last chorus of the combined voices comes floating from the darkness:

"Goin' to Peck's party, wanta come along?
Goin' to Peck's party, wanta come along?
Goin' to Peck's party, wanta come along?
We'll dance to the break of day."

The scene has been reversed. The view is now of the porch at the back of the Williams living room and takes in Laurey's bedroom, small, primitive, but feminine. There is a bed covered with a beautiful crazy quilt; and a dresser with souvenirs and toilet nick-nacks scattered over it.

Laurey is seated before the dresser combing her hair and humming bits of "The Miner Boy." She may hear Curly as he sticks his head in the living room still singing his lament:

"I passed my love's window, both early and late,
The look that she gave me, it made my heart ache—"

Laurey, smiling, pulls down the shade to her window. She is still combing her hair, looking younger and more glowing than before, as Aunt Eller comes in from the living room. Laurey is plainly agitated. Her talk with her aunt is rambling. She remembers when she wore her hair in pigtails, and the day she cut it off and got licked for it. She breaks into song when she can think of nothing else to say.

Laurey is full of dreams now. "Wish't I lived in the White House and had diamonds on my shoes, and a little nigger boy to fan me—when it uz hot . . . wish't I lived in Virginia or California. In California they's oranges growin', and snow fallin' at the same time. I seen a pitcher of it . . ."

Aunt Eller can see little sense to anything she is hearing and as much as says so. Which brings Laurey back to the present.

"Bet they'll be a hundred people at Peck's," she bets. "They'll come in buggies and surreys, a-horseback, in the wagon, and some'll come a-foot. Gracie Denham will come all the way from Cattoosie to be there, I bet. When she married Dan Denham, everybody thought—'good-by, good times'—for Gracie. She fooled 'em, though. How big is Indian Territory, Aunt Eller?"

"Oh, big!"

"It's a funny place to live, ain't it?"

"What's funny about it?"

"Well, take me. If paw and maw hadn't come here, I'd a been livin' in Missouri now, 'stid of here. I'd a-had education, I'll bet."

"There's more to life than education. I'd rather have a smoke-house full of meat, than a book full of writin'."

Laurey has finished with her hair and her mood has quieted. "I lied about the White House, Aunt Eller," she confesses, lying flat on her back on the bed and staring at the ceiling. "I'd ruther be married to a man—if he was a real good man—than to live in the old White House. . . ."

Now there is trouble. Aunt Eller has, with deliberate casualness, told of her invitation from Curly to go to Peck's party. The news stirs Laurey. She won't believe that. Aunt Eller can't go with Curly! She's got to go with her and Jeeter! She's got to! But Aunt Eller has made her plans. She and Curly will make out, with that fine rig Curly's hired.

Suddenly the look on Laurey's face startles Aunt Eller. Weakly she tries to continue her teasing:

"If you just *got* to go with Jeeter, they ain't no way out of it, I reckon. Well, me 'n' Curly, we'll make out—"

LAUREY (*quietly, strangely, sits on bed*)—Onct I passed a farm house and it was night. Paw and maw and me was in a covered wagon on our way to here. And this farm house was burnin' up. An' it was burnin' bright, too. Black night it was, like I said. Flames licked and licked at the red-hot chimbley and finally it fell, too, and that was the last of that house—an' that was turrible! I cried and cried. (*A sudden, slightly hysterical note in her voice.*) And the farmer's wife jist set there by the side of the road, moanin' and takin' on. Had on a sunbonnet, a *sunbonnet,* and at night! She kept sayin' over and over—"Now my home's burnt up. 'F I'd a-jist give him a piece of cold pork or sump'n. If I'd jist a-fed him!"— (*She shakes her head as if shutting him out. Her voice rises.*) Now ain't that silly!—Don't you listen to a word I said. Every onct in a while sump'n makes me think about it, the way that womern cried, and said whut she did. Don't you pay no attention to me—

AUNT ELLER—I b'lieve to my soul you got sump'n worryin' on yer mind. Never see you ack before like a chicken 'th its head cut off, Laurey.

Worried? Of course Laurey's worried! Worried to death. She hasn't got a thing to wear to the party. She will admit no more than that. Yet she cannot keep her mind entirely away from things that might happen, and she would have to leave that old farm! What if she had to leave! Things do happen! What if there was to be a prairie f'ar. Or a cyclone? What—what if Jeeter was to set fire to the house?

AUNT ELLER—Jeeter set the—what in the name of Jerusalem air you talkin' about! Jeeter set the— My goodness, get yer things ready, gonna start you right off to Vinita to the crazy house!

LAUREY—Well, I told you, anyway—

AUNT ELLER—Git 'em ready!

LAUREY—You don't have to listen.

AUNT ELLER—What if I'd put rat poison in the turnip greens? Now what on earth would Jeeter want to set the house on f'ar fer?

LAUREY—I just said he might.

AUNT ELLER—Might take a notion to rope a freight train, too. (*She makes for the door, slows her pace and turns around again.*) Now, whut do yo' mean, anyway—Jeeter set the house on f'ar?

LAUREY (*at window*)—They's a horse an' buggy turnin' off up the road this-a-way.

AUNT ELLER—I won't look till you tell me whut you're a-meanin'.

LAUREY—It's roan horse 'th a long tail. He's string-haltered. Look at the way he walks.

AUNT ELLER—Not *gonna* look, I tell you!

LAUREY—You know what a f'ar is, don't you? And you know Jeeter?

AUNT ELLER—That's jist it.

LAUREY (*gravely, queerly*)—Sump'n funny about him.

AUNT ELLER (*relieved*)—Well, I guess you don't mind that so much—goin' to parties with him, and all.

LAUREY (*her face white—in a low voice*)—I'm afraid to tell him I won't, Aunt Eller. Have you ever looked out there in the smoke house—whur he sleeps.

AUNT ELLER—Course I have, plenty of times.

LAUREY—Whut'd you see?

AUNT ELLER—Nuthin'—but a lot of dirt. Why, whut's out there?

LAUREY (*her voice tight with excitement, creating it*)—I don't know, sump'n awful.

AUNT ELLER—Laurey!

LAUREY (*as before*)—I know what I'm talkin' about.

AUNT ELLER—Why, I didn't have no idy you felt that a-way about him! Why, we'll run him off the place if you're skeered of him—

LAUREY (*with deep premonition, kneels to* AUNT ELLER)—Don't you do it! *That's* whut skeers me—he'd set the house on fa'r—like I told you!

AUNT ELLER—Land's sakes! Jist let me ketch him at it! (*She laughs.*) Now you've went and made all this up, and I don't believe a word of it—

LAUREY—You'll find out some day—

AUNT ELLER—Onct when you uz a little girl you know whut you done? Looked outa the winder and seen a cow standin' in the tool shed, and you said to yer maw, "I knowed it, I knowed it! I knowed the cow would eat the grindstone up!" But the cow didn't, though!

LAUREY (*rises, smiling*)—No, the cow didn't.

AUNT ELLER—Well, then. You didn't know's much's you thought you did.

A peddler has driven into the yard. Ado Annie Carnes is with him. Ado Annie is "an unattractive, stupid-looking farm girl, with taffy-colored hair pulled back from a freckled face," and she wears an unbecoming red gingham dress.

Ado Annie has taken the ride with the peddler because she wants to ask Laurey a favor: If she is going to Peck's party will she take Annie along? Laurey has lots of beaux and Annie hasn't any, so Annie thought she'd ast—

The suggestion is welcomed wildly. Laurey can think of nothing she'd rather do than take Ado Annie to the party, and, more than that, she will fix her up so fancy all the boys will fall over a wagon tongue lookin' at her!

Annie had better have a care about peddlers, though. They're a bad lot, Laurey warns. Got wives in every state in the union—and other places besides.

"Why, Alaska's jist full o' women a-livin' in ice-houses, and freezin' to death 'cause of peddlers' runnin' off and a-leavin' 'thout no kindlin' er nuthin'—"

"Aw!"

"A man *told* me! Shore as shootin'. He knowed a Eskimo womern that a peddler up there went off and left, and she had to sell her hair—a hundred hairs at a time—jist cut it right off—to keep from starvin' to death. Finally, she looked liked a ole shave head, bald-headed as a turkey buzzard, and she tuck cold and died."

"Who did?"

"The womern!"

"My goodness!"

Aunt Eller has brought the peddler in. "He is a little wiry, swarthy Syrian neatly dressed with a red bandanna around his neck. . . . His speech is some blurred European tongue with middle western variations."

The peddler is much impressed with the grand beauty into which Laurey has grown. Angel cake, that's what she reminds him of. Angel cake jist hot outa the overn. His flattery does not get him far, however, either with Laurey, though she is pleased in spite of herself, or with Aunt Eller, who remembers very distinctly the last time he was there and sold her an egg-beater that was guaranteed to do many things that no egg-beater on earth had ever done or could do . . .

Laurey can think of a lot of things she would like to have from the peddler's pack. She is running them over in her mind, her manner "a kind of abstracted ecstasy."

"Want some hairpins, a fine tooth comb, a pink un," she calls. "Want a buckle made out of shiny silver for to fasten onto my shoes! Want a dress with lace! Want pe'fume, face whitenin'! Wanta be purty, wanta smell like a honeysuckle vine!"

"Give her a cake of soap," suggests Aunt Eller, curtly.

"Want things I c'n see and put my hands on," continues Laurey, her mood rising. "Want things I've heard of and never had before—pearls in a plush box, diamonds, a rubber-t'ard buggy, a cut glass sugar bowl. Want things I cain't tell you about. Cain't see 'em clear. Things nobody ever heard of. Not only things to look at or hold in your hands. Things to *happen* to you!"

The peddler can only offer some nice silk garters as a substitute. Laurey decides that she will buy a pair of these for Ado Annie. And some face whitenin'? Has he any of that?

He has. "The best they is, Miss Laurey. Liquid powder. Smells like the Queen of Egyp'! Put it on you, they cain't no one stay away from you. Regler love drops! And only six bits a bottle—with a sponge throwed in."

Laurey tries the powder on Ado Annie with somewhat startling results. She hides all the freckles and much of Ado Annie.

Laurey is struggling to keep Ado Annie from rushing out of the house when suddenly a pistol shot rings out! It comes from the direction of the smoke house.

While the women are still staring helplessly at each other a second shot is heard. Laurey's face goes white.

"Curly!" she calls.

"Why, you're as white as a sheet," exclaims Aunt Eller, looking at her in alarm.

"Why'd you let him go out there whur Jeeter is?" demands Laurey.

"It couldn't be nothin', honey!"

"We got to go see!"

They are pushing out of the house in a scramble. Ado Annie lingers briefly to put on her garters. She joins them as the curtain falls.

Down by the barn the boys and girls are still gathering and singing. Martha is the soloist at the moment, raising a clear soprano in:

> "Hello, girls, listen to my voice,
> Don't you never marry no good-for-nothing boys,
> If you do your fate will be
> Hoe cake, hominy and sassafras tea.

"When a young man falls in love,
First it's honey and then turtle dove,
After he's married no such thing,
'Get up and get my breakfast, you good-for-nothing thing.' "

There are calls now for "Home on the Range" and also for "When I Was Single." Martha decides the latter song more appropriate to her mood.

"Oh, when I was single, oh, then, oh, then,
Oh, when I was single, oh, then,
Oh, when I was single, my pockets did jingle,
And I wish I was single again."

Calls for "Home on the Range" are renewed. Martha's voice grows tender in tribute to the prairie home:

"Oh, give me a home where the buffalo roam,
Where the deer and the antelope play,
Where seldom is heard a discouraging word
And the skies are not cloudy all day.

"Home, home on the range,
Where the deer and the antelope play,
Where seldom is heard a discouraging word
And the skies are not cloudy all day.

"I love these wild flowers in this dear land of ours,
The eagle I love to hear scream,
I love the red rocks and the antelope flocks,
A-graze on the mountain tops green."

Now they must have a song called "Idyho." The girls are familiar with this one and join lustily in the choruses:

"Remember what I promised you
When we set side by side,
Beneath that old persimmon tree
I said I'd be your bride.

"Way out in Idyho,
We're comin' to Idyho,
With a four-horse team and we'll soon be seen,
Way out in Idyho."

Photo by Vandamm Studio, New York.

"GREEN GROW THE LILACS"

"Back of the house containing the front room, and to be seen around the corner of the building, is a stretch of fence. Behind the fence is a row of cowboy farmers, leaning on their elbows mostly and listening to the baritone voice of another of their number . . ."

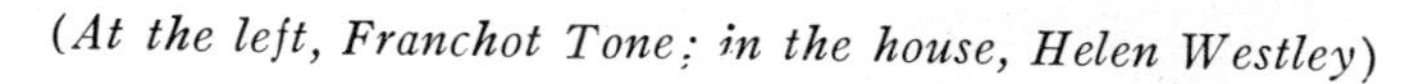

(At the left, Franchot Tone; in the house, Helen Westley)

The scene is back in the smoke house at the beginning of Curly McLain's visit to Jeeter Fry. It follows directly upon Curly's leaving the living room in the first scene.

"The smokehouse is a dark, dirty building where the meat was once kept. Now the floor is full of holes; at night field mice scurry about the room. The rafters are worn and decayed, smoky, covered with dust and cobwebs. On a low loft many things are stored—horse collars, plowshares, bridles, jars of fruit . . . On the walls, of unpainted two-by-twelves, soiled suits are hanging, also tobacco advertisements, an enlisting poster, a pink cover off the *Police Gazette,* a large framed picture of Dan Patch . . .

"Jeeter sits in a low chair looking at the post cards—the cover —then at Laurey's room, leaning forward now and then to spit at the spittoon. He is about thirty-five with a curious earth-colored face and hairy hands. He wears heavy brogans, a greasy pair of trousers, two shirts open at the neck and both dirty. He is always absorbed, dark and sullen."

Hearing a knock Jeeter puts his gun and his postcards hurriedly in the table drawer. He greets Curly gruffly, complainingly. His visitor has tied his horse to a peach tree, which anyone ought to know better'n to do. But Jeeter has turned the pony loose and he probably is a long way up the road by now.

Curly is not worried. A cow pony will stand for hours so long as his reins are draggin'. And, speakin' of cow ponies, Curly notices a mighty fine rope hangin' on Jeeter's wall. Reminds him a lot of the one he left tied to his saddle. But, of course, if it was *given* to Jeeter it couldn't be the same. Interesting things, ropes, Curly contends. You can do a lot with a good one. Will Parker, up by Claremore, can shore spin one. Spin rope and chew gum.

Jeeter could, if he wanted to, hang himself with a piece of rope like that tossed over a strong rafter like those in the smokehouse —hang himself as easy as falling off a log.

"Fact is, you could stand on a log—er—a chair if you'd ruther —right about here, see?" illustrates Curly, throwing the rope on a rafter with mounting enthusiasm, "and put this here around yer neck. Tie that good up there first, of course. Then, all you'd have to do would be to fall off the log—or the cheer, whichever you'd ruther fall off. In five minutes, er less, with good luck, you'd be dead as a door nail."

"Whut'd you mean by that?"

"The folks ud all gather around and sing. *Sad* songs, o' course. And some of 'em ud say whut a good man you was, and others ud say what a pig-stealer and a hound dog you was, and you'd orter been in the penitentiary long ago, fer orneriness."

JEETER—You better be keerful, now!

CURLY—*I* ain't sayin' it. I'm sayin' *they'd* say it. You know the way people talks—like a swarm of mud wasps. (*Looking about the room.*) So this is whur *you* live? Always like to see whur a man's a-livin' at. You got a fine place here, Mr. Jeeter. Matches you. (*He grins mischievously.* JEETER *gets up, goes over close to him, dangerously.*)

JEETER—I don't know who you air er nuthin'—but I think you better tell me whut you come bustin' in here fer, makin' free 'ith my things and talking the way you talk.

CURLY—Why, my name's Curly. Thought you knowed. Curly McLain. Born on a farm in Kansas. Cowpuncher by trade and by profession. I break broncs, mean uns. I bull-dog steers. I ain't never been licked, and I ain't never bin shot. Shot *at,* but not *shot.* I got a good disposition, too, and when anything seems like to me it's funny, why, I let loose and laugh till my belt breaks in two and my socks fall down. Whut on earth air *you* doin' 'th a pitcher of Dan Patch? (*He points to the picture.*)

JEETER (*nonplused*)—Got a right to have a pitcher of a horse, ain't I?

CURLY—Yeah, and you shore have. And that there pink pitcher there, now that's a pitcher of a naked woman, ain't it?

JEETER—Your eyes don't lie to you.

CURLY—Plumb stark naked as a jaybird! No. No, she ain't, not quite. Got a couple of thingumabobs tied on to her.

JEETER—That's a cover off the *Police Gazette.*

CURLY—Wouldn't do fer me to have sich a pitcher around.

JEETER—Whut's wrong with it?

CURLY—I never seen sich a pitcher. That ud give me idys, that would!

JEETER—Shucks, that ain't nuthin' to whut I got here! (*He draws out the postcards.*)

CURLY (*covering his eyes*)—I'll go blind! Whew! Lose my eyesight in a minute! (*Pushing them back.*) I wonder if we couldn't have a little game of pitch?

Jeeter is willing to play pitch, but first he must run through his dirty postcards until he finds a few favorites that are shore dingers. When he gets the playing cards from the table drawer Jeeter takes out a brace of pistols, too. The pistols interest Curly even more than the cards.

Now the game is on, but Curly's thoughts are not fixed on it. He talks to himself a lot with a kind of lyric warmth—"for he is stating something about his own life and his feeling for life."

"Outside the sun's jist crazy 'th the heat, beatin' on the prairie and the cornstalks," muses Curly. "Passed a field in the bottom this mornin' whur the backwater had been. Ground all cracked and blistered an' bakin' in the sun. Likin' it though! Likin' it good! Seen fields of wheat an' oats—fine as a fiddle. The crows went to honkin' at me when I went th'ough the Dog Crick timber, and I could see hundreds of squirrels friskin' in the blackjacks. I could smell them green walnuts, too, whenever old Dun ud tromp on 'em. Shore the purtiest mornin' in a long time! Felt like hollerin' and shoutin'. An' it's shore a funny end to a fine purty mornin' to find yerself shet up in a dark hole bent over a table a-fingerin' a pack o' cards 's greasy 's a ole tin spoon, ain't it? Yeah, that's the way it is, though, in this here life. Got to git used to it."

Now he has burst into song. The one about Sam Hall . . . "My name it is Sam Hall, and I hate you one and all, I hate you one and all, damn yer eyes!"

Jeeter is not greatly interested until Curly gets to the verse that has murder and hanging in it. "I must hang till I am dead, fer I killed a man they said, and I left him there for dead, damn his eyes."

A dog barks outside. From the window Curly watches the arrival of the peddler at the Williams cottage. The story of the song and the bark of the dog start a chain of associated ideas in Jeeter's mind. His tongue unloosed, he talks a lot about murder. Murderin' women, mostly.

There was the case of the feller who killed the girl he'd been keepin' company with after he found her in a barn loft with another feller. Killed her by drownin' her in the horse troft in her nightgown . . . And there was the case of the feller who killed the girl he'd got into trouble when she told him she was goin' to have a baby. "He wint jist hog-wild," this feller, "and found a piece of old rope in the tool box of the mowin' machine and tied her hands and feet with it and th'owed her right on top of a stack of hay and set f'ar to it. Burned her to death! Yeow, it's funny the things people do, like that."

Curly decides that he needs air, and goes to the door to get it. The voices of Aunt Eller and the women drift in. It is a reminder to Curly of their presence alone on the farm—with Jeeter.

The talk turns now to Jeeter's past. Where did he come from? Where did he work before?

The hired man is instinctively hostile, but he likes his own story. It goes back to many jobs for different people—people who were bastards to work for, though there were always ways of gettin' even—

Now Jeeter would turn the tables and make Curly talk—What's Curly doin' on the Williams place? What was his business up to the house? They haven't got nothin' Jeeter can think of that Curly would be wantin' unless it's one thing! An' it better not be that! He'd better stay away from that girl—

"You shore got it bad," sneers Curly. "So you're takin' her to the party tonight? Jesus! She's got a taste. I don't know if it's worth fightin' about if she'd ruther go with you. I step out—cheerful as anythin'. You're welcome. . . . Only—somebody ort to tell her whut you air. And fer that matter somebody ort to tell you onct about yerself."

JEETER—I've had jist about enough!

CURLY—If you'd like to *do* anything to me (*sits on table*), now's the best chanct you'll ever have. (*Softly.*) You've got two pistols, good uns, all loaded and ready to bark. They's a ax a-standin' in the corner. A bright sickle, right off the grindstone hangs over there on a nail and shines. Your hoe is sharp, your razor has got two edges onto it, and nary a one of 'em is rusty. A feller wouldn't feel very safe in here 'th you, 'f he didn't know you. (*Acidly.*) But I *know* you, Jeeter. I've knowed you fer a long time.

JEETER—You don't know a thing about me.

CURLY—The country's full of people like you! I been around. (*He laughs, without mirth. Then his voice rises dramatically. Rising.*) In this country, they's two things you c'n do if you're a man. Live out of doors, is one. Live in a hole is the other. I've set by my horse in the bresh some'heres and heered a rattlesnake many a time. Rattle, rattle, rattle!—he'd go, skeered to death. Skeered—and dangerous. Somebody comin' close to his hole! Somebody gonna step on him! Git his ole fangs ready, full of pizen! Curl up and wait! Fer as long's you live in a hole, you're skeered, you got to have pertection. You c'n have muscles, oh, like arn—and still be as weak as a empty bladder—less'n you got things to barb yer hide with. (*Suddenly, harshly, directly to* JEETER.) How'd you git to be the way you air, anyway—settin' here in this filthy hole—and thinkin' the way you're thinkin'? Why don't you git out an' do sump'n healthy onct in a while, stid of stayin' shet up here a-crawlin' and festerin'?

JEETER—Shet up, you!

CURLY—You'll die of your own pizen, I tell you!

Jeeter grabs for a gun in a kind of desperate frenzy and pulls the trigger. The bullet crashes through the wall across the room. Curly, taken by surprise, is leaning back out of sight of the window. Suddenly, in high excitement, though apparently calm and cool, Curly decides to do a little shooting on his own account.

"I wisht you'd let me show you sump'n," he says. "Jist reach me one of them pistols acrost here a minute. They's a knothole over there about as big as a dime. See it a-winkin'? See it? I jist want to see if I c'n hit it."

Jeeter does not move, but sits staring into Curly's eyes. Curly leans over, unhurriedly, with catlike tension, picks up one of the pistols and fires right over Jeeter's shoulder.

"Didn't make a splinter! Bullet right through the knothole, 'thout touchin', slick as a whistle, didn't I? I knowed I could do it. You saw it, too, didn't you?"

Outside the excitement of the women can be heard. Curly resumes his place at the table and goes on with the game, apparently intently interested in it. Laurey, Aunt Eller and the peddler, followed later by Ado Annie, rush in at the door, Aunt Eller gasping for breath, Ado Annie's face blanched with the whitening Laurey put on it.

AUNT ELLER—What's this? Who's been a-shootin'? Skeer the liver and lights out of a feller! Was that you, Curly? Don't set there, you lummy. Answer when you're spoke to!

CURLY—Well, I shot *once.*

AUNT ELLER—Whut was you shootin' at?

CURLY (*pointing*)—See that knot hole over there?

AUNT ELLER (*not looking*)—I see lots of knot holes.

CURLY—Well, it uz one of them.

AUNT ELLER—Don't tell me you uz shootin' at a knot hole!

CURLY—I was, though.

AUNT ELLER (*exasperated*)—Well, ain't you a pair of purty nuthins, settin' here a-pickin' away at knot holes 'th a pair of ole pistols and skeerin' everybody to death! Ort to give you a good Dutch rub and arn some craziness outa you! C'm here, you all—they ain't nobody hurt. Jist a pair of fools a-swappin' noises.

ADO ANNIE—Did someone shoot, Aunt Eller?

AUNT ELLER—Did someone *shoot!*

ADO ANNIE—Whut'd they shoot *at,* Aunt Eller?

AUNT ELLER—Yer grandmaw, silly! (*She goes out.*)

ADO ANNIE—My lands! (ANNIE *follows her out.* LAUREY *and* PEDDLER *stand in the doorway.*)

LAUREY (*after a moment*)—Curly.

CURLY (*crosses to her*)—Yeah.

LAUREY—Did you *hit* that knothole?

CURLY (*taking hat off*)—How's that?

LAUREY—I say, did you *hit* that knothole?

CURLY—Yeah, I—I hit it.

LAUREY (*cryptically*)—Well. That was good, wasn't it? (*She goes into the house.* CURLY *goes into the smoke house. Takes his rope and goes off singing, "Green Grow the Lilacs." The curtain falls.*)

ACT II

In the yard in front of Old Man Peck's house, which is flanked by a long open porch, the boys and girls have already got the party in full swing.

There is a square dance in progress; also quite a bit of "Hi, yi, yi-ing" and whooping it up.

Old Man Peck aims to stop the dancing and get the folks into the kitchen for the candy pull, which proves such a popular announcement that the yard is deserted when Aunt Eller and Curly arrive.

Aunt Eller is a little proud of the feller she's ketched in Curly and Curly likes the joke, too. But the smile goes out of his face a minute later when he discovers that Laurey and Jeeter haven't arrived yet. It takes considerable arguing on Aunt Eller's part to get Curly in the house. Jeeter's just a slow driver, Aunt Eller explains. That's why they're late.

When Jeeter and Laurey do arrive, with Ado Annie, Jeeter is in an ugly frame of mind. Largely because Laurey has insisted on Ado Annie's coming with them. More particularly because it seems he can never have Laurey to himself.

JEETER (*getting in front of the door*)—Mornin's you stay hid in yer room all the time. Nights you set out in the front room and won't git out of Aunt Eller's sight. I ain't seen you by yerself in a long time. Why ain't I? First time I seen you alone was last year's thrashin'. You was watchin' the chaff fly, and them knives a-cloppin' at the bundles. I come around the corner of the stack, and you stood there a-wavin' yer sunbonnet, to keep some of the dust offen you, and you ast me to git you a drink of water. I got you a drink of water. I brung the jug around. I give it to you. I *did* give it to you, didn't I?

LAUREY (*frightened*)—I don't know what you mean?

JEETER—Last time it uz winter when I uz sick that time, an' the snow uz on the ground. You brung me that hot soup out to the smoke house and give it to me, and me in bed. I hadn't shaved in two weeks. You ast me 'f I had any fever, and you put your hand on my head to see. Why'd you do that? Whut'd you tech me for? You won't git away from me. You've kep' outa my way, an' kep' outa my way. Cain't think o' nuthin' else; it's a killin' me. I cain't rest—cain't be easy—lay awake at nights. God damn you, quit a-tryin' to git away! I got you now! (*He grabs her, and tries to kiss her.*) So goddam purty!

LAUREY (*she frees an arm, and strikes him in the face, with desperate strength. He releases her, and stands, uncomprehending, tranced.*) Now lemme go! Lemme outa here, 'fore I holler and tell on you!

JEETER (*after a moment, slowly*)—You hit me. Like all the rest. I ain't good enough, am I? I'm a ha'd hand, ain't I? Got dirt on my hands, pig slop—ain't fitten to tech you. You're better, so goddam much better. Yeah, we'll see who's better, Miss Laurey, 'nen you'll wish't you wasn't so free 'th yer airs, you're sich a fine lady.

LAUREY—Air you makin' threats to me? Air you standin' there tryin' to tell me 'f I don't 'low you to stand there and slobber o'er me like a hog, why you're gonna do sump'n about it? Why, you're a mangy dog, and somebody ort to shoot you! (LAUREY *crosses to door.*) Yeah, I ort to 'low you yer own way, I reckon. Sich a great, big, fine strappin' man, so full o' dazzle, I ort to git down on my knees to him. Christ all hemlock! You think so much about bein' a ha'd hand. Well, I'll jist tell you sump'n, that'll rest yer brain, Mr. Jeeter. (*She crosses back to him.*) You ain't a ha'd hand fer me no more. Oh, an' I got better idys than that. You ain't to come on the place again, you hear me? Don't so much as set foot inside the pasture gate, or I'll sic the dogs onto you. Now then, next time you go makin' threats to people, you better think a few thinks first, and spit on yer hands fer good luck.

JEETER—Said yer say. Brung it on yerself.

Laurey starts to run into the house looking for Curly, but changes her mind. Jeeter delays his revenge for the moment.

Now Ado Annie appears. She's in trouble, and greatly excited about it. Her new garters are so tight they are about to kill her, and she jest cain't take 'em off and let her stockings fall down. Even if she would have all the boys runnin' after her, as Laurey says.

Furthermore, the boys are worryin' Ado Annie a lot. Sayin' things to her she doesn't understand. And she's afraid to ask them what they mean for fear they'll tell her.

Laurey has just asked Ado Annie to go in the house and send Curly out to her when the boys and girls come rushing out and fairly mob them. The boys are gay, and boisterous. Full of fun, slightly touched with likker and ready for another dance.

Now the fiddler has mounted the bench and is calling the figures:

"Eight hands up and circle to the West!"

Laurey has found Curly in the crowd and is clinging to him a little desperately, trying to tell him of her adventure with Jeeter, when Old Man Peck tears them apart, hauling Curly over to the men's side of the yard while the girls circle around Laurey and take her with them.

It is Peck's idea that there has been dancing enough and that now there should be some singing. When they get through singing they can all go out to the smoke house and git their ice cream.

Some of the girls would like to hear one of the old ballads. "The Dyin' Cowboy," for instance. But it is Peck's idea that they should start off with "The Chisholm Trail," to which each of them can add his own verse. Cord Elam starts it.

"Come along, boys, and listen to my tale
And I'll tell you of my troubles on the old Chisholm trail—"

They all yell the chorus in unison:

"Come a Ty yi, yippy, tippy, ti yi yae,
Come a Ty yi, yippy, yi yae."

"Goin' back West on the old Chisolm trail,
Ribbon on a heifer and a bull by the tail—"

The girls push Laurey into the circle and she adds a verse:

"Foot in the stirrup and a hand on the horn,
Best durn cowboy that ever wuz born."

Curly's contribution comes later:

"Well, I'm goin' to Oklahoma, gonna marry me a squaw,
And raise papoopsies for ma paw-in-law."

Once, when it looks as though everybody was running out of verses Laurey tries again to have a word with Curly. She's got to see him, she says. She's got to tell him something—

But again Old Man Peck and the crowd interfere. The singin' must go on.

One of the men produces a banjo and a reedy baritone and begins the narrative of the bronc buster who tried to ride Old Strawberry and found himself "settin' on nuthin' way up in the sky."

They try to get Aunt Eller to sing, but she escapes by tossing Ado Annie into the ring. Ado Annie has plumb forgot all the songs she ever knowed, but she manages finally to remember the one about the young man who found her "young and single and easy led astray."

> "The night is dark and dreary,
> A little incline to rain—
> O God, my heart is weary
> For my lover's gone off on a train."

The crowd is unkind to Annie as she concludes her lament, but the ice cream in the smoke house soon takes their minds off their teasing. They are parading out now, promenade style, singing lustily.

As the crowd disappears Laurey gets Curly away from his partner and drags him back into the yard.

"Curly," she calls, wildly, "I want to tell you sump'n; don't run away and leave me."

"Now whut on earth is ailin' the belle of Claremore?" demands the astonished Curly. "By gum, if you ain't a-cryin'."

"Curly, I'm 'fraid, 'fraid of my life!"

CURLY (*in a flurry of surprise and delight*)—Jumpin' toadstools! (*He waves his hat and finally throws it away wildly and puts his arms around* LAUREY, *muttering under his breath.*) Great Lord—!

LAUREY—Don't you leave me—

CURLY—Great Godamighty—!!

LAUREY—Don't mind me a-cryin', I cain't he'p it—

CURLY—Jesus! Cry yer eyes out—!

LAUREY—Oh, I don't know whut to do!

CURLY—Here, I'll show you. (*He lifts her face and kisses her. She puts her arms about his neck. He exclaims softly.*) Laurey,

Laurey! (*He kisses her again and again, then takes a step away from her disengaging her arms gently.*)

LAUREY (*in alarm*)—Curly— (CURLY *shakes his head as if coming out of a daze, gives a low whistle, and backs away.*)

CURLY—Whew! 'Bout all a man c'n stand in public—! Go 'way from me, *you!*

LAUREY—Oh, you don't like me, Curly—

CURLY—*Like* you? My God! Git away from me, I tell you, plumb away from me! (*He strides across the room and sits down on the stove.*)

LAUREY (*crying out*)—Curly! Yo're settin' on the stove!

CURLY (*leaping up*)—Godamighty! (*He turns round, puts his hand down gingerly on the lids.*) Aw! 'S cold's a hunk o' ice! (*He sits down again.*)

LAUREY (*pouting*)—Wish 't ud burn a hole in yer pants—

CURLY (*grinning at her understandingly*)—You do, do you?

LAUREY (*turning away to hide her smile*)—*You* heerd me.

CURLY—Laurey, now looky here, you stand over right there whur you air, and I'll set over here (*he brings bench down-stage and sits on it*) and you *tell* me whut you wanted with me.

Laurey tells him of Jeeter's threats; of his trying to kiss her and the rest of it. Curly is pretty mad about it. He would go after Jeeter and have it out with him, but is content to stay so long as Laurey explains that she has fired Jeeter and will have nothing more to do with him. That should about settle the Jeeter business.

"Now, quit yer worryin' about it or I'll spank you," Curly concludes, with a note of mastery in his voice. Then quite suddenly, he thinks of something else: "Hey, while I think of it," he shouts, "how about marryin' me?"

"Gracious, whut ud I wanta marry you fer?" protests the flustered Laurey.

"Laurey, please, ma'am—marry me! I don't know whut I'm gonna do, if you don't."

"Curly,—why, you—why, I'll marry you—if you want me to—"

The shock is a little startling, but Curly absorbs it successfully. He takes Laurey in his arms and kisses her gently. "I didn't think you would, I didn't dream you'd ever—"

"Sh!"

Curly puts a stool on top of the stove and lifts Laurey up to it. Then he lets down the oven door to provide a seat for himself. He is still a little confused by the things that are happening to him.

CURLY (*humbly*)—I ain't got no right to ast you—a good-fernuthin' cowpuncher like me—

LAUREY—Don't say things like that.

CURLY—If I'd ever a-thought! Oh, I'd crter been a farmer, and worked hard at it, and saved, an' kep' buyin' more land, and plowed and planted, like somebody—stid o' doin' the way I've done! Now the cattle business'll soon be over with. The ranches are breakin' up fast. They're puttin' barbed w'ar, an' plowin' up the sod fer wheat and corn. Purty soon they won't be no more grazin'—thousands of acres—no place fer the cowboy to lay his head.

LAUREY—Don't you worry none, Curly—

CURLY—Yer paw done the right way. He knowed. He could see ahead.

LAUREY—Pap ain't alive now to enjoy it. But we're alive, Curly. Alive! Enjoy all we can! 'Case things happen!

CURLY—Nuthin' cain't happen now—nuthin' very bad—if you —if you love me—and don't mind a-marryin' me. (*Puts arm around her.*)

LAUREY—Sh. I'll marry you. Somebody's comin', don't you reckon?

CURLY—I don't keer. When *will* you marry me?

LAUREY—Oh, purty soon. I'll have to ast Aunt Eller, first.

CURLY—I'll ast her myself! (*Gayly.*) Oh, I 'member the first time I ever seen you! You uz pickin' blackberries 'longside the road here years and years ago—you uz a little tyke— (*He laughs.*) You'd been a-eatin' berries as fast as you could pick 'em, and yer mouth was as black as a coal shovel!—'F you wasn't a sight! (*Kisses her.*)

LAUREY (*embarrassed*)—Curly!

CURLY—'Nen I seen you onct at the Fair—a-ridin' that little gray filly of Blue Starr's, an' I says to someone—"Who's that little thing with a bang on her forehead?"

LAUREY—Yeow, I remember. You was ridin' broncs that day, and one th'owed you.

CURLY—Did *not* th'ow me!

LAUREY—Guess you jumped off, then.

CURLY—Shore, I jumped off. Be the happiest man a-livin' soon's we're married. (*Frowning.*) Oh, but I'll shore be a unsettled man, though, you're so blamed purty, worried somebody'll run off with you! 'F I ever have to leave home to be gone all day, gonna shore tie you up to the hitchin' post, so you'll be there 'gin I get back, you hear? Ain't gonna take no chances!

LAUREY (*gravely, touching his hair shyly*)—I jist sit here and listen at you, and don't keer whut you say about me. Say I'm homely as a mud fence, you want to—why then, I *am* homely as a mud fence. 'F you say I'm purty why I'm purty as anything, and got a voice like Jenny Lind. I never thought of anything like this! But I always wondered and wondered, after the first time I seen you— (*Her eyes fill with tears, absurdly. The crowd steals in, one couple after another.*) And here we set, you and me, on an' old bench, like a pair of washpans, and I don't know whut's come over us to act so silly—and I'm gonna cry in a minute—and it's all your fault, you orten to a-made love to me this-a-way— (CURLY *puts his arms around her.*)

CURLY—Laurey, cry if you want to, then. (*He kisses her tenderly.*) Laurey—sweet— (*He hugs her.*)

The crowd, still paired off, sweeps around the house yelling hilariously. The two love birds are discovered! All signs point to a wedding. It is an event greatly relished in anticipation by the crowd.

The boys and girls are still dancing around Curly and Laurey when Jeeter Fry suddenly lurches into the yard. He has been drinking and has a bottle in his hand. He jumps on the bench and waves the bottle. Then down again and begins circling the lovers menacingly.

Curly starts for Jeeter, but Laurey holds him back. Old Man Peck sees and saves the situation. With a whoop he grabs the hands of the people nearest him. They form a circle that rapidly grows and little by little they surround Curly and Laurey and leave Jeeter at the edge of the yard.

Now they have hoisted Laurey and Curly on chairs and are circling around them, yelling. Someone starts a song:

"My girl's gone, oh, what'll I do?
. . . . .
I'll get another one pretty as you
. . . . .
Cain't get a redbird, bluebird'll do,
Skip to my Lou, my darling!"

The curtain falls.

Again the boys and girls are gathered down by the corral listening to Smoky tell in song the sad, sad case of the bronc buster whose horse fell on him and crushed in his head.

> "There was ba-lud on the saddle,
> And ba-lud all around,
> And a great big puddle
> Of ba-lud on the ground—"

Four verses of this before anybody would think of stopping Smoky. Then Cord Elam breaks in with the one about Old Paint.

> "My feet are in the stirrups, my bridle in my hand,
> Good-by, my little pony—my pony won't stand.
>
> "Good-by, Old Paint, I'm a-leavin' Cheyenne
> Good-by, Old Paint, I'm a-leavin' Cheyenne;
> I'm a-leavin' Cheyenne, I'm off for Montana,
> Good-by, Old Paint, I'm a-leavin' Cheyenne!"

We move on out to the open field, leaving the crowd behind. "A July moon makes silver tents of the mounds of unbaled hay which recede in irregular formation far into the distance, crossing a low hill. A gaunt wire rake, with enormous wheels, stands at one side. The sky is powdered with stars . . . a soft summer wind, creeping about the meadow, lifts the spears of grass that have escaped the sickle."

Curly and Laurey steal in cautiously. They are breathless and suspicious. They hear strange sounds, but lay them to the wind.

"We'll leave Ole Eighty standin' whur we tied her," Curly announces. "We cain't drive up to the house, 'cause 'f anybody's watchin' out fer us, they'd see us. We'll sneak acrost the hayfield and th'ough the plum thicket—and go in the back door. Come on now. Watch whur you step."

"Curly, if they catch us what'll happen?" whispers Laurey, taking Curly's hand, timorously. "Will it be bad?"

"You know about shivorees, honey. They git purty rough."

LAUREY—I'm a-feared.

CURLY—Don't be a-feared, honey. Aunt Eller says for shore nobody seen us gittin' hitched.

LAUREY—They mighta s'pected sump'n though. (*Her voice low.*) That's the ketch about gittin' married.

CURLY (*reassuringly*)—But here we air, honey. Married—and purty nigh home. And not a soul in sight.

LAUREY (*after a moment of registering this, relievedly*)—Yeah! We fooled 'em, didn't we?

CURLY—Shore we did.

LAUREY—Course. (*Her voice full of wonder.*) Curly—we're—we're married now.

CURLY (*softly*)—Yeah. Plumb hitched.

LAUREY—Was you skeered when the preacher said that about "Will you take this here womern—"

CURLY—Skeered he *wouldn't* say it.

LAUREY—I was skeered you'd back out on me.

CURLY—I *couldn't* back out on you—'f I wanted to. Could you me?

LAUREY (*smiling tenderly*)—Not if I tried and tried. (*They kiss and embrace for a moment. Then, still holding her hand,* CURLY *turns, looking out over the moonlit field.*)

CURLY (*lyrically, feeling the moment*)—Look at the way the hayfield lays out purty in the moonlight. Next it's the pasture, and over yonder's the wheat and the corn,—and the cane patch next, 'nen the truck garden an' the timber. Ever'thin' laid out fine and Jim Dandy! The country all around it—Indian Territory—plumb to the Rio Grande, and north to Kansas, and 'way over east to Arkansas, the same way, with the moon onto it. Trees ain't hardly a-movin'. Branch bubbles over them limestone rocks, you c'n hear it. Wild flower pe'fume smellin' up the air, sweet as anythin'. A fine night for anyone to remember for a weddin' night! A fine night—fer *anyone!* (*Caught up in the spell of the night and their feelings.*) Come on—

Curly and Laurey, hand in hand, have started off across the stubble. From back of the haystacks there is the sound of tittering, a good deal of shushing and broken giggles. Now from behind every mound of hay heads appear. "Dozens of men carrying noise-making instruments" come out into the open, pointing, staring, in the direction of the newlyweds, giggling and making mock of them.

"'Fine night to remember fer a weddin' night,'" sighs one.

"Tee, hee! Bet they'll go to bed in the dark!" suggests another.

"Be keerful, they'll hear you, you hoodlums! 'Whee!' 'High old times!' 'Ketch 'em in the act!' 'Don't give 'em too much time.' 'He shore got him sump'n there!' 'Couple of sections;

grazin' and timber and plowed land; money, scads of it and more comin'. An' she's a purty one, too.' 'Got a face fer kissin'.' 'An' that ain't all, brother!' "

Across the fields the men can see a light in the window of Laurey's room. Excitement grows with raucous comment and eagerness to be on with the party. Now they have started off toward the house, smothering their laughter.

A young farmer, flushed with drink, staggers out from in back of the largest stack of hay. He is reciting adventurous prose to himself—"Bridegroom a-waitin' and a-waitin'! Don't you wait now, Mr. Bridegroom! The moon's a-shinin'! Yer time has come—"

From the direction of the house weird noises begin to shatter the night air. Cord Elam rushes in to direct the crowd back to the right haystack—the one with the ladder against it.

A few men drag Curly in, struggling and angry, his hair in his eyes. His shirt has been ripped off in the struggle.

"Damn you, leave her alone," he shouts. "Don't one o' you put his hands onto her, I'll kill him—"

"Aw, nobody's a-hurtin' her, Curly—"

Now "a wide circle of men, shouting, whistling, beating their various noise instruments, advances across the stubble. In the middle of the group, walking along, is Laurey, in a nightgown, her hair down about her pale and shaken shoulders."

The crowd pushes Laurey over to the foot of the ladder.

"Right up the ladder with you, you purty thing!" calls the leader. "You ain't bashful, air you?"

The crowd chimes in. "Go on, boost her up!" "Right up on the stack!" "Make out it's a bed, why don't you?"

Laurey looks pleadingly toward the helpless Curly and then climbs the ladder. Next it is Curly's turn.

"Go on, Mr. Bridegroom! There's yer bride!" "She's all yours, cowboy!"

With bride and bridegroom on top of the stack the men throw the ladder down amidst great cheering and more noise.

Curly moves toward Laurey. She goes to his arms in dumb misery. "The men break out into derisive and lascivious guffaws."

"Give us a little kiss, honey-lamb—"

One, two, three straw babies are thrown up on the stack and fall at the feet of the unhappy pair.

Again the dancing, parading, shouting crowd shatters the night with a deafening noise.

"Suddenly a dark figure carrying a torch lurches out of the gloom."

The smell of burning hay is in the air. In the distance a stack is ablaze. Curly sees it first and calls to the men to stop the fire before the whole meadow goes.

The man with the torch is recognized as Jeeter Fry, drunk and reeling. He has broken into the open still carrying the torch before the men can catch him.

"Oh, you thought you had it over me so big, didn't you?" he sneers at Curly and Laurey. "And you, too, Missy—wanted sump'n purtier to sleep with— Yaah, you won't be a-havin' it long! Burn you to cracklin's!"

With the torch waving Jeeter dashes toward the stack and applies the flame. The men hesitate to close in on him. With a leap from the top of the haystack Curly is on Jeeter and the torch is sent flying across the field.

Now the men have come in and smothered the flames at the stack, and stamped out the torch. Jeeter has drawn out a knife and opened it. He throws himself upon Curly. In the struggle the two fall to the ground, gripping each other desperately. Suddenly there is a groan from Jeeter. He whimpers and lies very still—

Curly realizes that something has happened. With staring eyes he backs away. Jeeter is still motionless.

"Look at—look at him!" cries Curly. "Fell on it—stuck th'ough his ribs!"

Some of the men have bent inquiringly over Jeeter Fry. Shaken, horrified, Curly turns dazedly towards the stack of hay as the curtain falls.

A few evenings later, out in the moonlight, stretched along the fence; some of them sitting cross-legged on the ground, others leaning lazily against the bars; the boys and girls are again enjoying their evening songs. "The Dying Cowboy" is the cheerful choice of this particular gathering, and they take it with full chorus effect:

"Oh, bury me not on the lone prairie—
These words came low and mournfully
From the pallid lips of a youth who lay
On his dying bed at the close of day.

"Oh, bury me not on the lone prairie
Where the wild coyotes may howl o'er me

In a narrer grave jest six by three
Oh, bury me not on the lone prairie.

"Oh, bury me not and his voice failed there
But they took no heed to his dying prayer
In a narrow grave jest six by three
They buried him there on the lone prairie.

"And the cowboys now as they roam the plains
For to mark the spot where his bones were laid
Place a handful of roses on his grave
With a prayer to God that his soul be saved."

In the living room of the Williams house Ado Annie and Aunt Eller sit sewing and wondering about the unhappy Laurey in the next room. Laurey has eaten very little and slept practically not at all since the officers took Curly McLain away to the Claremore jail, and Aunt Eller is fairly wild with apprehension, knowing she can do little or nothing about it. Makes Aunt Eller bitter against marriage.

"Don't you ever marry," is Aunt Eller's advice to Ado Annie. "I did and look at me. First yer man—he'll die—like mine did. 'Nen the baby—she'll die. The rest of yer younguns'll grow up and marry and leave you, the way mine did. 'Nen you'll be all by yerself. Time you're old as me, you'll be settin' around, jist the way *I* am, 'th a wooden leg and a bald head, and a-rippin' up old flour sacks to make yerself a pair of drawers out of."

Trouble starts when you marry. Aunt Eller is sure of that. But, she concludes, trouble starts anyhow, so it doesn't make much difference whether you're married or not.

Aunt Eller is listening, now, at Laurey's door. And muttering to herself. They can't stick Curly—she's sure of that. He fought in self-defense—that's plain enough. Jeeter fell on his own knife, and died, as he ort to—that's plain enough, too. It ain't fair that they should hold Curly for any old hearin'—them town fools— And Laurey and Curly not *really* married yet—

Laurey has come from her room, "looking very pale and changed, a woman now."

Laurey can't sleep. And if a person can't sleep, what's the use goin' to bed? Laurey thinks she really ought to be in Claremore with Curly— She ought to be there to testify for him.

But, as Aunt Eller explains, Laurey couldn't testify for Curly, bein' his wife. They're sure to let Curly off, anyway.

"Why'd they have to th'ow Curly in jail? Anyone could see how it happened," moans Laurey.

"Shore they could, honey," comforts Aunt Eller. "Shore they could. But you know the way everybody feels about shivoreein'. They got a right to it somehow. And a thing like this a-happenin' in the middle of a shivoree—why, it looks *bad,* that's all. But Curly'll go free. Why, it's only been three days. They jest got to git eve'ything straight."

It is hard to break through Laurey's depression. There is too much she remembers; too much that just can't be forgot; some things a person just can't get out of his mind.

"Yeah, you've had yer troubles," agrees Aunt Eller, compassionately. "I know, Laurey. But they's been good things, too. You've had you a good home—"

"Paw and maw—"

"Yeah, right when you need them most, both gone. But you lived on, didn't you? You been happy since, ain't you? Course. You been strong about it. Oh! Lots o' things happen to a womern. Sickness, bein' pore and hungry even, bein' left alone in yer old age, bein' afraid to die— It all adds up. That's the way life is—cradle to grave. And you c'n stand it. They's one way. You got to be hearty. You *got* to be."

For a moment Laurey's mind is diverted. She's just a baby, she agrees, when she ought to be strong, like Aunt Eller. She'll try to sleep, now. And she'll promise to eat hearty—fried chicken and everything—tomorrow.

Out in the yard a dog begins to bark. It brings the women up standing and startled. Laurey starts excitedly for the window, Curly's name on her lips.

It couldn't be Curly, insists Aunt Eller, pulling Laurey away from the window. Old Shep wouldn't bark that-a-way if it were Curly—

A dark figure is seen to dash past the window, around the corner of the house and to the steps leading to Laurey's room. There is a noise back of Laurey's door. Aunt Eller grabs the fire shovel, takes her position and orders the intruder to come out.

It *is* Curly! Disheveled and worn, he comes through the door. Laurey rushes to his arms and clings convulsively to him. Aunt Eller is wildly joyous.

"My, oh, my! Look whut the ole cat's drug in!" she calls. "Thought we had him safe in jail, and here he turns up like a bad penny: Laws-a-me! Whutta you mean, tryin' to skeer us walleyed?"

LAUREY—Curly, what is it? (*With premonitory alarm.*) Whut's the matter? Everything's all right, ain't it? They've let you off, ain't they? Curly! Tell me and be quick, I—

CURLY (*crosses to* LAUREY)—No. They ain't let me off.

LAUREY—Curly! They couldn't a-sent you up! It wasn't yore fault. They couldn't. I won't let 'em—I won't, I—

CURLY—Sh! (*As they become silent again.*) They're after me. (*He goes swiftly across and pulls down the window shade.*)

AUNT ELLER—Who's after you, the old Booger Man?

LAUREY—Curly!

CURLY—When I clumb th'ough the fence jist by that little bridge, I seen lights 'way over towards Claremore. I knowed they'd got on to which way I was headin', so I run acrost the back of the—

AUNT ELLER—What *air* you jabberin' about? (*Light dawning on her.*) Oh! I mighta knowed a curly-headed cowhand like him ud come to a bad end! He's went and broke outa jail.

CURLY (*crosses to* LAUREY, *quickly*)—I *had* to see Laurey. I *had* to! I knowed she'd be a-worryin' about ever'thin', an' I couldn't stand it her a-worryin' and nobody to help her none—(*He takes* LAUREY *in his arms again.*)

AUNT ELLER (*swinging* CURLY *around—severely*)—Worryin'! I orter take a hick'ry to you and beat you plumb to a frazzle! Here you'd a-got off tomorrow, you crazy youngun—ever'body *said* so. Now you'll prob'ly git sent up fer five year fer breakin' loose—an' I hope you do! (*Turns him back to* LAUREY.)

LAUREY—Aunt Eller, they cain't send him up, *they cain't!*

AUNT ELLER—Oh, cain't they? You wait and see. (*To* CURLY.) Didn't you know they'd know where you was headin' fer, and find you?

CURLY—I didn't think.

AUNT ELLER—I reckon you hain't got nuthin' to think *with.* (*Giving him a swat.*) I'd like to give you a good beatin'! (*Smiling at him tolerantly.*) Aw, I reckon you jist had to see yer girl, didn't you?

CURLY—My wife.

AUNT ELLER (*crosses, puts shovel in fireplace*)—Yeow? Well, call her that 'f it does you any good. How fur back was it you seen 'em comin' after you?

CURLY—'Bout half a mile.

AUNT ELLER—You got jist about two minutes to tell Laurey good-by, then.

CURLY (*crosses to* AUNT ELLER)—They won't ketch me!

Hide me till mornin', Aunt Eller. I cain't let them take me now, Aunt Eller!

AUNT ELLER—You'll stay *right here* till they come. You've already caused enough trouble to last us all till doomsday. (*She pushes* CURLY, *crosses to window.*) Now then. Ado Annie, come on out in the kitchen, and git yerself sump'n to eat. Bet you're hungry.

ADO ANNIE—I hain't hungry, Aunt Eller. I jist had a piece of—

AUNT ELLER—Not hungry! Why, you're all fallin' to staves. Feel ever' rib you got! (*She shoves* ADO ANNIE *out and follows her. As she goes out:*) They'll come any minute now.

CURLY—Listen, Laurey, I had to see you 'fore the hearin' tomorrow. That's why I broke out. Fer whut if they'd send me up, and I not see you fer a long time?

LAUREY—Curly! *It couldn't be.* Don't say that.

CURLY—Anythin' can be. You got to be ready.

LAUREY (*alarmed*)—Have you heered anything, Curly? Tell me, whut'd you hear?

CURLY—Nuthin', honey. Ain't heard nuthin' but *good.*

LAUREY (*with glad relief*)—Oh, it's all right, then!

CURLY (*gravely*)—That ain't it. I'm shore myself, honey. Er, I was shore till I broke out. I never thought *whut* that might do. Sump'n's always happenin' in this here world. Cain't count on a thing. So you got to promise me sump'n. Whutever happens—*whutever* it is, you got to bear up, you hear me? (*Crosses to window. Smiling.*) Why, I'm a purty one to go a-losin' sleep over, ain't I?

LAUREY (*ruefully*)—Oh, a fine start *we* got, ain't it? (*With an effort, painfully working it out in her mind.*) Oh, I've worried about you, shet up in that filthy jail—

CURLY—Don't mind about that. (*Crosses to settee and sits.*)

LAUREY— —and I've thought about that awful night, too, till I thought I'd go crazy. Then I tried to figure out how I'd go on if sump'n happened to you. Oh, I've went th'ough it all, Curly, from the start. Now I feel shore of sump'n, anyway—I'll be growed up—like ever'body else. Why, I'll stand it—if they send you to the pen fer life—

CURLY (*with mock alarm*)—Here! Don't know's I like that very well! (LAUREY *bursts into a peal of amused, hearty, infectious laughter.*) The look on your face. 'S the first time I laughed in three days.

Curly is happy, too, for the moment. He jokes about wearing funny prison clothes. He makes fun of Laurey and pretends to doubt her liking for him. Then he drifts into a serious mood. He has been thinkin' a lot in jail. Everything's got to be different in the future. It has come to Curly that he will have to give up being a cowboy and become a farmer. Got to get his hands blistered a new way, now.

"They gonna make a state outa this," he sings, in a kind of visionary absorption. "They gonna put it in the union! Country a-changin', got to change with it! Bring up a pair o' boys, new stock, to keep up 'ith the way things is goin' in this here crazy country. Life jist startin' fer me now. Work to do! Now I got you to he'p me— I'll 'mount to sump'n yit! Come here, Laurey. Come here and tell me 'good-by' 'fore they come fer me and take me away."

"All we do is says 'Howdy' and 'So long!'" Laurey answers, wryly. And then adds, gravely: "Curly, if you come back tomorrow I'll be here a-waitin'. If you don't come back I'll be here a-waitin' anyhow."

"I'll come back, honey," Curly answers, confidently. "They couldn't hinder me 'th bird shot."

Outside there are the noises of a crowd's approach. Curly knows what that means. Laurey clings to him desperately. Aunt Eller comes to them, but not encouragingly. Curly will have to go back with the men. She's sorry, but that's the way it'll have to be.

It is Old Man Peck knocking at the door. Aunt Eller lets him in. The crowd stays outside. Peck has been deputized as a federal marshal and he has come for Curly. He ain't sidin' with the marshal, Peck explains, but Curly's hearin' ain't come up yet and he had no right to run away. Breakin' outa jail is agin the law.

The crowd grows anxious. They'd have Curly brought out and get started back for jail. Aunt Eller takes the matter up with them through the window. A fine lot of neighbors, they are! And the things she knows about them and what they done to the law! Well, she's mad now, Aunt Eller is, and she doesn't plan they should take Curly at all. What'd they want to be sidin' with a federal marshal for, anyway?

"You'd think us people out here lived in the United States," shouts Aunt Eller. "Why, we're territory folks—we orter hang together."

On second thought she changes "hang" to "stick" to the huge amusement of the crowd.

"Whut's the United States?" she goes on. "It's jist a furrin country to me. An' you supportin' it. Jist durty ole furriners, every last one of you!"

The crowd doesn't like that. Protests are many and a little shrill. Aunt Eller takes back the furriner charge. Neither is she askin' them to let Curly off. But they don't have to take him back tonight. They can take him in the mornin' jist as well!

There is wrangling in the crowd, now. The men are of two minds. Finally they agree to put it up to Peck. He's the boss.

AUNT ELLER (*turning back into the room to* OLD MAN PECK)—See there? They said it was all right to let Curly stay tonight.

OLD MAN PECK—No, they didn't, Aunt Eller.

AUNT ELLER—Did too. Cain't you hear nuthin'? (*Desperately.*) I'll take a blacksnake whip to you.

YOUNG FARMER (*who has been eavesdropping through the window*)—She's goin' to take a blacksnake whip to him.

THE CROWD—I guess the old lady put it over on you. Whut are you going to do, Mr. Peck?

OLD MAN PECK (*sheepishly*)—Well, I—if my men is gonna back out on me this-a-way—I reckon I better let Curly stay.

AUNT ELLER (*overjoyed*)—I knowed you'd see daylight, I knowed it, I knowed it. (CURLY *and* LAUREY *have risen. Hugging* AUNT ELLER.)

OLD MAN PECK—I was young onct myself—

AUNT ELLER—You ole devil—tell yer wife on you.

CURLY—D'you want me to stay, Laurey? (*She backs away, flushed and embarrassed and joyous at the same time, flings an arm about his neck and kisses him quickly, whirls over to* OLD MAN PECK, *gives him a quick hug and flies into her room.* CURLY *grins, pats* OLD MAN PECK *on the back and starts after her. When he reaches the door* OLD MAN PECK *speaks.*)

OLD MAN PECK—Curly, I'll be right after breakfast to fetch you. I'll be here bright and early. (CURLY *goes in and shuts the door behind him.*)

AUNT ELLER (*after the door is shut*)—Well, not *too* early. (*Picks up the lamp. Then gravely.*) Young uns has a turrible time, don't they? Yeah, they shore to git to be old-timers soon enough. Too soon. (*They go off.*)

CURLY (*heard singing from* LAUREY'S *bedroom*)—

Green grow the lilacs all sparklin' with dew,
I'm lonely, my darlin', since partin' with you.

AUNT ELLER (*with delight—to* OLD MAN PECK)—Listen to that fool cowpuncher! His weddin' night—and there he is a-singin'.

CURTAIN

AS HUSBANDS GO

A Comedy in Three Acts

BY RACHEL CROTHERS

IT was as late as March 5 that John Golden got around to producing Rachel Crothers' new comedy, "As Husbands Go." And he did not have a great deal to do with it then, having gone away to Florida and left the details of casting, rehearsing and presenting the play in Miss Crothers' hands, exactly as he had done with the same author's "Let Us Be Gay" the year before.

The real reason of the late arrival of "As Husbands Go," however, was the continued success of Frank Craven's "That's Gratitude," which had started in the late summer of 1930 and continued prosperously at the John Golden Theatre for seven months.

"As Husbands Go" proved to be one of those happy over-night successes of which all authors and producers dream. A light, pleasant, truthfully observing domestic comedy, it struck the husband and wife set squarely between the eyes, and added a public of both experienced and casual European travelers to its audiences immediately.

It is an old Crothers custom to back a comedy with a definitely serious purpose. In this instance the leader of our native lady playwrights seeks to reveal the witchery which the purple mists of Paris work on susceptible and romantic middle-aged ladies from America, and in contrast to call attention to the homely but steadfast virtues of an average American husband, slave to his job, his sense of duty and his true affections.

It is an honest, amusingly human study of character, was happily cast and well played. Its run continued well into the summer.

As Miss Crothers starts the adventure of her ladies from Dubuque in "As Husbands Go" they are sitting with two gentlemen companions, in the corner of a private room in a smart Paris café. There are padded leather wall benches back of them, a table before them, and a maître d'hôtel is placing a champagne cooler at their feet. Dance music is heard from an adjoining main room.

It is about 4 o'clock in the morning of a late summer day. The Americans are Lucile (Mrs. Charles) Lingard, "thirty-five—a very beautiful woman—slender and delicately lovely—now wearing one of her new French evening gowns and looking extremely smart and distinguished," and Emmie Sykes, a widow, "forty-five and very young indeed—pretty in a round-eyed, baby sort of way. She, too, is now wearing her new finery."

Lucile's escort is Ronald Derbyshire—"twenty-nine, a tall, good-looking Englishman, a writer with one successful novel to his credit," and Emmie's friend is Hippolitus Lomi—"60—small, dark, rather Latin in effect—a mixture of European parentage and an inheritance of many backgrounds."

The conversation of the four is desultory but centered chiefly on the fact that this is the last night Emmie and Lucile are to have in Paris and the resulting tragedy of their farewells with these two charming friends.

"It is time for the American women to go home again," sighs Hippie, which is short for Hippolitus. "You make us so gay with your pilgrimage to us—and then you set sail and leave us *desole*. Great fleets of you going back to your patient business men."

The men are ardent in thier protests of unquenchable affection. Emmie is positively torturing Hippolitus, according to Hippie, even though she has often assured him that it is absolutely impossible there should ever be anything more than friendship between them.

Ronald, between times, assures Lucile that not only is she, as always, the most beautiful woman in the room, but that life without her is quite seriously unthinkable.

LUCILE (*drawing away from him a little*)—We're losing our heads—we mustn't.

RONALD—I'm not losing mine.

LUCILE—It's been so sweet—so sweet! (*She closes her eyes.* RONALD *goes on talking to her—his lips close to her ear.*)

EMMIE (*rolling her eyes toward* LUCILE)—Look at that. I ought to be chaperoning her—but it's all I can do to take care of myself.

HIPPIE—Why do you make yourself so miserable? Why do you feel so guilty when you are happy? That is the most American thing about you.

EMMIE—Well—at least I haven't a husband. Lucile *has* you know. A perfectly good one. Though I don't know but that a daughter is a much worse handicap. Peggy thinks I simply oughtn't to lead my own life at all—you know—just *hers*. She thinks I ought to just revolve around her. (*The music is heard again.*) That's why it's so nice to come to Paris and revolve around myself for a change. (*She rises as* HIPPIE *rises to ask her to dance.*) Ooooh! I certainly am revolving around something now.

HIPPIE—Come and revolve with me.

EMMIE—I'd love to. (*They move towards the entrance.*) Where is that American woman she was talking about? I don't see her. They all look alike to me. I don't see any difference in *anybody*—and I hope nobody sees any difference in *me*. (EMMIE *laughs as* HIPPIE *takes her out.*)

RONALD (*to* LUCILE)—Do you want to dance, dear?

LUCILE (*dreamily—her elbows on the table—her chin in her hands*)—Not now.

RONALD—You're going to tell him—as soon as you get home—aren't you? You promise that—don't you?

LUCILE—Ronald—we only have a few hours more—we *must* face the truth.

RONALD—That's what we're doing. You love me. Everything else is so unimportant.

LUCILE—But Charles is so *good*. How can I hurt him? If we stop now—and keep this as a beautiful memory—

RONALD—Rot!

LUCILE—We *could*.

RONALD—We didn't go after this you know. It *came* to us. Either it's the most glorious thing that can ever happen to me—or nothing on earth is worth a damn.

LUCILE—But I can't believe you do love me like that, Ronnie.

RONALD—Why can't you believe it? You mean something to me that no one else ever has. I've never worked in my life as I have these last two months. If I have anything to say—you'll make me say it.

LUCILE—Oh, darling! That's too marvelous. *Me?*

RONALD—You! It's you! You're strange—subtle—inspiring, understanding. It isn't what you *say*—it's what you make me feel.

LUCILE—That I should make a man of genius do better work! That's the most marvelous thing that can happen to any woman. It justifies our love—doesn't it? Makes it gloriously right—doesn't it?

RONALD—Of course. (*Kissing her shoulder.*)

Ronald's passion mounts with contact and the thought of parting with Lucile, and she, drifting dangerously and seeking justification, glows with the excitement of her adventure.

"I've been awfully *good,*" Lucile protests. "Ronnie, I haven't even flirted. You're the little dream deep down in my heart come true. The little dream I've never dared even whisper to myself. You've given my soul wings."

"You're like a flower unfolding to the sun," murmurs Ronnie, kissing her arm and holding her close.

It is Ronald's firm conviction that he should follow Lucile to America just as soon as his book is finished and take her "decently and honestly" to himself. But that is exactly what he mustn't do, insists Lucile. He must wait until she comes back to him.

Now Emmie and Hippie have finished trying to dance in the crowd and Hippie has an idea. They will all go for a ride in the Bois and have their last breakfast together some place.

Emmie is agreed, but Lucile is hesitant. The men have gone to see if Emmie's car is all right and to give the women time to decide.

With Lucile's help in counting her francs Emmie manages the payment of the check. Then they take up the more pressing problems. Hippie swears he is going home with them on the same boat, reports Emmie, and she doesn't know how she can help it. She isn't quite sure she wants to help it. She doesn't propose to listen to any preaching from Lucile, either. If Emmie were to go home and tell all she knows— But Lucile denies that there is a thing to tell.

LUCILE—I haven't anything to be afraid of.

EMMIE—Not over *here!* They don't think anything of it over here. They're sorry for a woman who *doesn't.* But wait till you get home. I can see old Liberty now shaking her finger at me as we sail in— "Now, Emmie—you've had a good time—settle down and behave yourself."

LUCILE (*moving closer to* EMMIE)—Look at me. You haven't done anything you'll be sorry for?

EMMIE—No—but I may have left *un*done things I'll be sorry for. That's what I don't know. That's what I'm not sure of.

LUCILE—What do you mean?

EMMIE—Oh—stop that virtuous pose with me—Lucile—and own up. Now if you *have*—or *haven't*—don't you think it would have been better if you *had?* Better to just have an out and out affair with Ronnie—and let him be your—you know—while you're about it—and you'd go back to Charlie a great deal more contented.

LUCILE—Emmie! You don't know what you're saying.

EMMIE—I'm saying just what you're *thinking*. We aren't used to talking about it at home. Europe lets you out—and makes you real. Don't you suppose I know how you've been arguing with yourself—up and down and sidewise?

LUCILE—You don't—

EMMIE—You're flattered to death that a man does want you to be bad. You bet *I* am. It's been so long since a man has thought I *could* be bad—that I'm made over. And I don't mind telling you that I'm as confused as I can be—over here—as to what *is* good and bad. If I were going to stay over here I honestly think I'd just take a castle or something and live in it a while with him—and Peggy would never know anything about it.

LUCILE—Emmie—I didn't realize that you were in this kind of a—

EMMIE—Why shouldn't I have some fun? I'm not as old as Methuselah you know. Hippie knows. He sees things in me. Things I'd forgotten I had—have come out. I'm darned sick of just being Peggy's mother. Hippie says I have great individuality of my own—and *real* allure. And I have too. I can feel it myself—over here. And I can also feel it freezing up like *that*—the minute I get off the boat. (*Beginning to cry a little.*) I'm lonely—lonely—way down deep in the bottom of my soul. I want to live—and be loved—and understood—before I die. Why shouldn't I? Why shouldn't I?

LUCILE—But, Emmie—you *can't* let yourself go like this. Life doesn't let us off so easily.

EMMIE—Oh, life—poppycock! You never were as good looking as you are this minute because a man is making love to you. You've got twice the magnetism you have at home. No wonder you look Russian and things—because he's told you you do. Well, Hippie thinks *I* look things, too. And I do—when I'm with *him*. I've got a man in love with me, too—and it's just as thrilling as yours is. Now—I've told you *everything*. And if you don't tell me—I'll *know*.

LUCILE—There's nothing for you to know.

Still, Emmie feels that she is the one to be shocked. Her husband, at least, is perfectly dead. She is free to marry Hippie, if it weren't for her daughter, Peggy. Peggy is almost sure to look upon Hippie as something the cat brought in.

Lucile's confession expands to the declaration that Ronnie does want to marry her; that he is deeply, marvelously in love with her. He wants her to get a divorce and marry him immediately. But it isn't as easy as Emmie thinks. Furthermore, Emmie must never breathe a word of anything Lucile has told her to any living soul. . . .

The men are back. Emmie and Hippolitus have left for their ride and breakfast in the Bois. Which makes Ronald curious. Is Emmie going to marry Hippie? She must know it is her money—

Emmie is no fool, Lucile assures him. She knows. But she also knows that she is lonely and that she wants companionship. Why shouldn't she?

RONALD—But!—But! Have you just been amusing yourself with me this summer? If you have—it will smash something in me—my faith in life. I'll never write another word as long as I—

LUCILE (*putting her hand on* RONALD'S *cheek to make him look at her*)—You know I haven't. It's been the most wonderful thing in my life. I want to meet it full tide too.

RONALD—Then why do you hesitate? Are you going through with it—or not? Are you going to tell him decently and honestly that you're in love with somebody else? (LUCILE *turns away from him. He goes to her.*) Is that too much to expect?

LUCILE (*quietly—breathlessly as she pulls on her long gloves*) —I'm going to tell him—decently and honestly. I know I owe it to life to take care of this. I owe it to you— I owe it to myself— I owe it to him—to be strong—and honest.

RONALD—You'll tell him—the minute you're alone with him—won't you?

LUCILE—As soon as I can—Ronnie. It's going to be awfully hard. *Charles is so good.*

RONALD—The first minute you're alone with him.—Will you?

LUCILE—I'll try.

RONALD—Oh— (*Turning away—jealously—and throwing himself down at the table again.*)

LUCILE (*going to him*)—But, Ronnie—

RONALD (*hitting the table with his fist*)—Why do you say you'll *try?*

LUCILE—I—

RONALD—Either it's over *this minute* for him and you—or it's over for us—now—forever.

LUCILE—But—

RONALD—Will you?

LUCILE (*standing close to him—her hands on his arms*)—Yes.

RONALD—At once—as soon as—

LUCILE—Yes!

RONALD—That you're *not* his wife.

LUCILE—Yes.

RONALD—That you're going to marry me.

LUCILE—Yes. (*She bends down and kisses his lips in a long kiss. The music swells—the lights fade—as the curtain falls.*)

ACT I

IT is five weeks later, 5 o'clock in the afternoon of an October day. The living room of the Lingard house in the country near Dubuque, Iowa, has been put in its best order. "The room is large and cheerful—and comfortable. Not individual, but with a general effect of good style and good taste."

Charles Lingard is walking about the room satisfying himself that everything is as it should be. Charles "is forty-five—medium sized and unremarkable—but he becomes good looking as his slow charm grows apparent in his self-effacement and his wise tolerance. His smile illumines his face and reveals a rare sense of humor and great sweetness."

Charles agrees with Christine, the maid, that everything apparently, is all right. The piano should be open. Perhaps a slight twist to the couch would put it a bit more as it was, but generally speaking everything is fine.

"I've given them up for today," announces Christine. "It's five o'clock now. Traveling by motor is very uncertain business—especially with Mrs. Sykes. She may have changed her mind again."

"I don't think there is anything to make her change her mind between here and Chicago," Charles chuckles, taking three telegrams from his pocket. "We haven't had another one of these things yet today. (*Reading*) 'Docked on time. Marvelous crossing. Leaving New York now. Home Thursday. Love from us both.' Number two—'Delayed in New York. Leaving now. Arrive Chicago Thursday. Dubuque Friday.' Number three—'Delayed in Chicago. Leaving now. Home this afternoon.' They must be on the last lap now."

Christine has returned to the kitchen and Wilbur Lingard has come hesitantly into the hall. Wilbur is Charles' nephew. "He is twelve—a slender boy with a sensitive, intelligent face—shy—on his guard."

Wilbur is a little anxious as to what his status is going to be when the Lingard family is reorganized. Or where his Uncle Charles wants him to be when Lucile arrives. It will probably be just as well, thinks Uncle Charles, if Wilbur stays in the study until the time seems right to send for him. Wilbur will notice a great change in the house with Lucile in it.

"You'll see something happen," he tells the boy confidently, "the flowers will be a little sweeter than you thought they were. The things you think are chairs and sofas will take on a kind of a—something you didn't know they had—when she sits on them. They stop being ordinary. Understand? (*He looks keenly at* WILBUR. WILBUR *nods without speaking.*) I guess you do. If you don't—you will."

"Will she want me to call her Aunt Lucile?"

"She may—and she may not. She doesn't look like anybody's aunt. Let it take care of itself. You see, boy—the reason I haven't told her you were here—"

Peggy Sykes comes dashing in. Peggy is in a state of mind. She is "nineteen—slender—clean cut—and pretty in a fresh, healthy way."

She has a telegram announcing that her mother is bringing a friend home with her. Probably "some dame coming over to lecture or raise money for the cause—and working mother to a finish" is Peggy's bet. Well, mother has a surprise waiting for her, too. His name is Jake, he is six foot something, and Peggy has parked him outside for the time being. She has gone now to see if Jake is still standing.

Charles feels that perhaps there is a little more explanation due Wilbur, who is still hanging shyly about the room. He motions the boy to come to him.

CHARLES—I was going to say—the reason I haven't told her you were here—is that I didn't want her to associate you with your father in any way. She only saw him once—because—well—she's the kind of person you want to keep unhappy, disagreeable things away from. But she knows he died this summer. I did write her that—and I thought it was better for her just to find you here.

WILBUR (*standing before* CHARLES)—You mean she may not want me here!

CHARLES—I mean *this.* I want her to get you in her own way—without my bungling it. And I want to pound this into you. I didn't ask you to come and stay with me because you're my nephew—or because I thought it was my duty—or any of that nonsense. But because I took one look at you—and here we are. (WILBUR *turns to the fireplace—his back to* CHARLES.) I would have been lonely as hell rattling 'round this empty house this summer without you. (WILBUR *turns and shyly smiles at* CHARLES—*then goes and sits in the big chair at the right of the fireplace.*) You haven't the faintest idea how lonely I would have been—because you don't know what it is to be without *her*. So I'm greatly in your debt. See?

WILBUR—You say that just because— (*Lowering his eyes.*)

CHARLES (*rising and going to stand before* WILBUR)—Now see here. Your father has nothing to do with you. It's just an accident that he was your father. More of a one than being my brother. Brothers are nearer than fathers and children. You didn't know that—did you? I didn't either till a scientific fella told me the other day. But what I'm getting at is—that you're *on your own*—and you're somebody everybody is going to like.

WILBUR—Will *she?*

CHARLES—The joke is you won't know whether she does or not—you'll get such a kick out of liking *her*.

The travelers have arrived. Christine goes excitedly to the door. Charles as excitedly hurries Wilbur into the study.

Lucile is in the doorway. For a moment she hesitates, looking at Charles. Then she goes to him. "He closes his arms about her, kissing her lips, her face, her throat." His voice is husky as he holds her away from him and wonders if it is really she. Something, Charles insists, has happened to Lucile.

"I've never seen you so—you're more beautiful than ever," he enthuses.

"It's my hat," declares Lucile, flustered, but pleased. "Emmie's here, too."

He will not let her get away from him for a moment. It is too wonderful to have her home again. Lucile walks a little excitedly about the room, touching the furniture, noting the flowers, finding everything the same. "It is all so comfortable—and American," she comments.

"It's almost worth letting you go—to have you come back," repeats Charles.

"But you're looking awfully well—Charles," Lucile flutters on. "You can't pretend you've been lonely. Can you? You've got on splendidly without me—haven't you?"

Photo by White Studio, New York.

"AS HUSBANDS GO"

Charles: The more you keep on telling a woman she's the most wonderful thing in the world—the more you believe it yourself.

Ronald: You don't see a fault in her.

Charles: Certainly I do. I'm not an imbecile. Don't you suppose I know I think she's prettier than she is? . . . She is in love with somebody else—and I'm trying to find out whether he's enough in love with her—to make her *safe* with *him.*

(*Jay Fassett and Geoffrey Wardwell*)

"Oh, yes," Charles answers, with a slow smile. "The clock just stopped, that's all. Now it's begun again."

"You're a funny old dear," she agrees, looking deeply at him.

"God! What if something had happened to you?" he answers, quietly.

Again Lucile tries to call Emmie, but again Charles holds her back. He is eager to hear about Emmie, but in no hurry to see her. How is Emmie?

"Emmie's marvelous," admits Lucile. "She bought everything in Paris. There isn't a thing left. But, Charles—you must be awfully sweet to her now—kind."

"What's the matter with her?"

"You don't know Emmie."

"I've only known her twenty years."

"That's just it," answers Lucile, with a rising excitement which she tries to conceal. "That's just it. You think you know her too well—to really know her at all . . . You're so close to her—you take her for granted. There's another side to Emmie—entirely. It's the things we don't understand that are the most important. Try to understand her, Charles."

Charles is not altogether convinced that Europe has done anything to Emmie that it will be difficult for him to understand. When she comes, he greets her with that intimate affection that has always existed between them. He is amused and pleased at her grand earrings. But he does find it a little difficult to adjust himself to the thought of Hippie, after the women have told him.

Hippie, Emmie explains, is still with Peggy and the awful boy Peggy has with her—Jake something or other. And Peggy is behaving towards Hippie exactly as her mother had expected. As for Jake, Emmie is determined that she will soon "brush him out."

When Charles has gone to rescue Hippie and bring him into the house, Emmie and Lucile have a chance to readjust their homecoming plans. Lucile is distressingly nervous about them.

"You are so excited you are behaving like a lunatic," she says.

"You're the excited one," snaps Emmie. "Why Charlie doesn't know there's something the matter I can't *see*."

LUCILE—Be *careful!* If you keep on *thinking that*, you're going to *say* it.

EMMIE—I'm not going to say a thing. But I keep thinking how guilty you look.

LUCILE—Shut up, Emmie. And stop doing that to that bag. Behave yourself. Be *natural.*

EMMIE—How can anyone be natural with Hippie around? (*They both laugh a little—foolishly.*) And he looks so much more unnatural than I thought he was going to. Peggy hasn't taken her eyes off him *once.* (CHRISTINE *comes in from the hall.*)

LUCILE—Everything looks so nice, Christine. Just as though I'd never been away at all.

CHRISTINE (*going to the fire and picking up the crumpled telegram which* PEGGY *has thrown on the hearth*)—Yes'm. Thank you. There are a great many letters and telegrams and flowers—but Mr. Lingard put your purple asters there with his own hands. He's been nursing them all summer.

EMMIE—Oh, God!

LUCILE—Yes, they're lovely. We'll have tea now, and Mrs. Sykes and Miss Peggy will stay.

CHRISTINE—I thought they would. And will that other—

EMMIE—Yes. *He will!*

CHRISTINE—Yes'm. (*Stopping at the hall door.*) Will you have it here—or in the hall?

LUCILE—Right here.

CHRISTINE—Yes'm. (*She goes out, closing the door.*)

LUCILE (*rising and going quickly to* EMMIE)—Why did you say "Oh, God," like that before Christine?

EMMIE—I couldn't *help* it! Charles putting purple asters around in the same old places with his same old hands! What are you going to *do?*

LUCILE—I'm going to *scream.* That's what I'm going to do—if you don't stop being so stupid.

EMMIE—How do you actually *feel?*—yourself. Are you wavering or not? Everything seems sort of slipping away from me. The right to live—you know—seemed so much more so in Europe than it does over here. Peggy looked at his monocle *every second.* Why it didn't crack right in two—I don't see.

LUCILE (*laughing*)—You're too absurd.

EMMIE—I know I am. I'm just going to shut my eyes and try to remember how Hippie looked in Europe—and if Peggy says *one word—*

PEGGY (*coming in from the hall*)—Mother! Where in the name of all that's holy did you get it? What is it? *How* is it? *Why* is it?

EMMIE—Now Peggy Sykes—let me tell you something. He's a very distinguished person. Tell her, Lucile. His background and his culture are— You tell her how distinguished he is, Lucile.

LUCILE—Peggy can see that for herself, surely.

PEGGY—I can see a good deal for myself.

EMMIE (*uncomfortable under* PEGGY's *gaze*)—Now I've only had them plucked a tiny little bit. (*Touching her eyebrows.*) And I'm perfectly frank and open about my hair—and you are not going to get these earrings.

PEGGY—Mother, you're a fool! (PEGGY *and* LUCILE *laugh.* PEGGY *throws her arms around her mother's neck.*) Your hair was just beginning to be sweet with a little gray in it.

EMMIE—Hush!

PEGGY—Why did you let her out of your sight a minute, Lucile?

EMMIE—Out of *her* sight. You'd better ask *me* why I let her out of *my* sight.

Lucile has started toward the door, but she comes quickly back into the room, and sits down with elaborate innocence.

Peggy is crazy about Lucile, the way she looks and everything. She can hardly wait until she sees all the things she has bought.

Lucile and Emmie try to tell Peggy that this has not been a shopping tour of Europe at all. For the first time they have really felt and seen Europe itself.

"How did it feel?" asks Peggy, innocently.

"The things that are—interesting and stimulating—and satisfying are just *there.* It's all so effortless—so simple. Not strained and made and self-conscious as it is over here—it just is.

"What is?"

"That's just it," puts in Emmie. "You can't put your finger on it. The air is full of it."

"Of what?" pesters Peggy.

"It isn't something you go *out* for," explains Lucile. "It's life itself—over there."

"Absolutely," agrees Emmie. "It just oozes out—and you breathe it in."

"I advise you to let it all ooze out of you before you see anyone else," advises Peggy significantly.

Peggy's chief concern at the moment is a dinner party she has planned for Sunday night and the problem of Hippolitus. If he comes he is certain to be insulted, she warns.

Neither does Peggy take kindly to her mother's references to her Jake as a giraffe with a perfectly awful American voice. Jake, Peggy would have them know, teaches Greek in the Junior

Public High School, and has one of the best minds in the state. Also, she is going to marry him.

This announcement is almost too much for Emmie. To Peggy it is much less serious than her mother's "Hip-Hip affair." It is all that Lucile can do to quiet them before Mr. Lomi and Jake Canon are brought in by Charles. Hippie looks more Continental than ever. Jake is 21, 6 feet 2, shy, and much too big for the furniture.

Hippolitus is the perfect guest. He has seen enough of America to understand why Americans boast of it and he tactfully overlooks all of Peggy's none too subtle gibes. Jake drapes himself quietly in a chair and takes little part in the conversation.

Tea is served and the conversation flits in and out of the travelers' adventures abroad. Charles is effulgently happy to have his wife home again and says so. It is a matter of surprise to Hippie that Charles ever let Lucile get away in the first place. It also astonishes Hippie that Charles has never seen Europe. Charles is content, he says, to get his Europe from Lucile. Lucile always makes him see everything she's seen and do everything she's done.

"I think I'm going to get a bigger kick than ever out of Europe this time," declares Charles.

"What do you mean?" demands the suspicious Emmie.

CHARLES—There's something new and mysterious about you both. Is it Continental culture—or what?

PEGGY (*as she takes the plate of sandwiches and goes to her mother again, acquiring a very English accent*)—Oh—we realize that we seem very crude and raw to you—after your long life on the Continent of course. (EMMIE *refuses a sandwich and* PEGGY *goes back to* JAKE *who takes the plate and puts it on the piano.*)

LUCILE—Don't mind them, Hippie. Come and get your tea. Everything is funny to them. (HIPPIE *goes to sit beside* LUCILE *on the sofa.*)

EMMIE—But that's not so funny as you think. Everything is crude. I kept telling Hippie in Paris how magnificently beautiful America is—and now that I've been showing it to him— Well, it just *is* raw.

LUCILE (*with superior sweetness*)—If they'd just stop *building* New York and *let* it get old and mellow and soft and gray like Paris!

EMMIE—Absolutely. And as to Chicago— Well, it's just *embarrassing.*

PEGGY (*leaning against the piano as she drinks her tea*)—Look out—Jake comes from Chicago.

EMMIE—That's what I *say*.

CHARLES—I hope you apologized to Mr. Lomi for Chicago, Emmie.

LUCILE—Mr. Lomi's been saying delightful things about America all along the way.

EMMIE—Hippie's being polite. I know how he *feels*. If we were in Paris now we'd be having tea under the trees in the Bois—this minute—and dining out there later. And the lights would come out—not *blaze* out and hit you in the eye—but just—

LUCILE (*dreamily*)—Just—melt out.

EMMIE—Absolutely. It's all so soft, so subtle!

LUCILE—Paris is so gay and so sad!

EMMIE (*closing her eyes*)—With that gray mauve mist over it all—as Ronnie says. (*She opens her eyes in terror.*)

PEGGY—Who's Ronnie?

HIPPIE (*quickly but suavely*)—A young Englishman—a writer.

EMMIE (*relieved—but terrified*)—Yes—just a writer—one of those.

PEGGY—What did he write?

EMMIE—A— I don't remember.

PEGGY (*beginning to enjoy herself*)—Charlie—the culture has gone deep. Do *you* remember what the writer wrote—by any accident, Lucile?

EMMIE—Why are you so curious, Peggy?

PEGGY—Curious? What else is there to talk about? I'm just being polite about your travels. Don't you want us to ask questions so you can answer them?

CHARLES—Aren't you going to let us shine a little in reflected glory? *You* tell us about the illustrious young Englishman, Lucile.

HIPPIE—He is a friend of mine.

PEGGY—Oh! Maybe *you* can give us a little information. We might like to *read* his book. Might we not, Charles? How about you, Jake? Would you like to read a book?

JAKE (*with a grin*)—I might at that.

Peggy is persistent and finally Hippie relates that Ronnie has published one volume of poems, another of essays and one novel; that his name is Ronald Derbyshire. Emmie, it is also stated, for all her suspicious actions, is not at all hot and bothered concerning Ronnie, as Peggy suspects.

Charles can see that something has happened on this particular trip. Always before when Lucile and Emmie returned they were content to say that America looked pretty good to them after all. But this time they are different. Still, he is not worried, and very content to be a stay-at-home himself.

"If a man sees purple mists in his own backyard—need he travel into the unknown for his soul's sake?" demands Charles.

"It all depends upon what his soul demands," answers Lucile, studying her tea cup intently. "You prefer home-made things, Charles."

"Perhaps there's something wrong with me," Charles admits. "Perhaps I like what I have too well. . . . If I think my house and my wife the best in the world—what more can the world give me?"

"And if I think Jake's a work of art—what the hell does it matter what anyone else thinks?" demands Peggy.

Soon they are twitting Emmie about Ronnie again, and Emmie is threatening covertly to explode with the injustice if Lucile does not set her right with them all. But Lucile can't imagine what she is worried about. Now Emmie has flounced out of the room and come right back into it again as soon as the others leave Lucile alone.

"I'm not going to keep this up, you know," flares Emmie. "I saved the situation this time—but I am not going to keep on being the goat."

"Saved it? You made it," answers Lucile, with spirit. "Every time you open your mouth you—"

"Well—well, I'm not going to sit with my mouth shut forever. *Tell* him. For heaven's sake tell Charlie and get it over. We can't live sitting on powder. And I'm so sorry for him I could bawl when I look at him."

They have all gone now. Charles is back and still amused at Emmie's excitement over every reference to Ronnie. If Hippie is the real friend, why all the excitement about Ronnie? And if she is going to take Hippie—that's terrible too— How could Lucile ever have let Emmie get herself into that?

Lucile is spirited in her defense of Emmie and her interest in Hippie. Hippie understands Emmie. He has lifted her out of the humdrum routine everybody else has poked her into, insists Lucile. He makes her something she did not even know herself she could be. What else does life mean, anyway?

It might mean one or two other things, thinks Charles as he is reminded of Wilbur and of the death of Wilbur's father. He wants to talk about that to Lucile, but she is not in a mood to listen. She never even wants to see Wilbur. It would serve to bring back too many unpleasant memories of the boy's father to her. And she does want to go on explaining Emmie—and other things that are not only hard to tell, but are going to require all Charles' understanding—

"Now don't tell me Emmie is living in sin—with Hippie?" smiles Charles.

"If you'd only stop thinking everything is a joke—Charles," protests Lucile, seriously. "It *isn't,* you know."

CHARLES (*walking about as he talks*)—Dearest—if Emmie thinks this little man can keep her amused for the rest of her life—and she wants to pay his bills—why not? As you say—who knows what spells happiness for anybody else? I'm the luckiest devil on earth—and I *know* it. You're the loveliest thing God ever made, Lucile—and you get more so all the— (*Going toward her.*) It's a fact—you *are* more beautiful than when you went away. There's something radiant about you. Your eyes—your skin—are sort of luminous. Is it because you're so happy to be back? (*He comes closer to her. Her eyes shift. She is afraid to move—afraid to stand still.*) You bet I want Emmie to live. I want everybody to live. I've got more to be thankful for than any man going. What is it you want to tell me, dearest? (*Putting his arm about her and putting his head against her hair.*) *Make* me understand. If there's something in life that I don't know anything about—something it's going to take all I've got to see—you make me see it. (*He kisses her hair—slowly—tenderly.*) What is it you want to tell me, dear?

LUCILE (*slowly drawing away from him a little—and trying to smile*)—What is it—*you* want to tell—me?

CHARLES—Wilbur's in there. (*Nodding toward the library.*)

LUCILE (*startled*)—What?

CHARLES—I brought him home with me. He's been here all summer.

LUCILE—Charles—how could you?

CHARLES—I couldn't help it. The poor little devil didn't have any place to go. He's all right, Lucile.

LUCILE—How could he be—with that inheritance?

CHARLES—Pretty bad—I admit. A drunken loafer for a father and a silly half-cocked mother who isn't straight—I'll bet my hat—but in spite of that the kid has managed to be a— Wait till you see him. He's sound as a pippin—a regular fella. Likes to fish. We've fished our fool heads off.

LUCILE—Oh—

CHARLES—And always *here* when I got home from the bank. Next to having you here it was— Gosh—you don't know how it helped to fill up the cracks. I've sort of kidded myself that he *was* my son. I couldn't help keeping him till you got back and if you don't mind—I'd like to let him stay a little longer. Not just kick him out you know. (*He has walked away from her.*)

LUCILE (*a keen look coming into her face*)—If he kept you from being lonely—I'm glad. That's the one thing you've never forgiven me—not giving you a son—isn't it?

CHARLES (*turning back to her*)—Oh—now—

LUCILE—If you *didn't* have me—you'd like to have him—wouldn't you? (CHARLES *nods.*) Let's keep him, awhile—anyway.

CHARLES—You're just trying to be decent.

LUCILE—I mean it. I want you to have him.

CHARLES—You're—

LUCILE—Bring him out—let's see him.

CHARLES (*looking at her gratefully and unbelievingly and going to open the library door*)—Come out, Wilbur. She wants to see you. (*After a pause* WILBUR *comes into the room—going slowly to* LUCILE *with wistful eyes.*)

LUCILE (*putting her hands on his shoulders*)—Why—he actually looks like you—a little through the eyes. How do you do, Wilbur?

WILBUR—How do you do?

LUCILE—Call me Lucile. You need a new tie too. We'll snitch some from Charles' new ones. He tells me it's been wonderful to have you here this summer. We want you to stay on for a while. Will you? (*She has spoken to* WILBUR *with all her charm. He looks at* CHARLES*—speechless.*)

CHARLES (*who has stood near the door watching them*)—I guess you can manage that—can't you? You haven't got too many engagements, have you? (*He smiles to cover up the catch in his voice.*) You skip and spruce up for dinner. We will have to buck up now and mind our p's and q's. Got to have clean collars tonight—the queen will be at the table.

WILBUR—Thank you—for asking me. (*He goes out—smiling at* LUCILE.)

CHARLES (*going close to* LUCILE*—standing back of her*)—That's one of the sweetest things you ever did in your life, old girl. Well—that's my secret. Now tell me yours. I'll try and meet it as magnificently as you did. It seems to me there isn't anything in God's world I couldn't understand—with my arms around you. (*Putting his arms around her.*)

LUCILE (*her courage going*)—I'm awfully tired. Let's wait till after dinner. I'm going to get in the tub. (*She starts to go.* CHARLES *holds her.*)

CHARLES—You might give me a kiss. (*She turns back—kisses him lightly on the lips and goes hurriedly out.* CHARLES *stands looking at the door happily—as the curtain falls.*)

ACT II

Five weeks later Emmie has arrived suddenly at the Lingard home and sent Christine to bring Lucile to her. Emmie is in evening gown and coat. It is about 9 o'clock.

She had not expected to see Charles, but here he is and eager to know what all the excitement is about. Probably about Ronnie. Ronnie has arrived from Europe to visit Emmie. Emmie has just left him with Hippie and Jake. They are coming on later.

Charles is curious to know whether Ronnie looks as illustrious in America as he did in Europe, and what is his visit going to do to Hippie? It's great, thinks Charles, that Emmie should have two beaux and Peggy only one, but he thinks, too, that the situation should soften Emmie's feelings a little toward Jake. But, Emmie is still against Jake.

Lucile and Emmie have a chance to talk when Charles goes to fix drinks for the coming guests. Emmie has rushed on ahead, she explains, because she couldn't remember whether Lucile is supposed to have seen Ronnie since he arrived, or is meeting him tonight for the first time. She and Ronnie have signals agreed upon so she can flash the news to him.

Ronnie should have remembered, thinks Lucile. No, they are not supposed to have met before. Lucile has been with Ronnie, but no one has seen them together. They have taken a short drive in Lucile's car. She is sure no one has seen them. Charles suspects nothing. He still thinks it is Emmie who is exciting to Ronnie—and Emmie is getting tired of that.

Peggy and Jake are in. Hippie and Ronnie are still in the hall. Suddenly Emmie realizes that she has again forgotten her signals for Ronnie. She pulls Lucile into the library to set her right.

The excitement is continuously mystifying to Jake and Peggy, they admit. Ronnie and Hippie both after Emmie! And Ronnie doesn't seem a bit in love with her. Could it be a dual racket of some sort—

It occurs to Jake that it is Lucile. If Ronnie were interested in Lucile that would explain a lot.

"She's all lit up ever since your mother got that cable," suggests Jake. "Every time I see her she's more excited than the time before. You know—all kinda smoldery—underneath. Sparks sorta shoot out from her. (*Twiddling his finger to indicate the sparks.*) You get it you know—that is—a *man* does."

"*Lucile?* Jake, you're a wizard!" explodes Peggy, as the probability dawns upon her.

Immediately there is the thought of Charles. If Lucile were wrong it would kill Charles. Gee, life's hell, Peggy agrees. "Let's run straight," she says to Jake. "There's nothing in the other." And Jake's agreed.

Now Lucile and Emmie are back from the library and Charles is in with the drinks, singing gayly.

The men are coming in from the hall. Ronnie hesitates at the door and Emmie promptly forgets how she was to let him know whether or not he had seen Lucile before. There is an embarrassing second or two and then Lucille rises and goes to Ronald. Still they seem to hesitate before shaking hands, which amuses Charles—

"You don't seem to be quite sure whether you know each other or not," he suggests. A moment later he is introducing himself to Ronnie, and welcoming him to America. Congratulates him, too, on coming right through New York and seeing Dubuque first. Better to see New York last.

Now young Wilbur has come in with Jake and been introduced to Ronnie as Charles' pal. Wilbur is brightly pleased to report that he has been reading one of Ronald's books. A book of poems. He had found it in Lucile's car.

Lucile, after a vibrant second or two, remembers that Emmie had left the book in the car several days ago. Emmie remembers now, too, but she is a little puzzled when Peggy asks her to name her favorite verse.

Again little Wilbur is willing to help. One of the poems, he recalls, was marked—the one "about hoping you can—always—love 'er."

Hippie, fortunately, remembers that one too.

Charles is eager to do something to help make Mr. Derbyshire's visit pleasant. He will be glad to put him up at his golf club and he is delighted when he discovers that Ronnie is an ardent fisherman. There should be a good chance for some fishing. They can start early some morning, if Ronnie is game, and put in a whole day at it.

Charles is even enthused at the thought. It's great to meet a man who likes what he likes, and he has always found that when you find a real fisherman you find him a real man. They go to have a drink on that.

Lucile and Emmie have gone back to the library for further confidences. Hippie is about to join Charles and Ronald, but Peggy stops him. She would like to talk to him about Ronnie and his friendship for her mother. It doesn't seem reasonable. If it were Lucile, she could understand it. But Ronnie and Lucile don't even seem to know each other.

"Yes, they do," speaks up Wilbur.

"What?"

"Sure they do. I saw them together in Lucile's car this afternoon."

"Where?"

"On the back road by your place—I was on my bike."

Jake thinks they had better agree not to say anything about that, and Wilbur promises he won't. Jake and Wilbur have gone out when Peggy takes the matter up again with Hippie.

PEGGY (*going closer to* HIPPIE)—What is this?

HIPPIE—I do not know. I was not on my bike.

PEGGY—You do know. It isn't mother at all. It's Lucile.

HIPPIE—Are you not jumping very fast at conclusions?

PEGGY—If you want to do something that will save an awful lot of trouble—take Ronnie and *get out*—both of you.

HIPPIE—May I suggest that you are interfering in something you do not know anything about?

PEGGY—You don't have to know much to know Lucile is making a damn fool of herself. You don't have to know much to know that you and mother *married* would be an *impossible combination.*

HIPPIE—*That,*—it seems to me—is entirely for your mother to decide.

PEGGY (*fighting back her tears*)—You've flattered her—and fooled her—and made an idiot of her. *I won't have it.*

HIPPIE—Now, Miss Peggy— (*Soothingly and tactfully.*)

PEGGY—You wouldn't want to marry her without her money—would you?

HIPPIE—Certainly not.

PEGGY (*looking at him in amazement*)—What?

HIPPIE—Certainly *not*. Your mother and I would be an impossible combination without her money. With it—we are an exceptionally good one.

PEGGY—Bunk! She's as unsophisticated as a baby. *She* hasn't any continental standards. You'd be mixed up with other women in no time at all. She couldn't stand it—and I'm not going to let her—

HIPPIE—But, since you are so sophisticated, Miss Peggy—you ought to know that I have experienced a wide enough variety of life to find a secure and peaceful existence with your mother the greatest novelty of all—and a *perfect* finish.

PEGGY—You've got a nerve to say that to me.

HIPPIE—And your sophistication ought to tell you that it is because I have lived so much that I *know* I am truly deeply fond of her. If I were *not*—all the money in the world would not make her desirable to me. Your sophistication ought to tell you that the heartaches and miseries which Jake will bring to *you*—your mother will escape—with me.

PEGGY—You're not putting *Jake* and *you* in the same—

HIPPIE—Oh, yes. In his own way he will make you as unhappy as I have made many women.

When Charles brings Ronnie back into the hall their friendship has expanded. Now Charles would like very much to have Ronnie hear Lucile sing, and tell him exactly what he thinks of her voice.

"I might overrate it," Charles confesses. "I think everything about her is the most wonderful in the world. But you would know. You've heard everything."

"It is one of the voices that the world ought to hear," Ronald is agreed.

It is planned that someone is to ask Lucile to sing when she comes in. For some reason she has not sung at all since she got home, and Charles is worried. There is also another blunt question he would like to ask Ronnie.

"You can help me, more than anybody," explains Charles. "I don't often get the chance to have the opinion of a man of the world like you. Of course there's Hippie—but I don't think he could tell the truth about a woman. He'd have to say something agreeable. Now—has she got that strange mysterious something that *puts it over*—the spark that would draw the world to her? Has she got it for *you?*"

"Yes."

"And what am I to do about it?"

"What do you mean?"

"I think a woman who has the real thing ought to have a chance to try. Lucile wouldn't ask for it. She'd be afraid of hurting me. (*Rising.*) Ask her to sing now—please. You'll get a fresh impression. Then if you'll tell me what you think—I'll appreciate it. You stay here. I'll send her out."

Charles has gone into the library. A moment later Lucile appears, closing the door cautiously behind her and going to Ronnie.

RONALD (*tensely—scarcely able to speak*)—It's horrible that you haven't told him.

LUCILE—I told you how hard it would be.

RONALD—You've let me come into his house. I feel like a skunk you know—and I'm not.

LUCILE—And don't you think I've tried and tried and *tried?* And every time—he— (*She stands very close to him. He doesn't touch her.*)

RONALD—But it makes it beastly instead of honest.

LUCILE—You're blaming me.

RONALD—I'm not—but—

LUCILE—Do you care as much as you *thought* you did?

RONALD—Haven't I raced across an ocean and a continent to get to you as fast as I could ?—Do you care?—Is that why you haven't told him—because you—aren't *sure?*

LUCILE—I love you more than I *knew* I did, Ronnie. Oh, dearest, now that you're near me again—I can't give you up. I must have the courage to tell him. I *will.*

RONALD—You can't go on like this another day. The only decent thing we can do is to get out.

LUCILE (*moving away from him a little*)—Darling!

RONALD—We've got to.

LUCILE—But—

RONALD—Tomorrow— (*They speak in whispers.*)

LUCILE—Oh, that's too quick. I can't hurt him like that.

RONALD—What you're doing is much worse. It's horrible, Lucile. I can't stick it. If you love me—you'll come away with me tomorrow—or tonight—now. Why don't we do it now?

LUCILE—Oh, no. It couldn't be that way.

RONALD—It's torture to be near you—like this.

LUCILE—Darling—

Emmie has found them and warned them that they can't stand there talking when Lucile is supposed to be singing. The company is drifting back now, and Charles has another idea. Why can't he and Ronnie go fishing on Saturday? There is a dance at the Country Club at night. Could Ronnie manage both? Ronnie thinks he could. That, Charles explains to Lucile, will help keep things straight, and help Emmie from getting herself in an awful mess. He will have Ronnie fishing all day and Lucile can take him to the party, so he won't be left out in the cold. And now, will she sing "Ah, Love But a Day?"

Lucile runs over the accompaniment and starts the song. "Ah, love but a day and the world has changed." Her voice is tight and she cannot go on, even at Charles' urging. Still she makes another try. "Look in my eyes. Wilt thou change too?"

Ronald, standing at the end of the piano, is gazing at her until Emmie distracts his attention. Charles has caught the expression. As Lucile goes on with the song, "Charles, puzzled, looks from her to Ronald—and then at the others. The thing which the room is filled with begins to come to him. Lucile stops singing and rises faintly."

Charles quickly has his arm about Lucile and Jake has gone for a glass of water. It is air that Lucile needs, she thinks. She will lie down for a moment in the library.

After she has gone Charles and Ronnie look steadily at each other as Charles asks for a verdict. It isn't fair, thinks Ronald, to judge Lucile's voice by that song.

Now Emmie has decided to break up the party. It was silly for them to come in the first place. Ronnie is dead tired after the long journey and Lucile will be glad to be rid of them. Lucile's so temperamental.

They all say their good-bys to Charles, with an extra touch of affection in their parting. Peggy even throws her arms about his neck and embraces him with enthusiasm. "If it weren't for Jake I'd be in love with you," says Peggy.

CHARLES (*following them to the door*)—Thanks for those kind words. It's a date for tomorrow then, isn't it, Ronnie? Because tomorrow's sure to be a fine day—and if we postpone it—we might put it off too long.

RONALD (*calling back to him*)—Why, yes—surely—if you say so. (*Their voices die away as they call "Good night" to* CHARLES. *As* CHARLES *turns back into the room—leaving the hall door open*—LUCILE *comes in from the library.*)

CHARLES—They've gone.

LUCILE—Oh—without any food? How absurd! That's just like Emmie. (*Lightly, nervously, trying to be natural. She takes a handkerchief from the piano—her vanity case from the mantel —and goes to the couch to straighten a pillow.*) After I've gone to all this trouble! The whole thing was her idea anyway.

CHARLES—Are you all right now?

LUCILE—Perfectly.

CHARLES—What was the matter?

LUCILE—The room was smoky or something—I s'pose. I *couldn't* sing.

CHARLES (*going to the fire and standing with his back to* LUCILE)—Ronnie thinks you have a very rare voice.

LUCILE (*breathlessly—her back turned to him as she picks up the pillow*)—Did he say that?

CHARLES—He did. And he seems a very—honest chap—to me. Does he to you?

LUCILE—Why—yes.

CHARLES—That's important—isn't it?

LUCILE—What?

CHARLES—To be honest.

LUCILE—Of course. (WILBUR *comes in from the hall with a small book.*) What are you doing with that book, Wilbur?

WILBUR (*frightened and off guard for a moment*)—Uncle Charlie said he wanted to read it tonight. I thought he'd like me to bring it in from the car.

CHARLES—Yes—I do want to read it. Thanks, Wilbur. You can go to bed now. You must be sleepy. Good night, boy.

WILBUR—Good night, Uncle Charles. (*He looks at* LUCILE.) Good night! (LUCILE *doesn't answer.* WILBUR *goes out—leaving the door open.*)

LUCILE (*watching the book as* CHARLES *holds it*)—Let me have it, please. It's Emmie's. She didn't mean to leave it.

CHARLES—But it's surely meant to be read, isn't it?

LUCILE (*putting her hand over the book quickly as* CHARLES *opens the cover*)—No!

CHARLES—Oh!—Is there something she wouldn't want me to see?

LUCILE—Yes.

CHARLES—Sorry. (*He gives the book to* LUCILE.) If Emmie has anything she wants me to know—I s'pose she'll tell me.

LUCILE—Y-e-s—I suppose she will—when she's *sure*—herself. (*She goes to the door and turns to* CHARLES.) Good night, dear.

CHARLES—Good night. (*She goes quickly.* CHARLES *stands motionless a moment as the sickening pain comes into his face and body—then turns and goes slowly to fire—standing with his back to the audience. And the curtain falls.*)

It is eight o'clock the following evening. There is a grate fire from which the light shines across a corner of the Lingard library. Arm chairs stand before the fireplace, an unlighted bridge lamp above one of them.

Presently Charles and Ronald let themselves in through the door. They are still wearing their fishing togs, are dirty and disheveled and stiff with cold.

Charles lights the bridge lamp. A moment later he has found a bottle of Scotch and some glasses in a wall cupboard and poured them each a drink while they wait for Christine to fetch the White Rock. They have three of these before Christine gets back.

Now, with a highball added, they are beginning to melt into a comfortable conversational mood. Charles pours the drinks and is noticeably more generous with Ronald's than he is with his own. Gradually the day's adventure takes on a colorful, reminiscent glow.

CHARLES—I'm glad you weren't disappointed—and you certainly landed the big fellow as neatly as anything I ever saw done in my life.

RONALD—Think so? *God*—I'm cold! Might as well be drinking iced water.

CHARLES—Me, too—but keep at it. (*Giving* RONALD *a highball.*) Yes, sir—to land one that size on a thin line—that takes real fishing.

RONALD—He didn't put up a bad fight, did he? That's what I like. To see them jump like that. He was rather magnificent, wasn't he?

CHARLES—You can *fish!* You're all right! You're an all-round *man.* That's what I like about you. (CHARLES *stands beside* RONALD *before the fire—holding his glass in one hand and a sandwich in the other. Both men are beginning to be comfortable.*) You're a *man's man* as well as a woman's man. That's a great combination. I often wish I had it. To understand women is a wonderful thing. Now you've only been here two days and I expect you understand my own wife in some ways better than I do myself.

RONALD—What makes you say that?

CHARLES (*talking with his mouth full*)—You've got a poetic—romantic—sympathetic side to you—that *knows* that complex mixed up thing we call a woman's nature.

RONALD—I must get along now.

CHARLES (*taking* RONALD'S *glass*)—Yes. Just one more will fix us up.

RONALD—No more, thanks. No, really.

CHARLES—Just a drop for me then and I'm with you. (RONALD *turns to the fire to light a cigarette.* CHARLES *pours a large drink into* RONALD'S *glass and only a drop into his own.*) Is it beginning to get to your toes a little? You'll dance all right. That's another sympathetic thing about you. I can't dance. Lucile says I'm light on *my* feet, but not on hers. She says I don't respond to the music. Responsiveness—that's what a woman wants. Now that's what you've got.

RONALD (*having taken the long drink*)—I don't know about that. But you're a *man's* man—which is much more important.

CHARLES—Think so?

RONALD—Oh, much! Much more important for a man to be a man's man. That's what I like about *you.*

CHARLES—Well—I don't know. Of course any man—that *is* a man—is a man's man.

RONALD—No, I don't mean that. I mean a man—that *all* men recognize as a man—as an exceptional man—an outstanding—upstanding man. A man that a man knows is a man's man. That's what I call a man's man.

Charles had hoped, he admits, that they would have had a chance during the day to have a good talk about Lucile's voice. Ronald also had an idea they would have a good talk, but there didn't seem to be time.

Now, as man to man, Ronald is forced to admit he is a little disappointed in Lucile's singing. Didn't seem as good as it did in Paris. But, suggests Charles, she was too filled with emotion last night. Which, agrees Ronald, is exactly what he means—an artist controls emotion, and is not controlled by it. "The road to the stars is over stony ground," insists Ronald. "Anyone starting on a career needs courage, force, tenacity, great moral force—"

"You mean guts," suggests Charles.

"Yes," admits Ronald, with a bow. "That's what I mean—though I don't like to speak of a lady's guts—if you know what I mean."

"I get you. And what about her age? Do you think she's too old to begin? Of course she seems young to me. I'm forty-five. She's only thirty-five."

"My God! She couldn't be!" exclaims Ronald.

Their confessions continue volubly. Ronald is free to admit that even a woman's beauty is a strange thing. Largely depends on surroundings. Take Lucile—take Lucile in Paris—

"Lucile doesn't seem so beautiful to me right here as she did in Paris," admits Ronald. "Less glamour. Things seem to me somehow to be *just exactly as they are*. If you know what I mean."

"Glamour's a great thing," admits Charles, pouring Ronald another drink; "but you see—to me—she *has* all the things you think she hasn't got—and if I give her up to somebody else—I want to be sure he'd think she's just as wonderful as I do—and keep on thinking so—*forever*. Get me?"

Charles is worried. Now that he has found out that it is not a career that Lucile wants he is worried. She's not happy and he wants her to be happy. He wouldn't have her miss happiness just because she is married to him. If there's anyone Lucile wants Charles wants her to have him.

Ronald is again convinced that it is time for him to be getting on, but he has some difficulty finding the door knob in that side of the wall where there is no door. Nor does he do much better when he locates the catch to the wall cabinet, toward which Charles kindly directs him.

Ronald would also like to say a few words about American door knobs and other early American inventions that are really English, and Charles would like very much to hear him. It's a rare treat to Charles to hear a man of intellect talk. But for the moment they return again to Lucile.

CHARLES (*putting an arm about* RONALD'S *shoulders*)—You think I'm right—don't you—in expecting her to tell me—if she fell in love with another man?

RONALD (*leaning across the table*)—What would you do—if she *did* tell you she wanted someone else?

CHARLES—I'd want to see him.

RONALD—To—shoot 'im?

CHARLES—Oh, no. I'd want to know whether he could take care of her or not—so she'd have what she always has had. Women have to be taken care of—and the better you do it—the easier they think it is.

RONALD—Oh, hell—I want a woman to take care of *me.* I say it in all modesty— I've got a spark of genius—and *it* comes *first*—before any woman on earth. It's got to. God—it's life! Women come and go—but *it stays. It's what I live with.* When I find a woman who has made that spark burn brighter—that's the woman I want. I thought I'd found her once—my ideal woman—but it fades away somehow—it (*after a pause*) fades away. Was that party tonight or tomorrow night?

CHARLES—I think it was last night.

RONALD—Oh—well—that's all right. That's good. It's so comfortable here. Well— (*Holding up his glass.*) Here's to you, Charlie— (*They both drink.*) Lucile is perfect to you—isn't she? How do you do it?

CHARLES (*as they sit with their heads close together*)—The more you keep on telling a woman she's the most wonderful thing in the world—the more you believe it yourself.

RONALD—You don't see a fault in her.

CHARLES—Certainly I do. I'm not an imbecile. (CHARLES' *own tongue has loosened by now—his own heart has become a little too warm and confidential.*) Don't you s'pose I know I think she's prettier than she is? But she is a darn sight better looking than most wives. God—when I see them around the Country Club! I thought we were safe—but the whole bloomin' thing I thought we had—we haven't got at all. She is in love with somebody else—and I'm trying to find out whether he's enough in love with her—to make her *safe* with *him.*

RONALD—And if you thought he was—you'd give her up—to him—because you love her so. (*After a pause* CHARLES *nods—unable to speak.* RONALD *puts an arm across* CHARLES' *shoulders.*) Well, let me tell you something. When I first saw you I thought—no offense, mind you—I thought— Good God!—No wonder she—

CHARLES—No wonder she what?

RONALD—But let me tell you what I think *now.* I think any man that had the nerve to think he's more of a man than you are—and to crash into what you've made out of your love for a woman—oughtn't to be shot—but just *kicked* to death—and kicked long and hard and slow—so that he'd have time to know what a bloody-low-down skunk he is. I like you better than any man I ever saw in my life—or ever hope to see. Charlie, now that we're such good friends—and understand each other so well—I want to tell you something. I— (LUCILE *opens the door and comes in. She is in the gown she wore the last night she was in Paris. She stops aghast in horror—as she sees the men.* CHARLES *gets to his feet and pulls* RONALD *up.*)

CHARLES—It's all my fault if he's a little late, Lucile, I—

RONALD—Good evening, Lucile. How beautiful you look!

CHARLES—He'll be ready in no time at all.

RONALD—Ready for what? I tell you I've had the most marvelous time—

LUCILE—Don't! This is the most disgusting thing I ever saw.

CHARLES—But—darling—

LUCILE—*Don't!* I wouldn't have believed it was possible. You're beasts!—disgusting—loathsome *beasts!*

RONALD—I'm sorry about the party last night. (LUCILE *goes —closing the door with a bang.*) She seems to be displeased about something. Is anything wrong, Charlie?

CHARLES—*Not a thing!* (*They put their arms about each other as the curtain falls.*)

ACT III

It is twelve o'clock Sunday morning. In the Lingard living room Katie, the second girl, is putting a bowl of flowers on the piano when Emmie and Peggy Sykes come in from the hall.

Both Peggy and Emmie are eager, even anxious to see Lucile, who, so far as Katie knows, is in her room. Katie will call her.

Emmie would have Peggy go back to the car and wait for her with Jake and Hippie. But Peggy is inclined to stay. She is afraid to have her mother see Lucile alone. Lucile will probably put something else over on her. Probably Charlie doesn't know yet that neither Lucile nor Ronnie was at the party last night. And Peggy doesn't propose that they will get her mother in that, too.

Where did Lucile go with Ronnie, in place of bringing him to the club? Emmie would like to know that. And when she thinks of poor, innocent Charlie, totally unsuspicious as usual, she is doubly distressed.

Peggy is not so sure Charlie did not suspect something when Lucile tried to sing, but Emmie is sure he didn't. If he had he couldn't have spent the day fishing with Ronnie. But how could Ronnie have gone?

Christine is back to report that Lucile is not at home. She went out for a walk some time ago. And Mr. Lingard has gone to church, Christine thinks.

Now, Peggy insists, her mother will have to wait for Lucile and get herself out of the new mess quick. What, otherwise, is she going to say to Charles when he asks, "Why didn't *you* tell me, Emmie? Why did you deceive me, Emmie?"

Of course, Peggy is convinced, Charlie will blame Emmie for everything. If she had behaved herself in Europe Lucile would have, too. And Emmie cannot escape on the plea that she is not married. She is married, and has a grown-up daughter, and is forty-six, not forty-three, and she has acted very silly with Hippie—

Jake and Hippie, tired of waiting, are in to see what is happening. Everything is a bit confused. Hippie, learning the situation, is quite disappointed in Ronnie.

HIPPIE—If only he had been cautious until they got over it—Charlie would never have known. For I do not think it would have gone too far. I mean I do not think it would have gone so far as marriage. Oh—I am very disappointed in Ronnie. I have known him five years—but you can never tell what an Englishman in love will do. The honest shy ones are the most dangerous. This will hurt Charlie so much.

PEGGY—But you think it would have been all right for them to have an affair right here under Charlie's nose so long as they didn't let him find it out!

HIPPIE—You put it very bluntly, Miss Peggy. Oh, I am so very sorry.

PEGGY—It's a cute time for *you* to be sorry.

EMMIE—*Peggy!*

PEGGY—Oh, mother—the whole nasty mess is his fault—yours and his. If you hadn't done what *you've* done—this wouldn't have happened. (EMMIE *begins to cry.* HIPPIE *walks away towards the windows at right.*)

JAKE—I think that's going some, Peg.

PEGGY—It's the truth, isn't it?

JAKE—No— I don't see that your mother has anything to do with it. (EMMIE *takes her handkerchief away from her eyes to look at* JAKE *in surprise.*)

PEGGY—She has *everything* to do with it.

JAKE—She has a right to—to fall in love—if she wants to.

EMMIE (*pointing to* JAKE)—Even *he*—even *he*—treats me better than you do.

PEGGY—He doesn't care as much as I do.

JAKE—Oh, now—

PEGGY—She's my *mother!* How would you like to see your

mother help a woman have an affair and deceive and fool the best man in the world—and get mixed up herself with a queer *foreigner?*

EMMIE (*rising*)—I can't stand it! I won't marry you, Hippie. (HIPPIE *turns from the window. They all stare at* EMMIE.) I absolutely could not endure what I'd have to from Peggy the rest of my life if I married you. It isn't worth it. You'll just have to go home without me.

HIPPIE (*after a pause*)—Are you sure you mean that—Emmie?

EMMIE (*absolutely*)—I could live with one of you at a time and let you each think I couldn't live without you—but not both of you at once. I *couldn't.*

HIPPIE—If you had told me in Paris—to go—I should have thought of you always as a charming memory—but now that I have seen you here—day by day—now that I have come to really know you—and have seen how amiable you are—even with your own family—it is very hard to go—Emmie. (*His voice breaks with real emotion.*)

EMMIE—What can I do? She's my own flesh and blood.

HIPPIE—Yes—I know. (*He goes out quickly through the hall.* EMMIE *turns her back to* PEGGY *and sits on the sofa.*)

PEGGY (*after a long pause—very much ashamed of herself*)—If you don't want him in *spite* of everything I say—you don't want him much. (*Pause.*) I don't pay any attention to what you say about *Jake.* (*Another pause.* EMMIE *keeps her back turned.*) Don't you know your own mind?—I believe he really likes you, mother. If you've got to marry anybody—you'd be a nut to let him go. Regardless of everything about him that makes me sick at my stomach—I like him.

JAKE (*getting up from the couch*)—Atta girl!

EMMIE (*to* PEGGY)—You're the most outrageous—

Charles comes cheerfully through the hall. He has just passed Hippie and can't understand why Hippie didn't speak to him.

"I hope nothing's wrong," ventures Charles. "I've grown to like the little man enormously. Your foreign importations were a great success. Ronnie's one of the most delightful fellows I've ever seen in my life. I got to know him yesterday—alone all day with him. He's all there—a good sport—and a high-minded decent chap. (*Going to the fire and turning and looking genially at all of them.*) How was the party last night? Did you all have a good time? I haven't seen Lucile yet this morning. I've been to church and prayed for you all—especially for myself. I asked Lucile to take care of Ronnie at the party last night, Emmie—for fear you would neglect him. Did she?"

"Yes—I guess she *took care* of him all right," ventures Peggy.

If Emmie has turned Hippie down, that must mean she is going to take Ronnie, decides Charles. And probably that is just as well. An Englishman should be safer in the long run, though it would have been hard for Charles to choose between Hippie and Ronnie.

Now Lucile is back from her walk and testily surprised that they should be surprised at her having gone. Peggy, taking Jake with her, deciding to catch up with Hippie and apologize, stops long enough to embrace her mother and ask if she can tell the Frenchman everything is oke.

Charles is making a desperate attempt at being natural. He apologizes to Lucile for messing things up with Ronnie after the fishing trip. He will explain later. Now he wants to call Ronnie by phone and find whether or not he is up. Charles has a date with Ronnie for the afternoon, if Emmie doesn't mind.

Charles is in the library telephoning when Emmie demands an explanation from Lucile. Can Lucile be absolutely mad? Where was she last night with Ronnie? Why didn't they show up at the club? How could Lucile do such a—

LUCILE—Oh, don't—don't! You don't know what you're—

EMMIE—Then tell me where you were.

LUCILE—I was here—*here*—waiting and waiting upstairs for Ronnie—and then I came down here and opened that door and found them—*together*—Charles and Ronnie—*drunk*.

EMMIE—Oh—thank God! That's the best thing they could possibly have done.

LUCILE—Don't be an idiot! They were loathsome.

EMMIE—Well—why shouldn't they be? They're men.

LUCILE—He'd forgotten the party. They'd forgotten *me*—utterly—both of them.

EMMIE—That's the best thing they could do, too. What of it? You can't expect men to be thinking about you every minute—when you're not around. You're lucky if they think of you while you're with 'em.

LUCILE—You don't know what you're talking about.

EMMIE—What were they talking about? (*She kneels on the sofa facing* LUCILE *who is standing back of it.*)

LUCILE—I don't know.

EMMIE—What did they talk about *all day?*

LUCILE—That's just it.

EMMIE—Do you think Charles *knows?*

LUCILE—I don't know— I don't know— I don't know.

EMMIE—They must have got awfully chummy if they got drunk—*together.*

LUCILE—Something's happened. Ronnie was changed.

EMMIE—Changed—or just drunk?

LUCILE—Both. When I opened that door I tell you he had forgotten me as completely as if—

KATIE (*coming in from the hall with a letter*)—Here's a letter for you, Mrs. Lingard. (*She goes toward* LUCILE *with the letter.*)

LUCILE (*taking the letter quickly*)—Where did it come from?

KATIE—Mrs. Sykes' chauffeur gave it to me.

EMMIE—Henry?

KATIE—No—the other one. He drove up just now. (KATIE *goes out through the hall.* LUCILE *has opened the letter and is reading it—her back to* EMMIE.)

EMMIE (*watching her*)—What is it— (*Going towards her a little.*)—What is it, dear?—what—

LUCILE (*sitting slowly on the couch*)—He's gone!

EMMIE—Ronnie? (LUCILE *nods—too broken to speak*)—Lucile—darling—tell me. (*She drops on her knees beside* LUCILE.)

LUCILE (*reading*)—"If we had stayed over there—if I hadn't come over here—we might have gone on persuading ourselves that it was a great and enduring love—that would have inspired us both to the things we think we are meant for—and can reach. Great enough to justify itself for destroying something else. I have seen the magnificent sympathy of a big man—the shining glory of a selfless love that has enveloped you and made you perfect in its own beauty." (LUCILE *breaks and gives the letter to* EMMIE. EMMIE *gently takes it and continues reading.*)

EMMIE—"I have seen the fool and cad I was—and I'm thankful, Lucile, dear, that you have not had to come to see me as such yourself."

LUCILE—He *wasn't* a cad. He was big enough to run away. That's what he's done, Emmie— Oh, God!—Oh, God!—Oh, God!— That's what he's done.

Lucile has thrown herself on the pillows and is sobbing bitterly. Emmie tries to comfort her. It's Charlie who is responsible, Lucile realizes, as soon as she has controlled her sobs. Ronnie has seen how fine Charlie is— She is going to tell Charlie everything.

But Emmie is against that. It would not be fair to hurt Charlie so. Let Lucile thank God Charlie doesn't know. It would be like nearly killing him just to help her own conscience.

"The kindest thing you can do is not to tell him," Emmie repeats. "And after a while—I honestly believe—you'll love him more than you ever have. Ronnie was awfully young, Lucile. It would have been awfully uncertain—compared to *this*—and Charlie."

"He *did* love me—in Paris—didn't he?"

"Of course he did. Oh, Lucile—those days in Paris!"

"The charm—the beauty—the fun."

EMMIE—Will you ever forget the first night we dined with them in that adorable dirty little place on the river—and saw Paris in that dim—soft— (*She stops and sits again beside* LUCILE.) But I feel so guilty—having Hippie.

LUCILE—Don't be silly! I'm awfully glad for you—Emmie. You've been a brick. (*She kisses* EMMIE *on the cheek with honest love. I'm going to tell* CHARLIE. *She stands up.*)

EMMIE—No! (WILBUR *opens the hall door and comes in.*)

WILBUR—Uncle Charlie wants to know if you want him and Hippie to come in here.

LUCILE—No. I just want *him* to come—not Hippie. Come here, Wilbur. You tell Charlie I want him please, Emmie.

EMMIE (*going to the hall door*)—Don't, Lucille. Sometimes the very worst thing we can do—is do the thing—we ought to do. (EMMIE *goes out, closing the door.*)

LUCILE (*sitting on the sofa and putting out her hand to* WILBUR)—I'm sorry I was cross about the book last night. It didn't matter a bit—really.

WILBUR (*standing before* LUCILE)—That's all right.

LUCILE—When I first asked you to stay it was—for something else—but now I'd like you to stay—because Charlie wants you—so much. That is, if you'd like to stay. I mean *really* stay—forever—you know. Would you?

WILBUR (*swallowing the lump in his throat*)—Do *you* want me?

LUCILE—Yes.

WILBUR—If you and Uncle Charlie wanted me because you kinda liked to have me around—not just because you're sorry for me—that would be—

LUCILE—Would be what?

WILBUR—*Swell.* It makes all the difference if you kinda *belong.*

LUCILE—You do belong, Wilbur—to us.

WILBUR—Gee—that's—

LUCILE—It's swell—isn't it?

WILBUR—I guess yes.

LUCILE—I think so, too.

WILBUR (*seeing* LUCILE'S *disheveled condition and turning to look at the door*)—Uncle Charlie's comin'. Your nose is pretty red. (LUCILE *laughs suddenly and shows him her wet crumpled handkerchief.*) I got one. (*Very proudly he takes an immaculate handkerchief from his coat pocket where it had been folded in a perfect pattern.* LUCILE *takes it gratefully.*) Your hair's all kinda—I got a pocket comb, too. (*Taking a small comb from his pocket.*) It's clean.

LUCILE—That's wonderful. (*She leans against him with a sob.* WILBUR *blinks hard and shyly puts an arm about her shoulders—manfully patting her on the back.*)

WILBUR (*after a moment*)—You'd better keep on. He'll be here in a minute.

LUCILE (*combing her hair a little with the comb* WILBUR *has given her*)—How am I?

WILBUR—You look nice. (CHARLES *comes in from the hall carrying a Sunday paper.* WILBUR *starts for the library door.*)

CHARLES—Where are you going, Wilbur?

WILBUR (*keeping his back to* CHARLES)—Something's the matter with my bike— I gotta fix it. (*He goes out the library door.*)

LUCILE (*still on couch, at left*)—Charles, I have something to tell you.

CHARLES—That Ronnie's gone? Oh—Emmie told me that. And she's going to marry Hippie. That's great, isn't it? (*He pulls a chair a little nearer the window and sits to read his paper—pretending to be very interested in it.*) Have you read about the cyclone in Kansas? I'm tickled to pieces about Emmie, aren't you? (*He hasn't looked at* LUCILE *and he now opens the paper wide so that she is hidden from him—and protected from his eyes.*)

LUCILE—Charles—listen to me—

CHARLES—I'm listening, darling. Emmie seemed to want to tell me something—but I told her I didn't want to hear it. Um—three thousand people. *She* couldn't help it if Ronnie fell in love with her.

LUCILE—But—maybe—he—didn't.

CHARLES—Oh—it must have been pretty serious for him to come half way round the world to get her.

LUCILE—But when he got here—and saw—how fine—

CHARLES—Hippie is— I think it was damned decent of him to turn right around and go away again. Damned decent. Don't you? (LUCILE *rises and goes to the fire.* CHARLES *knows this but goes on talking with the paper still up.*) It must be an awful lot of fun for a woman to have a young fellow fall in love with her. Gosh! I can understand that all right. If I were a woman I know that's what I'd fall for.

WILBUR (*coming in from the hall*)—Dinner's ready.

CHARLES (*rising*)—Well, I s'pose it's the same old Sunday dinner—chicken—mashed potatoes and all. And I'm hungry. (*To* WILBUR.) How about you?

WILBUR (*radiantly happy*)—We got ice cream—with chocolate sauce.

CHARLES—You don't say. (*He looks at* LUCILE *who is still standing at the fire.*) Coming? (LUCILE *goes slowly towards the door—then turns to* CHARLES *and sinks against him in complete abandon.*)

LUCILE—Hold me—close! (CHARLES *puts his arms about her slowly and strongly. They start to the door. In the doorway* LUCILE *stops and turns to* WILBUR *holding out her hand to him. The three of them go through the door as—*

THE CURTAIN FALLS

ALISON'S HOUSE

A Drama in Three Acts

By Susan Glaspell

"ALISON'S HOUSE" was modestly produced by Eva Le Gallienne and the Civic Repertory Company the first of December, 1930. There were conflicting openings that night and few of the first line drama reviewers got down to Fourteenth Street for the first performance.

Those who were there received the play with an assortment of polite phrases in praise of certain of its virtues, coupled with the familiar predictions that it might please the Repertory subscribers and fit comfortably into Miss Le Gallienne's list of plays, but that much could not be hoped for it in the matter of popular approval.

Thereafter "Alison's House" was played on an average of once or twice a week, being given a total of twenty-five performances during the next five months.

In May the Pulitzer awards were made and, much to the surprise and a little to the distress of the experts, Miss Glaspell's drama was given the prize as "the original American play performed in New York which shall best represent the educational value and power of the stage."

There was more disagreement than usual over the award. Philip Barry's "Tomorrow and Tomorrow," Lynn Riggs' "Green Grow the Lilacs," Louis Weitzenkorn's "Five-Star Final" and the Kaufman-Hart "Once in a Lifetime" were generally preferred by the professional playgoers. As usual, their agitation sputtered briefly and subsided.

Miss Le Gallienne, having announced the closing of her season, agreed to play an extra week that "Alison's House" might have a fair start on a new, or regular, commercial career on Broadway.

Under the chaperonage of Lee Shubert the play was revived at the Ritz Theatre on May 11. Its first week was hugely successful, though there were again indications that the critics were right in doubting its wide popular appeal. A second week, with Gail

Sondergaard taking over the Le Gallienne rôle of Elsa, carried the play into a spell of hot weather and poor returns and it was withdrawn.

"Alison's House" is what drama critics most frequently describe as a literary play. Meaning, usually, that it is burdened with intelligence, a generally undramatic story and a superabundance of stiff dialogue.

The charge in this instance, I feel, is no more than partly true. There are dull stretches through Miss Glaspell's play. But it is also a drama of definite appeal to many whose sympathies and interest it will arouse. The dramatist's effort has been to re-create a spiritual influence wielded by a poet who, eighteen years after her death, achieved a righteous justification of her life.

The play is admittedly based on incidents taken from the life of Emily Dickinson, a gifted New Englander who was posthumously admitted to the ranks of the greater American poets. Miss Glaspell changes the locale to Iowa.

As the play opens it is nearing noon the last day of the nineteenth century, December 31, 1899. The library of the old Stanhope homestead in Iowa, on the Mississippi River, is in a state of some confusion. The Stanhope possessions are being packed preparatory to the family's moving.

Ann Leslie, secretary to John Stanhope, the present head of the family, is making typewritten record of various books and papers. "Ann is fair, sensitive looking. She wears a shirtwaist and blue skirt, in the manner of 1900. She is about twenty-three and has gentle manners."

When Richard Knowles arrives, Ann is the only one to receive him. Knowles is a reporter for the *Chicago Record-Herald* and he has come hoping to get a story about the breaking up of the Stanhope home. Everybody is interested, he thinks; at least everybody who knows anything about Alison Stanhope is interested, even though she has been dead eighteen years.

In fact, Alison Stanhope isn't dead, the reporter insists. Anything about her is alive. "She belongs to the world, but the family doesn't seem to know that," he says. True, Alison Stanhope's poems have been published, but where—and how—were they written? "The desk she sat at. The window she looked from. Is there a bird singing in that tree now? Well, no, probably not, the last day of December. But looking through the dead branches, to meadows sloping to the Mississippi, as she looked."

"You cared for the poems?"

"I'll never forget the day I got them—at the bookshop on the

Midway, and walked down through Jackson Park, and saw the lake—because she had seen the river. I write a little poetry myself."

Mr. Knowles is particularly eager to see Alison Stanhope's room before it is dismantled. It has not been touched since the day the poetess died, Ann explains. It is just the same now as it was then.

Whatever the family's feeling regarding the room, Reporter Knowles feels that it should be seen and described by someone who has some feeling about it.

Miss Leslie lacks authority to show anyone about the house, but Ted Stanhope, who has just come in, being a younger son and adventurous, is rather attracted by the idea of stealing a march on the family. Everybody is in the dining room counting dishes. Why not show the reporter what he wants to see? Ted and Knowles are on their way upstairs before anyone stops them.

Now the news has spread that there is a reporter in the house. Louise Stanhope has heard it. Louise is the daughter-in-law. She is one who would like to know all about anything that is happening and immediately take a hand in its correction, even if it isn't wrong.

Louise gets small satisfaction from Ann Leslie. And not much more from Mr. Stanhope, when she summons him and repeats her suspicions. Stanhope "is vigorous for a man of sixty-three, though troubled at the moment. One soon feels that he has a feeling for others that makes him tolerant, though firm."

Father Stanhope fails to see why he should become excited because of a reporter. Even if he has come to see the house, what of it? Having a distinguished person in the family naturally carries its own obligation. Father Stanhope would, if he could, go on with his work, but Louise is determined to carry her point. Ruthlessly she renews the attack:

Louise—Father, please let's try to do this without—stirring things up. Just because we're breaking up the house do we have to revive the stories about Alison?

Stanhope—To what stories about my sister do you refer?

Louise—Now please don't be vexed with me. You know as well as I do—the whole story they've harped on so long—that she was different—a rebel—goodness, I don't know what they do mean.

Stanhope—I think the worst they can say about my dear sister is that she was a great soul, and a poet. It isn't going to hurt my feelings to have it said again.

Louise—But you know how they talk—it makes the whole

family seem—different. And after Elsa— Oh, forgive me, but you know how the town does talk about Elsa. You can't run away with a married man—live with a man who has a wife and children and not be talked about.

ANN—In making the memoranda of these old contracts am I to— (STANHOPE *moves to her.*)

LOUISE—And they do link it up with something queer about Alison.

STANHOPE (*checking anger and speaking easily*)—That would be most unjust to Alison. She never lived with a man who had a wife and children.

LOUISE (*knowing she shouldn't say it*)—She wanted to, didn't she?

STANHOPE (*again checking anger, speaking humorously*)—Oh, we want to do a lot of things we don't do. I might want to ask my daughter-in-law to keep still. In fact, I think I shall.

LOUISE (*rather angry, and made the more persistent by it*)—Where did he go—this reporter?

ANN—Why, they went out—just a moment ago.

LOUISE—They? Who's with him?

ANN—He's with Ted.

LOUISE—Ted! He's already told him enough to fill a page. Where did they go?

STANHOPE (*as* ANN *peers at a paper*)—Well, where did they go, Ann—the roof—the cellar?

ANN—He wanted to see the Alison room.

LOUISE—And you dared—and Ted dared— Oh, what *management.* (*She moves to the door, but* STANHOPE *follows.*)

STANHOPE—No. Not up there. No disturbance in Alison's room. It is to keep its—serenity, the one day it has left.

There can be no serenity anywhere with reporters prowling about. That is Louise's opinion. And, seeing her children are Stanhopes, and must suffer the taunts resulting from any revival of old family scandals, Louise does not purpose letting the matter rest. Furthermore, in addition to what the children might suffer, Louise does not feel any too sure of her husband, Eben. Eben might also decide to shake everything loose. In such matters Louise thinks a family should stand together.

Louise has flounced out of the room, considerably to Father Stanhope's relief, before Ted Stanhope and young Mr. Knowles come downstairs to confess that they have invaded the sacred room. Father Stanhope is obviously displeased with Ted. Many people have wanted to see Alison's room, but few have been granted that privilege. Now, he supposes, Mr. Knowles will be writing a lurid story about it. Nor is he more than a little reassured by the reporter's apparent sincerity.

Aunt Agatha Stanhope wanders into the room as Mr. Knowles is still trying to explain his feeling towards Alison Stanhope as a world figure. Agatha "retains the manner of strength, though she is obviously feeble. She is carrying a china teapot and a sugar bowl." Agatha, too, is quite perturbed by the thought of anyone's prying into the Stanhope affairs, particularly as they may be concerned with her dead sister. The more they try to appease her fears the more nervously excited she becomes.

"I won't have people looking through Alison's room," she shrills, querulously. "I've guarded it for eighteen years." And then, as a crafty look steals into her eyes, she adds: "All right, look! Look again! See what you find."

Mr. Knowles realizes that he should be going, but there is still one question he must ask. Have all the poems of Alison Stanhope been published? Aunt Agatha turns sharply from the basket of straw into which she is preparing to pack the sugar bowl and tea pot.

"What's that?" she snaps. "What does he mean?"

STANHOPE (*soothing* AGATHA)—Never mind. (*To* TED.) I will answer your question, though I've answered it many times before. All of the poems of Alison Stanhope have been published.

AGATHA—Now. You see? He answered you, didn't he?

KNOWLES—In going through the house—going through the old papers—did you—

STANHOPE—It was one question you were to ask.

KNOWLES—Please, just this. It is a matter of public concern, you know. Did you find any papers—

AGATHA—What papers? What papers is he talking about?

STANHOPE—My sister is not equal to this. No, we found nothing that brings any new light to bear on the life of Alison Stanhope. Everything had been gone through long before.

AGATHA—Everything had been gone through long before.

KNOWLES—Thank you, sir. (*To* AGATHA.) Sorry to have disturbed you.

AGATHA (*sharply*)—You didn't disturb me.

KNOWLES (*to* ANN, *with a smile*)—Good-by.

AGATHA (*after* KNOWLES *goes out*)—Where did he come from? What does he want?

STANHOPE—It's nothing—nothing at all. (*To himself.*) We're lucky to get off this easy.

AGATHA—That's why I didn't want to move. Stirring it all up! I wish they'd let Alison alone.

STANHOPE—They will, my dear, in time.

AGATHA—Why can't they let her rest in peace?

STANHOPE—They will—soon. Though it wasn't in peace Alison rested.

AGATHA—What do you mean? I knew her better than you did.

STANHOPE—No, you didn't, Agatha. But never mind. Now you don't have to pack these things yourself.

AGATHA—Mother's tea set? I'll pack it myself, and take it with me myself.

ANN—Perhaps I could help you, Miss Agatha. (*To* STANHOPE.) Have I time?

STANHOPE (*nodding*)—We don't make much headway, anywhere. (*He sits at the table, discouraged.*) It's harder than I thought.

Aunt Agatha is still unhappy. Unhappy at the thought of being moved out of the old house, even though her brother insists he is taking her to his home in town so it will be easier for her to look after him. Nor is Aunt Agatha's mind made the more tranquil by the return of Ted and his repeated declaration that it is foolish for anyone to think they can keep Alison in a prison, seeing she really does belong to the world.

Ted is faced with the proposition of writing a letter to his English professor that will help him make his grade by revealing all the little intimate things about his dead and famous aunt. What kind of pen did she use? And where is the pen now? It is with difficulty that Father Stanhope succeeds in suppressing Ted, even temporarily.

Ann and John Stanhope return to the work of cataloging the books. It is a slow business. Each book is a memory of Alison, a reminder of her love for them, or of her reading aloud to them. It is fascinating work, too. They are too absorbed in it to see that Agatha, a strange light shining in her eyes, has taken the tea set from its bed of straw in the basket and put it where it cannot be seen. Nor do they see her when she takes the basket and starts, with cautious, hesitant steps, toward the door. When they do see her they call but she does not stop. They let her go. After all, it is her last day in the house.

Louise is back with suggestions that the workers may as well go ahead disposing of the furniture in the library now as to wait. She is just in time to catch one of Ted's questions as to whether or not Alison slept well. Such questions may not make sense to the family, Ted admits, but they will help get him his grade. His English prof is an Alison Stanhope fanatic. He has often taken Ted out and filled him up on wine to get him to talk about her.

"Your teachers at Harvard take you out and give you wine?" protests Louise.

"Only Styles. Ever since he heard I was her nephew. Nearly dropped dead first time he asked me. But it always ends telling me I got no soul—insensitive family—unworthy. He's crazy. Got to get this grade though."

And yet Professor Styles was conservative, Ted insists. He had never got him full but once and that was when he was trying to find out about Alison's love affairs. Nor is he interested in any of the rest of the family, however distinguished.

"He says the rest of the family is of interest only because it is so vacuous," reports Ted.

Now Eben Stanhope has arrived from town. He is Louise's husband, "self-assured in manner, though soon one feels the inner uncertainties, hesitations and the inner beauty."

Eben has closed his law office early because there was no interest in work this last day of the century. He has news that cousin Marion has some thought of inducing her club women to take over the Stanhope house and preserve it as a museum. But cousin Marion has thought that for two years, Father Stanhope reminds them. Father has decided to close with a prospect named Hodges who is more decided. Besides, Agatha would never submit to the house being turned over to the public.

Agatha, Father Stanhope repeats for the benefit of Eben as well as the rest of them, is, by the doctor's orders, to be kept from all excitement. Nothing must be said to agitate her. Everything possible must be kept from her. Her heart is more and more uncertain. It is quite important, thinks Father Stanhope, that they all work to make Agatha believe that she must leave the old house and go to town to live so she can take care of him.

Eben is as upset as the rest of them at the thought of giving up the old place. Spurred by the thought that this may be his last visit, memories of his and Elsa's childhood there crowd in upon him; memories of all the little understanding things that Alison used to do for them. "Alison won't tell," she'd say, when they had run off to the river. "Alison knows."

Eben is morbid. That's what Louise thinks. He shouldn't let his mind run on such things.

"Was Alison a virgin?" demands Ted, still struggling with his letter. The family all but fall upon him. Eben would like to do him physical violence. But Ted persists. He's just got to make his grade and his prof wants to know. Was Alison a virgin or wasn't she? And when he is violently informed that she was, Ted is still doubtful. How does anyone know?

Now Eben has exploded and has Ted by the collar, shaking him violently.

"You miserable little fool," he shouts. "And you're the baby Alison used to say got through from heaven. The hell you did! Didn't you get anything from her? (*Shaking him.*) Didn't you?"

"Say, leave me alone, will you? I guess I was only two years old when she died! What do I know about her?"

"Nothing, absolutely nothing, and never will. Why, that prof ought to kill you. If your soul wasn't a shriveled peanut something from her would have made you a human being."

Eben must have been drinking, Louise thinks, or he would not rave so. Even Father Stanhope admits that Eben's emotions are quite uncontrolled. Still, Eben persists:

"The last day we'll ever be in her house," he reminds them; "the last day it will be her house—how can we help but think of her—and feel her—and wonder what's the matter with us—that something from her didn't—oh, Lord, *make* us something."

Elsa Stanhope, wearing a coat, furs and hat, has stepped inside the door. "She has beauty, a soft radiance." She stands hesitant, looking at them inquiringly, before she speaks. Her voice is low and thrilling. She speaks, in endorsement of what Eben has just said. Then she turns to her father.

ELSA—Father, may I—come in? (*One hand, palm up. Goes out toward him, timidly, but eloquent.*)

LOUISE—Certainly you may not—not while— (*But is afraid to go on,* STANHOPE *is staring so strangely at his daughter.*)

TED—Hello, Elsa. How'd you get here?

ELSA (*gratefully*)—Hello, Ted. (*To her father.*) Perhaps I shouldn't have come. But Eben wrote me the place was being broken up and—

LOUISE—You wrote to her?

EBEN—Yes, I write to my sister.

ELSA—I had to be here once more. I thought—perhaps it's too much to ask—but I hoped you would let me stay here. Just tonight. It would—do me good.

LOUISE (*with a shrill laugh*)—Now that's—*funny.*

ELSA (*advancing a little to her father*)—It doesn't mean you forgive me, Father, if—if you don't. But won't you just do it—because Alison would do it? She'd take my hands. She'd say—Little Elsa. She'd say—Elsa has come home. (*From upstairs a wild cry from* JENNIE.)

JENNIE (*above*)—Mr. Stanhope!—Everybody!—Help! (EBEN *hurries out.*) Everybody—quick—the house—burning!

TED—Fire! I smelled it! (*He runs out,* LOUISE *goes, and* ANN. STANHOPE *does not pass his daughter without pausing a moment, looking at her. Outside a confusion of voices, a running about. Only* ELSA *remains as she was, as if she cannot move.*)

ELSA—Just as I stepped into the house. As if—as if— (*Shaking this off.*) Oh, no—no. (*She looks around the room. Softly.*) Don't burn. Don't! (*After a long moment, having looked from one thing to another, she goes to the books, runs her hands over them. Stands there. But at a noise of something falling upstairs, she becomes frightened, suddenly takes an armful of books. Is starting out, but stopped by a confident shout from* EBEN.)

EBEN (*from upstairs*)—It's all right. We're getting it! Two more buckets, Ted!

Elsa is sitting at the table, still holding the books in her arms, when Agatha appears in the doorway. She does not see Elsa, nor has Elsa heard her. Agatha is white, rigid and plainly distrait. She starts violently when Elsa drops one of the books on the table. Nor does she recognize Elsa as she stares, frightened, into her eyes.

Now the fire has been put out and Father Stanhope is excitedly searching the house for Agatha. He finds her with Elsa and tenderly explains to her that there is nothing to fear, now that the fire is out. Agatha seems more startled than pleased at the news.

Eben, coming excitedly from upstairs, is convinced the fire was set. There was charred straw in the closet that breaks through into Alison's room, and indications that coal oil had been poured on it. Someone has been trying to burn the house, that's plain.

They call Jennie, the hired girl, and question her. Jennie weepingly insists that she knows nothing about it. No one has been there, except the family.

There was that reporter, Louise reminds them. He had been upstairs. It is possible he wasn't a reporter at all. He might represent some hostility to the family.

Father Stanhope considers the suggestion ridiculous and Ann is quite sure Mr. Knowles was just what he represented himself to be. He had even showed her a poem he had written. Couldn't the fire have just happened? Straw, saturated with gasoline, doesn't just happen, snaps Louise.

They call Ted. What does he know about the reporter? What did they do while they were upstairs? "You were the only people in that part of the house and a fire was set," Father Stanhope reminds him.

TED—For—Pete's—sake! Talk about *me* being crazy! You think I set a fire to burn the house?

STANHOPE (*violently*)—No! I don't think anything of the kind! But what did you do up there?

TED—We looked at Aunt Alison's room. And he talked about her that crazy way people do talk about her. And that's all.

STANHOPE—Did you have any straw up there?

TED (*tolerantly*)—Oh, Father, what would I be doing with straw?

STANHOPE (*furiously*)—I don't know what you'd be doing with straw! You just might have some idea of making yourself useful!

TED—Useful enough to burn the house.

STANHOPE—Be still. (*Turning to* JENNIE, *who stands by the door, frightened.*) Who had straw upstairs?

JENNIE—Nobody. Nobody's I know of.

STANHOPE—Did you take coal oil upstairs?

JENNIE (*beginning to cry*)—I did not. I did not take coal oil upstairs.

STANHOPE—Very well, Jennie, I believe you. But who— (*In looking around, bewildered, his eye falls on the tea set. Slowly he moves over to it, then looks at his sister, who is still in that strange, fixed state. An idea comes to him that is a shock. Ponders, incredulous, but the idea is growing. To* EBEN)—Straw—you say? (*Moves nearer* AGATHA. *Speaks gently.*) Agatha, why did you unpack the tea set, after Ann had packed it for you?

JENNIE—Oh!

AGATHA—What? What's that you say? Tea set?

STANHOPE—Yes. Why did you unpack it, after Ann had packed it for you?

AGATHA—I can pack my own mother's tea set, can't I?

STANHOPE (*gently*)—But you let her do it for you. (*Silence, after which he speaks carefully.*) Agatha, what did you do with the straw the dishes were packed in?

AGATHA (*as a wail*)—O-h! I wish you'd all go away—and leave me here alone! Why couldn't you *let it burn?*

STANHOPE (*slowly*)—You love the house so much you would *burn* it—rather than—leave it?

AGATHA (*not speaking to any of them now*)—What could I *do?* I tried— I tried. Burn them? All by themselves. (*In a whisper.*) It was—too lonely. (*She falls back.*)

STANHOPE—Get brandy, quick. And the doctor. (LOUISE *goes out, and* TED.)

AGATHA (*resolutely sitting up*)—I don't want the doctor. (*But she again falls back.*)

ELSA—Are you all right, Aunt Agatha?

AGATHA (*looking up at* ELSA)—Couldn't take them away—and couldn't—*couldn't*—

THE CURTAIN FALLS

ACT II

At 3 o'clock the same afternoon the work of cataloging books and disposing of papers continues in the Stanhope library. Ann Leslie is at her typewriter, Father Stanhope is musing over a batch of old bills and receipts, discarding many and casting them into the fireplace. Interestingly trivial old receipts, some of them. One for a carriage, signed twenty-eight years before, reminds him that he used to take Ann's mother riding in that carriage. Reminds him also that Ann's mother was a lovely person.

Eben is down from the attic with the last of the papers that have been accumulating dust up there. Mostly old newspapers. Stories of James G. Blaine. Stories of the old hotel's burning, and of the suit the Baileys brought against the McMasters for stealing a stallion for breeding. Funny old papers. Some way they seem to belong to the house—

Nothing can be left as it was, Father Stanhope is again at pains to explain. Surely they must know that breaking up the old place is harder for him than for anyone. He was born there and grew up in that house. But Agatha can't be left alone there any longer. They must see that. And she won't leave so long as they keep the place. It is almost too bad it didn't burn.

Funny about the fire, they agree. Probably it was some old thing she cherished that Aunt Agatha did not want to take from the house. It might have been something about Alison. It could not have been any of Alison's poems. Those were all published—all that Professor Burroughs thought worth publishing.

Nor Alison's letters. Each has his own. Might have been Agatha's letters from Alison. If she wanted to burn those she should be allowed to.

Talk turns to the New Year's Eve celebration. Nobody wants to go to the dance. Even Ann had rather stay and help.

Eben doesn't want to go, even if Louise does. Eben is bored with dances these days. This being the last night in the old place, Eben thinks he had rather stay there.

Ted is back at his letter again and determined to ferret out more facts about his Aunt Alison's life. What flowers did she like best? And why did Aunt Agatha want to burn down the house? That reporter fellow would certainly like to have *that* story . . .

Mr. and Mrs. Hodges have called. The Hodges have been looking at the Stanhope house again and trying to make up their minds whether or not they could do anything practical with it if they should buy it.

Mr. Hodges, "a small, lean, shrewd-faced man," is still in doubt about buying, but Mrs. Hodges, who "is larger, and has a rather foolish face," thinks she sees possibilities in the place if they were to put a couple of piazzas on it and fix it up nice for summer boarders. The suggestion is something of a shock to Father Stanhope.

STANHOPE (*rather faintly*)—Summer boarders?

HODGES—That's how we calculate. Don't think a poor man like me'd buy this ramshackle old place for just my old woman and those two young uns, do you? But we'd have to fix it all up. Paint her a bright yellow, maybe, with green edgin'—somethin' you can *see*. Summer boarders wouldn't take to a gray house edged with red you can't tell for red.

MRS. HODGES—I could make that conservatory into a sun parlor where they could sit when it rained.

HODGES—But 'twould mean a big outlay, 'cause we'd have to cut it up into more rooms. (*The* STANHOPES *are silent.*)

MRS. HODGES (*feeling she must break the pause*)—Nobody could pay what'd be right to pay for rooms that big.

HODGES—Well, folks don't need rooms so big now.

MRS. HODGES—Hard to take care of.

HODGES—But it's in bad repair, Mr. Stanhope.

STANHOPE (*with effort*)—Oh, I don't think so. The roof needs just a little mending, but the foundations are good.

MRS. HODGES—Looks a good deal run down, Mr. Stanhope. (*Fearing she has been impolite.*) Of course, you haven't been living here yourself. You have your nice place in town. But for summer boarders 'twould need a lot of paint and varnish, and that new wall paper that's more lively-like.

HODGES—All those things cost. They cost.

STANHOPE—Certainly. But we feel our price is low. The house has—character.

HODGES—Character. (*Rubbing his chin.*) Well, maybe so. But *what* character? Not the character for summer boarders. That's what I tell the old lady here. And how do I know there'd be any boarders?

EBEN (*cheerfully*)—There might not.

HODGES—Just what I say. Folks like to go up the river nowadays, not down the river. And with the old Mississippi rising higher every year, seems like she'd wash this place away 'fore we could get dead and buried.

EBEN—Then you could have a house boat.

HODGES—How? (*Laughs loudly.*) Yes, that's a joke. (*To his wife.*) Summer boarders on a house boat.

STANHOPE (*courteous, but cold*)—Just why did you come in today, Mr. Hodges?

HODGES—Want to take one more look at her, 'fore we give her up. Try to figure out where we could put in partitions—modernize. Outside, too, needs a lot. Too many trees make a place gloomy.

EBEN—Those trees have been growing a long time.

HODGES—Well, then they've been growing long enough, haven't they? (*Laughing, waiting for* EBEN *to join him, but* EBEN *does not.*) And that lilac hedge—shuts the place in too much. What's the use of putting your money in a place nobody can see? Take out some of that tangled old stuff and put in flower beds in fancy shapes—heart-shaped, maybe—you'd be surprised the difference it would make.

EBEN (*softly*)—No, I wouldn't be surprised. (*Speaking more brightly.*) Now here's an interesting thing, Mr. Hodges. You aren't sure you want to buy, and we aren't sure we want to sell.

HODGES (*to* STANHOPE, *sharply*)—Not want to sell? But you made me a proposition and I've gone to the expense of getting a carpenter to figure on it.

STANHOPE—I will stand by what I said. But you will have to make up your minds. We have other possibilities for the place.

Mr. Hodges is surprised that anyone should really want to buy the place. He wouldn't think of it if it were not for his old woman, who is pretty difficult to manage once she gets ideas. Eben also tries to discourage Mr. Hodges, but without complete success. Leastways the Hodges think they will have another look upstairs, to see what can be done about cutting up the rooms. Summer boarders don't like large rooms.

Ann is taking the Hodges through the house when Father Stanhope confesses to Eben that he is deliberately selling the place to them because he knows they will destroy it. He wants it destroyed. As long as it remains anything like it is Aunt Agatha will keep coming back to it. It is imperative that Agatha should be protected, in mind as well as body. She is, as Eben says, old to transplant—and they are doing it very badly, with all the confusion. And now Elsa—

EBEN—She loves Elsa. Elsa doesn't harm anybody—except herself.

STANHOPE—She harmed all of us. She disgraced us.

EBEN—Maybe she couldn't help it.

STANHOPE—"Couldn't help it!" What a weak defense. Alison helped it—and so did I.

EBEN—What did you say, Father?

STANHOPE—Never mind what I said. The only person in this family who has any sense of family is Louise—and she's another family.

EBEN—Oh, Louise takes it too hard.

STANHOPE—She goes at it wrong, but she's the only one wants what I want.

TED (*hopefully entering the conversation*)—And what is that, Father?

STANHOPE—Hold a family together. Have some pride.

TED—I've got a great idea. Redeem family fortune. Fellow at school's worked out a new idea for putting on rubber tires. Like to go in with him, soon's our sentence expires at Cambridge.

STANHOPE—You will go in your father's office, which was his father's before him, and you will try and show more interest in the business than your brother does.

TED—Sometimes I think I haven't just the mind that makes a lawyer.

EBEN—Oh, I think you have.

STANHOPE—What do you mean? The law is a noble profession.

TED—Thought I might do better in some kind of a rubber wheel business.

EBEN—I tell you, Father, suppose I take a year off?

STANHOPE—Seems to me you've taken ten years off.

EBEN—Sometimes I feel I want something else.

STANHOPE—What?

EBEN—I don't know.

STANHOPE—And what about your family?

EBEN—Oh, that's why I'm going.

STANHOPE—You are not going.

EBEN—Probably not.

STANHOPE—Going where?

EBEN—I don't know. Somewhere—where things are different.

STANHOPE—Things are not different anywhere.

EBEN—Sometimes I think if I didn't have to do anything for a while—I could do something.

STANHOPE—What?

EBEN—Don't know yet.

STANHOPE—You have your children.

EBEN—Louise's.

STANHOPE—Well, you couldn't very well have had them alone, could you? Come, Eben, don't talk like a weakling. What if you aren't perfectly happy with Louise. I wasn't happy with your mother, either, but I didn't run away, leaving my children to shift for themselves.

EBEN—It isn't just Louise—or, I suppose not. It's things I used to think about when I was with Alison. And still think about—when she's with me.

STANHOPE—Alison didn't desert her family.

EBEN—No, but I don't write poetry.

STANHOPE—Oh, dear.

EBEN—Never mind, Father—guess I'm just talking foolishly, because the old place is being broken up.

STANHOPE—It's time to put your shoulder to the wheel.

EBEN—All right. Where's the wheel?

They have returned to the sorting and destroying of the papers when Louise descends upon them to learn whether or not Elsa is to be permitted to stay. If Elsa is to spend the night there Louise feels that she must leave. Elsa had run away with the husband of Louise's best friend, and there would be no facing her friend if Louise should spend even one night under the same roof with Elsa.

Father Stanhope is sorry, but Elsa is staying the night, and if Louise feels that way about it she will have to go back to town.

Louise does not think that she should be the one to be turned out, and she further thinks that at least Eben should go with her, which Eben refuses to do. This is bad enough, but when Louise also hears that Father Stanhope asked Ann, an outsider, to show the Hodges around the house in place of calling her she is hurt indeed.

Now the Hodges have finished their tour and are ready to close the sale. Of course nothing is exactly as he would have it, but Mr. Hodges is ready to pay a hundred and fifty dollars to bind the bargain.

The house is sold. Eben is a little bitter at the thought of it. Father Stanhope is clearly depressed. Then Jennie announces the return of Mr. Knowles, the reporter. It isn't any of the family he wants to see, however. It is Ann. He has come, Knowles explains, to ask Miss Leslie to take a walk with him, and it is a question he does not think should concern Father Stanhope or any of them, except Miss Leslie.

"You know, I think all your family have something of the spirit of Alison Stanhope," he says to Ted, when the others have gone back to the books. ". . . It's as if something of her remained here, in you all, in—in quite a different form. A playfulness."

"Golly, you think we're playful?" explodes Ted. "Why, man, we're going through the blackest page of our history. As for me, I can't decide which room to choose."

"Choose?"

"To hang myself."

It is Ted's notion that he might strike a bargain with Knowles. If Knowles will write him a theme—about playfulness, or suicide or something—he will help Knowles with Ann.

As it turns out, Ted's help is not needed. Ann is a little surprised at the return of Knowles, but after he has explained how very much he wanted to have a talk with her because it is the only way he can think of that will give him a chance to tell her anything about himself and also the only chance they will ever have to take a walk in that particular century—she is favorably impressed.

Father Stanhope has moved in from the alcove and stands with his back to them, reading a book.

"I was walking down there by the river," explains Knowles, "and I didn't know whether I was thinking of Alison Stanhope, or thinking of you. Well, guess you were part of the same thing. And I was thinking of the last day of the century getting dim.

(STANHOPE *is listening, though he has not turned.*) You know, how you think of a lot of things at once. I thought of how she used to walk where I was walking. (STANHOPE *turns, though they do not see him.*) And never will again. But it was as if her thoughts were there. They must have been hers—for they were better than mine. And it seemed to me if you would walk there with me—you and I together—well, that she wouldn't be gone.

"I think a walk might do you good," ventures Father Stanhope, coming down from the alcove. And when Ann has gone to get her things he turns to Knowles, the book he has been reading in his hand.

STANHOPE—This is a book my sister Alison loved and used.

KNOWLES (*taking it*)—Emerson's poems. (*Looking through it.*) Did *she* mark it? (STANHOPE *nods.*)

STANHOPE—I was going to take it for myself. But she loved to make her little gifts. So—for her—on the last day of her century—I would like to give it to you.

KNOWLES (*incredulous*)—You *would?* Oh, *thank* you, sir. (*Feeling the book as something precious.*) I can't tell you how—Why, I can hardly believe it! I never in my life heard of anything more generous.

STANHOPE (*a little embarrassed*)—Oh, no; not at all.

KNOWLES (*looking at the book, begins to read aloud what he sees*)—

"Hast thou named all the birds without a gun;
Loved the wood-rose and left it on its stalk;
At rich men's tables eaten bread and pulse;
Unarmed, faced danger with a heart of trust;
And loved so well a high behavior
In man or maid, that thou from speech refrained,
Nobility more nobly to repay?—
Oh, be my friend, and teach me to be thine!"

(*Pause.*) It's called Forbearance.

STANHOPE (*simply*)—Thank you. (*Holds out his hand for the book.*) I will read you one—because you are a poet. (*Turns a few pages.*)

KNOWLES—I'm afraid—

STANHOPE—It is called "The House."

"There is no architect
Can build as the muse can;
She is skillful to select
Materials for her plan;

"Slow and warily to choose
Rafters of immortal pine,

(*He glances up at the beamed ceiling above.*)

Or cedar incorruptible,
Worthy her design."

Some other things and then— (*Looking ahead.*)

"She lays her beams in music,
In music every one,
To the cadence of the whirling world
Which dances round the sun.

That so they shall not be displaced
By lapses or by wars,
But for the love of happy souls
Outlive the newest stars."

(*He hands back the book.*)

KNOWLES—Alison's house.

STANHOPE—Yes. (EBEN *comes from the alcove with more books.*)

EBEN—These all right for me, Father? (*They look at them,* ANN *returns.*)

ANN—All ready.

KNOWLES—Fine! Well—good-by. And thank you—again.

STANHOPE—Good-by.

ANN—I'll be back. (*They go out.*)

EBEN—Did you notice Ann?

STANHOPE—Yes, I noticed her. She never looked more like her mother.

EBEN—Happy.

STANHOPE—She's in love.

EBEN—In *love?* (*Laughing.*) Oh, come, Father! She doesn't know him.

STANHOPE—Neither did Alison know him!

EBEN—It must have been—pretty tough for Alison—giving him up.

STANHOPE—You'll never know. I know a little—no one will ever know the half.

Elsa has been asked to make her choice, also, of the books she would like to have. Her first choice is for the copy of "David Copperfield," from which Alison had read to them the time she had sprained her ankle jumping from the hayloft.

Now Aunt Agatha wants to come down to the library, though a doctor has said she should stay in bed. Shall they let her come? Father Stanhope will try to dissuade Agatha from making the effort.

"You staying long, Elsa?" Eben asks.

"No," she answers. "How could I? . . . I suppose I shouldn't have come."

EBEN—Far as I am concerned, you should. Father—

ELSA—He looks so much older.

EBEN—You made him older. Nothing ever hit him as hard.

ELSA—Oh, Eben, don't.

EBEN—Well, you've got to take it.

ELSA—Of course. But if only I could take it—all.

EBEN—You can't. That's why you had no right to do it. Alison didn't.

ELSA—No. But she was Alison. She had God.

EBEN—Afraid God left her pretty lonely at times.

ELSA—Yes, that's why she wrote about Him as if He ought to be more.

EBEN—How's Bill?

ELSA—Bill's all right. He misses the business, and his friends, and the children. I can see him missing them.

EBEN—Lucky he has enough to live on.

ELSA—Yes, but that isn't enough.

EBEN—But you're happy?

ELSA—Happy, and unhappy.

EBEN—What did you run away like that for? Why didn't you talk it over with me?

ELSA—You would have kept me from going.

EBEN—Of course I would!

ELSA—But I had to go, Eben. Don't you see? That was the way I loved him.

EBEN (*after watching her face*)—Wish I loved someone.

ELSA—I wish you did.

Now Agatha is downstairs, protesting volubly that she is no prisoner. Father Stanhope steadies her arm and helps her to the big chair Elsa has placed for her. Agatha is clutching a silk bag, which she holds closely to her.

Elsa draws up a footstool and is sitting at her Aunt Agatha's feet, listening as the old lady mumbles her protests and repeats her regrets at leaving the old house.

Eben, throwing discarded papers on the fire, builds up quite a blaze. The fire attracts Agatha.

AGATHA—Yes. Make it burn. (*Turning a little to see.*) Burn them. Burn them all. (*She clutches the bag.*) What are they?

EBEN—Old things we don't need any more.

AGATHA—Old things we don't need any more. (STANHOPE, *who has been watching her, can bear it no longer, goes out.*)

ELSA—You'll have your tea now, won't you, Aunt Agatha?

AGATHA (*after a moment of not coming from her own thought*) —What? No. No, I don't want it. (*She turns her head to the fire, taking the bag from her arm, holding it in her hands.*) Put on—old things we don't need any more. (*After an anxious look at her,* EBEN *puts more papers on the fire.*)

EBEN (*briskly*)—It's going to be fine for you up at Father's. That's going to be the most comfortable room you ever had.

AGATHA—If Elsa hadn't run away and left her father I wouldn't be turned out.

ELSA—I'm sorry, Aunt Agatha.

AGATHA (*quite differently*)—Little Elsa. (*With a low sob* ELSA *leans against her aunt.* EBEN *goes softly out. So they sit a moment,* AGATHA'S *hand on* ELSA'S *hair. But from this she goes into a curious, fixed state.*) Where is Alison?

ELSA—She isn't here. Though she seemed here, just a moment ago.

AGATHA—I have to take care of Alison.

ELSA—Yes. You always did.

AGATHA—I always did.

ELSA—Always.

AGATHA—But she—went away. How could I tell—what she wanted me to do? Who is looking at us?

ELSA—No one is looking at us. You and I are here alone.

AGATHA—You are Elsa?

ELSA—I am Elsa. (*With trembling fingers* AGATHA *undoes the string of her bag and takes out a small leather portfolio. Looks fearfully around, looks at the fire. She tries to rise.*)

ELSA—What is it, Aunt Agatha? I will do anything you want done.

AGATHA—You will—do anything—I want done?

ELSA—Why, yes, Aunt Agatha. I will do anything in the world for you.

AGATHA—Elsa will do it. Elsa.

ELSA—Yes. Elsa will do it.

AGATHA—Then— (*She holds out the leather case, but withdraws it. Then suddenly gives it.*) Take it! For—Elsa. (*She falls forward.*)

ELSA (*frightened*)—Aunt Agatha. (*She leans her back in the chair, though not letting go the small portfolio* AGATHA *has given her. Becomes more frightened as she looks.*) Aunt Agatha! What is it? Speak to me! (*After another moment of growing fear she runs to the door.*) Father! Eben! (EBEN *hurries in.*)

EBEN—What is it? (STANHOPE *enters.*)

ELSA—She—has she fainted?

STANHOPE (*bending over her*)—Agatha! Agatha! (*On the other side* EBEN *takes one of her hands, he is feeling for her pulse.* EBEN *lays his head against her heart.*)

EBEN (*looking up*)—Why, Father, I don't— (*Her eyes are closed.* STANHOPE *lifts one of the lids, looking at the eye.*)

ELSA—Has she—fainted?

STANHOPE—She has died. (ELSA, *who has not let go of the leather case, presses it against her breast.*)

EBEN—It is better.

STANHOPE (*who is kneeling by her*)—My sister! Agatha! Forgive me. (*Lifting his head, taking her two hands, looking into her face. Softly, as if putting her to sleep.*) Yes. Yes. Find Alison, dear. Find Alison.

CURTAIN

ACT III

Alison Stanhope's room, after eighteen years, still holds the atmosphere of a place that has been continuously occupied.

A friendly four-poster bed juts out from the wall, covered with a light, flowered counterpane. Alison's desk stands against the wall, and a small walnut stand at her bedside. An old bureau, an easy chair, an old-fashioned walnut table have settled familiarly into a carpet that is the color of gray-green moss. A fire has been built in the fireplace and the bed lamp is lighted.

It is a little after 10 when Elsa comes. "She waits a moment by the door, as if to be asked to enter. Then goes to the fire, holding out her hands. She looks at the clock, on the fireplace mantel. Winds, sets it, consulting her watch. Turns, standing uncertainly a moment. Goes slowly to the desk. Looks at a picture in a gold, oval frame, which hangs over the desk. She opens a drawer and takes out the portfolio her Aunt Agatha gave her. Stands there holding it. She is about to sit at the desk, but steps back from it, as if it is not for her to sit there. Goes to the table; putting the portfolio there; she goes to the mantel, where are two silver candle sticks. Lights them and takes them to the table. She sits down, and after holding the portfolio a moment, spreads it out as if to open the pockets. It is one of those flexible cases which doubles over. She is opening one side when there is a knock at the door."

It is Ann Leslie. She has been wanting to have a word with Elsa, to tell her how really glad she is that she came, and how glad Eben and Ted are, too.

Ann can understand how Elsa could have felt that she had to come and how she would feel that Alison would understand.

ELSA—I used to come to this room when things went wrong. "Come to Alison, dear," she'd say. Or "Whatever is wrong, Alison will make it right." If only she could!

ANN—Perhaps she can.

ELSA—I fear not. I have gone—out of her world.

ANN—I'm not sure she would think so.

ELSA—Perhaps not. For—really—you couldn't go out of her world. She was everywhere. She knew.

ANN—I didn't know her but—it does seem that way. What did I say? I didn't know her? But I do know her. Her poems let me know her. And now—tonight—I know her better than before. (ELSA *only waits in inquiry.*) Elsa, can you fall in love, all at once, with somebody you don't know?

ELSA (*looking at the picture over the desk*)—Ask Alison.

ANN (*following her look*)—Is that—his picture?

ELSA—Yes. It was always there—as long as I can remember.

ANN (*going to it*)—How strange the clothes look.

ELSA—Ours will look strange, too, in thirty years.

ANN—Why, I suppose they will. They seem so right now.

ELSA—Nothing stays right—forever.

ANN (*turning to her*)—Love does.

ELSA (*with a little laugh*)—Love doesn't have to clothe itself.

ANN (*coming back to her*)—Then you think it really can be love, though it happens, all at once?

ELSA—It has happened too often for me to say it can't be true. Though it wasn't that way with me.

ANN—You and Bill had known each other a long time.

ELSA—Since I had braids down my back. And he never used to be—different from anyone else. And then—all of a sudden—We had been dancing; we stopped by the door. We just looked at each other—stared, rather, and he said— "Why, Elsa!" We stood there, and then he said, "It is Elsa." And we went out to the veranda, and everything was different, because he was Bill and I was Elsa.

ANN—So it did happen suddenly, after all.

ELSA—And everything we had together in the past—when we used to slide down hill together—was there, alive, giving us a past we hadn't known we were making for ourselves.

ANN—I think it is a miracle, don't you?

ELSA—Yes, I think it is a miracle. Though it is a miracle you have to pay for, sometimes.

ANN—Always, perhaps.

ELSA—I don't know. Often it goes happily. It's nice that you don't have to hurt anyone.

ANN—But I do, I fear. He was almost engaged. Not quite, Elsa. His name is Richard.

ELSA—Richard is a nice name.

ANN—I shall never call him Dick. Richard, I think, is better for him. (ELSA *nods gravely.*) And to think it was Alison brought us together! That is like a blessing, don't you think?

ELSA—I do think so.

ANN—It was wonderful—down by the river, thinking of all that happened in this century that is going, of all that will happen in the century that is right here now, for us. (*She is lost in this a moment.*) Perhaps it seems cruel we should be sitting here talking of love, with poor Miss Agatha dead just across the hall.

ELSA—It is the way it is.

ANN—And it is strange. She was so good, but she does seem dead, and Alison, dead eighteen years, is here.

Ann also has an errand. In spite of all that has happened, of course Richard has to think of his paper. And of the Stanhope story, which is a much bigger story now, with Agatha's dying just as she was leaving the house where she and Alison lived together. Richard must have a picture of Agatha—

There is likely to be trouble about that, Elsa thinks. Only Father Stanhope, or Eben, would have the right to say—

But it is Elsa that Ann is appealing to. It has always been Elsa to whom she has felt that she could talk. Even after Elsa had—had—gone away Ann and the other girls, though they were shocked, had thought of her as being brave.

Elsa understands and is grateful. But, as to the picture— There is one, taken a long time ago, before Alison died, when Agatha was much younger—

"It never would have occurred to her to have one taken afterward," Elsa explains. "She thought she was just for Alison."

"She worshiped her."

"And guarded her, her whole life through. I'd really like to give it to you, for her own sake. Aunt Agatha, who lived always in this house, now wanted, for a moment, by the world. She was so good. And she will pass—so soon. I'd like to talk to your Richard, and tell him how good she was."

"Oh, *would* you, Elsa?"

"But I haven't the right to speak for the family."

Now Eben is there and he, too, feels at first that Father Stanhope is the only one who can decide about the picture. But with sudden impulse he agrees that Ann may give it to Knowles. Let Agatha have her one moment of youth.

Ann has gone. Slowly the spell of Alison's room has come over Elsa and Eben. They see it again as it was, with Alison there—

ELSA (*her hand on the chair by the fire*)—Here—she should be sitting.

EBEN—Unless— (*He goes over to the desk, puts his hand on that chair.*) Here. (*Standing back, as if looking at* ALISON.) She is sitting here with her papers—with her thoughts, and the words for her thoughts. She is wearing a white dress. The full skirt spreads out from the chair. The sleeves, too, are full, and her small hands hover over what she has. Her eyes— Heavens! have I forgotten them?

ELSA—They are clear—like golden wine.

EBEN—Her brown hair is parted in the middle, and held loosely at the neck. She is looking straight ahead, as if into something. But she is really waiting for the right word to come. They came, you can tell that. They were willing visitors. She didn't have to go out and pull them in. There is a knock on the door. It's me. I am crying. She makes a funny little face. She says— Tell Alison. I tell her Jimmy Miles has knocked over my mud house. She says— You can build a fort, and put him in it. She tells me the story of the bumble bee that got drunk on larkspur and set out to see how drunk you could get in heaven. And what became of her thoughts—the thought I interrupted?

ELSA—Oh, it waited for her, and the bumble bee came into it.

EBEN—And that was his heaven.

ELSA—Why not? (*They are both brighter.*) Then another knock. No, a pounding with fists— Alison— Alison. Little Elsa! Aunt Agatha won't give me a cookie because I pulled the cat's tail. She tells me Aunt Agatha can't help being like that, and that the cat would agree with her. And she says—what if I had pulled the tail off, and we laugh; and she writes me a little poem, about a cookie that had no tail. She gives me candy, and stands at the door so Aunt Agatha can't get in, but God, she says, could come down the chimney.

Elsa has turned again to the portfolio that Agatha had given her and is wondering what it holds when Father Stanhope comes. He stands in the door for a moment, and when he speaks it is as though he were talking to himself.

"I wish I could talk to Alison," he says.

He is sitting now before the fire. Agatha's funeral, he has decided, must be from the old house. They can straighten things around enough for that.

He is reminded of Agatha's death. Elsa was alone with her. Just what was it she said?

She had, Elsa explains, just held out the leather portfolio and said: "For Elsa." Then she had fallen back and died.

The portfolio—let them open it and see what is in it.

Eben protests that the portfolio is Elsa's. It is the family's, insists Father Stanhope. Let them open it—

There is a timid knock at the door. It is Jennie, the maid. She has come to find something—something she must find. Miss Agatha had told her, and she had given her promise.

"All these last days," mumbles Jennie, "after she got the idea—and couldn't—it was always the same—'Make the fire, Jennie. Put on more wood—make it burn'—and she'd sit by it —and couldn't."

Frantically Jennie searches the drawers of Alison's desk and finds nothing. Then she spies the portfolio. That is it. That is what she had promised—promised to burn—

But Agatha had changed her mind, Father Stanhope insists. She afterwards gave the portfolio to Elsa.

Then she wanted Elsa to burn it, persists Jennie. It must be burned. Jennie won't be able to sleep a wink until it is burned. She had given her promise—

"You will sleep, Jennie," Father Stanhope reassures her. "This is a family matter. You may rest assured I will see that the right thing is done."

"I looked after her—thirty years," wails the unhappy Jennie. "And I did for Miss Alison, when we had Miss Alison. What am I going to do now?"

"Of course you know we will always look after you, Jennie."

"But who—who will I look after?" Jennie is inconsolable.

Jennie has gone. Father Stanhope has taken the portfolio and spread it out on his lap. It is still Eben's idea that, as Agatha had given the portfolio to Elsa, it is Elsa who should open it, now or later, and see if its contents are for all of them.

Father Stanhope reluctantly agrees, after consideration, and Elsa unfastens the portfolio. In it she finds a slender package of old papers tied with a thread.

EBEN—Why, that's like—

ELSA (*feeling it*)—It's the paper Alison used for—for her—(*Taking out others.*) All tied—that same way.

EBEN—The way *she* tied them. Undo one of them. (ELSA *tries to untie the knot, has trouble with it.*)

STANHOPE—Break that thread! (ELSA *does so and unfolds a long sheet of old paper.*)

EBEN—Alison's writing!

STANHOPE (*sharply*)—What are they?

ELSA (*reading*)—Why—they are—they are—

EBEN (*reading over her shoulder*)—Are they—*poems?* (*He takes one from another package, then opens still another. As if he cannot believe it.*) All of them. (*He takes a package to his father.*) They are Alison's. They are poems. Poems we never saw. (STANHOPE *examines one.*) They are her poems, aren't they?

STANHOPE (*slowly*)—No one else—that ever lived—would say it just that way.

EBEN—But, Father—had you known about them?

STANHOPE—I did not know they existed.

EBEN—But *why?* (*Showing one he is himself reading.*) See? She never wrote a thing—more Alison.

STANHOPE (*reading it*)—Alison—at her best.

EBEN—Then I just can't understand it! Where have they been? Why? My God—was it *this* Aunt Agatha thought she must burn?

STANHOPE—I don't understand it.

ELSA (*who has been reading*)—O-h, I think I do.

EBEN (*about to speak to her, but she is deeply absorbed, turns again to his father*)—But, Father—this is of immense importance! Look at them! Why, I believe it's almost as many as we published! Coming now—when she has her place—you know all they say about her—now—so much later—all of these—but *why?*

ELSA—*Alison.*

For a moment Elsa leans her head heavily among the papers. Then Ted comes in. He has been delayed at the dance. He did not know about Aunt Agatha. He is terribly sorry not to have been there. Louise is coming back, too—

Ted has noticed one of the newly discovered poems that Elsa's arm has brushed to the floor. He recognizes Alison's writing. He thought all the manuscripts were at the State Historical Society! Gee! That's important, isn't it? What did Aunt Agatha want to hide them for? Gee!

It isn't easy to get rid of Ted, but he goes, finally. Eben would have his father go to bed, too, and let the poems rest until a better time. But Father is remembering Elsa's exclamation.

"Why did you say her name like that?" he demands.

"Because she was telling me her story," answers Elsa. "It's here—the story she never told. She has written it, as it was never written before. The love that never died—loneliness that never died—anguish and beauty of her love! I said her name because she was with me."

They are all sitting at the table now, reading the poems, commenting occasionally on what they read in low voices and "in beautiful excitement."

Gradually the lights are dimmed. The clock on the mantel strikes eleven. There is a moment's darkness. "When the lights rise Elsa still sits at the table, as if she had had a great experience, as if she had come to know something, and has the courage to know it. Eben has moved, and is standing by the fire. Stanhope sits as he was, bowed over the papers still in his lap. After a moment the clock strikes the half hour.

EBEN (*slowly, as if trying to realize it*)—And all of that—went on in this room.

STANHOPE—If I had known it was, as much as this—I would not have asked her to stay.

ELSA—You did ask her to stay?

STANHOPE—In this room I asked her to stay. He was below. He had come for her.

EBEN—I never really knew the story.

STANHOPE—She had gone East, with Father, to Cambridge. Thirtieth reunion of Father's class. She met him there. He was a teacher of English, at Harvard. At once they seemed to recognize each other. He was for her. She was for him. That was—without question. But he was married. He had children. They parted. But—they were one. I know that now.

EBEN—And it was after that—after all those years that—she played with us, Elsa—loved her flowers—comforted us and gave us the little presents.

ELSA—It was death for her. But she made it—life eternal.

EBEN (*so moved it is hard to speak*)—Never mind, Alison, we have found you.

ELSA—You will never be alone again. (*A knock,* TED *comes in.*)

TED—I want to get some of the poems. (*As no one speaks.*) Well, gee, I'm of the family, too, ain't I? If you don't want me here I'll take some of them down to the library.

STANHOPE—They will not be taken from this room.

TED—All right, then I'll read them here.

EBEN—Not now.

TED—They're mine as much as yours, aren't they?

STANHOPE—I will protect my sister. I will do—what Agatha could not do.

EBEN (*sharply*)—What do you mean?

STANHOPE—They were for her alone. She does not have to show her heart to the world.

ELSA—Father! You don't mean— Tell us you don't mean—!

STANHOPE—I mean that I am going to burn them in her own fireplace—before her century goes.

EBEN—Father!

ELSA (*gathering up the papers*)—No!

TED—And *I* say—no! They're ours, too, aren't they?

STANHOPE—I shall protect my sister, if it's the last thing I do on earth.

EBEN—She isn't just your sister, Father.

TED—I should say not. She's Alison.

STANHOPE—And she could help get you through Harvard, couldn't she? What luck! Send a wire to your teacher! Get your grade!

EBEN—Steady now, Father. There's been too much today. No decisions can be made tonight.

STANHOPE—If they're not made tonight, they will never be made.

Ted is excitedly obdurate. He represents, he insists, the younger members of Alison Stanhope's family. He will be alive when the others are gone. He should be the guardian of the poems. Defiantly he grabs some of the papers and stuffs them in his pocket. In a moment Father Stanhope has sprung at him and would strangle him if Eben did not interfere.

It is Eben who brings some sort of order out of the scene though he, too, must come to grips with Ted before Elsa, reminding them that they are in Alison's room, that their Aunt Agatha lies dead across the hall, shames them into some show of family respect. Elsa promises Ted to protect both the poems and all the family's interest. She knows their value better than any of them.

"Ted's exasperating," Elsa agrees, after both Ted and Eben have gone; "but of course you didn't mean it, Father. You couldn't mean it. It's Alison's heart. You wouldn't keep that from—living in the world she loved."

"Living in your world? Linked with—you? As if—"

"Don't say it, Father. She wouldn't. She would understand. Alison knew. And do you know, I think she would be glad?"

"Glad you ran away with a married man—living in shame and leaving misery behind you?"

"Glad I have my love. In spite of—all the rest. Knowing what it is to be alone, I think she would be glad I am not alone. What could I do—alone? How could I—Elsa—find victory in defeat? For, you see, I am not enough. She would know that. She would be tolerant. She would be gentle—oh, so gentle. If she were here now—in her own room—she would say— Happy? Are you happy? Be happy, little Elsa, she would say."

Eben is back with a bottle of sherry wine. He pours three glasses, that they may toast the new year—and Alison.

Again Father Stanhope insists that the poems shall be burned. Alison had not given them to the world—

"She didn't give the others to the world," counters Eben. "She was too timid of the world. She just left them, and we did the right thing, as in her heart she knew we would."

It is Ann who is able in the end to convince Father Stanhope. She has come, brought by Ted and Richard Knowles, who feels that he, too, being the only one from the outside who knows, should as a duty tell them how he feels.

"You were so good to me, always, I feel as if you were my father, though I know you're not really," says Ann, sitting on a stool at Father Stanhope's knee. "You were so good to Mother. (*Low.*) You loved her. And she loved you. Through years. And you denied your love, because of me, and Eben, and Elsa, and Ted. Well, here we all are—the children—Eben, Elsa, Ted and Ann. Can't you let us, now when you are old, and sad, tell you what to do—for us? Won't you let Alison's words pass on—as a gift to all love—let them *be* here—when you are not here?"

"Ann! Don't!"

ANN—I must. It is too important. I know that now. I know tonight, better than I would have known last night.

STANHOPE (*his hands falling at his sides*)—I cannot make it plain to you but she was of an age when people did not tell their love. She held it deep in her heart. Then can I let her tell it now, to serve you?

ANN—Yes.

STANHOPE (*turning his face away*)—I cannot bear—your youth.

ANN—Will you promise me to leave it to Elsa?

STANHOPE—Elsa? Why should I leave it to Elsa?

ANN—To a woman. Because Alison said it—for women.

STANHOPE—Alison was not like Elsa. Alison stayed.

ANN—Then let her speak for Elsa, and Mother, and me. Let her have *that* from it. For her own sake—let her have that from it!

EBEN—Yes. I think Father will leave it to Elsa. And now the rest of you, please go.

ANN (*making a move to go, but turning back*)—I don't want you to do it, because I have a great love for you, and I don't want you, when dying, to feel, I am guilty, I took life. (*She goes out.* TED *starts after her, but as* KNOWLES *steps forward* TED *stands in the doorway.*)

KNOWLES (*very simply, but as if the words have great mission*)—

"She lays her beams in music,
In music every one,
To the cadence of the whirling world
Which dances round the sun.

That so they shall not be displaced
By lapses or by wars
But for the love of happy souls
Outlive the newest stars."

EBEN (*after a little time*)—Enough for one night, isn't it? One thing we know. Aunt Agatha left the poems to Elsa. For the time being then, they are with Elsa. After—after the funeral we can decide just what to do. Good night, Father. (*No reply.*) Good night, Elsa.

ELSA—Eben, don't leave me.

EBEN (*with a nod as to say, it is better*)—Yes. (*He goes.*)

ELSA (*after a pause, low*)—I didn't know, Father, that you had gone through it, too.

STANHOPE—Did you think I was happy with your mother?

ELSA—No.

STANHOPE—And why did I stay? For you, and your brothers. Mostly for you.

ELSA—And then I—

STANHOPE—Then you—made it all nothing.

ELSA—I must seem—all wrong to you, Father.

STANHOPE—You are wrong. You did not think of others, and that is wrong. And don't you know what this would say? It would say— They are like that. They were always like that. Louise is right there.

ELSA—Oh, Father—Louise! Our little town! Is that the thing to think of—when Alison has spoken?

STANHOPE—Our little town is our lives. It's Eben's children.

ELSA—And what will be wrong with Eben's children—that they can't love, and understand? You do. Eben does. Have faith, Father. Trust them to understand.

STANHOPE (*as a cry from deep*)—Oh, Elsa! Why did you go away—and besmirch the name Alison held high? (*A sound from* ELSA, *a sobbing under her breath.*) And now—because of you—

ELSA—Don't, Father. Don't say it. She wouldn't. You ought to hurt me—some. But don't be that cruel—to make me feel—because of me—she can't go on. I loved, Father. I loved so much that—

STANHOPE—It is possible to love so much you can live without your love.

ELSA—I suppose it is possible, if you are a very great soul, or have a very stern sense of duty. But do you know, Father, I feel Alison wrote those poems for me.

STANHOPE—I feel she wrote them for me.

ELSA—And there will be those in the future to say, "She wrote them for me."

STANHOPE—I feel—something right, something that all the time had to be, in you and me, here alone in her room, giving back to her century what she felt and did not say.

ELSA—But she did say.

STANHOPE—For herself alone.

ELSA—How can you know that? And even so—what has been brought into life cannot be taken from life. (STANHOPE *goes to fire, puts on more wood.*)

STANHOPE—I never thought you and I would do another thing together. But she did love you. Then shield her. Join with me. What went on in this room—let it end in this room. It is right. (*He goes to the table and takes the portfolio.*)

ELSA (*standing between him and the fire*)—Father! The birds that sang thirty years ago. (*Her hands go out, as birds.*) The flower that bent in the wind. (*She bends, as in the wind. The clock gives the first stroke of twelve. He stands motionless, listening. She is choked with tears.*)—Happy New Year, Father.

STANHOPE (*mechanically*)—Happy— (*From a distance are bells in the village, whistles, a few shots. He looks around the room, hearing the bells. He looks long at* ELSA.) It isn't—what you said. Or even, what Ann said. But her. It goes. It is going. It is gone. She loved to make her little gifts. If she can make one more, from her century to yours, then she isn't gone. Anything else is—too lonely. (*He holds the poems out to her.*) For Elsa—From Alison.

ELSA (*taking them*)—Father! My father!

STANHOPE (*his arms around her*)—Little Elsa. (*He holds her close while distant bells ring in the century.*)

CURTAIN

FIVE STAR FINAL

A Melodrama in Three Acts

By Louis Weitzenkorn

THE last week in December, 1930, saw the production of two newspaper plays, Louis Weitzenkorn's "Five Star Final" and Claire and Paul Sifton's "Midnight."

The two were alike in theme insofar as both attacked that form of sensational journalism which formerly was known as "yellow." It has, of late years, been more commonly designated as the sin of the tabloids, those small and amazingly popular picture papers in the larger news centers.

"Midnight" sought to prove that the newspaper reading public has come to wallow in crime stories and the exciting and revealing details of sensational murder trials. As a result we have more and more, if not worse and worse, crimes directly traceable to these exhibitions of depravity.

"Five Star Final" savagely pinned the blame on the picture papers and, in argument, worked through the history of one specific case in which the exposure of a shooting stenographer's past brought tragedy into the lives of several eminently respectable persons.

Mr. Weitzenkorn's play was immediately accepted by both reviewers and public as a thoroughly exciting and emotionally gusty melodrama. Because of its basic truth and the author's intense feeling for his play it overcame to a noticeable extent the handicap of being biased and extravagant. Mr. Weitzenkorn had himself suffered an unhappy experience on the New York *Graphic*.

"Five Star Final," being played in nineteen scenes, demands a flexible stage and calls for the same technical expertness in production that "Grand Hotel" demands. The producer, A. H. Woods, saw that these were provided. The setting is a three-part stage. The chief scenes are played in the center section, with incidental scenes at either side. Thus, in those incidents in which the telephone plays an important part, and they are numerous in this play, both ends of the conversation are in sight, so to speak, and frequently a glimpse is given of the exchange operator making the wire connection.

The opening scene, played on the center stage, is that of Corcoran's speakeasy, or that corner of this resort in which the bar is located. It is a typical bar of the modern, or prohibition, saloon, being backed by a mirror, an assortment of variously shaped glasses and bottles of liquor supposedly hard to get. Its dull-toned mahogany top is shiny, and its decorative façade includes a brass rail and a brass cuspidor.

At one end of the bar is a glass-covered cheese. There is a table and chairs for drinkers who have time to sit down, and a bench near the door for those who pause on the way in or out. The wall carries a map of the United States on one side and a picture of an old-fashioned brewery on the other. There are the usual pictures of pugilists, etc., the etc. mostly legs.

Corcoran's, being close to the publication offices of several newspapers, is most frequently host to newspaper men. They come there seeking relaxation and a proper place for the exchange of confidences.

At the moment there are two *Gazette* men, Colby and Rooney, both in their late twenties, sitting at the table. Jerry, the bartender, wearing the slightly soiled apron of his profession, is putting in a lot of time back of the bar repolishing the polished glasses.

The reporter's talk is mostly shop talk. At the moment it vaguely covers the hard luck of one Julia Murphy, who has just been fired, and considers the possibility of a general shake-up to follow.

As to this latter possibility there appears to be no definite news. Even Ziggie Feinstein, the contest editor, who has just dropped in, knows no more than Colby and Rooney. He, however, has greater hopes for the rag that employs them than they have.

"The guy that owns this paper knows what the public wants." That's Ziggie's opinion.

At the moment Ziggie is engaged in the exploitation of a June Bride contest for which he has hopes. If you can buy a woman in Paris for two dollars, ventures Ziggie, why shouldn't a dame get married for the *Gazette* for a thousand?

Randall, the managing editor, a vigorous, well-set-up, taciturn man, with tired eyes and testy temper, is in. He would buy drinks for all of them, but they're satisfied with what they have. Colby and Rooney go back to their jobs. Ziggie sticks awhile in the hope that he may give the boss a few pointers.

Ziggie is convinced the June Bride contest needs a bit of jazzing. Let him run it his way and he can put on forty thousand circulation with it.

"What's the matter with it now?" demands Randall.

"Hell, boss, I got plenty niggers, but I can't get Jews and Catholics. You said you wanted all kinds."

RANDALL—I thought you said you ran the East Side.

ZIGGIE—That's all right. I got a couple of personal friends who'll do it. But the Church—

RANDALL—What church?

ZIGGIE—The Catholic and the other one—

RANDALL—What other one?

ZIGGIE—Oh, you know. The one that's like the Catholic only—

RANDALL—Oh!—the Episcopal.

ZIGGIE—Yeah, and listen, Unk. Hinchecliffe's offering the winner a house and lot out in Astoria. That's just gettin' rid of some of his bum real estate. And you can't get Christians in if you're going to give a house to a nigger.

RANDALL—Ah, you're a sweet headache after a hard day.

ZIGGIE—All right—let me do this other one.

RANDALL—What's the other one?

ZIGGIE—Taxicab contest. Race 'em in relays from the Bronx to City Hall. Give the winners new cabs, see?

RANDALL—And kill a hundred people?

ZIGGIE—All right, but every mockie running a cab will boost the *Gazette*.

RANDALL—You'll own this sheet some day.

ZIGGIE—My name's Ziggie.

RANDALL—You know—I've got a feeling people are fed up with dirt.

ZIGGIE—They never get fed up with dirt—that's where you go wrong. Why don't you give Hinchecliffe what he wants?

RANDALL—How do you know I'm not giving him what he wants?

ZIGGIE—Maybe I'm stepping in too deep.

RANDALL—I knew you had something on your mind. Come on now, talk!

ZIGGIE—Give him what he wants. Give him the legs. All this politics and tariff— Nobody reads that junk.

RANDALL (*goes to bar, pays for his drink, then goes over near bench, and after a long pause*)—Everybody thinks I'm trying to go highbrow, don't they?

ZIGGIE—I hear some talk.

RANDALL—Well, spread it around that I've only been taking a vacation. (*Goes to door.*) So long, Jerry. (*Goes out.*)

JERRY—So long, Mr. Randall.

ZIGGIE—Hey, Jerry, where you buying your Scotch these days?

JERRY—I'm getting it from Brooklyn.

ZIGGIE—What do you pay for it?

JERRY—Fifty-five a case.

ZIGGIE—Listen, I got some for fifty a case, and—

The lights are up on a second stage. It is a corner of the office of the Rev. Isopod, religious editor of the *Gazette.* The Rev. Isopod, a spare, pale man in dark clothes, is answering the phone. He does not know when he can get home but corn fritters will be quite all right for his supper. With which statement the Rev. Isopod also fades out.

There are two desks in Hinchecliffe's office, which is the third scene. Hinchecliffe is the proprietor of the *Gazette,* a large, confident, unctuous person of a successful business man mold. One desk belongs to him. The other to his secretary, a fairly colorless young person named Edwards.

At the moment Hinchecliffe is in conference with French, his circulation manager, and Brannegan, in charge of advertising. The *Gazette* is twenty thousand behind its last year's figures in circulation and Mr. Hinchecliffe wants to know why.

It is Mr. French's idea that the weather may have had something to do with it. Brannegan is convinced the fault lies with the editorial policy of the managing editor. The *Gazette,* points out Brannegan, has succeeded up to now because its policy has been sensational.

Hinchecliffe dislikes the word "sensational." The Hinchecliffe policy has been merely to develop "the human interest in life." "What I want definitely is an immediate lift in circulation, and I mean to get it," announces Hinchecliffe, finally. "These editing matters I'll take up with Mr. Randall."

BRANNEGAN—It's certainly time some things were taken up with Mr. Randall. Why should we be printing cables from the League of Nations, and reports of the procedure of the Polish Diet? We can't sell this paper unless we have something to sell.

HINCHECLIFFE—What's your idea?

BRANNEGAN—Randall is getting too swell for the chewing gum trade. What the hell's the use of kidding ourselves, Mr. Hinchecliffe? We're not selling papers on Park Avenue.

HINCHECLIFFE—I think you're on the right track, Brannegan.

BRANNEGAN—I know I'm on the right track. Look at this piece of slop we're running now! "Love Under the Sea!" Why can't we have stories about shop girls, servant girls, something that our readers know?

HINCHECLIFFE—That's exactly what I've had on my mind. Do you remember the Nancy Voorhees shooting?

BRANNEGAN—Oh, yes. I was in charge of the Bronx circulation for the *American* in those days.

FRENCH—Oh, yes, didn't she shoot a rich candy manufacturer she was working for?

HINCHECLIFFE—That's the case. Now, I've had an extremely good writer to develop a serial with the real inside story. I'm sure it's just what we need.

BRANNEGAN—Right on the line. She was a stenographer, wasn't she?

HINCHECLIFFE—Yes.

BRANNEGAN—Well, every stenographer in the country would eat up a story like that.

HINCHECLIFFE—Exactly.

BRANNEGAN—Sure, there's no doubt about it, Mr. Hinchecliffe. Our weak spot is the Editorial Department. I haven't anything against Randall personally, but I think he needs a jacking up.

HINCHECLIFFE—Well, that will be all for the present, gentlemen. There's nothing more to discuss, until Randall gets back. But I'd like to have you remain around the office. (*They all rise.*) I'll send for you later. Please marshal your ideas!

FRENCH—If I'm not in my office, Mr. Hinchecliffe, you can reach me in the Delivery Room. (BRANNEGAN *and* FRENCH *go out.*)

HINCHECLIFFE (*rises, and puts his glasses on*)—Oh, by the way, have you got the Nancy Voorhees serial there, Miss Edwards? (MISS EDWARDS *goes to him with serial, which he takes.*) Thank you. By the way, did you read it?

MISS EDWARDS—Yes, sir.

HINCHECLIFFE—What did you think of it?

MISS EDWARDS—I think that part about the illegitimate child is not made clear enough.

There are desks in Randall's office, next revealed. This is a room less modernistically but more characteristically furnished than that of Publisher Hinchecliffe. Randall has gone in largely

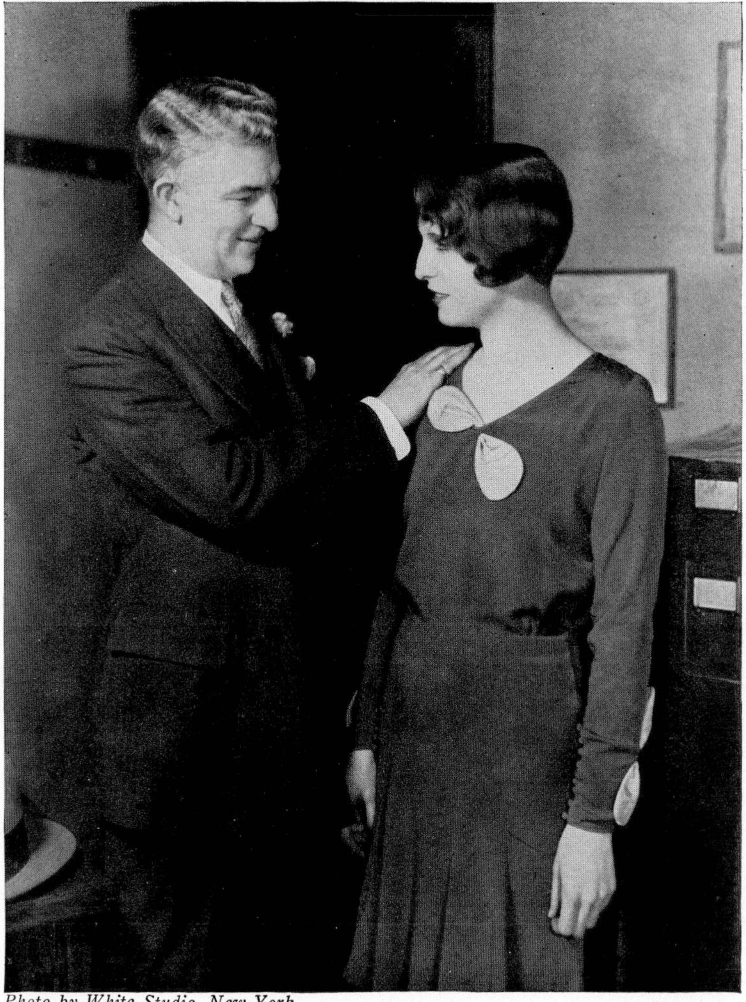

Photo by White Studio, New York.

"FIVE STAR FINAL"

Randall: I'm too old to be ashamed of myself. I'm going to be one newspaper man who gets out of this business with enough money to give me a decent old age. And now you've said your little say and I want you to go home and sleep it off, and forget it.

(*Arthur Byron and Helene Sinnott*)

for pictures. There is one of Al Smith, flanked by a couple of framed telegrams. There is also one of Tunney taking the long count in Chicago. There are pictures of Lloyd George, Mussolini and Woodrow Wilson.

Miss Taylor is Randall's secretary. She is of the alert, intelligent type who knows more about her employer than he knows about himself. She makes and breaks his appointments, listens to his soliloquies and tactfully sets him right, or tries to, whenever she thinks she sees him going wrong.

Miss Taylor also resents the recent discharge of Julia Murphy, fired, the office insists, because she was flat-chested. And she has her opinion of the developing plan to hire a girl from the Chicago *Daily News* because she comes with a reputation for being able to vamp stories out of shyster lawyers.

Randall, who is late, walks in to find Hinchecliffe there before him. The publisher has come for a policy conference. He suggests that French and Brannegan also be brought in and while he is waiting for them to be summoned he delivers himself of a few observations on the character of his managing editor.

Hinchecliffe has always liked Randall. Liked particularly the way he ran the *Gazette* during its formative days. But of late—

"My boy," throbs Mr. Hinchecliffe, "the life blood of a newspaper today is circulation. In our type of paper we must have mass circulation. Editors have a tendency to get on a pedestal above their readers."

"If I sat on a cigar box I'd be above ours," ventures Randall.

"There you have it, Randall," Hinchecliffe continues. "Now I've got something like seven million dollars involved in this paper which keeps me quite away from sentimentalism. Now we can raise our circulation, and at the same time, raise sex to a dignified standard."

"How?"

"For example, let us suppose a girl has been raped—"

"After an automobile ride."

"Exactly—and the police are searching for her assailant. I want a reporter to go to that girl's mother. I want the moral values brought out. I want to know if the mother ever warned the girl against riding with strange men. If she did warn her, then it's a lesson for other daughters. If she didn't warn her—then it's a lesson for other mothers. Which reminds me, Randall. I was just talking with Brannegan and French, discussing a new serial I have in mind. It's the inside story of the notorious Nancy Voorhees case. I'll let you have it so you can read it."

Brannegan and French are found by Miss Taylor and brought into the conference, still arguing. Mr. Hinchecliffe achieves a recapitulation. The *Gazette,* he thinks, has been, of late, a little formal. What they need is a wider appeal.

What they need, according to Randall, is ten more linotype machines so they can print the stock tables. What they need also is department store advertising. What they need is fewer frozen features and more comics.

"And what about the serials?" puts in French. "I'd like to see the sales pick up on the West Side."

HINCHECLIFFE—I was just mentioning the Nancy Voorhees serial to Mr. Randall.

BRANNEGAN—Now, that's the stuff.

HINCHECLIFFE—Well, Brannegan, you must admit that we haven't had much to build on except politics.

RANDALL—My God, there hasn't been a good murder in this town since the Snyder case.

HINCHECLIFFE—Randall, how well do you recall the Voorhees shooting?

RANDALL—I covered it for the old New York *Press.* She shot a fellow named Bill Rogers. They called him the "Chocolate King."

BRANNEGAN—It might be a good idea to have Randall write the serial himself.

RANDALL—Yeah, and play a pipe organ around the office, too.

HINCHECLIFFE—Well, now, now, gentlemen, let's get back to this story. It will certainly interest the new generation who never heard of it. I've had a very good writer working on it and I want to get it pointed up. Randall, I'd like to have you get Doctor Isopod to write a series of introductions for each installment.

RANDALL—Oh, Miss Taylor, send for Isopod.

MISS TAYLOR (*into the disc*)—Send for Isopod.

BRANNEGAN—Didn't the Voorhees woman have a kid or something by Rogers?

HINCHECLIFFE—I believe there was an incident of that kind. Now, Randall, that's where the moral lies. And I think Doctor Isopod is just the man to point it. I wish you'd use Doctor Isopod a little more. He gives us the tone I like. Now for instance, for this serial, there's that little thought from Saint Mark which he might use for a text— How does it go?—"For from within, out of the hearts of men, proceed evil thoughts, fornication, adulteries, murders—"

ISOPOD (*enters*)—You sent for me, Mr. Hinchecliffe?

HINCHECLIFFE—Oh, how do you do, Doctor Isopod? We have an idea or two we would like to suggest.

ISOPOD—I hope everything is satisfactory, Mr. Hinchecliffe.

BRANNEGAN—You're getting too cut and dried.

ISOPOD—Really, if you'll give me a chance to explain—

RANDALL—I think Brannegan's right. Now, what you ought to do, Isopod, is to turn out a dozen sermons on the woman caught in adultery. We're going to catch some every day from now on.

ISOPOD—Why, I should be very—

HINCHECLIFFE—Mr. Randall is jesting, Doctor Isopod.

RANDALL (*glances at the serial*)—Isopod, we've got a serial story on the Nancy Voorhees shooting. Do you remember the case?

ISOPOD—No, sir.

RANDALL—I didn't think you did. She was secretary to a man named Rogers. He got her pregnant and refused to marry her. Before the child was born she killed him, and the jury refused to convict a pregnant woman. Got that?

ISOPOD—Yes, sir.

HINCHECLIFFE—And the moral is, Doctor Isopod, that girls who work should not allow their employers to—to—ah—

RANDALL—What is the word, Doctor Isopod?

ISOPOD—Embrace them.

HINCHECLIFFE—Exactly. And mothers should demand that young girls who work give an account of their time. We might get a symposium on it; some interviews with Children's Court judges, and social workers.

FRENCH—And what will you do to promote it directly, Mr. Hinchecliffe?

HINCHECLIFFE (*takes out some post-cards from his pocket*)—I'm having it called "The Love-Mad Stenographer," and we're sending out a hundred thousand postal cards to the office girls of New York.

ISOPOD—Ah! A very good idea! A very good idea!

HINCHECLIFFE—Each card reads, "WARNING! DON'T FALL IN LOVE WITH YOUR BOSS!" And then follows with the announcement of the serial starting in the *Gazette*.

Both French and Brannegan are pleased with Hinchecliffe's ideas. French is so cheered he thinks he can sell five thousand extras on that night's prize fight at the Garden.

When the others have gone Randall sends the Rev. Isopod for

the Miss Carmody of the Chicago *News,* who is waiting to see him. Now he has them both before him. They wait while he talks with the night desk on his inner office phone.

RANDALL—Jamieson. Send out to the morgue and get the clips on Nancy Voorhees. . . . My God, didn't you ever hear of Nancy Voorhees? . . . Well, she shot a guy twenty years ago. Find out where she is now. I think she married after her trial. Ask the District Attorney's office to tell you. If they don't know try Headquarters, and see what pictures they've got. (*Hangs up receiver of the house phone. To* LUELLA.) So you're from Chicago, eh? Did they teach you to swipe pictures out there?

LUELLA—Sure, I've done everything.

RANDALL—I'll start you at forty a week, and if you're a good little girl—I'll give you fifty. (*To* MISS TAYLOR.) Put her on the payroll. (*To* LUELLA.) I've got a little job for you two. I'm going to team you up with a clergyman. (ISOPOD *gazes at her adoringly.*) It might be good for both of you. Pay attention, Isopod! You know that theatrical costumer on Fortieth Street?

ISOPOD—I'll find it.

RANDALL—Well, I want you to go there and hire the best clergyman's rig you can find. Don't spare expense. Collar button behind and everything.

ISOPOD—I have my own, sir.

RANDALL—You do as I say. (*Into phone.*) I'm listening. What?

ISOPOD—But, Mr. Randall—

RANDALL—Shut up! (*Over the phone.*) Get this. (*To* MISS TAYLOR.) Nancy Voorhees, married to Michael Townsend, Assistant Cashier, Metropolitan National. Lives one hundred eighty-four West One Hundred Seventy-second, fourth floor rear. Daughter, twenty. Got that? Fine, Jamieson. Get out the pica. (*Hangs up the receiver.*) Now listen, Isopod. You get yourself dressed, then drop around there daintily and graciously— I don't care how you do it—but I want you to get an appointment. If you can get me an interview with Nancy Voorhees, I'll give you a fifty dollar bonus. (RANDALL *rises.*) Now you listen. (*To* LUELLA.) Here's a woman who killed a man twenty years ago. We're starting to print a serial on the facts leading up to the murder. What I want to do is pump up interest in this serial through the news columns. And that's where you come in. You work with Doctor Isopod on this and while he's working on his angle you go to the people of the neighborhood, talk to the grocer, the butcher and the dressmaker—everybody she might have contact with. See what they think of her. Find out what church she goes to. Where's her daughter? What school did she attend? Was she ostracized? And both of you get this. I want to whoop this up and I *want* pictures. *Pictures.*

The lights are up in Ziggie's office. It is almost identical with the Rev. Isopod's cubby hole. The contest editor is also at the phone. He is talking to Police Commissioner Donovan. Ziggie is fixing up his taxi contest, a race from the Bronx to City Hall, and he wants the police to help clear the streets for it. A thousand cabs to start, three to win. An Irishman, a Jew and a Wop. Ziggie's got it all fixed.

The Townsend apartment, in the Washington Heights district of New York, is neatly but modestly furnished. It is evening. The family has finished its after dinner coffee. Michael and Nancy Voorhees Townsend are discussing the future plans of their daughter, Jenny, and her fiancé, Philip Weeks, with the young people.

This particular evening Philip and Jenny are going to the theatre. For the future they are going to be married as quietly and unostentatiously as a simple church wedding will permit and they are not going to Niagara Falls on their wedding tour. There is much too much water there.

The families of both the young people are reconciled to the marriage, although Philip's mother, being socially ambitious, is pressing the matter of formal announcements and selected guests.

"She had a list of guests drawn up," reports Philip. "They were all the people who had just missed the Social Register by six inches. So you see, Jenny, we'll be at least near-beer."

There is someone on the phone—a Rev. T. Vernon Isopod—about whom Michael Townsend is puzzled. No one of them knows him. But Philip thinks he is probably an assistant rector if he is looking for information about the wedding. Michael asks the Rev. Isopod up.

Philip and Jenny have been sent out to get the Wall Street editions of the papers while Mr. and Mrs. Townsend prepare their gift surprise for them. It is a Brunswick radio and it has, up to now, been concealed by a screen.

Now the children are back with the newspapers, are properly surprised and delighted with their radio and Michael is for organizing a dance. He and Jenny are waltzing while Philip and

Nancy look over the news. Philip, coming upon an *Evening Gazette* announcement, reads it aloud.

"The first true story of the sensational Nancy Voorhees case to start in the *Gazette* Monday. Turn to page 5."

Michael and Jenny stop dancing. Nancy's face goes white. Philip has turned to page 5.

"Beginning Monday the New York *Evening Gazette* will publish the first installment of the notorious Nancy Voorhees murder. . . . The first inside and authentic narrative of the beautiful stenographer who killed Candy Kid Rogers will be given to the readers of this newspaper."

"Stop reading that, Philip, and pay attention to me," demands Jenny. And Philip minds . . .

When Philip and Jenny leave for the theatre, the outside door has no sooner slammed after them than Nancy turns anxiously to her husband.

"Michael, what are we going to do?" she asks, helplessly.

"They don't know your name now," Michael answers, glancing hurriedly through the *Gazette* announcement; "they don't know where we live. We might go away somewhere."

"They'll find us."

"And lie doggo until it is all over."

"They have ways."

Perhaps, thinks Michael, if the newspaper knew what discovery would do to them; perhaps if a man like Doctor Isopod were to go to the editor, with the influence of his church behind him—

The buzzing of the doorbell indicates the arrival of Doctor Isopod. Michael brings him into the room. Michael and Nancy try to put their caller at his ease.

Soon they have told him such preliminary facts as interest him: That Michael is employed in a bank; that Nancy, being a lazy woman, devotes herself only to her home and her daughter.

"We've raised a pretty wonderful daughter," Michael puts in, pridefully.

"So I hear," encourages the Rev. Isopod. "They say she is beautiful. Does she take after her father or her mother?"

"After her—" begins Nancy, nervously.

"After her mother," interrupts Michael, quickly. "Nancy, where's that picture of Jenny?"

Now Doctor Isopod has the picture, which he trusts they will let him keep. They always like to have a photographic record of their married couples, he explains. And now, suddenly, Michael has come to the subject of their problem.

MICHAEL (*sitting on arm of chair*)—Doctor Isopod—we, Mrs. Townsend and I—were going to ask you for—

NANCY—Doctor, may I ask you something?

ISOPOD—Well, if there's anything I can do—

NANCY—Doctor, you've heard many people—I mean they come to you or Doctor Bevans, or someone in your church with their troubles, don't they?

ISOPOD—Yes, indeed they do—daily.

NANCY—If someone were to ask your advice—you would keep that secret?

ISOPOD (*chuckling*)—My dear Mrs. Townsend, it's the code of the church.

NANCY—Doctor, I— I'm in a desperate trouble, not for myself, but for my daughter, and her happiness.

ISOPOD—Ah, perhaps you had better speak to Dr. Bevans.

MICHAEL—You're an assistant at Saint Gregory's—you're a man of maturity—and understanding.

NANCY—Doctor, we haven't any time. As you know, Jenny is to be married tomorrow.

ISOPOD—I—I—am slightly bewildered, I must say.

NANCY (*goes to the radio and gets the* Gazette *and brings it down to* ISOPOD)—Here is a newspaper—look at this. (MICHAEL *crosses as* ISOPOD *scans the page.*) I'm Nancy Voorhees.

ISOPOD (*leaps to his feet, with the photograph under his left arm; drops the paper on a chair*)—Really, Mrs. Townsend!

NANCY (*rises*)—Jenny doesn't know about it. She thinks—she doesn't even know my name was Voorhees. She never even heard of the murder.

ISOPOD—I— I am still in the dark, Mrs. Townsend.

NANCY—Will you, representing Saint Gregory's, go to the editor of this newspaper and ask them not to print this awful thing?

ISOPOD—Really, it seems to me—

NANCY—I know what you think—it's not for my sake. I I don't want my daughter punished for what I've done. Surely if the church were to ask them— If they knew what they were doing!

ISOPOD (*taking her hand and reassuring her*)—Mrs. Townsend, I'll go immediately. I'll see what I can do. I suppose we shouldn't waste any time. (*Picks up his hat; turns to them abruptly.*) Oh, it just occurred to me. The bridegroom may have influence—his name I mean, it sometimes means so much to newspapers.

NANCY—His name is Philip Weeks. His father is a manufacturer of machine parts—

MICHAEL—Nancy, just a moment.

ISOPOD—Weeks, Weeks. Oh, thank you so much, and good-by. Good-by, Mr. Townsend.

NANCY—Good-by. (ISOPOD *goes out hastily.*) What were you saying, dear? Michael, do you think he can do anything? Oh, we didn't arrange to have him telephone or anything. (*Slumps into a chair.*)

MICHAEL—Nancy—

NANCY—What is it?

MICHAEL—Did it strike you as odd that Doctor Isopod didn't know Philip's name?

NANCY—Why, no,—why, Michael, what do you mean?

MICHAEL—Wouldn't a clergyman from a church where two people were to be married know the bridegroom's name?

NANCY—Michael, what are you trying to—

MICHAEL—He didn't even know Jenny's first name. He didn't— (*Pause. Crosses to the desk, takes up the phone.*) Hello, Wadsworth seven-five-two-O. (*Pause.*) Wadsworth seven-five-two-O. (*Loudly.*) Seven-five-two-O. (NANCY *picks up the* Gazette *from behind her.*)

NANCY (*starts up suddenly, reading from the paper*)—Michael! (*Rises.*) Michael!

MICHAEL—What is it?

NANCY—Religious Editor—The Reverend T. Vernon Isopod!

THE CURTAIN FALLS

ACT II

Late that night there was still nothing in the *Gazette* office that Editor Randall was satisfied could be used as a ballyhoo for the Voorhees story, which was scheduled to start Monday. The Rev. Isopod had not been seen since he started out on the story.

Randall, in his office, is sure of but one thing: he wants the Voorhees story played up; he wants Nancy Voorhees' picture, taken in prison, fixed up with bars, even if they have to paint them in; he wants room left in his City Edition for whatever Isopod may bring in, and he wants to see Luella Carmody.

Miss Carmody has not got very much on the Voorhees story, she reports. She has been combing the Townsend neighborhood. She discovered that Mrs. Townsend's daughter went to Hunter

College, where her record was pretty good and where she was known only as Miss Townsend. The Rev. Isopod? No, Miss Carmody hasn't seen the Rev. Isopod. Not since she rode down town in a taxi with him. Which was experience enough to convince her that she doesn't want to work with that guy any more. There's practically no skin left on her knees.

"I'll tell you what to do, Miss Carmody," instructs Randall. "Write the story along these lines: Nancy Voorhees, noted so and so—is one of the few women killers—blah-blah—who disappeared immediately from the spotlight and found a haven of refuge in the quiet family neighborhoods of, well, whatever it is. Get me? Work in about her daughter—and the contrast of Nancy's present life with that of the time of the killing."

"I understand."

"All right. Hop to it."

Luella has gone. Randall has given instructions to his night editor, Murphy, on how he wants the Voorhees story played up and made at least to look like something. He has gone out to the city room to see that this is done when Miss Taylor returns to the scene.

Miss Taylor is slightly unsteady and altogether disgusted. Arthur, the office boy, has an idea that she ought to go home, but the suggestion does not get very far with Miss Taylor.

She has answered the phone and discovered that the Rev. Dr. Isopod is at the other end of the wire. She would like to talk with the Rev. Isopod. "Say, listen, Pastor, what is the *Gazette* going to do with Nancy Voorhees?" she demands, confidentially. "Believe it? I'd believe anything. Wait a minute. (*To* ARTHUR.) God's little gift to mankind! What do you think, Arthur? He discovered a murderess, a murderess, mind you, and a woman with an offspring of adultery, trying to marry her daughter off to a young and innocent boy. Can you beat that for a gag?"

"Miss Taylor, tell him he'd better hurry over here."

"Listen, Pastor, listen very carefully. Mr. Randall says for you to get over here damned quick. And now do you know what I think you are? I think you're a great big little louse with a cross hanging on your belly. You know what I think Hinchecliffe is? I think he's the illegitimate son of Judas and Ruth Snyder. And you know what I think Randall is—? I—

Miss Taylor would also have added her opinion of Mr. Randall, but the Rev. Isopod hung up the receiver.

Randall has come back to his office, heard the report from

Isopod, dismissed Arthur for the night and discovered Miss Taylor.

"What are you doing here?" he wants to know. When she does not answer promptly he looks at her intently and draws conclusions. "You've been drinking, haven't you?" he asks.

MISS TAYLOR—Want to hear what I think?

RANDALL—I know what you think.

MISS TAYLOR—I think if we all lost our jobs we'd feel like a lot of bums that've been disinfected.

RANDALL—Do you want to lose your job?

MISS TAYLOR—I don't give a damn. You asked me for my opinion today, didn't you? (*Rising.*) Well, I'll give it and then you can fire me. (*Goes to him.*)

RANDALL—You're certainly full of sky-rockets, aren't you?

MISS TAYLOR—Look here, Mr. Randall, I've been with you a long time. You've done a lot for me, and now, all the time you've been doing something for me, you've been doing something for yourself.

RANDALL—What are you talking about?

MISS TAYLOR—You let this lousy rag seduce you with a lot of money.

RANDALL (*goes behind her back*)—You're drunk. Go home. (*She turns toward him.*) God damn it, I want to tell you something. I've been on enough papers and I've seen enough people to know that ideals won't put a patch on your pants. I know what you're driving at. You think this Voorhees story's a pretty filthy mess.

MISS TAYLOR—I think that woman suffered enough. She had a right to kill that man. And what we're doing is putting her on trial again, and sneaking around about it with morals and warnings. Can't you see what this might do to that family? (*Shouting.*) You ought to be ashamed of yourself!

RANDALL—I'm too old to be ashamed of myself. I'm going to be one newspaperman who gets out of this business with enough money to give me a decent old age. And now you've said your little say and I want you to go home and sleep it off, and forget it.

The Rev. Isopod arrives. He is filled with excitement and excuses and carries Jenny Townsend's picture. Randall is in no mood to listen to alibis. He is anxious to hear Isopod's report. Before Isopod starts that, however, Randall decides to tell his religious editor a few things every newspaperman should know. One of them is that he has no right to go out on a story and not keep in touch with his desk.

The Rev. Isopod, after several futile starts, manages to explain to Randall that he has found Nancy Voorhees; he has seen her in her flat; that her daughter Jenny is getting married the next day and that he has brought Jenny's picture. Randall is not visibly impressed. He looks long and earnestly at Jenny's picture. Miss Taylor moves forward, drawn by her interest in his reactions.

RANDALL—Well? Nancy's daughter is getting married tomorrow. What the hell's hot about that?

ISOPOD—But don't you see—

RANDALL—Those people don't even rate our social column.

ISOPOD—But don't you see, Mr. Randall?—This woman—this murderess—is marrying off her daughter of adultery to an unsuspecting young boy. This is really something for the *Gazette* to take up. I was shocked, Mr. Randall—shocked!

MISS TAYLOR—Oh, poop. (ISOPOD *gives her a mean look.*)

RANDALL (*glaring at her*)—Say, what do you think you are—a critic? (RANDALL *again looks at the picture.*) So that's her daughter.

ISOPOD—And probably as bad as her mother.

RANDALL—Infant damnation, eh?

ISOPOD—Exactly.

RANDALL (*to* ISOPOD)—Did you see her?

ISOPOD—No, she was out.

RANDALL—Who's the man she's marrying?

ISOPOD—His name is Philip Weeks. His father makes machinery equipment.

RANDALL—Weeks? Weeks? (*Into the phone.*) Murphy, this is what I want you to do. Go in with the first edition the way it is and let them run off enough for the trains. Then we'll replate with this Voorhees story. Find out the full name of a man named Weeks who makes machinery parts. His son's marrying the daughter of Nancy Voorhees! Isopod says Nancy is palming off the daughter on the kid. I've got a picture of the girl. I'll send it out. (*He hangs up and motions to* MISS TAYLOR. *She gets up.*) Miss Taylor, give this to Murphy. Tell him to make it big and put the other pictures around. (*To* ISOPOD.) What's the name of the church?

ISOPOD—Saint Gregory's.

RANDALL (*taking a pencil and paper, he draws a plan.* MISS TAYLOR *goes to him*)—Miss Taylor, give this to Murphy. The girl's to go there, see? The bridegroom here, if we get him. Nancy here, and the others where I've indicated. If Murphy doesn't understand, tell him to call me. And then do me a great favor and go home. (MISS TAYLOR *takes the layout and silently and sullenly goes out, leaving her handbag on the desk.*) What time is the wedding?

ISOPOD—I— I didn't learn that. I should say it would be around noon.

RANDALL—Well, find out, and let me see your lead when it's finished. And don't forget that text to precede "The Love-Mad Stenographer."

ISOPOD (*at the door*)—Yes, sir. Is that all?

RANDALL—Yeah. (*Picks up the pocket book, looks at it and then lays it on the desk. Takes the house phone.*) Murphy? What's happened in your little war? Two Americans? Get pictures. What about the fight story? Did he get the knockout? Put a couple of pictures on the last page. And listen, take a look at that damn drama page, will you? Griffin's been handing Flo Ziegfeld the top of his column every day. Find out who our Dramatic Editor is sleeping with.

There is a flash of Ziggie, the contest editor, in action. He is calling up Dinckie Ginsberg to give him a job from the circulation manager. Ziggie wants Dinckie to take a couple of the boys and use 'em on those Sixth Avenue babies who are buryin' the *Gazette* under all the other tabs on their news stands. Let them use their brass knuckles if necessary. There's twenty-five dollars in it for everybody.

In the Townsend apartment Nancy Townsend is still sitting up, though the hour is late. Jenny is back from the theatre, but Michael is still out. Michael had to go to the bank, Nancy explains to her daughter, though that doesn't altogether satisfy Jenny's suspicions that something is wrong.

The something that's wrong, Nancy insists, is that she is going to lose her daughter, but Jenny has a way of fixing that. She is going to have a lot of babies and give them all to her mother to take care of. And she isn't going to name a one of them after Phil's family.

Now Michael is back, looking pale and worn, and Jenny has gone to bed. The conference at the bank has not gone so well, though Michael will not go into details. Mr. Hollister, their branch manager, may help them, but Hollister is a very cautious man. Michael had never realized before how cautious he is. He had told Hollister the whole story.

Anyway, there should be others who can help them. Old friends they used to know. Michael had had a lot of friends twenty years before. What has ever become of them?

Michael is going through his address book, trying to remember the old friends as the lights fade.

In his office Randall is doing considerable excited telephoning. He has found the address of Arthur Loveland Weeks, 72 Central Park West. He has called Luella Carmody and got her out of bed. He wants her to go over to the Weeks address and get an interview with Mr. Weeks. What does Weeks think about his son's marrying the daughter of the woman who bumped off Candy Kid Rogers? She can tell them she is the society editor of the New York *Tribune*.

From her cubby hole high in the building the *Gazette's* telephone exchange operator perfunctorily makes and breaks the call connections.

Next morning, in his office, Randall is again busy with the phone. Miss Carmody is on the wire and reports the Voorhees wedding set for 12 o'clock.

"Very mysterious at the church," Randall relays to Jamieson, over the house phone. "This might be a damned good yarn. It looks as if Nancy is trying to gather her daughter into the money under another name—all right, I'll switch her over to you. (*Hangs up and speaks into the other phone.*) Oh, Miss Carmody, when I'm through talking to Jamieson give him what you've got. Now listen, I want you to hop up to the Voorhees home and ask them what's up. Maybe they know we're in on this and have switched the marriage to another church? What? Tell Jamieson to give you a camera man. Catch them coming out of the house if you can, or better still, set your camera for a flash and ring the doorbell. Have you got that? You've got their address. Hold on a minute. (*He jangles the hook.*) Put this call on the day city desk.

The last caller is Ziggie. He's got a great idea for another contest—a bathing beauty race to Hollywood—in airplanes!

In the Townsend apartment, there is natural excitement as the hour of the wedding approaches. Jenny and Philip have gone for the license. Suddenly there is a knock at the door. Mr. and Mrs. Arthur Loveland Weeks are calling.

Mrs. Weeks, a large and commanding woman, is inclined to take the lead. Mr. Weeks preserving a proper masculine dignity, is eager for as peaceful adjustment of the situation as possible. Weeks would, if he could, save everybody's feelings. Under the circumstances there seems but one thing to be done. The marriage must be canceled. The Weeks have not spoken to Philip because they believe it would be more proper for the parents—or the parent—of the girl to break off matters.

"I'm sure you both see our position?" suggests Mr. Weeks.

"I see yours," admits Michael, "but I don't yet see Philip's."

MRS. WEEKS—He will do as he is told. You must see that a marriage with a girl—

WEEKS—Isabelle, I have asked you to let me handle this.

MRS. WEEKS—Very well, then. But you're not on a diplomatic mission.

WEEKS (*to* MICHAEL)—Must we speak more plainly?

MICHAEL—Mr. Weeks, you must understand that my place in this matter—

NANCY—What are you saying, Michael?

MICHAEL—Nancy, dearest, you didn't let me finish. (*He assists her to a chair.*) My place, Mr. Weeks, is entirely outside that of my wife's.

WEEKS—I don't follow you.

MICHAEL—Very well, then. I'll give you a straight answer.

MRS. WEEKS—That's what I'd like to have.

MICHAEL—Madame, my replies will be at least courteous.

WEEKS—What were you going to say, sir?

MICHAEL—I was going to say that I, as a man outside my wife's misfortune, I am not conniving at anything for your son that I haven't done myself. Mrs. Townsend and I have been married for twenty years and her daughter is my daughter. Being as much an outsider as your son, I fail to see that Jenny is unequal to a marriage with the son of that lady.

MRS. WEEKS—Regardless of the necessity of being insulted, we shall stay here until we get what we came for.

WEEKS—Mr. Townsend, what you did was perhaps, a noble thing.

MICHAEL—You realize, do you not, what you are doing to my wife?

WEEKS—I am truly sorry. I would have avoided it if it were at all possible. Nevertheless, what you did, you did knowing all the circumstances. My son knows nothing.

MICHAEL—And if he did?

MRS. WEEKS—It doesn't matter whether he knows or not. It doesn't matter what he would like to do. He's not going to marry the daughter of a murderess. (WEEKS *checks her.* MICHAEL *starts, but restrains himself.* NANCY *rises. Pause.*)

MICHAEL (*goes to the door and opens it*)—I don't think there's anything more to be said. (*Pause.*)

WEEKS (*to* MICHAEL)—I'm sorry—Mrs. Weeks—we—are excited.

Again it seems to the Townsends that the only thing to do is to make every effort to stop the publication of the story. Nancy believes that if she were to go personally to see the editor something might be done. Michael is afraid they are not sufficiently important people to have any influence.

"Everything I touch falls apart," sighs Nancy. "I dragged you down and now it's Jenny."

"You haven't dragged us down," Michael replies, kissing her tenderly.

Michael goes to have a last try at Hollister at the bank. Nancy flies to the phone to call Canal Ten Thousand.

There are lights in both Brannegan's and Hinchecliffe's offices as the operator makes the connections. Brannegan is reporting the signing of a hundred line contract with the Anti-Sterility crowd at sixty cents a line. Hinchecliffe is pleased, though he deprecates the use of patent medicine advertising. He wishes they could afford to drop it.

Mrs. Townsend's call comes through to Mr. Hinchecliffe's phone and Miss Edwards takes it. Mr. Hinchecliffe refuses to speak to her. Let Miss Edwards tell Mrs. Townsend he is not in.

Nancy is switched to Randall's phone. Randall, also, is too busy talking over the house phone with Hinchecliffe, trying to explain how it is the *Gazette* has an overload of colored subscribers.

Nancy grows more and more hysterical. Now she is cut off. Then she is shifted from phone to phone. Finally she does get Randall, because Miss Taylor practically insists that he shall talk with her.

NANCY (*in phone*)—Is this Mr. Randall?

RANDALL—Yes, this is Mr. Randall.

NANCY—You know why I'm calling. Please listen to me. Are you listening?

RANDALL—Go on.

NANCY—Mr. Randall, I want you to stop this story. You don't know what it means. I'm not asking for myself. Please believe that. But you wouldn't punish an innocent person, would you?

RANDALL—I don't follow you.

NANCY—Mr. Randall, my daughter is being married today. She doesn't know anything about this. If you print this story it will ruin her life. Will you make this sacrifice? Will you, please?

RANDALL—Miss Voorhees, I would like to, but—

NANCY (*rises*)—There are so many other things to write about. Mr. Randall, do you hear what I'm saying?

RANDALL—Miss Voorhees, I can do nothing about it. It's published and the paper is on the street.

NANCY (*hysterically*)—What? WHAT?

RANDALL (*hangs up*)—Christ! I can't go on with this. If she calls up again, I'm not in.

In the Townsend apartment Nancy hangs up the receiver despairingly. Gradually her hysteria mounts. She paces back and forth across the room. At the desk she stops and takes a revolver from a drawer. After a pause she puts the revolver back. There is a look of determination on her face as she goes quickly into her own room. A moment later there is a bitter cry, half laugh and half sob, followed by a crash of glass and a groan from Nancy.

For a moment there is silence. Then Michael enters, calling Nancy. Getting no answer he goes into the bedroom. When he comes back into the room his face is twisted in agony. He has the poison bottle and a part of the broken glass. He takes a cocktail glass from the table and pours a part of the poison into it. He is on his way toward the bedroom when Jenny and Philip are heard in the hall outside. Michael puts the poison bottle in his pocket. He is still holding the cocktail glass.

Jenny is pleased to report that the State of New York has given its consent to her marriage. They also have their railroad tickets. But, where is Nancy?

Michael manages to stop Jenny as she starts for Nancy's room.

He tells them Nancy has thought of something she needs at the last minute.

Jenny notices the cocktail glass in Michael's hand. Why shouldn't they all have a cocktail? And she wants to hear her radio. She turns it on. A dance tune is playing. Now it is time, Michael thinks, that they should be running on.

PHILIP—I should telephone home, I think.

JENNY—Aren't you going to escort us?

MICHAEL—I'm going with Nancy.

JENNY—Dad, is there anything the matter?

MICHAEL—What could be the matter?

JENNY—You're evading me.

MICHAEL—Jenny, darling, we're all a bit nervous.

PHILIP—Do you know what I'd like to do?

JENNY—What, dear? Oh, that's a nice song.

PHILIP—I'd like to get on the train and go get married in Canada.

MICHAEL—You mustn't do that, Philip. (JENNY *sways rhythmically and hums with the music.*)

PHILIP—Why not?

MICHAEL—Your mother and father will be at the church. You must see them before the wedding.

PHILIP—That's just the reason I'd like to go away.

JENNY—But why, dear?

PHILIP—I don't know. This business is catching. I didn't know getting married was so serious. (*Claps his hands to* JENNY'S *dancing.*)

MICHAEL—Look, it's eleven-thirty. You children run along.

JENNY—But mother will be back any moment. I want to see her first. (MICHAEL *is hardly able to control himself. He is guarding the door and the poison. Suddenly the phone rings. He dashes to it, and lays his drink on desk.*)

MICHAEL—Hello? What? (*A pause.*) Oh, Nancy, Nancy. I'd wondered what had become of you. The children are here waiting for you. What? Where? Where, dear? Right. Immediately. (*He hangs up the phone and turns to* JENNY *and* PHILIP.) Now, Jenny, you must go. Nancy is in a shop around the corner and she forgot to take money with her. I've got to join her. (*He laughs hysterically.*) Just like a woman, isn't it?

JENNY—You'll meet us in Saint Gregory's? (PHILIP *gets his hat and goes to the outside door.*)

MICHAEL—Yes, yes. In the vestry, isn't it?

JENNY—That's it.

MICHAEL (*at the door*)—Well, Philip. I'm going to call you my son, now (*shakes hands warmly*), for the first time.

PHILIP—Thanks, Mr. Townsend.

MICHAEL—Now about a little kiss, Miss Jenny? (JENNY *comes to him. He puts his arms tenderly about her and holds her tightly to him.*) Come now, out with you both. (*He shoves them towards the door and opens it. They go out.*)

JENNY—Don't be long, Dad. (*The door closes.*)

MICHAEL—I won't, Jenny. And mind you give the right answers.

Michael is laughing bitterly as he closes the door. The telephone is ringing. He takes the receiver off the hook and lays it on the table. The radio is broadcasting, "Let a Smile Be Your Umbrella." Nervously Michael picks up his pipe and raps the ashes out of it. He takes up his cocktail glass, hesitates a moment and then walks quickly into Nancy's room.

A few moments later Luella Carmody appears on the fire escape and comes through a window into the room. She is followed by Rooney, the camera man.

"You know what it means if we're caught? Burglary!" mutters Rooney.

"Oh, hell! We got a newspaper behind us, haven't we?" answers Luella. "Let's look around. I got to get pictures."

Luella has reached the desk and is making a quick search of the drawers. Rooney, finding nothing to shoot, has tried the door to Nancy's room. He takes a hurried look inside and then draws back with a startled exclamation—

"Jesus! God Almighty, look; will ya look!"

Luella goes into the room and comes rushing back a second later. Rooney shuts off the radio. Luella grabs the phone and calls Canal Ten Thousand.

The light in Randall's office flashes on as she gets the connection.

RANDALL (*at his desk, into phone*)—Hello.

LUELLA—This is Miss Carmody, Mr. Randall. Nancy Voorhees and her husband have just committed suicide.

RANDALL (*after a pause, breathless*)—How do you know?

LUELLA—I'm in the apartment with Rooney.

RANDALL—Jesus!

LUELLA—What do you want me to do?

RANDALL—Hold on a minute. (*He rings the house phone.*) Jamieson. Hold up your next edition and get ready for an extra. I've got a call here from Miss Carmody. Nancy Voorhees and her husband are dead. Suicide. Put the best rewrite man you have on it and I'll have the call switched. (*Back into the phone.*) Miss Carmody, I'm having you switched to the City Desk. Give them all you have. Then get back here and write me a new story for the five star final.

There is a flash of a cheap room in an apartment hotel in the Forties. A single bed against the wall, a dressing table littered with empty liquor and ginger ale bottles and cigarette butts. Outside in the street newsboys are calling an extra. "Read all about the big suicide!"

Trixie, a neighbor, is calling on Pearl, the roomer. It has been a hard night for both of them. What they need is coffee and lots of it.

The calls of the newsboys attract them. They buy a couple of *Gazettes*. They are fascinated by what they read: "Former Beauty in Suicide Pact." . . . "Nancy Voorhees, notorious murderess of twenty years ago, is found dead with her husband in Washington Heights flat. Police believe tragedy was suicide pact."

"Well," ventures Pearl, "it takes guts, anyhow . . ."

"I think it's lousy," counters Trixie. "What do they wanna dig up a woman's past like this for?"

"They gotta have something to print, don't they?"

"Yeh, but why do they spill a lot of dirt on a woman? I wish to God I had the guts to do what she did. . . ."

"Yeah, we're a lot of damn saps, we are. All a guy has to say is love, and the next morning we wake up in a strange hotel."

There is another flash of an apartment of a colored couple. Minerva is at an ironing board working and singing, "I Hate to See the Evening Sun Go Down." Harold, her fat husband, is sitting near in his shirt sleeves reading the *Gazette* suicide extra. Seein' Harold ain't doin' nothin' Minerva thinks he might read her the news about the two white folks what took poison.

"Nancy Voorhees, notorious killer of two decades ago, committed suicide today," lazily reads Harold. "Husband, Michael Townsend, also killed himself in what police believe was a death pact. Photo, copyrighted 1930 *Gazette*."

When Minerva doesn't understand exactly what a death pact is

Harold shows her the picture. "Dat am a death pact," he elucidates, wisely.

"You hear of people killin' themselves for a lot of reasons," Minerva admits, "but you nevah heah of a man who killed hissel' from work."

Which, Harold insists, shows she is just gettin' mean agin.

In Corcoran's speakeasy Randall is sitting at a table alone, staring dejectedly, bitterly, into space. There is an empty glass before him. He has been drinking steadily.

Mike, the policeman, is asleep in the arm chair. Jerry, the bartender, is dozing back of the bar. Randall calls for more liquor.

All night, Randall confesses, he has been trying to get drunk. The whiskey Jerry sells wouldn't tip an egg over. No wonder the Federal dicks are always pinching speakeasy proprietors.

Jerry thinks perhaps a little gin and lemon would be a good thing to change to. Randall is willing to try anything, but he has a feeling that he will never be able to get drunk again. . . .

Randall has started for the door and turned back. He leans over the bar and faces Jerry seriously.

"Did you ever kill a man, Jerry?" he demands.

"God!" ejaculates the startled Jerry.

RANDALL (*laughing hysterically*)—Did you ever kill a man?

JERRY (*still bewildered*)—You're joking, Mr. Randall.

RANDALL—D'ye ever killa woman, Jerry? (*Continues hysterical laughter. After a pause he returns to the table, sits down and finishes his drink.* JERRY *stares at him.*) I don't mean poisoning 'em with your rotten liquor.

JERRY—Say, Mr. Randall, you ain't sick, are you? I seen people drink a lot and not get drunk, and got sick. You'll excuse me for talkin' like this?

RANDALL—Yeah, I'm sick. I got a pain that'll last me a long time.

JERRY—Why're you talking about killin' people. You never killed anybody. (*Laughing.*) I knew a guy once who killed his wife.

RANDALL—Yeh? Tell me about it.

JERRY (*leaning over the bar*)—He caught her in bed with a dude guy. He was a ham actor. The dude guy busted him in the jaw and beat it. Then the dame laughed at him an' he smashed her head in. An' can you believe it—he only got five years.

RANDALL—How did he feel after?

JERRY—He used to get drunk and cry. I guess he loved her or something. I never saw such a man. He used to say if she'd come back he wouldn't care who she slept with.

RANDALL—What happened to him?

JERRY—Damned if I know. He ran outa money, I guess. Stopped coming here.

RANDALL—Ran outa money, eh? My God, Jerry, I never thought about it before. What do people do who are in trouble and they haven't money to buy liquor? There must be lots of them in the world. That's why this prohibition stink can't succeed. (*Laughs.*) The old duel goes on, Jerry, doesn't it? (*Laughs.*) God gives us heartaches and the devil gives us whiskey. (*Drinks.*)

There is a flash of the telephone exchange operator of the *Gazette* as she puts an outside call on Mr. French's wire.

They want more papers in Harlem. French thinks the Delivery Room better send another five thousand copies up there. Also there should be additional allotments for Brooklyn and East New York . . . French would talk with Randall, but Randall isn't in. He tells Miss Taylor that Randall has done a great job. Circulation's up a hundred thousand.

Luella Carmody is telephoning from a booth. She gets Colby the rewrite man on the wire. Sure, she'll meet him at the Astor when he gets through . . . The bodies of the Townsends have been removed to the morgue. The funeral will be held from an undertaking establishment and the burial will be in Woodlawn Miss Carmody reports.

In the Townsend apartment Jenny Townsend and Mrs. Weeks are seated. Mr. Weeks is standing between them. Jenny is trying hard to convince them that she has not seen Philip since he left them at the church. Until she has seen him she will not answer any of their questions as to whether or not she and Philip are married, or whether they are planning a second ceremony.

The Weeks are hopelessly at sea. Philip has not been home, they do not know where he is. But of one thing Mrs. Weeks is firmly convinced:

"There can be no marriage," says she.

"I want to hear that from Philip, not from you," replies Jenny.

"He'll do as we say."

"Don't you think, Jenny, you are acting selfishly toward him?"

"If Philip loves me he'll marry me in spite of everything," calmly declares Jenny. "And if he doesn't I might as well know it now."

When a man from the undertaker's is announced the Weeks decide to leave. They cannot talk before a stranger.

The undertaker's man has come to see about carriages. Probably two will be enough. And he would like to check up the coroner's report. He is mumbling it aloud—

"Place of death: Boro of Manhattan; full name, Nancy Townsend; report of death by B. J. Finkle"—as the scene blacks out.

Ziggie, the contest editor, is having some trouble over the phone getting his winning bride to stand for the ceremony.

"Listen," he is saying, "you tell her it's got a fifty-foot front, yeh. And the house has everything—with a back porch. Now, listen, Herschel. I know her mother wants her to get married. What more does she want? You tell that schotschin to get a good guy that wants a start in life. And listen, Herschel, go over to the Scholem Aleichem Literary Association and offer five dollars for everyone that'll go in the contest. They don't have to win the prize. No, no marriage. Just to fill up the damn hall."

By promising the bride a good guy, not much over forty, and by throwing in a vacuum cleaner, Ziggie is able finally to complete the bargain.

Randall is back in his office. His mood is sullen, his attitude determined. He is brusque with Miss Taylor, orders Murphy to drop the Voorhees story and is all set for Hinchecliffe when the *Gazette's* owner walks in.

Hinchecliffe has sent for Brannegan and French and is prepared for a conference. Also he is thinking seriously of taking a short European trip. Mrs. Hinchecliffe feels that an ocean voyage would do her a lot of good.

Randall thinks it must be nice in England at this time, but he is not sure if Hinchecliffe wants him to get a minimum rate from the Cunard line or is only trying to duck the Voorhees thing.

Hinchecliffe is frankly upset. He thinks maybe the Voorhees serial should be dropped, but on the other hand—

HINCHECLIFFE—Let's not be too hasty. I know you are touched by what has occurred. Nevertheless a great newspaper transcends the individual.

RANDALL (*rises*)—You know God damned well that these people committed suicide because we dug up that old story.

HINCHECLIFFE—Randall, there are several ways of looking at this. You have been in this business long enough to allow that sentimentality—

RANDALL—It's not sentimentality. It's damn good sense. (*The door opens and* BRANNEGAN *and* FRENCH *enter, followed by* ISOPOD *and* ZIGGIE.) And if you print this serial now—

BRANNEGAN—Did you send for us, Mr. Hinchecliffe?

FRENCH—Randall, I want to congratulate you. We had a bigger sale today than we had when the United States entered the war.

HINCHECLIFFE—Gentlemen, we have a little question on our minds. We were discussing the advisabliity of dropping the serial story.

FRENCH—You mean the Voorhees thing?

BRANNEGAN—We've got the biggest thing in years and sewed up.

RANDALL—Does it ever occur to any of you that a story like this would be a boomerang?

BRANNEGAN—Boomerang, hell!

HINCHECLIFFE—Just how do you mean, Randall?

BRANNEGAN—Give me this circulation for three months and I'll jump the advertising rate ten cents a line.

HINCHECLIFFE—Let's hear what Mr. Randall has to say.

RANDALL—I'm not going to argue with the Counting Room. But I'm saying this and flatly. I *won't* run that story.

BRANNEGAN—That's between you and the owner. (*Sits in chair right of* TAYLOR'S *desk.*)

HINCHECLIFFE—Perhaps we can find a middle course.

BRANNEGAN—There's no middle course. We must run this serial.

It is Ziggie's opinion that a great thing can be made out of the Voorhees serial by rewriting it in the first person and making it Nancy Voorhees' own story.

"It's a cinch, boss," insists Ziggie, explosively. "Look, this girl ain't got a nickel, see. Now the mother's dead and nobody can deny anything. We print this yarn in the first person, give the dame a thousand dollars and everything's jake. We can send Isopod (Randall paces up and down in disgust) up to spill a few sympathy tears and hand her the dough. Nancy Voorhees' own story, exclusive in the *Gazette*.

HINCHECLIFFE—I think— I think we can give the daughter a little more. What do you say, gentlemen? Eh! Randall?

RANDALL—You've heard my opinion.

BRANNEGAN—I think Feinstein's got a good idea.

RANDALL—Yeah—well? All the practical wisdom in the world doesn't repose itself in the heads of the business department.

BRANNEGAN (*rising*)—Listen, Randall—keep personalities out of this.

RANDALL (*sharply to* BRANNEGAN)—You wait till I finish. No one can ever accuse me of trying to run a school of journalism newspaper. I'm not a crusader nor an uplifter. And the only reason I'm in this business is to make money for myself by making it for the paper.

HINCHECLIFFE (*rising*)—Now, gentlemen—now let's not have any excitement. You're a very amenable man, Mr. Randall. But I think in this instance you are being guided by emotion.

RANDALL—Emotion or brains doesn't count. At least I have a guide. And you ought to know God damned well, Brannegan, that for every moron who will buy the *Gazette* because of a first person story by Nancy Voorhees there will be an intelligent advertising man who will be offended. By God! There are some things in life which transcend dollar-getting.

BRANNEGAN—See here, Mr. Randall.

HINCHECLIFFE—Gentlemen—I insist, we must modify this tone. I want calm advice, not excitement.

Miss Taylor is in to announce that Miss Townsend is in the outer office asking to see Mr. Hinchecliffe or Doctor Isopod. Both Hinchecliffe and Isopod are convinced that it would be extremely unwise to see her. Randall is not only of a contrary opinion, but equally determined. He sends for Miss Townsend, in defiance of their advice. Brannegan, French and Ziggie get out, but Randall manages to hold Hinchecliffe and Isopod.

Jenny Townsend is not hysterical when she enters the room and faces them. She has come, she says, to see Mr. Hinchecliffe. Hinchecliffe greets her affably, but would postpone an interview—

HINCHECLIFFE—Miss Townsend, you caught us at a very busy moment. Wouldn't you like to wait for me in my office? There we could be quiet and talk things over, calmly.

RANDALL—To hell with that stuff. You've got a proposition to make this girl. That's what we were talking about. Let's get it over with. (JENNY *turns inquiringly to* RANDALL. *Pause.*)

HINCHECLIFFE—Miss Townsend, let me begin by saying how sorry—how dreadfully sorry—we all are for your misfortune. You see, Miss Townsend, newspapers are huge, impersonal machines. They are the great mirrors that reflect the world as it passes. We are not responsible for the actions of people—we merely hold this mirror up so they may see their follies.

JENNY (*very quietly to* HINCHECLIFFE)—Mr. Hinchecliffe, why did you kill my mother? (*Pause.*)

ISOPOD—Miss Townsend, may I as a clergyman put into words the meaning of these sad necessities? If you'll allow me—

JENNY (*ignoring him*)—Mr. Hinchecliffe, why did you kill my mother?

HINCHECLIFFE—Miss Townsend, do you think—that you could ever begin to understand the position of so complex a machine as a great newspaper? It is impossible now to be impersonal or—

JENNY—Mr. Hinchecliffe. Why did you kill my mother?—I want an answer from all of you. (*Turns around to all.*)

RANDALL (*goes to her*)—I'll tell you. By God! I'll tell you.

HINCHECLIFFE—You are only adding to everybody's confusion, Randall. I don't know why you choose a time like this.

RANDALL—You're going to know a great many things before this day is over. Right now I'm talking to Miss Townsend, and if you know anything about me, you'll keep damn quiet. Miss Townsend, we killed your mother and Michael Townsend for purposes of circulation. He killed them and I killed them and the smaller fry aided and abetted the murders to amuse a gang of white illiterates and nigger pot rastlers. That's the answer—that's the only answer there is.

JENNY—Answer? Answer? Do you know that yesterday my mother and father were living? We had a future, all of us. And then you sent this man sneaking in on us in his priest's uniform. A Minister of Christ. (*To* RANDALL.) What is he doing here?

RANDALL—Miss Townsend, for God's sake, stop. Will you believe that—I—

JENNY—What? That you're sorry? Do you think I care what you feel? You've smashed us. You've killed my mother and father. You've driven away from me the only other human being I love. And now you say you're sorry. (*Hysterical sobs from* JENNY.) Where is my mother now? (*To* HINCHECLIFFE.) Would you have done this to the daughter of John D. Rockefeller? Who are you to condemn people to death?

PHILIP (*heard outside*)—Get away from that door, God damn you— (*Enters and rushes to* JENNY.) Jenny—

JENNY—Philip, they killed them. That Minister—the Minister who telephoned. Philip, I'm going crazy. A clergyman—a clergyman— And that man—he owns this paper. (*Working into a fury.*) He kills people. (*She opens her purse, snatches revolver and aims it at* HINCHECLIFFE.)

PHILIP—Jenny, don't! Please, for God's sake, don't. (PHILIP *wrests the weapon away from her, as she collapses in his arms. Pause. Quietly:*) What's the use? You or I could kill any one of them, and then they'd kill us. It never ends—it never ends.

JENNY (*sobbing*)—Oh, Nancy—Nancy—you were so beautiful. Your face—all burned.

PHILIP (*he puts the revolver in his side pocket*)—Jenny, please. (*He escorts her to a chair by the table. Turning to them.*) You needn't be frightened. There won't be any more murders and it won't do any good to tell you what you've done. You'll go on doing it, hunting down little, unimportant people who can't fight back. You'll go on pulling the clothing off women and selling their naked bodies for two cents. You've grown rich and nobody has dared rise up and crush you out. (*Threateningly.*) But if you ever mention my name or my wife's name in your rotten paper again I'll kill you. (*They go out.* MISS TAYLOR *closes the door behind them.*)

RANDALL—All right. Isopod—get out— Go on, get out! (ISOPOD *goes out and closes the door.* RANDALL *and* HINCHECLIFFE *face each other.*) Now, Hinchecliffe, what are you going to do with this Nancy Voorhees serial?

HINCHECLIFFE—We have plenty of time to decide that, Randall.

RANDALL—We're going to decide that right here and now.

HINCHECLIFFE—Has this paper changed owners, Mr. Randall? I'm going to tell you exactly what this newspaper's going to do. We have already announced this serial to our readers. We're going to print it and we're going to print it in the first person. And if you have any qualms about following the policy of the *Gazette*—

RANDALL—There's just one difference between you and me, Hinchecliffe. You thought up these murders and I committed them. I did it for wages. You did it for circulation.

HINCHECLIFFE—Now, look here, Randall.

RANDALL—No. I'm through taking your money and I'm through running a lousy vaudeville for soda jerkers and elevator boys. That's whom we killed these people for. For fat hired girls. This is your engine, Hinchecliffe, and I'm handing it back to you, but before I go (*steps right up to* HINCHECLIFFE), and to appease the hatred of God, if only by a comma, I'm going to tell you what you are.

HINCHECLIFFE—You must be completely mad.

RANDALL—I am. All my life I'll be mad—for all my life I'll see that girl standing there and asking me why I killed her mother. Well, I want you to enjoy that picture with me. I want you to wake up in the night and see your own squashy, putrid little soul. I want you to know that every human being who works for you knows what a hypocrite you are. We all know it, and God help us, we take your money and do your work because we're afraid to starve.

HINCHECLIFFE—I assume that you have said all you care to say, Mr. Randall. You may turn your office over to Mr. Murphy, just as soon as you possibly can. (HINCHECLIFFE *goes out.*)

RANDALL (*picks up his hat, puts it on, picks up his fountain pen from the desk, and puts it in his pocket*)—Miss Taylor, have Arthur collect my things, and bring the stuff up to my apartment.

MISS TAYLOR—Mr. Randall, what are you going to do?

RANDALL—The future hasn't had time to get here yet. (*Pats* MISS TAYLOR'S *cheek and goes to the door.*) I've learned that ideals won't put a patch on your pants. I'm going to be one newspaperman that gets out of this business with enough money to give me a decent old age. (*Laughs. He goes out. Voices heard outside:*) "What you read, Mister?" etc.

CURTAIN

OVERTURE

A Drama in Three Acts

BY WILLIAM BOLITHO

MEN of his profession spoke of William Bolitho as the most brilliant of the younger journalists of his time. He had come from a variety of early adventures, culminating in long service in the British army during the great war, into newspaper work. For some years he served as foreign correspondent of the *New York World.* Later his contract stipulated that he should spend alternate six-month periods in America, and during this time his column of essays on the *World* became one of the most widely discussed and generally quoted of newspaper features.

He had several books to his credit before he decided to write a play. "Overture," in fact, was the last literary work on which he concentrated and he was still busy revising his first draft when he died Avignon, France, in June, 1929.

When the play was brought to the stage it passed through the hands of at least two directors, Marc Connelly and Gabriel Beer-Hofmann. The author's widow also served as adviser. It was produced under the auspices of Bela Blau, Inc., at the Longacre Theatre, New York, on Dec. 5, 1930. The reviews ranged from the esctatic to the moderately enthusiastic type. Audience response was equally varied. But there was general agreement that the drama provided a purposeful, well-written and moving entertainment in the theatre.

As "Overture" opens it is about two years after the war and Germany is passing through a secondary revolution. The scene is the Municipal Council Chamber of Herfeld (Muhlheim in the printed version of the play), "a largish town in the heart of the German western industrial area."

Not only Herfeld, but practically every town in the vicinity has been affected by these minor revolutions. Every town, in fact, "has its own revolution, under its own leaders, with its own program and its own shabby little history. Here is bloodshed; there, none; a little, much, or none at all."

"Three towns on an arc, on the west side of Herfeld are, at

this moment, in the hands of the Bolshevists and their attitude towards events in our town is important. There are fairly compact little Red armies in each of these places, quite well armed, and above all a disciplined central command. This group, or rather still higher powers of the 3d Internationale, have sent a delegate, Maxim, to observe and mix in the situation in Herfeld, with power to call in an intervention of the Communist neighbors, which he will do only if the Herfeld revolution submits to his and his party's control, if he may abstain. He has been elected a member of the Herfeld Workman's Delegation, which has demanded to be heard in protest today by their Mayor and Council, who have approved an emergency law halving the workers' pay, and increasing their hours, with various other hardships."

The Council Chamber is a long hall paneled in solid oak. It is on the second floor and overlooks, from a high double window, the courtyard below, where the citizens are in the habit of gathering to hear speeches on holidays.

There is a long table with seats for eight Councilors, and a throne seat for the Mayor.

At the moment a large, or at least a broad, scrubwoman is busy with bucket and brush cleaning a floor "paved with something that makes all footsteps noisy, like stone flagging."

Peters is the first Councilor to arrive. He is "a brisk, nervous little man, spats, pressed trousers, bearded like Burgomaster Max of Brussels."

Councilman Peters thinks to put in the time while he awaits the assembling of his colleagues finding out from the scrubwoman, Mrs. Lopper, just how times are from her point of view. Mrs. Lopper, "with a face almost as large and expressionless as a plowed field," is frank to assure Councilman Peters that times are very hard indeed, especially for an old working woman. What she, what all the people want, is the good old times back again. She, for one, is sick of potatoes—potatoes and margarine, which is practically all the people have had since the war. What they want is ham and beer and the free spreads the Council used to give the voters at the shooting matches.

"You ask me what the people want," repeats Mrs. Lopper, and follows with a straight answer. "Kaiser or no Kaiser, republic or town council, or trades, union rates, or valuta, or treaties, or anything. What we want is to know if the good old times will ever come back."

Councilman Peters cannot promise the good old times back,

and if he can't, insists Mrs. Lopper, the rest of it "has no more taste in it than potatoes."

But, if the Councilors can make no such promise, insists Peters, neither can the Communists, led by the impossible delegate, Maxim. Nor can Captain Ritter. And since neither of these prophets can help the people it is, thinks the Councilor, a villainous thing for them to go about stirring the people up.

It is Mrs. Lopper's idea that Captain Ritter is the only one of them who really wants to help. No man can call him a villain. An officer and a gentleman born, a hero whom the Councilor himself, and the Mayor, took pride in seeing the Kaiser decorate —Captain Ritter is no villain and no disturber.

"Do you still believe in the Bible and the Holy Book of Daniel, Mr. Councilor?" demands Mrs. Lopper. "That says, 'The latter days shall come to pass.' I believe *that's* what it's all about. What it's all about *is* that the likes of the Captain are part of it. There's something queer about most of the veterans, as they call them. As to *what* sort of people they are, that's one thing. Those who started young and went right through, what's left of them don't match the times. They are not up to date, like Communists and Capitalists."

Now two other Councilmen have arrived—Thomas, "with a thick neck and a blood pressure," and Kraus, "a depressed whiskered individual." Mrs. Lopper gathers her buckets together and leaves them.

Arriving in ones and twos, engaging in much excited conversation, the Council gathers quickly, and is quickly organized. At the Mayor's suggestion the reading of the minutes is dispensed with and the report of Councilman Kraus asked for. Councilman Kraus is unhappy to report that despite every influence he could bring to bear a majority of the Council had, as the Mayor knows, decided to receive a delegation of the workers. Furthermore, it is understood that the delegation will include one Captain Ritter, who certainly does not belong in it.

Immediately the Council is in tumult. It will not hear anything from Captain Ritter, "that imbecile"; neither Ritter nor the Communists. In the midst of which the delegation of workers, headed by Ritter, has pushed its way past the attendant at the door and stands more or less deferently facing the agitated Council.

They are six in number. "Ritter is a specimen of that practically extinct breed, never very common in Germany, the officer and gentleman. As it is only two years after the war, he is still youngish. He is wearing a field gray tunic, worn but well cut, as the veterans did in Germany for a long while after the war."

Katie Tauler, standing next to Ritter, "is very young but will never now be an old maid. She wears a tight silk bodice, which displays almost innocently part of her most desirable charms, an arty velveteen skirt, trench boots. A little studio Bolshevik on active service of the cause, who has the cause, Marxianism, ambulance driving, jazz, pajama parties (it is 1920) love and women's votes all mixed up and exciting. At the present moment she is in love with Ritter. But a few months ago she was the free companion of Maxim.

"Maxim is so icily cold he sometimes appears burning hot. He wears an extremely badly cut, evilly woven coat and trousers of some substitute for cotton. A fountain pen protrudes like an ill-chosen ornament on his breast. He wears a Latin Quarter Red tie and carries a wide-brimmed black hat.

The others are Doctor Levy, "the editor of the local moderate Socialist *Workman's Friend,* a threadbare, short-sighted journalist, bony and ill-nourished, with a very poor complexion"; Rubens, a blacksmith, "naturally wide in the shoulder, with terribly impressive hands, which do not symbolize his essentially sentimental weak and incorrigibly pious trick of phrase," and Pepper, an "old, haggard miner," dressed, as is Rubens, "as abominably as any poor," just as they come from dirty work.

The Mayor addresses the workers. It has been agreed by vote, he says, to receive them. It is the Council's desire to keep closely in touch with the working part of the Community. The government, the Fatherland, has been forced, in these disastrous times, to ask for hard sacrifices, and it is the regrettable duty of the Council—

"Just a moment, Mr. Mayor," interrupts Ritter, in an eager, loud, distinct voice; "we have not exactly come to listen, but to give you a message."

The Council is disturbed. Several are shouting. Ritter is a bandit, shouts one. He should, insists Councilor Kraus, be ashamed of himself; a member of one of the most respected families, with such a father as he had, to try deliberately to bring blood and ruin on his home community!

"You are a rat of your class," shrills Councilor Jung.

"What class is that?" retorts Ritter.

JUNG—If this is a question of capital and labor, how are you standing where you are?

RITTER—You forget, Jung, my father, unlike you, was stupid enough to put his whole fortune into patriotic loans. You can't say I am a capitalist.

JUNG (*firmly*)—How can it be that you, an officer in such a regiment as the Third Royal—I don't know how many times decorated—should so lose your sense of decency as to stand where you are?

RITTER—One word: that's all, Jung, and you, Mayor, since the war ended I have seen where my duty lies as clearly as I did in the war.

KRAUS (*intervening, hissingly*)—Rather different company, eh, Captain? Instead of the trenches, bumming coffee from house to house of your father's servants—instead of those who were your equals, officers of breeding, creatures like that beside you.

RITTER (*sneering back and exchanging a contemptuous smile with* MISS TAULER)—You mean Comrade Tauler, the duly accredited representative of the Women Workers' Council?

KRAUS—Yes, your fellow worker. Your secretary, isn't she?

KATIE TAULER—We are mated together, if that's your meaning, and it interests you.

KRAUS (*more and more vigorous*)—You, a Ritter, slumming with a draggle tail.

PETERS (*first Councilor*)—Oh, order, Mr. Mayor. What's the decency or sense in all this?

JUNG—Shut your mouth, Peters.

MAYOR (*at last*)—Silence. This is my ruling. First we hereby communicate to you, without entering into any further discussion of your qualifications to represent the workers, trusting you to communicate it to them in the honorable desire for pacification, that the Emergency Law on Pay and Hours goes into operation at once within this district. This is no time to stand on forms. For God's sake, for your country's sake, for all of our sakes, try to get them to take it as it should be taken, as a sacrifice imposed by absolute necessity alone, and the whole economic ruin of the country.

MAXIM (*coldly*)—In short, half pay and twelve-hour day.

MAYOR (*earnestly*)—For a period of from ten to fifteen years. Now, again this is no time to stand on form. I take it on myself to say we will listen to anyone of you except Mr. Maxim and Captain Ritter, whose qualifications to be heard are disputed.

LEVY (*making a retort which no one except* MISS TAULER *smiles or nods at*)—Anything to say before sentence of death is pronounced, eh?

Photo by White Studio, New York.

"OVERTURE"

General: ". . . Take the female prisoner to the window and show her what death is."

(*The girl, Barbara Robbins; the General, Carlos Zizold*)

BLACKSMITH RUBENS (*steps forward and starts, with a suggestion in his tone of the preacher, that is, with anxiety coated with oil*)—Mr. Mayor and all comrades and Councilors, we, the people, I mean, most earnestly beg to request that this law be not carried out. We've all read about how the capitalists, I mean, the government, says it is necessary. But you know now in all fairness—Doctor Levy will tell you better than I that it is not at all that this law is necessary. Things have been much exaggerated. As each one of you know, figures can be twisted to mean anything. So, for God's sake, don't give slavery, and what is more, half pay. Do you know what that means to a decent working man's family at present? It is not too much to say that we are living in hard times, and if you strictly understand this is not a definite threat, we cannot and will not stand for this law. (*This has made no impression on anyone. But* PEPPER, *the knotted old tree of a miner, claps his hands vigorously, and shakes hands with* RUBENS. *Evidently a sort of a ritual.*)

MAYOR—Now, let us be quick.

PEPPER—I know you, Mr. Mayor, and I know you are not so bad as we say, unless you have changed, that is. Look here, Mr. Mayor, the people, they are just like a horse. Now you, the riders, always found it was a good horse, isn't that so? Answer me that. But didn't you, all these black years, load up that horse and work that horse, in winter and summer, late and early, all night, too, in a manner of speaking. Well, we miners say, and we are not threateners, not like those of the new pits (*turning to* MAXIM) not that I have anything against you or the Communists, Comrade. They do what they think right in the new towns out there, and we have our way of thinking. In fact, we think the old horse can work no further and no harder. Lawful rest and lawful corn is what it must have. (*A pause, looking for words.*) We've gone through the war, and these two years were worse than the war. No, we can't go through another fifteen years, still worse, there's no sense in that. Even a dog . . .

JUNG (*brutally*)—We are not talking about horses and dogs, but wages and hours.

MAYOR (*smoothly*)—Economic necessities, Mr. Pepper. Has anyone anything more to say?

MISS TAULER (*stepping up and blushing, delivers something she has evidently learnt by heart*)—Speaking before you, in this, your solemn meeting, I, as the accredited and elected representative of the Women's Workers' Council for health, reform and life, bring you our united message. A final message, indeed. We refuse and repudiate the monstrous and inequitable attempt to place new and unheard of burdens on the innocent and overcharged shoulders of . . . er . . . us, the working women, mothers, sisters and wives.

Miss Tauler is flushed of face as she finishes, but will accept no comfort from Maxim.

Now Ritter has taken the floor again, even against the clamor of the Councilors. Pushing out his chin defiantly he moves toward the window. Facing them he opens the window and the excited murmur of the crowd below bursts upon them. The Mayor, Kraus, move to stop him, but he is already addressing the crowd. Some cannot hear. "Speak up!" they shout.

RITTER (*louder*)—That is not much use. You know, all of you, that your delegates met. As a matter of fact we stayed together all night. (*A roar of idiotic laughter and cheers.*) We decided—(*jerkily, yet firmly*) to present a solemn protest. And solemn *warning* (*silence*) to these people, these poor people here. After all, they are to be pitied, too. (*With finger.*) They do not understand with what dreadful, stern and unconquerable forces—they in their miscalculation have opposed themselves. People! People! People! these men who think they are so cunning, and who in business anyway, are so calculating, have made a terrible mistake. They have had the simplicity, the ignorance, the madness, to imagine that the old, beautiful, powerful things are quite dead. That there is no longer any force of life in those great things—justice, liberty, justice. If the cunning man leaps too far, he misses his goal and falls into—stark folly. They have pushed cynicism too far. They have done a mad thing. This wicked law of theirs (*throws his hand at Council, particularly aimed at* MAYOR, *who brushes his face absently*) is above all a stupid law. (*Voice rises almost to a shout.*) What, is it possible, I do not say for an intelligent man, but for a cunning man so to delude himself as to think that the people, that deep and fundamental humanity, the reservoir of all civilization, all history and all social possibility can be used, at the will of a few privileged individuals, as if it were a mere natural source of power, and not the holiest and most venerable part of mankind? As it most certainly is, I swear it.

KRAUS (*quietly*)—You scoundrel.

RITTER (*looking at him, very loftily*)—I give you back the word you have chosen yourself. Scoundrels, do you think you can not only mock, not your unhappy God, but the people? Do you think that after we have suffered the war, when you have drained our blood in gallons, in metric tons, you can furthermore, without punishment or the slightest practical difficulty, now reduce us to slavery? People— (*a formidable roar*) their law kindly, most benevolently states that—it—is—only for fifteen years. Shall I answer them? (*Piercing cries and deep protests.*) I tell them, not for fifteen years, not for ten years, not for one single year. Even such few days as we had to spare, that they could swindle us out of, are gone to the last minute.

MAYOR (*coolly*)—Well, get it out of you as fast as you can.

RITTER (*answering sneer for sneer*)—Don't fret, Mr. Mayor, we will make it all quite clear and short to you. (*Dropping his voice.*) This is our answer to you. (*Raising it again.*) Go and burn your law in hell. We are going to live.

MAYOR (*interjecting loud enough to be heard outside, and getting up nonchalantly and approaching the speaker*)—Of *course;* who says no to that?

RITTER (*with a lofty smile*)—We are going to live free, do you hear? If we starve, we starve, free men. If we die, we die . . . (*Renewing surge of voices.*) "Allow me to present to you his worship, the Mayor." (*Billowing of crowd. Distinguishable shouts of Old Paunch. A woman is screaming, "Bellyful, bellyful." Evidently a nickname. Another voice, raucous and trembling—"That is where the money goes. Untie your bag, let go the swag."* RITTER *sensationally changing his voice in the silence he has now induced suddenly with his hand.*) Mr. Mayor of this town, will you let me tell you what has been your mistake? Your greatest mistake? You have thought you could mock the people, once more. It cannot be done again, not so many times. Even a rat or a mouse could not be taken in so many times. We went to the war for you. All right. We left our brothers there, millions of them. All right. We left our arms and legs there. All right. You deceived us. The joke was at our expense. We paid. But now you have exceeded the bounds of possibility, excuse me, Mr. Mayor. You are now mocking at reality, and our answer is— (*Inaudible in roar.*) Liberty, justice, these are more real than the rows of figures in your check book. (MAYOR *makes a half tolerant, half contemptuous gesture.*) Our answer is then, no. But it is quite a long answer, a boring answer, do you hear? For tonight, tonight, tonight, do you hear, all of you—we, the people, robbed and abused, are coming to take our own. I advise you to keep out of our way.

Ritter is thoroughly aroused now. The sneers and jibes of Mayor and Council do not reach him. He is ready to meet them on any ground. The flag is hoisted! The fight for liberty and justice is again on! They had better run from it while they may.

"Who will meet me tonight and argue with these people like a soldier?" he demands. "Who is fond of his wife? Who has a sweetheart? Whose wife is justice? Whose sweetheart is liberty? Let's swear an oath here to have them out of it, or die this very night. That's all, Mr. Mayor, and honorable Councilors."

The Mayor dashes for the window in the hope of holding the crowd. He is greeted with gleeful shouts of his nickname "Paunchy!" and "Bellyful!" They invite him, dare him, to come down to them. "There are two or three obscene squawks of trumpets." Finally they decide to listen.

The Mayor appeals for understanding. The Council has, he says, explained to the people's delegation how reluctantly the Councilors were forced to pass along to them the government's decision that had been forced upon them. The Mayor is in hopes they will understand and that they will now depart peaceably to their homes.

Now Maxim, the Communist, has also pushed his way to the window. He is shouting to the people.

"Workers, come up and talk to him yourself!" he yells. "Yes, get a ladder! Come up! Come up!"

Katie adds her excited plea. There are answering calls from below. Ritter and Katie, their arms about each other, stand at the window enjoying the struggles of the people to get up. Soon they are able to reach out helping hands as the first of the mob, two flushed boys, reach the ledge of the window and jump into the room.

Gradually the pyramids at the window are built up with the hot and eager faces of those citizens who are able to make the climb. Having got that far they are at a loss just what to do next.

The Mayor and the Councilors are contemptuous, but a little frightened. Kraus keeps calling upon the Mayor to close the session. This the Mayor threatens to do. The Council has been fair with Ritter and his delegation, he says. Unless this fairness is respected the session will be closed.

Ritter admits the justice of the Mayor's attitude and good-naturedly urges the crowd back into the courtyard. Soon the window is closed again and a silence settles over the chamber that is strangely heavy. The Councilors are still staring at the workers' delegates with "implacable resentment, as if something unpardonable had passed between them."

The Mayor, recovering his equanimity, again turns upon Captain Ritter. The Mayor would know, if possible, exactly where Ritter stands and why he stands there. It is still a good deal of a mystery.

It is plain enough to Captain Ritter, however. It is not a question of idealism so much as it is one of common sense. The Captain had gone to war believing his Kaiser to be right. When he came back from the war he discovered that many things he had taken for granted were quite wrong. Particularly the caste spirit.

"The people ought to rule," insists Ritter.

"But we *are* the people," replies the Mayor.

"No, I mean the real people," explains Ritter; "the poor, the workers. The majority. If you had been about among them as I have these last years, Mr. Mayor (isn't that so, Comrade Tauler?), you realize that their right is not only legal and—by ordinary justice, but according to the very deepest justice. I find it hard to explain that. Now look here, I had a suspicion of it in the war, living and dying with the men, the rank and file. You, who had your own reasons for not taking an active part in the war, staying behind, munition work and all that, don't know what a chance you missed of seeing a frightfully important truth. You would have seen the people there face to face, and you would have seen, seen, mark you, with the evidence under your own eyes, how *good* they are. Generous, faithful. They and not us, and not you of the merchant and business class, are the salt of the earth. By that right the earth belongs to them. You see what I mean?"

The Mayor believes he does see, but it does not in any way change his convictions. What, he demands, of the present situation?

Well, in the present situation, Ritter declares it to be the right of the workers to be treated as brothers, and to share what there is to share with their so-called superiors. It is not communism, insists the Captain, certainly not communism as Comrade Maxim preaches it.

"I just want a plain, decent world of brotherly kindness to come out of all the past miseries and mistakes." Ritter is earnest in this belief. Nor is his threat to use force in behalf of the people a threat of armed revolution. He is, he believes, doing the just and the right thing in defending the Fatherland by defending the rights of the people.

The Mayor loses patience. Let Captain Ritter beware. The moment he offers armed resistance to the forces of law and order he is walking straight into a terrible trap. Even if he gain a temporary advantage the people will not be able to hold it. And in the end he will surely lose his life.

Now Maxim, the Communist, would have a word.

"Comrade Ritter has told you, quite right, quite true," says Maxim, "that before you of the capitalist class impose your last eccentricity of injustice on the working class you have always exploited mercilessly, there are a lot of things to happen. Now I tell you, Mayor, before your trap closes, that you boast about, a further considerable quantity of unpleasant things are going to happen. I suppose you to be hinting that you have troops up your sleeves. Some of our present class—traitor government's hired bandit troops, off-scourings of the old régime. Well now, even if you have, I too, speaking always in humble discipline, have troops at my disposal. It is the will of the Communist Party, to which I have the honor to belong, which now holds Celsenkirchen, Bochum, Essen and Dusseldorf on your west, that the oppressed proletariat of this town is not left at the mercy of an ignoble reprisal. Against your troops I set the Red Army."

"God, I wish you would do it," vehemently declares Jung.

In that statement of Maxim, the Mayor finds still greater reason why Captain Ritter should see on which side he belongs. Let him agitate to his heart's content. Let him set himself up for election if he will. That will give him an outlet for his emotions, and it will not be suicide. Soon the Council will be settling its accounts with Maxim. It would be unpleasant to have to destroy Ritter, too.

Ritter is still defiant. Let the Councilors either withdraw their proposal by nightfall or be prepared to see the people take over the control of affairs from their hands. And they had better hurry about making their decision, because the people are determined and it will be difficult to hold them in check.

With this defiance ringing in the ears of the Councilors, Ritter shepherds the workers' delegation toward the door. Maxim and Katie hold back long enough to light their cigarettes.

Now the workers are gone and the Mayor, the situation well in hand, faces his glumly attentive colleagues. For their private ears he has further information. His reason for taking the attitude toward the would-be revolutionists that he did is due to the fact that he has been officially informed that already there are four battalions of picked Government troops, Swastika battalions, already approaching the town. In Berlin, it would appear, the authorities are losing their tempers, and they are ready to intervene, firm and hard. The next town to go into revolt will in all probability be made an example of, and General von Hueffer will strike with all his energy. To any who recall von Hueffer's record before Amiens and the Canadian divisions that will mean much.

There is no doubt in the Mayor's mind that Captain Ritter will succeed in raising the population. Ritter is an officer of the first quality, a brave, even rash, leader and a tactician of unusual ability. There is also danger that Maxim may be able to bring over Red battalions from the neighboring towns. Still, the Mayor would discount the threat of Red intervention. At least the mob will not master the situation without a fight. That much the Mayor is prepared to promise. He also has a plan that he feels the Councilors would be wise to follow.

MAYOR—. . . I propose to you that we all leave town, this afternoon. It looks like being a very lovely afternoon. We will go each to his home after this meeting, and each will make his own arrangements. Personally I am getting my chauffeur to drive me and my wife with enough luggage for a week, eastwards possibly as far as Dresden where I understand all is perfectly quiet. Anyone who wishes to imitate my route will sooner or later come to General von Hueffer's lines. The town clerk downstairs in the office will make out passes, which I will sign before we leave the building. That is all, gentlemen.

JUNG (*musingly*)—It is running away, of course.

MAYOR (*sharply*)—A romantic conception, dear Jung. Things are going to be extremely unpleasant here. Now I feel it is more our real duty to go than to stay. But let everyone do as he pleases. Just one last detail. I will summon our small force of guardians of the police and give them their orders—for tonight. (*Rings. Attendant appears.*) George, tell the police lieutenant to come up with his squad. You will find them waiting in the Clerk's office. (*A silence.*)

JUNG—Are you going to let them—do their duty, too?

MAYOR (*earnestly misunderstanding on purpose*)—Mr. Jung, that is not my idea, though I can hardly honestly say I disapprove of it. I have been instructed that if there is to be any development at all, things are absolutely to be brought to a head. General von Hueffer will make no attempt to move towards a decision, unless the revolt is absolutely clear cut and flagrant.

Then only he will move. He will either fight or abstain. There are very obvious reasons for this also connected with the International situation and our disabilities under—the—er—Treaty—hum. That is, you understand, he will not bring his troops to act as simple police, to keep grumbling crowds circulating, to keep his men hanging about in an indefinite situation exposed to the moral and tactical disadvantages of a mere occupation. He brings with him not the Riot Act, but Martial Law, with all its rigors and all its solutions. It is to the advantage of ourselves and the town that he should come in, and lance the abscess once and for all. Is that not so? Of course, we hate the whole beastly business. Yet in the circumstances, as realists, we have only one course. Why, it is even forced upon us as administrators of the law.

JUNG—Then the police not only remain . . .

MAYOR—They not only remain, but they will have to protect this Municipal building. (*Enter six policemen, in uniform, with chests of medal ribbons. One or two of them limp. All are hard, decent, thin, quiet-looking veterans of the war. They stand uneasily at attention.*) Lieutenant.

LIEUTENANT—Yes, sir. (*Salutes and steps out.*)

MAYOR (*kindly*)—Lieutenant, I had you all up here because I have rather a bad job for all the lot of you.

LIEUTENANT (*frozen*)—Yes, sir.

MAYOR—Lieutenant, there may be an attack on this place tonight. The Workers' Delegation, Captain Ritter especially, made certain threats of it.

LIEUTENANT (*uncertainly*)—Captain Ritter, sir?

MAYOR (*passing on*)—Now these are your orders. You are soldiers, that is, ex-soldiers, aren't you?

LIEUTENANT—Yes, sir.

MAYOR (*firmly*)—Then take your orders. You are to get out the machine gun and all the ammunition. (*He pauses.*) Then you are to keep them at bay.

LIEUTENANT—Keep them at bay, sir?

MAYOR—Yes, keep them out.

LIEUTENANT—You mean fire on them, sir?

MAYOR—Now, Lieutenant, please understand, I don't want you to sacrifice yourself, or fight to the death exactly. You must put up a good show, that is all. I am afraid you must use your own discretion as to how far to push things. You ought to be able to keep them out altogether. If indeed they come. It is not at all certain they will come, Lieutenant.

LIEUTENANT (*considering*)—Yes, sir. (*After a pause.*) Will you be back of us, sir?

MAYOR—Yes, yes, we'll be back of you, never fear. Now go about it. (LIEUTENANT *salutes and exeunt.*) Anyone else desires to speak? No? (*Raps table.*) Then the meeting is adjourned. (*All rise and start chattering on way to door as curtain falls.*)

ACT II

The following morning the Council Chamber shows some results of a first engagement in which the workers have captured the town. Hardly one of the framed photographs of former mayors decorating the walls is without the mark of a shattering bullet hole.

Captain Ritter is seated in the Mayor's chair at the Councilor's table intensely absorbed in poring over stacks of papers. Diagonally across from him, so the light from the tall windows may fall upon her sewing, Katie Tauler is at work on a large red flag.

Ritter is much too busy to notice Katie. In fact, up to now, he has not realized that she is there, not having heard her come in. He is willing, however, once his attention is attracted, to stop working for a moment. When he had left her at four in the morning she was still dancing in the square.

Now, as Ritter stands back of Katie's chair, hands resting affectionately on her shoulders, he hears her praise of him as a quite wonderful man in a fight, one brave enough to face machine guns in the hands of police without flinching. All the others had ducked when the volleys were fired at them, or over their heads. All but Ritter. Even Comrade Maxim had ducked, though with a certain dignity.

It was with his looks and his voice, insists Katie, that Ritter had cowed the police, even though they had all the guns back of their sandbags on the balcony. It was not his eloquence. Probably they did not hear half he said. It was just the way he looked.

And now all the police are in the cellar with a Red guard over them. Decent fellows, Ritter insists. He plans to let them go as soon as he can explain to his other officers.

Katie would sew a gold star on her flag, but it is not a Soviet star. Ritter would not like that. This, he reminds Katie, is not a Bolshevist revolution they are fighting. Her star is a secret star, Katie explains. It stands for their own private evening star at which they gazed from the window of an inn the night that was the beginning of their romance.

It is a memory that Ritter also holds as rather precious. He would grab Katie now and tell her so, but she eludes him. She is eager to nail the flag she has sewn over the fireplace. He is too nervous to be of much help. The ladder shakes uncertainly, even when he tries to steady it for her, until she finally drops both hammer and nails and finds herself practically fallen into his arms.

RITTER—Surrender, surrender, Katie, or suffer the extreme penalty of martial law. (*He catches her and forces a kiss, knocking her cap off, carries her to the couch and stumbles on to it.*)

KATIE—You're crazy! For God's sake let me go! Let me go, I say! (RITTER *finally releases her.*)

RITTER—Say you're sorry.

KATIE—Sorry for what?

RITTER—Never mind about what. Insolence to a superior officer. (*Attacks her again, ruffling her hair.*) Say you're sorry, say you're sorry.

KATIE—I'm sorry, I'm sorry. All right, I'm sorry . . . (*She pulls down her dress. They sit side by side.*)

RITTER (*murmuring to her*)—Oh, Katie, the feel of your body in my arms, it always makes me quite drunk. It intoxicates me. There is some sort of magnetism in your skin that passes into me and sets me on fire all through.

KATIE (*locking her arms around his neck*)—Darling.

RITTER (*nearly panting*)—It works at a distance too, almost as strong. I remember as you stood near the window, that night of the star, and you were all marked out. All your nakedness.

KATIE—Oh, Karl, that night. The night air came and came into me like a mist. I have never known such sweetness when I felt your arms round taking me, when I did not notice your coming.

RITTER—You remember that silly short nightgown the innkeeper's daughter lent you?

KATIE—How burning hot the sheet seemed to be. It was so coarse, almost like a hair shirt.

RITTER (*almost stifles her and bares her shoulder, kissing it*)—Katie, it is forever, isn't it?

KATIE—Of course it is forever, silly boy. How would I live without you?

RITTER (*gravely and almost a trifle scared*)—Katie, I have

told you so often what you were to me. Every day it is stronger. Why, I believe that even the cause beside you is not really important in me. That is not quite right. I mean that the whole inner blood of the cause to me is just you. Why, I do believe (*wonderingly*) that if I had to choose between you and the cause —I would desert it without a second's wait. Isn't it dreadful to love so much? The danger of death is nothing to the danger of loving as we do. If you were to die or get lost somehow, I can't conceive how impossible everything in the world would be. You are my whole fortune in the world, I couldn't trust without you, or hope anything without you. There is no other value or meaning except when you are in my mind.

KATIE—Darling, I don't exist except when I feel your breath on me.

RITTER—I know how it is. You are the whole real self in me now. Do you know how I live, when I have to leave you for an hour or a minute? I have you with your fresh, scented little body just like that night, inside my head. There we are, yes, locked with our arms round each other, lying.

KATIE (*earnestly*)—Karl, I swear I will never leave you.

RITTER—Life or death?

KATIE—Life or death.

RITTER—You needed to swear.

KATIE—It does me good to swear it over and over. It puts a great peace in my mind. Forever and ever and ever, Karl. You swear too.

RITTER—I swear.

KATIE—Yes, but you are quite, quite certain? Oh, Karl, Karl.

RITTER—Come here closer and I will prove it much better.

KATIE—No, Karl, no, Karl (*feebly*), not here.

RITTER—Yes, yes, I must. My flesh and blood can't stand this love for you, the touch of you, the scent of you, your arms and neck . . .

KATIE—Karl . . . (*Scared.*) Karl, be careful, for God's sake. (*A noise at door. Hastily disengaging herself* KATIE *goes to ladder again and pretends to be busy.*)

The interruption is by Levy, the journalist. He is wearing a derby hat and he carries a rifle. On his arm is a red flannel band. Levy has just come from the office of his newspaper. There is a new deal there, too. The paper he has just issued is to be No. 1 of the *New Era*.

As the rest of the delegates arrive they are all carrying rifles and all are decorated with the red arm band. Maxim is among them. Ritter insists, with a wave of his hand, that Maxim shall take the Mayor's chair.

Ritter is ready with his report. Following the tragedy, or comedy, of last night's victory he has stationed his outposts. The motor service has been organized and every member of the defense corps has been ordered to fall in on parade at 11 o'clock. As for arms, they have the 150 rifles contributed by their Communist brothers, through Comrade Maxim; there are many revolvers and the arms seized from the police. Everything is in order. The main thing is now to know when Comrade Maxim's troops may be expected to arrive.

As for that Comrade Maxim is not certain. There are one or two matters to be settled first. Most important of these is the disposition of the captured police. What is to be done with them?

So far as Captain Ritter is concerned the police are to be set free, "with a present of mixed kicks on the behind."

In that case Comrade Maxim regretfully reports that no assistance whatever can be expected from his Communist brothers. He will recommend that they stay where they are.

"Unless those six yellow dogs, sworn enemies of the cause of their own class—they serve the capitalist régime, you know—are taken out within the next hour and given their deserts, I and my party reluctantly wash our hands of this enterprise," announces Maxim.

Whether the police shall be shot or hanged matters little to the Comrade, so long as they are destroyed. War is war, and revolution is revolution—a hundred times as serious as war. "There is no place for comic opera romanticism in it," announces Maxim, and continues with vehemence:

"What do you expect me to do? Trudge behind you with a guitar on the quest of the Holy Grail? Now listen, Ritter, you are playing at a grim game and we, the united proletariat, are in no mood for joining you. We have a program; you have none. We have a technique, the only one, which is terror."

"I know the use of terror," answers Ritter. "I use it to conquer an enemy in arms."

MAXIM (*indulgently—as if speaking to an intelligent child*)—You would pitilessly exterminate an enemy as long as he held his rifle?

RITTER—Of course. I am a soldier, unlike you, Mr. Maxim.

MAXIM—Just so. And spare him when he surrenders. Just

so. Well, if that is war, mind I do not admit, on your word, for perhaps it was owing to some miscomprehension, some generous miscomprehension that you ended as a Captain and not a General. Then, well, revolution works just the opposite. We are scientists, not poets, sir. We kill those of our enemies in our power, pitilessly and sometime perhaps we know how to yield to those arms that are superior. In short, we have the will to win, at any cost. Now you? (RITTER *says nothing, thinking.* MAXIM *continues.*) Now I am not afraid to call this an ultimatum. For a start, abolish those police. Then we shall see. I will then bring up a certain number of Red Guards under my own leadership of course. Probably later I shall issue orders to abolish such bourgeois as are left behind, in carefully dosed batches.

RITTER—Yes, wholesale massacres. I don't understand you. But you don't understand me. You even said I had no program. I thought we had the same, but anyhow here's mine. I will fight —fight, I said, for decency. For four years I did that. I know now I was wrong. The cause of the people is the only decent one. I fight for justice, liberty, fair dealing . . .

MAXIM—Words! You have the distinction, permit me to tell you, to have gone more brilliantly and magnificently astray than anyone I have ever known. Justice? A bourgeois comparison. Liberty. Worse. Fairness—not even a healthy bourgeoise concept. Let me correct you. The people, the real class-conscious proletariat want your ideals no more than they want the economic system of the capitalists you are kindly helping to destroy. First we want the blood of the bastards, do you understand that? Then when they have drunk and bathed in that essence of reality, blood, we will reshape the world. I even believe you would commit suicide in the strange beauty of the world we are going to create, Captain. But never mind about that. I am no schoolmaster for charming boys. Will you let me baptize your infant revolution with terror and fright, make your mob of amateur rioters into strong, steel men? Or—

LEVY (*very distressed and frightened*)—Or?

MAXIM (*settling back again, absently*)—Nothing, Doctor Levy.

A boy comes to report, confusedly, that one Schmidt and his gang are everywhere running into soldiers moving in. A distressingly unsoldierlike report that irritates Captain Ritter considerably. He will himself investigate. And be back for supper, he smiles at Katie, as he leaves.

The delegates are restless and troubled with Ritter away. But they will stick with him, and nothing the sneering Maxim can say changes them. Maxim turns then to Katie. Surely these workers have not taken her in with their "misty, hazy, flouey, sugar foam stuff." He would take Katie to a place he knows, "the foxes' den," and talk things over with her. Just talk. Of course Maxim understands, as Katie prompts him, that the rest is all finished between them.

"Don't worry, you fellows," Comrade Maxim calls, as he and Katie leave the delegates; "any reënforcements that blasted Mayor can send up here Ritter will deal with . . . Why, at the very worst he would hypnotize them all like he did the machine gunner last night . . . Don't worry!"

But the delegates *are* worried. Levy is certain of his feelings. He is firmly on the side of Ritter. Pepper is not so sure that the workers need either Maxim or Ritter. Rubens, the blacksmith, is disturbed by the thought that both Ritter and Maxim want bloodshed. Rubens doesn't want blood. He had rather submit to the new laws than shed blood.

Levy would remind them that there are some things more precious than life. Liberty and justice, for example.

"Comrade Maxim misinterpreted, I feel certain, the real philosophy of the Communists, Lenin anyway," declares Levy. "The cause of the people in all its forms, from the moderately left position I and my paper have always unswervingly taken up, is always founded on justice, after all; a purer rather than a different concept than that of some of our middle class thinkers. All, in fact."

The argument is still on as the curtain falls.

Hours later, in the Council Chamber, Levy, Rubens and Pepper are crowded around Katie Tauler, reading a printed slip she has laid on the table. The men have rifles slung over their shoulders. There are signs to indicate that there has been fighting.

The suspicion is confirmed by the arrival of Captain Ritter. His uniform is muddy and torn. His head is roughly bandaged with a dirty piece of sheet. He is carrying his rifle, and is plainly excited.

Ritter's excitement, it transpires, is due to the defeat his citizens' army has suffered, a complete and ignominious defeat in which most of his fighting men had turned and run like rats at the first sight of the enemy. The ambulances likewise had driven off hurriedly with all the nurses, spilling Katie out near the canal.

It was from the canal that she had fished the paper she has brought in with her. It had been dropped from an airplane. The paper is still wet, but they can make it out. It is an order from General Conrad von Hueffer demanding that four leaders of the revolution shall be delivered up without arms immediately. Otherwise there will be a bombardment and a house to house visitation. Two hours after sundown anyone found with arms will be shot out of hand. This is no bluff, Ritter agrees, unless "Wolfy" von Hueffer has changed completely since the war.

There is not much time, but Ritter thinks there is enough to permit the carrying out of his plan. Let them start immediately blowing up the mines and send word to von Hueffer that the destruction will stop when his soldiers withdraw.

Pepper is all against that. The mines are the people's work. Maxim is also opposed. "The instruments of production are sacred," shouts he; "they belong to me, to the people."

All right, agrees Ritter, if they will have it, let them cut cards to see which four shall remain as hostages. Or toss coins. They are all in it, except Katie. Ritter draws the line at Katie.

First place Ritter assigns himself, as leader, without consent. That leaves three to fill. Levy is the second to volunteer. Only Rubens, the blacksmith, is panic-stricken with the thought that all four will likely be shot.

Now Katie has insisted that she will stay with Ritter, whatever comes. And Maxim. Ritter twits Maxim into joining the four. Surely, he, too, would be a leader! Maxim makes the fourth, to the hysterical relief of Rubens.

"Now the rest of you clear out like hell," seriously advises Ritter. "If you can find anyone who has the guts to go under a flag of truce to tell what makes you happy, do so. It will probably save you a shell in your bedroom tonight. I know old Hueffer."

Still, Rubens thinks the people would feel safer if there was a written confession of some sort, something set down in black and white.

Levy dictates the paper and Ritter writes it. "We, the undersigned four leaders, under the terms imposed by General von Hueffer declare ourselves solely responsible for what has happened to the exclusion of any other person—"

Rubens will be the messenger. He will get the paper to the general himself if possible. He is fawningly grateful to the volunteers.

"You are dying for the holy cause of the people," he assures them.

"We're not dying for you, you dirty coward," answers Katie.

They push Rubens out of the room. The four are alone now—Ritter, Katie, Maxim and Levy. But not for long. Maxim decides suddenly to withdraw.

RITTER (*half contemptuous again*)—Do you mean you are going to run?

LEVY (*hysterically*)—You would be a coward and buy your life with those of those thousands of poor devils?

MAXIM—I am going, if that is what you mean. Surely I explained my way of thinking to you. But come now, hurry. Don't let us indulge in any romantics. Are all of you coming with me? Are you, Ritter? (RITTER, *no answer, kissing his girl greedily and tenderly.*) Katie, are you coming? Katie, don't be crazy. Come along with me. (*Commandingly.*) If you were ever in earnest about the revolution, if any of you were not playing at love for the people, come. Can't you see that that and that only is the way to win?

RITTER—Katie, you had better go. I love you forever, truest death and life friend.

KATIE—I am adoring you.

MAXIM (*stiltedly*)—It is my duty, as I conceive it, to say you are playing into the hands of the reaction. The people? Those cowards and traitors? They are no good. The people we must die for are the people of the future. Come on now. I can put you all safe for days, until my friends smuggle us out. Then, Ritter, you will fight another battle, with another sort of troops.

RITTER—You are quite right, Maxim, I put things, some things, above even the revolution and the people.

MAXIM (*bitterly calm*)—Those things are bourgeoise sentimentality. (*No one answers.* LEVY *wipes his glasses. In a sudden harsh scream.*) Come on, you damn fools. There's no time. (*Another shaking of the place, rattling of the window, roar, and high from the distance. The electricity dims, as it does at a lightning flash.* LEVY *goes and sits down heavily on the couch. The two go towards the window. No one notices* MAXIM. *Talking to an audience in the air.*) They are not fools. They are ghosts, creatures of a superstitious fairy tale. (*Checks himself.*) Well, you can't be expected to see that. Good-by, Levy. Good-by, Ritter. (*They each shake hands stiffly.* KATIE *refuses.*) May I say that I honor your behavior very highly? You can't see my point, but I see yours. We must find a substitute for romanticism when we remake the world for the workers. It is a great force. (*The door closes.* LEVY *on couch. A faint echo of a march by a regimental band draws the two to the window.*)

KATIE—Do you see? The soldiers are marching in. (*From now onward there is an accompaniment, with pauses of band music through the night, as detachment after detachment of the invaders approach in the distance, fade out of earshot, and are followed by others. Old nostalgic march tunes. Squeezing* RITTER'S *hand as he gazes meditatively—listening.*) Poor old Levy wants you to say something to him. (RITTER *goes over to* LEVY, *leaving* KATIE.)

LEVY (*stretching himself out as if he was ill*)—I can't face execution. You don't know how brutality—to be tied and stared at and battered—shocks me. It makes me sick.

RITTER—Do you mean to say you are going to go with Maxim? I don't want to put pressure on you, but you know what that means to the poor devils in this town. Von Hueffer . . .

LEVY (*without the least resentment*)—I am not going to run. It is a question of the manner of death that appalls me most.

RITTER—Yes. A man can choose his own way of dying for his ideal. Yes, Levy. (RITTER *goes slowly back to the window.* KATIE *and he stand side by side with their fingers entangled.*)

KATIE—The music is coming back again. (*Pause.*) Why, there must be thousands of them. (*A lilting unmistakable tune rather louder than any that have passed before.*)

RITTER—That's the fortieth regiment march past. I wonder if those are the boys who got my ear. (*Dabs at it ruefully.*) I used to have a lot of friends in that regiment. They were a fine crowd till they went to the Eastern front. The new ones are not the same quality. None of the old discipline. Therefore, none of the old dash. I suppose all the best men have been dead these five years. The best are always unlucky, have you noticed? I sometimes think it is a sort of slur on me that I was left. (*Laughing.*) Well, I've gained whole years on them all anyway, years of days . . . and nights. (*They look at each other and embrace.*)

There is a rumbling that indicates the tanks are coming in. Tanks are a kind of hobby with Captain Ritter. They do not frighten him as they do many soldiers. Give him a few sticks of dynamite and one or two determined fellows and he knows a way of dealing with the brutes . . .

Now Katie is feeling frightened, too, at the thought of death. Ritter would comfort her, too, as he has comforted Levy.

"Being frightened has no sense, my little star," he says to her with gentle persuasiveness. "It is not as if we were going to live forever. That is how I see it always. Why, to hear people like Maxim—and they call themselves hard realists—you would think that death meant the loss of the certainty of a million years of bliss, instead of five or six,—more or less drab. Is it not romantic to see that, and to accept it at a glorious moment? When my men ran away this afternoon, Katie, it wasn't death that frightened me but a stupid, meaningless ugly life. Just think now here together we are not being caught, but escaping. No more worry about who's right, who's wrong, no more fear of sickness, or betrayal or fatigue. Why, think, Katie, some of those fellows that left us will die of cancer some day. No more getting old. To die like this knowing I am loved, is my eternal compensation for all my work, all my suffering. All the cold and marching of my life. My blessed little child.

KATIE (*dreamily*)—Go on, my darling. I am not frightened now.

RITTER—You see, it is in a sort of way godlike to be dead. "For the nature of the gods must ever of itself enjoy repose supreme." It goes on: "Through endless time, far withdrawn from all concerns of living men, free from all our pains, free from all our perils, strong in the resources of our own." How is it? Yes, "needing naught." Needing naught but each other, my little cat. (*Eagerly, as if urging her to something good.*) You see, my Katie, it can only be one of two things. Socrates said that, I remember, in my last year of high school—and it's honest iron common sense, do you see? It's either sleep. Dreamless sleep. I will sleep with you in my arms, the curves of your body fitting into me, as we used to do. My hands forever holding your breasts, and no sun or cockcrows to disturb us. Why, I could step straight into such a bed this moment. (*Kisses.*)

KATIE—Millions of years in a dreamless bed.

RITTER—Millions of years? More than that, more than that. Billions and billions of years, even after the sun gets cold again, and the earth freezes. Even when our star itself flickers out from old age, we shall have only started our night together.

KATIE—Oh, my darling, our dust will all mix up together if they bury us in the same— (*hesitates at the word "grave"*) earth.

RITTER—Or else, listen Katie, this is even better. There may be something else. I would never say it before all those people. Their minds are closed. I believe there *may* be something else. That makes me so happy. I can hardly express it. If there are other worlds, which will we live in forever as we are now? Do you like the sea? We never saw the sea together. Why, there might be vast oceans to come, and forests, and clearings, where, when we want to rest from traveling, we can live in forever, and love.

While Ritter is talking Levy has twisted himself around until he has reached the revolver in his pocket. Now there is a report and as Katie screams suddenly, sharp and shrill, Levy falls half off the sofa, dead.

Ritter has "pulled the body out, straight and decent," and covered it with his officer's tunic, when there is a great clattering on the stairs. The doors are thrown violently open and through them bursts Rubens, the blacksmith, "panting as though he were suffocating with the effort."

One glance at the room adds to Rubens' panic. Where is Levy? Where is Maxim? Do they realize what it means to the people if von Hueffer's demands are not complied with?

"They won't count as carefully as you, blacksmith," Ritter promises the craven one.

They are waiting the coming of the guard. Katie is again beset with fears of death. Nor can Ritter comfort her.

"There is something eating away at me, inside, in my head," pleads Katie; "like a disease making me live. Even if I grow old, even with a cancer. Oh, can't you see that it is a cancer, this life that won't let me die? I'm horrible, I'm vile, I'm rotten with fear. Do you hear? I must live, even with a cancer. Even if I'm alone for evermore!"

Suddenly the doors are flung open with a crash. One huge soldier leads others into the room, pushing and cuffing Rubens before him. A youngish officer follows the group. In his hand he has Rubens' paper.

From the paper the officer counts off the names. Ritter, Tauler—a woman; Levy, Maxim? Where are Levy and Maxim? They show him Levy's body. Maxim, Ritter explains, signed the paper but is not there. Who is the man Rubens, the Lieutenant wants to know. Just nobody, Ritter answers. Rubens continues to plead hysterically for his life and to blubber openly.

"We'll have to look into this business about Maxim," declares the Lieutenant. "The General wanted him more particularly.

(*After hesitation.*) Well, take him out, Sergeant, and throw Mr. Nobody downstairs as hard as you like."

Katie is sent to the guardroom, though she clings to Ritter until the soldier forces them apart.

The Lieutenant and Ritter are alone.

"Hello, Ritter," says the officer, as though he was seeing his prisoner for the first time. "You remember me?"

The curtain falls.

ACT III

It is early morning. Captain Ritter and the Lieutenant have apparently spent a good part of the night debating the virtue of such military tactics as were displayed in the recent engagement between the soldiers and the citizen mobs. There are guards back of Ritter's chair, at the door.

It is Ritter's contention that von Hueffer's position was really weaker than his and that, given a few hundred, even a small handful, of his old troops he (Ritter) could have easily beaten the General and his so-called trained men.

Nor would the tanks that von Hueffer held in reserve have stopped Ritter. He knows how to handle those "fancy agricultural machines" quite effectively. True, psychologically von Hueffer had the better of the argument. The citizen army was not, in fact, anything of which a military man could boast. Citizen armies never are.

"The people are not much good as soldiers, and that is a fact," Ritter admits.

"Rats!" agrees the Lieutenant. "Guts to them is something like a rifle—a weight to throw away so they can run faster."

"Well, I didn't run, and I'm the people," objects Ritter.

"You the people be damned!" replies the Lieutenant, with some heat. "You are simply a proof of what I always say. That the working class have no heart, no guts, unless they are officered by us."

Nevertheless, Ritter still contends that if he had only fifty, or a hundred, men of the old sort he would have chased von Hueffer and all his soldiers as far back as the suburbs of Berlin. In fact, he thinks he could have done it with old Guttman, and Schmidt, and a couple of tough Pomeranian fellows!

There is a clatter of arms, the guards come to attention and General von Hueffer enters the room. He is "tailored, undecorated, wears a black monocle; an ascetic, old face, resembling portraits of old von Moltke." In the midst of the squad of soldiers following him is Katie Tauler.

The General has taken his place in the Mayor's chair, the guard is put at ease. Ritter tries to wave encouragement to Katie, but her eyes are fixed on the ground and she is hedged in by her guard.

General von Hueffer would have Ritter know that in this unpleasant business he would shed the minimum of blood. But so far as Ritter is concerned there is but one course for him to pursue. Ritter, as an officer and as a leader, will have to go. Also the six policemen. Ritter did them a bad service, the General insists, in distracting them from their duty. Nor will he listen to Ritter's plea that he and not the policemen was responsible.

The formal cross-examination is brief. Karl Ritter, over thirty, an officer in the reserve, an ex-captain in the Third Royal, disbanded . . . charged with revolution and incitement to ditto . . . admits the charges . . . refuses to name accomplices . . . and would, asked if he has anything to say, add, "Long live the people; long live the cause," but that is officially stricken out.

To the indictment is added: "Sentence confirmed and duly carried out by shooting, six o'clock, seventh, sixth 1921." The General signs the paper.

General von Hueffer turns to Katie Tauler. Katie meets his first queries with spirited rejections. His men, she says, would not write down the things she would wish to say to him.

"Just a minute, just a minute, Miss Tauler," the General interrupts, and continues in a wheedling tone, "I wish to spare all unpleasantness, but I must do my duty. You both understand that. (*Sincerely.*) A horribly unpleasant duty. I have to put aside all personal consideration for my own feelings. Now, er, my duty is to ask you the same question, as I have asked Captain Ritter. (*Claps hands together and then flicks finger at her. Slowly, says:*) Do you, Miss Tauler, know the present address of Maxim?"

"Refuses," Ritter answers for her, before the guard can silence him.

Von Hueffer is not discouraged. He would remind Miss Tauler that there has been gossip connecting her name with that of Maxim. She did know him, did she not?

Katie admits that she knew Maxim very well at one time; that he was kind to her and that their relations were altogether pleasant until she left him for the man who was her real lover; the lover who had lifted her to heights she never knew existed; the Karl Ritter with whom she is prepared to die.

It is Katie's boast, now that she has found her tongue, that however the General may sneer, there is as much that is fine and heroic in the make-up of a modern woman as there was in the women of an older day; modern women are made of sterner stuff; they know the rights of love and hold them sacred; they hold that the finest things are not subject to law, which Katie remembers as one of Karl's finest sayings. Karl is the finest talker in the world, Katie assures General von Hueffer; beside him Maxim was only glittering and cold; between her love for Karl, the sort of thing a person dies for, and the passing fancy that held her to Maxim, there is a million years of distance.

GENERAL—Yet you talk about dying. I may be densely old-fashioned, but I have always believed that the object of love was to live and not to die.

KATIE—When you have such memories as we have had together, Karl and I, the only thing to do not to be false to such beauty is to die. The travels we've seen together. The woods. The evenings, and moon rises and dawns. The talks all day. The long walks fighting together, against the poor people's ignorance, for the cause, visiting them in their homes, being given their trust.

GENERAL—Why, after all you speak of them very kindly, seeing they deserted you both in the final hour. Excuse me saying so, basely deserted you.

KATIE—I suppose what you say is true. I did feel bitter about it. But now that I have taken the great decision, all that seems very far away from me.

GENERAL—But all the same to die—you so young. It is such a waste, all your life before you.

KATIE—Oh, I have thought about all that.

GENERAL—I quite understand your viewpoint. If it was necessary. The only beautiful deaths are necessary ones. Otherwise it is a waste.

KATIE—But it is necessary. You have decided to kill us.

GENERAL—Not if you give me Maxim's address.

RITTER—She doesn't know Maxim's address.

KATIE—I don't know it, and I wouldn't give it to you if I did know it. We have decided.

GENERAL—Yes, still I am convinced. I have special reason to know that you do know it. My dear young lady, allow me just to plead with you not to throw your life stupidly away. You know death is a very shocking and awful thing. A very ugly thing. (KATIE *looks at him mutely.*) You think of death too much in the abstract. You have thought of dying like—like Juliet died, or like Romeo. In a matter of fact, that would be nothing. But death by being ignobly executed . . . Firmly I am going to give you a look at real death. It is cruel perhaps to do so. But I only have a choice of two cruelties. (KATIE *is already uneasy and looks around desperately.*)

RITTER—General . . .

GENERAL—Excuse me, Ritter, it is you that are at fault, not me. You are going quietly to allow this girl, this very charming and beautiful girl, to die. I am going to rip the deceptive veils from—what is coming—so that she can at any rate see clearly what it is she has chosen. (*Turning to* OFFICER.) What time is it?

OFFICER (*reading from wrist watch*)—Nearly five, sir, three minutes to five. (*There is a trampling of iron-shod feet somewhere in the courtyard.*)

GENERAL—I fancy you must be a little slow. I ordered those six to be shot at five precisely.

RITTER—Poor devils.

GENERAL—Yes, Captain, poor devils, and I am anxious that Miss Tauler here shall not be a poor devil, in precisely the same way. I am trying to save her life. Do you dare try to stop me? (RITTER *lowers his head with a deeply worried frown and makes no answer.*) Sergeant. (SERGEANT *salutes.*) Take the female prisoner to the window and show her what death is. I fancy, Miss Tauler, you are not quite, quite fully aware of what your decision really means.

RITTER (*hoarsely and anxiously*)—General, sir, she does not know the address.

GENERAL—That would be a great pity for her. Take her over, Sergeant.

The tall Sergeant has grabbed Katie in his long arms and is carrying her to the window against her shrill protests. Ritter calls excitedly to her not to look.

From below the sound of men marching across the courtyard. The condemned, the Sergeant reports, have been lined up. Muffled cries of "Mother!" and "God!" mingle with the orders of the officers.

The General has leaped to his feet and is pounding the table.

"Hurry, hurry, hurry!" he shouts, excitedly. "Make her look, Sergeant!"

The Sergeant forces his hands under Katie's chin and lifts her head. Suddenly she jerks her head away, her eyes starting and staring with morbid curiosity. There is a volley. Katie screams and covers her eyes. One of the men is writhing on the ground; the volley had failed to kill him.

"They didn't hit the last one, not properly," the Sergeant reports.

"Didn't I tell you, Hofmann," shouts Ritter, his voice hard and unnatural; "didn't I tell you! They are not soldiers! They are nothing but . . . nothing but a miserable band of—plow hands—and station loafers!"

Katie Tauler turns from the window and fixes her gaze on General von Hueffer. Slowly and deliberately, refusing to look at Captain Ritter, she walks to the table and faces the General.

"Well, what do you want?" she demands, coldly.

"Give me Maxim's address."

"If I tell you will you let me go? Will you let us both go?"

"No, my dear, only you."

The Sergeant has closed the window, shutting out the noises from the court. There is an intense silence. Then Katie turns to Ritter, "I must tell," she says . . .

A corporal has written down the description of the house in which Maxim is hiding and been dispatched to find him.

"As soon as you have satisfied yourself of his identity, pull him out and shoot him against the door," orders von Hueffer.

KATIE (*now in a sneering rage, rather common, you notice*)—What makes you think that Maxim is waiting there for your murderers to come and take him?

GENERAL (*coldly and scornfully*)—Why, what makes you think he would not feel secure there?

KATIE (*this stab deflects her mood into an anguished surrender. She says to him horror-stricken*)—Don't you ever feel sorry at all? Aren't you a human man?

GENERAL—Not when I am in uniform. Now, Tauler, follow the escort out. You will be detained for a short time still, but be quite calm. You will be released in the course of the morning. I advise you.

RITTER (*calls out*)—Cheer up, Katie, and good-by.

KATIE (*leaning across the table trying to catch at the* GENERAL'S *sleeve*)—Please, sir, please! But you *must* listen to me, for three little single minutes. Please, sir! This is a good man you are killing, a good man. If you let him go with me, we will go away together and no one in the world will ever hear of us again. We are only small people, sir. We are not dangerous people. If you only knew all the things we had planned, and never anyone killed from end to end of them. (*Motions to* SERGEANT *who approaches slowly.*) He cannot be killed, you hear . . . you hear, you devils, I love him! I've damned myself. You've damned me, you devils. Simply because I am too ill to die. Give me the devil's pay. Don't kill him, don't kill him . . . (*They have hemmed her in.*)

RITTER—Oh, get her out of this. (*She is half trailed limply to the door. At the doorway she makes a last scuffle. No one looks around. The door closes on her, shouting.*)

KATIE—Kill me, kill me! (*Silence.*)

GENERAL—Well, Ritter, I am very sorry indeed. You have brought all this on your own head.

RITTER (*is led nearer to the table in his old position*)—Am I expected to be ashamed of what we did?

GENERAL—My dear sir. I have no mission to reform the world. Well, I regret it infinitely, believe me, but I must now make out the final orders. Call up the chaplain, Sergeant. And warn the firing squad for duty. Let them be ready. Where do I sign, Hofmann? (OFFICER *pushes execution warrant across.* SERGEANT *goes out to give the orders.*)

RITTER (*to* GENERAL)—The quicker the better now. I am tired of the lot of you. I am tired of the whole world. You are all indecent, senseless people. (*His guards make a threatening gesture to him, one raises his fist at the insult thrown at the* GENERAL.)

HOFMANN (*very sharp and fierce*)—Keep your blasted hands down, what's your name! Don't let me see you dare to think of raising your hand against an officer! (*To* GENERAL *who raises his eyebrows gently.*) Excuse me, sir. (*Deeply apologetic.*) I was once brother officer to Captain Ritter.

GENERAL—Quite right, very proper. Oh, I'm not objecting.

CHAPLAIN (*enters. In uniform, with dog collar, and a short, absurd stole over his shoulders. He salutes* GENERAL)—Why, hello, Ritter. I am very sorry indeed to see you.

RITTER (*all very calm and indifferent now*)—Hello, Padre. I have not seen you for many a day.

HOFMANN—Will you have a drink, old man?

RITTER—Yes, I would like a drink. (HOFMANN *goes to the*

cupboard—finds a glass, and fills it. RITTER *dabs his head repeatedly as if in an involuntary reaction to a twinge of pain.*)

HOFMANN (*holds drink up to his lips*)—Would you like a few prayers, old man?

RITTER—Yes, I would like a few prayers.

CHAPLAIN (*begins out of Anglican prayer book*)—I know that my Redeemer liveth and that He shall stand at the latter day upon the earth, and though after my skin, worms devour this body, yet in my flesh shall I see God. Whom I shall see for myself and not another.

RITTER (*falling in between two soldiers.* GENERAL *and* HOFMANN *standing at salute.* GUARDS *at door at word from* SERGEANT *present arms.* CHAPLAIN *precedes*)—I shall not be sorry to be alone for the next million years. (*He smiles. Then as he is turned he catches sight of the flag with the star which* KATIE *hung so high that no one has noticed it. He salutes it with a large sweeping variety of the gesture of salute—somewhat as if tossing a light ball into the air with a bent elbow he has used before.*)

CHAPLAIN (*in a solemn natural voice*)—Man that is born of woman hath but a short time to stay and is full of misery. He cometh up and is cut down like a flower. (*He has no book. Keeps hands clasped unostentatiously in front of his chest, in a subdued military version of the sacerdotal gesture.*) He fleeth as if it were a shadow and never continueth long in one stay . . . etc. (*They march on slowly and disappear. Noise of feet on the stairs. Silence.* HOFMANN *gets up and goes to the window and looks out with his hands in his pockets.*)

GENERAL (*goes on writing*)—Orderly.

ORDERLY—Yes, sir.

GENERAL—Get a ladder, and get that thing down. Up there, you see. Pull that thing down. All right.

CURTAIN

THE BARRETTS OF WIMPOLE STREET

A Drama in Three Acts

By Rudolf Besier

KATHARINE CORNELL read the manuscript of Rudolf Besier's play, "The Barretts of Wimpole Street," while she was on a boat that was taking her down the Atlantic and through the Panama Canal to California.

By the time her boat had arrived at Havana she had decided she wanted to own the play. She did not, she says, at first consider herself as particularly suited to the rôle of Elizabeth Barrett, a statement that will cause some wonder in the minds of all those who have been, or later will be, witness to her perfect embodiment of that rôle.

She had made arrangements to acquire the American rights to the play before it was produced in London. Around its production she later built up her entrance into the theatre-world as an actress-manager. She selected the company, with the help and advice of her husband, Guthrie McClintic, who staged the play for her. She attended to so much of the finances as she felt an actress-manager should. And she achieved the success of her stage career when the play was first produced in Cleveland the night of Thursday, January 29, and later in New York, at the Empire Theatre the night of February 9, 1931.

Week after week, from the date of its opening, "The Barretts of Wimpole Street" played to as many people as the Empire holds. As we are sending this volume to its publishers, the play still is running through the summer, with Saturday performances eliminated and Wednesday and Thursday matinées substituted, a change in theatrical customs also suggested and probably ordered by the actress-manager.

Mr. Besier's play is probably as near the perfect biographical romance as any the stage has seen, or is likely to see, for years on years. It clings sufficiently close to the established facts of Robert Browning's and Elizabeth Barrett's life story to achieve at least a suggested authenticity, and still is able to build artificially a plot that is both sentimentally moving and dramatically stimulating to all imaginations.

The room in which the action of "The Barretts of Wimpole Street" takes place is Elizabeth Barrett's bed-sitting room which she once described in a letter to a friend. "The bed, like a sofa and no bed," she wrote, "the large table placed out in the room, toward the wardrobe end of it; the sofa rolled where a sofa should be rolled—opposite the armchair; the drawers crowned with a coronal of shelves (of paper, deal, and crimson merino), to carry my books; the washing table opposite turned into a cabinet with another coronal of shelves; and Chaucer's and Homer's busts on guard over their two departments of English and Greek poetry; three more busts consecrate the wardrobe. In the window is fixed a deep box full of soil, where are springing up my scarlet-runners, nasturtiums and convolvuluses, although they were disturbed a few days ago by the revolutionary insertion among them of a great ivy root with trailing branches so long and wide that the top tendrils are fastened to Henrietta's window of the higher story while the lower ones cover all my panes."

It is a large, square room, comfortably furnished with English furniture of the period. There are books everywhere. The table top carries also a copy of the London *Times,* and a large writing portfolio of embossed leather.

The year is 1845. The time is about 8:30 on the evening of May 19. Elizabeth Barrett, of medium build, of dark brown hair and eyes, is reclining on a couch liberally supplied with cushions and covers. Dr. Chambers, an amiable, thick-bodied man, making one of his periodical examinations, finds Elizabeth's pulse inactive and an increasingly low vitality a disturbing factor.

It is Elizabeth's opinion that not much else should be expected of a person who has been confined to one room for years on end. Perhaps if the doctor would prescribe something really exciting for a change, results would follow.

She is not, Elizabeth insists, overdoing in the matter of her mental activities. She is not working with her Greek more than a few hours a day, and she is doing comparatively little writing for the *Athenæum* and other papers. Furthermore, if it were not for her scribbling and her study Elizabeth hesitates to think of how utterly unbearable her life might become.

It is Dr. Chambers' opinion that the Barrett home and family life exert a fairly depressing influence and that this should be changed. He would, if he could, prescribe some sort of change that would get his patient quite away from her dismal surroundings and away from English winters and springs. Italy is really the place for her.

Miss Barrett is quite agreed as to that. Italy is her heavenly dream, but to one who has taken no more than a few steps, and those with assistance, since a fall as far back as Christmas, dreams of Italy are not particularly cheering.

Even now, when the doctor urges her to try again to walk a little, with his help, Elizabeth finds her knees an altogether insufficient support and has to be helped back to her couch.

Neither can the patient report that she is doing well with her dieting. Particularly she has been distressed by the dark beer called porter which her father has suggested and Dr. Chambers has approved. Elizabeth detests porter, and surely nothing a person thoroughly detests can be of any value as a strength-builder.

It is hard for Dr. Chambers to conceive of any human being who cannot enjoy a pint of porter with his meals, but if she insists, he will, as a concession, permit her to substitute hot milk for the beer.

The family has finished dinner. Dr. Chambers has gone to talk with Mr. Barrett in the study. Wilson, the maid, has cleared away Elizabeth's dinner things from a side table, including the hated glass of porter, and taken Flush, Elizabeth's spaniel, for its evening run.

And now of the family of Barrett sisters and brothers ready to troop in for the evening visit with the invalid, Henrietta is first to arrive. Pretty, spirited, quick of speech and action, Henrietta is in a rebellious state of mind. Dinner has been another depressing experience. Papa was in one of his very worst moods.

"The nagging mood is bad enough," ventures Henrietta, her eyes flashing her resentment; "the shouting mood is worse, but don't you think the dumb mood is the worst of all?"

"Yes, perhaps," agrees Elizabeth. "But they all frighten me."

"I don't believe there were more than a dozen remarks all through dinner," continues Henrietta, sitting at the foot of Elizabeth's sofa; "and most of them were frozen off at the tips. Papa would just turn his glassy eyes on the speaker. You know? For the last twenty minutes or so the only sound in the room was the discreet clatter of knives and forks. Directly dinner was over he ordered the port to be taken to his study, and thank heaven he followed it almost at once."

ELIZABETH—Dr. Chambers is with him now.

HENRIETTA—Oh, Ba, I do hope for all our sakes, his report of you isn't too good.

ELIZABETH—But, Henrietta—!

HENRIETTA (*all contrition, moves and sits on sofa, takes* ELIZABETH'S *hand*)—Forgive me, dearest—it was odious of me to say that. You know I didn't mean it, don't you?

ELIZABETH—Of course I do, you silly child. But what you said makes Papa an inhuman monster. And that's wickedly untrue. In his own way he cares for all his children.

HENRIETTA (*rises*)—In his own way! No, dear, what I meant was that good news of any kind would be sure to aggravate him in his present mood. (*Sits on sofa again.*) I don't know why it should, but it does. (ARABEL MOULTON-BARRETT *enters, closing door after her.*)

ARABEL—Oh, you're here, Henrietta. I've been looking for you everywhere. Papa has just sent you this note from his study.

HENRIETTA—Me? Oh, dear! When he starts sending notes from his study, look out for squalls! (*Opens note and reads.*) "I have heard this morning that your Aunt and Uncle Hedley, and your cousin Bella, have arrived in London earlier than was expected. They are staying at Fenton's Hotel. Your cousin Bella and her fiancé, Mr. Bevan, propose to call on you tomorrow at 3 o'clock. You and Arabel, will, of course, be there to receive them, and if Elizabeth is well enough you will bring them upstairs to see her. I have written to invite your Aunt and Uncle and Cousin to dinner next Thursday.—Papa." (*With emphasis.*) Well!

ARABEL—I understand now why Papa seemed so—so displeased at dinner.

HENRIETTA—Vile-tempered, you mean!

ARABEL—Is it necessary always to use the ugliest word?

HENRIETTA—Yes, Arabel—when you're describing the ugliest thing! (*To* ELIZABETH.) Oh, but Papa is quite impossible! He got this letter from the Hedleys at breakfast. Why couldn't he have spoken then? Why couldn't he have spoken at dinner? Heaven knows he had time enough!

ARABEL—I'm afraid he was too displeased.

HENRIETTA (*with a grimace*)—Displeased! Oh, of course we all know that he hates being ordinarily polite to anyone, and now he's simply bound to show some kind of hospitality to the Hedleys. No wonder he was—displeased!

Henrietta's particular rage is due to the fact that she is expecting a friend at the same hour the Hedleys are calling. She neither wants to put the friend off, nor does she welcome Arabel's suggestions as to how the problem may be met. She flounces out of the room in emphasis of that decision.

It is foolish, Arabel thinks, for Henrietta to feel so. She knows, as they all know, that their father will never permit a marriage in his family. She must remember what a scene there was two years before when young Mr. Palfrey had wanted to marry her. Papa's prejudices in the matter do not worry Arabel particularly. Men have never appealed to her that way. Nor should they worry Elizabeth—a conclusion on Arabel's part that wins a quick little laugh from Elizabeth.

"Oh, of course, today anything of that kind is quite out of the question, my poor darling—Papa or no Papa," declares Arabel; "but even when you were younger and stronger, I don't ever remember your having had little affairs with gentlemen."

"Perhaps the gentlemen never gave me the chance," Elizabeth whimsically suggests.

Now Henrietta has dashed back to apologize to Arabel, and Elizabeth, adding to the reëstablished cordiality, insists that next day when Captain Surtees Cook calls on Henrietta, and Bella and her fiancé are in to see the family, that Arabel shall bring Bella and her young man up to see her, which will leave Henrietta to entertain Captain Cook in the drawing room.

But, Elizabeth adds, they will all have to get out by half past three, for then Robert Browning is calling. This news is received with excited exclamations by both Henrietta and Arabel.

Henrietta—Of course I know you've been corresponding with Mr. Browning for months. But then you write to so many literary people whom you absolutely refuse to see.

Arabel—Has Papa given his permission?

Elizabeth—Of course.

Henrietta—But why? Why have you made an exception of Mr. Browning? I've heard he's wonderfully handsome, but—

Elizabeth (*laughing*)—Oh, Henrietta, you're incorrigible!

Arabel—I know he's been most anxious to call. Mr. Kenyon told me so.

Henrietta—But you said yourself only a short time ago that you didn't intend to receive him.

Elizabeth—I didn't—and I don't particularly want to now.

Henrietta—But why?

ELIZABETH—Because, my dear, at heart I'm as vain as a peacock! You see, when people admire my work, they are very likely to picture the poetess as stately and beautiful as her verses. And it's dreadfully humiliating to disillusion them.

HENRIETTA—Don't be silly, Ba. You're very interesting and picturesque.

ELIZABETH (*laughing*)—Isn't that how guide books usually describe a ruin? As a matter of fact, Mr. Browning has been so insistent, that out of sheer weariness, I've given way. But I don't want an audience to witness the tragedy of his disillusionment! So mind, Arabel, Bella and her Mr. Bevan must be out of the room before he arrives.

Now the family arrives in order—first Octavius, a good-looking young fellow in his twenties, given to stuttering slightly; then Septimus, a year older than Octavius; then Alfred, Charles, Henry, and George, each a little older than the other, each solicitous as to Elizabeth's continued health and the report of Dr. Chambers, and all of them plainly distressed but politely resigned to the news of the Hedleys coming to dinner.

Henry, also, has news that tends to offset in a measure the prevailing family gloom. Papa, says Henry, has arranged to go to Plymouth on business next week and does not expect to return for at least a fortnight!

There are smiles and murmurs of satisfaction at this announcement. Henrietta is so joyous that she flings her arms about the neck of her brother, George, and kisses him. She would also polka around the room with him, if George did not accept the suggestion as being quite childish. So Henrietta is compelled to "polk" by herself, which she does with great enthusiasm, humming "Little Brown Jug" by way of providing her own music. The others are enjoying the dancing with amused smiles and Octavius has even gone so far as to clap his hands, when the door is suddenly opened and Edward Moulton-Barrett enters the room.

"An awkward silence falls. Henrietta stops dead in the middle of the room. Barrett stands just inside the room with a perfectly expressionless face."

Nor does the expression change when Elizabeth greets her father pleasantly with a "Good evening, Papa." Barrett is standing in front of the fireplace. His appearance is military, his voice is cold, his expression measured, his steel gray eyes look steadily before him.

Photo by Vandamm Studio, New York.

"THE BARRETTS OF WIMPOLE STREET"

Browning: I'm neither mad nor morbidly impressionable—I'm as sane and level-headed as any man alive. Yet all these months, since I first read your poems, I've been haunted by you—and today you are the center of my life.

(Brian Aherne and Katharine Cornell)

BARRETT—I am most displeased! It is quite in order that you should visit your sister of an evening, and have a few quiet words with her. But I think I have pointed out, not once, but several times, that in her very precarious state of health it is most inadvisable for more than three of you to be in her room at the same time! My wishes in this matter have been disregarded—as usual! (*A pause.*) You all know very well that your sister must avoid any kind of excitement. Absolute quiet is essential, especially before she retires for the night. And yet I find you romping around her like a lot of disorderly children— I am gravely displeased. (HENRIETTA *gives a nervous little giggle.*) I am not aware that I have said anything amusing, Henrietta.

HENRIETTA—I—I beg your pardon, Papa.

BARRETT—May I ask what you were doing when I came into the room?

HENRIETTA—I was showing Ba how to polk.

BARRETT—To—polk?

HENRIETTA—How to dance the polka.

BARRETT—I see. (*A long pause.*)

OCTAVIUS (*nervously, starting towards* ELIZABETH)—Well, B-Ba, I think I'll say g-good night, and—

BARRETT (*interrupting*)—I should be grateful if you would kindly allow me to finish speaking.

OCTAVIUS (*stepping back*)—Sorry, sir. I thought you'd d-done.

BARRETT (*with frigid anger*)—Are you being insolent, sir?

OCTAVIUS—N-no, indeed, sir. I assure you—

BARRETT—Very well.

ELIZABETH—As I am really the cause of your displeasure, Papa, I ought to tell you that I like nothing better than a little noise occasionally. It's delightful having all the family here together, and can't possibly do me any harm.

BARRETT—Perhaps you will forgive my saying, Elizabeth, that you are not the best judge of what is good or bad for you. And that brings me to what I came here to speak to you about. Dr. Chambers told me just now that you had persuaded him to allow you to discontinue drinking porter with your meals.

ELIZABETH—It needed very little persuasion, Papa. I said I detested porter, and he agreed at once I should take milk instead.

BARRETT—I questioned him closely as to the comparative strength-giving values of porter and milk, and he was forced to admit that porter came decidedly first.

ELIZABETH—That may be, Papa. But when you dislike a thing to loathing, I don't see how it *can* do you any good.

BARRETT—I said just now that you are not the best judge of what is good or bad for you, my child. May I add that self-discipline is always beneficial and self-indulgence always harmful! Believe me, Elizabeth, I have nothing but your welfare at heart when I warn you that if you decide to discontinue drinking porter, you will incur my grave displeasure.

The impulse of rebellion rises in Elizabeth at her father's insistence upon the porter, despite Dr. Chambers' attitude. Even though he may see that a tankard is brought to her bedside, as he says he will do, Elizabeth will not drink it.

Thereupon Mr. Barrett orders Henrietta to go to the kitchen and fetch a tankard of porter at once. Henrietta refuses. It is sheer cruelty to force Ba to drink the stuff. But Henrietta's rebellion is also short-lived. Even though she might stand out against her father's angry demand that she obey at once, she cannot stand Elizabeth's plea that she go at once and thus bring the distressing scene to an end.

Now the family has been dispersed, at Papa's suggestion, each of them filing solemnly and dutifully past Elizabeth's couch and wishing her an affectionate but formal good night.

Henrietta is back with the porter, which Barrett takes from her and places on the mantel. Henrietta is also dismissed. Barrett has moved over to the sofa and is looking down wonderingly at Elizabeth, whose eyes are wide and fearful as they follow him.

Barrett cannot understand that look in Elizabeth's eyes. His voice grows gentle as he inquires the cause of her apparent fear of him. Surely she must know how dear she is to him; how it would hurt him if she were really frightened of him. If she loves him she cannot be afraid, for love casts out fear.

"You love me, my darling?" he pleads, anxiously. "You love your father?"

"Yes," whispers Elizabeth.

"And you'll prove your love by doing as I wish?"

"I don't understand. I was going to drink—"

"Yes, out of fear, not love," corrects her father. "Listen, dear. I told you just now that if you disobeyed me you would incur my displeasure. I take that back. I shall never in any way reproach you. You shall never know by word, or deed, or hint of mine, how much you have grieved and wounded your father by refusing to do the little thing he asked."

Elizabeth is desperate now. Let her have the porter. She will drink it and forget it. "I can't forgive myself," she says, "for having made the whole house miserable over a tankard of porter."

He hands her the tankard and she drinks it straight-off, though with apparent effort.

Now Barrett is ready to say his good night, too. But before he goes he will, if Elizabeth wishes it, say a little prayer with her. To her whispered "Please, Papa," he kneels at the foot of her couch, clasps his hands, lifts his face and shuts his eyes.

"Almighty and merciful God," he prays, "hear me, I beseech Thee, and grant my humble prayer. In Thine inscrutable wisdom, Thou hast seen good to lay on Thy daughter, Elizabeth, grievous and heavy affliction. For years she hath languished in sickness, and for years, unless in Thy mercy Thou take her to Thyself, she may languish on. Give her to realize the blessed word that Thou chastisest those whom Thou lovest. Give her to bear her sufferings in patience. Take her into Thy loving care tonight. Purge her mind of all selfish and bitter, and unkind thoughts, guard her and comfort her. These things I beseech Thee, for the sake of Thy dear son, Jesus Christ, Amen."

Barrett has gone. Wilson is back with Flush. Elizabeth sinks unhappily into her couch. She is tired. Tired of "this long, long, gray death in life," which gives no promise of ever ending.

Wilson is quite distressed at her mistress' melancholy. Outside, she reports, the night is quite warm and there is such a lovely moon. Perhaps, Elizabeth thinks, she could see the moon, if Wilson will draw back the curtains and raise the blind . . . Yes, she can see it, just above the chimneys. If Wilson will just put out the lamp and leave her now, Elizabeth will be quite all right. She doesn't want to go to bed just yet. . . .

Elizabeth's quickened breathing has become audible. Now her whole body is racked with sobs. The only sound is her strangled weeping as the curtain falls.

The following afternoon Elizabeth Barrett's room is bright with the sunshine that streams through the windows of drawn curtains and raised blinds. Everything is back in its place, including the lamps, and there is a bowl of tulips in the center of the large table. The tea table, near the couch on which Elizabeth is lying, reading a book with intense absorption, holds the last of Elizabeth's lunch, an untouched sweet.

There is a verse in the book Elizabeth is reading that, in the evident hope of clarifying its meaning, she reads aloud:

"With flowers in completeness
All petals, no prickles,
Delicious as trickles
Of wine poured at mass-time—"

It is the "All petals, no prickles, delicious as trickles of wine—" that stops her.

She is still worried about it after Wilson has come to clear the luncheon things and has given her her physic. Absent-mindedly she has gone through with the regular routine. Remembering that there is to be company she has asked Wilson to keep the door open that the room may be freshened. She would like to have a window raised, but that, of course, is strictly against orders. And then she goes back to her book. Finally she agrees to try the puzzling verse on Wilson. She reads it all, slowly, carefully. Does Wilson know what it means?

Wilson thinks it is just lovely but it doesn't mean anything to her. But, for that matter, poetry never means anything to Wilson, not real poetry such as Miss Barrett writes. This, as it happens, isn't Miss Barrett's poem. It was written by Mr. Browning.

Wilson has gone for a walk and taken Flush. Octavius is home unexpectedly, having been delegated by his anxious and proper Papa to represent the men of the Barrett family when Bella Hedley and her Mr. Bevan call. There is also Elizabeth's conspiracy to clear the way for Captain Cook and Henrietta which Occy is told about and warned to make possible. It seems a good time, too, for Elizabeth to protest to Occy, in favor of the family, that they are all, from her observation, living their lives like so many automata. They rise, dress, eat their breakfast, go to work, return home, dine and retire with a regularity that must surely be taking everything out of life that makes life worth while for them.

"Oh, I admit we're a pretty spineless lot," admits Octavius. "But what would you? We're none of *us* particularly gifted, and we're all of us wholly dependent on Papa, and must obey or be broken. You're not c-counseling sedition?"

"No—but not resignation," insists Elizabeth. "Keep your souls alive. What frightens me is that you may become content with a life which isn't life at all. You're going that way, all of you, except Henrietta."

Octavius sees little to be gained by defiance. Henrietta gets "more kicks than ha'pence," he reminds her and Elizabeth's experience with the porter should have shown her how foolish it is to rebel. But, Elizabeth persists, their lives are before them, while her life is finished . . .

When Bella Hedley and her Mr. Bevan arrive, Bella is discovered to be a sweetly simpering young woman with a pronounced lisp and he a modified dandy of the period boasting a fringe of immature Galways.

Bella is effusive in her greeting of her dear Elizabeth, and most unhappily moved to find her old playmate become "so fwail, so spiwitual." Mr. Bevan is formally honored at being able to kiss the hand that has penned so much that is both noble and eloquent.

Elizabeth, for her part, is sure they are both to be congratulated on their engagement. Miss Hedley has found that she adores Elizabeth's poetry, particularly her "Lady Gewaldine's Courtship" as her dear Ha'wy reads it aloud. Mr. Bevan is also a great admirer of Miss Barrett's verse. He does not quite approve of Mr. Tennyson, because it grieves him at times to find that poet's attitude toward sacred matters all too often an attitude tinged with doubt. But there is never a line of Miss Barrett's that he would object to even dear Bella reading.

A part of Miss Bella's errand is to ask Henrietta to be one of her bridesmaids, and she is quite surprised to hear Henrietta admit, rather bitterly, that it must all depend on their father's permission. It is entirely possible, Henrietta insists, that he will refuse for no rhyme or reason, except that he happens to be out of temper.

"He once owned slaves in Jamaica," is Henrietta's explanation, "and as slavery has been abolished there, he carries it on in England."

Octavius' hurried reminder that tea must be ready saves a somewhat awkward situation and sends them all below stairs. All but Henrietta, who must stay behind to apologize to Elizabeth again for speaking so unkindly of their common family problem. It was only her own misery that spurred her tongue—her misery and a wild happiness as well. Captain Surtees Cook has asked her to marry him! Elizabeth is thrilled by the news.

HENRIETTA—And, of course, I accepted him—and said that I couldn't. And I had to tell him that we must never see each other again. When he calls here tomorrow we shall have to—

ELIZABETH—You're not talking sense, child. What really has happened?

HENRIETTA—I don't know—except that we both love each

other terribly. Oh, Ba, what *are* we to do? Surtees has only just enough money to keep himself decently. And I haven't a penny of my own. If I only had your four hundred a year, I might defy Papa and leave the house, and marry Surtees tomorrow.

ELIZABETH—And what earthly good is that money to me? I'd give it to you, and how gladly—

HENRIETTA—I know you would, darling. But that's utterly impossible. Think what your life would be like, when Papa knew that you had made it possible for me to marry? (*With sudden urgency.*) But, dear, is there anything, anything at all to be said for Papa's attitude toward marriage? Can it possibly be wrong to want a man's love desperately, and to long for babies of my own?

ELIZABETH—No. But who am I to answer a question like that? Love and babies are so utterly remote from my life—

HENRIETTA—Yes, I know, dear. You're a woman apart. But it's natural to an ordinary girl like me, and what's natural can't be wrong.

ELIZABETH—No—and yet the holiest men and women renounced these things—

HENRIETTA—I daresay. But I'm not holy—and come to that, neither is Papa—not by any means—

Mr. Browning has called. Wilson has announced him, and Elizabeth, grown suddenly self-conscious, declares she cannot see him. Let Wilson tell Mr. Browning that she is very sorry, but that she is not well enough to receive him.

Henrietta will not have this. Elizabeth is acting like a silly school-girl, insists Henrietta. She will bring Mr. Browning up herself. And she does.

The poet, as he enters Elizabeth's room, is tall and handsome. His manner suggests at the moment a carefully restrained impulsiveness inspired by a very sincere joy at being there and meeting Elizabeth Barrett at last. It is a pleasure, he feels, that she never would have granted him had he not been so tiresomely persistent.

For her part, Elizabeth is at pains to explain that she has not been at all well through the winter; that even now her doctor obliges her to live in what must seem to him to be a hot-house temperature.

Mr. Browning's inspection of the room is also satisfying. It is exactly as he had been picturing it for months, thanks partly to the descriptions he had been able to drag from their mutual friend, Mr. Kenyon, and partly to his imagination.

"Directly I had read your brave and lovely verses," explains Mr. Browning, "I was greedy for everything and anything I could get about you."

ELIZABETH (*smiling*)—You frighten me, Mr. Browning.

BROWNING—Why?

ELIZABETH—Well, you know how Mr. Kenyon's enthusiasms run away with his tongue. He and I are the dearest of friends. What he told you about me, I quite blush to imagine.

BROWNING—You mean, Miss Barrett, about you—you yourself?

ELIZABETH—I feel it would be hopeless for me to try to live up to his description.

BROWNING—He never told me anything about you personally that had the slightest interest for me.

ELIZABETH (*puzzled*)—Oh?

BROWNING—Everything he could give me about your surroundings and the circumstances of your life I snatched at with avidity, but all he said about *you* was quite beside the point, because I knew it already and better than Mr. Kenyon, old friend of yours though he is.

ELIZABETH—But, Mr. Browning—do my poor writings give me so hopelessly away?

BROWNING—Hopelessly—utterly—entirely—to me. I can't speak for the rest of the world.

ELIZABETH—You frighten me again.

BROWNING—No?

ELIZABETH—But you do. For I am afraid it would be quite useless my ever trying to play-act with you.

BROWNING—Quite useless.

ELIZABETH (*smiling*)—I shall always have to be just myself.

BROWNING—Always.

ELIZABETH—And you, too, Mr. Browning?

BROWNING—Always—just myself. But really you know, Miss Barrett, I shan't be able to take much credit for that. Being myself comes to me as easily as breathing. It's play-acting I can't manage—and the hot water I've got into in consequence. If life's to run smoothly we should all be mummers. Well, I can't mum.

ELIZABETH—I can well believe that, now I've met you. But isn't it extraordinary? When you are *writing*, you never do anything else but play-act.

BROWNING—I know—

ELIZABETH—You have never been yourself in any one of your poems. It's always somebody else speaking through you.

BROWNING—Yes, and I shall tell you why. I am a very modest man. (*Quickly.*) I am, really.

ELIZABETH—I didn't question it, Mr. Browning.

BROWNING—So modest I fully realize that if I wrote about myself—my hopes and fears, hates and loves, and the rest of it—my poems would be unutterably dull.

ELIZABETH—Well, Mr. Browning, since we are pledged to nothing but the truth, I shan't contradict that until I know you better.

BROWNING (*laughing*)—Bravo!

ELIZABETH—Oh, but those poems of yours, with their glad and great-hearted acceptance of life, you can't imagine what they mean to me. Here am I—shut in by four walls—the view of Wimpole Street, my only glimpse of the world. And they troop into the room and round my sofa, those wonderful people of yours, out of every age and country and all so tingling with life. No, you'll never begin to realize how much I owe you.

BROWNING (*with emotion*)—You—you really mean that?

ELIZABETH—Why, why, Mr. Browning—

BROWNING—But, of course, you do, or you wouldn't say it. And you'll believe me when I tell you that what you have just said makes up to me—oh, a thousand times over for all the cold shouldering I've had from the public.

ELIZABETH (*fiercely*)—Oh, it infuriates me. Why can we never know an eagle for an eagle, until it has spread its wings and flown away from us for good?

It is Browning's opinion that it may be his style that is largely to blame for his unpopularity. Elizabeth is reluctant to agree, and yet there are passages that are a little puzzling. For example, that passage from "Sordello—"

Browning, taking the book from her and reading the verse she indicates, is himself puzzled. It is, to be sure, a passage torn from its context. Still—he puzzles over it again.

"Well, Miss Barrett, when that passage was written only God and Robert Browning understood it," he admits, laughing with her. "Now only God understands it." He is ready to pitch the book into the fire.

Elizabeth recovers her "Sordello," which, she insists with spirit, is not to be despised because of a few "spots on the sun." It may be, as Mr. Browning insists it is, a colossal failure as an attempt, but she loves it. She, too, is always making colossal attempts—and always failing. Yet they are agreed in this: That one such failure is worth a hundred small successes.

"You think so, too?" Mr. Browning grows ardent at the thought. "But of course I knew that. Miss Barrett, you smiled when I told you that Mr. Kenyon had no need to describe you, because I knew you through and through already. And what you have just said about success and failure proves to me finally how right I was. All Kenyon did was to fill in the background, I had painted the portrait with the true soul of you, ardent and lovely, looking out of it."

"Ardent and lovely. And you think you know me." Elizabeth smiles bitterly. "Oh, Mr. Browning, too often impatient and rebellious."

"Well, what of it?" he is quick to answer, moving his chair close to the side of her sofa. "I've no love for perfect patience under affliction. My portrait is the portrait of a woman, not of a saint. Who has more right to be impatient and rebellious than you?"

Mr. Kenyon must have painted her background with a gloomy brush, thinks Elizabeth. He doubtless told Mr. Browning that she is a dying woman; that her family life is one of unrelieved gloom. Does he find her, then, so pitiable an object?

"I find you," says he, "as I expected to find you—full of courage and gayety. And yet—in spite of what you say, I'm not at all sure that Kenyon's colors were too somber."

Elizabeth would protest, but there is no stopping Browning now. "No, no—listen to me," he goes on, his ardor mounting. "These colors are not yet dry. They must be scraped off. The whole background must be repainted. And if only you'll allow it, I must have a hand in that splendid task.

"No, listen, I'll dip my brush into the sunrise, and the sunset, and the rainbow. You say my verses have helped you—they're nothing. It's I—I, who am going to help you now. We've come together at last, and I don't intend to let you go again."

"But . . ."

"No, listen to me. Give me your hands!" He has bent forward and taken her hands in his. "I've more life in me than is good for one man," he says. "It seethes and races in me. Up to now I've spent a little of that surplus energy in creating imaginary men and women. But I've still so much that I have no use for, but to give. Mayn't I give it to you? Don't you feel new life tingling and prickling up your fingers and arms and right into your heart and brain?"

"Oh, please, Mr. Browning, please let go my hands!"

Elizabeth is a little frightened. Her voice is shaken. Obediently he opens his hands. For a moment she leaves hers in his open palms. When she withdraws them it is to press them to her cheeks as she looks at him with a disturbed smile.

Mr. Browning, Elizabeth admits, is rather an overwhelming person. But he will not let her say again that she is frightened of him. It is life that frightens her, and that shouldn't be. But, she insists, when life becomes a series of electric shocks—

ELIZABETH (*lightly*)—No wonder I hesitated about meeting you, much as I wanted to. You'll laugh at me, Mr. Browning, but when my maid told me you had arrived, I was so panic-stricken that I all but sent down word that I was too unwell to receive you.

BROWNING—I think I must have been about as nervous as you, at that moment.

ELIZABETH—You, Mr. Browning?

BROWNING—Yes, yes, and I'm anything but a nervous man as a rule. But that moment was the climax of my life—up to now. Miss Barrett, do you remember the first letter I wrote you?

ELIZABETH—Yes, indeed. It was a wonderful letter.

BROWNING—You may have thought I dashed it off in a fit of white hot enthusiasm for your poems. I didn't. I weighed every word of every sentence—and of one sentence in particular—this sentence: "I love your books with all my heart, and I love you, too." You remember?

ELIZABETH (*lightly*)—Yes—and I thought it charmingly impulsive of you.

BROWNING (*almost with irritation*)—But I tell you there was nothing impulsive about it. That sentence was as deeply felt and as anxiously thought over, as any sentence I've ever written.

ELIZABETH—I hope I may have many readers like you. It's wonderful to think I may have good friends all the world over, whom I have never seen nor heard of.

BROWNING—I am not speaking of friendship—but of love. (ELIZABETH *about to make a smiling rejoinder, he continues:*) No, it's quite useless your trying to put aside the word with a smile and a jest. I said love—and I mean love.

ELIZABETH—But really, Mr. Browning, I must ask you—

BROWNING—I'm neither mad nor morbidly impressionable—

I'm as sane and level-headed as any man alive. Yet all these months since first I read your poems, I've been haunted by you—and today you are the center of my life.

ELIZABETH (*gravely*)—If I were to take you seriously, Mr. Browning, it would, of course, mean the quick finish of a friendship which promises to be very pleasant to both of us.

BROWNING—Why?

ELIZABETH—You know very well that love, in the sense you apparently use the word, has no place, and can have no place in my life.

BROWNING—Why?

ELIZABETH—For many reasons—but let this suffice. As I told you before, I am a dying woman.

BROWNING (*passionately*)—I refuse to believe it. For if that were so, God would be callous, and I know that He's compassionate—and life would be dark and evil, and I know that it's good. You must never say such a thing again. I forbid you to.

ELIZABETH—Forbid, Mr. Browning?

BROWNING—Yes—forbid. If you forbid me to speak of you as I feel, and I accept your orders, as I must—isn't it only fair that I should be allowed a little forbidding as well?

ELIZABETH—Yes, but—

BROWNING (*with sudden gayety*)—Dear Miss Barrett, what a splendid beginning to our friendship. We have known each other a bare half hour, and we've talked intimately of art, and life, and death and love. And we've ordered each other about, and we've almost quarreled. Could anything be happier and more promising? Well, with your permission I'm going now. (*Rising, puts chair back.*) Mr. Kenyon impressed upon me to make my first visit as short as possible, as strangers tire you. Not that I'm a stranger—still I can see that you are tired. When may I call again? (*Puts on cape and moves to sofa.*)

ELIZABETH (*a little dazed*)—I don't quite know.

BROWNING—Will next Wednesday suit you?

ELIZABETH (*as before*)—Yes, I—I think so. But perhaps it would be better—

BROWNING—Next Wednesday then.

ELIZABETH—But—

BROWNING—At half past three, again?

ELIZABETH—Yes— but I—

BROWNING (*bowing over her hand*)—Au revoir, then. (*Kisses her hand.*)

ELIZABETH—Good-by.

BROWNING (*crossing and turning*)—Au revoir.
ELIZABETH—Au revoir.
BROWNING—Thank you.

The door has closed behind him. Elizabeth sits up and clasps her face with both her hands. Then, wonderingly, adventuresomely, she slips off the couch and rises unsteadily to her feet. She reaches timorously for the back of the big chair. Leaning on that she manages another step or two which brings her to the table. From there she half falls, half walks into the curtains, supporting herself by the draperies.

She is looking down into the street after the departing Browning, "her face alive with excitement and joy, as though she were a young girl," as the curtain falls.

ACT II

Three months later, another bright, sunshiny day, Elizabeth's room has undergone certain orderly changes in appearance. Most of the bottles and carafes that belong to a sick room have disappeared. Books and papers are still in some disorderly profusion, but there are flowers and a general atmosphere of changed living conditions.

Dr. Chambers and Dr. Ford-Waterlow are with Elizabeth, who is obediently, smilingly, confidently walking up and down the room before them. It is a performance that delights Dr. Chambers and fills Dr. Ford-Waterlow with wonder and satisfaction. Three months before he had been called in consultation by Dr. Chambers, and at that time he had found Miss Barrett in a very low condition. The change in her is remarkable. Dr. Chambers, he insists, has done wonders.

Dr. Chambers, however, disclaims the credit. He has had a great deal of outside help. The real healer is Miss Barrett herself. Just as he had begun to feel, three months before, that she was ready to slip through his fingers she suddenly had developed a wish to live, and a wish to live, Dr. Chambers has often noticed, is worth a dozen physicians.

Elizabeth is pleased to report to Dr. Ford-Waterlow that she is now able to visit her friends, and that she has had several delightful drives in the park. Her chief difficulty is in getting down stairs and she has not yet been able to negotiate the upward journey.

With so much gained, it is the opinion of both physicians that serious thought must be given to the future. Another winter in England must, if possible, be avoided. Dr. Ford-Waterlow thinks that by October she will be able to travel south—to the Riviera, or, better still, to Italy.

To Elizabeth the thought is thrilling. As the doctor suspects, there are no practical obstacles to stand in the way. She has her own small income. There is, of course, as Dr. Chambers has already informed his colleague, the matter of her father's consent. Dr. Ford-Waterlow is prepared to speak plainly to Mr. Barrett about that.

The doctors have left her, and Elizabeth is thrilled anew with the thought of Italy—of Rome! Florence! Venice! Vesuvius! Raphael! Dante! Sordello!

In her excitement she throws her arms about the neck of Arabel, as that surprised sister comes through the door. Nor will she permit herself to be discouraged by Arabel's reminder that Papa may not consent. Anyway, Arabel doubts that it was wise for Elizabeth to keep her Italian plan secret from her father, and then spring it suddenly on him. But that was Dr. Chambers' advice, Elizabeth reminds her. . . .

Bella Hedley is in. And Henrietta. Henrietta is wearing the bridesmaid's dress that Bella has ordered for her, and is very lovely in it. Bella prettily fears that Henrietta may draw all the attention of the men at the wedding wight away fwom the poor little bwide. And she never would have had so "pwetty" a "bwidesmaid" if she hadn't spoken to Uncle Edward herself—

"*Spoken* to Papa," interjects Henrietta. "I like that. Why, you sat on his knee and stroked his whiskers."

"And why not?" demands Bella. "Isn't he my uncle? Besides that I think he's most fwightfully thwilling. I adore that stern and gloomy type of gentleman. It's so exciting to coax and manage them. And so easy—if you know how! And I weally think I do. What I can't understand ith his extwordinary attitude towards love and mawwiage, and all that. And didn't he mawwy himself—and what's more have eleven children? (*There is an uncomfortable silence, as the sisters bow their heads.*) Oh, have I said anything vewy dweadful?"

"No, dear, but perhaps not quite nice," ventures Arabel. "When God sends us children, it's not for us to inquire how and why."

Bella thinks it quite wonderful that despite Uncle Edward's extraordinary ideas his whole house is fairly seething with romance. There's Henrietta and Captain Surtees Cook. There's George who, Bella is sure, has quite a thwilling understanding with his cousin, Lizzie. There is Occy, who has made her own Mr. Bevan fwightfully jealous. Finally there is Elizabeth "and the handsomest poet in England." What a wonderful lot Flush must have learned about poetry since Mr. Browning has been coming to see Elizabeth at least once every week. "For," adds Bella, archly, "when two poets are gathered together they talk about whymes and wythms all the time. Or don't they? I'm fwightfully ignorant."

"Oh, no, my dear," laughs Elizabeth; "on the contrary you are 'fwightfully' knowing."

"Bella, I regret to say it," solemnly declares Arabel, "but I think you are one of the few girls I know who would have benefited entirely under Papa's system of upbringing."

"Ooh—what a thwilling thought. He was always fwightfully strict, wasn't he? Did he whip you when you were naughty? How fwightfully exciting it would be to be whipped by Uncle Edward."

She has barely finished this observation when the door opens and Edward Barrett steps inside. The family is immediately on the alert, but Bella is not at all startled.

BELLA—Oh, Uncle Edward—uncle, dear, if I had been your little girl instead of Papa's would you have been tewwibly severe with me? You wouldn't, would you, or would you?

BARRETT—Would—wouldn't—wouldn't—would—are you trying to pose me with some silly riddle?

BELLA—No, no, no! (*She pushes him into a chair.*) It's like this—but why that gloomy frown, Uncle Edward? (*Passes her fingers lightly over his forehead.*) There—there, all gone. (*She sits on his knee.*) Arabel said it would have done me all the good in the world to have been bwought up by you. She thinks I'm a spoilt, fwivolous little baggage—and— (HENRIETTA *moves upstage.*)

ARABEL (*rising*)—Bella— I never said anything of the sort!

BELLA—I know you didn't, but you *do.* (*To the others.*) And *you* do and *you* do. But *you* don't, Uncle, do you?

ARABEL—Really, Bella.

BARRETT (*speaking to* BELLA *but at the others*)—If my children were as bright and affectionate and open as you are, I should be a much happier man.

BELLA—Oh, you mustn't say such things or they'll hate me.

BARRETT (*the two are quite withdrawn from and oblivious of the others*)—And you are a distractingly lovely little creature.

BELLA—Anything wrong in that?

BARRETT (*thickly*)—I didn't say so.

BELLA—Then why do you look at me so fiercely—do you want to eat me up?

BARRETT—What's the scent you have on?

BELLA—Scent? Me? (*Coyly.*) Don't you like it?

BARRETT—I abominate scent as a rule—but yours is different.

BELLA—Nice?

BARRETT—It's very delicate and subtle—still, I should prefer you not to use it.

BELLA—Why?

BARRETT—Never mind.

BELLA (*triumphantly*)—I never use scent. I haven't a dwop on me. Oh, Uncle, you're a darling! You've called me bwight and open and affectionate, distwactingly lovely, and fwagwant, all within a few minutes. You may kiss me. (*He kisses her roughly on the mouth twice. Suddenly he pushes her abruptly from his knees, and rises, she looks a trifle scared.*)

BARRETT (*brusquely*)—There, there, child, run away now, I want to speak to Ba.

They have all gone. Mr. Barrett is relieved. He will feel even better after Bella is married and living mostly in the country. True, he is fond of her. Isn't she his niece? But she is a disturbing influence in the house. He has seen Elizabeth's brothers following her about with their eyes. Faugh!

However, it is with Elizabeth that her father wants to talk. Her doctors have just left him. Their report is excellent. He is astonished and gratified, even though she will probably never again be a normal woman. That optimistic fool of a Chambers has admitted that.

As for that Dr. Ford-Waterlow, even if he is one of London's cleverest physicians, as Elizabeth has heard, "he needs some amazing qualities to counterbalance his execrable manners."

"But even this medical phenomenon was unable to account for the sudden improvement in your health," Barrett adds. "He put it down to Chambers' ministrations—which is, of course, errant nonsense."

"Perhaps the wonderful weather we've been having has most to do with it. I always thrive in warmth and sunshine."

"Rubbish! Last summer was sweltering, and you have never been worse than then. No—to my mind there is only one whom we have to thank—though this Doctor what's-his-name was pleased to sneer when I mentioned HIM."

"HIM?"

"I mean Almighty God. It amazes me, Elizabeth, that you on whom this miracle of recovery has been worked should ascribe it to mere earthly agencies. Haven't I knelt here night after night and implored our all-loving Father to have compassion on His child? It amazes me. It grieves me unspeakably. That is all I have to say for the present."

There has been no reference to the doctors' suggestion about Italy for the winter. Elizabeth, nervously anxious, is finally forced to bring the subject to her father's attention. Dr. Chambers is sure she will be fit to travel by October—

Barrett is furious. At last the precious plot is laid bare! How many months has it been hatching? The doctors know about it, Elizabeth's brothers and sisters know about it, Mr. Kenyon, Mr. Horne, even the charlatan Browning, have been let into the secret, but he alone has been shut out "treated like a cypher, ignored, insulted—" They probably feared that he would nip the plan in the bud at once.

Nor will he listen to explanations from Elizabeth. The whole miserable business is abundantly clear, and he is cut to the quick that she, the only one of his children that he trusted implicitly, should be capable of such underhand conduct.

BARRETT—If returning health must bring with it such a sad change of character, I shall be driven to wish that you were once more lying helpless on that sofa. There is nothing more to be said. (*He once more turns to the door.*)

ELIZABETH (*with dignified and restrained passion, rises and walks toward him. He stops*)—But there is something more to be said, and I must beg you to listen to me, Papa. How many years have I lain here? (*He slowly turns to face her.*) Five? Six? It's hard to remember, as each year has been like ten. And all that time I've had nothing to look forward to, or hope for, but death.

BARRETT—Death—?

ELIZABETH—Yes, death! I was born with a large capacity for happiness—you remember me as a young girl? And when life brought me little happiness and much pain, I was often impatient for the end.

BARRETT—You shock me! Elizabeth! (*Steps toward her.*)

ELIZABETH—And now this miracle has happened. Day by day I am better able to take and enjoy such good things as everyone has a right to—able to meet my friends—to breathe the open air, and feel the sun, and see grass and flowers growing under the sky.

When Dr. Chambers first spoke to me of Italy, I put the idea away from me—it seemed too impossibly wonderful! But as I grew stronger it came over me like a blinding revelation, that Italy wasn't an impossibility at all, that nothing really stood in the way of my going, that I had every right to go.

BARRETT—Right!

ELIZABETH—Yes! Every right! If only I could get your consent. So I set about consulting my friends, meeting all obstacles, settling every detail, so as to have a perfectly arranged plan to put before you, after the doctors had given you their opinion. In my eagerness I may have acted stupidly, mistakenly, tactlessly. But to call my conduct underhand and deceitful is more than unkind— (*Turns downstage and sits on sofa.*) It's unjust, it's cruel.

BARRETT (*more in sorrow than in anger*)—Self! Self! Self! No thought, no consideration for anyone but yourself, or for anything but your pleasure.

ELIZABETH—But, Papa—

BARRETT—Didn't it even once occur to you that through all those long dark months you proposed to enjoy yourself in Italy, your father would be left here utterly alone?

ELIZABETH—Alone?

BARRETT—Utterly alone. Your brothers and sisters might as well be shadows for all the companionship they afford me. And you—oh, my child, don't think that I haven't noticed that even you, now that you are stronger and no longer dependent on me, are slowly drawing away from your father.

ELIZABETH—It's not true.

BARRETT—It is true, and in your heart you know it's true.

ELIZABETH—No!

BARRETT—New life, new interests, new pleasures, new friends—and little by little I am being pushed into the background. I, who used to be your whole world—I, who love you—who love you.

ELIZABETH—But, Papa—

BARRETT (*with a silencing gesture, in a measured tone*)—No. There is nothing more to be said. (*Crosses up to window, looks out, then turns.*) You want my consent for this Italian jaunt. I shall neither give it nor withhold it. To give it would be against my conscience, as encouraging selfishness and self-indulgence. To withhold it would be a futile gesture. You are at liberty to do as you wish. And if you go, I hope you will sometimes spare a thought for your father. Think of him at night stealing into this room which once held all he loved. Think of him kneeling alone beside the empty sofa, and imploring the Good Shepherd to—

Wilson's knock at the door is an interruption. The maid comes to announce Mr. Browning. This is another thorn in Barrett's side. He will not stay and meet "that fellow." Hasn't he always made it a point never to inflict himself upon any of his children's friends?

Mr. Browning is joyously thrilled at Elizabeth's receiving him standing. It is the fourth time. He is also delighted to hear of the wonderful report of the doctors. Yet, he never doubted that she would turn the corner one day.

And Italy? What about Italy? The doctors are agreed, Elizabeth reports, that she should be fit to travel by October, if there is no relapse.

"Relapse?" he repeats, scoffingly. "There isn't such a word! October! Extraordinary! For you know October suits my own plans to perfection."

"*Your* plans?"

"Don't you remember my telling you that I had thought of wintering in Italy myself? Well, now I have quite decided. You see, I have practically made up my mind to remodel 'Sordello.' I should never be able to grapple with the task satisfactorily in England. Impossible to get the Italian atmosphere in a land of drizzle and fog. May I call on you often in Italy? Where do you intend to stay? (ELIZABETH *laughs.*) Why are you laughing?"

"In Italy I am afraid you will need seven-league boots to call on me," sighs Elizabeth.

She tells him of her father's feelings in the matter and that under the circumstances she doubts that she will be able to go. He finds it difficult to listen and more difficult to understand. Elizabeth tries seriously to point out her father's real need of her; of his lack of sympathy with any of his other children; of his real devotion.

"You tell me I don't understand," Browning finally bursts forth. "You are quite right. I don't. You tell me he is devoted to you. I don't understand a devotion that demands favors as if they were rights, demands duty and respect, and obedience and love, demands all and takes all, and gives nothing in return. I don't understand a devotion that spends itself in petty tyrannies and gross bullying. I don't understand a devotion that begrudges you any ray of light and glimpse of happiness, and doesn't even stop at risking your life to gratify its colossal selfishness. Devotion! Give me good, sound, honest hatred, rather than devotion like that!"

"Mr. Browning, I must ask you—"

"Forgive me, but I won't be silent any longer. Even before I met you, I was aware that sickness wasn't the only shadow in your life. And all these months, even though you never once breathed a syllable of complaint, I felt that other shadow deepening, and I've stood by and looked on, and said nothing. I might find you tired and sick after hateful scenes I could picture only too vividly—and I must pretend to know nothing, see nothing, feel nothing! Well—I've done with pretense from today on! I refuse any longer to let myself be gagged and handcuffed. (*He leans on back of sofa.*) It's not just your comfort and happiness which are at stake now. It's your very life—and I forbid you to play with your life! And I have the right to forbid you!"

ELIZABETH (*desperately*)—No—no—no—oh, please don't say any more.

BROWNING (*with compelling ardor*)—The right—and you won't deny it—you're too utterly candid and true. (*Sits on sofa.*) At our first meeting you forbade me to speak of love—there was nothing more than friendship between us. I obeyed you—but I knew very well—we both knew—that I was to be much more than just your friend. Even before I passed that door, and our eyes first met across the room, I loved you, and I've gone on loving you—and I love you more now than words can tell—and I shall love you to the end and beyond. You know that? You've always known?

ELIZABETH (*brokenly*)—Yes— I've always known. And now for pity's sake—for pity's sake—leave me. (*Rising.*)

BROWNING (*with a firm grasp of both her hands, rises and comes around end of sofa*)—No!

ELIZABETH—Oh, please—please—let me go. Leave me. We must never see each other again.

BROWNING (*maintaining his grasp*)—I shall never let you go—I shall never leave you! (*Draws her into his arms.*) Elizabeth! Elizabeth!

ELIZABETH (*struggling feebly in his embrace*)—No—no—Oh, Robert, have mercy on me.

BROWNING—Elizabeth, my darling— (*He kisses her and at the touch of his lips her arms go around his neck.*)

Elizabeth—Oh, Robert—I love you—I love you—I love you. (*They kiss again, then she sinks onto the sofa and he sits holding her hands.*)

Browning—And yet you ask me to take my marching orders, and go out of your life?

Elizabeth—Yes, Robert, for what have I to give you? I have so little of all that love asks for. I have no beauty, and no health—and I'm no longer young—

Browning—I love you.

Elizabeth (*speaking with restrained spiritual ecstasy*)—I should have refused to see you after our first meeting. For I loved you then, though I denied it even to myself. Oh, Robert, I think Eve must have felt as I did when her first dawn broke over Paradise—the terror—the wonder—the glory of it. I had no strength to put up any kind of resistance, except the pitiful pretense of mere friendship. I was paralyzed with happiness that I had never dreamt it was possible to feel. That's my only excuse—and God knows I need one—for not having sent you away from me at once.

Browning—I love you.

Elizabeth (*continuing as before*)—My life had reached its lowest ebb. I was worn out, and hope was dead. Then you came. Robert, do you know what you have done for me? I could have laughed when Dr. Chambers said that I had cured myself by wanting to live. He was right, oh, he was right. I wanted to live—eagerly, desperately, passionately—and all because life meant you—you (*he leans down to kiss her hands*)—and the sight of your face, and the sound of your voice, and the touch of your hand. Oh, and so much more than that! Because of you the air once more was sweet to breathe, and all the world was good and green again.

Browning (*rising from kissing her hands*)—And with those words singing in my ears, I'm to turn my back on you and go?

Elizabeth—But, Robert, can't you see how impossible—

Browning—I've never yet turned my back on a friend or an enemy. Am I likely to turn it on you?

Elizabeth—But how is it all to end? What have we to look forward to? And how—

Browning—I love you, and I want you for my wife.

Elizabeth—Robert, I can't marry you. How can I, when—

Browning—Not today or tomorrow. Not this year, perhaps, or next. Perhaps not for years to come—

Elizabeth—I may never be able to marry you.

BROWNING—What then? If you remain to the last beyond my reach, I shall die proud and happy in having spent a lifetime fighting to gain the richest prize a man was ever offered.

ELIZABETH—Oh, Robert, put aside your dream of me and look at me as I am. I love you too well to let you waste your manhood pursuing the pale ghost of a woman.

BROWNING—Do you think I'm a boy to be swept off my feet by an impulse, or a sentimental dreamer blind to reality? There's no man alive who sees things clearer than I do, or has his feet more firmly planted on the earth. And I tell you in all soberness that my need of you is as urgent as your need of me. If your weakness asks my strength for support, my abundant strength cries out for your weakness to complete my life and myself.

Once more Elizabeth tries to make him see how unhappy their love would make him if they tried to keep it secret and what a great wrong she would be doing him if she were to become his wife. Let them say good-by today, while there is nothing but beautiful memories to last to the end of their lives. He cannot even believe it is she who is speaking. Where is her courage? Has cowardice suddenly overcome her?

"Here's life—*life*—offering us the best that life can give," he cries out, "and you dare not grasp at it for fear it will turn to dust in your hands. We're to dream away the rest of our lives in a tepid sadness, rather than risk utter disaster for utter happiness. I don't know you—I never thought you were a coward."

ELIZABETH (*proudly and indignantly*)—A coward? I? (*With a sudden change of voice.*) Yes, I am a coward, Robert, a coward through and through—but it's not for myself that I am afraid.

BROWNING (*going swiftly to her and taking her in his arms*)—I know that, my darling.

ELIZABETH—What's another disaster, great or small, to me who has known little but disaster all my life? But you are a fighter, and you were born for victory and triumph. If disaster came to you through me—

BROWNING—Yes, a fighter. But I'm sick of fighting alone. I need a comrade at arms to fight beside me.

ELIZABETH—Not one already wounded in the battle.

BROWNING—Wounded, but undefeated, undaunted, unbroken!

ELIZABETH—Yes, but—

BROWNING—Then what finer comrade could a man ask for?

ELIZABETH—But, Robert— (*He bends down and kisses the protests from her lips.*)

BROWNING—No.

ELIZABETH—But, Robert.

BROWNING—No. (*He is still kissing away her protests as the curtain falls.*)

ACT III

Several weeks later there is a slight commotion in the hall outside Elizabeth's room. It is occasioned by Elizabeth's first effort to climb the stairs unassisted. Arabel, who has preceded her sister, is urging Wilson to help Elizabeth, but the help is neither needed nor accepted and Elizabeth is proud of the stair-climbing feat, even though it has taken all her breath.

Arrived in the room, and having put aside her outdoor wraps, Elizabeth finds letters awaiting her on the table. One is from Mr. Browning. It was written the evening before—to wish her good night. Another is from her father, from Dorking, and contains not only the rather disturbing information that he will be home the following day, but also that he has rented a furnished house in Surrey to which he plans to move the family within a fortnight.

"Whether we shall eventually make it our permanent home I have not decided," reads Mr. Barrett's letter, "at any rate, we shall spend the winter there. You will benefit by the country air and the complete seclusion of your new surroundings. I have felt for some time now that your present feverishly restless mode of life in London, will if continued, affect you harmfully, both physically and morally."

"He finishes," adds Elizabeth, with a wry smile, "with a characteristic touch of humor. He signs himself 'Your loving Papa.' "

There is to be no discussion of the proposed move, the letter warns Elizabeth, and her father's decision is irrevocable.

It will be harder on Elizabeth and Henrietta than any of the others, Arabel thinks. They have all been conscious of the way things have been progressing between Elizabeth and Mr. Browning and Arabel is terribly sorry that nothing can really ever come of that romance. . . .

Mr. Browning has called. He has taken Elizabeth in his arms, and noticed the tired look in her eyes. Something, he knows, knowing her, is wrong. What is it? Has her father returned?

Elizabeth indicates the letter. Browning reads it. The fact that it is a crumpled letter, indicating anger on the part of its recipient, pleases him. Furthermore, he is not at all alarmed by its contents. It simply means that they must be married at once.

Elizabeth insists that he must be a little mad; she cannot marry him; she never can marry him. A suggestion to which he makes emphatic answer.

BROWNING (*passionately*)—You can and you shall! You'll marry me if I have to carry you out of this house and up to the altar. Do you seriously imagine I'm going to allow myself to be elbowed out of your life, now? And just to satisfy the selfish jealousy of a man whom I no longer believe to be sane? You ought to know me better by this time.

ELIZABETH (*quickly breaking in*)—Oh, Robert, it's not only Papa who stands between us. It's I—it's I—

BROWNING—We've been into that a hundred times already, and—

ELIZABETH—Yes—and now we shall go into it once again, and frankly, and for the last time. Robert, it's no use deceiving ourselves. However much stronger I become, I shall always remain an invalid. You tell me that you want me, sick or well. And it's wonderful of you to say this. But I—Robert, I'm not generous enough—I'm too proud if you like. As your wife, I should be haunted by the thoughts of all the glorious things you would have enjoyed but for me—freedom—adventure—and passionate love, I could never really satisfy.

BROWNING—Oh, no, listen—

ELIZABETH—Oh, Robert, I should be haunted by the ghosts of your unborn children. When I read that letter my world seemed to fall to pieces. But now I thank God that it came while we're still free, and have the strength to say good-by.

Browning goes on with his plans, quite matter-of-factly. Saturday, while the family is attending a planned picnic with the Hedleys, he and Elizabeth will go to Mary-le-Bone church and be quietly married by the vicar. Then, not to crowd too much excitement into one day, Elizabeth shall return home and rest there quietly for a few days. The following Saturday they will take the boat train at Vauxhall and sail from Southampton. There is but one other thing for her to see to: she must arrange to have Wilson go with them. Nor will he listen to any further protests.

"Suppose I were to die on your hands?" suggests Elizabeth.

"Are you afraid, Ba?" he asks, quietly.

"Afraid? I? You know I am not afraid," she answers. "You

know that I would sooner die with you beside me, than live a hundred lives without you. But how would *you* feel if I were to die like that? And what would the world say of you?"

"I should be branded as little less than a murderer, and what I should feel, I leave you to imagine."

"And yet you ask me to come with you?"

"Yes. I am prepared to risk your life and much more than mine, to get you out of this dreadful house into the sunshine, and to have you for my wife."

"You love me like that?"

"I love you like that."

Still Elizabeth pleads for time. She can't decide on the instant. A few hours and she will let him know. Before she sleeps that night she will write him her decision.

Browning has gone. There is a knock at the door. It is Henrietta come to plead that she be allowed to bring her Captain Cook in to meet Elizabeth. The Captain has just been receiving his adjutancy at the hands of Queen Victoria at St. James Palace and is in his full regimentals. Elizabeth will never have another chance to see him at such fine advantage.

The Captain, a modest little man, handsome in his uniform and carrying his headgear under his arm, is greatly honored to meet Henrietta's sister. At some pains, too, when Henrietta has gone to fetch the sword he has left in the hall, to suggest stammeringly his deep interest in Henrietta. Elizabeth is deeply sympathetic, but, as she explains, quite powerless to help.

Henrietta is back with the sword, and is kneeling before Captain Cook, fastening it on so that Elizabeth may get the full effect, when Barrett opens the door.

Elizabeth and Henrietta stare at their father in some consternation. Captain Cook stands stiffly awaiting the introduction that follows. Captain Cook, Henrietta explains, is a great friend of her brothers, George and Occy. Which makes it a little hard for Mr. Barrett to understand why he should call at a time of day when George and Occy are least likely to be home.

Captain Cook a moment later retires in some confusion. Henrietta would see him to the door but her father stops her. The servant will see to that. There are explanations to be made that may account for the presence of Captain Cook.

Both Elizabeth and Henrietta try to explain the casual friendship of Henrietta for the soldier, but their father is unyielding in his suspicions. When Henrietta, with a show of defiance, takes responsibility for the visit on herself, Barrett, with rising anger, accuses her of having carried on a secret love affair with Captain Cook. To force such a confession from her he has grabbed her by the wrists and twisted her to her knees.

Nor will he believe her when she protests the purity and naturalness of her love. Nor listen to the pleas of Elizabeth that he release her sister. When Henrietta clasps his knees and begs forgiveness, he throws her from him and finally forces her to take oath on a Bible that she will neither see nor have any communication with Captain Cook again. After which she is sent to her room and warned to remain there until she has his permission to leave.

Now Barrett has turned to Elizabeth for some explanation of her attempted interference with his will.

BARRETT—Have you anything to say to me, Elizabeth?

ELIZABETH (*in a dead voice*)—No.

BARRETT—Then I must leave you under my extreme displeasure. I shall not see you again, I can have nothing to do with you, until God has softened your heart, and you repent of your wickedness and ask His forgiveness—and mine. (*He picks up his Bible and goes out. The moment he closes the door,* ELIZABETH *gets up with an air of decision, crosses and pulls bellrope. A pause, then* WILSON *enters.*)

ELIZABETH—Shut the door, please. (*Impulsively, as* WILSON *does so:*) Wilson, are you my friend?

WILSON (*bewildered*)—Your—friend, Miss?

ELIZABETH—Yes, my friend. I am in dire need of friendship and help at the moment.

WILSON—I—I don't quite understand, Miss Ba—but I'm that fond of you, I'd do anything to help you.

ELIZABETH—You would? And I know I can trust you?

WILSON—Yes, indeed, Miss.

ELIZABETH—Wilson, next Saturday I am going to marry Mr. Browning.

WILSON (*with a gasp*)—Marry—

ELIZABETH—Hush! We're to be married at Mary-le-Bone Church. Will you come with me?

WILSON—Me, Miss— Yes, Miss—and gladly—

ELIZABETH—Directly afterwards I shall return here for a few days and—

WILSON (*in boundless amazement*)—Here! With Mr. Browning!

ELIZABETH (*with an hysterical laugh*)—No—no—no! Just

alone with you. Then on the following Saturday I shall join Mr. Browning, and we're going abroad. We're going to Italy. Will you come with us?

WILSON (*in a whisper*)—To Italy—?

ELIZABETH—Yes—will you come with me?

WILSON—Well, Miss, I can't see how I can help myself. Not that I 'old with foreign parts—I don't. But 'usband or no 'usband, you'd never get to Italy alive without me.

ELIZABETH—Then you'll come? Then you'll come! Oh, I am so glad! I'll tell Mr. Browning— (*Goes to desk and takes out writing materials.*) I'm writing to him now. And I shall want you to take the letter to the post at once. Go and put on your things—I'll have finished by the time you're ready.

WILSON—Yes, Miss. (WILSON *has gone.* ELIZABETH *is at the desk writing feverishly as the curtain falls.*)

The following week finds Elizabeth excitedly preparing for flight. Wilson has packed most of the books. The room is stripped and orderly. Flush has been fitted with his leash. Elizabeth has written nine letters to the members of her family and placed them on the mantel over the fireplace. Her coat and hat are hanging in the wardrobe. But there is still an hour and a half to wait. It seems an endless time to the nervous Elizabeth.

There is no one in the house except Miss Henrietta, and she is getting ready to go out. Still Elizabeth is desperately anxious. Is Wilson sure she made definite arrangements with the livery stable man? Wilson is sure. The cab is to be at the corner of Wimpole Street at half past three punctual. It will take them no more than ten minutes to drive to Mr. Hodgson's library and there Mr. Browning will meet them and take them in charge—"Your 'usband, Miss Ba," Wilson reminds her.

There is nothing that Elizabeth can think of that will help to keep her mind occupied. She has taken the letters from the mantel and put them in the desk. She has reread that one she has written to her father. There is nothing to add to it. She wishes there were. She is most thankful that she will be miles and miles away when her father reads his letter. Wilson, for her part, would be glad to be there.

Suddenly Henrietta bursts into the room. She is in bonnet and hat, and she brings a letter. Elizabeth quickly turns her own letters face down in some little confusion, but for the moment Henrietta is too concerned with the letter she has just had from the postman, to think of anything else. It is addressed to Elizabeth, but it is in Captain Cook's handwriting.

The letter contains a message for Miss Elizabeth and encloses a second note for Henrietta. Captain Cook has been ordered with his regiment to Somerset and he positively must see Henrietta before he goes. He would have written her directly but he feared his letter might have been intercepted.

Henrietta reads her own note. A look of determination settles in her eyes. She has given her Bible oath to her father never to write or see Captain Cook again. This is the day she is going to break that oath. From now on she is going to lie to her father frequently and freely whenever he asks her concerning the word of honor she has given him. Henrietta is fearfully unhappy, torn between love and hate. Elizabeth can only sympathize with her and bid her, above everything else, not to lose her courage—

Wilson, her face white with fear, comes running through the door. The Master has just come in. Someone must have told him—

Elizabeth quickly gets her hat and coat out of sight. And two steamer rugs that Wilson had forgotten to pack. Henrietta cannot understand why Elizabeth is so pale, and so excited. What does it mean? It means nothing more than that this is the first time in ten days that her father has been to see her, Elizabeth explains. Scenes of forgiveness are always likely to be trying.

When Mr. Barrett strides into the room they are prepared to meet him calmly. His first questions are directed at Henrietta. Where has she been? Where is she going? Has she kept her oath? Is she going to keep it?

In answer to all of which queries Henrietta lies gracefully, and is dismissed. Barrett turns to Elizabeth.

"Do you know why I am back so early?" he asks.

"No, Papa," she answers, her voice hardly more than a whisper.

"Because I could bear it no longer." His voice is low and intense. "It's ten days since I last saw you."

"Am I to blame for that, Papa?"

BARRETT—You dare to ask me such a question? Weren't you a party to your sister's shameless conduct? Haven't you encouraged her? And did you expect to go scot-free of my displeasure? (*Stopping himself with a violent gesture, comes down below sofa.*) I've not come to speak about that—but to put it behind me,—to forget it! I wonder, my child—have you been half so miserable, my child—have you been half so miserable these last ten days, as your father?

ELIZABETH—Miserable, Papa?

BARRETT—Do you think I can be happy when I am bitterly estranged from all I love in the world? Do you know that night after night I had to call up all my will-power to hold me from coming here to forgive you?

ELIZABETH—Papa—

BARRETT—All my will-power, I tell you—all of my sense of duty, and right, and justice. But today I could bear it no longer. The want of your face and your voice became a torment. I had to come. (*Sits on sofa.*) I am not so strong as they think me—I had to come—and I despise myself for coming, despise myself, hate myself—

ELIZABETH (*crossing to sit next to him on sofa, puts head on his shoulders*)—Oh, Papa, can't you see, won't you ever see, that strength may be weakness, and your sense of justice, and right, and duty may be mistaken and wrong?

BARRETT (*in a low, tense voice, taking her hands from his shoulders*)—Mistaken and wrong? What do you mean? (*Quickly stopping her from speaking.*) No, be silent. Don't answer me. Mistaken or wrong? You don't know what you're saying.

ELIZABETH—If you'll only listen to me, Papa, I—

BARRETT—No.

ELIZABETH—But, Papa—

BARRETT—No! (*Goes away from her to fireplace and stands half turned away. A pause. His voice is calm as he continues*)—If there were even a vestige of truth in what you say, my whole life would be a hideous mockery. For always, through all misfortunes and miseries, I've been upheld by knowing beyond a doubt what was right, and doing it unflinchingly, however bitter the consequences. And bitter they've been—how bitter God only knows. It's been my heavy cross that those whom I was given to guide and rule have always fought against the right I knew to be the right, and was in duty bound to impose upon them. Even you? Even your mother.

ELIZABETH (*in a whisper, turning to him*)—My mother?

BARRETT—Yes, your mother. But not at first. You—you, my eldest child, were born of love, and only love. But the others—long before they came the rift began to open between your mother and me. Not that she ever opposed me—never once. Or put into words what she felt. She was silent, and dutiful, and obedient. But love died out, and fear took its place—

ELIZABETH (*in a whisper, staring before her*)—Oh, dear God, what she must have suffered.

BARRETT—She? She? And what of me?

ELIZABETH—You? Oh, Papa, then you loved her after her love for you had died?

BARRETT (*embarrassed, looking aside*)—Love? What's love? She was my wife. You—you don't understand—

ELIZABETH (*in the same horrified whisper*)—And all those children—born in fear! Oh, it's horrible—it's horrible—! (*With a shuddering sob, covers her face with her hands.*)

BARRETT (*aghast and embarrassed, taking a couple of steps toward her*)—Ba, my dear—don't—don't. I shouldn't have spoken—I shouldn't have told you all that. Forget it, my child. (*Goes to her.*) Take your hands from your face. (*Gently takes her wrists, she starts away from him with wide, frightened eyes.*) Don't look at me like that. (*In a low, thick voice, averting his eyes.*) You don't understand. How should you? You know nothing of the brutal tyranny of passion, and how the strongest and best are driven by it to Hell. You would have abetted your sister in her—

ELIZABETH (*fiercely*)—Henrietta's love—how dare you speak of it in the same breath as—

BARRETT (*brutally*)—Her love? You ignorant little fool! What do *you* know of love? The lust of the eye—the lowest urge of the body!

ELIZABETH (*starting to rise*)—I won't listen to you.

BARRETT (*taking her hands and putting her down again*)—You must—you shall! Do you suppose I should have guarded this house like a dragon from this so-called love, if I hadn't known from my own life all it entails of cruelty and loathing, and degradation and remorse? With the help of God, and through years of tormenting abstinence, I strangled it myself. And so long as there's breath in my body, I'll keep it away from those I was given to protect and care for. You understand me?

ELIZABETH (*in a low voice, looking him full in the face*)—Yes—I understand you.

BARRETT (*turns away from her. She sits quite still, looking straight before her*)—This has been a hateful necessity. I had to speak plainly, but we must turn over this ugly page and forget what was on it.

ELIZABETH (*drawing her hand from his*)—I shall never forget what you said!

BARRETT—Never—perhaps that's just as well. (*With sudden urgency, sits next to her on sofa.*) But, for God's sake, my darling, don't let this raise any further barrier between us! Your love is all I have left to me in the world.

ELIZABETH—You had Mamma's love once—you might have had the love of all your children.

BARRETT—Yes, if I'd played the part of a coward, taken the easier way, shirked my duty. I'd rather be hated by the whole world, than gain love like that.

ELIZABETH—Oh, Papa, you don't know how I pity you.

BARRETT (*roughly*)—Pity? I don't want your pity, but if I should ever lose you, or if I should ever lose your love— (*He seizes her unwilling hands.*) Ba, my darling, next week we shall have left this house, I've grown to loathe it—even this room has become hateful to me. In our new home we shall draw close to each other again. There will be little to distract you in the country—nothing and no one to come between us. (*He draws her stiffening form into his arms.*) My child, my darling, you must look up to me and depend on me, lean on me. You must share your thoughts with me, your hopes, your fears, your prayers. I want all your heart and all your soul. (*He draws her passionately close to him. She leans away from him, her face drawn with fear and pain.*)

ELIZABETH (*sobbingly*)—I can't bear it—I can't bear any more. Let me go, Papa—please let me go. (*He releases her, she stands aside, her arm covering her face.*)

BARRETT—Forgive me, dear—I was carried away. I'll leave you now.

ELIZABETH (*in a whisper*)—Please.

BARRETT (*rising*)—Shall I see you again tonight?

ELIZABETH (*as before*)—Not tonight.

BARRETT—I shall pray for you.

ELIZABETH (*half to herself*)—Pray for me? Tonight? Yes, pray for me tonight—if you will.

Barrett has gone. Elizabeth, tremulous with excitement, repeats again and again, the one phrase: "I must go—I must go at once—"

Wilson comes to report that her master is in the study. It is an hour before the cab will be at the corner, but Elizabeth cannot wait. Even if she has to walk the streets she cannot wait.

"Wilson," she says, "things have passed between my father and me which force me to leave this house at once. Until today I have never really known him. He's not like other men—he's dreadfully different. I—I can't say any more. If you draw back, you need never reproach yourself. But I must go now."

Now Wilson is in Elizabeth's arms emotionally pledging a lasting loyalty. She goes to get her hat and coat.

Slowly, wonderingly, Elizabeth draws from her bosom her wedding ring, takes it from the ribbon on which it is strung and puts it on her finger. She looks at it for a moment and then draws on her glove.

Now Wilson is back tiptoeing and whispering. Elizabeth picks up Flush and sends Wilson on ahead to see that her father's study door is shut.

"If you bark now, Flush, we're lost," she says.

A moment later she has followed Wilson into the hall, closing the door softly behind her.

The lights are dimmed. Darkness follows. An hour or two have passed. Then the room is gradually lightened.

Arabel is the first of the family to arrive. She notices the room's emptiness. The reading lamp is missing from the desk. She brings it in and sees the letters.

Now she has found and read her own letter. Her excitement results in little gasping explanations.

"Oh—! No! No! Married—! No! Oh-oh—! Married! Gone—"

Suddenly Arabel is shrieking with hysterical laughter. This brings the rest of the Barretts trooping in. Nothing they can do has any effect on what Octavius describes as Arabel's "high strikes."

"She's married—she's gone—married—gone—" Arabel keeps repeating.

It is Henrietta who finally takes command. Grabbing Arabel by the shoulders she shakes her vigorously. Arabel is finally able to blurt out her news—that Elizabeth has married Mr. Robert Browning! And to indicate the letters on the desk.

Now the whole family is threatened with the high strikes, followed by the awful thought: Who shall give Papa his letter? Henrietta will see to that? Henrietta would love to give Papa that letter.

A moment later Barrett strides into the room. He has heard their hideous noise. What is the meaning of it? Where is Elizabeth?

"Do you hear me?" he shouts, turning to Henrietta. "Where is your sister?"

Arabel has risen, fearfully, and grabbed Henrietta's arm. But

Henrietta frees herself quickly from Arabel's grasp and steps forward.

"She left you this letter," she says, handing it to him.

"Left me? What do you mean?"

"She left letters for all of us—this is yours." And, as he, bewildered and fearful, starts reading the letter, Henrietta springs forward and seizes his arm, continuing passionately and entreatingly—"You must forgive her, Papa—you must forgive her—not for her sake—but for yours! I thought I hated you—but I don't! I pity you—I pity you! And if you have any pity on yourself, forgive her!"

He looks at her steadily for a moment then pushes her aside. He opens and reads the letter. No one stirs. Nothing but the fury of his thickened breathing shows his emotions. He starts as if to collapse, HENRIETTA *and* OCTAVIUS *go to him, he pushes them aside. He turns and walks up to the window quite steadily, but his gait gives the impression that he is blind. He stands in front of the window, his back to the room, his hands tightly clasped behind him grasping the letter. The movement of his shoulders shows that he is breathing quickly and heavily. No one stirs.*

BARRETT (*half to himself, turning from the window*)—Yes—yes—her dog. (*An ugly smile flickers across his face.*) Yes—I'll have her dog—Octavius!

OCTAVIUS—Sir?

BARRETT—Her dog must be destroyed! At once! (*Slightly raising his voice.*) You will take it to the vet—tonight! You understand me? Tonight! (*A pause.*) You understand me!

OCTAVIUS (*desperately*)—I really d-don't see what the poor little beast has d-done to—

BARRETT (*ominously*)—You understand me?

HENRIETTA (*vainly trying to control the triumph in her voice*)—In her letter to me, Ba writes that she has taken Flush with her!

(BARRETT'S *face becomes once more a still white mask. He stands perfectly still staring straight before him, and mechanically tearing the letter into little pieces which drop to his feet as the curtain falls.*)

"GRAND HOTEL"

A Drama in Three Acts

By Vicki Baum

(Translation by W. A. Drake)

ANOTHER of those accidental sensations that provide the highlights of any theatre year followed the production of the German play, "Grand Hotel," at the National Theatre in mid-November.

It had been staged in Berlin by Max Reinhardt as "Menschen im Hotel" at the Deutsches Theatre, a playhouse celebrated for its revolving stage. Over there it was not a great success. As a possibility among plays it had been peddled in America, in a translation by W. A. Drake, and had been turned down by several producers. Principally because they did not think it could be done without a revolving stage and would be too expensive with one.

A Clevelander named Harry Moses, whose wife for years has been an ardent theatre lover, had backed Leo Bulgakov in a season of revived plays. One of these was also a translation by Mr. Drake. Mrs. Moses was a member of the Bulgakov company. Drake met Moses and showed him his translation of "Grand Hotel." Moses took it to Herman Shumlin, who had, the year before, scored so great a success with "The Last Mile."

With Mr. Moses' financial backing, Mr. Shumlin agreed to do the German play, and stage it on a series of pivotal platforms. The morning after its production its sweeping success was town talk.

"Grand Hotel," should, I think, be accepted as a satisfying adventure in the theatre rather than judged as a drama conforming in any accepted sense to playwriting standards. It is an adventure that inspires in the auditor's mind a sense of actual contact with life. He becomes a first-hand observer of episodes in many lives woven into a single pattern and displayed in a sort of universal Grand Hotel.

In the opening scenes of the play there is much bustle. As

much bustle, in fact, as a traveled person would naturally expect of any Grand Hotel anywhere.

The first view the audience has of the scene discloses an operator stationed at the nerve center of the institution, the telephone switchboard. Her busy hands respond automatically to the monotonous cadences of her voice, plugging in, breaking off the dozens of calls with which she is engaged; calling this person to that booth, and putting that one in touch with such outside connections as might lead around the world or no farther than around the corner.

"Grand Hotel. Hold the wire. Grand Hotel. Hold the wire. I am connecting you with 126 . . . He arrived this evening . . . Fourteen checked out an hour ago . . . The gentlemen do not wish to be disturbed . . . Senf, your connection in booth 2."

The light over the telephone operator's head blacks out. The light in booth 2 flashes on. Mr. Senf, somewhat excited, is talking with a nurse at a hospital . . . Mrs. Senf, we gather, is expecting a baby . . . Mr. Senf is suffering a painful impatience.

"Grand Hotel. Hold the wire. Grand Hotel . . . Mr. Bloom's room does not answer . . . Mr. Preysing . . . Long distance call to Fredersdorf . . . Booth 3."

Mr. Preysing fills up booth 3. . . . Mr. Preysing is manifestly worried . . . Mr. Preysing's stock is down another twenty-three points, which means that unless the merger with Saxonia goes through there will be trouble . . . Mr. Preysing will do what he can . . . Mr. Preysing is expecting Justice Zinnowitz.

In booth 4 Fräulein Flaemmchen is explaining to an impatient listener that she is at the Grand Hotel because Justice Zinnowitz told her to come there and take a friend's dictation. . . . Flaemmchen will therefore be unable to keep any other date that evening. . . . After all, Flaemmchen has to make her living.

In booth 6 Kringelein has succeeded in raising his friend Kampmann back home. . . . Kringelein is in Berlin, at the Grand Hotel, and he would like to have Kampmann tear up the will he (Kringelein) made before his operation. . . . Kringelein has seen a great specialist in Berlin and he knows now that he can live but a little while. . . . Kringelein has turned all his assets into cash, his life-insurance, his old-age pension, everything—and he probably never is going back to Fredersdorf again. . . . "You plague and bother and save and all of a sudden you're dead," says Kringelein. . . . He is at the Grand Hotel, where all the very best people stop. . . . He has even seen Preysing, his boss—and there is music all day long. . . ."

"Grand Hotel. Grand Hotel. Hold the wire."

In booth 5 Baron von Gaigern is in need of money. . . . With money the Baron can go on with the business in hand. . . . He has met Madame Grusinskaia. . . . He has played bridge with her orchestra leader, Witte, whose room is next to hers. . . . Tonight, at the theatre or after, Baron von Gaigern expects to complete the deal with Grusinskaia; but, first the Baron needs money. . . .

In booth 1 Suzanne has some difficulty making Mr. Meierheim, the impresario, understand that Mme. Grusinskaia has decided not to dance tonight. . . . No, Madame will not dance! Madame is crying; Madame is very tired. . . . Perhaps Herr Meierheim had better hurry over.

"Grand Hotel. Just a moment, please. . . ."

There is a babel of voices. Now everyone seems to be talking at once. The lights go out. Nothing but a confused ringing of bells is heard. It grows fainter. An orchestra is playing.

When the lights are on we are standing facing the clerk's desk in the lobby of the Grand Hotel. A busy lobby, conventionally furnished.

Through the revolving door from the street visitors, guests, clerks, bellboys pass in and out. The orchestra is playing in an adjoining grillroom. Drinks are being served at a pair of round tables in the corner. The elevator at the end of the desk, just beyond the pillar, is actively in service.

A nervous lady is trying to get accommodations on a train that does not happen to have the conveniences she demands. A gentleman is trying to have his theatre seats changed so he will be farther forward than they have put him. The assistant clerk is having some difficulty finding out over the desk phone whether Mme. Grusinskaia's car is to be brought or not to be brought. First it is and then it isn't.

The Baron von Gaigern runs into Herr Witte in the lobby and learns something of Mme. Grusinskaia's present temper. The great dancer is very difficult at times. Mr. Witte has come to the lobby for quiet. To room next to Mme. Grusinskaia is to be always on the run . . . Herr Witte would change his room if he did not fear he would hurt the madame's feelings . . . The Baron would gladly change rooms with Herr Witte . . .

Kringelein has been trying for some time to attract the attention of the clerk . . . Kringelein has a complaint. He does not like his room. He wants a better room . . .

Justice Zinnowitz would like to leave directions for his expected secretary . . . The nervous lady decides to take the train whether there is a diner or not . . . The old gentleman is finally convinced that his theatre seats are not so bad, but will the show be any good?

Kringelein would like to call the clerk's attention again to the fact that he does not like his room. It is very small and very inexpensive, but he does not want a small, inexpensive room. He wants a fine, big room, like Mr. Preysing's . . .

Flaemmchen has reported to the clerk . . . She is Justice Zinnowitz's secretary . . . She will wait for Justice Zinnowitz in the lobby.

What Herr Kringelein wants is a better room . . . A real Grand Hotel room . . . Not later; now! . . . "I have no time. I cannot wait," explains the unhappy Kringelein. "Every day counts, every hour, every minute. I came here because I want to live here two weeks—or three— God only knows . . . I will pay you what you ask . . . I want to live well . . . Just as other people do; just as Mr. Preysing does. Exactly as he does. I want to live here awhile, do you understand? I've got the money. I am sick. I am tired. And you give me a tiny little room, where the water pipes make a racket. . . ."

Herr Witte overhears . . . They can, if they will, give the young man his room, if it is so important . . . Both the clerk and Baron von Gaigern protest . . . Witte insists again . . . He prefers that Kringelein should have his room . . . Kringelein is greatly impressed . . . He will be neighbor to Mme. Grusinskaia, the famous lady who has her pictures in all the papers . . . The famous dancer and owner of the Sergei pearls! . . . Kringelein can hardly believe his ears . . . A grand room with bath—with a private bath all his own!

Now Baron von Gaigern is being even more kind to Kringelein . . . He would have Kringelein meet him in the lobby later and join him in a cocktail . . . To drink a cocktail with a real baron! . . . Kringelein's step is high as he goes to his room to pack and change.

Preysing has met Zinnowitz and been introduced to Flaemmchen, the secretary . . . He will be ready presently for the dictation . . . Meantime Flaemmchen can wait in the lobby and order what she likes for herself . . .

A chauffeur comes through the revolving doors . . . He sees Baron von Gaigern.

CHAUFFEUR—Have you time now, sir?

GAIGERN—Well, what is it?

CHAUFFEUR—May I see you just a minute, sir?

GAIGERN—Cigarette out of your mouth when you speak to me. How many times must I tell you that? You're giving us away. Where's the money?

CHAUFFEUR—Here's a hundred.

GAIGERN—I've got to have more money. I'll rush it. It costs like the devil to live here.

CHAUFFEUR—Finish the job and then you'll get more money. You've had plenty already. We know how that goes. Always money. We want results. You've been dragging this out for weeks.

GAIGERN—I can't rush it. I send her orchids every day. I . . .

CHAUFFEUR—You send her orchids. What's the idea? Are you in love with her?

GAIGERN—Don't be a fool. I play the part of an infatuated admirer. I had hoped to get into her room through her orchestra leader, Witte. But he has changed his rooms at the last minute with some funny provincial. Now I've got to get on good terms with him. That will take time.

CHAUFFEUR—Tomorrow night she'll be leaving.

GAIGERN—Tomorrow I'll do it.

CHAUFFEUR—Tonight!

GAIGERN—Tomorrow.

CHAUFFEUR—Tonight! I'll have the car here about 12.

GAIGERN—I'll do my best. Give me some more money.

CHAUFFEUR—Tonight at 12 I'll give you all the money. You were to get sixty thousand. You've had six already, Mr. Baron.

GAIGERN—I'll do what I can. You may go now, thanks.

CHAUFFEUR—Thank you, sir.

MEIERHEIM (*entering hurriedly*)—Madame Grusinskaia is still here?

SENF (*the manager*)—Madame is still here, Mr. Meierheim.

MEIERHEIM—My God! The performance soon starting. Quick! Quick! Bring her car!

SENF—Madame Grusinskaia's car.

CLERK (*ringing desk bell*)—Madame Grusinskaia's car.

BELLBOY (*at the door*)—Madame Grusinskaia's car.

(*The curtain falls.*)

Mme. Grusinskaia's room is as typical of a Grand Hotel as the lobby. A chaise longue. A dressing table. An armchair. A clothes rack in front of the door leading to Witte's room.

Suzanne, a "silent, faded and elderly factotum of Grusinskaia," awaits her mistress. She has brought Madame's ballet shoes. Madame may want to practice before the performance.

There is to be no performance, Madame announces, coming from her dressing room. A handsome Russian, in negligee, her eyes a dull, steady black in a white mask. There will be no performance. Has she not canceled the order for her car?

Another box of orchids arrives for Madame. Without any card. But surely from the same young man who had followed them to Nice, and sits in the theatre, night after night, applauding.

Herr Witte has been summoned from the lobby. He hears from Suzanne that Madame has a touch of stage fright and will not dance.

"No, it is more than that," Grusinskaia corrects, "I am afraid, Witte, terribly afraid."

"It will pass, Lisaveta." Witte is reassuring. "In Brussels you were just as tired, after the rough passage from England, but then you danced so wonderfully, and we had such an ovation—"

"But last night there was no applause. And if I dance tonight—" Grusinskaia becomes suddenly determined. "No, I will not dance. I am so tired—here—and here—" She indicates her heart and her forehead. "Witte, let us cancel the engagement."

WITTE—Madame has never canceled.

SUZANNE—One cannot cancel!

GRUSINSKAIA—Oh, yes, one can! One can cancel; one can quit entirely. Now is the time. I feel it. "Assez!" everything tells me "assez," enough, enough. (*She takes from jewel casket the loop of pearls.*)

WITTE—You are only overwrought, Lisaveta.

GRUSINSKAIA—No, Witte, I feel—everything growing cold around me . . . (*Presses pearls against her forehead.*) The Grand Duke Sergei is dead . . . His pearls are dead. And we are dead, too. (*Sits at dressing table.*) Passe! Finished.

SUZANNE—No, no, Madame, everything is as good as it always was.

GRUSINSKAIA—No, everything is threadbare now—the Russians—the pearls—Grusinskaia, oh . . . (*She throws her pearls at her feet.*)

SUZANNE (*picking up pearls*)—Mon Dieu! The pearls! If something were to break!

WITTE—Please, Lisaveta.

GRUSINSKAIA—They don't break. They hold together and bring me bad luck. This is no life for me any more. Ballet shoes—divertisements—attitudes . . .

WITTE—Madame will certainly have a great success tonight.

GRUSINSKAIA—I shall have no success tonight—nor tomorrow—I'll never again have any success. No. This is the end. I am going to retire from the stage. That is all. (*The phone rings.*)

SUZANNE (*at phone*)—Yes. One moment. The chauffeur is calling, Madame. He is waiting with the car.

GRUSINSKAIA—I don't want it! I didn't tell them to send it.

SUZANNE—He came of his own accord. He knew it was time to take you to the theatre.

GRUSINSKAIA—I won't go. I want to be left alone. Send the car away.

SUZANNE (*into the phone*)—Madame does not want the car now.

GRUSINSKAIA—I am very unhappy, Witte. I am tired. I am so alone . . .

SUZANNE—Come, Madame must dress.

WITTE—It is time, Lisaveta. You must go to the theatre.

GRUSINSKAIA—I won't have you say "must"—my heart is so tired. Witte, please help me.

WITTE (*sits beside her*)—Lisaveta, if I only could. How can I help you?

The door has been flung open. Meierheim, the impresario, dashes in. He is excited, too. It is no more than an hour before the performance and Madame is still in negligee! It is enough to give a manager a stroke!

"I am not coming. I am canceling the engagement."

Meierheim is not impressed. Grusinskaia *will* dance. There

are obligations. There are promises. People are not paying thirty marks to see understudies dance.

"Madame, you will dance," declares Meierheim with some authority. "You are too great an artist to go on being temperamental. You cannot disappoint your public. The theatre is jammed to the rafters. I simply will not hear of a cancellation. There has been a line in front of the box office since six o'clock. Come! Quick! Get dressed!"

"Is there really a full house tonight?" Grusinskaia is sitting up quite brightly now.

"Doesn't Meierheim say so? The Crown Prince made reservations! Two foreign ministers! Mary Wigman came from Dresden just to see you. Max Reinhardt is bringing a couple of American millionaires. And now, shall Desprez take your place?"

"All right. Wait for me in the lobby. I'll be ready in ten minutes!"

There are not ten minutes to spare, according to Meierheim. The start must be made at once. And let her not forget the pearls. How careless they all are with those pearls. Not dance with them? Of course she will dance with them!

By the time Meierheim can get to the phone and order the car again the parade has started—Grusinskaia, Suzanne, Witte, Meierheim.

The lights fade. The curtain falls.

Back in the lobby we pick up the scene where we left it with Flaemmchen ordering something. She has a champagne flip, but needs a light for her cigarette. Baron von Gaigern can furnish this, and does. He thinks, perhaps, he has met Flaemmchen in Baden-Baden. But Flaemmchen knows better. She has never been in Baden-Baden. Besides, that is an old, old game.

Flaemmchen is pleased to have Gaigern sit and talk with her, but she cannot dance with him because she is waiting for someone. Later in the evening, perhaps— But later in the evening Gaigern has an engagement to go to the theatre and see Grusinskaia dance. He is very, very fond of Grusinskaia, Gaigern admits, but for the moment he likes Flaemmchen's type quite as well. So well that he would like her to promise that she will meet him there tomorrow—

The elevator has brought the Grusinskaia party to the lobby. The hotel manager has discovered that he has a telegram for Mme. Grusinskaia. Madame has read her telegram and discovered it to be a notice of cancellation from Budapest.

The news is displeasing to Madame. She has been stealing a covert glance or two at Gaigern, but now her anger has put other things out of her mind. Of one thing she is convinced—all her bad luck can be traced to those Sergei pearls. She has said before and she now repeats she will not dance with those pearls again. Let Suzanne take them at once back to her room! . . .

The chauffeur is back. He reports formally to Gaigern. It is time to leave for the theatre. But Gaigern is not going to the theatre this night. The pearls are not in the theatre. Let the chauffeur come back at 12, and be waiting at the south door.

Gaigern is able now to rejoin Flaemmchen. He introduces her a moment later to Kringelein. Kringelein has finally changed rooms and is quite happy over the new arrangement. He has everything he wants now.

"I had the amusement guide book sent up," he tells them. "I'd like to see something. Have a big time. Drink champagne, for instance. It's expensive, I know. I looked on the card. You can't get it for less than twelve marks. That makes no difference. I want to eat caviar, too—for the first time in my life. (FLAEMMCHEN *laughs.*) I see the lady is laughing."

FLAEMMCHEN—Have caviar if you like. But it tastes like herring.

KRINGELEIN—Caviar and champagne may mean nothing to you, but to me they mean a great deal. You see, sir, I am ill, and all of a sudden I got a fear, such a fear, of missing life. I don't want to miss life . . . do you understand?

FLAEMMCHEN—Funny. You speak of life as if it were a train you wanted to catch.

KRINGELEIN—Yes, and for me it is going to leave any minute. I am not at all well.

GAIGERN—Well, Mr. Kringelein, what do you say? Let's have a really big night, would you like that?

KRINGELEIN—Yes, indeed, Baron.

GAIGERN—And Flaem comes along, don't you, Flaemmchen?

FLAEMMCHEN—No, worse luck, I've been engaged for the evening.

KRINGELEIN—Can a person engage you just for the evening?

FLAEMMCHEN—Yes, to take dictation—a Mr. Preysing.

KRINGELEIN—Preysing! Of course! It would be Preysing! That's just like him.

FLAEMMCHEN—Do you know him?

KRINGELEIN—Do I know him! Do I know him! (PREYSING

and ZINNOWITZ *enter from the corridor.*) I know him through and through! I'd give a good deal—to settle my accounts with him—

PREYSING (*to* RECEPTION MAN *as they cross over to the grill room*)—I engaged the conference room for 7 o'clock. (*To* ZINNOWITZ.) We can talk there without being disturbed. We shall need you very soon, Miss Flaem. (KRINGELEIN *rises on hearing* PREYSING'S *voice, stops short and listens.*)

KRINGELEIN (*to* PREYSING)—I have the honor, Your Excellency!

PREYSING (*scarcely glancing at him*)—How-do. (*To the boy.*) If a telegram comes (*to* ZINNOWITZ) from Manchester (*to the boy*) bring it to me immediately. Come, Zinnowitz!

OTTERNSCHLAG (*an acquaintance*)—That's no way to catch up with life, Mr. Kringelein! (*The lights go out. The curtain falls.*)

SCENE V

A bellboy shows Preysing and Zinnowitz into a small conference room. It is a bare room, filled for the most part with a long conference table surrounded by large chairs.

Preysing is extremely anxious about the approaching meeting. Zinnowitz is more optimistic. He has seen the Saxonia people. If word should come from Manchester, as they expect it will, that Burleigh & Son are willing to enter into an association with Preysing's firm, everything will go off smoothly. Otherwise, of course, with the stock dropping as it is, there may be trouble.

The merger, according to Preysing, must go through. His firm is solid, but in a bad way temporarily. Some way, the merger must be consummated.

Preysing has phoned the clerk to send Flaemmchen up. He wants to start dictating his speech for the conference. He cannot talk without notes.

Zinnowitz leaves Preysing with the advice that if he has to lie a little about the willingness of Burleigh & Son to come into the deal he had better do so than risk the chance of failure. But Preysing, being an honorable man, a married man, with a family and children, does not want to lie . . .

Flaemmchen finds a typewriter on the table. Her youth and prettiness burst a little startlingly on Preysing. He had not noticed her before.

Even after he has begun the dictation of his speech, which Flaemmchen is taking at the typewriter rather than by shorthand,

Preysing is compelled to stop occasionally to wonder about Flaemmchen. She really is very pretty for a typist.—

How, Preysing wonders, did her hands get so sunburned?

"That's from skiing," admits Flaemmchen. "A gentleman friend of mine took me to Switzerland last month."

"He took you to Switzerland, eh?" The suggestion has possibilities.

A knock at the door and the voice of the bellboy in the corridor interrupts the dictation. The boy brings a telegram. Preysing opens it with feverish haste. It is from Manchester. Reading it, Preysing goes suddenly white, and drops into a chair. The telegram falls from his hand. Flaemmchen picks it up and reads:

"Deal definitely off—Brosemann."

"Oh, is that something terrible?" she asks, innocently. "Don't we need to go on with the dictation now?"

Preysing is on his feet again, annoyed at her inquiry.

"Nothing of the sort!" he snaps.

FLAEMMCHEN—But you are so pale. Do you want some water? (*She hands him a glass of water.*)

PREYSING (*drinks*)—Thank you. (*Takes telegram from her.*) Who gave you permission to read the telegram?

FLAEMMCHEN—You are right. I'm sorry. (*Crosses to typewriter table—sits.*)

PREYSING—As a matter of fact, the telegram isn't important at all. What my agent, Brosemann, is telegraphing about is nothing at all. (*He crosses room and gulps hard.*) The fool! On the contrary the telegram brings very good news. Very good news . . . Come, let's get my report finished. Where were we?

FLAEMMCHEN—"Namely with the consequent large increase in profits for such participation in the world market. Period—"

PREYSING—What? Oh, yes. Period. Write. "The Fredersdorf woolen mills at this very time are developing such brilliant prospects of this sort that—" (*Crosses to* FLAEMMCHEN.) Do you see, Miss Flaem? It's stated that way so as to fool anybody who might accidentally get hold of it. It's a code. Yes, a code. That's what it is . . . Where were we?

FLAEMMCHEN—"Such brilliant prospects . . ."

PREYSING—"Such brilliant prospects of this sort. (*Picks up telegram from the floor.*) That it is obvious that the merger—between the two concerns can bring only the finest results—" (*The typewriter machine is still clicking as the lights fade and the curtain falls.*)

In Kringelein's room the Baron von Gaigern is watching his new friend unpack his recently transferred suitcase. It is a neatly furnished hotel room of the better grade, and Kringelein is well pleased with it.

The concern of both at the moment is how Kringelein and Gaigern can get the most out of their evening. They will go to a theatre, and then to a night club and from then on the night will probably take care of itself.

A porter brings in the Kringelein trunk and, before he goes, stops to lock the door that connects with the room occupied by Mme. Grusinskaia.

It happens that Mme. Grusinskaia has the room one side of Kringelein and Herr Preysing has the room the other side. They are identical rooms so far as their furnishings are concerned. Kringelein is proud when he thinks of that.

But about the evening's festivities—Kringelein hasn't any dress clothes. Never had any. Does not think it would pay him to buy any for—so short a time.

That, concludes the Baron, is false reasoning. If he wants to live a little while, and have a good time, he must look right and dress right. Tonight he can wear the best he has. Tomorrow he shall go to a good tailor and be outfitted. Meantime he must go to the barber, be shaved and have the hair cut around his forehead.

This, decides Gaigern, must be done immediately before the barber shop is closed.

The Baron has hustled the somewhat confused Kringelein through the door and on his way to the barber shop before he knows what really is happening. Gaigern follows after and closes the door.

A moment later Gaigern is back. Nervously he lets himself in and approaches the door leading to Mme. Grusinskaia's room. He has produced a set of skeleton keys and is fumbling with the lock as the lights fade.

Mme. Grusinskaia's room is in darkness until the connecting door opens slowly and the beam of Gaigern's flashlight picks out the furniture and rests finally upon the dresser. He crosses to this, fumbles quietly through the drawers, produces a jewel casket and from this lifts the Sergei pearls and slips them into his pocket.

A rattling at the door disturbs the Baron. He has barely time to switch off his light and conceal himself behind a costumer hung with clothes. The door opens and a chambermaid enters.

She straightens the articles spread over the dresser, turns on the mirror light, stirs up the pillows on the sofa and goes into the adjoining bedroom.

A moment later she has called the hall porter to know why the door of the adjoining room was open. The porter does not know.

Now the phone is ringing. Someone from the theatre is trying to get in touch with Mme. Grusinskaia. Or Madame's maid. The chambermaid is explaining that neither is there when Suzanne, in some excitement, walks in. She, too, has been searching for Mme. Grusinskaia and cannot find her.

Something had happened at the theatre. Mme. Grusinskaia had made her appearance, as usual. There was no applause. Shortly there was a hiss. When the curtain was lowered Herr Witte had taken Madame to the dressing room and Suzanne had run for a doctor. At the end of the intermission they went to call her and Madame had disappeared. Now, no one knows where she is. She may have done harm to herself!

Meierheim has dashed in. He is both excited and angry. An artist—to desert—right in the middle of the performance! Well, it will cost Grusinskaia a suit for breach of contract—

Witte has joined the group. He is too anxious to care what happened to his orchestra. He left the concert-master leading and Desprez, the substitute, dancing for Grusinskaia. Now he would send the manager back to the theatre.

"Meierheim, do me a big favor and go back to the theatre," pleads Witte. "If Madame comes home she will need rest. Her nerves—"

"Her nerves! Her nerves!" screams the excited Meierheim. "All she has to do is dance, I take the risk. She has ruined me, and who is she, anyway? An out-of-date dancer that no one gives a damn about any more."

They are still quarreling when Grusinskaia appears quietly in the door. She has thrown a cloak over her ballet costume.

Now they have swarmed about her. Suzanne and Witte are solicitous. Meierheim is ready to carry his protests personally to the author of them. Grusinskaia puts them all off. She wants to hear no more of what has happened tonight. She wants to be alone.

It is difficult for them to understand, but one by one they are induced to leave her. Slowly she raises her head. There are tears of self-pity in her eyes. Before the mirror she mutters: "Poor Gru! Poor Gru!" Putting her coat aside she takes a dancing position. She tries a few steps and collapses. "Never!

You cannot dance again! You cannot dance again! Finished—finished—" she murmurs.

Grusinskaia has taken her robe and is turning toward the bedroom when she sees Gaigern's reflection in the mirror. As he steps out from behind the costumer, the dancer backs away and then stops, as though she were more curious than afraid. She has recognized Gaigern.

He has come, Gaigern tells her, just to be in her room because he loves her. She stares at him a long moment, and then suddenly throws herself on the couch and is sobbing passionately. He has come to the couch and is bending solicitously above her.

"Poor Grusinskaia," he murmurs. "Does it do you good to cry? Are you afraid? Shall I go? Poor, poor little thing. Has somebody harmed you? Were the people bad to you? Are you afraid? Do you cry because I love you? You poor little . . ."

"I was so alone," she sobs; "always alone—nobody—and suddenly you were there and said that word." She is sitting up now, looking frankly at him. "No, I am not afraid. It is strange."

GAIGERN—You were crying, it tore my heart to hear you sob like that.

GRUSINSKAIA—Nerves, just nerves. Monsieur is to blame. Monsieur frightened me. You are the one who sent me those orchids? Such a fright. You must forgive me, I have had a bad evening. I am very tired. Do you know what it is to be tired—tired of a routine existence?

GAIGERN—I'm afraid I don't. There is no routine for me. I always do exactly what I feel like doing, at the moment.

GRUSINSKAIA—So—you feel like walking into a lady's room, you walk in?

GAIGERN—Yes. (*He sits on couch at her right.*)

GRUSINSKAIA—Why do you look at me like that?

GAIGERN—Because you are beautiful. I did not know you were so beautiful, and . . .

GRUSINSKAIA—And what else?

GAIGERN—No, I mean it. You are so appealing, so soft, so little, so fragile. I feel like taking you in my arms and not letting anything more happen to you, ever.

GRUSINSKAIA (*involuntarily closing her eyes*)—And . . . and . . .

GAIGERN—How tired you are!

GRUSINSKAIA—Yes—tired . . .

GAIGERN—So alone.

GRUSINSKAIA—Yes, alone . . . always alone. (*In Russian.*) Na ceveri, decome stoite odenoke na goloy varshini sosna.

GAIGERN—You mustn't speak Russian to me.

GRUSINSKAIA—Man, strange man . . .

GAIGERN—Am I quite strange to you?

GRUSINSKAIA—Not quite strange now. It's as if I had been expecting you. You know, once when the Grand Duke was alive, I found a young man hiding in my room—a young officer—

GAIGERN—And . . . ?

GRUSINSKAIA—He disappeared. Later he was found shot.

GAIGERN—I never knew it was so dangerous to be found in a room in which a woman is alone. A woman—one loves. (*Touches her hand.*)

GRUSINSKAIA (*drawing away from him*)—No. No. No. Who are you—man?

GAIGERN—A man who loves you—that is all, a man who has forgotten everything else for you.

GRUSINSKAIA—You love me. You know I haven't heard that word for a long time. I was so cruelly alone. How is it that you —let me look at you. Your hands. Your eyes. Why do you love me?

GAIGERN—Don't you know that I've followed you all over Europe—for weeks? I heard you cry—I saw you in the mirror. You are so beautiful—I have never seen a woman as beautiful as you. What kind of a woman are you?

GRUSINSKAIA—Well, I'm just old-fashioned. I am from another world, another country than yours. That is it. We were drilled like little soldiers, we dancers, in the school of the Imperial Ballet, in St. Petersburg. No rest, no leisure, no stopping, ever. And then, whoever is famous is alone. Then one isn't a person any more, not a woman! One is just a symbol of success that is driven round and round the world. And what it means to hold on to success, five years, ten years, fifteen years! On the day success ends, life ends for such as I. Are you listening to me?

GAIGERN—Yes, yes.

GRUSINSKAIA—Do you understand me? Oh, how I wish you would understand.

GAIGERN—I do understand—let me be good to you. Let me stay here with you.

GRUSINSKAIA—I think you must go now. The key is in the door.

GAIGERN—No. I am not going. You know I am not going.

GRUSINSKAIA—I wish to be alone.

GAIGERN—That is not true. You were in despair before I came. If I left you, you would feel worse than you did before. (*Closer to her.*) You must not be alone. You must not cry, you must forget. Tell me that I can stay with you, tell me . . . (*Face to face.*)

GRUSINSKAIA (*whispering*)—Just for a minute. (*She is in his arms as the lights fade. The curtain falls.*)

ACT II

The next morning, in the conference room, delegates representing the Saxonia corporation are assembled. They include Gerstenkorn, an older man of the executive type; Schweimann, who is younger, and Dr. Waitz, legal counsel.

Mr. Preysing, it appears, is already ten minutes late, and the Saxonians are inclined to resent both the waste of time and the attitude of indifference which Preysing's lateness indicates.

Talking among themselves the delegates are free to admit their belief that Preysing's Fredersdorf company is in a bad way. Two months will probably see it on the market, unless Burleigh & Son in Manchester enter into a selling agreement with Fredersdorf. In that case the combination would be strongly competitive.

Preysing soon joins them, but prefers not to discuss business until Justice Zinnowitz arrives. Another delay. While they are waiting Gerstenkorn would like to find out, if possible, how recently Preysing has been in England; what he thinks of the situation there and what, specifically, is his firm's connection, if any, with Burleigh & Son. Preysing refuses to commit himself. He prefers to talk about the advantages Saxonia would enjoy if the proposed merger with Fredersdorf is carried out.

The Saxonia delegates are not greatly interested in the report of business done by Fredersdorf Woolen Mills, nor in its trade possibilities. They have been all over that. What they want to know is about Manchester—

Gerstenkorn and Preysing are arguing with great fervor, each accusing the other of having started negotiations looking to a merger, when Justice Zinnowitz' arrival temporarily saves the situation.

Calmly, at Preysing's insistence, Zinnowitz takes charge of the meeting and begins a restatement of the facts.

"Gentlemen, the situation is quite clear," recalls Zinnowitz.

Photo by Vandamm Studio, New York.

"GRAND HOTEL"

"When the lights go on we are facing the clerk's desk in the lobby of the Grand Hotel. Could be any Grand Hotel." (Kringelein, coat on arm, is at the desk. The Baron von Gaigern, with hat and cane, sits at table. Near him, sitting demurely in the corner, Flaemmchen is waiting.)

"When the preliminary negotiations for the merger of Fredersdorf and Saxonia were begun, on June 11 of this year—"

"Thank God we're beginning at the beginning," sighs Gerstenkorn.

"It was fully understood and agreed," Zinnowitz continues, "that the existing situation was to be accepted by both parties as the basis for trading."

Zinnowitz' voice trails through the dimming lights as the scene is blacked out.

In Grusinskaia's room, brightened by the morning sun, the dancer is adding casually to her toilet before her dressing table. Seated facing her, quite wrapped up in the process, is the Baron von Gaigern.

Amused by his interest, Grusinskaia is suddenly reminded that she does not even know her friend's name.

GAIGERN—My name is Felix Amadeus Benvenuto, Freiherr von Gaigern. My mother called me Flix.

GRUSINSKAIA—Flix. And how do you live? What kind of a person are you?

GAIGERN—There's not much to be said about me. I am a prodigal son, the black sheep of a white flock. I am a mauvais *sujet* and I shall die on the gallows.

GRUSINSKAIA (*laughing*)—Really?

GAIGERN—Really. I haven't a bit of character. I can't organize myself, and I am good for nothing. At home, I learned to ride and play the gentleman. At school, I learned to pray and lie. In the war, to shoot and hunt cover. That is all.

GRUSINSKAIA—So what do you do?

GAIGERN—I am a gambler, yet it would never occur to me to cheat. By all right I belong in jail. Yet I run at large. Happy as a pig, and enjoy all of life that pleases me.

GRUSINSKAIA—And what else do you do?

GAIGERN—I am also a criminal, a hotel thief.

GRUSINSKAIA (*laughing*)—And what else? Perhaps a murderer?

GAIGERN—Perhaps, yes. I even came here prepared for that last night. (*Takes revolver out of right pocket, shows it to her and puts it back.*)

GRUSINSKAIA (*softly*)—You make bad jokes.

GAIGERN (*takes both her hands*)—Please, look at me. (GRUSINSKAIA *looks at him.*) That way—quite calmly. You must believe me. You must believe that I love you; that I have never known what love is, until last night. You must believe me. (*He kisses her hands.*)

GRUSINSKAIA—What is the matter?

GAIGERN (*takes pearls out of his pocket, lays them in her lap*)—There.

GRUSINSKAIA (*with a little cry of pain*)—Ah! (*Awkward silence.*) Did you come here—just—to do that? This is horrible! (*She rises, leaning on dresser.*) You may keep the pearls. (*She drops them on dresser.*) I do not want them any more. I make you a present of them.

GAIGERN—I don't want the pearls!

GRUSINSKAIA—I will not denounce you.

GAIGERN—I know . . .

GRUSINSKAIA—So . . .

GAIGERN (*turns and takes a step toward her*)—Yesterday, I was a thief. Now . . .

GRUSINSKAIA (*turning away*)—Now you must go. I give you the pearls, but now you must go.

GAIGERN (*crosses to her*)—I will not go. You must listen to me. You must believe me. I am not an impostor. I haven't always been a criminal. I am really a Baron,—I was in fearful difficulties. I was threatened. I was desperately in need of a large sum of money. I would have chanced hanging for it. That is why I wanted your pearls. I followed you around. I found myself falling in love with you, but I forced myself not to think of you. I managed to get into your room, and now . . .

GRUSINSKAIA—And now . . . ? (*He sinks in chair, face in hands.*)

GAIGERN—I can't go through with it. Extraordinary. (*After a struggle, she bends over him and strokes his head.*) Do you understand? (*Looks up at her.*)

GRUSINSKAIA (*hugging him closely*)—Yes. Yes. Yes!

Grusinskaia is ready to believe Gaigern when he says that now he wants to be good to her—madly good. She is crying softly on his shoulder and assuring him that everything is to be all right when the telephone rings.

It is Suzanne warning Madame of an approaching rehearsal. Grusinskaia will be ready. Grusinskaia *wants* to rehearse now. She wants to dance. She must dance.

Early in the morning she will be leaving Berlin. Can't Gaigern come with them? It would be better—better for them both.

Grusinskaia is convinced of that. Money? She has money. She will give him money.

Gaigern will go with Grusinskaia. He promises that much. But he will not take money from her. He will find money, some way. He still has a whole day to do that.

"I shall dance, and you will be with me," Grusinskaia sighs happily as she sinks in his arms. "And then—listen—" Her voice grows tremulous and high. "After that you will come with me to Lake Como. I have a little house in Tremezzo. Everything is beautiful there, marvelous. I will take a vacation, six weeks, eight weeks; we will be insanely happy and lazy. And then you will go with me to South America. Do you know Rio?"

Suzanne is again on the phone. Grusinskaia answers—holding Gaigern close to her as she does so. Suzanne can come now when she will.

Gaigern has made his final promises. He will be on the train. He will do nothing foolish. He loves Grusinskaia—

Gaigern has gone. Grusinskaia turns happily to the telephone. She would call Witte. She has just thought of a wonderful new dance. She will need music for that.

She also gets Meierheim on the phone. Exultantly she informs the manager that she will be at rehearsal at 11, and advises him to hurry over.

Now she is hurrying Suzanne with the dressing and the ordering of the car. And now she has turned to the telephone again to call Gaigern.

There is nothing she has to say to Gaigern when she gets him. Except a joyous "Good morning!" And tell him again that she is happy.

She is doing that as the lights fade and the curtain falls.

The scene in the conference room has changed but little, but the atmosphere is greatly different. The air is thick with tobacco smoke. The table is littered with ash trays, coffee cups and the remains of a lunch.

Gerstenkorn, Schweimann and Waitz are huddled together examining a document. Preysing and Zinnowitz eye them anxiously.

The document is the agreement with Manchester which Preysing has produced at the eleventh hour. It is complete, with signatures, and entirely changes the existing situation. Now Saxonia is eager to sign the other agreement with Fredersdorf. They would not have wasted the whole day in conference, if they had known . . .

The Saxonians have left to catch their train for home. Preysing is wilted, but happy. Zinnowitz resents having put in a day talking when Preysing had the Manchester agreement all the time.

But that's the trick. Preysing did not have the Manchester agreement, because there is none! Preysing has bluffed the Saxonians into signing a merger on the strength of an agreement that does not exist. The fact that he discovered they were trying to bluff him is what inspired his courage. If bluff is what the world wants, Preysing will be as good a bluffer as anyone. Now, as Zinnowitz reminds him, he must hurry to Manchester and put through that merger on the strength of what he has done with Saxonia. Preysing is just a little hysterical with the thought of what he has done.

"I'd like to tear loose tonight," Preysing admits. "I'd like to drink cocktails, wine, go out! Do something! Things I have never done in my life. It came over me in a flash. They were out to get me! Then I turned the trick on them, one of their own tricks. They want Manchester! I'll give them Manchester, but I'll make them bring it to me themselves. It's crooked, but it makes miracles happen. Bluff's the thing. It's intoxicating! I'm ready for anything tonight!"

Suddenly Preysing recalls Flaemmchen, the stenographer. He would like to do some more dictating. He must send a report of the conference to his father-in-law. He thinks Flaemmchen is a very pretty girl. He agrees with Zinnowitz that she is much too pretty for an office. He will go downstairs and find Flaemmchen. He needs a drink, anyway.

"I don't know a thing about women," admits Zinnowitz, as they leave the room. "I've been married twenty-six years."

The lights are out. The curtain is down.

The dance floor of the Hotel Grill includes a bar at one end in front of which tables have been placed. The dancers are in the habit of frequenting that section of the room when they are thirsty or while they are waiting for their engagements.

As we enter several couples are dancing past or near the bar. Back of the bar a white and a Negro bartender are mixing drinks. Kringelein, his eyes shining with the excitement of his adventure, stands at one end of the bar. Flaemmchen is dancing with a stranger. Waiters are passing in and out with orders. It is all very exciting to Kringelein. He is particularly thrilled when Flaemmchen recognizes him and compliments him on his new clothes.

Flaemmchen is interested in Kringelein. Happy to drink a Louisiana Flip with him. Would be happy to dance with him if Kringelein could dance. But he can't. She's in there, she explains, because she had an engagement with someone who evidently has forgotten her. She dances away with a gigolo who has been watching her.

The Baron von Gaigern joins Kringelein at table. The Baron is sorry he is late, sorry he disappointed Flaemmchen, but he has had a hard day—and he is broke. Twenty-four marks is the sum total of his fortunes. He is likely to stay broke unless he can raise enough to get in a game. Winning a stake is his last chance, and he is desperately in need of funds.

Kringelein is not quite sure whether he should take the Baron seriously or not, but it would give him great pleasure to loan the Baron two, three hundred marks if that would help. It would, Gaigern agrees. And takes it.

Flaemmchen is through dancing with her gigolo, and has joined Kringelein and Gaigern. She is forgiving with Gaigern for his tardiness. She can see that he has had a hard day. She will hear the rest as they dance.

Kringelein is not left entirely alone when they are gone. His old friend, Otternschlag, joins him. Otternschlag is a good deal of a pessimist. He has put a varied and exciting past behind him and is convinced there was nothing in it. Life's a mess with Otternschlag.

"So now you're staying at the Grand Hotel," ruminates the pessimist. " 'Grand Hotel' you think. 'Most expensive hotel' you think. God knows what kind of miracles you expect from such a hotel. You will soon see what there is to it. Like everything else. One comes, stays awhile, goes away. Transients. What do you do in the Grand Hotel? Eat, sleep, loaf around, do business, flirt a little, dance a little. Yes, but what do you do anywhere? A hundred doors to one hall and nobody knows anything about the person next to him. When you leave another takes your room, sleeps in your bed. End."

Preysing and Zinnowitz have appeared and discovered Flaemmchen dancing with Gaigern. Preysing would take the young woman away immediately, but Gaigern is opposed to that. He promptly dances her out of reach again. Preysing is forced to wait at an adjoining table.

Now the dancers are back and Kringelein, delighted at the chance to be somebody before his old boss, Preysing, has gone to the bar to order drinks for them.

Flaemmchen is flushed with the success of her dance with Gaigern, but the Baron is serious. He would ask a favor of her, which she would, quite evidently, be happy to grant. But it is not a favor for himself. Gaigern wants her to be good to Kringelein. He wants her to dance once with Kringelein.

Flaemmchen is willing. She, too, is sorry for Kringelein. But she cannot quite understand what has come over Gaigern since yesterday. Nor is she altogether pleased with his confession that since yesterday he has fallen in love—and has been amazed to find that this time it is the real thing. . . .

Preysing would have something to say about Kringelein's dancing with Flaemmchen. He has risen promptly from his place at an adjoining table and stopped them as Flaemmchen puts her arm in Kringelein's and started away with him.

PREYSING (*coming down between* KRINGELEIN *and* FLAEMMCHEN—I must speak to you, Miss Flaem! Business. A dictation job.

FLAEMMCHEN—Fine. When does it start? Tomorrow morning?

PREYSING—No. Right now.

FLAEMMCHEN—Why, I'm busy right now. Do you gentlemen know one another? Mr. Kringelein, Mr. Preysing, Baron von Gaigern. (GAIGERN *rises stiffly, bows to* PREYSING, *who bows to* GAIGERN, *ignoring* KRINGELEIN.)

PREYSING (*to* KRINGELEIN)—Mr. Kringelein will be a good friend and not accept this invitation.

KRINGELEIN (*fairly rigid*)—I could not think of not accepting it.

PREYSING—So. Now I understand. You have reported sick at the plant, have you not? Leave of absence, with pay. And you are here in Berlin, having a high time. Indulging in diversions which ill befit your position and which are very far beyond your means. Quite extraordinary, Mr. Kringelein! We shall look into your books.

FLAEMMCHEN (*coming between them*)—Now, children! No fighting. Do that in your office. We're here to have a good time. Come, Mr. Kringelein! Let's have our dance.

KRINGELEIN (*as he is whirled away by* FLAEMMCHEN)—Does the world belong to you, Mr. Preysing? Haven't I any right to live?

FLAEMMCHEN—Come! Come! This isn't a place to fight.

This is a place to dance. (*To* PREYSING:) Will you please leave us alone?

PREYSING—Very well, Miss Flaem. I will not interfere with your pleasure. I will wait ten minutes for you. If you don't come then, I shall have to get somebody else.

FLAEMMCHEN (*somewhat intimidated*)—Yes, Mr. Preysing.

KRINGELEIN—Come on! Let us dance.

PREYSING (*to* GAIGERN)—I wonder if he is not an embezzler. An embezzler, here dancing at the Grand Hotel!

GAIGERN—Oh, leave the poor devil alone! Death is staring him in the face!

PREYSING—I did not ask your advice.

GAIGERN (*rising, sticking monocle in eye*)—Nevertheless, I think it would be better if you went away.

PREYSING—We shall see who remains here the longer. (*They stare at each other.*)

GAIGERN (*shrugging his shoulders and replacing his monocle in his pocket—and sits*)—As you wish.

The Baron von Gaigern's chauffeur has appeared and would like to see the Baron. Gaigern is gone when Flaemmchen and Kringelein dance in from the hall and pause for a moment before their table.

"You must look at my face, not at the floor," prompts the amused Flaemmchen. "You are trembling."

"I never danced before," explains Kringelein, happily embarrassed.

"Why, you are doing very well," insists Flaemmchen, sympathetically.

"I am happy, Miss Flaem."

"Really?"

"For the first time in my life I am happy."

A moment later the music has stopped. Now Flaemmchen must go to Mr. Preysing. That's business. A person has to earn a living.

"I'm just another desk slave, Mr. Kringelein," sighs Flaemmchen.

He takes her reluctantly to Preysing's table.

"It was wonderful—thank you very much," he says.

"I'm glad you liked it."

Preysing rises to meet them, flushed with anger.

"Well, here you are at last, Miss Flaem," he begins. "You may go, Mr. Kringelein."

"I'm not taking orders from you here, Mr. Preysing," shrills Kringelein, defiantly.

PREYSING—What is this insolence? It's unheard of.

KRINGELEIN—Do you think you have free license to be insulting? Believe me, you have not. You think you are superior but you are quite an ordinary man, even if you did marry money, and people like me have to slave for three hundred and twenty marks a month.

PREYSING—Get out of my way, sir, or . . .

FLAEMMCHEN (*coming between them*)—Oh, please, please. (PREYSING *turns upstage.*)

HEAD WAITER (*entering*)—Pardon me, gentlemen, but we are closing.

KRINGELEIN (*crossing to* PREYSING)—I have a big account to settle with you, Mr. Preysing. I've been looking forward to this a long time. You don't like to see me here enjoying myself? But if a man is working himself to death, that's not worth talking about. That's what he's paid for. You don't care whether a man can live on his wages.

PREYSING—We pay the regular scale, and there's the sick fund—the old age fund—

KRINGELEIN—What a scale! And what a fund! When I had been ill four weeks you wrote me a letter saying I would be fired if I was ill any longer. Did you write that, or did you not?

PREYSING (*turning away from him*)—I don't remember every letter I write. Anyhow, here you are on sick leave with pay. And living like a lord, like an embezzler!

HEAD WAITER—Gentlemen, we are closing.

KRINGELEIN (*going up to him*)—You are going to take that back! Right here, in the presence of the young lady. Who do you think you're talking to? (FLAEMMCHEN *picks* KRINGELEIN'S *hat from table.*) You think I am dirt. If I am dirt, you're a lot dirtier, Mr. Industrial Magnate Preysing!

PREYSING—You're fired!

FLAEMMCHEN (*taking a step toward* KRINGELEIN)—Oh, no, no!

PREYSING—What do you want of me? I don't even know who you are. (FLAEMMCHEN *puts hat in* KRINGELEIN'S *hand.*)

KRINGELEIN—But I know who you are. I keep your books. I know all about you. If one of your employees was as stupid on a small scale as you are on a big one—

PREYSING (*furious, takes* KRINGELEIN *by the coat, shakes him, and flings him against the bar*)—Enough, shut your mouth. You're fired! You're fired!

KRINGELEIN (*breathlessly*)—You fire me? You threaten me? But you can't fire me. You can't threaten me! You can't do anything more to me! (*Clinging to bar and edging along.*) Not a thing more! Do you hear! I am ill—I am going to die! Do you understand? I am going to die very soon. Nothing can happen to me any more. Nobody can do a thing more to me. (*Hysterical.*) By the time you fire me I'll be dead already!

With a convulsive sob Kringelein bolts through the door. Preysing stands for a moment spellbound. Flaemmchen has picked up Kringelein's hat and is starting after him, calling: "Mr. Kringelein! Mr. Kringelein!" The lights are out. The curtain has fallen.

The lobby of the Grand Hotel is again very much alive. Guests are coming and going and the staff is busy waiting on them. Flaemmchen has come in from the grill and reported to Preysing seated at a table.

Preysing has a plan to their mutual interest which he wishes to submit to Flaemmchen. He will have to make a trip to Manchester as a result of his deal with the Saxonia people and he wants her to come along. He will need a secretary. He will have a good deal of dictating to do, and he will want company as well. He is very nervous, Preysing admits, and if he had someone who would take care of him, and be nice to him, he would feel better about going.

Flaemmchen understands him perfectly. But she will have to think over his proposition, even though Preysing assures her that she may name her own price. He thinks there might also be time for a week or two in Paris.

Flaemmchen is reluctant to agree—but for a thousand marks, and something additional for the clothes she would need if Preysing wants her to look nice, she thinks, perhaps—

Then it is agreed and Preysing is enthused. He would begin the celebration immediately. They might go to a theatre tonight, and he could get Flaemmchen a room in the hotel, near to his, so that if he should want to do any dictating later she would be within call. . . .

Gaigern is in and glad to hear that Mme. Grusinskaia has not yet left for the theatre. From Witte he also learns that the rehearsal has been wonderful. Grusinskaia has seldom worked better or with more enthusiasm. She is like a charged dynamo. It is Witte's opinion that the dancer has either found wings, or a great love.

"You speak like a man who knows human nature," ventures Gaigern.

"I know women and men," answers Witte, confidently.

Now the descending elevator has brought Grusinskaia, followed by Suzanne, to the lobby. Grusinskaia is on her way to the theatre and has only a moment to speak to Gaigern in passing. She quickly gives Witte a few additional instructions and sends him and Suzanne to the car to wait for her.

GAIGERN—Beloved!

GRUSINSKAIA—Where have you been all day? I have had such a longing to see you.

GAIGERN—I too. I was chasing all over town.

GRUSINSKAIA—Are you coming to the theatre? Oh, I shall dance tonight, how I shall dance. I want to feel that you are in the theatre.

GAIGERN—I can't, I can't.

GRUSINSKAIA—What are you going to do this evening?

GAIGERN—Gamble.

GRUSINSKAIA—Flix, don't be silly, let me give you some money.

GAIGERN—No.

GRUSINSKAIA—Stubborn boy. (SUZANNE *enters from revolving door.*) I am worried about you.

GAIGERN—Don't be, please.

SUZANNE—Madame, it is time to go.

GRUSINSKAIA (*to* SUZANNE)—All right. (*She takes* GAIGERN's *hand.*) Does de vanya.

Grusinskaia has gone. Kringelein comes down in the elevator. He is faultlessly dressed in evening clothes. He is almost a perfect copy of Gaigern. The Baron, surveying him, is pleased. He gives a final touch to Kringelein's tie and then, offering his arm, calls:

"Ready?"

"Ready!" answers Kringelein, proudly. Together they walk toward the door. The lights fade. The curtain is down.

In a room devoted to gambling a huge gaming table occupies most of the space. A large lamp above the table confines the strongest light of the room to the table and to the faces of the players.

The game is baccarat. Otternschlag is dealing. Before each of the players are piles of banknotes. Both Gaigern and Kringelein are playing, Gaigern with the practiced air of a veteran, Kringelein with the flushed face and excitement of a novice. Gaigern loses consistently. Kringelein wins with every turn of the cards.

Gambling and champagne are making it a great night for Kringelein. For the first time he is meeting life. He insists on buying more and more champagne for the crowd. He insists on backing Gaigern when he loses. He finally takes the deal himself, and wins everything.

Witte comes from the opera house. He has a message for Gaigern from Mme. Grusinskaia. Gaigern is to know that the train goes at six twenty-seven. Mme. Grusinskaia is leaving Berlin in triumph. She is even now being tendered a farewell banquet by the French ambassador. But she would have Baron von Gaigern know about the train.

"I shall be on that train. Punctually." That is Gaigern's return message.

Kringelein continues to win. The others decide there is no use trying to play against his phenomenal luck. But if they will not play Kringelein would have them stay and drink champagne with him. For the first time in his life he has gambled, he has danced, he has tasted life!

"Life, gentlemen, is a wonderful thing. But very dangerous." Kringelein is of a mind to address his laughing friends, who insist that he is as drunk as a lord. "One must have courage for life, then it is wonderful. You do not know that because you are healthy and happy, but I . . . believe me, man must know death. Not until then does a man know anything about life. . . . To life, gentlemen! Every glass high! To life! The splendid, dangerous, mighty, brief, brief life, and the courage to live it. Gentlemen, I have lived only since last night. But that little while seems longer than all the time before. It doesn't matter that life be long—but that one live it entirely—that one—"

Kringelein suddenly collapses. Clutching wildly at his heart he falls in a heap. The others surround him excitedly. They take off his coat, unfasten his collar. Otternschlag produces a hypodermic needle and gives him an injection of morphine.

Gaigern has noticed Kringelein's coat. From the inner pocket a wallet bulges. In it are all of Kringelein's winnings. Gaigern transfers the wallet to his own pocket.

Gradually Kringelein recovers his strength. He goes now in search of his coat—and his money. He misses the pocketbook! He is excited at the thought of his loss! The others try to help him find it. Gaigern joins the search. Only Otternschlag is suspicious. He eyes Gaigern intently as he insists Kringelein's money must be found.

OTTERNSCHLAG—Kringelein's fourteen thousand marks must be got back to him at once.

KRINGELEIN—Fourteen thousand marks. Fourteen thousand two hundred marks! You don't know what that means to a man like me. (OTTERNSCHLAG *turns and looks at* KRINGELEIN.) It means twenty years in which one has lived like a dog— (GAIGERN *turns upstage toying with cards on the table.*) It's my life! Nobody gives you anything. You have to buy everything, and pay cash for it and pay dear. I want to pay for my last days with that money. Every hour costs money, every minute. I have nothing, nothing but that pocketbook. I have nothing, nothing but those fourteen thousand two hundred marks— (KRINGELEIN *leans against back of settee, tremulously continues*)—I must have them back. I must have my money. There are plenty of rich people—plenty of Preysings—who would rob a poor devil like me. (GAIGERN *turns and watches* KRINGELEIN *intently.*) Please, Baron, help me find my money. Help me. Get it back for me, Baron. (*There is a moment's silence.* OTTERNSCHLAG *looks from one to the other.* GAIGERN *slowly crosses to lower end of settee. From his coat he takes* KRINGELEIN'S *pocketbook and tosses it on lower end of settee.*)

GAIGERN—There's your pocketbook.

KRINGELEIN—Did—you—have my pocketbook, Baron?

GAIGERN—I was afraid you might be robbed. Good night, Kringelein.

Gaigern is gone. Kringelein is puzzled. He can't understand the Baron. The lights fade. The curtain is down.

ACT III

Four rooms face a section of the Grand Hotel corridor. They are numbered from 168 to 171. There is an entrance from the elevator near and a small telephone desk for the floor clerk.

From the elevator come Flaemmchen and Preysing. She is assigned to room 171, and he room 170. Kringelein has room 169. He comes now, leaning a little heavily on the arm of Otternschlag. He cannot understand why he collapsed. His friend assures him it is because he lives much too intensely.

Grusinskaia, followed by Suzanne and Witte are the elevator's next load. They are preceded by a bellboy carrying baskets of flowers. Grusinskaia's room is 168.

The dancer is radiant and ready to be moving. She is sure, she tells Witte, that the Baron von Gaigern will be on the train. Gaigern is a real man, she thinks; one must admire him. Yet she is very anxious about him. If Witte should see Gaigern he might send him to her.

Baron von Gaigern's chauffeur appears. He is looking for Gaigern. The porter would put him out but Anna, the chambermaid, identifies him. She knows he is the Baron's chauffeur. She always lets him wait.

It is not for long. The elevator soon brings Gaigern up. The chauffeur greets him belligerently. Gaigern, says the chauffeur, has messed up the job. If he thinks he is going to sneak out on the friends who have backed him he is all wrong.

GAIGERN—You shall be paid back and then we're through.

CHAUFFEUR—Have you got the money—six thousand marks?

GAIGERN (*laughing*)—I gave my last twenty pfennigs to the lift-boy.

CHAUFFEUR—You've got nothing to laugh at. You're in a bad way.

GAIGERN—Yes, desperate.

CHAUFFEUR—Stay with us. Something else will turn up. (*Grabbing his arm.*) We'll still count you in—

GAIGERN (*releasing himself with a jerk*)—I don't want to be counted in.

CHAUFFEUR—Don't be a fool.

GAIGERN—Listen to me. It is past one. At six twenty-seven I am going to catch a train, no matter what happens.

CHAUFFEUR—If you pay the money back.

GAIGERN—I'll have it, I tell you—

CHAUFFEUR—How are you going to get it?

GAIGERN—I'm going to try something tonight.

CHAUFFEUR—You don't get out of this hotel until you produce the money. You can take that as final— (*Turns slightly to left, then back to* GAIGERN, *suddenly changing his tone.*) What have you got in mind? Do you need tools?

GAIGERN—No—yes—for emergencies.

CHAUFFEUR (*quickly slips him a pair of picklocks from his pocket*)—Good enough?

GAIGERN—I have five hours yet. I will get the money.

CHAUFFEUR (*patting him on the arm*)—That's the way to talk.

GAIGERN—Right. (*Sees maid approaching.*)—On your way now.

CHAUFFEUR (*very loud*)—Very well, Baron.

From Anna, the chambermaid, Gaigern learns that Preysing's room is 170 and that the lady who came with him is in 171. The lady is not Preysing's wife. Anna is convinced of that. She is too pretty.

Gaigern has started for his room when Anna disappears down the corridor. He turns quickly, listens at both Preysing's and Flaemmchen's doors. Satisfied, he tries the knob of Preysing's door. It is locked. He takes out his picklock and is letting himself in as the lights fade.

Flaemmchen, in her room, has taken her kimono from her suitcase and is preparing to undress when she notices the knob of the door leading to Preysing's room is being turned. Preysing would like to see Flaemmchen. It is possible he might be able to help her.

He is in the room before she can stop him, though she tells him she much prefers to undress without assistance. She also would be much pleased if he would go back to his own room and wait. Preysing is slightly irritated by Flaemmchen's attitude. If she is to continue with her agreement he feels she must be conciliatory.

Preysing is sitting in the armchair. Flaemmchen joins him. She sits on the arm of the chair and submits to his caresses, but she will not call him by his first name, which Preysing considers would be much more friendly.

"You're a funny little creature, Flaemmchen," Preysing insists. "I can't make you out."

"Not funny at all," Flaemmchen explains. "One doesn't get friendly just off-hand. Of course I can go to England with you, and everything. We agreed. But there mustn't be anything left hanging over. Names are like that. I meet you next year; I say, 'How do you do, Mr. Preysing.' And you say, 'That is the young lady who was my secretary in Manchester.' All quite proper. But . . . suppose I met you when you were with your wife and I called out, 'Hello, Baby' . . . How would you like that?"

"Oh, you're so sweet . . . Your body is so slender—and young—"

Flaemmchen, complaining of being cold, has recovered her

kimono when Preysing is suddenly startled by sounds in his own room. The progress of his ardors is halted. He remembers his money! All his money is in his room!

He has crossed quickly to the door of his own room and is slowly opening it when the lights fade. The curtain falls.

In Preysing's room, which is still dark, a flashlight picks out the various objects of furniture and finally lights on Preysing's coat on the bed. Gaigern, emerging from the shadow, comes quickly forward, transfers the wallet to his own pocket and turns just as Preysing, opening the door leading to Flaemmchen's room, is silhouetted in the light.

Suddenly Preysing turns on the switch and the room is lighted. Gaigern is revealed making his way toward the hall door.

"Excuse me, I must have made a mistake," he explains. "The wrong door—"

"We'll soon see if you've made a mistake," answers the excited Preysing.

Now Preysing has discovered the loss of his wallet and demanded its immediate return. Gaigern hands it over without a word.

"I had to do it," he explains. "It is a matter of life and death. You do not understand. I must get some money tonight."

"Indeed? Must you, Baron? But you aren't going to! You're going to jail, Baron. You are a thief."

Preysing is yelling now, as he maneuvers toward the telephone. Gaigern is trying to keep him still at all costs. Preysing grows more and more vociferous.

As he reaches the telephone Gaigern is upon him with a drawn revolver, and a threat to use it if Preysing does not shut up.

Suddenly Preysing, apoplectic of face, reaches back of him, grabs the lamp, pulls it from the socket and hurls it at Gaigern.

There is a crash, sounds of a struggle and suddenly a pistol shot, followed by the thud of a falling body. Then Preysing's excited voice:

"Fire, will you?"

Preysing has switched on the lamp over the head of the bed. Gaigern is stretched out on the floor.

Flaemmchen, hushed and terrified, comes from her room and joins Preysing beside the body. As she recognizes Gaigern she becomes hysterical and must smother her screams.

"He was going to shoot me," protests Preysing. . . . "It was self-defense. . . . They must believe me! . . ."

Flaemmchen can stand no more. Hysterically she is making her way out of the room. Preysing springs to the door and locks it. He has put his hand over her mouth to stifle her screams. He is struggling with her when there is a knock on the door.

Kringelein is outside. He demands to know what is going on. Flaemmchen manages to get away from Preysing and to the door. She unlocks the door and calls to Kringelein.

Now Kringelein is inside and bending over the body of the dead Baron, amazed at the suddenness of his friend's passing and the simplicity of death. . . .

Flaemmchen has gone to Kringelein, is clinging to him, appealing for his help. He takes her past Preysing and into the hall.

Now he is back again to fetch Flaemmchen's clothes. He has, he says, telephoned for the police. They will be right along. Can he do anything for Preysing before the police come? In spite of certain disagreements Kringelein would be glad to do anything—send a telegram to Mrs. Preysing, perhaps? No. Arrange the details for the police investigation?

Preysing—You cannot leave. I need you. You must stay here if the police come. As a witness.

Kringelein—My testimony will soon be given.

Preysing—The man was a burglar. He was going to steal my money. Everything is still there on the floor. I have touched nothing.

Kringelein (*looking at pocketbook and bank notes scattered about on the floor*)—Possibly, possibly he was going to steal your pocketbook . . . But one does not kill a man about a pocketbook.

Preysing—What are you going to do with her? Miss Flaem. The woman was working with the man under cover. She enticed me into her room so that he could come here and rob me. I will say that in court. They will lock up the girl.

Kringelein—The lady is in my room. I came to get her clothing so that she can be dressed when the police come.

Preysing—Listen, Kringelein, if we shut this door no one need know that I was with the lady. Miss Flaem spent the night with you. She knows nothing. You also know nothing, Mr. Kringelein, and all goes well. You will not be questioned. Nor will Miss Flaem.

Kringelein—Your Excellency has killed a man.

Preysing—But that hasn't anything to do with it.

Kringelein—It has everything to do with it.

PREYSING—Mr. Kringelein, you are from Fredersdorf. You know my father-in-law. You know my wife. I have children. I lose everything if this story about Miss Flaem comes into court. Kringelein, take the affair of the lady upon yourself. You have nothing to do but hold your tongue. Go away—take her with you. Travel. Travel far. . . . Take her away—she was with you the whole night—you travel with her—you.

KRINGELEIN (*scornfully*)—The police will be here immediately, Your Excellency.

PREYSING—Here, here. I'll give you money. How much do you want? You need money.

KRINGELEIN—No, thank you very much. I have enough.

PREYSING—I beg you, Mr. Kringelein. I beg you to help me. I beg you. My fate depends on you. And when you come back to Fredersdorf I will see if your position cannot be improved . . . so that you need never worry again.

KRINGELEIN—Many thanks. Many, many thanks, Mr. Industrial Magnate Preysing. I'll never come back to Fredersdorf. You can keep your position, and you don't have to worry about me, worry about yourself. In a minute the police will be here.

PREYSING—The police!

KRINGELEIN (*bending over* GAIGERN, *softly, to himself*)—He looks content. It cannot be so hard.

PREYSING—They are coming . . .

KRINGELEIN—You must be steady now, Mr. Preysing.

The knock on the door is repeated. The lights fade. The curtain is down.

Through the darkness floats the sound of Grusinskaia's voice. The lights reveal her sitting before her dressing table. She is humming a Russian tune. It is three o'clock in the morning. Suzanne has the packing done and is tired. But Grusinskaia is not tired. She is gay. She thinks, perhaps, she will do her hair differently. Suzanne laughs at that. Once, she remembers, Madame had said that when a woman falls in love the first sign is that she does her hair differently. . . .

This endless packing and unpacking. One hotel, then another hotel. Then the theatre—

"Do you know what, Suzanne?" decides Grusinskaia, "we are going to take a holiday soon. We are going to Tremezzo, and we are going to live for six weeks like respectable people. I am going to live like a real woman. Perfectly quiet, perfectly simple . . . perfectly happy."

"Yes, Madame."

"We are going to have a guest, Suzanne."

"Certainly, Madame."

It is late. The packing is all done. Suzanne can go now and rest until a half an hour before bus time. . . .

The hotel operator answers the phone and is sure she has given Mme. Grusinskaia the room of Baron von Gaigern. She is ringing, but there is no answer.

Grusinskaia reluctantly hangs up the phone. Again she is humming the plaintive Russian melody. But there is a far away look in her eyes and her voice wavers.

The lights are out. The curtain is down.

Back in the lobby of the Grand Hotel. It is very early—five-thirty in the morning. Scrubwomen and porters are busy putting the place to rights, finishing tasks with vacuum cleaners and mops.

The clerks are arranging for the departure of guests and the bellboys are delivering the morning papers.

A policeman stands guard at the door. The killing in room 170 is responsible for that. One of the night clerks relays the news to Senf, the superintendent, who has just arrived after spending the night at the clinic, where Mrs. Senf is hoping to present him with an heir. The police, explains the clerk, are still upstairs.

"Man, that's something for the reputation of the Grand Hotel," ejaculates Senf. "The suicide last week—and now this murder—and it all gets into the papers. But I'm sorry about the Baron. He was all right."

"It seems he was a hotel thief and an impostor."

"I don't believe it. He was a real gentleman. I know people."

Five bellboys have marched in military precision to take their stations. Senf inspects their appearance, their hair, their faces, their nails, their boots. They are dismissed, with reservations.

The elevator brings Kringelein and Flaemmchen from the floor above. They have been dismissed by the police commissioner for the present and may go their ways.

"Poor Baron," sighs Flaemmchen. "I can't get him out of my mind. Killed—"

"He was friendly to me as no man ever was," adds Kringelein. ". . . He laughed, poor devil, and then a man like Preysing kills him."

"I didn't like Preysing right off," admits Flaemmchen.
"Then why did you have anything to do with him?"
"For money."
"Yes, of course, for money."
"Do you understand that?"
"Of course."
"Most people don't."

Meierheim, Madame Grusinskaia's manager, comes hurrying down the corridor with Witte, the conductor. Meierheim is looking for Grusinskaia. She may be on her way down, as Witte reports, but she is late, as usual, and there is serious danger of their missing the train. . . .

Flaemmchen is still explaining her affairs to the sympathetic Kringelein. She would hold nothing back.

FLAEMMCHEN—Preysing would have given me a thousand marks—I've got to have money. I'm too good looking for an office. There is always trouble. Money is so important, and anyone who says it isn't is just lying.

KRINGELEIN—I never knew what money really meant until I started to spend it. Do you know (*he is silent for a moment*) I can hardly believe that anything so beautiful should come to me from Preysing.

FLAEMMCHEN—I was afraid of him.

KRINGELEIN—You needn't be afraid of anything now. I'll take care of you. Will you come with me?

FLAEMMCHEN—With you?

KRINGELEIN—You will have a good time with me. I've got enough money, fourteen thousand two hundred in my pocket, eight thousand four hundred that I won. It will last a long time. I can win more. We'll travel. We'll go to Paris.

FLAEMMCHEN—Will we go to Paris? I always wanted to go to Paris!

KRINGELEIN—Yes, to Paris, anywhere you want. Here, I'll give you part of the money I won, three thousand four hundred. Later you can have all.

FLAEMMCHEN—Later?

KRINGELEIN—When I . . . when it's all over. It will not be long. Will you stay with me until . . . ?

FLAEMMCHEN—Nonsense, I know a doctor who cures the most hopeless cases. We will go to him.

KRINGELEIN—You will have a better time with me than with Preysing. Wouldn't you rather stay with me than with him?

FLAEMMCHEN—Oh, yes, much.

KRINGELEIN (*taking her hand*)—Do you like me better?

FLAEMMCHEN—Yes. You are good.

SENF—Your bill is ready, Mr. Kringelein.

KRINGELEIN (*rising*)—Yes, all right. (*Pointing to* FLAEMMCHEN.) And the lady's, too?

SENF—Yes, all right.

KRINGELEIN (*at desk paying bills*)—Order me a cab, please.

CLERK (*to bellboy*)—Cab for his excellency, Mr. Kringelein.

At the door they meet Otternschlag, bustling in. He is surprised that Kringelein is leaving. Yes, says Kringelein happily, he is on his way to Paris.

Otternschlag is a little solicitous. If it should happen that Kringelein should be troubled again with those heart pains—

Kringelein has forgotten all about heart pains. He is busy now. He must gather in Flaemmchen and hurry for the train. The bellboys take up the call:

"Cab for Mr. Kringelein!"

Flaemmchen takes his arm and they nod a farewell to Otternschlag as they go through the revolving door.

The elevator has deposited Grusinskaia, followed by Suzanne and a bellboy with bags. Meierheim meets them impatiently, but Grusinskaia pays little attention to him. She is anxious about another matter.

"Why isn't he here?" she demands of Witte. ". . . He is not in his room, either. Is he not traveling with us?"

"He will come later, Lisaveta."

MEIERHEIM—What are you waiting for? Have you got all the bags in the car? Hurry, we'll just make the train.

GRUSINSKAIA—I must wait. I am expecting someone.

MEIERHEIM—Impossible, not another minute. You've got a rehearsal in Prague at noon. Come, Madame!

GRUSINSKAIA (*to* WITTE)—Where can he be?

WITTE (*helping her toward revolving door*)—Go, Lisaveta, don't wait any longer.

MEIERHEIM (*takes out watch*)—Four minutes past! The train leaves at six twenty-seven. Out! March!

WITTE (*urging her forward*)—You must go, Lisaveta. He will be there. He will certainly be there.

GRUSINSKAIA—Witte, stay here. Look around. Bring him with you. Come on the next train. Tell him that he must travel with us. Must! Must! (MEIERHEIM *is seen through revolving door hurrying her away.*)

BELLBOY (*to* SENF)—You are wanted in the phone room, sir. An important message . . . from the hospital . . . something about a baby.

SENF—What? My God!

CLERK (*to* OTTERNSCHLAG)—Is the doctor leaving? Or does the doctor wish to engage the room for today again?

OTTERNSCHLAG—I shall remain for the time being.

A man has come through the revolving door and approached the desk. He wants a room. The clerk assigns him to 170, a large room with bath.

Witte has returned from the corridor. He has not found the Baron von Gaigern. He hurries to join the others.

From behind the clerk's desk the voice of the telephone operator can be heard.

"Grand Hotel! . . . Just a minute please! . . . Grand Hotel! . . . Hold the wire . . . Grand Hotel . . . Grand Hotel . . ."

The curtain is down.

THE PLAYS AND THEIR AUTHORS

"Elizabeth the Queen." A drama in three acts by Maxwell Anderson. Copyright, 1930, by the author. Copyright and published, 1930, by Longmans, Green & Co., London, New York and Toronto.

Maxwell Anderson, who has figured in previous volumes of this series, first as collaborator with Laurence Stallings in the writing of "What Price Glory" and later as the author of "Saturday's Children" and "Gypsy," took to playwriting after he had some success as a teacher in the universities of North Dakota and Southern California, and as a newspaper man, chiefly an editorial writer, in San Francisco and later in New York. Atlantic, Pa., was the scene of his birth; his father was a Baptist minister; he is married and the father of three children. He has spent considerable time in Hollywood of recent years.

"Tomorrow and Tomorrow." A drama in three acts by Philip Barry. Copyright, 1930, by the author. Copyright and published, 1930, by Samuel French, New York, Los Angeles and London.

This is the fifth of Philip Barry's plays to be included in the Best Plays series, the others being "You and I," "The Youngest," "Paris Bound" and "Holiday." He was born in Rochester, N. Y., is a Yale man but took his drama courses at Harvard with Prof. George Pierce Baker. Out of college he was for a time an attaché at the American Embassy in London and later a writer of advertising copy in New York before his success as a dramatist settled definitely the matter of his life work. He is married, a proud father and he does much of his writing in Cannes, France.

"Once in a Lifetime." A comedy in three acts by Moss Hart and George S. Kaufman. Copyright, 1930, by the authors. Copyright and published, 1930, by Farrar & Rinehart, New York.

George Kaufman is an old contributor to the records of this year book of American drama. Moss Hart is a newcomer. Mr. Hart first wrote "Once in a Lifetime," and had offers for it from four different managers. When it came to signing the contract he thought his chances would be better with Sam H. Harris, who had suggested Mr. Kaufman for such rewriting as might be to the comedy's advantage. Hence the combination that resulted in one of the first hits of the 1930-31 season. Mr. Hart, born in 1906 in New York, has been writing plays and sketches ever since he was a high school freshman. At first these were mostly Jewish sketches and many were produced in the Y.M.H.A. in the Bronx. He sold a play called "The Hold-up Man" to Augustus Pitou when he was serving Mr. Pitou as a confidential secretary, but not until the play was in rehearsal did he dare confess to his employer that he was the author. He has tried many jobs, including that of being a house detective in a cloak and suit business. He likes writing best.

Mr. Kaufman, as practically each volume of the year book since 1921-22, when he made his first appearance with Marc Connelly and "Dulcy," has recorded, is a Pittsburghian by birth. He took up newspaper work (if being a columnist can reasonably be called work), after he had tried stenography and low-pressure salesmanship. Later he became dramatic editor of the New York *Times*, a position he held right through the years of his greatest success as a playwright. Last fall he quit his newspaper job to act a part—that of the disillusioned playwright, Lawrence Vail—in his own (and Mr. Hart's) comedy.

"Green Grow the Lilacs." A comedy in three acts by Lynn Riggs. Copyright, 1930, by the author. Copyright and published, 1931, by Samuel French, New York, Los Angeles and London.

Lynn Riggs was born in what is now the state of Oklahoma when it was still known as the Indian Territory, his place of birth being a farm near Claremore. He stayed around home as a youth and then decided to go places. This took him as far as the Pacific Coast on the West and brought him as far east as New York. Before he had settled down to writing he had also seen Paris. In fact he began the composition of "Green Grow the Lilacs" in the Café de Deux Magots, which certainly sounds like the Left Bank. He is something of a poet and his verse was published in the *Poetry Magazine* and the *Smart Set* magazine before he had written a long play. He had two years at the University of Oklahoma and his jobs have been varied and numerous, ranging from the driving of a delivery wagon for a grocery store to the singing of second tenor in a touring quartet on the Chautauqua circuit. His first New York production was that of an early play, "Big Lake," done by the students of the American Laboratory in 1927. His next was "Roadside" (known originally as "Borned in Texas"), which Arthur Hopkins brought out last year and which lasted but two weeks. He is 32 years old, aims to write many more plays and will later try a novel.

"As Husbands Go." A comedy in three acts by Rachel Crothers. Copyright, 1931, by the author. Copyright and published, 1931, by Samuel French, New York, Los Angeles and London.

Rachel Crothers, with such satisfaction as must reasonably follow the experience, read in several of the more important home newspapers last winter that she had achieved the distinction of being America's foremost woman playwright. Her record of successful plays produced fully justifies the honor conferred. Miss Crothers has also been named with the selected ten in three of the volumes that preceded this one—for her "Nice People" (an award, incidentally, with which she did not agree), "Mary the Third" and "Let Us Be Gay." Miss Crothers was born in Bloomington, Ill., and both her parents were doctors. She took an active interest in dramatics during her school years, and after she was graduated from the Illinois State Normal College came East to study and later to teach in the Wheatcroft School of Acting in New York. She has written many plays and both cast and staged a majority of them.

"Alison's House." A drama in three acts by Susan Glaspell. Copyright, 1930, by the author. Copyright and published, 1931, by Samuel French, New York, Los Angeles and London.

Susan Glaspell, winner of the 1930-31 Pulitzer prize, drifted into playwriting when she was living in Provincetown, Mass., and was one of the organizers of the Provincetown Players. This was the group from whose ranks Eugene O'Neill was later to emerge and grow until he was heralded as America's greatest dramatist. In 1916, which was the first year of the Provincetowners' activities, Miss Glaspell wrote several short plays, including "Trifles," which brought her both fame and compliments. A year later she tried a full length play with her husband, the late George Cram Cook. This was called "Suppressed Desires," a satire on the psychoanalysis cult just then gaining prominence. "Bernice" and "The Inheritors" followed, the latter finding its way into the repertory of Eva Le Gallienne's Civic Repertory Theatre two years ago. Miss Glaspell was born in Davenport, Ia., attended both Drake University in Iowa and the University of Chicago. Out of college she turned to newspaper work and did considerable political reporting for a Des Moines paper. She scored a success with her first novel, "The Glory of the Conquered," and for years was both happy and successful as a writer of short stories. Two of these shorter pieces, "Poor Ed" and "The Hearing Ear," were selected by Mr. O'Brien for his "Best Short Stories" issue of 1917. "The Comic Artist," a comedy written by Miss Glaspell and Norman Matson, is scheduled for production the coming season.

"Five Star Final." A drama in three acts by Louis Weitzenkorn. Copyright, 1930, 1931, by the author. Copyright and published, 1931, by Samuel French, New York, Los Angeles and London.

Louis Weitzenkorn hails from Wilkes-Barre, Pa., where he was born in May, 1893. He was a student at the Pennsylvania Military College at Chester, Pa., and later graduated from Columbia University in New York. By 1914 he was a reporter on the New York *Tribune,* going from there to the *Times,* and from the *Times* to the *Call,* a socialist daily, on which he read copy and conducted a column headed "The Guillotine," devoted mostly to verse. About this time Herbert Bayard Swope, then executive editor of the late New York *World,* discovered Mr. Weitzenkorn and took him away from the *Call,* making him a reporter and eventually the feature editor of the Sunday *World.* From there he went to the New York *Graphic,* an evening tabloid newspaper, and it was his experience in this job that so stirred his emotions and his resentments as to make the writing of "Five Star Final" practically obligatory if his soul was to be saved. Two years ago he had a first play produced, a suburban tragedy of young married life called "First Mortgage."

"Overture." A drama in three acts by William Bolitho. Copyright, 1930, 1931, by Sybil Bolitho Ryall. Copyright and published, 1931, by Simon & Schuster, Inc., New York.

William Bolitho was born and grew up in South Africa. When he started out to see and to make what he could of and from a world that fascinated him his experiences included that of stoking a British liner. Arriving in England he was one of those eager and courageous young men who made up the first lines of defense in France, was seriously wounded at the Somme and spent a year in a military hospital in Scotland as a consequence.

In London he became the special correspondent of the New York *World*. In 1928 he made his first trip to America, and thereafter, by agreement, was to spend six months in the offices of the *World*, doing a daily essay on subjects of his own selection, and six months resuming contact with and study of Europe from a correspondent's point of view. He had written several books, "Leviathan," "Murder for Profit," and "Twelve Against the Gods" among them. "Overture" was his first and only play. He was still at work upon it when he died at his home in Avignon, France, in June, 1930.

"The Barretts of Wimpole Street." A drama in three acts by Rudolf Besier. Copyright, 1930, by the author. Copyright and published, 1930, by Little, Brown & Co., Boston.

Rudolf Besier was born on the island of Java in 1878 and educated at Elizabeth's College, which is in Guernsey, Isle of Jersey, and at Heidelberg, Germany. He has written many plays, but few of them have reached America, the last of these being one called "Secrets" written with the English authoress, May Edginton, and played here in 1922 with Margaret Lawrence in the cast. Mr. Besier's drama entitled "Don" was produced by Winthrop Ames at the New Theatre in 1909. Later Mrs. Fiske played his "Lady Patricia" at the Empire, after Mrs. Patrick Campbell had done it at the Haymarket in London. "The Prude's Fall" was done over here with William Faversham and Emily Stevens in the leading rôles, but under the title of "A Lesson in Love." Mr. Besier is described as a most retiring person, seldom appearing in London and being content to spend most of his time at his home, which continues to be on the Isle of Jersey. His excessive height, variously estimated as being from six foot six to six foot eight, is probably responsible for the development of a devastating self-consciousness. He has promised Guthrie McClintic, however, that he may drop over to America any day now for cocktails and tea. He is, as Mr. McClintic recalls him, "the tallest, the most amiable, and, in a way, the most detached author I have ever encountered." Mr. McClintic, incidentally, is Katharine Cornell's husband and the first man she engaged when she became an actress-manageress last fall. He staged "The Barretts."

"Grand Hotel." A drama in three acts by Vicki Baum. English adaptation by W. A. Drake. Copyright, 1930, by the author. A dramatization of Miss Baum's novel, "Menschen im Hotel."

Vicki Baum is a German writer who was born and lived her early years in Vienna. She is the wife of Richard Lert, conductor of the Berlin State Opera, and is herself a musician carefully educated for a career at the Vienna Conservatory. Frau Baum took to writing when the hard years following the war made the earning of more income quite necessary. She has written three novels about the stage and stage people, and three short plays for children. "Menschen im Hotel," in a dramatization which Frau Baum made from her own story and which Max Reinhardt remade to suit the uses of one of his trick stages in Berlin, inspired the writing of "Pariser Platz 13," which evidently concerns a beauty parlor, for "Beauty Parlor" is the English title Herman Shumlin, producer of "Grand Hotel," has chosen for it. She has other plays in mind, and a musical comedy for which Vincent Youmans hopes to write the score. When Frau Baum is at home with her husband and her two young sons she lives in Grunewald, a suburb of Berlin.

William A. Drake, who made the adaptation of "Grand Hotel," is also the adapter of an American version of Gorky's "Night Lodging" known as "At the Bottom." It was while he was working with the Leo Bulgakov Associates in the production of the Gorky piece that Mr. Drake met Harry Moses, a Clevelander who had backed the Bulgakov enterprise. Mr. Drake was working on "Grand Hotel" then and called it to Mr. Moses' attention. The latter's interest in the play resulted in his meeting Mr. Shumlin and their agreement to do "Grand Hotel" together. Mr. Drake is at present adapting "Phaea," a second German play similar in form to "Grand Hotel," which Mr. Moses promises to produce in 1931-32.

PLAYS PRODUCED IN NEW YORK

June 15, 1930—June 15, 1931

(Plays marked with asterisk were still playing June 15, 1931)

THE SONG AND DANCE MAN

(16 performances)

A comedy in four scenes by George M. Cohan. Revived by the author at the Fulton Theatre, New York, June 16, 1930.

Cast of characters—

Curtis .... Harry Lillford
Charles B. Nelson .... Robert Middlemass
Joseph Murdock .... Jack Leslie
"Hap" Farrell .... George M. Cohan
Crowley .... Jack Williams
Jim Craig .... Edward F. Nannary
Jane Rosemond .... Mary Philips
Mrs. Lane .... Eda Von Buelow
Leola Lane .... Isabel Baring
Freddie .... Manuel Duarte
Miss Davis .... Jane Thomas
Tom Crosby .... Joseph Allen
Anna .... Harriet Keen

Scenes 1, 2 and 4—Nelson's Apartment. Scene 3—Nelson's Business Office.

"The Best Plays of 1923-24."

FIND THE FOX

(3 performances)

A farce in three acts by Frank Martins. Produced by Odin Enterprises at Wallack's Theatre, New York, June 20, 1930.

Cast of characters—

Harry Sherwood .... Noel Warwick
Ruth Palmer .... Nina Walker
Ito .... Edward Colebrook
Mary Turner .... Peggy Worth
Edward Palmer .... Arch Hendricks
John Palmer .... W. H. Niemeyer
Mortimer Cooke .... G. Gurnie-Butler
Miranda Allen .... Mae Park
Alec Davis .... Phil Maher
Jeremiah McLaughlin .... Ben H. Roberts
Ike .... Bob McClung
Barnett .... Ray Earles

Acts I, II and III.—Greystone Manor, Meyersdale, N. Y.

MYSTERY MOON

(1 performance)

A musical comedy in two acts. Lyrics and music by Carlo and Sanders, book by Fred Herendeen. Produced by James M. Graf in association with Paul M. Trebitsch at the Royale Theatre, New York, June 23, 1930.

Cast of characters—

Lee Foo..Curtis Karpe
"Flash" Darrell....................................Arthur Uttry
Mildred Middleton..................................Kitty Kelly
Queenie North....................................Winfred Barry
Smith Banks...Harry Short
Don Bradley....................................Arthur Campbell
Lola Harriott...................................Frances Shelley
May Delight.......................................Maude Brooks
Goldie Del Monte...................................Pauline Dee
Premiere Danseuse....................................."Juliana"
Ernie Valle..Ernie Valle
James Boyd..............................Frank J. Marshall, Jr.
Gladys St. James...............................Virginia Watts
Pearl Lindy....................................Marjorie Gaines
Bessie Van Neer................................Virginia Dawe
Sam Martin.....................................Charles Lawrence
Joe Hendricks....................................Frank Shannon
Ben Flint....................................Harrison Brockbank
Doris Flint...Jane Taylor
Constable Smedley Baker...........................Larry Woods

Acts I and II.—The Scene of the Play Represents the Stage and Interior of the Portal Palace Theatre, Portal, North Dakota.

A touring musical comedy company plays a North Dakota theatre that is run by a gang doubling in dope peddling. During its frightening adventures the company loses its soubrette, kidnaped by the son of the theatre's owner.

EARL CARROLL'S VANITIES

(215 performances)

Musical revue assembled by Earl Carroll. Music by Jay Gorney, E. Y. Harburg, Harold Arlen and Ted Keohler. Produced by Earl Carroll at the New Amsterdam Theatre, New York, July 1, 1930.

Principals engaged—

Jimmy Savo
Jack Benny
Herb Williams
John Hale
Harry Stockwell
Louis Barrison
Billy Rolls
Murray Bernie
Dorothy Britton
Naomi Ray

Patsy Kelly
Thelma White
Eileen Wenzel
Betty Veronica
Faith Bacon
Claiborne Bryson
Collette Sisters

Staged by Earl Carroll, Priestly Morrison and LeRoy Prinz.

WHO CARES

(32 performances)

Musical revue with skits by Edward Clarke Lilley, Bertrand Robinson, Kenneth Webb and John Cantwell; lyrics by Harry Clarke; music by Percy Wenrich. Produced by The Satirists, Inc., at the 46th St. Theatre, New York, July 8, 1930.

Principals engaged—

Florenz Ames
Percy Helton
William Holbrook
Frank Allworth
Grant Mills
Robert Pitkin
John Cherry
Bobby Edwards
Peggy O'Neill
Margaret Dale
Mignon Laird
Dorothy Martin
Sibylla Bowman
Mary Ridgley
Templeton Brothers
Don Lanning

Staged by George Vivian, E. Clarke Lilley and William Holbrook.

LADIES ALL

(140 performances)

A comedy in three acts by Prince Bibesco, adapted by Elmer Harris. Produced at the Morosco Theatre, New York, July 28, 1930.

Cast of characters—

Nancy.. Violet Heming
Julie.. Germaine Giroux
Ann.. May Collins
Bob.. Walter Woolf
Chic.. Preston Foster
James.. William David

Acts I, II and III.—Nancy's Barn Studio Near Westport.

Bob, a ladies man de luxe, finds himself a favored guest at Nancy's barn studio in Westchester County. Sometime during the night one of the three attractive ladies in the house slips into his room, slips out again and leaves him mystified as to her identity, but very much in love with her. When accused each of the three first denies, then admits that she was the visitor. Still puzzled Bob is content when the departure of the other two candidates leaves Nancy to him.

DANCING PARTNER

(119 performances)

A comedy by Alexander Engel and Alfred Grunwald, adapted by Frederic and Fanny Hatton. Produced by David Belasco at the Belasco Theatre, New York, August 5, 1930.

Cast of characters—

Lord George Hampton....Henry Stephenson
Lord Robert Brummel....Lynne Overman
Lady Hartley....Charlotte Granville
Roxy....Irene Purcell
The Hon. Gwendolyn Davenham....Claudia Morgan
Armand Perichol....Auguste Aramini
Raquin....Jules Epailly
Henri Symeux....Ivan Servais
Rita-Vera....Suzanne Caubaye
Gina....Patrice Gridier
Fanchon....Germaine De Renty
Annette Lebrun....Mauricette Ducret
Pierre....Gustave Rolland
Louis....Paul Heron
Nervous Flight Passenger....Thomas Reynolds
Vickie....Clare St. Clair
A Pilot....Percy Woodley
A Floor Maid....Marie Durand

Mannequins, Tourists, Guests, etc.

Scene 1.—A Private Room in the Hotel Claridge, Paris. 2—An Intimate Corner in the Hotel Claridge. 3—Hotel Splendide-Royale, Biarritz. 4—Cabin of a Passenger Airplane. 5—A Room in the Hotel Splendide-Royale, Biarritz.

Staged by David Belasco.

Lord Robert Brummel, having had his successes with the yielding sex, is convinced pure women are scarce. When his rich uncle insists that he shall marry Roxy, Lord Robert declines the honor until he is convinced that Roxy is all her sponsors claim for her. To prove his point Lord Robert wagers that, masquerading as a gigolo, he will seduce Roxy within a month. When he fails, having fallen in love with her, he is glad to go through with the marriage.

SUSPENSE

(7 performances)

A melodrama in three acts by Patrick MacGill. Produced by Charles Dillingham (by arrangement with Hutter and MacGregor, of London), at the Fulton Theatre, New York, August 12, 1930.

Cast of characters—

Nobby....Henry Vincent
Spud....Bernard Savage
Officer....Perry Norman
N. C. O. ....Frank Horton
Pettigrew....John Halloran
Scruffy....Charles Dalton
Corporal Brown....Alfred Ayre
Lomax....Seth Arnold
Brett (Alleluia)....Herbert Ranson
Sergeant McLusky....Reynolds Denniston
Captain Wilson....Lionel Pape
Young Soldier....Charles Dill
Other Soldiers—William Evans, Burney Howard, Jack Morgan, Jack Fifer, George Anderson, Joseph Bodell, John Hewitt

Acts I and II.—Dugout Recently Taken from the Germans. Act III.—On a Duckboard.

Staged by Reginald Denham.

A detail of enlisted Britishers is quartered in a dugout beneath which the Germans are laying a mine. The tap, tap of the sappers' drills forces the men to a variety of emotional reactions. At the crucial moment they are relieved, but on the way to billets, while apparently safe, the detail is destroyed by shell fire.

THROUGH THE NIGHT

(8 performances)

A comedy in three acts by Samuel Ruskin Golding and Paul Dickey. Produced by Pilgrim Productions, Inc., at the Masque Theatre, New York, August 18, 1930.

Cast of characters—

Howard Talbott....George MacQuarrie
Cram....Henry W. Pemberton
Camilla Del Val....Francesca Destinn
Inez Talbott....Helen MacKellar
De Witt Clinton Pomeroy....John Westley
Bob Hedges....Robert Hudson
Tony Collister....Noel Tearle
Mrs. Prentiss....Margaret Pitt
Inspector Cardigan....Charles T. Lewis
Kelly....George Spelvin

Acts I, II and III.—The Home of the Talbotts in Suburban New York.

Staged by Samuel Golding and Paul Martin.

Inez Talbott, unhappy wife of Howard Talbott, blue-nosed crime commissioner, captures Tony Collister, who she thinks is a notorious society burglar the police are after. Charmed by Collister's suave ways she hides him in her boudoir. As it turns out Tony is an insurance company detective and he unmasks Talbott as a master crook.

TOPAZE

(16 performances)

A comedy in three acts by Marcel Pagnol, adapted by Benn W. Levy. Return engagement at the Barrymore Theatre, New York, August 18, 1930.

Cast of characters—

Topaze....Frank Morgan
Ernestine Muche....Barbara Barondess
Muche....Hubert Druce
Tamise....Harry Davenport
Le Ribonchon....George Spelvin
Suzy Courtois....Catherine Willard
Baroness Pitart-Vignolles....Essex Dane
Castel-Benac....Clarence Derwent
Butler....Leslie Smith
Roger de Berville....Nicholas Joy
First Stenographer....Aldeah Wise
Second Stenographer....Dauna Allen
Gendarme....Stapleton Kent
An Old Man....Halliam Bosworth

(Pupils at Pension Muche)

Cordier....Warren McCollum
Durant-Victor....Freddie Stange
Pitart-Vignolles....Peter Boylan
Seguedille....Harry Murray
Tronche-Bobine....James McGuire
Jusserand....George Canto-Janis
Bertin....James Guinane
Blondet....Richard Offer
Bleriot....Joseph McGarrity
Mentez....Martin Postal

Act I.—Classroom in the Pension Muche. Act II.—Small Salon at the Home of Suzy Courtois. Act III.—Office of M. Castel-Benac.
Staged by Stanley Logan.

"Topaze" had previously run from February 12, 1930, to June 28, 1930, at the Music Box Theatre.

HOT RHYTHM

(68 performances)

A colored revue in two parts. Sketches by Ballard Macdonald, Will Morrissey and Edward Hurley; music and lyrics by Porter Grainger and Donald Heywood. Produced by Max Rudnick at the Times Square Theatre, New York, August 21, 1930.

Principals engaged—

Al Vigal
Mel Duncan
George Wiltshire
Arthur Bryson
Eddie Rector
Johnny Lee Long
Dewey Markham
Sam Paige

Simms and Bowie	Hilda Perleno
Nora Green	Ina Duncan
Edith Wilson	Laura Duncan
Mae Barnes	Inez Seeley
Revella Hughes	Madeline Belt

Staged by Will Morrissey and Nat Cash.

THE 9TH GUEST

(72 performances)

A mystery melodrama in three acts by Owen Davis. Produced by A. H. Woods (by arrangement with S. M. Biddell) at the Eltinge Theatre, New York, August 25, 1930.

Cast of characters—

Jason Osgood....................................William Courtleigh
Mrs. Margaret Chisholm............................Thais Lawton
Hawkins...Robert Vivian
Dr. Murray Chalmers Reid.......................Berton Churchill
Tim Salmon...Frank Shannon
Sylvia Inglesby.......................................Grace Kern
Peter Daly...Owen Davis, Jr.
Hank Abbott...Allan Dinehart
Jean Trent...Brenda Dahlen

Acts I, II and III.—The Bienville Penthouse.
Staged by Owen Davis.

Hank Abbott summons a group of guests to dinner in his penthouse. When they are all locked in the room with no chance of escape a butler hired from an agency turns on the radio. The radio informs the assembled guests that they are doomed to die by 1 o'clock. The ninth guest is Death. One by one all are picked off, save the young lovers, Peter Daly and Jean Trent. It is Peter who unmasks Hank Abbott as a madman loaded with revenge germs.

TORCH SONG

(87 performances)

A drama in three acts by Kenyon Nicholson. Produced by Arthur Hopkins at the Plymouth Theatre, New York, August 27, 1930.

Cast of characters—

Otto...Larry Oliver
Ruby Nellis...Henriett Kay
Ivy Stevens...Mayo Methot
Howard Palmer.......................................Reed Brown, Jr.
Fred Geer..John Junior
Joe Kramer..Hal K. Dawson
"Tink"..Paul Porter

Cass Wheeler....................................Guy Kibbee
Edna Kinsey....................................Dennie Moore
Carl Loomis....................................Russell Hicks
Capt. Dwight Mellish....................................Frank Andrews
Mary Mellish....................................Aphie James
Betty Secrest....................................June Clayworth
Lottie....................................Pearl Hight

Prologue—"Paradise Rose Gardens" Roadhouse, Near Cincinnati. Act I.—Lobby of the "Riverview House," Pomeroy, Ohio. Acts II and III—Howard's Room, "Riverview House."

Staged by Arthur Hopkins.

Ivy Stevens, a singer of torch songs at the Paradise Rose Gardens near Cincinnati, is deserted by her lover, Howard Palmer, a traveling salesman, when he marries his employer's daughter. Ivy accepts the consolation offered by the Salvation Army and throws herself enthusiastically into religious work. A year later in a hotel in Pomeroy, Ohio, she meets Howard Palmer again. He is about to go out with some of the town girls. Ivy, pleading for the salvation of Howard's soul, is carried over into a reawakening of her love for him. She blames God for her second fall and in disgust is about to leave the army when she is reclaimed by an earnest worker in the cause.

CAFÉ

(4 performances)

A comedy in three acts by Marya Mannes. Produced by William A. Brady in association with John Tuerk at the Ritz Theatre, New York, August 28, 1930.

Cast of characters—

Josef....................................Edouard la Roche
The Fungus....................................Robert Chandler
Bernard....................................Ernest A. Treco
Emil....................................Allan Parr
Stout Lady....................................Claire Sorgus
Gigolo....................................Fred Newton
Andree....................................Renee Cartier
Paul....................................Leon Hartl
Boulevardier....................................Georges Des Lions
1st Checker Player....................................Ramon Lion
2nd Checker Player....................................Arnold Makowski
Letterwriter....................................Sam Byrd
Young Cocotte....................................Vivian McGill
Rolf Gates....................................Philip Leigh
Sally Burch....................................Georgia Caine
Maurice Larned....................................Rollo Peters
Algerian....................................Frank de Silva
French Painter....................................Victor Achison
Older Cocotte....................................Flora Dupree
German Husband....................................Albert Jacob
German Wife....................................Martha Brevka
Jane Geddes....................................Frances Fuller
Knitting Woman....................................Rosa Des Lions

Her Husband....................................Gregory Lebedeff
Post Card Vendor....................................Albert Simard
Zizi....................................Zrara Romanyi
Ruth....................................Lota Sanders
Marie....................................Theodosia Dusanne
Gendarme....................................Paul Rigaud
Louise....................................Marie Pitot
Jules....................................Henri Murguier
Lucien....................................François Cabuchon
Charlotte....................................Helene Cambridge
Albert....................................Edouard Dennee
Georges....................................Leonce Rousselot
Edouard....................................Pierre Latouche
Julien....................................Robert Leguillon
Felix....................................Armand Faure
1st Charwoman....................................Eugenie Daudet
2nd Charwoman....................................Marguerite Orme
Old Masquerader....................................Georges Des Lions
Nursie....................................Vivian McGill
Onlooker....................................Raymond Leon
Singer....................................Athy Dimitrieff
Lavisse....................................Albert Duchartris
Billy Geddes....................................King Calder
Le Diable....................................Jules Broussard
l'Ange....................................Arline Kazanjeau
Thunderbolt Jackson....................................Columbus Jackson
Alice....................................Marjorie Gateson

Acts I, II and III.—The Café des Anges in the Latin Quarter of Paris.

Staged by José Ruben.

Maurice Larned, artist, in Paris, living on the west bank, is trying to find himself, after having left a misunderstanding wife and child in America. He meets Sally Burch, they are mutually attracted, and all is well until Jane Geddes, another younger and lovelier artist person from Akron, Ohio, arrives and also wants to know life with Maurice. She is followed by the deserted wife, who makes her own fight for the uncertain husband. When the fighting is over Maurice stays on in Paris with Sally Burch and Paris has claimed another victim in Jane.

UP POPS THE DEVIL

(148 performances)

A comedy in three acts by Albert Hackett and Frances Goodrich. Produced by Lee Shubert at the Masque Theatre, New York, September 1, 1930.

Cast of characters—

John....................................James G. Morton
Biney....................................Albert Hackett
Polly Griscom....................................Mildred Wall
Drunken Man....................................Henry Howard
Anne....................................Sally Bates
George Kent....................................Brian Donlevy
Mrs. Kent....................................Florence Auer
Steve Merrick....................................Roger Pryor

Kelly....................................Jack Klendon
Luella May Carroll.......................Janet McLeay
Gilbert Morrell..........................John Marston
A Laundryman.............................Spencer Barnes
Mr. Platt................................George W. Callahan
Mrs. Platt...............................Mabel Montgomery

Acts I, II and III.—A Studio Apartment in an Old House in Downtown, New York.

Staged by Worthington Miner.

Anne and Steve Merrick have been living together for a year. Now their problem is whether or not to marry. Steve wants to write. Anne wants him to write. Steve tries to write while Anne earns a living for both of them. Steve can't write because of his housekeeping duties and numerous distractions, including a visiting neighbor, an attractive Southern girl. Steve and Anne finally split up, but are eventually brought together again in time to legitimatize their expected infant.

SECOND LITTLE SHOW

(63 performances)

A revue in two acts, assembled by Dwight Deere Wiman. Music by Arthur Schwartz, lyrics by Howard Dietz. Produced by William A. Brady, Jr., and Dwight Deere Wiman, in association with Tom Weatherley, at the Royale Theatre, New York, September 2, 1930.

Principals engaged—

Al Trahan	Ruth Tester
Jay C. Flippen	Gloria Grafton
Davey Jones	Helen Gray
Ned Wever	Kay Hamill
Joey Ray	Eleanor Moffett
Gus Hyland	Yukona Cameron
Jack Mason	Kay Lazelle
Tashamira	Dorothy Waller

Staged by Dwight Deere Wiman, Dave Gould and Monty Woolley.

THAT'S THE WOMAN

(29 performances)

A play in two acts by Bayard Veiller. Produced by Charles Dillingham at the Fulton Theatre, New York, September 3, 1930.

Cast of characters—

District Attorney Rogers..................George Probert
Richard Morris............................Gavin Muir
Mercer Trask..............................A. E. Anson
Judge Watts...............................Oswald Yorke

Mrs. Norris....................................... Effie Shannon
Clerk of the Court....................................... Henry Osgood
Isadore Fishbaum....................................... Albert Hayes
Thomas Erskine....................................... Austin Fairman
Margaret Erskine....................................... Phœbe Foster
John Dwight....................................... Gordon Weld
Isobel Dwight....................................... Helene Sinnott
Constance Irving....................................... Lucile Watson
James....................................... Jules Farrar
Mona Lisa....................................... Helen Eby-Rock
William Rodney....................................... Arthur Behrens
Miss Welch....................................... Betty Boice

Act I.—Scene 1—Supreme Court. 2—Norris's Apartment. 3—Erskine Home. Act II.—Scene 1—Norris's Apartment. 2—Trask's Office. 3—Supreme Court.

Staged by Lester Lonergan.

Richard Norris is about to be convicted of a murder on circumstantial evidence. His only defense is that he was walking in the park at the time the murder was committed and he will make no other. Mercer Trask is induced to come out of retirement to save Richard. He quickly decides the young man is shielding a woman. The trail he uncovers leads him to Margaret Erskine, attractive and married. He can't break Margaret until he produces a girl of the streets whom he has bribed to swear that she was with Richard the night of the murder. Margaret's vanity rebels. She goes to court as Richard's alibi.

THE UP AND UP

(72 performances)

A comedy in three acts by Eva Kay Flint and Martha Madison. Produced by Edward A. Blatt and M. J. Nicholas at the Biltmore Theatre, New York, September 8, 1930.

Cast of characters—

Red Grace....................................... Ruth Conley
Fat Grace....................................... Lotta Burnell
Punk....................................... Percy Kilbride
Alice....................................... Mabel Grainger
Maizie....................................... Ruth Hunter
Albert....................................... Roy Le May
Bee....................................... Sylvia Field
Doggie....................................... Donald MacDonald
Mr. Thompson....................................... Vincent York
Ike....................................... William Foran
Curly....................................... Pat O'Brien
Block....................................... Harry Wilson
Kaplan....................................... Jacob Frank
Kid Regan....................................... Anthony Blair
Policeman....................................... Clyde Franklin
Cinia....................................... Elizabeth Taylor
Dunn....................................... James Baber
Grady....................................... Charles C. Wilson
Joe Ryan....................................... Frank Dae

Act I.—Doggie's, 103rd Street. Act II.—Phone Room, 99th Street. Act III.—Doggie's, 118th Street.

Staged by Howard Lindsay.

Doggie, a cheap speakeasy proprietor, and Bee, a girl who yearns to be "legitimate," are living together, expecting to be married when Doggie's wife dies. Doggie's a liar and Bee leaves him for Curly, a square-shooting proprietor of a bookmaking establishment. Bee changes her mind a second time, decides it is Doggie she loves and gives up Curly's riches to go back to him.

THE LONG ROAD

(24 performances)

A drama in four acts by Hugh Stange. Produced by Herman Gantvoort at the Longacre Theatre, New York, September 9, 1930.

Cast of characters—

Bess Thomas....................Helen Brooks
Carolyn Lovett....................Marion Wells
Doctor Tom Lovett....................Otto Kruger
2nd Lieut. Henry Dale....................Kirk Ames
Captain Jack Beecher....................Howard Miller
Sergeant Spike Black....................Claude Cooper
Corporal Shorty Davis....................Edgar Nelson
Miss Faucett....................Julia Cobb
Marcelle....................Jeanette Fox-Lee
Private Blink Jones....................John Lynds
Sergeant Maidvale....................Arthur Porter
Regimental Runner....................Ronald Savery
Sentry....................Walter Owens
Signal Sergeant....................Walter Munroe
Colonel Edwards....................Joseph Greene
Captain Dodd....................Ray Earles
Ambulance Sergeant....................Harry Wallace
Captain Wedgecombe (British)....................W. Messinger Bellis
Gassed Soldier....................William Edwards
Another Gassed Soldier....................Harold Clarke
Bugler....................Arthur Nulens
Walking Wounded—Ray Earles, James Eakens, Walter Owens, William Edwards, Arthur Nulens, Harold Clarke, Randall Fryer, James Coyle.

Acts I and IV.—Living Room, Doctor Lovett's Home, Brooklyn. Act II.—First Aid Tent, Sanitary Detachment, Training Camp. Act III.—Scene 1—Kitchen of an Estaminet in British Sector Near Ypres, Belgium. 2—Same Kitchen, Now Headquarters.
Staged by Hugh Stange.

Dr. Tom Lovett, simple soul, greatly loves his wife, Carolyn. When he goes to war Carolyn turns to Jack Beecher, who is more her kind, for comfort and sympathy. Dr. Tom goes overseas. When he hears Carolyn is going to have a baby he knows he is not the father. Beecher, become a captain, is brought in wounded, dictates a last letter to the woman he loves and Lovett learns the truth. After the war Dr. Tom goes home. The baby is dead and Carolyn repentant. They decide to start afresh.

THAT'S GRATITUDE

(197 performances)

A comedy in three acts by Frank Craven. Produced by John Golden at the John Golden Theatre, New York, September 11, 1930.

Cast of characters—

Robert Grant....................Frank Craven
Thomas Maxwell....................George W. Barbier
Dr. Lombard....................James C. Lane
Bell-Boy....................George Wright, Jr.
Lelia Maxwell....................Thelma Marsh
William North....................Ross Alexander
Mrs. Maxwell....................Maida Reade
Delia Maxwell....................Myrtle Clark
Nora....................Helen Mehrmann
Clayton Lorimer....................Gerald Kent

Prologue—Hotel Room in The Dana House, Iowa. Acts I, II and III.—Home with the Maxwells. Hutchinson, Kansas.
Staged by Frank Craven.

Robert Grant, small-time theatrical manager, hears Thomas Maxwell groaning in pain in an adjoining hotel room. He goes to his rescue with a pint of prescription liquor and the two become friends. Maxwell takes Grant home with him. Grant outstays his welcome and becomes embroiled in the Maxwell family affairs. Helping out a boy who is engaged to a homely Maxwell girl and wants to marry her pretty sister Grant takes the homely one off the boy's hands, has her face treated by a plastic surgeon and makes her a successful prima donna. After which he would marry her. But she runs away with a beautiful but dumb tenor. That's gratitude.

INSULT

(24 performances)

A drama in three acts derived by J. E. Harold Terry and Harry Tighe from the Dutch (Dolle Hans) of Jan Fabricius. Produced by Lee Shubert at the 49th Street Theatre, New York, September 15, 1930.

Cast of characters—

Sidin....................Ali Taieb Boucari
Adinda....................Mona Li
Jolanthe....................Lydia Sherwood
Major De Weert....................D. A. Clarke-Smith
Does De Weert....................James Raglan

Kees Witte....................................Roland Hogue
Hans Hartman..................................Leslie Perrins
Sarbini.......................................H. H. McCollum
A Messenger...................................Ali Taieb Boucari
A Fusileer....................................John Gray
A Sergeant....................................James Vincent

Acts I and II.—Veranda of the Controller's House. Act III.—Guardroom of the Barracks.
Staged by D. A. Clarke-Smith.

Does De Weert, a civil governor in the Dutch West Indies, stupid but likable, is married to the beautiful Jolanthe who loves Hans Hartman, a handsome half-caste. Does De Weert's father, loathing half-castes, goads Hans into striking him and has him condemned to death for insubordination. Jolanthe confesses her love, her husband manages to have himself killed by the natives and Hans is executed.

WITH PRIVILEGES

(48 performances)

A comedy drama in three acts by Ruth Welty and Roy Hargrave. Produced by Hyman Adler and Philip Gerton at the Vanderbilt Theatre, New York, September 15, 1930.

Cast of characters—

Sarah Heppleby.................................Marie Hunt
Carl Westcott..................................Roy Hargrave
Aleppo...Lionel Jay Stander
Mary Rhodes....................................June Justice
Mr. Reisner....................................Frank Manning
Rachel Stein...................................Joan Madison
Miss Furst.....................................Madeline Grey
Mahlenheim.....................................Moss Fleisig
Pedro..Saul Z. Martell
Exterminator...................................Thomas V. Morrison

Acts I, II and III.—Kitchen in a Rooming House in Which the Roomers Are Privileged to Get Their Own Breakfasts.
Staged by Henry Stillman.

Carl Westcott, penniless but ambitious architect, and Mary Rhodes are roomers in the same house. Mary loves Carl, but Carl takes after Mary's roommate, Rachel Stein, who has been deserted by another man. Carl asks Rachel to go to Atlantic City with him, Rachel accepts, thinking to make her former lover jealous. When the ruse fails Rachel kills herself by jumping off the roof. After which Mary wins Carl and Carl wins $5,000 for an architectural design.

THE RHAPSODY

(16 performances)

A drama in three episodes by Louis K. Anspacher. Produced by George M. Cohan at the Cort Theatre, New York, September 15, 1930.

Cast of characters—

Lodar Baron....................................Louis Calhern
Delphine....................................Julia Hoyt
Doctor Hollister....................................John R. Hamilton
Marjorie Kellam....................................Natalie Schafer
Kaspar Wahl....................................Craig Williams
Austin Kellam....................................John T. Doyle
Anton....................................Adrian Rosley
Max Krueger....................................Curtis Karpe
Henry Bergh....................................Josef Adler
Elizabeth Trumbull....................................Aline McDermott

Acts I, II and III.—Drawing Room of Lodar Baron's Apartment Atop of His Office Building in New York City.
Staged by Sam Forrest.

Lodar Baron, an Austrian composer of light music with high artistic ambitions, has come through the years following the war obsessed by an urge to kill a brutal German superior who had humiliated him. His mistress and a friendly psychologist seek to rid his mind of the obsession. Baron is finally brought face to face with his enemy, whom he shoots with a gun from which the doctor had removed the bullets. As a further aid to the composer's recovery the mistress, Delphine, releases him to his true love, Marjorie Kellam.

SYMPHONY IN TWO FLATS

(47 performances)

A comedy in three acts by Ivor Novello. Produced by the Messrs. Shubert at the Shubert Theatre, New York, September 16, 1930.

Cast of characters—

PRELUDE

David Kennard....................................Ivor Novello
Lesley Fullerton....................................Benita Hume

PROLOGUE

Peter Innes....................................Anthony Hankey
Mason....................................Frederick Oxley
Mrs. Plaintiff....................................Lilian Braithwaite
Salmon Pryde....................................Ethel Baird
Beryl Plaintiff....................................Ann Trevor

David Kennard.......................................Ivor Novello
Lesley Kennard.......................................Benita Hume

THE FLOOR ABOVE

Mabel.......................................Minnie Raynor
Leo Chavasse.......................................Ivan Samson
Lesley Kennard.......................................Benita Hume
David Kennard.......................................Ivor Novello
Jean Burton.......................................Netta Westcott
Miss Trebelli.......................................Maidie Andrews

THE FLOOR BELOW

Salmon Pryde.......................................Ethel Baird
Porter.......................................Una Venning
Mrs. Plaintiff.......................................Lilian Braithwaite
Beryl Plaintiff.......................................Ann Trevor
Peter Innes ("Curly").......................................Anthony Hankey
George Park.......................................J. Lister Williams

Prelude—Point of Vantage at the Chelsea Arts Ball. Prologue—Empty Studio. Act I.—Scene 1—Floor Above (Andante). 2—Floor Below (Allegro). 3—Floor Above (Ritardo). Act II.—Scene 1—Floor Below (Pizzicato). 2—Floor Above (Lento). 3—Floor Above (Lento E'Adagio). Act III.—Scene 1—Floor Below (Finaletto). 2—Floor Above (Finale).

Staged by Raymond Massey.

David Kennard and Lesley Fullerton meet at a fancy dress ball, fall in love and decide to marry, despite Lesley's engagement to Leo Chavasse. David, an ambitious composer, enters a prize symphony competition and turns Lesley over to Leo during the weeks of his preoccupation. When David suffers blindness from eye strain Lesley and Leo tell him he has won the prize, Leo furnishing the money. David finds out the truth over the radio; also the truth about his wife and his friend, and casts them off. Later there is a reconciliation. Running parallel to this story is a comedy being enacted by the family living on the floor below. Mrs. Plaintiff, dependent on her daughter Beryl's income, strives valiantly to keep Beryl from marrying until she herself becomes engaged. Then she works as hard to hurry the daughter off.

LUANA

(21 performances)

A musical comedy in two acts adapted by Howard Emmett Rogers from Richard Walton Tully's "The Bird of Paradise." Music by Rudolph Friml; lyrics by J. Kiern Brennan. Produced by Arthur Hammerstein at Hammerstein's Theatre, New York, September 17, 1930.

Cast of characters—

Keipia.......................................George Djimos
Mahuna.......................................Marguerita Sylva
Hewamena.......................................William Pringle

Meikia..Lillian Bond
Hoheno..Donald Novis
Luana...Ruth Altman
Paul Wilson...Joseph Macaulay
Captain Hatch...George Nash
Sergeant Cavanaugh..Pat O'Dea
"Sure-Fire Thompson"......................................Harry Jans
Jimmy Smith...Harold Whalen
Mr. Sawyer..Harry C. Bradley
Diana Larned..Diana Chase
Robert Dean...Robert Chisholm
Polly Hatch...Doris Carson
Major Andrews...Harold Ten Brook
Lemuele...Ferris Martin
Hula Dancer...Swani Lani
Hawaiian Children................Joseph, John and Michael Rayia
Saki..Peter Goo Chong

Act I.—Scene 1—Outside of Luana's House, Puna. 2—Road Near Dean's Shack. 3—Bathing Pool. Act II.—Scene 1—Interior of Luana's House. 2—Exterior of Moana Hotel, Waikiki Beach, Honolulu. 3—At the Base of Pelée. 4—Volcano.

Staged by Arthur Hammerstein, Howard Rogers and Earl Lindsey.

Luana discovers on her twenty-first birthday that she is the princess of her tribe and that her people expect her to assume their leadership. Eluding the honor, Luana marries Paul Wilson, an American doctor. When Wilson, gone native, later deserts her, Luana throws herself into the crater of Pelée in expiation of her sins.

CINDERELATIVE

(4 performances)

A comedy in three acts by Dorothy Heyward and Dorothy DeJagers. Produced by Lionel A. and Jack Hyman at the Comedy Theatre, New York, September 18, 1930.

Cast of characters—

THE PROLOGUE

The Boy...Derek Fairman
The Girl..Dorothea Chard

THE PLAY

Penfield Manton...Edward Hogan
Agatha Manton...Marjorie De Voe
Carter..G. Lester Paul
Paul Manton...Richard Irving
Jonathan McCallister, "The Boy"...........................Derek Fairman
The Girl..Dorothea Chard
Horace J. Hill..Jonathan Hole
Marcia Lyman..Frances Sheil

Prologue—Elevator in a Paris Apartment. Acts I and II.—Living Room, Paul Manton's New York Home. Act III.—Suite 1234, Hotel Pocahontas.

Staged by Herschel Cropper.

The Girl, living unhappily with her divorced mother in Paris, is eager to see her father in America. She also hopes to keep her identity secret until she discovers whether or not her father likes her. She takes the name of a friend, an expected bride, and, with the help of the prospective groom, has a lively time for a week. Trying to run away because she thinks her father does not like her she is revealed as her true self and welcomed to the paternal arms.

NINA ROSA

(137 performances)

A musical comedy in two acts by Otto Harbach; music by Sigmund Romberg; lyrics by Irving Cæsar. Produced by the Messrs. Shubert at the Majestic Theatre, New York, September 20, 1930.

Cast of characters—

Tom....Frank Horn
Dick....George Kirk
Harry....Zachary Caully
Chinaman....Richard Koch
Yana....Belle Sylvia
Corinna....Armida
Bob Wilson....George Anderson
Silvers....Don Barclay
Jimmy Blakeley....Jack Sheehan
Don Fernando....Clay Clement
Pablo....Leonard Ceeley
Jack Haines....Guy Robertson
Nina Rosa Stradella....Ethelind Terry
John Craig....Stanley Jessup
Elinor Haines....Marion Marchante
Cholo....Katherine Skidmore
Chico....Victor Casmore
Gaucho Dancer....Stephen Cortez
Chiquita....Peggy
Dolores....Evlyn Klein
Mona....Mona Soltis
Ramido....John Tomney
Maca....Judy Lane
Enta....Sybil Comer
Paca....Norma Leyland
Spirit Dancers....Yo-Hay-Tong, Kalil-Ogly
Gauchos....Arthur Singer, Walter Palm, Roy Vitalis, Edwin Drake
Peddler....Alfred Russ

Acts I and II.—Near Cuzco, Peru, South America.
Staged by J. J. Shubert and J. C. Huffman.

Jack Haines, a mining engineer working in Peru, falls in love with an attractive native girl, Nina Rosa, and proposes taking her back to the States with him. He is violently opposed by Pablo, a vicious hombre, who takes a lot of whipping before he stays whipped.

A FAREWELL TO ARMS

(24 performances)

A drama in three acts adapted by Laurence Stallings from the novel of the same name by Ernest Hemingway. Produced by A. H. Woods at the National Theatre, New York, September 22, 1930.

Cast of characters—

Rinaldi	Crane Wilbur
Cesare	Joseph Downing
Brundi	Frank Coletti
Cavalcanti	Alberto Calvo
Captain	Jack La Rue
Priest	Rene Roberti
Major	Louis Veda
Miss Ferguson	Katherine Warren
Catherine Barkley	Elissa Landi
Lieutenant Frederick Henry	Glenn Anders
Sergeant Bonello	Albert Ferro
Aymo	Frank Farrara
Piani	Tino Valenti
Britisher	Albert Froom
Staff Colonel	Jules David
First Orderly	Hendryk De Paule
Second Orderly	Joseph Kashioff
Wounded Man	Vati Dono
Porter	Paul Cremonesi
Stretcher Bearer	Ricardo Calvo
Mrs. Walker	Carrie Lowe
Miss Gage	Jane McKenzie
Miss Van Campen	Florence Earle
Doctor	Armand Cortez
Medical Captains	Ricardo Bengali Juan Villasana
Valentini	Mortimer Weldon
Manager	Fritz Ulm
Waiter	Ralph Desmond
Two Girl Refugees	Helen Kim Dorothy Paule
Sergeants of Infantry	John Genaro Antonio Berri
Colonel Gaglairdi	C. Sager Czaja
Officer of Carabinieri	Harold Huber
Second Officer	Joseph Scotti

Acts I, II and III.—On the Italian Front and in a Milan Hospital.
Staged by Reuben Mamoulian.

Catherine Barkley and Frederick Henry, two disillusioned warriors in the hospital service on the Italian front, she a nurse, he an ambulance driver, meet and are mutually attracted. Henry is wounded, moved to a Milan hospital and is there nursed back to health by Catherine. They separate when Henry returns to the front. They are reunited during the Caporetto retreat. Catherine dies in childbirth bearing Henry's son.

UNCLE VANYA

(16 performances)

A comedy in four acts, adapted by Rose Caylor from Chekov's original. Revived by Jed Harris at the Booth Theatre, New York, September 22, 1930.

Cast of characters—

Marina....................Kate Mayhew
Michael Astroff....................Osgood Perkins
Ivan Voinitski (Uncle Vanya)....................Walter Connolly
Sonia....................Zita Johann
Alexander Serebrakoff....................Eugene Powers
IIlya Telegin....................Eduardo Ciannelli
Helena....................Lillian Gish
Mme. Voinitskaya....................Isabel Irving
A Servant....................Harold Johnsrud

Act I.—An August Afternoon in the Garden of the Serebrakoffs' Country Estate, the Late Nineties. Acts II and III.—In the House. Act IV.—Vanya's Study.
Staged by Jed Harris.

This was a supplementary engagement, following the run of the play from April 15, to June 21, 1930. The original cast was restored with the exception of Zita Johann, who replaced Joanna Loos.

FINE AND DANDY

(255 performances)

A musical comedy in two acts, book by Donald Ogden Stewart; music by Kay Swift, lyrics by Paul James. Produced by Morris Green and Lewis E. Gensler at Erlanger's Theatre, New York, September 23, 1930.

Cast of characters—

Joe Squibb....................Joe Cook
Wiffington....................Dave Chasen
Mrs. Fordyce....................Dora Maughan
Maribelle Fordyce....................Nell O'Day
Nancy Ellis....................Alice Boulden
George Ellis....................Joe Wagstaff
Mr. Ellis....................George A. Schiller
Edgar Little....................John W. Ehrle
Miss Hunter....................Eleanor Powell
Aunt Lucy....................Laura Clairon
Office Boy....................Jimmy Hadreas
Clergyman....................Jack Burley
Hugo Giersdorf....................Herman Ergotti
Johann Giersdorf....................Paul Brack
A. Giersdorf....................Frank Naldi
P. Giersdorf....................Frank Innis

A Clerk..Joe Clayton
The Old Man...George Neville
Insurance Agent..Joe Lyons
Ukulele Mike...Jack McClusky
Harmonica Player..Joe Clayton
First Workman...John R. Hall
Second Workman..Dick Erskine
Third Workman..Joe Riley
Fourth Workman ....J. Rousseaux
Fifth Workman..Frank Naldi
Sixth Workman...Ben Bernard
Seventh Workman...Billy Randall
Eighth Workman ....Scott Jensen
J. Newton Wheer..Pat Walshe
Foreman..David D. Morris
Miss Hargrave...Eleanor Etheridge
R. V. Wilkins..Walter Fehl
The Four Horsemen......Murray Evans, Jack Flaherty, Joe Reilly, Jack Burley
The Colt..Pat Walshe
Tommy Atkins Sextet............Merriel Abbott Specialty Dancers

Act I.—Scene 1—Machine Room of the Fordyce Drop Forge and Tool Factory. 2—Caddy House of the Country Club. 3—A Sand Trap in a Golf Course. 4—Joe's Office. 5—In Front of Squibb's Finance Chart. 6—On the Way to the Graduation. 7—Garden of the Fordyce Night School. Act II.—Scene 1—Employees' Picnic Grounds. 2—Interior of a Bank. 3—Mrs. Fordyce's Garden.

Staged by Morris Green, Frank McCoy, Dave Gould and Tom Nip.

Joe Squibb, proud to be a working man if he does not have to work much, becomes general manager of the Fordyce Drop Forge and Tool factory when the widow who owns it falls captive to his brash charms. Joe revolutionizes the picnic schedules and does other things to the works, retiring from active participation at 11.15 P.M.

* ONCE IN A LIFETIME

(305 performances)

A comedy in three acts by Moss Hart and George S. Kaufman. Produced by Sam H. Harris at the Music Box, New York, September 24, 1930.

Cast of characters—

George Lewis...Hugh O'Connell
May Daniels...Jean Dixon
Jerry Hyland..Grant Mills
The Porter..Oscar Polk
Helen Hobart..Spring Byington
Susan Walker...Sally Phipps
Cigarette Girl..Clara Waring
Coat Check Girl..Otis Schaefer
Phyllis Fontaine..Janet Currie
Miss Fontaine's Maid...............................Marie Ferguson
Miss Fontaine's Chauffeur............................Charles Mack
Florabel Leigh...Eugenie Frontai
Miss Leigh's Maid......................................Dorothy Talbot
Miss Leigh's Chauffeur..................................Edward Loud
Bellboy..Payson Crane

Mrs. Walker.................................Frances E. Brandt
Ernest.................................Marc Loebell
Herman Glogauer.................................Charles Halton
Miss Leighton.................................Leona Maricle
Lawrence Vail.................................George S. Kaufman
Weisskopf.................................Louis Cruger
Meterstein.................................William McFadden
First Page.................................Stanley Fitzpatrick
Second Page.................................Edwin Mills
Three Scenario Writers..........Kempton Race, George Casselbury, Burton Mallory
Rudolph Kammerling.................................Walter Dreher
First Electrician.................................Jack Williams
Second Electrician.................................John O. Hewitt
A Voice Pupil.................................Jane Buchanan
Mr. Flick.................................Harold Grau
Miss Chasen.................................Virginia Hawkins
First Cameraman.................................Irving Morrow
The Bishop.................................Granville Bates
The Sixth Bridesmaid.................................Frances Thress
Script Girl.................................Georgia MacKinnon
George's Secretary.................................Robert Ryder

Act I.—Scene 1—In a Hotel Room. 2—On a Pullman Car. Acts II and III.—Herman Glogauer Studio, Hollywood.

Staged by George S. Kaufman.

See page 110.

THE GREEKS HAD A WORD FOR IT

(253 performances)

A comedy in three acts by Zoe Akins. Produced by William H. Harris, Jr., at the Sam H. Harris Theatre, New York, September 25, 1930.

Cast of characters—

Schatze.................................Dorothy Hall
Jean.................................Verree Teasdale
Polaire.................................Muriel Kirkland
Waiter in the Night Club.................................Jack Bennett
Louis Small.................................Don Beddoe
Dey Emery.................................Hardie Albright
Boris Feldman.................................Ernest Glendinning
The Russian Woman.................................Helen Kingstead
Jones.................................Harold Heaton
Justin Emery.................................Frederic Worlock
Stanton.................................Gordon Stout
Waiter.................................John Walpole
Bellows.................................Ethel Hamilton

Act I.—Scene 1—Small Backroom of a Night Club. 2—Music Room in Boris Feldman's Apartment. Act II.—Schatze's Sitting Room in an Apartment Hotel on Central Park West. Act III.—Parlor of a Private Suite in the Ambassador Hotel, New York.

Staged by William Harris, Jr.

Schatze, Jean and Polaire are three ex-Follies on the make. Three mistresseers of the tonier apartment hotels, they have an understanding that they are one for all and all for one so long as none of them cheats. Jean takes a fancy to Dey Emery, a millionaire's son, but Dey prefers Polaire and that causes some conflict. Jean finally compromises by taking Dey's father, Justin. When the elder Emery wants to marry Jean she agrees, but at her wedding, drinking wine with her old-time buddies, who are about to leave for Paris with some big aviation officials, Jean decides suddenly to go along with Schatze and Polaire and leaves Emery to find himself another bride.

FRANKIE AND JOHNNIE

(61 performances)

A melodrama by John M. Kirkland. Produced by the author at the Republic Theatre, New York, September 25, 1930.

Cast of characters—

The Count	Kenneth Burton
Danny	Arthur Griffin
Frank	Jack H. Clifford
Mike	Edward Kelly
Floria	Gene Ravette
Ethel	Marion Blau
Fifi	Regine Valdy
Ike	Jerome Cowan
Laura	Irene Lorraine
Ray	Herbert Spencer
Gertrude	Ethel Clifford
Lou	Valerie Valaire
Walsh	Will T. Chatterton
Pansy	Josephine Evans
Nellie Bly	Roberta Beatty
Waiter	Cliff Heckinger
Jake	Edward J. Wright
A Fancy Man	Manuel Duarte
Frankie	Anne Forrest
Curley	Don Rowan
Johnnie	Frank McGlynn, Jr.
Dana	Ike Ball
George	Jack McDowell
Will	William Hart
Joe	J. Taylor Brownlaw
Ralph	Neil Stone
Brinn	Myrtland La Varre
McCarthy	Ben Roberts
Hitchcock	Roger Bacon

Acts I, II and III.—Danny's Alton House, a Waterfront Resort in St. Louis, Mo., in 1849.

Staged by Lee Elmore.

Frankie loved Johnnie. She was a prostitute in St. Louis and he was a card sharp who took money away from unsuspecting gamblers because he looked like a hick. When Johnnie came off the river boats with $13,000 Frankie wanted him to go to California and become a man. But Nellie Bly wanted him to stay in St. Louis and have a party. Johnnie made Frankie believe that he had lost his money and she agreed to make more for him. When she learned that he had spent all he had on Nellie Bly Frankie shot Johnnie dead.

ROADSIDE

(11 performances)

A comedy in three acts by Lynn Riggs. Produced by Arthur Hopkins at the Longacre Theatre, New York, September 26, 1930.

Cast of characters—

Pap Rader.......................................Frederick Burton
Buzzy Hale.......................................Jack Byrne
Hannie Rader.......................................Ruthelma Stevens
Red Ike.......................................Gilbert Squarey
Black Ike.......................................Kendall Foster
Texas.......................................Ralph Bellamy
Town Marshal.......................................Roderick Baybee
Neb.......................................Frank I. Frayne
Judge Snodgrass.......................................Harry Hermsen
Mrs. Foster.......................................Anne Tonetti

Acts I and III.—By the Side of a Road Through the Woods in Indian Territory. Act II.—Scene 1—The Same. 2—Courtroom in Verdigree Switch.

Staged by Arthur Hopkins.

Texas, a roving playboy from the state whose name he has adopted, gets roaring drunk in the Indian Territory, maims his guards, shoots up the courtroom and breaks out of jail. On the roadside he meets Pap Rader and his daughter, Hannie. Texas falls in love with Hannie, but his assurance and boastfulness lead her to make sport of him. Out of chagrin Texas gives himself up. There being no jail left to put him in, he takes to the road again, meets the Raders a second time, wins Hannie and decides to stay with them.

NINE TILL SIX

(25 performances)

A drama in three acts by Philip and Aimee Stewart. Produced by Lee Shubert at the Ritz Theatre, New York, September 27, 1930.

Cast of characters—

Mrs. Pembroke.......................................Auriol Lee
Miss Roberts.......................................Gwendolyn Hammond
Freda.......................................Norah Balfour

Gracie Abbot..Prunella Page
Mrs. Abbot..Elwyn Harvey
Clare Pembroke..Viola Lyel
Daisy..Merle Tottenham
Violet..Audrey Cameron
Lady Avonlaye..Estelle Thebaud
Bridget Penarth..Ann Macgregor
Gwladys..Sybil Davidson
Carry..Edith Harcourt
Beatrice..Wyn Clare
Judy..Jeanne Stuart
Helen..Petra Charpentier
M'selle..Eliz Gergley

Acts I, II and III.—Millinery and Dressmaking Shop in Regent Street, London.

Staged by Auriol Lee.

Mrs. Pembroke, the capable proprietress of a millinery and dressmaking establishment in Regent Street, London, adds two young girls to her staff of apprentices. One, Gracie Abbot, is the daughter of working people, the other, Bridget Penarth, the daughter of a lord who wishes to add to her spending allowance. Bridget manages to keep the girls dissatisfied because of her superior ways and advantages, and is indirectly responsible for two of them, Freda and Gracie, taking gowns from the stock. Gracie only borrowed hers, but Freda confesses to stealing. The understanding Mrs. Pembroke, after lecturing the girls, gives them another chance.

ONE, TWO, THREE

(40 performances)

A comedy in one act by Ferenc Molnar. Produced by Gilbert Miller at the Henry Miller Theatre, New York, September 29, 1930.

Cast of characters—

Nordson..Arthur Byron
Nordson's Secretary..George H. Trader
Nordson's Valet..Norbert Humphreys
Lydia..Audray Dale
Anton Schuh..John Williams
Miss Kuno..Aldeah Wise
Miss Posner..Eileen Byron
Miss Brasch..Joan Carr
Miss Petrowitsch..Natica de Acosta
Dr. Pinsky..Frederick Roland
A Haberdasher..Johnnie Brewer
Mr. Osso..J. P. Wilson
Mr. Ciring..George Fogle
Dr. Wolff..Harold Thomas
A Barber..Isidor Marcil
Count Von Dubois-Schottenburg..Reginald Mason
Dr. Faber..Robert Noble
Kaldoorian..Donald MacMillan
Miss Lind..Fifi Laynee

Karl.......................................Forbes Herbert Dawson
Felix...Colin Hunter
Colleon...Maurice Cass
Kristian..Frank Rothe
Ferdinand.......................................Carl Del Mel

Scene—Nordson's Private Office in a Central European Capital.
Staged by James Whale.

THE VIOLET

By Ferenc Molnar

Cast of characters—

Miss Roboz......................................Natica de Acosta
The Producer-Manager................................A. P. Kaye
John...Johnnie Brewer
Miss Markus.....................................Aldeah Wise
The Composer...............................Reginald Mason
Miss Rakolnoki.......................................Joan Carr
Miss Szell...Sue Moore
Ilona Stobri......................................Ruth Gordon

Scene—The Office of a Producer-Manager.

Nordson, who fancies himself as a German Napoleon of business, learns that Lydia, the daughter of his richest and most important American client and a visitor in his home, has married a socialistic taxi driver. Lydia's family is expected the same day the discovery is made and Nordson, feeling responsible for Lydia, decides that the taxi husband must be made into a respectable son-in-law within the hour. He marshals his vast resources, hires tailors and haberdashers by the dozen, pays handsomely for an adoptable father of title for the boy and manages the stunt successfully.

"One, Two, Three" was preceded by "The Violet," also a Molnar one-acter, relating the adventure of a theatre manager who is tired of the advances of the girls he hires for his shows and turns his office over to an amorous composer. Just as the composer is getting along handsomely with Ilona Stobri the manager decides to resume his old job.

MRS. MOONLIGHT

(321 performances)

A drama in three acts by Benn W. Levy. Produced by Charles Hopkins at the Charles Hopkins Theatre, New York, September 29, 1930.

Cast of characters—

Tom Moonlight.......................................Guy Standing
Minnie..Haidee Wright

Edith Jones....................................Kathryn Collier
Sarah Moonlight....................................Edith Barrett
Percy Middling....................................Leo G. Carroll
Jane Moonlight....................................Katherine Standing
Willie Ragg....................................Vernon Kelso
Peter....................................John Ross

Acts I, II and III.—The Living Room of Tom Moonlight's Home in England.

Staged by Charles Hopkins.

Sarah Moonlight, being the victim of a wish she had made on a charmed necklace, is unable to lose the youth she once prized so greatly. At 28 she still looks 18 and everybody is beginning to notice it. Fearing the consequences as the years go on, Sarah runs away. In ten years, after her husband has married a second time, she returns as her own niece and helps her daughter avoid an unhappy marriage. Disappearing again she comes back when she is 70, is with her husband when he dies and shortly follows him into the shadows.

MR. GILHOOLEY

(31 performances)

A drama in three acts adapted by Frank B. Elser from the novel by Liam O'Flaherty. Produced by Jed Harris at the Broadhurst Theatre, New York, September 30, 1930.

Cast of characters—

A Beggar....................................Joseph Shea
Seumas Hanrahan....................................Charles Kennedy
Mick Friel....................................John A. Butler
Sean Macaward....................................P. J. Kelly
Mr. Gilhooley....................................Arthur Sinclair
A Street Walker....................................Eileen Burke
A Girl....................................Helen Hayes
Cissy....................................Maire O'Neill
Pollard....................................Barry Macollum
Tom Shaughnessy....................................Clement O'Loghlen
Mrs. Davin....................................Kate McComb
Mr. Davin....................................Ralph Cullinan
A Trunkman....................................Jimmy Scott
Maggie....................................Peggy Doran

Act I.—Scene 1—Street Corner in Dublin. 2—Gilhooley's Room in Mrs. Davin's Boarding House. 3—Hall at Mrs. Davin's. Acts II and III.—Flat in Dublin.

Staged by Jed Harris.

A Girl (Nellie Fitzpatrick) finding herself hungry and penniless in Dublin, accosts Mr. Gilhooley in front of a pub and begs him to help her. Gilhooley buys her food and takes her to his room. She warns him that though she is willing to play the game she can never love him, being still in love with a young man who had deserted her in London. Gilhooley accepts these terms, but later grows furiously jealous of the unseen lover. The night he discovers that Nellie has been out hunting for her lost love Gilhooley strangles her to death and shoots himself.

BAD GIRL

(85 performances)

A drama in three acts, adapted from Vina Delmar's novel of the same name by the author and Brian Marlow. Produced by Robert V. Newman at the Hudson Theatre, New York, October 2, 1930.

Cast of characters—

Eddie........Paul Kelly
Dot........Sylvia Sidney
Edna........Charlotte Wynters
Jim........William Pawley
Maude........Sascha Beaumont
Sue........Joan Winters
Pat........Lawrence Bolton
Ted........Walter Vaughn
Miss Parsons........Eleanor Merlin
Miss Brown........Grace Morse
Miss Lambert........Joan Harmon
Doctor Stewart........Martin Howe
Mrs. Lensky........Angela Jacobs
Mrs. Vernon........Emily Graham

Act I.—Scene 1—Eddie's Room. 2—Edna's Apartment. Act II.—Scene 1—Dot and Eddie's Living Room. 2—The Hospital. Act III.—Scene 1—The Hospital. 2—A Taxi.

Staged by Marion Gering.

Eddie and Dot, having given in to their love, marry and settle down in a flat in the Bronx. When Dot discovers that she is to have a baby she is at first inclined to avoid the responsibility, fearing that Eddie does not want the child. Later she changes her mind and on the way home from the hospital discovers that Eddie is crazy about being a father.

STEPDAUGHTERS OF WAR

(24 performances)

A drama in three acts, adapted by Kenyon Nicholson from the novel of Helen Zenna Smith. Produced by Charles Frohman, Inc., at the Empire Theatre, New York, October 6, 1930.

Cast of characters—

Georgine Toshington (Tosh)........Olive Reeves-Smith
Madge Meredith (The Bug)........Viola Frayne
Etta Potter (Etta Potato)........Dorothy Patten

Bertina Farmer (The B. F.)........................Lucille Lisle
Kit Evans..................................Katherine Alexander
Patricia Hammond (Skinny)........................Ellen E. Lowe
The Commandant...............................Eda Heinemann
Geoffrey Hilder..............................Warren William
Sarah..Alice Belmore Cliffe
Tony Farraday................................G. P. Huntley, Jr.
Audrey Farraday..............................Florence Vroom
Aunt Katherine..................................Ethel Griffies
Fanny Evans.................................Winifred Fraser
Barbara Evans...................................Mary Arbenz
Martha Edwards..............................Philippa Bevans
Florence Preston..............................Enid Menhinick

Acts I, II and III.—Behind the British Front in Flanders; and at Folkstone and Wimbledon.
Staged by Chester Erskin.

Kit Evans, senior member of an ambulance-drivers' unit in France, fed up with war and disillusioned as to its glories, finds herself suddenly recalled from a long overdue leave. Turning back at Folkstone she surrenders to a romance of the moment and permits Captain Geoffrey Hilder to spend the night with her. Later Kit resigns her commission, but in order to help a sister returns to the front. She is in love with Hilder but engaged to a home boy. Hilder, badly wounded, confesses that he is no more than a ghost of a man, but Kit, feeling that she belongs more to the dead than the living, asks him to marry her.

ROMEO AND JULIET

(44 performances)

Shakespeare tragedy in four acts. Revived by the Civic Repertory Theatre, Inc., at the Civic Theatre, New York, October 6, 1930.

Cast of characters—

Escalus, Prince of Verona........................Jacob Ben-Ami
Paris...Blake Scott
Montague.......................................Harold Moulton
Capulet...Walter Beck
An Old Man....................................Joseph Kramm
Romeo..Donald Cameron
Mercutio..................................J. Edward Bromberg
Benvolio......................................Robert F. Ross
Tybalt.......................................Robert H. Gordon
Friar Lawrence...............................Sayre Crawley
Friar John....................................Joseph Kramm
Balthasar.......................................Arnold Moss
Samson.......................................Herbert Shapiro
Gregory..Robert Lewis
Peter..Burgess Meredith
Abraham..Lee Hillery
An Apothecary................................Howard da Silva
Page to Capulet................................Edith Evans
Page to Paris................................Gordon Wallace
Page to Mercutio..............................Vernon Jones

An Officer....................................John Saltzman
Lady Montague....................................Mary Ward
Lady Capulet....................................Alma Kruger
Juliet....................................Eva Le Gallienne
Nurse to Juliet....................................Leona Roberts
1st Watchman....................................Morris Morrison
2nd Watchman....................................Marc Lawrence
3rd Watchman....................................David Kerman
Drummers............Gordon Wallace, Sean Dillon, Richard Waring
Pages.........William Steinhorn, Edward Kogan, Lawrence Levin, Mary Sarton, Joyce Neitchie
Dancers.......Estelle Sheer, Jane Kim, Elizabeth Schonberg, Mary Tartar, Sean Dillon, Peter Raily, Charles Martin, Allan Weaver, John Saltzman, De Witt Kiernan

Act I.—Scene 1—A Public Place in Verona. 2—A Street. 3—Capulet's House. Act II.—Scene 1—Capulet's Orchard. 2 and 5—Outside Friar Lawrence's Cell. 3—A Street. 4—Capulet's Garden. 6—Juliet's Room. Act III.—Scenes 1 and 4—Friar Lawrence's Cell. 2—Hall in Capulet's House. 3—Balcony, Juliet's Room. 5—Hall Capulet's House. 6—Juliet's Room. Act IV.—Scene 1—Hall in Capulet's House. 2—Juliet's Room. 3—A Street in Mantua. 4—Outside Friar Lawrence's Cell.

Staged by Eva Le Gallienne.

Resuming the repertory season of her company Miss Le Gallienne's first week included revivals of "Romeo and Juliet," "The Cradle Song," and "The Lady from Alfaqueque," preceded by Arthur Schnitzler's one-act play, "The Green Cockatoo," with the following cast:

Cast of characters—

Prospere (Host of the Green Cockatoo)..............Egon Brecher
Grasset....................................J. Edward Bromberg
Lebret....................................Robert H. Gordon
Sergeant....................................Joseph Kramm
Grain....................................Burgess Meredith
Scaevola....................................Howard da Silva
Jules....................................David Kerman
Henri....................................Jacob Ben-Ami
Leocadie....................................Beatrice de Neergaard
François, Vicomte de Nogeant....................Harold Moulton
Albin, Chevalier de la Tremouille..................Gordon Wallace
Michette....................................Ria Mooney
Flipotte....................................Sala Staw
Emile, Duke de Cadignan............................Walter Beck
Marquis de Lansac....................................Paul Leyssac
Guillaume....................................Sayre Crawley
Rollin....................................Donald Cameron
Severine, Marquise de Lansac......................Estelle Scheer
Maurice....................................Herbert Shapiro
Etienne....................................Arnold Moss

The Action Takes Place in Prospere's Wine-Room, "The Green Cockatoo," in Paris on the Evening of July 14, 1789.

BROWN BUDDIES

(111 performances)

A negro musical comedy by Carl Rickman; music by Joe Jordan and Millard Thomas. Produced at the Liberty Theatre, New York, October 7, 1930.

Cast of characters—

Spider Bruce....................John Mason
Mathews....................Thomas Moseley
Hamfat....................“Little Ferdie” Lewis
Mammy Johnson....................Ada Brown
Jessie Watkins....................Alma Smith
George Brown....................Andrew Tribble
Ukulele Kid....................Putney Dandridge
Bill Jones....................Walter Brogsdale
Pete Jackson....................Maurice Ellis
Deacon Siccomore....................Shelton Brooks
Mabel....................Ethel Jackson
A Woman....................Nancy Sharpe
Sam Wilson....................Bill Robinson
Betty Lou Johnson....................Adelaide Hall
A Policeman....................Sam Jones
A Trumpeter....................Hank Smith
Lieutenant Pugh....................Wm. E. Fountaine
Houstin Charlie....................Joseph Willis
Captain Andrews....................James A. Lillard
Medical Officer....................Carroll Tate
Orderly....................Pete Thompson
A Guard....................Edgar Brown
Privates Red and Struggy....................Red and Struggy
Y.M.C.A. Man....................Thomas Wye
A Corporal....................Archie Toms

Act I.—Scene 1—Street in the Mud Flats of East St. Louis. 2—Outside the Barracks. 3—Aboard a Transport. Act II.—Scene 1—Y.M.C.A. Entertainment Hut. 2—A Road to the Front. 3—A Forest Trail. 4—Street in East St. Louis. 5—Home of Captain Andrews in East St. Louis.

Wartime adventures of a group of enlisted colored men, led by Sam Wilson.

MARIGOLD

(13 performances)

A comedy in three acts by L. Allen Harker and F. R. Pryor. Produced by Simon Ord at the 49th Street Theatre, New York, October 8, 1930.

Cast of characters—

Robina Macfarraline....................Marie Shields
Miss Valencia Dunlop....................Marguerite Cellier
Miss Sarita Dunlop....................Winifred Ord
Mrs. Pringle....................Jean Clyde
Marigold....................Sophie Stewart
Peter Gloag....................Edmond Beresford
Madam Marly....................Yvette Pienne
James Payton....................Walter Roy
Archie Forsyth....................Ellis Irving
Major Andrew Sellar....................Lionel Gadsden
Mordan....................William Aldous
Nigel Lumsden....................Gordon Petrie
Bobbie Townsend....................John Lauriston
St. Leger Carrington....................Royston Taylor

Act I.—Manse Parlor at Paradykes. Acts II and III.—Archie's Quarters in “The Rookery,” Edinburgh Castle. Time: 1842.
Staged by Norman Page.

Marigold, whose parents separated when she was an infant, is reared by her Aunt Maggie. When she is of marriageable age she is affianced to the dour but rich James Payton. During her engagement Marigold meets Archie Forsyth of the Dragoons and falls in love. When Archie invites her to Edinburgh to watch a Queen Victoria procession from the balcony of his quarters she runs away and arrives the night before. Nor, being a simple child, can she see why she cannot stay there unchaperoned. Aunt Maggie follows after and everything is made right, including Marigold's release from Payton and her engagement to Archie.

PRINCESS CHARMING

(56 performances)

A romantic opera in two acts adapted by Jack Donohue from the original of Martos, Wimperis and Wylie; music by Albert Sirmay and Arthur Swartz. Produced by Bobby Connolly and Arthur Swanstrom at the Imperial Theatre, New York, October 13, 1930.

Cast of characters—

Baron Sigman.......................................Roy Gordon
Lieutenant of the *Elyria*..............................John Kane
2nd Lieutenant................................Ernest McChesney
Marie..Betty Gallagher
Wanda Navarro..................................Jeanne Aubert
Irving Huff......................................Victor Moore
Princess Elaine of Novia.........................Evelyn Herbert
Captain Torrelli of the Cruiser *Elyria*.............Robert Halliday
Ivanoff.....................................Douglass Dumbrille
Christian II. of Elyria.........................George Grossmith
Aide de Camp to the King.......................Howard St. John
Attorney General...................................Paul Huber
Lord Chamberlain to the King.....................Raoul de Tisne
Lulu..Dorothea James
Page...Duke McHale
Veronique..Yvonne Grey
Colette..Irene Bostick
Anastasia......................................Frances Markey
Marguerite.......................................Wilma Roeloff

Act I.—Scene 1—Crystal Room in the Palace of the Elyrian Embassy in Novia. 2—Outside the Embassy. 3—On Deck the Cruiser *Elyria*. Act II.—Scene 1—In the Throne Room, Royal Palace, Elyria. 2—Exterior of Baron Sigman's Castle. 3—Bedroom of the Countess Wanda Navarro at Baron Sigman's Castle. 4—Garden of the Sigman Castle.

Staged by Edward Clark Lilley and Bobby Connolly.

Princess Elaine of Novia, having been promised in marriage to Christian II of Elyria, finds her way blocked by a revolution and a passport denied her. She marries Captain Torrelli of the cruiser *Elyria* in order to get the passport and with the intention of divorcing him as soon as she is safely in Elyria. After she hears the Captain sing she decides she prefers to remain his wife, a matter that is finally adjusted to the satisfaction of everyone, including Irving Huff, representing a New Jersey insurance company that has taken on the princess as a risk and promised to deliver her safely to Christian of Elyria or forfeit a quarter million dollars.

SOLID SOUTH

(31 performances)

A satirical comedy in three acts by Lawton Campbell. Produced by Alexander McKaig at the Lyceum Theatre, New York, October 14, 1930.

Cast of characters—

Geneva.......................................Elizabeth Patterson
Bam...Bette Davis
Leila Mae...................................Jessie Royce Landis
Major Bruce Follonsby.........................Richard Bennett
Patience......................................Georgette Harvey
Rex...Owen Davis, Jr.
Elijah..Richard Huey
Edward V. T. B. Garrison......................Moffat Johnson
Jasper..Lew Payton
Acts I, II and III.—Living Room of the Follonsby Home in a Southern City.
Staged by Reuben Mamoulian.

Major Bruce Follonsby is a non-reconstructible fire-eater of the old South. Still hates the damnedyankees and considers even a casual reference to "Uncle Tom's Cabin" an insult to the lost cause. When Edward V. T. B. Garrison and his son Rex, representing big business in Pittsburgh, invade Alabama and make love to Major Follonsby's widowed daughter-in-law and his granddaughter the old man wants to shoot them until he learns that Garrison stands ready to buy the Follonsby acres and retire its owners.

GIRL CRAZY

(272 performances)

A musical comedy in two acts by Guy Bolton and John McGowan, music by George Gershwin, lyrics by Ira Gershwin. Produced by Aarons and Freedley at the Alvin Theatre, New York, October 14, 1930.

Cast of characters—

Danny Churchill....................................Allen Kearns
Molly Gray....................................Ginger Rogers
Pete....................................Clyde Veaux
Lank Sanders....................................Carlton Macy
Gieber Goldfarb....................................Willie Howard
Flora James....................................Eunice Healy
Patsy West....................................Peggy O'Connor
Kate Fothergill....................................Ethel Merman
Slick Fothergill....................................William Kent
Sam Mason....................................Donald Foster
Tess Parker....................................Olive Brady
Jake Howell....................................Lew Parker
Eagle Rock....................................Chief Rivers
Hotel Proprietor....................................Jack Classon
Lariat Joe....................................Starr Jones
The Foursome.................................... { Marshall Smith, Ray Johnson, Del Porter, Dwight Snyder }
Antonio and Renee Demarco, "Red" Nichols and His Orchestra,

Act I.—Scene 1—Exterior of the Custer House, Custerville, Ariz. 2—Dude Ranch. 3—Gieber's Election Headquarters. 4—Outside the Custerville Post Office. 5—Barroom at the Dude Ranch. Act II.—Scene 1—Hotel Los Palmas, San Luz, Mexico. 2—The Railroad Station, San Luz. 3—Outside the Dude Ranch.

Staged by Alexander Leftwich; dances by George Hale.

Danny Churchill, being sent to Arizona by his millionaire father in the hope the fresh air will cure his thirst for liquor and women, makes the trip in Gieber Goldfarb's taxi. In Custerville, Ariz., a womanless town, Danny jazzes things up by starting a dude ranch and importing a Broadway chorus. Gieber Goldfarb, running for sheriff, runs into many comic difficulties.

TWELFTH NIGHT

(65 performances)

A comedy in three acts by William Shakespeare. Produced by Kenneth MacGowan and Joseph Verner Reed at the Maxine Elliott Theatre, New York, October 15, 1930.

Cast of characters—

Feste....................................Lewis Martin
The Duke Orsino....................................Coburn Goodwin
Curio....................................Kirk Henty
Valentine....................................Henry Richards
Viola....................................Jane Cowl
Sea Captain....................................Robert Lowe
Sir Toby Belch....................................Walter Kingsford
Maria....................................Jessie Ralph
Sir Andrew Aguecheek....................................Arthur Hohl
Olivia....................................Joyce Carey
Malvolio....................................Leon Quartermaine
Antonio....................................Gordon Burby
Sebastian....................................Jerry Bowman
Fabian....................................Harry Sothern
First Officer....................................Henry Richards

Second Officer....................................Derek Fairman
Priest..Robert Lowe
Sailors } ....{ Derek Fairman
Pages } { William Qualey
Lords............................Alfred Flanders, George Wilcox
Ladies in Attendance.....Elise Breton, Jane Traylor, Evelyn Evans
Musicians...........Harry Waller, Marietta Bitters, Harry Thorne

Act I.—Scene 1—Duke's Palace. 2—A Sea Coast. 3, 5—Olivia's Garden. 4—Duke's Palace. 6—A Sea Port. 7—A Street. 8—A Cellar in Olivia's House. Act II.—Scene 1—Duke's Palace. 2, 4—Olivia's Garden. 3—A Street. Act III.—Scene 1—A Cellar in Olivia's House. 2—Olivia's Garden.

Staged by Andrew Leigh.

A version of the Shakespeare comedy shortened as to playing time by the use of a novel scenic background. A book of heroic proportions is set up on the stage. With each turning of a page a new scene is revealed. Feste, the clown, has charge of the scene book.

THREE'S A CROWD

(272 performances)

A revue in two acts compiled by Howard Dietz, lyrics and music by Mr. Dietz, Arthur Schwartz and others. Produced by Max Gordon at the Selwyn Theatre, New York, October 15, 1930.

Principals engaged—

Fred Allen
Clifton Webb
Wally Coyle
Earl Oxford
Harold Moffett
Lou Wood
Fred MacMurray
Alan Jones
Parcy Launders

Libby Holman
Tamara Geva
Margaret Lee
Portland Hoffa
Marybeth Conoly
Joan Clement
Amy Revere
Rene Du Plessis
Herb Montei

Staged by Hazzard Short; dances by Albertina Rasch.

BLIND MICE

(14 performances)

A comedy in three acts by Vera Caspary and Winifred Lenihan. Produced by Crosby Gaige at the Times Square Theatre, New York, October 15, 1930.

Cast of characters—

(Those Who Stay Home Saturday Night)

Fannie..Hallie Manning
Freda...Julia Colin
Jane..Frances Vicory

Verne..Helen Brady
Loretta..Betty Breckenridge
Emily..Libby Ferguson
A Serious Girl..................................Mary Alice Collins
Elsie Schmidt..................................Mary V. Heinlein
Lou Vavck.......................................Jane Seymour

(Those Who Go Out Saturday Night)

Ellen..Geraldine Wall
Baby...Olive Shea
Addie..Virginia Stone
Beatrice..Eunice Hunt
Daisy...Cyrena Smith
Scottie..Fern Peterson
Agnes Thorpe.....................................Mildred McLeod
Mae Thorpe.......................................Claiborne Foster
A New Girl...Rita Davies
Miss Johnstone......................................Percita West

Acts I, II and III.—Recreation Room on the Second Floor of Rolfe House, a Residential Club for Self-supporting Girls.
Staged by Winifred Lenihan.

Mae Thorpe, restless and unhappy in a residential home for working girls, and madly in love with a boy named Boyd, agrees to spend a week-end with him in a borrowed flat. She discovers that she is in trouble about the time she learns that Boyd has married his boss's daughter. Mr. Moses, the owner of the drug-store in which Mae works, wants to marry her, even after he knows all, and Mae agrees. The plot of this play is developed with the aid of the telephone. Neither Boyd nor Mr. Moses appear, the cast being exclusively feminine.

GARRICK GAIETIES

(Second Edition)

(12 performances)

A topical revue in two acts, rearranged for touring purposes. Produced by the Theatre Guild at the Guild Theatre, New York, October 16, 1930.

Principals engaged—

Albert Carroll
Sterling Holloway
Philip Loeb
Doris Vinton
Ruth Chorpenning
Katherine Carrington
William Holbrook
Roger Stearns
Louis Simon
James Norris
Rosalind Russell
Neal Caldwell
Donald Burr
Imogene Coca
Edwin Gilcher
Neila Goodelle
Otto Hulett
Robert La Branch
Edgar Stehli
Alice Bankert
Bunny Bremer
Mary Brown
Irene Carroll
Anna Marie Cotter
Anne Delphin
Giner Meehan

Sylvia Miller	Emily Thompson
Mildred Muller	Kathleen Whitcomb
Dot Stemme	Viola Wilson

Staged by Philip Loeb.

LONDON CALLING

(13 performances)

A comedy in three acts by Geoffrey Kerr. Produced by John Golden at the Little Theatre, New York, October 18, 1930.

Cast of characters—

Staight....St. Clair Bayfield
Jenny Fall....Penelope Hubbard
Henry Dayton....Walter Wilson
Mary Dayton....Emma Bunting
Chauncey Knayling....Graham Velsey
Anne Hunter....Helen Flint
Carl Merodini....Edward Leiter
Willie Craft....Charles Lawrence
George Craft....Geoffrey Kerr
Blewes....Dallas Welford
Mrs. Craft....Anne Sutherland

Acts I and III.—Mrs. Craft's Apartment, Park Avenue. Act II.—George Craft's Furnished Apartment, East 49th Street.
Staged by Dan Jarratt.

George and Willie Craft, brothers, have been separated since childhood. Their American mother has kept Willie in New York with her while their English father has had George with him in London. George pays Willie and his mother a surprise visit. The boys become great pals until their friendship is threatened by Anne Hunter, a designing lady. They decide to give Anne the go by, George comes to like America and Mrs. Craft hears London calling as a reconciliation with her husband threatens.

CANARIES SOMETIMES SING

(24 performances)

A comedy in three acts by Frederick Lonsdale. Produced by Charles B. Dillingham at the Fulton Theatre, New York, October 20, 1930.

Cast of characters—

Geoffrey Lymes....Robert Loraine
Ann Lymes....Mary Merrall
Ernest Melton....Athole Stewart
Elma Melton....Yvonne Arnaud

Acts I, II and III.—In the Country House of the Lymes.
Staged by Athole Stewart.

Geoffrey Lymes, playwright, feels that he is living as caged a life as his pet canary. Ann Lymes, his somewhat flighty wife, has little sympathy with or understanding of his needs. Ernest and Elma Melton spend the week-end with the Lymes. They are also mismated. The cheerful Mrs. Melton takes a great fancy to Mr. Lymes, and Mrs. Lymes is stricken with an interest in Mr. Melton. An agreement looking to a general domestic readjustment is adopted, but later modified. Mrs. Lymes will get her freedom but Mr. Melton will hang on, and Mr. Lymes will go to live with the Meltons as a paying guest.

PAGAN LADY

(152 performances)

A drama in three acts by William Du Bois. Produced by Morris Green and Lewis E. Gensler in association with Erlanger Productions, Inc., at the 48th Street Theatre, New York, October 20, 1930.

Cast of characters—

Dingo Mike....................Russell Hardie
Nellie....................Jane Ferrell
Dr. Heath....................Leo Donnelly
Dot Hunter....................Lenore Ulric
Jerry Willis....................Richard Terry
Gwen Willis....................Elise Bartlett
Malcolm Todd....................Thomas Findlay
Tola....................Ralph Morris
Ernest Todd....................Franchot Tone

Acts I, II and III.—Veranda of the Hotel Chautauqua on the Beach at Mandarine, a Small Tourist Town on the East Coast of Florida.

Staged by John D. Williams.

Dot Hunter, living with Dingo Mike in Florida, becomes interested in Ernest Todd, son of the evangelist, Malcolm Todd, and himself headed for the church. Ernest is also fascinated with Dot. The night Dingo is away Dot and Ernest swim to a near-by island, returning next morning. Ernest is conscience stricken. Dot gives him back to the church confident that his outlook on life will thereafter be both more tolerant and more intelligent.

SIEGFRIED

(23 performances)

A drama in four acts, translated by Philip Carr from the French of Jean Giradoux. Produced by The Civic Repertory Theatre, Inc., at the home theatre October 20, 1930.

Cast of characters—

Muck....................Harold Moulton
Eva....................Margaret Mower
Servant....................Arnold Moss
Baron Von Zelten....................Egon Brecher
Schmidt....................Sean Dillon
Mrs. Hoepful....................Agnes McCarthy
Keller....................Joseph Kramm
Kratz....................Burgess Meredith
Mr. Patchkoffer....................Howard da Silva
Mrs. Patchkoffer....................Edith Lane
Meyer....................Robert Ross
Genevieve....................Eva Le Gallienne
Robineau....................Donald Cameron
Siegfried....................Jacob Ben-Ami
Jacques de Fongeloy....................Robert H. Gordon
General von Waldorf....................Walter Beck
General Ledinger....................Paul Leyssac
Sergeant....................Herbert Shapiro
Orderly....................Burgess Meredith
Pietri....................J. Edward Bromberg
Schumann....................Howard da Silva

Acts I and III.—Waiting Room of an Official Building. Act II.—Siegfried's Study. Act IV.—Waiting Room of a Frontier Railway.
Staged by Eva Le Gallienne.

Siegfried, desperately wounded, is picked up on the battlefield by Eva, a German nurse, taken to the fatherland and nursed back to health. His mind restored save in the matter of memory the recovered soldier becomes the dominant leader of the community. Baron von Zelten, suspicious of Siegfried's origin, convinced that he is French, sends for Genevieve, who recognizes in Siegfried a brilliant young scholar who was her fiancé before the war. Eva fights to keep Siegfried in Germany, where his work is of supreme importance. Genevieve succeeds finally in taking him back to France.

SISTERS OF THE CHORUS

(32 performances)

A comedy in three acts by Martin Mooney and Thompson Burtis. Produced by Raymond Productions, Inc., at the Ritz Theatre, New York, October 20, 1930.

Cast of characters—

Blanch Page....................................Enid Markey
Maxine Laverne.................................Edna Hibbard
Hubert DuFrayne...................................Jean Malin
Betty Gilbert...................................Sonia Karlov
Theodore Kane.................................Henry Crosby
Billy Clark....................................Allan Hughes
Anne Page...................................Dorothea Chard
Barney Hutchinson.........................Albert Van Dekker
Louis Gordon..............................William C. Green
Charles Lawrence................................Charles Laite
A Canvasser...................................Jimmie Collins
Acts I, II and III.—Apartment in the West Fifties Occupied by Three Chorus Girls.
Staged by John Hayden.

SWEET STRANGER

(24 performances)

A comedy in three acts by Frank Mitchell Dazey and Agnes Christine Johnston. Produced by Paul Streger at the Cort Theatre, New York, October 21, 1930.

Cast of characters—

Charles...Frank H. Day
Albert Rustin..................................Ralph Morgan
Mrs. Sturdevant.................................Viola Roache
J. W. Marvin...................................Clyde Fillmore
Betty Marvin........................Gertrude Coghlan Pitou
Ann Norton.....................................Linda Watkins
Miss Saunders.......................................Mel Efird
Holloway..Lloyd B. Nolan
Preston...J. Ascher Smith
Staged by Worthington Miner.

Ann Norton, hungry and broke, reading of the exciting lives rich men's mistresses live, determines to have a try at being a mistress. She selects for the experiment J. W. Marvin, credited with being a wealthy "pushover" who changes his favorites frequently. Invading the Marvin offices to offer herself Ann discovers that Marvin is about to sail away with another lady. Marvin turns Ann over to his chief executive, Albert Rustin, with instructions to look after her. Rustin accepts the responsibility and he and Ann are attracted to each other. When Marvin returns and proposes setting Ann up in an apartment Rustin protests violently. Ann is too nice to be anything but his wife.

THIS ONE MAN

(39 performances)

A drama in three acts by Sidney R. Buchman. Produced by Arthur Lubin and Richard W. Krakauer at the Morosco Theatre, New York, October 21, 1930.

Cast of characters—

Marvin Holland	Paul Guilfoyle
Doctor Camp	Dean Raymond
Molly Holland	Constance McKay
Eugene Vignon	Boris Marshalov
An Attendant	Charles Harrison
Saul Holland	Paul Muni
Jig	Mike Donlin
Dan	William Franklin
Pop	Billy Fay
Mr. Chambers	George Spear
First Questioner	Robert Griffin
Second Questioner	Victor Kilian
Mr. Wilkes	Carroll Ashburn

Act I.—Scene 1—Living Room of the Holland Home. 2—The Hideout. Act II.—Scene 1—Study of the Home of Mr. Chambers. 2—A Questioning Room. Act III.—Scene 1—With Marvin. 2—With Saul.

Staged by Leo Bulgakov.

Saul and Marvin Holland are brothers. Saul is strong, handsome, wicked, cruel, and the family idol. Marvin is frail, sensitive, fine, and rather despised for his weaknesses. Sharing the idolatry of Saul Marvin becomes convinced that he is possessed of Saul's soul; that Saul cannot become a complete man until he (Marvin) dies. When Saul, escaped from prison, is recaptured after a bank robbery during which murder has been done, Marvin takes the crime on his own shoulders, is convicted and sentenced to the chair over Saul's excited protests. When Marvin is executed Saul's heart softens.

LEW LESLIE'S BLACKBIRDS

(57 performances)

A colored revue in two acts, by Flourney Miller, music by Eubie Blake, lyrics by Andy Razaf. Produced by Lew Leslie at the Royale Theatre, New York, October 22, 1930.

Principals engaged—

Flourney Miller	Jazzlips Richardson
Mantan Moreland	Berry Brothers
Broadway Jones	Blue McAllister

Ethel Waters
Neeka Shaw
Mercer Marquise
Buck and Bubbles
Cecil Mack's Choir
Minto Cato

Staged by Lew Leslie.

HIS MAJESTY'S CAR

(12 performances)

A comedy in three acts adapted by Fanny and Frederic Hatton from the Hungarian of Attila Von Orbok. Produced by the Messrs. Shubert at the Ethel Barrymore Theatre, New York, October 23, 1930.

Cast of characters—

Andre Dornik....................Theodore St. John
Mrs. Dornik....................Gertrude Maitland
Lily Dornik....................Miriam Hopkins
Ernest Dornik....................C. H. Croker-King
Robert Bardon....................Edward Crandall
Peter Hahn....................Hugh Miller
Miss Marks....................Lillian Brennard Tonge
Madelaine....................Marcella Swanson
Geo. Sappo....................William Kershaw
Reporter....................Emile Littler
Cameraman....................Wells Richardson
A Major-Domo....................James Dunn
Mitzi....................Peggy Conklin
Strohn....................Herbert Standing
Von Werden....................Arthur Barry
The King....................Anthony Kemble-Cooper
The Baroness....................Louise Bateman
The Countess....................Isabel Atwill
Alvarez....................Roman Arnoldoff

Act I.—Dining Room at the Dorniks. Act II.—Lily's Boudoir. Act III.—Reception Room in the Palace of the Minister of Finance.
A Small Kingdom in Central Europe.

Staged by Stanley Logan.

Lily Dornik, being with Robert Bardon, her fiancé, the day he is invited by an automobile salesman to take a ride in the king's car before it is delivered to the royal garage, is astonished the following day to receive presents and flowers from many distinguished citizens. Rumor has spread that she is the king's newest favorite. On advice of Robert, Lily does not deny the rumor and capitalizes it by accepting all the clothes and jewels tradesmen send. She also helps her father and her brother to good jobs. Finally the king, hearing of what is going on, determines to visit his favorite mistress. The king is charmed with Lily and Lily, thinking him a lieutenant in the army, falls in love with the king. After that it is easy to confirm the rumors.

SWEET CHARIOT

(3 performances)

A comedy in three acts by Robert Wilder. Produced by Michael Mindlin at the Ambassador Theatre, New York, October 23, 1930.

Cast of characters—

Lola....................Fredi Washington
Delia....................Vivian Baber
King....................Alex Lovejoy
Futch....................Harrison Blackburn
Marius Harvey....................Frank Wilson
Troll....................Percy Verwayne
Ship's Captain....................Martin Mallory
Port Officer....................Clay Cody
First Negro....................Dixie Reid
Second Negro....................Hubert Browne
A Worker....................Clara Smith
Peter....................Billy Andrews
First White Man....................Victor Esker
Second White Man....................George Dreyden

Act I.—Scene 1—Office of Marius Harvey in the Negro District of a Southern Seaport. 2—Pythian Mall. Act II.—Scene 1—Smoking Cabin of the S.S. *Black Star* off the Coast of Africa. 2—Courtyard of a Settlement on the African Coast. Act III.—The Courtyard.

Marius Harvey, colored exhorter, promotes a black man's empire in Africa and sells fake stock in a steamship company on the side. Fired by his own eloquence Harvey turns zealot and renounces his crooked partners. He takes a boatload of blacks to the promised land but British authorities refuse to let them land. Later, when hospitable territory is found, the disappointed pilgrims turn on Harvey and desert him. He is left with only his faithful Lola to stick by him.

ROAR CHINA

(72 performances)

A drama in two acts by S. Tretyakov, translated from the German of Leo Lania by Ruth Langner. Produced by the Theatre Guild, Inc., at the Martin Beck Theatre, New York, October 27, 1930.

Cast of characters—

Coolie....................Y. W. Woo
Wang Fu, a Commission Man....................Seungman Ahn
Li Tai, a Merchant....................Von Wang

Hall, an American Exporter........................William Gargan
Burns, a Reporter........................Harry Cooke
Ama, a Procuress........................Grace Chee
Mrs. Tourist........................Eva Condon
Mr. Tourist........................Erskine Sanford
Chang, a Boatman........................H. L. Donsu
Pei Fu, an Old Boatman........................Lee Tung-Foo
A Fo, the Eldest of the Boatman's Guild........................Frank Sinne
Ho Sung, a Boatman........................Paul Fung
1st Boatman........................Ivan Achong
2nd Boatman........................H. T. Tsiang
3rd Boatman........................Henry Leong
4th Boatman........................Richard Wang
Bonze........................Arthur Leon
Low Ba, the Police Captain........................Charlie Fang
Mate of H.M.S. *Europa*........................Edward Trevor
Mrs. Smith........................Winifred Hanley
Cordelia, Her Daughter........................Sanchia Robertson
Lieutenant Cooper........................Eric Blore
Mr. Smith........................Reynolds Denniston
Captain of H.M.S. *Europa*........................Edward Cooper
Chinese Boy........................Peter Kwan
Johnson, a Lieutenant........................Charles Cardon
1st Policeman........................James Lee
Ho Chin Ling, Ho Sung's Wife........................Irene Wong
Ho San San, Her Daughter........................Elsie Wu
The Missionary........................Edwin Brandt
Mme. De Brochell........................Adrienne Lachamp
M. De Brochell........................Athy Dmitrieff
The Daoyin of the City of Wan Hsien........................Sam Kim
A Student Interpreter for the Daoyin........................Y. Y. Hsu
Chang Yuen, Chang's Wife........................Helen Kimm
Ho Sung's Son........................James Yoon
A Fo's Daughter........................Siang Pan
Chang's Son........................Dorothy Woo

Acts I and II.—On a Quay in the Harbor of Wan Hsien and on the Deck of the H.M.S. *Europa* Anchored in the Harbor During the Summer of 1926.

Staged by Herbert Biberman.

Hall, an arrogant American exporter in China, is tipped out of a boat and drowned during a scuffle over the fee. The commander of a British warship, speaking for the Anglo-Saxon race in the Far East, demands that the boatman be caught and executed by dawn. If he is not caught two other boatmen shall be killed in his stead. The authorities and citizens of the village protest. The Britisher will not yield. When the escaped boatman is not caught two innocents are garroted in his place, inspiring an incipient rebellion.

THE NOBLE EXPERIMENT

(16 performances)

A drama in three acts by Michael Grismaijer. Produced by Durandy and Miller at the Waldorf Theatre, New York, October 27, 1930.

Cast of characters—

Alexa Jovanovitch.................................Gordon Richards
Steel Workers............John Connolly, Harry Bond, Jack Stone, Harold Cook
Ilia...Sidney Satvro
Milan..Don Darcy
John...Thomas McQuillan
Nick Medich.......................................James LaCurto
George....................................George Gurnie-Butler
Julia...Traeie McCann
Tony.......................................Edward T. Colebrook
Joe...Garland Kerr
Katie Orlovitch...................................Anne Lubow
"Red" Mike..................................G. Gordon Hamilton
Kid Marco...James T. Morey
Mary..Helen Shea
Milla..Gelda Oakleaf
The Sheriff.......................................Hugh Thompson
Kelly...Jerry Cavanaugh
Judge Ben Fardy...................................G. Swane Gordon
First Red...Richard K. Keith
Second Red.......................................Edwin G. O'Connor
Maggie..Ruth Edell
Maria..Florence Ferguson
Jovan..Jess Sidney
Jack..Maynard Holmes
Students, Workers, etc.: Virginia Barrie, Elaine Roemer, Virginia Toland, Joveta Velveen, Elenora Barrie, George Spelvin.

Prologue—Steel Workers' Camp in Michigan. Acts I and II.—Speakeasy of Katie Orlovitch in the Same Town. Act III.—Private Office of Katie and Alexa in Their "Club des Aristocrats."

Staged by Don Mullaley.

PUPPET SHOW

(7 performances)

A drama in three acts by Samuel Ruskin Golding. Produced by Pilgrim Productions, Inc., at the Belmont Theatre, New York, October 28, 1930.

Cast of characters—

Anthony Davies.....................................J. W. Austin
Lionel Gordon...................................Daniel Makarenko
Estelle Plant.....................................Doris Underwood
Alfredo Martinez................................Octavio Valentini
Suzanne Carleton.................................Anne Seymour
Max Pinkus...Milton Wallace
Rhoda Strong.....................................Eunice Stoddard
Neil Cummings..................................Donald Blackwell
Leland O'Malley..................................Reginald Goode
Clerk of Court......................................C. A. Carroll

Acts I, II and III.—In the Study of Anthony Davies.

Staged by Samuel Ruskin Golding.

Anthony Davies, playwright, visualizes the characters in a drama on which he is working. They move about the stage, frequently arguing with him as to his right to make them do and say the things they do. The story with which they are concerned is that of the arrest and trial for murder of Rhoda Strong, who, in a fit of mental aberration, shoots and kills her husband, Neil Cummings, under the impression that she is killing the woman with whom he is threatening to run away.

ON THE SPOT

(167 performances)

A melodrama in three acts by Edgar Wallace. Produced by Lee and J. J. Shubert, in association with Mr. Wallace and Lee Ephraim, at the Forrest Theatre, New York, October 29, 1930.

Cast of characters—

(Prologue)

A Priest..John Wheeler
Interne...John Adair
Shaun O'Donnell..............................Mike Sullivan
Officer Ryan.....................................George Spelvin
Capt. Harrigan...................................Stanley Wood
A Nurse..Jeanne Winters

(The Play)

Tony Perrelli......................................Crane Wilbur
Minn Lee...Anna May Wong
Keriki...Suezo Tckero
Angelo..John Gallaudet
Con O'Hara...................................George Drury Hart
Marie Pouliski...................................Glenda Farrell
Jimmy McGarth......................................Alan Ward
Detective Commissioner John Kelly.................John M. Kline
Mike Feeney.....................................Arthur R. Vinton

Prologue—An Impression. Brothers Hospital, Chicago. The Play—Tony Perrelli's Apartment on Michigan Avenue, Chicago.

Staged by Lee Ephraim and Carol Reed.

Tony Perrelli, the leading racketeer and rum runner of Chicago, has ordered two of his gang, Jimmy McGarth and Con O'Hara, to kill Shaun O'Donnell as a warning to Mike Feeney, who was invading the Perrelli territory. Feeney demands revenge. He will agree to cry quits if Perrelli will put the boys who did the O'Donnell shooting on the spot by sending them into the Feeney territory where they can be killed. Perrelli agrees. Minn Lee, Perrelli's half-caste Chinese mistress, loves McGarth, gives herself to him and commits suicide as soon as she hears of his death. Perrelli is accused of her murder and arrested.

THE LAST ENEMY

(4 performances)

A drama in three acts by Frank Harvey. Produced by the Messrs. Shubert at the Shubert Theatre, New York, October 30, 1930.

Cast of characters—

Dr. Alexander McKenzie............................George Merritt
James Churchill...................................Donald Eccles
Janitor...Cecil Ramage
Thomas Perry......................................O. B. Clarence
Clara Perry.......................................Gwen Day Burroughs
Cynthia Perry.....................................Jessica Tandy
Nancy...Peggy Eccles
Jerry Warrender...................................Derrick de Marney
Harry Graham......................................Robert Douglas
Wilson..Allan Wade

Acts I, II and III.—In the Antarctic, at the Perry's and at Warrender's Lodging.

Staged by Nicholas Hannen.

Dr. Alexander McKenzie and James Churchill freeze to death in the Antarctic. On the way to heaven they meet a celestial guide who explains life to them. Thanks to Adam's request for company, he says, each human being is a divided entity. Each Adam has an Eve somewhere in the world, and each Eve has an Adam. A man may be the spiritual father of his affinity's children without even being aware of their existence. Back on earth Cynthia Perry is having a time choosing between two soldier lovers, Jerry Warrender and Harry Graham. The night Jerry becomes crazed with liquor and tries to seduce Cynthia it is James Churchill, her spiritual father, who hears her call. His spirit walks through a bolted door and saves her. A year later, however, Cynthia marries Jerry.

THE MAN IN POSSESSION

(98 performances)

A farce comedy in three acts by H. M. Harwood. Produced by Lee Shubert at the Booth Theatre, New York, November 1, 1930.

Cast of characters—

Mrs. Dabney.......................................Frances Ruttledge
Esther..Evelyn Moore
Paul Dabney.......................................Paul Gill
Claude Dabney.....................................Harman Phelps
Raymond Dabney....................................Leslie Banks
Clara...Mabel Buckley
Crystal Wetherby..................................Isabel Jeans
Mr. McAlister.....................................David Keir
Lord Bellairs.....................................Tracy Holmes
Sir Charles Cartwright............................J. Neil More

Act I.—Dining Room of the Dabneys' House in Highgate, Near London. Acts II and III.—Mrs. Wetherby's House in Park Street, London.

Staged by H. M. Harwood.

Raymond Dabney, having sold a motor car that did not belong to him, spends several months in the workhouse. On his release his father refuses to continue his support unless he agrees to leave London. Raymond likes London and decides to stay there on his own. He gets a job as a sheriff's officer and is assigned to the home of Crystal Wetherby, a widow in debt. Raymond's perfect Cambridge manners and ardent love making attract Mrs. Wetherby, who happens also to be his brother's fiancée, and when Raymond agrees to take his father's $2,000 and clear out if she will run with him she jumps at the chance.

ELIZABETH THE QUEEN

(147 performances)

A drama in three acts by Maxwell Anderson. Produced by the Theatre Guild, Inc., at the Guild Theatre, New York, November 3, 1930.

Cast of Characters—

Raleigh.......................................Percy Waram
Penelope.......................................Anita Kerry
Captain Armin.......................................Philip Foster
Cecil.......................................Arthur Hughes
Bacon.......................................Morris Carnovsky
Essex.......................................Alfred Lunt
Elizabeth.......................................Lynn Fontanne
A Councilor.......................................Charles Homer
Burghley.......................................Robert Conness
The Fool.......................................Barry Macollum
Mary.......................................Mab Anthony
Tressa.......................................Edla Frankau
Ellen.......................................Phœbe Brand
Marvel.......................................Royal Beal
A Man-at-Arms.......................................John Ellsworth
A Courier.......................................Charles Brokaw
A Captain of the Guards.......................................Edward Oldfield
A Courtier.......................................Robert Caille
A Herald.......................................Vincent Sherman
Burbage.......................................Whitford Kane
Heming.......................................Charles Brokaw
Poins.......................................Curtis Arnall
Ladies-in-Waiting..........Lois Huntingdon and Annabelle Williams
Guards, Men-at-Arms: James Wiley, James A. Boshell, Curtis Arnall, Perry King, Thomas Eyre, Michael Borodin, George Fleming, Stanley Ruth, Nich Wiger, Henry Lase and Guy Moore.

Act I.—Scene 1—Entrance Hall Before the Council Chamber in the Palace at Whitehall. 2—Queen's Study. 3—Council Chamber. Act II.—Scene 1—Interior of Essex's Tent in Ireland. 2—Queen's Study. 3—Council Chamber. Act III.—Queen's Apartments in the Tower.

Staged by Philip Moeller.

See page 445.

AS GOOD AS NEW

(56 performances)

A comedy in three acts by Thompson Buchanan. Produced by Charles Dillingham at the Times Square Theatre, New York, November 3, 1930.

Cast of characters—

Tom Banning....................................Otto Kruger
Mrs. Violet Hargrave...........................Vivienne Osborne
Detective Franklin.............................Owen Martin
Donald McArthur................................Lionel Pape
Mrs. Eleanor Banning...........................Marjorie Gateson
Detective McIntyre.............................Walter F. Scott
Mr. D'Arcy.....................................Sardis Lawrence
Bob Freeman....................................Kenneth Haviland
Andrews..Fred Lennox
Mary Banning...................................Dorothy Libaire
Tommy Banning..................................Billy Quinn
Bill Townsend..................................Ben Smith
Maid...Gwladys Hupton
Mr. Bradford...................................Montague Shaw
Mrs. Bradford..................................Faye Martin

Act I.—Living Room in Tom Banning's Private Apartment. Acts II and III.—Tom Banning's Pent House Near Sutton Place.
Staged by Stanley Logan.

Tom Banning, indulging an afternoon flirtation with his wife's best friend, Violet Hargrave, in a hideaway apartment, is surprised by Mrs. Banning and two detectives. With the evidence in her hands Mrs. Banning is dissuaded temporarily from making her divorce plans public because of the resulting scandal. When the Banning children are told of their parents' intentions Mary, a daughter of marriageable age, announces that if sex is so important a factor in the success or failure of marriage she intends to make sure she wants to marry her intended, Bill Townsend, by living with him first. Tommy, the Banning son, runs away from home to avoid the humiliation of accepting a stepmother. In order to save their children the Bannings thereupon agree upon a reconciliation.

ROOM OF DREAMS

(13 performances)

A comedy in three acts adapted by Daniel Coxe from the Viennese by Ernest Raoul Weiss; translation by James Burrell and Anne MacDonald. Produced by the New York Theatre Assembly at the Empire Theatre, New York, November 5, 1930.

Cast of characters—

Angustine....................................Kathryn Card
Maxime Delaujan..............................Walter Greenough
Adrienne Delaujan............................Elsie Lawson
Theodule Emontin.............................Fred Sullivan
Lucien Germond...............................Maurice Burke
Jacqueline Emontin...........................Lee Patrick
Marinette....................................Czara Romanyi
Francine.....................................Ruzzka Yanka
Antoine......................................Nat Davis
A Taxi Driver................................Lester Cole
Acts I and III.—Adrienne's Salon. Act II.—A Room in Lucien's Apartment.
Staged by Kenneth Webb.

Lucien Germond loves Adrienne Delaujan, his friend's wife, very much and lives in a dream world with her in an apartment which he has furnished in exact duplication of her own. The night Adrienne agrees to inspect the apartment her husband, Maxime, gets tight and is brought there by his friend. Lucien gets Maxime tighter and sends him home. Because of the similarity in rooms Maxime is next morning convinced that he has been home all the time, and therefore learns nothing of Adrienne's visit to Lucien.

THE VANDERBILT REVUE

(13 performances)

A revue in two acts assembled by Lew Fields, sketches by Kenyon Nicholson, Ellis O. Jones, Sig Herzig, and E. North; music and lyrics by Dorothy Fields, Jimmy McHugh, Jacques Fray, Mario Braggiotti and E. Y. Harburg. Produced by Lew Fields and Lyle D. Andrews at the Vanderbilt Theatre, New York, November 5, 1930.

Principals engaged—

Paul Everton
Richard Lane
Franker Woods
Richard Ryan
Billy Stephens
Charles Barnes
Joe Penner
Teddy Walters
Jimmy Ray
Harry Dixon
Joe Lennon
Rene de Bouche
Gus Schilling
Dalsky's Russian Choir

Lulu McConnell
Evelyn Hoey
Eileen Poe
Francesca Braggiotti
Francetta Malloy
Dorothy Humphries
Dorothy Dixon
Adeline Seaman
Charlotte Ayers
Tonia Ingre
Wallace Sisters
Juliana
Stella Royal
Jean Carpenter

Staged by John E. Lonergan, Jack Haskell and Theodore J. Hammerstein.

THE WELL OF ROMANCE

(8 performances)

An operetta in two acts by Preston Sturges, music by H. Maurice Jacquet. Produced by G. W. McGregor at the Craig Theatre, New York, November 7, 1930.

Cast of characters—

Ann Schlitzl.....Laine Blaire
Wenzel.....Tommy Monroe
Frau Schlitzl.....Lina Abarbanell
Gertrude.....Elsa Paul
Mildred.....Mildred Newman
Louise.....Louise Joyce
His Excellency, the Grand Chancellor.....Louis Sorin
Her Serene Altesse, the Princess.....Norma Terris
Poet.....Howard Marsh
Lieutenant Schpitzelberger.....Louis Rupp
Second Lieutenant.....Syuleen Krasnoff
Third Lieutenant.....Eugene Racine
General Otto, Baron Von Sprudelwasser.....Max Figman
A Gypsy.....Edis Phillips
Joseph.....Joseph Roeder
A Waiter.....Pat Walters
First Guardsman.....Rowan Tudor
Second Guardsman.....James Libby
Butterfly.....Lo Iven (front) Ruth Flynn (rear)
Specialty Dancers—Dorothy Kamdin, Etna Ross, Betty Nylander and Grayce Heath.
Act I.—Exterior of an Inn. Act II.—Covered Courtyard.
Staged by Benrimo; dances by Leon Leonidoff.

The Princess has been bidden by her king to accept General Otto as her husband. To arouse some interest in the affair she drinks from the well of romance, which presumably stirs the human passion of love. Her companion at the well, however, happens to be the Poet. Love attacks them simultaneously, and although it turns out that the Poet is really the King disguised as a tenor, it requires the better part of another act to clear the way to the consummation of the royal romance.

MR. SAMUEL

(8 performances)

A comedy in three acts adapted by Winthrop Ames from the French of Edmond Fleg. Produced by George C. Tyler, in association with Erlanger Productions, Inc., at the Little Theatre, New York, November 10, 1930.

Cast of characters—

Harris....................................Brinsley Shaw
White....................................Harry Redding
Miss Rosenthal..........................Geneva Harrison
Samuel Brisach.........................Edward G. Robinson
Kasen....................................Charles Ritchie
Cato.....................................Charles H. Doyle
Lemler...................................Sam Silverbush
Nathan...................................Harry Joyner
Joseph...................................Manart Kippen
Simon....................................Wallis Clark
Roland...................................Robert Hudson
Russell..................................Thomas Coffin Cooke
Philip Baird.............................Fairfax Burgher
Irving Van Ingen........................H. Dudley Hawley
Junior Baird.............................Eddie Wragge
Lillian Baird............................Betty Hanna
Maud Ruben...............................Gladys Lloyd
Judith...................................Adelaide Prince
Anna.....................................Kate Byron
Maid.....................................Jeanne Wardley
Estelle..................................Teresa Dale
Head Waiter..............................Alexis M. Polianov
Dr. Weil.................................France Bendtsen
Señor Pradella..........................Henry Mortimer

Act I.—Office of Samuel Brisach. Acts II and III.—His Apartment.

Staged by Clifford Brooke.

Samuel Brisach dominates his family and his firm. During a business depression his brothers and his son, making up the firm, turn against him and would take the business out of his hands. In the argument that follows Brisach suffers a heart attack and collapses. He is strong enough next day, however, to get to a telephone and from there he directs a Wall Street buying campaign that saves the firm and turns a net profit of a million.

BIRD IN HAND

(65 performances)

A comedy in three acts by John Drinkwater. Revived by Lee Shubert at the 49th Street Theatre, New York, November 10, 1930.

Cast of characters—

Joan Greenleaf...........................Daphne Warren Wilson
Alice Greenleaf..........................Olga Slade
Thomas Greenleaf.........................Walter Edwin
Gerald Arnwood...........................Ronald Dare
Mr. Blanquet.............................Eliot Makeham
Cyril Beverley...........................John Warburton
Ambrose Godolphin, K.C...................Frank Petley
Sir Robert Arnwood.......................Arthur Ridley
Barmaid..................................Gwen Lowrey

Acts I and III.—Bar Parlor. Act II.—Beverley's Bedroom.

Staged by John Drinkwater.

There were two return engagements of the English comedy that ran through the season of 1929-30. See "Best Plays of 1928-29."

LIGHT WINES AND BEER

(40 performances)

A farce comedy in three acts by Aaron Hoffman. Produced by the Stanhope Productions Co., at the Waldorf Theatre, New York, November 10, 1930.

Cast of characters—

John Miller.....Charles Horn
Gus Rausch.....Ralph Hertz
The Bum.....McLain Gates
Fritzie Zimmer.....Helene Salinger
Tim.....George Sullivan
Ted Schloss.....Fred Herrick
Nick Schloss.....Sam Bernard, 2d
Jim Knowles.....David Andrada
Rudolph Zimmer.....Al Shean
Mrs. Mahoney.....Sarah Camp
Katie Zimmer.....Louise Kirtland
William J. Parker.....Herbert Warren
Sweeney.....George Gilday
Jack.....James Spelvin
Doyle.....Oscar Ames
Officer Kelly.....Ralph Hudson

Acts I and III.—Nick & Rudolph's Café, New York City. Act II.—Living Room in Rudolph's Home.
Staged by Charles Sinclair.

Produced in August, 1923, as "The Good Old Days," with Charles Winninger and Charles Bickel in the leading comedy rôles of Schloss and Zimmer. See "Best Plays of 1923-24."

MADE IN FRANCE

(5 performances)

A farce comedy in three acts by Jack Larric. Produced by Laura D. Wilck at the Cort Theatre, New York, November 11, 1930.

Cast of characters—

Flora Richmond.....Joan Blair
Morton.....Arthur Stenning
Ada Hawley.....Ethel Intropidi
James.....Leslie Denison
Yvette.....Lya de Putti
Henry Tuttle.....Harland Tucker

Tom Hawley....................................Hobart Cavanaugh
Donald Colby....................................Stanley Ridges
Acts I, II and III.—In the Reception Hall of a Château near Bar-le-Duc, France.
Staged by Dickson Morgan.

Yvette, who knew many doughboys during the war, wrote three of them after the armistice that she had borne them twins. When they all arrive the same summer ten years later and demand to see their offspring Yvette is comically upset. She finally produces a pair of war orphans. It turns out she has adopted these children and paid for their support with the money the alleged papas sent her from the States.

THE TYRANT

(13 performances)

A romantic drama in five scenes by Rafael Sabatini. Produced by Charles L. Wagner at the Longacre Theatre, New York, November 12, 1930.

Cast of characters—

Panthasilea Degli Speranzoni..........................Lily Cahill
Giulia..Ada Sinclair
Count Guido Degli Speranzoni....................Herbert Ranson
Santafiora......................................Byron Russell
D'Aldi..George Riddell
Gianluce Della Pieve........................Robert Henderson
Del Campo..J. S. Murray
Paviano...Burr Caruth
Seneschal of Solignola............................C. E. Smith
Prince Ercole Sinibaldi........................Averell Harris
A Swiss Guard...............................Henschel Cropper
Capello.......................................Arthur Metcalfe
Niccolo Macchiavelli..........................Cecil Reynolds
Ramirez...John Park
Scipione...Arthur Geary
Ferrante..Lloyd Taylor
Cardinal Remolino..........................Frederick Rudin
Mariano...Hugh Gordon
Chamberlain..John Lyons
Gasparo...Walter Plinge
Micheletto da Corella........................Charles Ashley
Simonetta.....................................Patrick Glasgow
Agabito Gherardi.............................Arthur Marlowe
Cesare Borgia......................................Louis Calhern
Gino..J. Harold Machon
Giovanni.......................................James Maurier
Counselors of Solignola........Herbert Hasluck, Clay Cody, Victor Bozart, Ed Douglas, Cecil Clovelly
Ladies of Assisi.........Billy Williams, Helen Milligan, Florence Metcalfe, Clara Stager
Gentlemen of Assisi.........Iven Ross, Ed Smythe, Martin Lane, Victor Esker
Monks.........................Gregory Deane, Walter Williams
Swiss Guards.......John W. Kramer, Ivan Ramer, Leslie Pearsall
Lackeys....Willie Watson, Hugh Pollock, Edward Field, Sam Smith
Pages.............................Leslie Bailey, Edward Brown

Executioners......Daniel E. Washington, Ben Small, Hubert Brown
Scene 1—Hall in the Castle of Solignola. 2—Antechamber in the Communal Palace at Assisi. 3—Torture Chamber in the Communal Palace. 4—Bedroom in the Pieve Palace. 5—Hall in the Castle of Solignola.
Staged by Horace Sinclair.

Count Speranzoni of Solignola agrees with his Counselors that Cesare Borgia, who has been overcoming many smaller states in middle Italy, must be restrained. The plan is to have Count Guido's daughter, Panthasilea, trap Borgia with her beauty. He will then be taken captive and held as a hostage. Borgia sees through the plan, permits the girl to go through with it, enjoys her love and then goes on with his plan to take Solignola. They poison his wine, but the girl drinks the cup and dies in his arms.

* GRAND HOTEL

(257 performances)

A drama in eighteen scenes, translated by W. A. Drake from the German of Vicki Baum. Produced by Herman Shumlin at the National Theatre, New York, November 13, 1930.

Cast of characters—

Senf...Walter Vonnegut
Preysing.....................................Siegfried Rumann
Flaemmchen...................................Hortense Alden
Suzanne......................................Raffaela Ottiano
Baron Von Gaigern............................Henry Hull
Kringelein...................................Sam Jaffe
Desk Clerk...................................Walter Baldwin
Witte..Lester Alden
Dr. Otternschlag.............................Romaine Callender
Justice Zinnowitz............................Harry D. Southard
Reception Manager............................Frank W. Taylor
Chauffeur....................................Joseph Spurin-Calleia
Meierheim....................................William Nun
Grusinskaia..................................Eugenie Leontovich
Porter.......................................Fred Eckhart
Chambermaid..................................Audrey Bauer
Inspectress..................................Florence Pendleton
Gerstenkorn..................................Harry Hanlon
Schweimann...................................Stephen Irving
Waitz..Richard Lloyd
Gigolo.......................................Milton LeRoy
Acts I, II and III.—Thirty-six Hours in the Grand Hotel in Berlin.
Staged by Herman Shumlin.

See page 355.

HELLO, PARIS

(33 performances)

A musical comedy in two acts, adapted by Edgar Smith from Homer Croy's novel of the same title; music by Russell Tarbox and Michael Cleary. Produced by the Messrs. Shubert at the Shubert Theatre, New York, November 15, 1930.

Cast of characters—

Opal Peters....Eileen Dougal
Clark McGurley....Glen Dale
Ide Peters....Ethel Wilson
Lady Wolvertress....Claire Hooper
Aunt Minnie....Stella Mayhew
Ed Eggars....Nat C. Haines
Wheel Wilson....Roy Peck
Ross Peters....Jack Good
Lem Putt (The Specialist)....Chas. "Chic" Sale
Gracie Jones....Mary Adams
Pike Peters....Chas. "Chic" Sale
Tony....Louis La Granna
Clearwater Band Drummer....Charles Garland
The Trombonist....Harry Sanger
The Baritone....Freddie Packard
Captain....Lois Deppe
Bill Jones....J. Clifford Rice
Newsboy....Don Morrell
Fleurie Capel....Georgie Hayes
Captain S.S. *Ile de France*....Roy Peck
Marquis De Coudray....Maurice La Pue
Deck Steward....Freddie Packard
A Passenger....Helen Thompson
Another Passenger....Jimmy Ardell
A Devoted Husband....Charles Garland
His Very Sick Wife....Iris Hold
Ship's Officer....J. Clifford Rice
Major Domo....Roy Peck
Mons. Ville....Ray Ronheimer
Antoine....J. Clifford Rice

Act I.—In Clearwater, Okla.; New York and on Board the *Ile de France*. Act II.—In and around Paris.
Staged by Ben Holmes.

A sketchy revue type of musical comedy built on certain characters and episodes lifted from Homer Croy's "They Had to See Paris." Pike Peters having struck oil takes his family on a continental jaunt during which they enjoy many adventures.

MARSEILLES

(16 performances)

A comedy in three acts adapted by Sidney Howard from the French of Marcel Pagnol. Produced by Gilbert Miller at the Henry Miller Theatre, New York, November 17, 1930.

Cast of characters—

Escartefigue..Hubert Druce
Marius..Alexander Kirkland
Picquoiseau...Arthur Lysons
Engineer of Ferryboat...............................Ted Fetter
An Arab Rug Seller..................................Henry de Koven
Fanny...Frances Torchiana
Cesar...Dudley Digges
Panisse...Guy Kibbee
Monsieur Brun.......................................Douglas Wood
A Malay Girl..Enid Raphael
Honorine..Alison Skipworth
A Gendarme..Jefferson Lloyd
Petty Officer Goelec................................Colin Hunter
Suzanne...Natica de Acosta
Arabs...Ris Hassan and Hassan Farss

Acts I, II and III—Cesar's Bar on the Quay of the Old Harbor of Marseilles.

Staged by Gilbert Miller.

Marius, son of Cesar, proprietor of a small bar near the quay at Marseilles, hungers for adventure and the far countries. His father would keep him at home. So would Fanny, who loves him. Cesar offers a job and a home. Fanny offers herself. Marius accepts Fanny's offer, and is willing to stay and marry her. But Fanny knows she cannot hold him against the sea and his dreams. She lets him go and agrees to marry Panisse, the merchant, who promises her a maid and a hundred thousand francs.

SWEET AND LOW

(184 performances)

A revue in two acts by David Freedman; music by Billy Rose. Produced by Billy Rose in the Forty-sixth Street Theatre, New York, November 17, 1930.

Principals engaged—

George Jessel
James Barton
Jerry Norris
Roger Davis
Moss and Fontana
Arthur Treacher
Fannie Brice
Paula Trueman
Hannah Williams
Shirley Richards
Peggy Andre
Lucille Osborne

Staged by Alexander Leftwich.

PRESSING BUSINESS

(16 performances)

A comedy by Alfred H. White and P. William Tell. Produced by Algeo Production Co., Inc., at the Republic Theatre, New York, November 17, 1930.

Cast of characters—

Lapidus....................................Mark Adams
Fanny Small................................Mildred Elliott
Izzy Small.................................Bernard Gorcey
Beatrice...................................Edith White
Walter Chase...............................William Myron
Abie Goodman...............................Alfred H. White
Peggy O'Day................................Nina Walker
Ben Goodman................................Alan Lowe
Mrs. Wilkinson Chase.......................Muriel C. Rogers
Peter O'Day................................Andrew Mack

Act I.—Rear of Second Hand Clothing and Pressing Shop, Greenwich Village. Acts II and III.—Show Room and Office in Goodman & Small's.

Izzy Small and Abie Goodman, tailors, start a cloak and suit business on small capital and suffer many irritating adventures. Ben Goodman loves Peggy O'Day, Abie's ward. They have been reared as brother and sister, though Peggy has been brought up a Catholic because of Abie's promise to her father. Abie, Izzy and the cloak and suit business explode, but Peter O'Day, Peg's long-absent father, turns up with a happy ending.

SMILES

(63 performances)

A musical comedy in two acts by William Anthony McGuire; music by Vincent Youmans; lyrics by Clifford Grey, Harold Adamson and Ring Lardner. Produced by Florenz Ziegfeld at the Ziegfeld Theatre, New York, November 18, 1930.

Cast of characters—

Holy Joe...................................Tom Howard
Pierre.....................................Edward Raquello
Tony.......................................Adrian Rosley
Dick.......................................Paul Gregory
Madelon....................................Lorraine Jaillet
First Sailor...............................Gil White
Slim.......................................Frank Coletti
Izzy Cohen.................................Pat Mann
Arline.....................................Arline Aber
Charline...................................Charline Aber
Doughface..................................Bernard Jukes
Bob Hastings...............................Fred Astaire
Larry......................................Larry Adler
Mackin.....................................Joe Lyons
Mother Jones...............................Mary Collins
Smiles.....................................Marilyn Miller
Dot Hastings...............................Adele Astaire
Lillian....................................Jean Ackerman
Clara......................................Clare Dodd
Mrs. Hastings..............................Georgia Caine
Gilbert Stone..............................Eddie Foy, Jr.
Officer Dennis O'Brien.....................Harry Tighe
Sankee.....................................Charles Sager

Pat....................................Kathryn Hereford
Chang Lang Foo....................................C. Sager Czaja
Miss Parker....................................Ruth Morgan
Kiki....................................Hilda Moreno
Betty....................................Ruth Patterson
Ann....................................Katherine Burke
Mrs. Brown....................................Jean Ackerman
Mr. Brown....................................Gil White
Mr. Green....................................Louis Delgardo
Ensemble—Virginia Bruce, Betty Dumbris, Marian Dodge, Caja Eric, Georgia Ellis, Marcel Edwards, Dorothy Flood, Maurine Holmes, Meredith Howard, Neva Lynn, Marjorie LaVoe, Rose Mariella, Christine Maple, Peggy Peacock, Blanche Satchel, Helen Walsh, Gertrude Dahl.

Prologue—Outskirts of a Deserted Village in France, 1918. Act I.—Scene 1—East Side, New York City. 2—Interior Salvation Army Mission. 3—Bar in the Hastings' Residence at Southampton. 4—Garden on the Hastings' Estate. Act II.—Scene 1—Café Le Berry, Paris. 2—Street in Montmartre. 3—Bedroom in the Hotel Crillon. 4—Steamship Dock, N. Y. 5—Roof Garden of the Hastings' City Home, New York.

Staged by Ned Wayburn and William Anthony McGuire.

Holy Joe, Pierre, Tony and Dick, four war buddies, come upon Madelon, aged 10, in a shell-torn retreat in France, 1918. They rename her Smiles and take her back to America after the armistice. Smiles grows up to become a Salvation Army girl, but quits the army for society as represented by Bob and Dot Hastings. In the end she returns to Dick, her favorite adopted father.

TONIGHT OR NEVER

(232 performances)

A comedy in three acts by Lili Hatvany. Produced by David Belasco at the Belasco Theatre, New York, November 18, 1930.

Cast of characters—

The Prima Donna....................................Helen Gahagan
The Faithful Dog....................................Ferdinand Gottschalk
The Man Servant....................................Robert Greig
The Maid....................................Greta Meyer
His Excellency....................................Warburton Gamble
The Unknown Gentleman....................................Melvyn Douglas
The Marchesa....................................Katherine Stewart
The Marchesa's Maid....................................Agnes de Dome
The Waiter....................................Edmund Loewe

Acts I and III.—Room in the Prima Donna's House. Act II.—Apartment in the Hotel Royale.

Staged by David Belasco.

The Prima Donna, restless and tired of hearing her music master, The Faithful Dog, complain that she will never sing until she has experienced love and suffering, deliberately seeks out the young gigolo who has been following her. After the visit, which lasts the night through, the Prima Donna gives an inspiring performance at the matinée and learns that the gigolo is really a scout for the Metropolitan Opera Company and eager to marry her.

ART AND MRS. BOTTLE

(50 performances)

A comedy in three acts by Benn W. Levy. Produced by Kenneth Macgowan and Joseph Verner Reed at the Maxine Elliott Theatre, New York, November 18, 1930.

Cast of characters—

Michael Bottle....................G. P. Huntley, Jr.
Judy Bottle....................Katharine Hepburn
Sonia Tippet....................Joyce Carey
Parlormaid....................Elise Breton
George Bottle....................Walter Kingsford
Celia Bottle....................Jane Cowl
Charlie Dawes....................Lewis Martin
Max Lightly....................Leon Quartermaine

Acts I, II and III.—Second Floor Spare Room in Mr. Bottle's Home.

Staged by Clifford Brooke.

Judy and Michael Bottle are artists reared in the belief that their mother had died when they were babes. When they are grown Mrs. Bottle, who had really run away with Max Lightly, an artist, returns and promptly wins their understanding confidence. She has considerable difficulty holding this when she discovers that Judy is in love with the same Max who had successfully broken up the family twenty years before and will not be turned from him. Nor Michael from his model, Sonia. So Mrs. Bottle dutifully withdraws and leaves her family to their own problems.

THE VINEGAR TREE

(229 performances)

A comedy in three acts by Paul Osborn. Produced by Dwight Deere Wiman at the Playhouse, New York, November 19, 1930.

Cast of characters—

Max Lawrence....................Warren William
Augustus Merrick....................H. Reeves-Smith
Winifred Mansfield....................Katherine Wilson
Louis....................Walter Colligan
Laura Merrick....................Mary Boland
Leone Merrick....................Helen Brooks
Geoffry Cole....................Allen Vincent

Acts I, II and III.—Living Room of the Merricks' Country Estate.

Staged by Winchell Smith.

Laura Merrick, restless as she realizes in her forties that her husband is still years older than she is, lives largely in an imaginative past in which a handsome young artist figured prominently one purple afternoon. Mrs. Merrick now believes that artist to have been the same Max Lawrence, who is week-ending with the Merricks, and lays her plans accordingly. She is greatly distressed when her own daughter seems about to take Max away from her, but is reasonably content in the end when she makes the discovery that the artist with whom she had spent the afternoon was really Laurence Mack, pianist, and not Max Lawrence, painter.

AN AFFAIR OF STATE

(23 performances)

A comedy in three acts by Robert L. Buckner. Produced by Benjamin David at the Broadhurst Theatre, New York, November 19, 1930.

Cast of characters—

Josef....................Dennis Gurney
Nikola....................Leonard Carey
Otto....................Wilfrid Seagram
Alexa....................Florence Eldridge
Von Platz....................Moffat Johnston
Aunt Augusta....................Jessie Busley
Bergdorf....................A. Trevor Bland
Eric....................Clifford McLaglen
Fritz....................Edward Leiter
Hilda....................Margaret Mullen

Acts I, II and III.—Summer Palace of the Archduchy of B——, near the Danube.
Staged by Moffat Johnston.

Otto and Alexa, ten years the rulers of the Archduchy of B——, are facing a crisis. Their constituency, having nothing else to worry about, is plotting a revolution. If, on the other hand, the people could be promised an heir to the throne it would probably settle their minds. Von Platz, the chancellor, thinks the situation could be met if the royal couple would consider inviting the advice and assistance of, say, a handsome young army captain. The archduchess, however, rather fancies a certain young lieutenant. The situation is accepted both delicately and patriotically by all concerned and in due time the archduchess is able to announce that the country is about to be saved.

SCHOOLGIRL

(28 performances)

A comedy by A. W. Pezet and Carman Barnes. Produced by Henry B. Forbes at the Ritz Theatre, New York, November 20, 1930.

Cast of characters—

Naomi Bradshaw....................................Joanna Roos
Gerry Bradshaw....................................Dot Matthews
Dave Montague....................................Michael Barr
Mary Gresham....................................Virginia Stone
Nicky....................................Levin Houston
Boggsy....................................Walter Rivers
Louise Bradshaw....................................Beatrice Hendricks
Cornelia....................................Elizabeth Taylor
George Bradshaw....................................Charles Waldron
Janet Livingston....................................Helen Claire
Celia Morgan....................................Hilda Haywood Howe
Margie Morgan....................................Elda Voelkel
Miss Merry....................................Annot Willingham
Belinda....................................Margie Woods
Rena Fairchild....................................Lois Jesson
Paula....................................Ernestine Hornady

Acts I and III.—Living Room of the Bradshaw Home. Act II.—Naomi's and Janet's Room, South Fields Boarding School.
Staged by A. W. Pezet.

Naomi Bradshaw, in love with Dave Montague, is ready to run away and marry him before either is through school. Her plans are frustrated and she is sent away to boarding school as a protection. In school she learns a lot about girls she never knew before, climbs out a window, meets Dave, spends the night with him and climbs back only to be discovered by the school authorities. At home Naomi admits her sin but refuses to try to make it right by marrying Dave. She is not as sure as she was that she loves him. Dave and Naomi go back to school with a promise of some sort of adjustment after Dave is out of college.

OH, PROMISE ME

(145 performances)

A farce comedy in two acts by Howard Lindsay and Bertrand Robinson. Produced by Sam H. Harris at the Morosco Theatre, New York, November 24, 1930.

Cast of characters—

Luther Bowen....................................Donald Meek
Flo Bowen....................................Eleanor Hicks

Elsie Carpenter....................................Mary Philips
Connie Clark....................................Eleanore Bedford
Mark Reed....................................Lee Tracy
Mr. Brown....................................Chester Clute
Mrs. Brown....................................Rosamund Carpentier
Louise....................................Jeanne Greene
Jasper B. Ogden....................................Edward H. Robins
Bell Boy....................................Eddie Hodge
Marshall Durant....................................Frank Sylvester
Judge Hawley....................................Frazer Coulter
Court Clerk....................................Arthur Davies
Court Stenographer....................................Jack Morgan
Court Attendant....................................William Nelson
Mr. Siegel....................................Harry Hornik
Henry Dietz....................................Clarence Bellair

Act I.—Bowen Apartment. Act II.—Scene 1—Room in a Connecticut Hotel. 2—Court Room.

Staged by Howard Lindsay and Bertrand Robinson.

Mark Reed, a self-educated lawyer, having won a sensational murder trial, is eager for another chance at publicity. Connie Clark, in love with Mark, agrees to frame the flirtatious elderly person who is her boss, Jasper B. Ogden. Ogden invites Connie to go on a business trip with him. When he calls at the house to confirm her acceptance she manages to force him into a compromising situation and yells for witnesses. The lawyer brings suit for a quarter million damages, the case is won on perjured testimony and everybody is happy except Jasper B. Ogden.

SCARLET SISTER MARY

(24 performances)

A drama in five scenes adapted by Daniel Reed from the novel by Julia Peterkin. Produced by Lee Shubert at the Ethel Barrymore Theatre, New York, November 25, 1930.

Cast of characters—

Maum Hannah....................................Beatrice Terry
Mona....................................Anita Rothe
Tressie....................................Denise Morris
Sister Mary (Called Si May-e)....................................Ethel Barrymore
Budda Ben....................................Horace Braham
Cinder....................................Estelle Winwood
June....................................John Roseleigh
July....................................Walter Gilbert
Cousin Andrew....................................Leo Kennedy
Big Boy....................................Herbert Gentry
Doll....................................Georgie Drew Mendum
Tussie....................................Blanche Collins
Luke....................................Burke Clarke
Gadsen....................................Wilbur Cox
Gracey....................................Marjorie Main
Reverend Duncan....................................Marcel Dill
Brer Dee....................................Daniel Bagnell
Unex....................................Albert Ridge
Daddy Cudjoe....................................William B. Mack
Seraphine....................................Ethel Barrymore Colt

Thatcher...Marcel Dill
Brunton..Alan Campbell
Wade...Charles Quigley
Big Boy (at Age of 30)...............................Theodore De Corsia
Unex (at Age of 20)..................................Malcolm Soltan
The Heaven Gate Singers—Mabel Ridley, Helen Dowdy, Sylvia Allen, Frank Jackson, William Raymond, Alice Cannon, Bertha Powell, Sam H. Gray, Toussaint Duers, Joseph Christian.
Flower Girls—Erma Smith, Corrine Harris, Julia Smith.

Scene 1—Dooryard at Maum Hannah's. 2 and 3—July and Mary's Home. 4—Crossroads at Heaven Gate Church. 5—Sister Mary's Home.

Staged by E. M. Blyth.

Sister Mary, marrying the lovable and lustful July, bears him the infant Unexpected. July runs away with Cinder and Sister Mary, after a period of lonesomeness, decides to take life at its current value. Wanting children she has them, taking their fathers as they appeal to her. After twenty years little Unex returns to his home to die. In his death Sister Mary sees a vision which assures her the Lord has listened to the pleading of her son and that she will be accepted and understood at the throne of grace.

FIRST NIGHT

(86 performances)

A drama in three acts by Frederick Rath. Produced by Richard Herndon at the Eltinge Theatre, New York, November 26, 1930.

Cast of characters—

Joe..Tom Burton
Larry..Walter Powers
Hogan..Al Guin
Joan Reid..Emily Graham
Robert Martin..Henry Wadsworth
Warden Ross..Edwin Cushman
Governor Moore.......................................John F. Morrissey
Bartlett Harvey......................................William Bonelli
Inspector Owens......................................George MacQuarrie
Frank Pisano...Harold Huber
The "Duke"...Wallace Widdecombe
George...Richard N. Gregg
Betty..Ronnée Madson
Stanley Reid...Donald Blackwell
First Reporter.......................................Spencer Kimbell
Second Reporter......................................Britton Diller
Third Reporter.......................................Frank Stringfellow
Berg...Jack A. Clifford
Connelly...Louis E. Miller
Barnes...Alf Helton
Irene Barnes...Edith Broder
Kerr...Phil M. Sheridan
Hicks..Robert C. Schnitzer
Rizzo..Salvatore F. Zito

Sharpe.......................................Spencer Kimbell
Convict.......................................Perry Norman
Acts I, II and III.—On the Stage and in the Auditorium of Sing Sing Prison.
Staged by Milton Stiefel.

Joan Reid writes a play from the evidence presented in a murder trial in which her brother Stanley was convicted of murder in the first degree and sentenced to the chair. The play is given first at Sing Sing and the Governor of the state is invited. Recognizing that an attempt is being made to influence his decision in Stanley Reid's case the Governor tries to stop the play, but is induced to sit it through on the promise that there is much new evidence in the last act. He stays. The play proves young Reid circumstantially innocent. The Governor agrees to the pardon.

THIS IS NEW YORK

(59 performances)

A comedy in three acts by Robert E. Sherwood. Produced by Arthur Hopkins at the Plymouth Theatre, New York, November 28, 1930.

Cast of characters—

Waiter.......................................Bruno Wick
Mrs. Krull.......................................Virginia Howell
Senator Harvey L. Krull.......................................Robert T. Haines
Hauser.......................................Sam Wren
Emma Krull.......................................Lois Moran
Mr. Murchard.......................................Allen Atwell
Joseph Gresham, Jr. ....Geoffrey Kerr
Lucille.......................................Henrietta Ravenell
Phyllis Adrian.......................................Audrey Dale
Harry Glassman.......................................Robert Barrat
Jean Doran.......................................Ruth Hammond
Babe Savito.......................................Murray Alper
Sheila Lavery.......................................Lota Bonner
Judge Gohagan.......................................Raymond Bramley
Milt Fleisler.......................................William T. Carpenter
Pete.......................................Frank Layton
Conway.......................................Thaddeus Clancy
Elevator Boy.......................................Boris Nicholai
Kavanaugh.......................................Tom Fadden
Sztineck.......................................Martin Noble
Reporter.......................................Charles A. Richards
Camera-Man.......................................W. W. Watson
Act I.—Sitting Room in the Krulls' Suite in the Hotel Roosevelt. Acts II and III.—Living Room in Phyllis Adrian's Apartment, Central Park West.
Staged by Arthur Hopkins.

Senator Harvey L. Krull and Mrs. Krull of Dakota are in New York on a lecture tour. They are disturbed by a rumor that has seeped through the press that their daughter Emma, at school in the East, has become engaged to Joseph Gresham, a Broadway playboy. Called to account, Emma admits the charge and is not at all frightened by her father's threat that she must renounce Gresham. She is much more concerned about Gresham's confession that he has been paying Phyllis Adrian's rent. Emma calls on Phyllis, who threatens blackmail. While she is there a bootlegger's mistress jumps out a window and is killed. Emma is held as a material witness. The scandal breaks; the Senator is forced to stand back of his daughter; Miss Adrian's blackmailing scheme is kicked in the head; Emma marries Joe, who promises to go West and help reëlect the Senator before settling down in New York.

A KISS OF IMPORTANCE

(24 performances)

A comedy adapted by Arthur Hornblow, Jr., from the French of André Picard and H. M. Harwood. Produced by Arch Selwyn in association with Erlanger Productions, Inc., at the Fulton Theatre, New York, December 1, 1930.

Cast of characters—

Fred....................Johnnie Brewer
Arthur Dupin....................Ivan Simpson
Mlle. Thomas....................Alice Burrage
Comte de Cerisay....................Frank Henderson
Christian Saint Obin....................Basil Rathbone
Gilbert Laurent Courcel....................Montague Love
Isabelle de Corquefon....................Ann Andrews
Octave de Corquefon....................Frederick Kerr
Albertine....................Marjorie Hollis
Gardener....................George Wright, Sr.
Act I.—Dupin's Office on the Avenue Kleber, Paris. Acts II and III.—Salon of de Corquefon's Château in the Country.
Staged by Lionel Atwill.

Gilbert Courcel loves the wife of his political opponent, the aging Octave de Corquefon. Isabelle, bored with her home life, agrees to marry Gilbert if a divorce can be arranged. Christian Saint Obin, young and handsome, agrees to serve them as a professional co-respondent, visit the de Corquefon estate, make love to Isabelle, be caught by Octave and thus furnish evidence for the divorce. Christian complicates matters somewhat by taking his time, after he arrives at the estate. Forced finally into action by the impatient lovers he does so good a job of love making that Isabelle changes her mind about the divorce. She had rather cling to Octave if she can also live near Christian.

ALISON'S HOUSE

(41 performances)

A drama in three acts by Susan Glaspell. Produced at the Civic Repertory Theatre, Inc., New York, December 1, 1930.

Cast of characters—

Ann Leslie....................Florida Friebus
Jennie....................Leona Roberts
Richard Knowles....................Robert Ross
Ted Stanhope....................Herbert Shapiro
Louise....................Josephine Hutchinson
John Stanhope....................Walter Beck
Eben....................Donald Cameron
Elsa....................Eva Le Gallienne
Miss Agatha....................Alma Kruger
Hodges....................Howard da Silva
Mrs. Hodges....................Mary Ward

Acts I and II.—Library of the Old Stanhope Homestead in Iowa, on the Mississippi. Act III.—Alison's Room.
Staged by Eva Le Gallienne.

See page 222.

THE MERCHANT OF VENICE

(15 performances)

A comedy by William Shakespeare in three acts. Revived by Charles Dillingham in association with Erlanger Productions, Inc., at the Times Square Theatre, New York, December 2, 1930.

Cast of characters—

The Duke of Venice....................Frank Howson
Prince of Morocco....................Louis Polan
Antonio....................Hugh Buckler
Bassanio....................Geoffrey Wardwell
Salanio....................Geoffrey Harwood
Salarino....................Philip Robinson
Gratiano....................Albert Hayes
Lorenzo....................John Halloran
Shylock....................Maurice Moscovitch
Tubal....................Henry Alexander
Launcelot Gobbo....................Maury Tuckerman
Old Gobbo....................Noel Ainley
Leonardo....................Sylvia Ware
Balthazar....................Charles Hanna
Stephano....................Lucille Lisle
A Page....................Vera Krug
Portia....................Selena Royle
Nerissa....................Judith Elder
Jessica....................Dorothy Tree
Madrigal Singers........Randall Fryer, Wallace Banfield, Walter J. Owens, J. H. Eakin

Act I.—Scene 1—Venice. A Public Place. 2—Belmont. A Room in Portia's House. 3—Venice. Before Shylock's House. 4—Belmont. 5—Venice. Act II.—Scene 1—Venice. Before Shylock's

House. 2—Belmont. 3—Venice. A Street. 4—Belmont. Act III.—Scene 1—Venice. A Court of Justice. 2—Belmont. Portia's Garden.
Staged by Andrew Leigh.

The version used by Mr. Moscovitch during the long run of his revival in London. It is arranged in three acts and liberally cut.

OVERTURE

(41 performances)

A drama in three acts by William Bolitho. Produced by Bela Blau, Inc., at the Longacre Theatre, New York, December 5, 1930.

Cast of characters—

Mrs. Lopper....Lois Arnold
Peters....Armand Cortes
Thomas....William Foran
Jung....Pacie Ripple
Attendant....Bjorn Koefoed
The Mayor....Frederick Roland
Kraus....Daniel Makarenko
Felder....Richard Freeman
Lindermann....Martin Malloy
Karl Ritter....Colin Clive
Katie....Barbara Robbins
Maxim....Pat O'Brien
Doctor Levy....Maurice Cass
Rubens....Joseph Robison
Pepper....N. R. Cregan
1st Student....Ward Vernon
2nd Student....J. P. Gould
A Girl....Lee Burgess
Lieutenant of Police....Royal C. Stout
Heiber....Frederick Backus
1st Delegate....William Boren
2nd Delegate....Bjorn Koefoed
A Sergeant....Daniel Hamilton
Lieutenant Hoffman....John Hoysradt
General von Hoeffer....Carlos Zizold
Corporal....Harry Selby
Chaplain....Bjorn Koefoed
Acts I, II and III.—Council Chamber in the Town of Herfeld, Germany.

See page 286.

THE NEW YORKERS

(168 performances)

A musical satire by Herbert Field, suggested by Peter Arno and Ray Goetz; music by Cole Porter. Produced by E. Ray Goetz at the Broadway Theatre, New York, December 8, 1930.

Cast of characters—

A Nurse....Marjorie Arnold
Dr. Cortlandt Jenks....Paul Huber
Alice Wentworth....Hope Williams
Felix....Charles Angelo
Dr. Windham Wentworth....Richard Carle
Lola McGee....Ann Pennington
Gloria Wentworth....Marie Cahill
Alfredo Gomez....Maurice Lapue
James Livingston....Barrie Oliver
Mona Low....Frances Williams
Al Spanish....Charles King
Jimmie Deegan....Jimmie Durante
Oscar Gregory....Lew Clayton
Grover Monahan....Eddie Jackson
Butch McGeehan....Tammany Young
Burns....Ralph Glover
Dopey....Billy Culloo
May....Kathryn Crawford
Attendant at Sing Sing....Donald McGinnis
Plague....Stanley Harrison
Mildew....Oscar Ragland

Prologue and Epilogue—Consulting Office of Dr. Cortlandt Jenks, New York. Act I.—Scene 1—Club Toro, New York. 2—A Cellar. 3—Amendment Import Company. 4—In Front of Reuben's. 5—Reuben's, That's All! 6—Before a Park Avenue Apartment House. 7—Salon in the Wentworth Home. Act II.—Scene 1—Lounge at Sing Sing. 2—Street in New York. 3—Lawn of Al's Home in Miami.

Staged by Monty Woolley; dances by George Hale.

The revue type of musical comedy strung on the slender plot of Alice Wentworth's dream, Alice being a tired and disgusted society girl hailing from Park Avenue, "where bad women walk with good dogs." Dr. Jenks gives Alice an opiate and she dreams two acts of foolishness, taking her all around the town and as far south as Miami.

PETTICOAT INFLUENCE

(98 performances)

A comedy in three acts by Neil Grant. Produced by Gilbert Miller at the Empire Theatre, New York, December 15, 1930.

Cast of characters—

Richard Chalfont....John Williams
Peggy Chalfont....Helen Hayes
Daincourt....Mary Heberden
Reggie Melcombe....Reginald Owen
The Countess of Darnaway....Valerie Taylor
Lord Algernon Raytoun....Eric Cowley
The Earl of Darnaway....Henry Stephenson
Talbot....Henry Vincent

Act I.—Room in Colonel Chalfont's London Flat. Acts II and III.—Drawing Room in the Mayfair Residence of the Earl and the Countess of Darnaway.

Staged by Gilbert Miller.

Richard Chalfont has been expecting an appointment as the governor of Arba. When he hears the place has gone to an incompetent named Lord Algernon Raytoun, because he happens to be the uncle of a cabinet minister's wife, he is sorely disappointed but resigned. Peggy Chalfont, his wife, refuses to take the defeat as gracefully. Discovering by accident that the minister's wife is having an affair with the minister's secretary she deftly uses the information to her husband's advantage, causing the cabinet minister to cancel Lord Algernon's appointment and give it to Chalfont.

BABES IN TOYLAND

(33 performances)

A musical comedy by Glen Macdonough; music by Victor Herbert. Revived at the Imperial Theatre, New York, December 20, 1930.

Cast of characters—

Uncle Barnaby....William Balfour
Frances....Frances Moore
Betty....Betty Flanigen
Tom Tom....Ruth Gillette
Hilda....Mary Wilson
Gonzorgo....Jack Cameron
Roderigo....Robert Darrell
The Widow Piper....Jayne Waterous
Bo Peep....Margaret Byers
Jill....Ethel Lynne
Peter....Florence Little
Bobby Shaftoe....Mabel Thompson
Jack....Betty Hayden
Sallie Waters....Eleanor Gilmore
Curly Locks....Dorothy May
Tommy Tucker....Lydia Lucke
Simple Simon....Frances Baviello
Little Red Riding Hood....Gertrude Waldon
Miss Muffett....Lillian Morris
Boy Blue....Billie Williams
Jane....Betty Byron
Alan....Charles Barnes
1st Dandy....Frank Yannelli
Contrary Mary....Dorothy Kane
Inspector Marmaduke....Bert Matthews
Master Toymaker....Leslie Stowe
Grumio....Joseph Knight
Max....Frank Yannelli
The Brown Bear....Harry Knabenshue
The Giant Spider....Bernie Sager
A Fairy....Dene Dickens
Santa Claus....Edward Bird

Act I.—Scene 1—Country Fête in Mary's Garden. 2—Garden Wall Back of the Garden. 3—Spider's Forest. Act II.—Scene 1—Christmas Tree Grove in Toyland. 2—Street in Toyland. 3—March of the Toys. Act III.—Scene 1—Master Toymaker's Workshop. 2—Street in Toyland. 3—Temple of the Palace of Justice in Toyland.

Staged by Milton Aborn; ballet by Virginie Mauret.

Interested with Mr. Aborn in this revival were the Messrs. Shubert, who expressed the hope that the operetta would hereafter be an annual Christmas event in honor of all children.

BALLYHOO

(68 performances)

A musical comedy by Harry Ruskin and Leighton K. Brill; music by Louis Alter. Produced by Arthur Hammerstein at Hammerstein's Theatre, New York, December 22, 1930.

Cast of characters—

Sam	Don Tomkins
Ruth	Jeanie Lang
Manager	Neil Moore
Harry	Al Downing
Flora Fay	Grace Hayes
Whitey Duke	Andy Rice, Jr.
Goldie La Marr	Janet Reade
Brown, Smith, Jones } Runners	Three Slate Brothers
Larry	Jack Colby
Betty	Patricia Murphy
A Gourmand	Chaz Chase
Vera	Floria Vestoff
Drum Major	J. Mardo Brown
Q. Q. Quale	W. C. Fields
Shorty	William Blanche
Landlord	Neil Moore
Cowboys	{ Slate Brothers Al Downing
Bill Collector	James Cushman
Reporter	Harvey Murray
Mr. Miner	Arthur Cardinal
Mr. Pidgeon	Gus Wicke
Photographer	Herbert Weber
Camera Man	Craig Kershaw
Sound Man	Herb Lund
Bank President	Anthony O'Dea
Junior	Max Hoffman, Jr.
The King	Richard Lambert
Jim	Douglas Alene
Sam	Charles Evans

Ted Black's Band—Al Giroux, Samuel Kahn, Sherman Brande, Bill Doerflinger, James Bander, Fred Barber, Sam De Bonis, Walter Jewhurst.

The Cheer Leaders—Raymond Clark, Charlie Fowler, Herb Hall, Fred Shawhan.

Girls, Boys

Act I.—Scene 1—Street in New York. 2—Dance Hall in New York. 3—Street in Shamokin, Ohio. 4—Public Square, Shamokin. 5—Room in Commercial Hotel, El Toro, N. M. 6, 7 and 8—Corridor. 9—Patio of Hotel, Butte, Ariz. Act II.—Scene 1—Back Stage, Opera House, Salome, Ariz. 2—Railroad Station, Salome, Ariz. 3—Stage, Opera House, Salome, Ariz. 4—First Trust Bank, Hollywood. 5 and 6—Sound Stage, Colossal Studios. 7—Café, Hollywood. 8—Quayle's Pharmacy, Beverly Hills. 9—Ruth's Beverly Hills Home.

Staged by Reginald Hammerstein; dances and ensembles by Earl Lindsey.

Q. Q. Quayle, promoter, is running a "bunion derby" from a New York night club to Hollywood. He carries a troupe of entertainers with him, and has some trouble eluding sheriffs and creditors. Also his leading woman, who is greatly attached to him. Arrived in Hollywood most of his actors get into the movies one way or another.

LIFE IS LIKE THAT

(32 performances)

A comedy in three acts by Jo Milward. Produced by Curtis W. Emery at the Little Theatre, New York, December 22, 1930.

Cast of characters—

Tong.................................Hanaki Yoshiwara
Elizabeth Courtney..............................Mary Morris
Charlie Reed....................................Alan Davis
Delories.....................................Helen Shipman
May Addison....................................Doris Covert
William Courtney.............................Edward Pawley
Jane Barton.................................Peggy Shannon
Jimmie......................................James K. Rogers
Dr. Ramsey.................................William H. Barwald

Acts I, II and III.—In the Pent-house of William Courtney in the East Fifties.
Incidental music by Clifford Lang, Jack Hyman, Hazel Chisholm and Helen Kaminsky.
Staged by Paul Edouard Martin.

Bill Courtney is hiding from a terrifying wife, Elizabeth Courtney, in a pent-house, accompanied in a way by Jane Barton, who understands him, and Delories, a showgirl friend. Mrs. Courtney manages finally to make the pent-house and takes a shot at Bill, missing Bill but killing his Chinese servant. The doctor agrees to call the shooting accidental because if he doesn't Delories will not have anything more to do with him. Bill and Jane go to Russia in search of contentment and adventure.

INSPECTOR GENERAL

(7 performances)

A farce comedy in three acts adapted by John Anderson from the Russian of Nicolai Gogol. Revived by Jed Harris at the Hudson Theatre, New York, December 23, 1930.

Cast of characters—

Hospital Commissioner............................Josef Lazarvici
Luka Lukitch......................................Frank Conlan

A Servant, Mishka....................................Theodore Hart
The Mayor....................................Claude Cooper
Lyapkin-Tyapkin....................................Eugene Powers
Shepkin....................................Eduardo Ciannelli
Bobchinsky....................................Edward Rigby
Dobchinsky....................................Owen Meech
A Constable....................................Joseph Sauers
Police Superintendent....................................Con MacSunday
Anna....................................Lina Arbarbanell
Marya....................................Dorothy Gish
Osip....................................J. Edward Bromberg
A Waiter....................................William Challee
Ivan Alexandrovitch Hlestakov....................................Romney Brent
A Maid....................................Bessie Traub
Another Constable....................................William Dorbin
A Merchant....................................Harold Johnsrud
The Sergeant's Wife....................................Flavia Arcaro

Acts I and II.—Scene 1—The Mayor's House. 2—Hlestakov's Room at the Inn.

Staged by Jed Harris.

The mayor and other public officials of a small town in provincial Russia hear they are likely to be visited by an Inspector General from Petersburg. Because of the state of their accounts they are thrown into a fever of fear. Thinking the Inspector may travel incognito they decide a stranger at the inn, who happens to be an impecunious bookkeeper indulging a travel adventure, is the Inspector. They wine, dine and bribe him for days and then discover their mistake. The regular Inspector arrives in the midst of their confusion.

PURITY

(12 performances)

A drama in three acts by Rene Wachthausen, adapted by Barre Dunbar and Ralph Roeder. Produced by Lee Shubert, at the Ritz Theatre, New York, December 25, 1930.

Cast of characters—

Gustave....................................Jan Linderman
A Park Guard....................................Frank Horton
A Lady with a Dog....................................Helene Girard
Yvonne....................................Peggy Conklin
An Old Man....................................James Moore
A Lady....................................Loretto Shea
A Man About Town....................................Walter Fenner
Henri....................................Richard Bird
Victoire....................................Florence Reed
A Little Girl....................................Frances Tannehill
Jeanne....................................Marcella Swanson
Henriette....................................Pearl Ramoy
Julie....................................Muriel Robinson
A Walking Advertisement....................................Edward M. Favor
M. Leon....................................Malcolm Williams
Madame Michaud....................................Maude Odell

Act I.—Scene 1—The Square des Innocents, Paris. 2—Room on

the Top Floor of a Lodging House in a Poor Quarter. Act II.—The Room. Act III.—On the Banks of the Seine.
Staged by Stanley Logan.

Mme. Victoire, a charwoman taking her ease in the park, meets Henri, 20, jobless, friendless and half starved. Sympathetically interested in him Mme. Victoire takes Henri to her own poor lodgings, fills his stomach and makes him comfortable. Thereafter she practically adopts him. Henri rewards her kindness by spending her savings and eluding work. In his coat Mme. Victoire discovers an impassioned love letter from Henri's current mistress and the flare of her jealousy shocks her into the realization that her love for the boy is not maternal but physical. She tries to commit suicide but is drawn back to continue her life of sacrifice. Better that she should stick by Henri and suffer than die and desert him.

KING LEAR

(4 performances)

A tragedy in four acts by William Shakespeare. Revived by the Chicago Shakespeare Society, headed by Fritz Leiber, at the Ambassador Theatre, New York, December 25, 1930.

Cast of characters—

Lear, King of Britain....................Fritz Leiber
King of France....................Howard H. Inches
Duke of Burgundy....................William J. Maloney
Duke of Cornwall....................Thayer Roberts
Duke of Albany....................Ralph Menzing
Earl of Kent....................Lawrence H. Cecil
Earl of Gloster....................Philip Quin
Edgar....................Hart Jenks
Edmund....................John Burke
Old Man....................Robert Strauss
Physician....................Frank Peters
Fool....................John Forrest
Oswald....................Lionel Ince
A Captain....................J. Augustine Keogh
Herald....................Walter Plinge
Goneril....................Virginia Bronson
Regan....................Ingeborg Torrup
Cordelia....................Mary Hone

Act I.—Scene 1—Room in King Lear's Palace. 2—Hall in Gloster's Castle. 3—Before the Duke of Albany's Castle. Act II.—Scene 1—Heath. 2—In Front of Gloster's Castle. 3—Heath. 4—In Front of Gloster's Castle. Act III.—Scene 1—Heath. 2—Before Albany's Castle. 3—Heath. 4—Tent in the French Camp. Act IV.—An Encampment.

During this visit of the Chicago Shakespeare Society to New York Mr. Leiber and his players also presented "Hamlet," "The Merchant of Venice," "Julius Cæsar," "Macbeth," "As You Like It" and "Richard III."

ELEKTRA

(8 performances)

A tragedy in three acts by Sophocles, adapted by Hugo von Hofmannstahl. Produced by Carl Reed in association with Elizabeth Marbury at the New Yorker Theatre, New York, December 26, 1930.

Cast of characters—

Clytemnestra....Katina Paxino
Elektra....Marika Cotopouli
Chrysothemis....Popy Panayiotou
Ægisthus....Yannis Apostolides
Orestes....Alexis Minotis
Foster-father of Orestes....Char. Spiliopoulos
Waiting Woman....Maria Thiveou
Train Bearer....Lela Patrikiou
Young Serving Man....Chr. Tsaganeas
Old Serving Man....Takis Syrakos
Cook....Nicos Thiveos
Overseer of Women....Despina Georgiou

Acts I, II and III.—The Courtyard of the Palace, Near the Servants' Quarters.

Staged by Marika Cotopouli.

The Von Hofmannstahl version presents Elektra as a distrait and disheveled child completely submerged in her grief over the murder of her father, Agamemnon, by Clytemnestra, his queen, and her lover. After "conversing with her father's shadow," and swearing an oath of vengeance Elektra tries first to induce her sister, Chrysothemis, to assist her. That failing, and the report of her brother Orestes' death having reached her, Elektra is about to undertake the wiping out of Clytemnestra as her own task when Orestes appears, is quickened to the deed and dispatches the guilty queen. Elektra's joy is savage.

THE TRUTH GAME

(107 performances)

A comedy in three acts by Ivor Novello. Produced by Lee Shubert at the Ethel Barrymore Theatre, New York, December, 27, 1930.

Cast of characters—

Rosine Browne....Phœbe Foster
Max Clement....Ivor Novello
Sir George Kelvin....Gerald McCarthy

Harris....................................Gwen Day Burroughs
Evelyn Brandon....................................Billie Burke
James Hubbard....................................Burton McEvilly
Atkins....................................Jean Fullarton
The Lady Joan Culver....................................Viola Tree
Sir Joshua Grimshaw....................................Albert Garcia Andrews
Lord Straffield....................................Forbes Dawson
Vera Crombie....................................Dorothie Bigelow

Act I.—Scene 1—Outside Rosine's House in Curzon Street, Mayfair. 2—Rosine's House in Curzon Street. Acts II and III.—The Hall, Cleveland Manor.

Staged by G. Hamilton Gay.

Max Clement, meeting Rosine Browne under romantic circumstances, immediately announces his love and an intention of marrying her. Rosine is touched by his love but unable to marry him. Being a widow if she marries she loses her income. Finally she succumbs to the lure of poverty and love only to learn that Max is the distant cousin of her late husband who is to inherit her money. Rosine calls everything off at this discovery and then changes her mind a second time.

THE LIFE LINE

(17 performances)

A comedy in three acts by Gretchen Damrosch. Produced by Leo Bulgakov at the Vanderbilt Theatre, New York, December 27, 1930.

Cast of characters—

Bronson Cutler....................................Carrol Ashburn
Lilly....................................Helene Ambrose
Blair....................................Eunice Stoddard
Jay Dadmun....................................Lewis Leverett
Gildersleeve....................................Harry Green
Pyle....................................Robert Parsons
The Reverend Dr. Trusedale....................................Shepherd Strudwick
Mrs. Irving Ives....................................Rosalind Ivan
Mr. Irving Ives....................................Herbert Delmore
Mr. Mario Tinzeel....................................Akim Tamiroff

Acts I, II and III.—In the Library of Mr. Cutler's House.

Staged by Leo Bulgakov.

Bronson Cutler, successful as a big business man, has promised his young minister that he will help the next person in trouble who appeals to him. The next person happens to be Mrs. Irving Ives, whose husband is evidently chasing after a younger flame. Cutler advises Mrs. Ives to leave her husband, which she does, and takes up her residence in the Cutler house. This drives Mrs. Cutler out and reveals the fact that it is the Cutler daughter who loves Ives. There are farcical complications and a final reversion to some sort of domestic peace.

MIDNIGHT

(48 performances)

A drama in three acts by Claire and Paul Sifton. Produced by the Theatre Guild at the Guild Theatre, New York, December 29, 1930.

Cast of characters—

Joe Biggers	Harold Vermilyea
Ada Biggers	Harriet MacGibbon
Mrs. Weldon	Josephine Hull
Stella Weldon	Linda Watkins
Arthur Weldon	Clifford Odets
First Reporter	Tom H. A. Lewis
Messenger Boy	Charles Powers
Edward Weldon	Frederick Perry
Second Reporter	Harold Bolton
Third Reporter	Samuel Rosen
Bob Nolan	Glenn Anders
Gar Boni	Jack LaRue
Richard McGrath	Francis Pierlot
Elizabeth McGrath	Maude Allan
Edgar Ingersoll	Fred Sullivan
Policeman	Neal Stone
Dr. Mannheim	Royal Dana Tracey
Woman Reporter	Zena Colaer
Photographers	Louis Veda James Parker
Plunkett	Robert Strange
Treadwell	William R. Kane

Acts I, II and III.—Living Room of the Weldon Home.
Staged by Philip Moeller.

Arthur Weldon, florist, serving as foreman of the jury trying a woman for having killed her lover, is largely responsible for having held the jury to a verdict that sends the defendant to the electric chair. The night of the execution he is tormented by hordes of newspaper reporters begging for a statement and by the woman's attorney seeking a last-minute stay. Weldon, honest citizen, refuses to have anything more to do with the case, in the papers or out of them. The law is the law and should be upheld. As the hour of midnight heralds the electrocution of the murderess, Stella, Weldon's daughter, slips weakly into the back door of the house, a smoking revolver in her hand. She has shot and killed her Italian lover, who threatened to desert her. Weldon still persists the law should take its course, but Bob Nolan, tabloid reporter, convinces both Weldon and the district attorney that Stella is entitled to a break.

QUEEN AT HOME

(16 performances)

A comedy in three acts by Shirley Warde and Vivian Crosby. Produced by John Henry Mears at the Times Square Theatre, New York, December 29, 1930.

Cast of characters—

Frederick Porter.................................Arthur Aylsworth
Granny Hunnewall.................................Jessie Crommette
Sula.................................Lillian Brown
Emma Porter.................................Rosemary King
Berta Lee.................................Clara Palmer
Ada Hunnewall.................................Suzanne Willa
Jennifer Lee.................................Sylvia Field
Larry Scott.................................William Carey
Snip Haviland.................................Elizabeth Mears
Roy Carrington.................................Franklyn Fox
Acts I, II and III.—Living Room of Jennifer Lee's Home at Teaneck, N. J.
Staged by the authors and Courtenay Savage.

Jennifer Lee is an actress and a hit in a new Broadway play. Unhappily married to Roy Carrington she is much in love with Larry Scott. To add to her troubles she has a house filled with disagreeable relatives and a girl friend, Snip. Jennifer bears her burdens with some grace and finally Snip frames Carrington, helping Jennifer to be rid of him. With this encouragement Jennifer also throws the relatives out.

FIVE STAR FINAL

(175 performances)

A melodrama in three acts by Louis Weitzenkorn. Produced by A. H. Woods at the Cort Theatre, New York, December 30, 1930.

Cast of characters—

Miss Taylor.................................Helene Sinnott
Arthur.................................Alvin Kerr
Luella Carmody.................................Laurie Jacques
Ziggie Feinstein.................................Allen Jenkins
Hinchecliffe.................................Berton Churchill
French.................................Henry Sherwood
Brannegan.................................Frank Dae
Miss Edwards.................................Madeleine Marshall
Exchange Operator.................................Lillian Bronson
Rev. T. Vernon Isopod.................................Alexander Onslow
Colby.................................Kenneth Dana
Rooney.................................Bruce MacFarlane

Jerry..P. J. Kelly
A Policeman..Mike D'Arcy
Randall...Arthur Byron
Nancy Voorhees Townsend........................Merle Maddern
Jenny Townsend.....................................Frances Fuller
Michael Townsend..................................Malcolm Duncan
Philip Weeks..King Calder
Mrs. Arthur Loveland Weeks.......................Kathryn Keys
Mr. Arthur Loveland Weeks.........................Sydney Booth
Pearl..Amy Dennis
Trixie ....Dorothy McElhone
Harold..Richard Huey
Minerva...Georgette Harvey
Undertaker ....Fred House

Act I.—Scene 1—Office of Mr. Randall, Managing Editor of *Evening Gazette.* 2—Office of Mr. Hinchecliffe, Owner of *Evening Gazette.* 3—Rev. T. Vernon Isopod's Office. 4—Corcoran's Speakeasy. 5—Brannegan's Office. 6—A Re-write Booth. 7—Randall's Office. 8—Townsend Apartment. 9—Drugstore Booth. 10—Randall's Office. 11—Townsend Apartment. Act II.—Scene 1—Randall's Office. 2—French's Office. 3—Townsend Apartment. 4—Randall's Office. 5—Weeks' Apartment. 6—Hinchecliffe's Office. 7—Randall's Office. 8—Townsend Apartment. Act III.—Scene 1—Hotel Bedroom. 2—Minerva's Flat. 3—French's Office. 4—Corcoran's Speakeasy. 5—Drugstore Booth. 6—Townsend Apartment. 7—Ziggie's Desk. 8—Randall's Office.

Staged by Worthington Miner.

See page 254.

MEET MY SISTER

(167 performances)

A musical comedy in a prologue, epilogue and two acts adapted by Harry Wagstaffe Gribble from the French of Berr, Verneuil and Blum; music and lyrics by Ralph Benatsky. Produced by the Messrs. Shubert at the Shubert Theatre, New York, December 30, 1930.

Cast of characters—

PROLOGUE

President of the Divorce Court...................Donald Campbell
Assessor to the Court..............................Niska Stefanini
Clerk of the Court...................................Graham Velsey
Eric Molinar...Walter Slezak
Dolly Molinar...Bettina Hall
Her Maid...Kay McKay
Her Butler...Boyd Davis
Her Footman...George Spelvin

ACT I

Eric Molinar...Walter Slezak
Charles..Boyd Davis
Henriette...Kay McKay
Dolly, the Countess Ste. La Verne....................Bettina Hall
Marquis De Chatelard...........................George Grossmith

ACT II

Irma...Olive Olsen
Otto H. Finkel..Harry Welsh
A Waiter...Julius Campo

Prologue—Divorce Court in Paris. Act I.—Countess La Verne's Library in Her Château, Near Paris. Act II.—Finkel's Shoe Store at Nancy. Epilogue—Divorce Court.
Staged by William Mollison; dances by John Pierce.

Eric and Dolly Molinar appear in a divorce court and try to convince the judge that they are incompatible. He wants to hear the whole story so they go back to the beginning when the Countess Ste. La Verne engaged the young Prof. Molinar to catalogue her library. The professor was girl shy and avoided the countess, who had fallen deeply in love with him. She pursued him then to Nancy, where he had gone to teach school, and placed herself on his social level by buying herself a job in a shoe store. There she captured him and became Mrs. Molinar. Then they quarrel. The judge helps to patch up the quarrel.

COLONEL SATAN

(17 performances)

A comedy in three acts by Booth Tarkington. Produced by George C. Tyler in association with Erlangers, Inc., at the Fulton Theatre, New York, January 10, 1931.

Cast of characters—

Colonel Aaron Burr....McKay Morris
Mr. Frederic Vanderberg....Ben Smith
Augustus Lally, Esquire....Arthur Treacher
Bobiche....Louis Casavant
Charles....Montague Shaw
M. Le Marquis d'Azyr-Romorantin....Aristides de Leoni
M. de Saulcy....Arthur W. Row
Bastide....Harro Ten-Brook
Victor....Roman Arnoldorff
A Lackey....Charles Renault
Mme. La Baronne de Bannalac....Jessie Royce Landis
Mme. La Duchesse de St. Pol-de-Lean....Mme. Burani
Zephire....Elvira Trabert
Mlle. Tou-Tou....Renee Cartier

Acts I and III.—Obscure Wineshop, Called "La Mouche," in Paris, 1811. Act II.—Salon of Mme. de Bannalac.
Staged by Stanley Logan.

Aaron Burr, living in the garret of a wineshop in Paris in 1811, accidentally becomes a part of a conspiracy engineered by La Baronne de Bannalac to dethrone the Emperor Napoleon and return Louis XVIII. His first night's introduction to the group convinces him that the Baroness, discovered to be the current mistress of the prefect of police, is really conspiring to round up certain famous royalist plotters. Burr makes fevered love to the Baroness, has a part in her exposure, fights a duel with a fiery young friend of Alexander Hamilton, and, finally, because of the continued interest of the Baroness, stands in a fair way of obtaining the passport that eventually brought him back to the United States in 1812.

PHILIP GOES FORTH

(97 performances)

A comedy in three acts by George Kelly. Produced by Laurence Rivers, Inc., at the Biltmore Theatre, New York, January 12, 1931.

Cast of characters—

Mrs. Randolph....................................Thais Lawton
Edna....................................Donna Pasdeloup
Philip....................................Harry Ellerbe
Mrs. Oliver....................................Cora Witherspoon
Mr. Eldridge....................................Thurston Hall
Cynthia....................................Madge Evans
Mr. Haines....................................Harold Webster
Miss Krail....................................Dorothy Stickney
Mr. Shronk....................................Harry Gresham
Hazel....................................Mary Gildea
Mrs. Ferris....................................Marion Barney
Bassett....................................Ralph Urmy

Act I.—Upstairs Sitting-room in the Home of Mr. Randolph. Acts II and III.—At Mrs. Ferris', in New York.
Staged by George Kelly.

Philip, out of college, quarrels with his father as to his future activities. Father wants Philip to go into father's business. Philip insists that something tells him he has the playwriting gift. He demands his right to express himself, which means to go to New York and become a great dramatist. With his allowance cut Philip goes to New York, gets himself a job as a salesman and writes plays nights. He makes good as a salesman but is a joke as a would-be dramatist. Many influences, including some met in a theatrical boarding house, induce Philip to reconsider and there is a reconciliation with his father.

SITA

(8 performances)

A favorite drama of India credited to the authorship of Valmiki, sage and poet. Produced by the India Academy of America at the Vanderbilt Theatre, New York, January 12, 1931.

Cast of characters—

Durmukha....................................Sj. Amalandu Lahiri
Rama....................................Sj. Sisir Kumar Bhaduri
Kanchuki....................................Sj. Sital Pal
Basishtha....................................Sj. Jogesh Chowdhury
Lakshmana....................................Sj. Biswanath Bhaduri
Urmila....................................Sreemati Bela
Sita....................................Sreemati Prova
Bharata....................................Sj. Tarakumar Bhaduri
Kausalya....................................Screemati Usha
Valmiki....................................Sj. Manoranjan Bhattacharyya
Lava....................................Sj. Soilen Chowdhury
Kusha....................................Sj. Rrabinda Bose
A....................................Screemati Kanka

Act I.—Terrace in the Interior of the Palace. Act II.—Scene 1—Chamber in the Palace. 2—Hermitage of Valmiki. Act III.—Royal Court.
Staged by Sisir Kumar Bhaduri.

This, the oldest Sanskrit epic known, credited to the authorship of Valmiki, India's legendary poet, tells of King Ram, ancient ruler of India, whose wife, Sita, was ordered banished by the high priests because, having been kidnaped and forced to live in the palace of a savage king, Ravana, she is pronounced unchaste. Sita, retired to the forest, gives birth to twin sons who grow up to hate their father because of his treatment of their mother. One son goes to the king's palace to fight with the king. A reconciliation follows and the high priests are willing to have Sita back if she will take oath that she has always been faithful to Ram. She meets the insult by praying the earth to open and receive her if she has remained unstained in thought and action all her life, which the earth does.

* TOMORROW AND TOMORROW

(183 performances)

A drama in three acts by Philip Barry. Produced by Gilbert Miller at the Henry Miller Theatre, New York, January 13, 1931.

Cast of characters—

Gail Redman....................................Harvey Stephens
Eve Redman....................................Zita Johann
Ella....................................Marie Bruce
Nicholas Hay....................................Herbert Marshall
Samuel Gillespie....................................Osgood Perkins
Jane....................................Adele Schuyler
Walter Burke....................................John T. Doyle
Christian Redman....................................Drew Price
Mary....................................Eileen Byron
Miss Frazer....................................Mary Elizabeth Forbes
Miss Blake....................................Alice MacIntosh

Acts I, II and III.—Living Room of Gail and Eve Redman's House in Redmanton, Indiana.
Staged by Gilbert Miller.

See page 74.

ANATOL

(45 performances)

A comedy in two acts by Arthur Schnitzler, adapted by Harley Granville-Barker. Produced by Bela Blau, Inc., at the Lyceum Theatre, New York, January 16, 1931.

Cast of characters—

Max....................Walter Connolly
Anatol....................Joseph Schildkraut
Hilda....................Dennie Moore
Emily....................Anne Forrest
Bianca....................Elena Miramova
Gabrielle....................Patricia Collinge
Waiter....................Oswald Yorke
Mimi....................Miriam Hopkins
Franz....................Roger Ramsdell
Lona....................Ruthelma Stevens

Act I.—Scene 1—Wine Garden on the Outskirts of Vienna. 2—Emily's Sitting Room. 3—Max's Rooms. 4—An Arcade. Act II.—Scene 1—Private Room in Sacher's Restaurant. 2—Anatol's Apartment.

Staged by Gabriel Beer-Hoffmann.

A sequence of events in the affairs of a lady's man about to wed. He has his hour with Hilda, Emily, Bianca, Gabrielle, Mimi and Lona, finds them still sighing for or glad to be rid of him, manages them variously and retires to matrimony a greatly puzzled and considerably worried young man.

* YOU SAID IT

(168 performances)

A musical comedy in two acts by Jack Yellen and Sid Silvers; music by Harold Arlen; lyrics by Jack Yellen. Produced by the Messrs. Yellen and Holtz at the Forty-sixth Street Theatre, New York, January 19, 1931.

Cast of characters—

Hal Foster, '30....................Henry Slate
Fuzzy Shawowsky, '32....................Benny Baker
Eddie Brown, '30....................Oscar Grogan
Frank Pennell, '31....................Syd Slate
Douglas Richardson, '31....................Allan D'Sylva
Frank Murphy, '30....................Jack Slate
Kewpie Andrews, '32....................Hughie Clarke
Loren Brooks, '31....................Kendall Capps
Tommy, '33....................Tommy Miller
Grace Carroll, '31....................Billie Leonard
Florence Hart, '30....................Betty Sundmark
Hattie Hudson, '32....................Peggy Bernier

Helen Holloway, '30 .... Mary Lawlor
Walter Prescott, '30 .... Walter Petrie
Bob Smith, '30 .... Stanley Smith
"Pinkie" Pincus .... Lou Holtz
Fanny .... Lyda Roberti
Willoughby Pinkham, '33 .... George Haggerty
Gladys Dorsey .... Paula Sands
Nicholas Holloway .... John T. Dwyer
Lord Hemingway Potts .... Vic Ethridge
Scotty .... Vic Munro
Squires .... J. Francis Robertson
Dr. Fairbairn .... John Walsh
Prof. Healy .... Bryan Davis
The Nurse .... Betty Nylander

Six John Boyle Dancers
Merry-Makers Quartette—The Campus Four

Act I.—Scene 1—Railroad Station at Kenton. 2—Campus Walk. 3—On the Campus. 4—Hollow Oak Lane. 5—Hollow Oak. 6—Campus Walk. 7—Alpha Chi Fraternity House. Act II.—Scene 1—On the Campus. 2—Campus Walk. 3—In Front of the Dean's Office. 4—Room in the Medical Laboratory. 5—On the Way to the Glen. 6—The Glen, on Cap-burning Night.
Staged by John Harwood and Danny Dare.

Pinkie Pincus matriculates at Kenton College, organizes all the college rackets, including the laundry, the baggage delivery, the Greek restaurant, etc., takes a hand in the love affairs of the dean's daughter by stealing the evidence that would have convicted her fiancé of bootlegging, manages to keep out of a lot of work and sends money home.

GREEN GROW THE LILACS

(64 performances)

A folk-play in six scenes by Lynn Riggs. Produced by the Theatre Guild, Inc., at the Guild Theatre, New York, January 26, 1931.

Cast of characters—

Curly McClain .... Franchot Tone
Aunt Eller Murphy .... Helen Westley
Laurey Williams .... June Walker
Jeeter Fry .... Richard Hale
Ado Annie Carnes .... Ruth Chorpenning
Peddler .... Lee Strasberg
Old Man Peck .... Tex Cooper
Cowboy .... Woodward Ritter
Another Cowboy .... Paul Ravell
Old Farmer .... William T. Hays
Young Farmer .... A. L. Bartolot
Marthy .... Jane Alden
Fiddler .... William Chosnyk
Banjo Player .... Everett Cheetham
Other Farmers: Carl Beasley, Joe Wilson, Roy Ketcham, Gordon Bryant, Everett Cheetham, Elmo Carr, Tommy Pladgett.
Cowboys: Slim Cavanaugh, Chick Hannan, Norton Worden, Jack Miller, Pete Schwartz, J. B. Hibbard.
Girls: Jean Wood, Lois Lindon, Orlando Lee, Alice Frost, Faith Hope, Eleanor Powers, Peggy Hannan.

"Green Grow the Lilacs" Is Laid in Indian Territory in 1900. Oklahoma, Which Was Admitted as a State in 1907, Was Formed by Combining Indian and Oklahoma Territories.

Scene 1—Williams' Farm House. 2—Laurey's Bedroom. 3—Smoke House. 4—Porch of Old Man Peck's House. 5—Hayfield Back of Williams' House. 6—Living Room of the Williams' House.

Staged by Herbert J. Biberman.

See page 147.

CAMILLE

(57 performances)

A drama in four acts by Alexander Dumas, fils, translated by Henriette Metcalf. Produced by the Civic Repertory Theatre, Inc., at the home theatre, New York, January 26, 1931.

Cast of characters—

Baron de Varville....Robert H. Gordon
Nanine....Alma Kruger
Nichette....Josephine Hutchinson
Marguerite Gautier....Eva Le Gallienne
Olympe....Beatrice de Neergaard
Saint Gaudens....Paul Leyssac
Prudence....Leona Roberts
Servants....Richard Waring and DeWitt Kiernan
Gaston Rieux....Harold Moulton
Armand Duval....Morgan Farley
Guests....Joseph Kramm and Jack Saltzman
Count de Giray....Donald Cameron
Gustave....Robert F. Ross
M. Duval....Jacob Ben-Ami
Arthur....Gordon Wallace
The Doctor....Walter Beck
Anais....Estelle Scheer
Servant....David Kerman
Guests in Third Act: Peter Railey, Richard Waring, Arnold Moss, Antonia Warren, Joan Van Seyfertitz, Morris Morrison, Howard da Silva.

Act I.—Scenes 1 and 2—Marguerite Gautier's Boudoir. Act II.—Living Room in Marguerite's Villa at Auteuil, Near Paris. Act III.—Salon in Olympe's House in Paris. Act IV.—Marguerite's Bedroom. Period: 1875.

Staged by Constance Collier.

The familiar version of the Dumas tragedy in which Armand Duval's love for Marguerite Gautier, a lady of some prominence on the wrong side of the Seine, is interrupted by the conspiracy of his father to save him. Marguerite, deliberately blasting the passion of her young lover, later calls him back when she knows that she has not long to live. The play was first produced in Paris nearly eighty years ago, and has been played in America by practically every great actress specializing in emotional rôles.

SHE MEANS BUSINESS

(8 performances)

A comedy in prologue and three acts by Samuel Shipman. Produced by James Elliott Productions, Inc., at the Ritz Theatre, New York, January 26, 1931.

Cast of characters—

Doris Roberts....................Ann Davis
Charlotte B. Evans....................Peg Entwistle
Allen T. Evans....................Wallis Clarke
William Brighton....................Herbert Rawlinson
John Roberts....................Ernest Glendinning
Edgar Lawson....................Ivan Miller
Margie....................Desiree Foster
George Forbes....................Houston Richards
Jane Barton....................Ruth Donnelly
Groff....................Edwin Walter
Aiken....................Tom Tempest
Holbrook....................Bennett Southard
Reubens....................Lee Kohlmar
Ware....................Robert Cummings
Walter Norman....................Douglas Wood
Mary....................Kate Byron

Prologue and Acts I and II.—Show Room of John Roberts' "Ladies' Bag Establishment." Act III.—Drawing Room at the Roberts'.

Staged by Frederick Stanhope.

Doris Roberts loves her husband, John, even though he is a good deal of a cad. Together they build up a ladies' bag business and share it 50-50. Then John decides a wife's place is in the home and Doris goes home. John proceeds to take up with an office wife and ends by running away to Europe with her. The business goes to pot until Doris again steps in and saves it. John comes home and would like to start afresh by taking over the recovered business, but one experience is enough for Doris.

* PRIVATE LIVES

(150 performances)

A comedy farce in three acts by Noel Coward. Produced by Charles B. Cochran at the Times Square Theatre, New York, January 27, 1931.

Cast of characters—

Sybil Chase....................Jill Esmond
Elyot Chase....................Noel Coward
Victor Prynne....................Laurence Olivier

Amanda Prynne....................................Gertrude Lawrence
Louise..Therese Quadri
Act I.—Terrace of a Hotel in France. Acts II and III.—Amanda's Flat in Paris.
Staged by Noel Coward.

Elyot Chase, arriving with his bride, Sybil, at a hotel on the French Riviera, discovers that Amanda, his first wife, from whom he has been divorced for five years, is in the adjoining apartment with Victor Prynne, her second husband, whom she also has just married. Elyot and Amanda, meeting on the terrace, gazing at the moon, listening to the hotel orchestra play sentimental tunes, suddenly realize that they are still desperately in love with each other and that any attempt to go through with a second marriage would be a failure. Between cocktails and dinner they run away to Amanda's flat in Paris. The next week they spend in alternately making love and quarreling. Then Victor and Sybil catch up with them and they are forced to run away a second time.

Mr. Coward having refused to play more than the three months originally scheduled for the run of "Private Lives," Mr. Selwyn arranged with Madge Kennedy and Otto Kruger to continue the run, beginning with the performance of May 11, 1931. Audrey Pointing, Robert Newman and Juliana Taberni were also added to the cast.

AS YOU DESIRE ME

(142 performances)

A drama in three acts by Luigi Pirandello, adapted by Dmitri Ostrow. Produced by Lee Shubert at the Maxine Elliott Theatre, New York, January 28, 1931.

Cast of characters—

Moto..Goo Chong
Mop..Mary Miner
Carl Salter...............................Douglass Dumbrille
The Unknown One..............................Judith Anderson
Young Man.....................................Maurice Ramon
Another.......................................Hugh Cairns, Jr.
Boffi..José Ruben
Lena...Vera G. Hurst
Salesio...Philip Leigh
Bruno Pieri....................................Brandon Peters
Maid...Charlotte Orr
Inez...Katherine Warren
Masperi.......................................Mortimer Weldon
Another Woman....................................Amy Jonap
Doctor..John O'Meara
Nurse..Charlotte Orr
Act I.—Salter's Apartment in Berlin. Acts II and III.—The Villa of Bruno Pieri, Not Far from Milan.
Staged by Marcel Varneli.

The Unknown One is recognized by Boffi, a painter, dancing in a Berlin cabaret. He believes her to be Lucia Pieri, the wife of his best friend. Lucia had been captured and violated by enemy troops during the great war, and has been missing for ten years. Finding her, Boffi seeks to induce her to return to her family. Lucia at first denies her identity, declaring that because of the degradation to which she has fallen she can never recover any part of her past. Agreeing finally to return to the home of Bruno Pieri she is greeted a little hesitantly as Lucia. Again she persists that she can only recover her past, can only be again as they see her, as they desire her to be. When a beast of a man she had lived with in Berlin appears with another Lucia, a mad woman, and doubt again assails the minds of her alleged kin, the Unknown One leaves them and takes to the open road.

THE STUDENT PRINCE

(42 performances)

A musical comedy in four acts, adapted by Dorothy Donnelly; music by Sigmund Romberg. Revived by the Messrs. Shubert at the Majestic Theatre, New York, January 29, 1931.

Cast of characters—

1st Lackey....Zachary Caully
2nd Lackey....Frazer McMahon
3rd Lackey....Irving Green
4th Lackey....Lynn Eldredge
Von Mark....William Pringle
Dr. Engel....Hollis Davenny
Prince Karl Franz....Edward Nell, Jr.
Ruder....Lee Beggs
Gretchen....Marion Weeks
Toni....Adolph Link
Detlef....Charles Chesney
Lucas....H. C. Howard
Von Asterberg....Charles Angle
Nicolas....George Del Rigo
Kathie....Eliz Gergely
Lutz....George Hassell
Hubert....Gus Alexander
Grand Duchess Anatasia....Marie Stoddard
Princess Margaret....Margaret Adams
Captain Tarnitz....Alexander Callam
Countess Leyden....Gustava Malstrom
Baron Arnheim....Jerry Maxwell
Rudolph Winter....Kaji Nansen
Freshman....Harold E. Bomgardner
Captain of the Guard....Dave Morton

Prologue: Ante-chamber in the Palace at Karlsberg. Acts I and IV.—Garden of the Inn of the Three Golden Apples. Heidelberg. Act II.—Sitting Room of Prince Karl, at Inn. Act III.—Room of State in the Royal Palace at Karlsberg.

Staged by Edward Scanlon.

The "Alt Heidelberg" romance, concerned romantically with the adventure of Prince Karl Franz the year he spent at the University of Heidelberg, and fell in love with Kathie, the pretty daughter of the Inn of the Three Golden Apples.

* IN THE BEST OF FAMILIES

(154 performances)

A farce in three acts by Anita Hart and Maurice Braddell. Produced by Thomas Kilpatrick at the Bijou Theatre, New York, February 2, 1931.

Cast of characters—

Bronson Hamilton..............................Charles Richman
Edwards..............................Johnnie Brewer
Millicent Hamilton..............................Grace Filkins
Sarah Mooreside..............................Florence Edney
James Hamilton..............................Derek Fairman
Charles Hamilton..............................Kendall Foster
June Kingsley..............................Mary Arbenz
Derek Hamilton, 2nd..............................David Morris
Mrs. Poppy Davis..............................Leonore Sorsby
Helen Hamilton..............................Enid Romany
The Reverend Dr. Fairfield..............................Perry Norman
Jeanette LaRue..............................Marian Warring-Manley
Hilda..............................Mele Efrid
Col. Derek Hamilton..............................Alfred Brown

Acts I, II and III.—Suburban Home of the Hamiltons, Roslyn, Long Island.
Staged by Jo Graham.

Bronson Hamilton, conservative banker, is awakened in the middle of the night by the furious ringing of his front door bell. He thinks it indicates the arrival of his somewhat fast son, Derek Hamilton, Jr., but discovers it to be an abandoned baby in a basket. A note left with the baby reads: "I want my son to be with its father." There are six males in the Hamilton household, including the butler, and all are suspected during the following action. The infant turns out to be the offspring of Grandpa Hamilton, whose last holiday had been spent in French Lick Springs.

ROCK ME, JULIE

(7 performances)

A drama in three acts by Kenneth Raisbeck. Produced by Morris Green and Lewis Gensler at the Royale Theatre, New York, February 3, 1931.

Cast of characters—

Steven Moorhead.................................Paul Muni
Janet Satterlee.................................Jean Adair
Joseph Satterlee.........................Thomas Coffin Cooke
Stella Satterlee Purss..........................Betty Hanna
Raymond Purss..................................Herbert Yost
Mrs. Archer Satterlee..........................Wanda Lyon
Archer Satterlee.........................James Spottswood
Guy Dexter.......................................Otto Hulett
Winifred Satterlee Dexter..................Dorothy Sands
Charlotte Satterlee..........................Helen Menken

Act I.—Living Room of the Satterlee House in Illinois. Act II.—Hilltop Overlooking the Mississippi. Act III.—Satterlee Living Room.

Staged by James Light.

Charlotte Satterlee has been away from the Satterlee homestead in Illinois for twelve years. Her family believes that she has been carving out a career as a singer in New York. Charlotte returns home suddenly. She has been a failure in the East and is going to have a baby. She finds a foster brother, Steven Moorhead, grown into a man who has worshiped the memory and the reports of her. Charlotte thinks perhaps she might marry Steven and thus provide a name and a home for her child. Steven shies away from the adoption of an illegitimate child, even after he discovers that he also is one. Charlotte's mother finally whips up her daughter's courage and sends her away to solve her own problems.

* THE BARRETTS OF WIMPOLE STREET

(148 performances)

A drama in three acts by Rudolf Besier. Produced by Katharine Cornell at the Empire Theatre, New York, February 9, 1931.

Cast of characters—

Doctor Chambers.............................George Riddell
Elizabeth Barrett Moulton-Barrett...............Katharine Cornell
Wilson...Brenda Forbes
Henrietta Moulton-Barrett....................Margaret Barker
Arabel Moulton-Barrett..........................Joyce Carey
Octavius Moulton-Barrett.....................John Halloran
Septimus Moulton-Barrett..................William Whitehead
Alfred Moulton-Barrett......................Vernon Downing
Charles Moulton-Barrett.....................Frederick Voight
Henry Moulton-Barrett..........................Basil Harvey
George Moulton-Barrett.......................Leslie Denison
Edward Moulton-Barrett.....................Charles Waldron
Bella Hedley...............................Dorothy Mathews
Henry Bevan................................John D. Seymour
Robert Browning...............................Brian Aherne
Doctor Ford-Waterlow.......................Oswald Marshall
Captain Surtees Cook..........................John Buckler
Flush...Himself

Acts I, II and III.—Elizabeth Barrett's Bed-Sitting-Room at 50 Wimpole Street, London, in 1845.
Staged by Guthrie McClintic.

See page 317.

DOCTOR X

(80 performances)

A mystery melodrama in three acts by Howard Warren Comstock and Allen C. Miller. Produced by William and Harry Brandt at the Hudson Theatre, New York, February 9, 1931.

Cast of characters—

Miss Warde....................................Alixe Walker
Marshall Stevens..............................Leslie Adams
Neil Merlin...................................George Blackwood
Prof. Graham Wells............................Robert Lowing
Eleanor Stevens...............................Florence Shirley
Mavis...Eden Gray
Dr. Xavier....................................Howard Lang
Ben...Barry Macollum
Jessie..May Vokes
Prof. Rowitz..................................Boris Marshalov
Leyden Duke...................................J. W. Austin
Prof. Haines..................................Charles Edwards

Act I.—Scene 1—Office of Marshall Stevens, Managing Editor of *N. Y. Ledger*. 2—Dr. Xavier's Laboratory in East Orange, N. J. Acts II and III.—The Laboratory.
Staged by Josephine Victor.

A mysterious murderer who signs himself Doctor X has baffled a lot of murder sleuths, including the famous Dr. Xavier, criminal psychologist. The search narrows. The murderer has a habit of gnawing his victim, indicating to Dr. Xavier that he is probably one who was once shipwrecked and maddened by the thought or act of eating human flesh. He invites all shipwrecked suspects to a séance, puts pulse-indicators on them and enacts a murder. But the wires become crossed and it takes a lot of shrewd deducing to locate the real killer.

AMERICA'S SWEETHEART

(135 performances)

A musical comedy in two acts by Herbert Fields; music by Robert Rodgers; lyrics by Lorenz Hart. Produced by Laurence Schwab and Frank Mandel at the Broadhurst Theatre, New York, February 10, 1931.

Cast of characters—

S. A. Dolan, General Manager of Premier Pictures....John Sheehan
Larry Pitkin.......................................Gus Shy
Madge Farrell.......................................Inez Courtney
Michael Perry.......................................Jack Whiting
Geraldine March.......................................Harriet Lake
Denise Torel.......................................Jeanne Aubert
Paula.......................................Vera Marsh
Dorith.......................................Dorothy Dare
Lottie.......................................Sue Moore
Miss Mulligan.......................................Virginia Bruce
Telephone Operator.......................................Alice Burrage
Dolores.......................................Francetta Malloy
A Stenographer.......................................Terry Carroll
Mr. Corrigan.......................................Jay Ford
Mr. Clark.......................................Fred Shawhan
Mr. Goulding.......................................Herbert Hall
Mr. Butler.......................................Bud Clark
Mr. Carey.......................................Charles Fowler
Georgia, Georgiana and Georgette................Hilda, Louise and Maxine Forman
A Booking Agent.......................................Al Downing
Radio Announcer.......................................Raoul De Tisne
A Policeman.......................................O. J. Vanasse

Act I.—Scene 1—Cafeteria on the Lot of Premier Pictures, Inc. 2—Corridor of Main Executive Building. 3—Private Conference Room. 4—Cabin in the Tennessee Mountains. 5—Before the Casino at Agua Caliente. 6—Back Porch of Madge's Bungalow. 7—Reception Room at the Beverly-Wilshire Hotel. Act II.—Scene 1—Casting Office at Premier Pictures, Inc. 2—Silver Screen, Hollywood Theatre. 3—Roof Garden at the Embassy Club. 4—At the Bungalow. 5—Grauman's Chinese Theatre, Hollywood.

Staged by Bobby Connolly and Monty Woolley.

Michael Perry and Geraldine March, from the Middle West, invade Hollywood to get Geraldine into the movies, which they succeed in doing. Shortly she is a new screen sensation and somewhat uppish toward Michael, who pushes her into a fountain and retires in something like a huff. Later, when the talkies arrive, Michael advances by leaps and bounds and Geraldine, because of a lisp, is left behind. Michael is generously forgiving, however, and gets Geraldine into the showing of his first big success.

SHE LIVED NEXT TO THE FIREHOUSE

(24 performances)

A farce in three acts by William A. Grew and Harry Delf. Produced by L. Lawrence Weber at the Longacre Theatre, New York, February 10, 1931.

Cast of characters—

Joe Callahan.......................................Lawrence O'Sullivan
Bunker.......................................Clifford Jones
Nell O'Leary.......................................Elda Voelkel
Ike Peyton.......................................Roger Gray
Charley Sweeney.......................................Harry Short
Lem Onderdonk.......................................John Henry

Dutch....................Ralph Hertz
Smoky Flynn....................Henry Jones
Seth Watt....................George Harvey
Capt. Steve O'Leary....................Victor Moore
Mrs. O'Leary....................Lotta Linthicum
Mrs. Callahan....................Patricia O'Connor
Harlan Smith....................William Frawley
Lieut. Buckridge....................William Gargan
Delilah Smith....................Ara Gerald
Sue Sweeney....................Lois Jesson

Acts I and III.—The Firehouse. Act II.—Delilah's Kitchen.
Staged by William B. Friedlander.

Delilah Smith, married to Harlan Smith, traveling salesman, lived next to a firehouse in the 1900s. Harlan Smith spent all but one day a month on the road. Delilah acquired the habit of entertaining the fire company during the long, lonesome evenings. This took the laddies' minds off their duties, but they helped a lot with the housework. One night, when all the boys had been over to Delilah's, including Capt. O'Leary, Harlan Smith came home suddenly. He was followed quickly by all the firemen's wives. They found the fireboys variously hidden, variously occupied, and variously garbed. At which time a fire broke out. Delilah explained later that she couldn't afford a maid and just had to do something.

HOBO

(5 performances)

A drama in eleven scenes by Frank Merlin. Produced by James Elliott at the Morosco Theatre, New York, February 11, 1931.

Cast of characters—

Ohio Slim....................Joseph Sweeney
K. C. Shorty....................Barney Flynn
St. Louis Blackie....................Paul Kelly
Willie Perkins....................Martin Tarby
1st Brakeman....................James Young
2nd Brakeman....................Charles P. Thompson
Dan Williams....................Al Rauh
Alice....................Josephine Evans
Delia....................Maud Turner
Nancy....................Gwyn Stratford
Miss Clara....................Valerie Bergere
Reverend Wilkins....................Dudley Clements
Organist....................Tatiana Amazar
Nellie....................Charlotte Henry
Deacon Benner....................Harry North
Officer Hayes....................Victor Kilian
Dying Man....................Clarence Chase
Judge Halsey....................James C. Morton
Mr. Jordan....................Alfred Jenkins
Clerk of Court....................George Averill
Miss Dalton....................Joan Harmon
Deputy Sheriff....................D. J. Sullivan
A Waiter....................William Hertz

Frank....................................Ricardo Bengali
Joe......................................Don Rodalito

Scene 1—Jungles Near Greensboro. 2—Railroad Yards, Springfield. 3—26 Railroad Avenue, Springfield. 4—The Tent, Springfield. 5—Outside the Jail, Springfield. 6—Inside the Jail, Springfield. 7—Courtroom, Springfield. 8—Same as Scene 5. 9—Same as Scene 6. 10—Box-car, 20 Miles West of Springfield. 11—Inside the Box-car.

Staged by Frank Merlin.

St. Louis Blackie has long been a social rebel agin the gov'ment and agin life. Arrested by railroad police in Springfield he claims citizenship and names an address in Railroad Avenue as being that of his sister. The officer takes him there. The place is a parlor house. Nancy, whom Blackie picks out as a sister, goes through for him and he is released. That night Blackie, questioning the message of a tent revivalist, is arrested for having broken up the meeting. About to be freed, his judge remembers that the county needs road work done and sentences him to six months' labor. With Nancy's further help Blackie escapes and gets out of town on another freight, leaving Nancy wondering whether or not she will ever see him again.

TOPAZE

(8 performances)

A comedy in four acts by Marcel Pagnol. Revived in its original French version by J. A. Gauvin at the Forty-ninth Street Theatre, New York, February 16, 1931.

Cast of characters—

Topaze....................................M. Arnaudy
Castel-Vernac.............................Paul Asselin
Muche.....................................Berger
Tamise....................................E. Hemme
Le Noble Vieillard........................Robert Charlys
Roger De Berville.........................Maurice Remy
Le Maitre D'Hôtel.........................Daniel Lorys
L'Agent...................................Gaston Robet
Sequedille................................Le Petit Arnaudy
Pitard-Vergnioles.........................Le Petit Jacques
Suzy Courtois.............................Mme. Suzanne Rissler
Ernestine Muche...........................Dolly Fairlie
Le Baronne Pitard-Vergnioles..............Marguerite Garcya
1re Dactylo...............................Simone Clairem
2me Dactylo...............................Helene Petrov

Act I.—La Pension Muche. Act II.—Le Salon de Suzy Courtois. Acts III and IV.—Le Bureau de M. Topaze.

See "Best Plays of 1929-30."

DEATH TAKES A HOLIDAY

(32 performances)

A drama in three acts by Alberto Casella, adapted by Walter Ferris. Revived by Lee Shubert at the Ambassador Theatre, New York, February 16, 1931.

Cast of characters—

A Maid....................................Frances Amherst
Fedele....................................Thomas Bate
Duke Lambert....................................Julian Royce
Alda....................................Eleanor Stuart
Duchess Stephanie....................................Olga Birkbeck
Princess of San Luca....................................Irby Marshall
Baron Cesarea....................................Wallace Erskine
Rhoda Fenton....................................Charlotte Andrews
Eric Fenton....................................Roland Bottomley
Corrado....................................Alan Willey
Grazia....................................Helen Vinson
His Serene Highness, Prince Sirki, of Vitalba Alexandri
Philip Merivale
Major Whitread....................................Frank Greene
Acts I, II and III.—Great Hall in the Castle of Duke Lambert.
Staged by Laurence Marston.

These thirty-two performances represent two return engagements of two weeks each. The original run began in December, 1929, and continued for 180 performances. (See "Best Plays of 1929-30.") In one change of cast Viva Birkett played the Princess, Ralph Locke the Duke, Frances Amherst Johnson the Duchess Stephanie and Rosalie Vale the maid.

HEAT WAVE

(15 performances)

A drama in three acts by Roland Pertwee. Produced by Stratford Productions, Ltd., at the Fulton Theatre, New York, February 17, 1931.

Cast of characters—

Hugh Dawltry....................................Basil Rathbone
George March....................................Henry Daniel
Philippa March....................................Selena Royle
Irene March....................................Betty Lawford
Nicholas Fayne....................................Mackenzie Ward
Dr. Muir....................................Lionel Pape
James Weysmith....................................Hugh Buckler
Mrs. Weysmith....................................Hilda Plowright
Mameena....................................Enid Raphael
Everard....................................Frank Henderson
Duckworth....................................Arthur Stenning

Bahadur....................................W. Wana Singh
Dawltry's Boy..............................William Cooray
Club Servant...............................K. A. Fernando
Club Servant...........................Fred K. Chandrasakara

Act I.—The Club. Act II.—Hugh Dawltry's Bungalow. Act III.—George March's Bungalow.

Staged by Stanley Bell.

Hugh Dawltry is a social outcast in an oriental town under British rule. Because of which he takes rather handily to drinking. Irene March, younger sister of Philippa March, goes voluntarily to Dawltry's cabin with the idea of forcing her love upon him. She is followed by her sister Philippa, who really loves Dawltry, and sent home. George March in turn follows his wife, finds her with Dawltry, believes the worst and shoots Dawltry. It turns out to be only a flesh wound, and when Dawltry clears himself of the charge for which he was ostracized Philippa leaves her cad of a husband and goes over to Dawltry.

THE GANG'S ALL HERE

(23 performances)

A musical comedy in two acts by Russel Crouse, Oscar Hammerstein, 2d, and Morrie Ryskind; music by Lewis E. Gensler; lyrics by Owen Murphy and Robert A. Simon. Produced by Morris Green and Lewis Gensler at the Imperial Theatre, New York, February 18, 1931.

Cast of characters—

Mr. Horace Winterbottom..........................Tom Howard
Julie Winterbottom...............................Gina Malo
A Man..Jack Bruns
A Woman..Anita Avila
A Girl.......................................Phyllis Cameron
A Young Man......................................Hal Morton
Another Woman....................................Elsie Duffy
Another Man..................................Harry Anderson
His Wife.......................................Ethel Britton
"Baby Face" Martini............................Jack McCauley
Andy Lennox......................................Jack Barker
Hal Le Roy...Hal Leroy
Professor Cavanaugh..............................Eddie Moran
Doctor Indian Ike Kelly............................Ted Healy
Stooges....................Paul Garner, Jack Wall, Dick Hackins
Big Casino..Ben Wise
Little Casino.....................................Joe McKeon
Le Jongleur de Notre Dame.....................Monsieur DuPont
Swiss Bell Ringer..................................Dr. Faust
Two on the Aisle.................Johnnie Dale and Rheta Stone
Dr. T. Slocum Swink..........................Thomas F. Tracy
Longfellow }
Whittier   }....................................Shaw and Lee
Peggy..Ruth Tester
Hotel Manager.....................................Jack Bruns
"Willy" Wilson..................................Zelma O'Neal

Hector Winterbottom....John Gallaudet
Dancers....Gomez and Winona
Chief of Police....Earl Gilbert
Street Vendor....Joe Verdi
A Sailor....Bert Fay
Hotel Proprietor....Albert F. Hawthorne
Ballet Soloist....Gertrude Stanton
Lyric Quartet: Robert Duenweg, Jack Bruns, Harry Anderson and Joseph Vitale
Tilly Losch Ballet: Joan English, Senta Stephany, Marie Grimaldi, Catherine Laughlin, Jeanie Lavera, Katherine Gallimore, Anita Avila and Alice Kellerman

Act I.—Scene 1—On the Boardwalk at Atlantic City. 2—Peacock Alley, Ritz Carlton Hotel, Atlantic City. 3—Winterbottom Suite. 4—Doctor Kelly's Office. 5—Approach to a Private Boathouse. 6—The Boathouse. Act II.—Scene 1—Square in Nantucket. 2—Lobby of the Wilson Hotel. 3—Wing of Hotel. 4—Dock. 5—Deck of Revenue Cutter. 6—Street. 7—Night Club.

Staged by Oscar Hammerstein 2d; dialogue by Frank McCoy; dances by Dave Gould and Tilly Losch.

Baby Face Martini and his mob have a scheme to put old Horace Winterbottom, millionaire bootlegger of Atlantic City, on the spot. Ike Kelly and his gang are drawn into the plot with comic results. The mutual interest of Hector Winterbottom and Peggy Kelly, in each other and the score, serves to bring about a domestic finish.

THE GREAT BARRINGTON

(16 performances)

A comedy in three acts by Franklin L. Russell. Produced by Oliver D. Bailey at the Avon Theatre, New York, Feb. 19, 1931.

Cast of characters—

Phœbe....Kathryn March
Prescott Barrington, the 12th....H. Dudley Hawley
Bishop....Alf Helton
Katie....Anne Revere
St. Bernard M. Blackwood....Charles Dalton
Mrs. Prescott Barrington, the 12th....Eleanor Woodruff
Wolfert Van Doorn, the 14th....Gene Gowing
Prescott Barrington, the 13th....Edmund George
Annabelle Barrington....Natalie Shafer
Jacqueline Van Doorn....Suzanne Caubaye
Peter Van Doorn....J. Malcolm Dunn
John Jones....George Lamar
Prescott Barrington, the 1st....Otto Kruger
Ogu....George Probert

Acts I, II and III.—Home of Prescott Barrington, the First, Along the Hudson, Built in 1629.

The Prescott Barringtons, 12th, in 1930 are snooty about their ancestry and have preserved the Barrington cabin, built on the Hudson in 1629 as an emblem of ancestral distinction. The Barringtons are visiting the cabin when the ghosts of Prescott

Barrington, 1st, his Indian friends and enemies, also drift about the place. The ancestral Barringtons were nothing to be proud of. Prescott the First finally commits a couple of murders, packing the bodies in a closet of the cabin wherein they are discovered by the current snooties.

AN AMERICAN TRAGEDY

(137 performances)

A drama in three acts adapted by Patrick Kearney from the novel of Theodore Dreiser. Revived by J. J. Leventhal at the Waldorf Theatre, New York, February 20, 1931.

Cast of characters—

(In the Prologue)

Clyde Griffiths....................Roy Hargrave
Elvira Griffiths....................Gertrude Ritchie
Asa Griffiths....................Richard Barrow
Hester Griffiths....................Marjorie Brown
A Young Tramp....................Hilton Josephs
A Girl....................Lora Hays
A Young Man....................Tom Rutherford
Another Girl....................Juliana Taberna
A Girl....................Consuelo Flowerton

(In the Play)

Mrs. Samuel Griffiths....................Marie Burke
Bella Griffiths....................Dorothy Garnier
Gilbert Griffiths....................Anthony Pawley
Samuel Griffiths....................Raymond Barrett
Clyde Griffiths....................Roy Hargrave
Sondra Finchley....................Dorothy Watson
Jill Trumbull....................Consuelo Flowerton
Whiggam....................Bert Wilcox
Roberta Alden....................Ruth Nugent
Stuart Finchley....................Tom Rutherfurd
Bertine Cranston....................Lora Hays
Harley Baggott....................Irvin Norvig
Dr. Glenn....................Richard Barrow
Mrs. Peyton....................Gertrude Ritchie
An Innkeeper....................Bert Wilcox
A Deputy Sheriff....................Joseph Lighthill
Orville Mason....................Walter Cartright
Alvin Belknapp....................Joseph Egginton
Reuben Jepson....................Philip Van Zant
Burton Burleigh....................Bert Wilcox
Bailiff....................Robert Emory
Clerk of Court....................Bert Emmors
Judge Oberwaltzer....................William Balfour
Foreman of Jury....................Joseph Lighthill
A Guard....................Hilton Josephs
Mrs. Asa Griffiths....................Gertrude Ritchie
Reverend MacMillan....................William Balfour
Second Guard....................Robert Emory
Third Guard....................Harry Watts

Prologue—A Street. Act I.—Scene 1—Home of Samuel Griffiths, Lycurgus, New York. 2—Clyde's Office. 3—Roberta Alden's Room. Act II.—Scene 1—Griffiths' Home. 2—Roberta's Room. 3—Dr. Glenn's Office. Act III.—Scene 1—Clyde's Room. 2—Big

Bittern Lake. 3—Camp Near Twelfth Lake. Act IV.—Scene 1—Supreme Court. 2—Auburn Prison.
Staged by George Greenberg.

See "The Best Plays of 1926-27."

THE VENETIAN GLASS NEPHEW

(8 performances)

A little opera by Eugene Bonner; libretto based on a novel by Elinor Wylie, adapted by Ruth Hale. Produced by Walter Greenough at the Vanderbilt Theatre, New York, February 23, 1931.

Cast of characters—

Peter Innocent, Cardinal Bon....................Dodd Mehan
Rosalba Bernis....................Mary Silveira
Chevalier De Chastelneuf....................George Houston
Virginio....................Louis Yaeckel
Alvise Luna....................Edgar Stehli
Angelo Querini....................Raymond Huntley
Count Carlo Gozzi....................Gage Clarke
Maria Loredan....................Lee Burgess
Bianca Contarini....................Joan Carter-Waddell

Six Masquers:

Columbina Pisani....................Dorothy Johnson
Isabella Moncenigo....................Gretchen Haller
Zerbinetta Tron....................Adele Sanderson
Pedrolino Zorzi....................Florence Rand
Arlechino Bembo....................Roy Mace
Scaramuccia Balbi....................Norman Oberg

Act I.—Scene 1—Palazzo Querini, Venice. 2—House of Alvise Luna, Venice. 3—Palazzo Querini. Act II.—Scene 1—Garden of Querini's Villa, Altichiere. 2—Workroom of the Brothers Dubois. 3—House of Virginio and Rosalba, Venice.
Staged by Walter Greenough.

Cardinal Bon wishes for a nephew but fears one of flesh and blood might be tempted into sin. His friend the Chevalier de Chastelneuf, a magician of parts, thereupon has a full-grown nephew blown of Venetian glass and supplied with lungs and a heart. Trouble arises when Virginio, the glass one, falls in love with Rosalba Bernis, who is frankly fleshly. Unhappy because she cannot even hug Virginio without breaking his arm, Rosalba agrees to walk into a fiery furnace and have herself baked into porcelain. After which she and Virginio live happily.

A WOMAN DENIED

(37 performances)

A drama in three acts adapted from the Italian of Gennaro Mario Curci by Jean Bart. Produced by Jimmie Cooper at the Ritz Theatre, New York, February 25, 1931.

Cast of characters—

Paolo Vanni....................................McKay Morris
Sandro....................................Donald Douglas
Lina....................................Genevieve Belasco
Lewis....................................Horace Sinclair
Don Carlos Von Weigand....................................Jules Epailly
Barbara....................................Mary Nash
Gomez....................................Donald Kirke
Riccardo Vanni....................................Herbert Braggiotti
Acts I, II and III.—Studio of Paolo Vanni, Paris, France.
Staged by Lee Elmore.

Paolo Vanni, an Italian artist struggling in Paris, picks up Barbara at a ball and, because she is drunk and clings to him, carries her into his studio. As she lies before the fire drying out Paolo is inspired to paint her as "The Drunkard." The painting brings him fame. When Barbara is sober he does her as "The Madonna." This gets him into the academy. Thereafter he can paint nothing successfully without the help of Barbara as model. He loves her but is intent upon remaining true to his wife in Rome. Barbara seeks to devil Paolo into taking her into his life, and might have succeeded if she had not been strangled by another model, young Sandro, who thought she had also deceived him.

PAGING DANGER

(4 performances)

A comedy in three acts by Claire Carvalho and Leighton Osmun. Produced by Staton and McKay at the Booth Theatre, New York, February 26, 1931.

Cast of characters—

Dawson....................................Henry Mortimer
Mrs. Dawson....................................Ann Dere
Kenneth Holden....................................Ray Collins
Ronnie Van Horn....................................Eric Dressler
Marie....................................Dolores De Monde
Mrs. Stafford....................................Betty Blythe
Shanley Jones....................................Gordon Westcott
Jeanette....................................Renee Cartier
Dominick....................................Joseph Errico

Miss Maynard....................................Natalie Norris
Mrs. Wellington Jones....................Edna Archer Crawford
Mr. Parkinson.................................William Dorbin
Monsieur Picard..............................George Le Soir
Brant...Ross Snow
Acts I, II and III.—Home of Ronnie Van Horn, Westchester, N. Y.

Ronnie Van Horn, son of a millionaire, gets drunk just after reading a work on will power. While drunk he is assailed by the idea that he can make Marie, the parlormaid, believe she is a princess. To convince her that she is he sends her out to buy herself a Rolls-Royce and a lot of diamonds. Marie takes Ronnie at his word, just to teach him a lesson. Ronnie's social climbing sister also accepts Marie as a princess and invites all her society friends to meet her. When the deception is exposed it turns out that Marie really is a princess, that the butler is her uncle, and the housekeeper her aunt. They are all members of the Russian nobility forced into service by the war.

GREATER LOVE

(8 performances)

A drama in three acts by Bruce Spaulding (Mary Hay) and Anthony Baird (Nella Steward). Produced by Martin Jones at the Liberty Theatre, New York, March 2, 1931.

Cast of characters—

Pamela Cornish..............................Catherine Proctor
Glen Cornish....................................Edith Meiser
Peter Cornish.......................................Mary Hay
Stephen Gordon................................John Breeden
Colin Cornish...................................Fred Sullivan
Clara...Muriel Stone
Oliver Cornish..............................Douglas Gillmore
Cynthia Wiman................................Brenda Dahlen
Holden Simms.....................................Jack McKee
Acts I, II and III.—Living Room of the Cornish Home, Westchester, Pennsylvania.
Staged by Gabriel Beer-Hoffman.

Oliver Cornish, facially disfigured in the war, returns to his home to discover that he is repellent to all the members of his family save his twin sister, "Peter," and his ne'er-do-well father. Cynthia Wiman, his fiancée, breaks her engagement and marries another man. "Peter" makes every sacrifice to protect her brother. The father finally kills himself. Vienna surgeons make Oliver whole and handsome again and he would run away with Cynthia, despite her treatment of him, but "Peter" also saves him from that.

PRIVILEGE CAR

(47 performances)

A melodrama in three acts by Edward J. Foran and Willard Keefe. Produced by Saul Abraham and William Fields at the Forty-eighth Street Theatre, New York, March 3, 1931.

Cast of characters—

J. B. DeWitt....................................Gordon Gunnis
Grab....................................William Foran
Cornets....................................Alan Bunce
Emptyhead....................................Elisha Cook, Jr.
Hawk....................................J. Hammond Dailey
Dan....................................Frederick Malcolm
Baraboo Slim....................................Harry Tyler
Jim Colton....................................William Corbett
Nell....................................Claire Devine
Jean Steel....................................Ruth Easton
Brady....................................James Meighan
Mayme Taylor....................................Lee Patrick
Parrish....................................Paul Guilfoyle
Mrs. Long....................................Genevieve Paul
Mr. Long....................................Tom Leeds
Freeman....................................J. Harry Jenkins
Workman....................................Frank Horton
Larson....................................Carl Judd
Trainman....................................James T. Ford

Acts I, II and III.—Privilege Car of Colton & Steel Circus.
Staged by Melville Burke.

"Cornets," a youthful adventurer from upstate New York, joins a band trouping with the Colton & Steel circus, falls in love with Jean Steel, niece of the proprietor and heir to half the show, and finds his way blocked by a variety of tough grafters, including Parrish Hawkins, son of the privilege car man and but recently out of jail. Young Hawkins manages to have a charge of rape shifted from himself to Cornets; a mob threatens the circus and Cornets has a difficult time clearing himself and taking Jean away with him.

GIVE ME YESTERDAY

(72 performances)

A drama in three acts by A. A. Milne. Produced by Charles Hopkins at the Charles Hopkins Theatre, New York, March 4, 1931.

Cast of characters—

The Rt. Hon. R. Selby Mannock, M.P....................................Louis Calhern
Lady Jane Mannock....................................Gladys Hanson

Arthur Mannock....................................Edward Crandall
Freda Mannock......................................Jane Wyatt
Digby..Robert Vivian
Edward Eversley....................................Edward Rigby
A Maid...Natalie Browning
Bertie Capp..Eric Blore
John Reader..Hugh Miller
Lord Carchester....................................Montague Shaw
Nite...Lawrence Vivian
Squier...Peter Donald, Jr.
Buteus Maiden......................................Nancy Kelly
Sally..Sylvia Field

Act I.—Cavendish Square. Act II.—Wildwood, Yorkshire. Act III.—In the Center of Cavendish Square.
Staged by Charles Hopkins.

The Rt. Hon. R. Selby Mannock, M.P., having married the politically-minded and inordinately ambitious Lady Jane, is brought suddenly face to face with what success has done to him when a boytime playmate recalls his past and the girl he left behind in Yorkshire. On a campaign tour in his old home country the Hon. Mannock dreams dreams of his youth. Next day he meets Sally, the girl. Their love is as strong as ever. The Hon. Mannock promises to go back to London, arrange everything and come back for Sally. In London he finds an appointment as Secretary of the Exchequer awaiting him and again success closes in on him.

BLOSSOM TIME

(29 performances)

A musical comedy in three acts adapted by Dorothy Donnelly from the original of Willner and Reichert; music adapted by Sigmund Romberg from the melodies of Franz Shubert and H. Berte. Revived by the Messrs. Shubert at the Ambassador Theatre, New York, March 4, 1931.

Cast of characters—

Kupelweiser..Harry Rabke
Vogl...Joseph Wilkins
Von Schwind..Joseph Toner
Binder...Maurice Tyler
Erkman...Trueman Gaige
Domeyer..Walter Wahl
Greta..Marice Christie
Bella Bruna..Gladys Baxter
Count Sharnoff.....................................Joseph Lertora
Mitzi..Greta Alpeter
Kitzi..Marie Starner
Fritzi...Mary Wilkins
Franz Schubert.....................................John Charles Gilbert
Kranz..Robert Lee Allen
Baron Von Schober..................................Clifford Newdahl
Violinist..Howard Samples
Mrs. Kranz...Evelyn Reide
Novotny..Robert O'Connor

Mrs. Colburg....................................Millie Freeman
Dancers: Gerry Dean, Stella Doyle, Georgia MacTaggart, Herta Rittell, Inez Goetz, Peggy Baldwin
Show Girls: Peggy Scevioure, Dorothy Drum, Agatha Phillips, Marie Craigin, Ann Johnson, Eleanor Lewis
Act I.—Prater Park in Vienna. Act II.—Drawing Room in the House of Kranz. Act III.—Franz Schubert Lodgings.
Staged by Edward Scanlon.

See "The Best Plays of 1921-22."

* AS HUSBANDS GO

(124 performances)

A comedy in three acts by Rachel Crothers. Produced by John Golden at the John Golden Theatre, New York, March 5, 1931.

Cast of characters—

Lucile Lingard....................................Lily Cahill
Ronald Derbyshire....................................Geoffrey Wardwell
Emmie Sykes....................................Catharine Doucet
Hippolitus Lomi....................................Roman Bohnen
Maître D'Hôtel....................................François Steyaert
Waiter....................................Bruno Wick
Charles Lingard....................................Jay Fassett
Wilbur....................................Buddy Proctor
Christine....................................Mathilde Baring
Peggy Sykes....................................Marjorie Lytell
Jake Canon....................................Robert Foulk
Prologue—A Café in Paris. Acts I, II and III.—Living Room in the Lingard House, Ten Miles from Dubuque, Iowa.
Staged by Rachel Crothers.

See page 186.

THE ADMIRABLE CRICHTON

(56 performances)

A satirical comedy by Sir James Matthews Barrie. Revived by George C. Tyler in association with the Erlanger interests at the New Amsterdam Theatre, New York, March 9, 1931.

Cast of characters—

The Earl of Loam....................................Hubert Druce
Hon. Ernest Woolley....................................Ernest Glendinning
Rev. John Treherne....................................J. C. Dunn
Lord Brocklehurst....................................Gerald Hamer
A Naval Officer....................................Harry Joyner
Mr. Crichton....................................Walter Hampden
Tompsett....................................William Dale
Lady Mary Lasenby....................................Fay Bainter
Lady Catherine Lasenby....................................Mary Hone
Lady Agatha Lasenby....................................Phyllis Connard
Countess of Brocklehurst....................................Effie Shannon
Fisher....................................Oriel Ross

Tweeny....................................Estelle Winwood
Servants at the Earl of Loam's by the Following Ladies and Gentlemen: Guy Cunningham, Clay Cody, Sybil Campbell, Vivian MacGill, Madge North, Norma Lytell, Judith Elder, George Smithfield, Alice Earhardt, Maurice Lord, Charles Chase.

Acts I and IV.—Reception Room in Lord Loam's House. London. Acts II and III.—On the Island.

Staged by William Postance.

First produced in 1903 with William Gillette as the perfect butler, William Crichton, who proves himself much the best man of the party when the Earl of Loam's family is wrecked on an out-of-the-way tropical island. The Earl is a great stickler for social equality in London, but on the island he would assume a leadership Crichton soon proves he is not fit to hold. After three years away from civilization Lady Mary Lazenby is flattered by Crichton's proposal of marriage, but next act they are rescued and once back in London everybody reverts to type. The play was adapted to the screen by Cecil DeMille under the title of "Male and Female."

SIMPLE SIMON

(16 performances)

A musical comedy by Ed Wynn and Guy Bolton; music by Richard Rodgers; lyrics by Lorenz Hart. Revived by Ed Wynn at the Majestic Theatre, New York, March 9, 1931.

Cast of characters—

Fingy (Bluebeard's Henchman)........................Albert Baron
Bert Blue (Bluebeard)..............................Gil Squires
Olee King (King Cole)........................William H. White
Gilly Flower } ....(Jack and Jill)............ { Laine Blaire
Jack Horner } { David Breen
Policeman....................................Paul Butterworth
Simon (Keeper of Information and Newspaper Shop).....Ed. Wynn
Gladys Dove...................................Frieda Mierse
Jonah (Genii)........................Master George Offerman
Popper..James McKay
Elaine King (Cinderella)......................Margaret Breen
Tony Prince (Prince Charming)....................Jack Squires
Otto Prince...................................Harry Shannon
Sal..Wini Shaw
The Horse.......................Joseph Schrode—Pete La Della
Première Danseuse..............................Harriet Hoctor
The Giant Head...................................Frank De Witt
The Frog.......................................William Ferry
Peter Pan...Renee Rivir
Little Boy Blue.................................Ruth Simmons
Red Riding Hood.................................Mimi Sherman
Wolf...Irma Montague
Goldylocks...................................Frances Williams
Puss in Boots...........................Virginia MacNaughton
Three Bears..........Muriel DeLova, Peggy Driscoll, Betty Blake
Hansel...Flora Taylor
Gretel..Muriel Harrison

Jazz..........Laine Blaire
Dog..........Jerrie Cragin
Dish..........Patricia Palmer
Bo-Peep..........Marie Shea
Fairy Goddesses..........Billie Seward, Buff Bullard, Barbara Hamilton, Jerry Rogers, Adele Smith, Lulu Gray
Snow Queen..........Villi Milli
Rapunsel..........Frieda Mierse

Act. I.—Scene 1—Coney Island. 2—Ferryman Alley. 3—Boundary Line Between Dulina and Gayleria. 4—Hunting Room in King Cole's Palace. 5—Forest at Christmas. 6—Fairyland in the Woods. 7—In the Clouds. Act II.—Scene 1—Corner Drug Store in Dullville. 2—Outside the Walled City. 3—Kissing Forest. 4—Inside the Citadel. 5—Ferryman Alley. 6—Magic Hall.

Staged by Seymour Hicks.

See "The Best Plays of 1929-30."

GRAY SHADOW

(39 performances)

A melodrama in three acts by Roger Wheeler. Produced by Edward Sargent Brown at the New Yorker Theatre, New York, March 10, 1931.

Cast of characters—

Uriah Fogg..........Le Roi Operti
Old Patch..........Joseph Kennedy
Toby Rumple..........George W. Williams
Pokey..........Lon Carter
Dr. Peabody..........Lewis Waller
Joe Pepper..........Claude Cooper
Mrs. Melley..........Rebekah Garden
Diana Trent..........Annabella Murray
Martin Scott..........Richard Nicholls
Gray Shadow..........William Townshend
Luigi..........John Fulco
Inspector Matthews..........Rupert H. Clarke
Jim..........James Marr

Act I.—Village Churchyard in Tyebridge. Acts II and III.—Dr. Peabody's Library at Holden House.

Staged by Edward Sargent Brown.

The Gray Shadow is a ghostly somebody who has schemed to collect one hundred and fifty thousand dollars on the life insurance policies of old Edward Holden, recently murdered as a part of the Gray Shadow's conspiracy. The Shadow is baffled in the end, but by whom or what this reporter did not wait to see. He thinks, however, that Diana Trent, a pretty ward who had taken quite a shine to a young insurance company investigator, Martin Scott, came in for a good share of the money as well as all Martin's love.

NAPI

(21 performances)

A comedy in three acts adapted by Brian Marlow from the German of Julius Berstl. Produced by L. Lawrence Weber at the Longacre Theatre, New York, March 11, 1931.

Cast of characters—

Meneval	Albert Van Dekker
Constant	Dallas Welford
Lackey	H. H. Gibbs
Officer of the Day	Stephen Courtleigh
Margot	Bernice Elliott
Lady-in-Waiting	Vera Fuller Mellish
The Empress	Frieda Inescort
Marshal Duroc	Averell Harris
Dr. Corvisart	Wallis Clark
Aristide Latouche	Ernest Truex
Jeanne Duval	Beatrice Blinn
La George, of the Comédie Française	Peggy Shannon
Prince Sapieha	Frank Wilcox

Acts I and III.—A Room in the Tuileries. Act II.—Boudoir of La George.
Staged by Ernest Truex.

Aristide Latouche, clerk in a lace shop in Paris, bears so striking a resemblance to Napoleon Bonaparte that Marshal Duroc, of Napoleon's staff, conceives the idea of having Latouche impersonate the Emperor. It is Duroc's scheme to send the fake Napoleon to the apartment of La George of the Comédie Française where he is to break off the Emperor's affair with the actress. As he emerges from the George apartment Latouche will probably be assassinated by Napoleon's enemies, but this will bring the enemies into the open so Duroc may cause their arrest. Latouche unwittingly agrees to the program, but after he meets the actress he changes his plans. On her invitation he stays the night in her apartment. Next morning the assassins do attack him, but he escapes. Thereupon the Empress Josephine, relieved to find there really is a second Napoleon, helps Aristide out of his scrape.

THE HOUSE BEAUTIFUL

(108 performances)

A drama in three acts by Channing Pollock. Produced by Crosby Gaige at the Apollo Theatre, New York, March 12, 1931.

Cast of characters—

Guy Stayton.....Roy Gordon
Elbert Baxter.....Ray Walburn
Jennifer Davis.....Mary Phillips
Archibald Davis.....James Bell
Hulda.....Ellen E. Lowe
Nina Baxter.....Helen Flint
Dr. Brink.....Joseph Baird
Sam Dreyer.....Lionel Stander
Martha Wiley.....Jane Seymour
Richard Davis.....Reed Brown, Jr.
Richard, the Boy.....Norman Williams
Vivian Baxter.....Annie Laurie Jacques

Acts I, II and III.—Home of the Davises, West Hills, N. J.
Staged by Worthington Miner.

Archibald and Jennifer Davis marry on Archibald's $40 a week as a bond salesman and buy a lot in West Hills, N. J. On the lot they build a house which grows, in Jennifer's vision, into a house beautiful because love and loyalty dwell there. Jennifer visions Archie as a true knight errant and sees him, a modern Sir Galahad, buckling on his armor each morning to catch the 8.20 and fare forth into the wicked city to meet the Black Knight, who is his boss. Archie is tempted by grafters and assailed by his own sense of failure, but he never loses caste with Jennifer. When he dies she waits patiently to join him in that heaven to which she visions him ascending.

MIRACLE AT VERDUN

(49 performances)

A drama with screen accompaniment in seven scenes by Hans Chlumberg; translated by Julian Leigh. Produced by the Theatre Guild at the Martin Beck Theatre, New York, March 16, 1931.

Cast of characters—

Smith.....Caryl Gillin
Jackson.....Robert Middlemass
Sharpe.....J. W. Austin
Marshall.....Thomas A. Braidon
Miss Greeley.....Shirley Gale
Dorothy.....Valerie Cossart
Violet.....Hilda Case
Verron.....Owen Meech
Mme. Verron.....Marion Stephenson
Remusat.....Jules Epailly
Lerat.....Carlos Zizold
Mme. Lerat.....Miriam Elias
Mme. Duvernois.....Germaine Giroux
Dr. Paetz.....Edward Arnold
Frau Paetz.....Helene Salinger
Von Henkel.....Con Macsunday
Frau Von Henkel.....Joan Grahn
Fritzchen.....David Gorcey
Brohl.....Max Willenz

Spaerlich.......................................Sydney Stavro
Heydner...Claude Rains
Pillwein, an Austrian...........................John Hoysradt
Old Italian.....................................Salvatore Zito
Young Italian...................................Ari Kutai
Old Japanese....................................J. Kunihara
Young Japanese..................................Hanaki Yoshiwara
First Priest....................................Juan de la Cruz
Second Priest...................................Douglas Garden
Mazas, Tourist Guide............................Georges Magis
Vernier, Cemetery Attendant.....................Edouard La Roche
Messenger.......................................Claude Rains

A Company of the Resurrected

Wittekind.......................................Hans Hansen
Hessel..Alexander Ivo
Weber...Jacob Bleifer
Sonneborn.......................................Walter Dressel
Schroeder.......................................George Brant
Lehmann...Michael Rosenberg
Schmidt...Anthony Baker
Vaudemont, the Captain..........................John Gerard
André Verron....................................Peter Wayne
Morel...Clement Wilenchick
Dubois..Ali Youssoff
Roubeau...Akim Tamiroff
Baillard..Percy Woodley
General Larmarque, French War Minister..........Carlos Zizold
General Von Gadenau, German War Minister........Max Willenz
French Officers.................Alexander Danarov, John Hoysradt
German Officers..............Joseph Lazarovici, Francis Schaeger
Vernier, Cemetery Attendant.....................Edouard La Roche

Scene 2—Celebrations in Paris and Berlin—1934

Premier Delcampe................................Jules Epailly
Interrupter.....................................Georges Magis
Radio Announcer.................................John Hoysradt
Reich Chancellor Overtuesch.....................Edward Arnold
Interrupter.....................................Jacob Bleifer

Scene 3—Bedrooms in Paris, Berlin, London

Premier Delcampe................................Jules Epailly
Odette Lefevre..................................Germaine Giroux
Reich Chancellor Overtuesch.....................Edward Arnold
Frau Overtuesch.................................Helene Salinger
Lord Grathford, English Prime Minister..........J. W. Austin
Leeds, His Valet................................Thomas A. Braidon

Scene 4—A Field on the Suippe

The Resurrected Look Upon the World

Mme. Vadinet....................................Miriam Elias
Jacques, an Apprentice..........................John Hoysradt
Jeannette.......................................Germaine Giroux
Policeman.......................................Georges Magis
Pastor..Juan de la Cruz
First Villager..................................Edouard La Roche
Second Villager.................................Hilda Case
Third Villager..................................Martin Cravath
Morel...Clement Wilenchick

Scene 6—Quai D'Orsay

The World Looks Upon the Resurrected

Lord Grathford, Prime Minister of England.......J. W. Austin
Michel Delcampe, Premier of France..............Jules Epailly
Dr. Overtuesch, Chancellor of the German Reich....Edward Arnold
Lamparenne, Prime Minister of Belgium...........Claude Rains
General Lamarque, French War Minister...........Carlos Zizold
General Von Gadenau, German War Minister........Max Willenz
Clarkson, American Ambassador...................Robert Middlemass
Bertolotti, Italian Ambassador..................Salvatore Zito

Yoshitomo....................................J. Kunihara
Cardinal Dupin, Archbishop of Paris..............Juan de la Cruz
Superintendent General Palm.....................Douglas Garden
Chief Rabbi Dr. Sorgenreich......................Sidney Stavro
Professor Dr. Steppach, Scientific Authority........Con Macsunday
The Secretary..............................Thomas A. Braidon
A Young Prelate..................................Ari Kutai
Tsatanaku, Japanese Premier...................Hanaki Yoshiwara
Representatives of Various Nations
Roumania.................................Robert Deviera
Yugo-Slavia................................Joseph Green
Poland...................................Lucien Girardin
Czecho-Slovakia.............................Mario Majeroni
Trolliet } ......of Lamparenne's Group....... { Edouard La Roche
Charrier } { Georges Magis

Scene 7—Petit Cimetière at Verdun

Staged by Herbert J. Biberman.

An ex-soldier in the German army named Heydner revisits the battlefields in France in 1934 during the celebration of the twentieth anniversary of the great war. At the little cemetery of Verdun, where French and German soldiers were buried in the same grave, Heydner rests near the shaft erected to the unknown dead while the other tourists go on to other parts of the burial ground. As his thoughts grow reminiscent and bitter he sees an angel of the Lord appear and announce the resurrection of the dead. Thereafter soldiers arise from their graves and march away to take their old places in the world. In succeeding adventures they find the world, after the lapse of years, completely readjusted to their loss. Disillusioned and unhappy they return to their graves. Heydner awakens and rejoins the tourists, on their way to the evening celebration in Paris.

THE WONDER BAR

(76 performances)

A continental cabaret drama in two sections, adapted from the German of Geza Herczeg and Karl Farkas by Irving Ceasar and Aben Kandel; music by Robert Katscher. Produced by the Messrs. Shubert in association with Morris Gest at the Bayes Theatre, New York, March 17, 1931.

Cast of characters—

Richard.....................................Gustav Rolland
Marcel.....................................Auguste Armini
Prince Nikolas Engalitcheff.............Prince Nikolas Engalitcheff
Mary Evans.................................Jean Newcombe
Elmer Evans................................C. Jay Williams
Sonya....................................Antonina Fechner
Billie....................................Dagmar Oakland
Rosette.....................................Adriana Dori
Martha.....................................Elvira Trabert

Helen Brown....................................Laura Pierpont
Edgar Banks....................................Henry Crosby
Monsieur Al....................................Al Jolson
Inez....................................Trini
Ramon Colmano....................................Rex O'Malley
Lord Cauldwell....................................Arthur Treacher
François Vale....................................Stuart Casey
Oscar Wayne....................................Clarence Harvey
Liane Duval....................................Wanda Lyon
Pierre Duval....................................Vernon Steele
A Gendarme....................................Roman Arnoldoff
Monsieur Simon....................................Adrian Rosley
Electra Pivonka....................................Patsy Kelly
Charlie....................................Al Siegal
A Rajah....................................Mohammid Ibrahim
Count Rugtoffsky....................................Michael Dalmatoff
Signora Medea Columbara...............Signora Medea Columbara
Benno Bondy....................................Hugo Brucken
Mrs. Soloman....................................Bertha Walden
Sam Soloman....................................Leo Hoyt
Pascal....................................Armand Cortez
Baroness Rosseau....................................Marie Hunt

Acts I and II.—The Wonder Bar, a Parisian Night Club.
Staged by William Mollison.

Monsieur Al, proprietor of the Wonder Bar, a popular night club in Paris, has considerable trouble with Ramon Colmano, gigolo and dancer, who has tired of his dancing partner, Inez, and plans to desert her for Liane Duval, a married woman from whom he already has stolen a valuable necklace. Ramon carries out his threat, takes Liane away with him, makes a dancer of her and otherwise ruins her life. A year later Ramon and Liane return to the Wonder Bar looking for a job. Al gives them the job and also gets even with Ramon.

THE SILENT WITNESS

(80 performances)

A drama in three acts by Jack De Leon and Jack Celestin. Produced by Lee Shubert at the Morosco Theatre, New York, March 23, 1931.

Cast of characters—

Anthony Howard....................................Anthony Kemble Cooper
Sylvia Pierce....................................Kathleen Lowry
Lady Howard....................................Ann Shoemaker
Sir Austin Howard, Bart....................................Lionel Atwill
Doreen Smith....................................Kay Strozzi
Gordon Smith....................................Fortunio Bonanova
Inspector Robins....................................Reginald Barlow
Mr. Justice Bond....................................Thurlow Bergen
Arthur Drinton, K.C....................................Jerome Lawler
Sir John Lawson, K.C....................................T. Wigney Percyval
Clerk of the Court....................................Francis Compton
Henry Hammer....................................Harold De Becker
Augustus Percy Carlton....................................Herbert Standing
Colonel Grayson....................................George Graham

Horace Ward....................................Geoffrey Harwood
Inspector Phillips....................................Milano Tilden
Act I.—Sir Austin Howard's Study. Act II.—The Old Bailey. Act III.—Private Office of Colonel Grayson in Scotland Yard.
Staged by Harry Wagstaffe Gribble.

Anthony Howard, having strangled Doreen Smith when he discovers that she has been playing him false, rushes home in a state of nerves. Confessing what he has done to his father and mother, Sir Austin and Lady Howard, the boy is on the point of collapse when Sir Austin agrees to meet the police and try to save his son. Anthony goes to trial for the murder and is about to prove an alibi when new and damaging evidence suddenly places his life in danger. Still further surprising evidence from a silent witness results in his acquittal.

GETTING MARRIED

(48 performances)

A comedy without intermission, by George Bernard Shaw. Revived by the Theatre Guild at the Guild Theatre, New York, March 30, 1931.

Cast of characters—

Mrs. Bridgenorth....................................Margaret Wycherly
William Collins....................................Henry Travers
The General (Boxer)....................................Ernest Cossart
Lesbia Grantham....................................Irby Marshall
Reginald Bridgenorth....................................Hugh Buckler
Leo....................................Dorothy Gish
The Bishop....................................Reginald Mason
St. John Hotchkiss....................................Hugh Sinclair
Cecil Sykes....................................Romney Brent
Edith Bridgenorth....................................Peg Entwistle
Oliver Cromwell Soames (Anthony)....................................Ralph Roeder
Mrs. George Collins....................................Helen Westley
The Beadle....................................Oscar Stirling
The Scene is in the Norman Kitchen in the Palace of the Bishop of Chelsea. The Action of the Play is Continuous, but the Curtain is Lowered Once to Allow for an Intermission.
Staged by Philip Moeller.

Cecil Sykes and Edith Bridgenorth are about to be married when each discovers new and possibly irksome responsibilities in the married state. Cecil, knowing Edith to be an impulsive young radical, worries for fear he will be constantly in trouble settling suits for libel that may be brought against her. Edith discovers how difficult it is to divorce even a terrible husband under the British law. In seeking to compose or otherwise adjust their problems relatives and friends of the young people bring to a conference table their experiences and their beliefs. These serve to confuse rather than clarify the drawing up of a proper marriage contract. In the midst of the muddle Edith and Cecil decide to take the traditional chance. They run away and are duly married.

LADY BEYOND THE MOON

(15 performances)

A comedy in two acts by William Doyle. Produced by Ramsay Streett, Inc., at the Bijou Theatre, New York, March 31, 1931.

Cast of characters—

Courtland Prentiss.............................John Goldsworthy
Gareth St. John.................................Allen Connor
Thyrle Krone...............................Donald McClelland
Sallie Ward.......................................Ione Hutaine
Mrs. James St. John-Cushman....................Valerie Bergere
Emily Mott-Payne................................Olive Valerie
Jimmie Cushman................................Ramon Racomar
Mr. Ward.....................................Joseph Lawrence
Mrs. Ward......................................Georgia Harvey
Wendell..Albert West
Acts I, II and III.—On the Terrace of the Courtland Prentiss' Villa at Lake Como, Italy.
Staged by William Streett.

Sallie Ward, thinking to surprise her fiancé, Thyrle Krone, who has been studying music for three years in Berlin, goes to Europe and comes upon Thyrle unexpectedly at Lake Como. Sallie also reads a rumor that Thyrle is about to marry his accompanist, Emily Mott-Payne. Thinking to be revenged upon something or somebody Sallie marries Courtland Prentiss, her host, but discovers that she cannot go through with her bargain. Next day she learns that Thyrle has no intention of marrying anybody but her and flies away to Berlin with him. The husband of one awful night agrees to arrange for an annulment of his marriage.

RIGHT OF HAPPINESS

(11 performances)

A drama in three acts by Roy Daavidson. Produced by DuRoy and LeMiastre, Inc., at the Vanderbilt Theatre, New York, April 2, 1931.

Cast of characters—

Dr. Bertram Wardell..........................Herbert Rawlinson
Mary...Anne Bryan
Dr. Tusack..Alan Floud
Ruby Cartier.....................................Ruth Holden

Nikolas....................Robert DuRoy
Helen Wardell....................Anne Sutherland
Myra Wardell....................Georgine Cleveland
Sonia....................Tamara Nicoll
Hilda Spangle....................Ada May Talbot
Carl Hammer....................Robert McAfee
Acts I, II and III—In the Home of Dr. Wardell.
Staged by Benrimo.

Dr. Bertram Wardell is entertaining in America two Russian protégés, Nikolas and Sonia. Nikolas has a crooked spine and the doctor has been promising for some years to see if it cannot be straightened. By the time he gets around to it, however, Nikolas is too old. The boy, overhearing his fate, becomes embittered. He will, he decides, grab happiness where he may. When he tries to seduce the doctor's wife, however, her screams arouse the house. Nikolas is abashed and contrite as well as disappointed. He starts next day for Russia. He does not know that he is the illegitimate son of Dr. Wardell, born of the doctor's student days and nights in Moscow. Which has something to do with explaining the doctor's reluctance to operate and also why he has taken so great a personal interest in trying to keep Nikolas pure.

THE WISER THEY ARE

(40 performances)

A comedy in three acts by Sheridan Gibney. Produced by Jed Harris at the Plymouth Theatre, New York, April 6, 1931.

Cast of characters—

Jack Taft....................G. Albert Smith
Dario....................Eduardo Ciannelli
Bruce Ingram....................Osgood Perkins
Gladys Williams....................Charlotte Wynters
Mrs. Gertrude Evans....................Julia Hoyt
Trixie Ingram....................Ruth Gordon
Alfred Leete....................Geoffrey Bryant
Jerry Goodrich....................Ben Lackland
Marion Wheeler....................Terry Carroll
A Steward....................Joseph Spree
Acts I and II.—Living Room of Bruce Ingram's Penthouse Apartment, New York City. Act III.—The Sitting Room of the Bridal Suite Aboard the S.S. *Olympic*.
Staged by Jed Harris.

Bruce Ingram has lived a life filled with women and adventure. Deciding to settle down and marry, he selects his ward, Trixie Ingram, as the lady to be honored. Trixie, who has played about a bit herself, is in love with Bruce but doubtful of his constancy. To bring matters to an issue Bruce gives a farewell party to which are invited three of Trixie's suitors and three of his own ex-mistresses. At the end of the party he sings the praises of love and loyalty and carries Trixie away to the bridal suite of the *Olympic*. A few days later they find one of Trixie's boys and one of Bruce's ex-mistresses on board. There are misgivings, but finally Trixie and Bruce agree that their mutual doubt of each other will probably keep both of them true.

JOY OF LIVING

(16 performances)

A comedy in three acts by Rudolf Lothar and Hans Backwitz. Produced by G. Fred Womrath and George W. Lederer at the Masque Theatre, New York, April 6, 1931.

Cast of characters—

Marx...Taylor Holmes
Adam...Donald Brian
Ly...Betty Hanna
Moses..Bernard Gorcey
Acts I, II and III.—The Home of Gustaf Marx in Berlin.
Staged by Harry Butler.

Marx, a German plumber, makes a fortune in stocks. While drunk he meets Adam, who has just lost a fortune in the same stocks. Marx proposes that Adam serve as his butler and Adam accepts the job. Ly, a Russian refugee, bent on suicide, drifts into the Marx home. Both master and man try to gain her favors, Marx for the adventure, Adam because he falls in love. Ly takes Adam and Adam wins a good part of his lost money back on tips from Marx.

THE RAP

(61 performances)

A drama in three acts by John P. Leister. Produced by Nava Productions, Inc., at the Avon Theatre, New York, April 6, 1931.

Cast of characters—

Frederick Harrington.............................George Spelvin
Dugan..Ernest Anderson
Carter...Jack Marvin
Garrison...Paul Harvey
Clarke...Edwin Vickery
Henry..Richard N. Gregg
Anne Stewart.....................................Louise Flood

Sloane..Eugene Keith
Buchannan..Walter McCall
Acts I, II and III.—Office of Frederick Harrington, a Lawyer, Office Building, Lower Manhattan, New York.
Staged by J. J. White.

Frederick Harrington, former district attorney, working at night on a vice investigation, is returning to his office and his confidential secretary, Anne Stewart, with sandwiches when he is shot by an unknown gunman through the glass door. Carter, a reporter, helps Detective Garrison with the investigation. Suspicion first centers on Anne, who had been throttled by the gunman, but shifts to Dugan, whom Carter accuses of having forced an ex-convict to do the killing. Dugan commits suicide by jumping out a window and Garrison, fearing further exposure at the hands of Carter, kills the reporter as he is telephoning his paper.

THE GREAT MAN

(7 performances)

A comedy in three acts by Paul Hervey Fox. Produced by Lew Cantor at the Ritz Theatre, New York, April 7, 1931.

Cast of characters—

Don Esteban De Montorio...........................John Westley
Commandant Lima.............................Edward F. Nannary
Señora Isabel Castano..............................Madeline Grey
Miguela...Valerie Valaire
Donna Fernanda De Montorio......................Nedda Harrigan
Lisa De Montorio.....................................Carla Hunter
Don Carlos De La Zara..........................Theodore Hecht
Belshazzar..John Kearney
Darby Mullins..William Norton
Jeremy..Gordon McCracken
Captain O'Malley......................................Walter Woolf
Mr. Wick...John Bohn
Mr. Jones...Ralph Sanford
Act I.—Patio in the Home of the Governor, in Seaport Town in Central America. Acts II and III.—The Harbor Fort.
Staged by Jo Graham.

Captain O'Malley, a buccaneering adventurer along the Central American coast, ties up at a seaport town and sends for the governor's wife, renowned for her beauty. Donna Fernanda is flattered and rather taken with O'Malley, but her young niece, Lisa, gets in the way of her romance. Lisa, having been threatened with a convent, is determined to marry O'Malley, and follows him so persistently he is finally forced to take her away with him when the authorities heave in sight.

PETER IBBETSON

(37 performances)

A drama in four acts by John Raphael and Constance Collier. Revived by Lee Shubert at the Shubert Theatre, New York, April 8, 1931.

Cast of characters—

Madge Plunket	Helen Tenney
Diana Vivash	Mary Newnham-Davis
Guy Mainwaring	Everett Ripley
Charlie Plunket	Patrick Glasgow
Mrs. Glyn	Alice John
Mrs. Deane	Valerie Taylor
Mr. Lintot	Clifford Walker
The Bishop	Stephen Wright
Footman	Lloyd Taylor
Colonel Ibbetson	George Nash
Peter Ibbetson	Dennis King
Raphael Merridew	Henry Carvill
Lady Gray	Nancy Lewis Waller
Mary, Duchess of Towers	Jessie Royce Landis
Misses Fenwick	Phyllis Wilbourn, Mabel Gore
Achille	Joseph Romantini
Major Duquesnois	Wallis Clark
A Sister of Charity	Eileen Byron
Victorine	Henriette Amiard
Mme. Seraskier	Jeanne Guise
Mimsey Seraskier	Anna Marie Barrie
Gogo Pasquier	Freddie Stange
M. Pasquier de la Mariere	Richard Lambart
Mme. Pasquier de la Mariere	Jean Fullarton
Crockett	Henry Carvill
Prison Chaplain	Clifford Walker
Turnkey	Philip Cary Jones
Warden	Lloyd Taylor
Governor	Charles Mussett

Guests: Josepha Chekova, Maxine Arnold, Claire Stange, Mary Lane, Mildred Spencer, Reneice Buck, Jack Daniels, John B. Riley, Peter Martin, Helen Walpole.

Staged by Constance Collier.

Peter Ibbetson and Mary, Duchess of Towers, meet years after they were playmates and realize their complete and never ceasing love one for the other. To overcome the distress of a forced separation they revive their childhood game of "dreaming true." By going to sleep with their hands back of their heads and their feet crossed, and thinking very hard of where they want to be, they are able to project themselves into a dream world where they can meet. Even after Peter is sent to prison for life, when he kills his uncle for an insult to his mother, it is possible for him to bear his fate happily because some part of each day he spends with his true love in dreamland.

DRACULA

(8 performances)

A drama adapted by Hamilton Deane and John L. Balderstone from the novel by Bram Stoker. Revived by O. E. Wee at the Royale Theatre, New York, April 13, 1931.

Cast of characters—

Wells.....Alfreda Sill
Jonathan Harker.....Arnold Daly
Dr. Seward.....William Melville
Abraham Van Helsing.....Maurice Morris
R. M. Renfield.....Edward Forbes
Lucy Seward.....Marcella Gaudel
Butterworth.....William Olathe Miller
Count Dracula.....Courtney White

Act I.—Library of Dr. Seward's Sanatorium, Purley, England. Act II.—Lucy's Boudoir. Act III.—Scene 1—Sanatorium. 2—A Vault.
Staged by Ira Hards.

See "The Best Plays of 1927-28."

* PRECEDENT

(72 performances)

A drama in three acts by I. J. Golden. Produced by Sidney Harmon at the Provincetown Theatre, New York, April 14, 1931.

Cast of characters—

Delaney, a Labor Organizer.....Royal Dana Tracey
Mrs. Delaney.....Ellen Hall
Preston, Pres. Queen City Railway Co.....Walter Green
His Secretary.....Lee Nugent
Graham, Editor *Gazette*.....William Gregory
Stewart.....Frank Ford
Riley, Queen City District Attorney.....William Bonelli
Mrs. Evans.....Nell Harrison
Police Officer.....James Wright
Maybelle Jones.....Louise White
Rossman.....John Bennett
Fremont, Editor *Dispatch*.....Clyde Franklin
Jim.....Ira Silver
Judge McInerny.....Kirk Brown
Callahan, Defense Attorney.....Charles Harrison
Judge Hunter, State Supreme Court Justice.....Geo. Farren
Governor.....Ben Roberts
Travers.....Charles Newsom
Mrs. Compton.....Elwyn Harvey
Dr. Harris.....Jess Sydney
Ketcham.....George Price

Act I.—Queen City. 1916. Scene 1—Delaney's Home. 2—Preston's Office. 3—Preston's Office, Day of Preparedness Parade. 4—Queen City Jail. 5—Maybelle Jones' Room. 6—A Courtroom. Act II.—Fremont's Office. Act III.—Governor's Library. Epilogue—In Front of a Prison Cell, Fifteen Years Later.
Staged by Walter Hart.

Delaney, a labor organizer, is threatening to organize a strike against the Queen City Railway Co. Preston, president, and other officers of the company determine to frame Delaney. When, later, a preparedness day parade is held in Queen City a bomb is thrown which kills ten persons. Through the connivance of Railway Company officials and Riley, district attorney, who owes his election to the company, Delaney is arrested and enough perjured testimony bought to convict him. He is tried and sentenced to death. Fremont, crusading newspaper editor, works with Callahan, attorney for Delaney, to dig up new evidence that proves Delaney to have been a mile from the scene of the bombing the day of the parade, and to expose the perjured testimony at the trial. The governor refuses a pardon, but commutes Delaney's sentence to life imprisonment. Delaney is still waiting for justice at the play's end.

SIX CHARACTERS IN SEARCH OF AN AUTHOR

(13 performances)

A comedy "in the making" translated from the Italian of Luigi Pirandello by Edward Storer. Revived by Tom Van Dycke at the Bijou Theatre, New York, April 15, 1931.

Cast of characters—

The Characters

The Father.......................................Eugene Powers
The Mother.......................................Doris Rankin
The Step-daughter................................Eleanor Phelps
The Son..Paul Guilfoyle
The Little Boy...................................Buddy Proctor
The Little Girl..................................Bebe Gilbert

The Actors

The Manager......................................Walter Connolly
The Leading Man..................................L'Estrange Millman
The Leading Lady.................................Gladys Wilson
The Juvenile.....................................Kirke Lucas
The Ingénue......................................Kate Byron
The Character Woman..............................May Gerald
Second Woman.....................................Consuelo Flowerton
Third Woman......................................Fanny Davenport
The Character Actor..............................Louis Lytten
Second Man.......................................Conrad Catsen
The Property Man.................................Clinton Corwin
The Stage Manager................................John Brown
Madame Pace......................................Ina Rorke

Scene—The Stage of a Theatre.
Staged by William W. Schorr.

See "The Best Plays of 1922-23."

MELO

(67 performances)

A drama in three acts adapted by Arthur Pollock from the French of Henri Bernstein. Produced by Lee Shubert at the Ethel Barrymore Theatre, New York, April 16, 1931.

Cast of characters—

Romaine Belcroix.....Edna Best
Marcel Blanc.....Basil Rathbone
Pierre Belcroix.....Earle Larimore
Christiane.....Ruth Abbott
Jeanne.....Marion Wells
Dr. Remy.....Harry Davenport
A Priest.....Fuller Mellish
François.....Stapleton Kent
A Professional Dancer.....John Worthington
A Gigolo.....Pierre Vistaud
A French Woman.....Henriette Douvier
Another French Woman.....Marie Maurier
A Maitre D'Hôtel.....François Amiard
A Man.....Robert Noble
Another Man.....Arthur Stenning

Act I.—Scene 1—Garden of Belcroix's Home Near Paris. 2, 4—Marcel Blanc's Studio, Paris. 3—Russian Cabaret. Act II.—Scene 1—Living Room of Belcroix's Home. 2—Marcel's Studio. 3—Pierre's Bedroom. 4, 5—On the Terrace of a Small Café. Act III.—Scene 1—Terrace of Small Café. 2—Home of a Priest. 3—Marcel's Studio.

Staged by Marcel Varnel.

The Belcroix, Romaine and Pierre, are living happily in a suburb of Paris when Pierre's boyhood friend and fellow student at the conservatoire, Marcel Blanc, comes to visit them. Romaine and Marcel are immediately attracted, each to the other. Especially Romaine. After many visits Romaine and Marcel know that they love each other helplessly. Marcel, a great violinist, is leaving on a concert tour. When he returns to Paris he will expect Romaine to be freed from his old friend, Pierre. Romaine can think of no way to be rid of her trusting husband except by poisoning him, which she tries. Caught in the act she realizes that she can neither go with Marcel or go back to Pierre. She throws herself in the Seine. Pierre and Marcel thereafter patch up their friendship, both mourning the dead Romaine.

COMPANY'S COMING

(8 performances)

A farce comedy in three acts by Alma Wilson. Produced by Stanley Sharpe at the Lyceum Theatre, New York, April 20, 1931.

Cast of characters—

Susie.....Leila Bennett
The Nameless One.....James La Curto
Mrs. Janney.....Frieda Inescort
Mr. Janney.....Lynne Overman
Mrs. Driver.....Frances Neilson
Mr. Thompson.....Sidney Riggs
Bobby Gordon.....James Spottswood
Mrs. Patterson.....Francesca Hill
Mr. Patterson.....William Black
Mrs. Boyd.....Mona Lester
Miss Mallory.....Rosalind Russell
Mr. Boyd.....William Boren
Mr. Fields.....Wilfred Clarke
Sergeant.....William Crimans
Police Officer.....Ellsworth Jones
Messenger.....Hy Glanz

Acts I, II and III.—A Furnished Apartment in a "Converted Dwelling" in Philadelphia.
Staged by Zeke Colvan.

Mr. and Mrs. Janney find themselves broke with a bridge party thrust upon them suddenly. Mrs. Janney pawns the cup on which he has won two legs as a tennis champion, expecting to get it back before the tournament on Saturday. The ticket is mislaid and the Janneys are thrown into a panic from which they are extricated at the eleventh hour. Then it rains so there cannot be any tournament.

YOUNG SINNERS

(16 performances)

A comedy in three acts by Elmer Harris. Revived by George Sharp at the New Yorker Theatre, New York, April 20, 1931.

Cast of characters—

Madge Trowbridge.....Mary Angel
Bud Springer.....Carl Frank
Betty Biddle.....Virginia Lloyd
Jimmie Stephens.....Morgan Galloway
Marie.....Sylvia Lee
Constance Sinclair.....Dorothy Appleby
Mrs. Sinclair.....Vessie Farrell
Baron von Konitz.....Alfred A. Hesse
Gene Gibson.....Jackson Halliday
John Gibson, His Father.....George Lessey
Trent.....Arthur Bowyer
Manager Apartment House.....W. W. Shuttleworth
Alice Lewis.....Astrid Alwynn
Tom Maguire.....Walter Wilson
Maggie Maguire.....Cynthia Blake
Tim.....Arthur Scanlon

Act I.—Scene 1—Sinclair Home in Florida; 2—Gene's Apartment in New York. Acts II and III.—Living Room of Gene's Camp in the Adirondacks.

See "Best Plays of 1929-30."

SCHOOL FOR VIRTUE

(7 performances)

A comedy in three acts by Arthur Ebenhack. Produced by Edward Casey at the Longacre Theatre, New York, April 21, 1931.

Cast of characters—

Bud Heasley....................................Buford Armitage
Tom Raydon....................................Robert W. Craig
Ray Graylen....................................Clarence Rock
Ron Sinton....................................William Atlee
Bill....................................J. C. Osborne
Clarinda Robbins....................................Evelyn Wade
Marg....................................Shirley Booth
Mrs. Taylor....................................Barbara Graft
Grocery Boy....................................Leopold Badis
Ladies of the Evening: Elma Mirian, Merry Wagner, Ruth Baumon and Betty Worth
Acts I, II and III.—Apartment of Bud Heasley.
Staged by Victor Morley.

Clarinda Robbins, deeply in love with Bud Heasley who, when she was quite young, had saved her life in Bucyrus, Ohio, comes to New York in search of him. She finds Bud a fast young leader of the Greenwich Village gin set, casts herself in his way and refuses to move when he seeks to save her from his friends and her less reliable impulses. Seeing he cannot be rid of her Bud undertakes to instruct Clarinda in the ways of being a good girl in a wicked community and ends by falling in love with her.

THE BELLAMY TRIAL

(16 performances)

A drama in three acts adapted by Frances Noyes Hart and Frank E. Carstarphen from Mrs. Hart's novel. Produced by E. E. Clive at the Forty-eighth Street Theatre, New York, April 22, 1931.

Cast of characters—

Mr. Farr (The Prosecuting Attorney)....................Fred Eric
Court Clerk....................................Nat Foss
Court Attendant....................Alexander Leftwich, Jr.
Doctor Stanley....................................Herbert Belmore
Mr. Lambert (for the Defense)....................E. E. Clive
The Judge....................................Ralph Roberts
Melanie Cordier....................................Clara Mahr
Douglas Thorne....................................Ian Emery
Mrs. Daniel Ives....................................Viola Roache
Elliott Farwell....................................Wilfred Seagram
Luigi Orsini....................................Henry Sherwood

Stephen Bellamy....................................Phillip Tonge
Doctor Gabriel Barretti............................Charles Esdale
Patrick Ives.......................................Ben Hoagland
Susan Ives...Ellen Southbrook
Randolph Phillips..................................Hannam Clark
Margaret Dunne.....................................Philippa Bevans
Acts I, II and III.—The Courtroom at Rosemont, N. Y.
Staged by E. E. Clive.

Stephen Bellamy and Susan Ives have been indicted and are on trial for the murder of Madeleine Bellamy, whose body had been found in the gardener's cottage of the Thorne estate with a knife wound in the heart. The trial covers a period of two days during which numerous witnesses testify for the state and the defense. The jury returns a verdict of not guilty five minutes after Mrs. Daniel Ives, mother of Susan, has confessed the murder. She resented Mrs. Bellamy's attempt to break up her daughter's home.

BRASS ANKLE

(44 performances)

A drama in three acts by DuBose Heyward. Produced by James W. Elliott at the Masque Theatre, New York, April 23, 1931.

Cast of characters—

Agnes Burton.......................................Ruth Gates
Ruth Leamer..Alice Brady
Larry Leamer.......................................Ben Smith
June Leamer..Jeanne Dante
Lee Burton...Percy Moore
Clara..Trixie Smith
Jake Darcy...Eddie Redding
Pink Jones...Bert Swor
Rev. Latterby......................................Joseph Sweeney
Mrs. Garrett.......................................Caroline Newcombe
Dr. Wainwright.....................................Lester Lonergan
Luke Jackson.......................................Al Rauh
A Neighbor...Roberta Bellinger
Acts I, II and III.—Living Room in the Leamer Home in Rivertown. A Village in the Deep South.
Staged by Harold Winston.

Ruth Leamer discovers with the birth of her second child that she has Negro blood. Larry Leamer, an ardent defender of the superiority of the white race, is crushed by the tragedy. Sensing the criticism of his friends and the resulting social ostracism of himself and family Larry hysterically proclaims his parentage of the black baby. Ruth, to save both her husband and her young daughter, calls the neighbors together and announces that she has had a Negro lover, who was the parent of her colored offspring. Larry, in rage, kills both Ruth and the infant.

DEVIL IN THE MIND

(11 performances)

A drama in six scenes adapted by William L. Laurence from the Russian of Leonid Andreyev. Produced by Leo Bulgakov Associates, Inc., at the Fulton Theatre, New York, May 1, 1931.

Cast of characters—

Dr. Anton Kerjan.................................Leo Bulgakov
Prof. Semyonov...................................Ian Wolfe
Alexey Savelov...................................Bruce Elmore
Tanya Savelov....................................Barbara Bulgakova
Sasha..Muriel Campbell
Alexander Fedorovitch............................Gage Clarke
Darya..Barbara Benedict
Vasilievne, Nurse................................Daisy Johnson
Another Nurse....................................Barbara Benedict
Dr. Sergei Pryamoy...............................Curtis Arnall
Masha..Mary Halsman
Dr. Ivan Petrov..................................Harold Johnsrud
Third Physician..................................A. O. Huhn
Orderly..Nicholas Baranoff

Scenes 1 and 4—Dr. Anton Kerjan's Study. 2 and 3—Alexey Savelov's Study. 5—Ante-Room of the State Hospital for the Criminal Insane. 6—Dr. Kerjan's Room in the Hospital.

Staged by Leo Bulgakov.

Dr. Anton Kerjan, having devoted a professional lifetime to the comparative study of ape men and men apes in an effort to discover and justify the super-man, finds himself slipping physically and mentally. His friend, Prof. Semyonov, eminent psychiatrist, advises his taking a long rest and also his seeking the society of the opposite sex. Dr. Kerjan's repressions are largely responsible, the professor believes, for his disturbed state. Dr. Kerjan flouts his friend's advice. A short time later Kerjan kills Alexey Savelov, husband of the woman he loves, is sent to an asylum for the insane and is there beset with doubt as to whether he murdered his friend because he was insane, or pretended insanity as an excuse for killing. When Tanya Savelov, his love, tells him she is convinced that he is indeed insane, Kerjan begins to believe it himself.

BETTY, BE CAREFUL

(8 performances)

A comedy in three acts by Willis Maxwell Goodhue. Produced by Gerald F. Bacon at the Liberty Theatre, New York, May 4, 1931.

Cast of characters—

Adeline West....................................Carolyne McLean
J. Cheever West....................................Edmund Elton
Elizabeth West....................................Margaret Mullen
Judy West....................................Mary Murray
Rollin North....................................Alan Goode
Benito Calles....................................Frederic Tozere
Bernie O'Kelley....................................Edgar Nelson
Pearl Meacham....................................Helene Dumas
Act I.—An Uptown Apartment. Acts II and III.—No. 68 Commerce Street.
Staged by Earle Boothe.

Elizabeth West, having been judged 98 per cent perfect in a physical culture contest, determines that she owes it to society to produce a perfect child. She selects her sister's beau, Rollin North, himself a 93 per cent perfect man, as the most likely father for her child. Rollin protests. Judy West, Elizabeth's sister, protests even harder, and J. Cheever West, their father, conspires to toss Elizabeth into contact with Benito Calles, an athletic but shy Argentinian. Benito, having been advised that American girls appreciate rough treatment, takes two drinks and, when Elizabeth approaches, hits her over the head with a boxing glove. This gives Elizabeth a slight attack of aphasia and she has no clear recollection of what happens during the second act. Therefore she is very glad to marry Benito.

THE MIKADO

(16 performances)

An operetta in two acts by W. S. Gilbert and Arthur Sullivan. Revived by the Civic Light Opera Company at Erlanger's Theatre, New York, May 4, 1931.

Cast of characters—

The Mikado of Japan....................................William Danforth
Nanki-Poo....................................Howard Marsh
Ko-Ko....................................Frank Moulan
Pooh-Bah....................................Herbert Waterous
Pish-Tush....................................William C. Gordon
Yum-Yum....................................Hizi Koyke
Pitti-Sing....................................Ethel Clark
Peep-Bo....................................Margaret Bickel
Katisha....................................Vera Ross
Act I.—Courtyard of Ko-Ko's Official Residence. Act II.—Ko-Ko's Garden.
Staged by Milton Aborn.

The last previous revival of "The Mikado" was made in 1927 by Winthrop Ames. In that cast John Barclay was the Emperor,

William Williams the Nanki-Poo, Fred Wright the Ko-Ko, William C. Gordon the Poo-Bah, and Lois Bennett the Yum-Yum. See "Best Plays of 1927-28."

HER SUPPORTING CAST

(32 performances)

A comedy in three acts by Harold Sherman. Produced by Philip Gerton at the Biltmore Theatre, New York, May 4, 1931.

Cast of characters—

Eleanor Curtis....................................Mildred McCoy
Gregory Lloyd.......................................Otto Hulett
Henry Duncan..............................Dodson L. Mitchell
Jeff Reekie...Jack Hartley
Acts I, II and III.—The Living Room of Eleanor Curtis' Apartment.
Staged by Russell Medcraft.

Eleanor Curtis, determined to capitalize her attraction for men, manages to be all things necessary to Gregory Lloyd, Henry Duncan, and Jeff Reekie. After extracting from the trio so much as each had to give, Eleanor calls them together and pays them back with the money she has made by carefully not following the advice of the broker, Henry Duncan. Eleanor thinks then to be free, but Gregory Lloyd, her prize fighting mate, throws her across his shoulder and carries her away.

* RHAPSODY IN BLACK

(40 performances)

A "symphony of blue notes and black rhythm" assembled by Lew Leslie. Produced by Blackbirds Productions, Inc., at the Sam H. Harris Theatre, New York, May 4, 1931.

Principals engaged—

Ethel Walters
Valaida
Avis Andrews
Eloise Uggams
Cecil Mack's Choir
Pike Davis' Orchestra
Joseph Steel
Blue McAllister
Al Moore
Berry Brothers
Eddie Rector
Samuel Gray
Dennis Dean
Ernest Allen
Staged by Lew Leslie.

A colored musical comedy without a chorus. Specialties alternated with songs by Cecil Mack's choir.

LONG PLAY TOURNAMENT

(5 performances)

Conducted by Walter Hartwig, under the auspices of the Manhattan Little Theatre Club, Inc., for a Samuel French prize of $1,000 and a silver cup awarded by the *Theatre Arts Monthly Magazine*. Held at the Craig Theatre, New York, May 11-15, 1931.

MONDAY, MAY 11

The Pyramid Players of Brooklyn, N. Y., present "Paradise," by Thomas Malloy and Pascal Biancardo.

The Cast—

Babe	Gladys King
Estelle	Jeanne Stucchio
Sadie	Terry Esposito
Jeanne	Dorothy Wolkind
Annette	Anne Pompa
Minerva	Edith Quinn
Dolly	Mazie Travers
Angela	Marie Pocaro
Pauline	Edna Joyce
Valenti	Lou Ladimer
Dummy	Frank Breschitz
Father	Ralph Boykin
Mother	Betty Reilly
Mitzi	Irene Rounds
Pearson	James McDonough
Garcia	Thomas Menagh
Eugene	Roland Chabot
Waiter	Paul Cort
Hecker	Pat Buchanan
Mickey	John Goodell
Doc'	Elliott Oakwood
Musician	William Paige
Big Boy	Dan Williams
Reid	Gus Bua
Harding	George Carlow
Preacher	Ralph James
Check Room Man	Ralph Lamberson

Acts I and II.—Paradise Dance Hall. Act III.—Sadie's Flat.
Directed by Pascal Biancardo.

TUESDAY, MAY 12

The Henry Players of the Playhouse of the Henry Street Settlement, Manhattan, present "The Mighty Nimrod," by Charles O'Brien Kennedy.

The Cast—

Cush, King of Shinar, Grandson of Noah and Father of Nimrod	Alex Kestenbaum
Dosha, Wife of Nimrod	Sara Manney
Keturah, Queen of Shinar and Mother of Nimrod	Ruth Silverman
Tubal Cain, Ironmonger and Dictator of Shinar	Edwin Clare
Nimrod, a Hunter	Robert Finch
Lud, Elam } Two City Men from Babel	Lawrence Braunstein, Murray Resnick
Ozem, a Master Assassin from the West	Nathan Hirsch
Dinah, Zilpah } Two Ladies from Hebron	Ruth Hamowitz, Janet Ant
Two Assistant Assassins	Joseph Rubin, Sol Krassner

Two Desirable Citizens........................ { Walter Reichberg / William Bispham }

Acts I and II.—Nimrod's Home in Shinar. Act III.—The Hall of Arrows in Nimrod's Palace on the Euphrates.

Directed by Charles O'Brien Kennedy and Eva M. Fay. Settings Designed by Frances von Bernuth and Executed in the Players' Workshop Under the Supervision of Frederick H. Little.

WEDNESDAY, MAY 13

The Morningside Players of Columbia University, Manhattan, present "If Booth Had Missed," by Arthur Goodman.

The Cast—

Abraham Lincoln....................................D. E. Plugge
John Wilkes Booth....................................M. Manisoff
Lloyd....................................Joseph Marra
Payne....................................T. D. Du Plantier
Sambo....................................Arthur Goodman
Thaddeus Stevens....................................George Glascow
Benjamin Butler....................................George U. Denny
Benjamin F. Wade....................................Samuel R. Moore
Theodore Tilton....................................George Goetz
Henry W. Davis....................................W. H. Gottlieb
George H. Pendleton....................................E. H. Hartzell
Mrs. Lincoln....................................Mary Lou Plugge
Edwin M. Stanton, Secretary of War..........Richard E. Lambert
Major Rathbone, Lincoln's Aide....................William Raphael
Call Boy....................................Franklin Irving
Tad Lincoln....................................Sidney A. Diamond
John Hay / John Nicolay } Lincoln's Secretaries.............. { Earl J. Currie / William Lovejoy }
Gideon Wells, Secretary of the Navy................A. H. Sanders
General Ulysses S. Grant..................S. Kennard Brookmire
William H. Seward, Secretary of State..............Richard Davis
Henry Stanberry, Attorney-General................T. D. DuPlantier
Hugh McCulloch, Secretary of the Treasury..........Joseph Marra
William Dennison, Postmaster-General.............Milton Forman
Andrew Johnson, Vice-President................Harold B. Putney
Chief Justice Chase....................................E. H. Hartzell

Act I.—Scene 1—White House Lawn. 2—Ford Theatre. Act II.—The White House. Act III.—The Senate Chamber.

Directed by Milton Smith.

THURSDAY, MAY 14

The Beechwood Players of Scarborough-on-Hudson, N. Y., present "Technique," by Eunice Burton Armstrong and Henry Stillman.

The Cast—

Marcia Thayer....................................Lucy Clarkson
John Thayer, Her Husband............................Judson Laire
Philip Thayer, Her Son.......................James W. Chapman
Betty Thayer, Her Daughter.......................Barbara Bement
Nancy Faulkner, Her Married Daughter............Beulah Koelsch
Tom Faulkner, Her Son-in-law......................Philip N. Ober
Minnie Lou Sanborn, Nancy's Friend..............Letitia Marshall
Dave Prentiss, Betty's Friend..........................T. Eliot Weil
Taxi Durante, Betty's Friend....................Paul R. B. Pierson
Dinah, Marcia's Old Family Servant................Dorothy Scott
Genie Moreland, a Neighbor..............................Mae Shults

The Action Takes Place in John Thayer's Study in His Country House on the Outskirts of a Medium-sized City.

Directed by Parker Fennelly and H. Tilden Swan.

FRIDAY, MAY 15

The Wigwam Players of Lapeer, Michigan, present "Sideshow," by Carl Beitell Smith.

The Cast—

Mamie....Elizabeth Sullivan
Betty....Margaret Sullivan
Larry Hogan....Kenneth Henderson
Pete....Howard Stone
Mike....Cyril Hardwicke
A Balloon-Man....Howard Jones
A Woman....Loretta Locher
A Man....Harry Larson
First Child....Jean Zemmer
Second Child....Marie Gustke
First Sheik....Arthur Forshaw
Second Sheik....Tom Sanders
Mary Baker....Nell Jane Damon
Eddie Baker....Clinton E. Lunt
Emma....Ethel Dodds
Lulu....Frances Vincent
Dot....Dorothy McDermid
Sally....Esther Ostrom
Slim....Marvin LaDuc
Hal....Harry Larson
Lois Baker....Jane Miller
Circus People, Citizens, Hangers-on, etc.—Emily Francis, Rose Gustke, Elizabeth K. Towne, Dorothy Southworth, Kathryn Miller, Lillian White, George Young, James Mack, Henry Gently, Roy Fuller.

Acts I and II.—A Circus Lot and Dressing Tent. Act III.—Living Room in Hogan Home.

Directed by Carl Beitell Smith.

The Samuel French prize of $1,000 was awarded Arthur Goodman's drama, "If Booth Had Missed," presented by the Morningside Players of Columbia University. The judges were William G. King, John Chamberlain, John Whedon, Carl Carmer, and Arthur Edwin Krows. Honorable mention was given to "Technique" by the Beechwood Players of Scarborough.

PERFECTLY SCANDALOUS

(5 performances)

A comedy in three acts by Hutcheson Boyd. Produced by Ray Gallo at the Hudson Theatre, New York, May 13, 1931.

Cast of characters—

Philip Moreno....Theodore Hecht
Frances Drake....Ann Dere
Sydney North....Henry W. Pemberton
Viva North....Natalie Schafer
Fay North....Jeanne Greene
Oliver Drake....Grant Gordon
Antonio....Himself

Acts I, II and III.—Library, Sydney North's Apartment, Manhattan.

Staged by Robert Webb Lawrence.

Sydney North's nephew, Oliver, is living with Uncle Sydney and Viva, his attractive second wife, in Park Avenue. Oliver is fond of Uncle Sydney's adopted daughter, Fay, but not at all conscious of being in love with her. In fact Oliver is not conscious of much until Aunt Viva takes him to a night club and lets him get a little tight. Then Oliver realizes that he is in love with Fay. The fact that the family thinks for a time that Oliver slept in Aunt Viva's room the night he was tight, and also believes the worst, accounts for complications.

* OLD MAN MURPHY

(32 performances)

A comedy in three acts by Patrick Kearney and Harry Wagstaffe Gribble. Produced by Robert V. Newman at the Royale Theatre, New York, May 18, 1931.

Cast of characters—

Margaret Murfree....................Gertrude Fowler
Elinor Murfree....................Peggy Conklin
Dudley Weatherbee....................Walter Vaughn
Hopkins....................John M. Troughton
Charles Murfree....................Henry O'Neill
Mike Donovan....................Roy Roberts
Henry Stonehill....................William E. Morris
Patrick Murphy....................Arthur Sinclair
Widow Donovan....................Maire O'Neill
Larry Heffernan....................Lawrence O'Sullivan

Act I.—The Murfree Home. Act II.—Scene 1—Widow Donovan's. 2—The Murfree Home. Act III.—Widow Donovan's. The Play Is Laid in a Middle Western City.

Staged by Harry Wagstaffe Gribble and Lawrence Bolton.

Patrick Murphy of County Wicklow, Ireland, learns that his son, Charles, is running for the office of mayor of a Western city in America. Patrick sails immediately to take charge of the campaign. He finds Charles married to a dominating woman who was Maggie Mulligan, born in "The Patch," but who became Margaret Murfree in real society across the tracks. Patrick wades in, gets a little drunk and finally takes the affectation out of the Murfrees and helps swing the votes of the Patch to Charles.

H.M.S. PINAFORE

(17 performances)

An operetta in two acts by W. S. Gilbert and Arthur Sullivan. Revived by the Civic Light Opera Company at Erlanger's Theatre, New York, May 18, 1931.

Cast of characters—

The Right Hon. Sir Joseph Porter, K.C.B.,
First Lord of the Admiralty....................Frank Moulan
Capt. Corcoran, Commander of H.M.S. *Pinafore*....Joseph Macaulay
Ralph Rackstraw....................Howard Marsh
Dick Deadeye....................William Danforth
Bill Bobstay....................William C. Gordon
Josephine....................Ruth Altman
Little Buttercup (Mrs. Cripps)....................Fay Templeton
Hebe....................Ethel Clark
Sailors: Charles Froom, Edward Taylor, Bert Melrose, Hobson Young, Charles Maduro, Edward Lambert, Felix Noonan, Allen Ware, Frank Murray, Martin Lilienfield, Frank Dowling and Harrison Fuller.
First Lord's Sisters, His Cousins and His Aunts: Misses Frances Moore, Olga Schumacher, Roslyn Shaw, Patricia Clark, Florence Little, Edith Artley, Eleanor Gilmore, Gertrude Waldon, Frances Baviallo, Margaret Bickel, Mabel Thompson, Flora Bell, Helen Hosp, Isabel Norwood, Belle Flower, Rosa Rubenstein, Mary Joe Matthews, Georgina Dieter and Marie Pittman.
Acts I and II.—Deck of H.M.S. *Pinafore,* off Portsmouth, England.
Staged by Milton Aborn.

This revival was distinguished by the engagement of Fay Templeton to sing her old rôle of Little Buttercup. Miss Templeton received nightly ovations for the two weeks of the engagement and announced her final retirement the closing night. She was also a feature of the last previous revival of the opera, made at the Century Theatre, New York, in 1926 by the Messrs. Shubert.

THE HONOR CODE

(24 performances)

A comedy in three acts by Mark Linder. Produced by Jack and Charles Linder at the Vanderbilt Theatre, New York, May 18, 1931.

Cast of characters—

Pietro Piccichanti....................E. L. Fernandez
Lillian Piccichanti....................Betty Kashman
Ciro....................Frank S. Marino
Gasper....................Vincent Rondinone
Rosario Piccichanti....................Valerie Bergere
Luigi Piccichanti....................Antonio Maiori
Abe Levine....................Sam Liebert
Joe Morello....................Jack Harwood
Sam....................Charles H. Doyle
Costello....................Antonio Filauri
Nick....................Michael Alvin
Cashier....................Gloria Eller
Theresa....................Sadie Banks
Dopey Frank....................Harry Jackson
Tony....................Victor Adams
Angelina....................Miriam Battista
Tom....................Gordon Hamilton
Farfarello....................William E. Blake
Captain Curley....................Herbert Warren

Wandering Musicians........................ { Joe Webb / Anthony Romaine
Novelty Entertainer..............................Nick Bakarich
Blondy..Beth Milton
Acts I and III.—Piccichanti's Home. Lower East Side of New York City. Act II.—Costello's Spaghetti and Wine Cellar.
Staged by Mark Linder.

Pietro Piccichanti wrongs his niece, Lillian Piccichanti, and is thereafter haunted and hounded by the forces of law and morals until the girl is revenged.

* BILLY ROSE'S CRAZY QUILT

(32 performances)

A revue in two acts assembled by Billy Rose. Produced by Mr. Rose at the 44th Street Theatre, New York, May 19, 1931.

Principals engaged—

Phil Baker
Ted Healy
Tom Monroe
Lew Brice
Stewart and Vale
Fannie Brice
Tamara
Ethel Norris
Marion Bonnell
Gomez and Winoana
Staged by Billy Rose.

* A MODERN VIRGIN

(29 performances)

A comedy in three acts by Elmer Harris. Produced by the Messrs. Shubert at the Booth Theatre, New York, May 20, 1931.

Cast of characters—

Eddy...Boris Nicholai
Richard Chiltern..............................Nicholas Joy
Rob Winslow.................................George Houston
Tweed.....................................Fred Irving Lewis
Hazard.......................................Roger Pryor
Yvette.....................................Andree Corday
Aunty Weeks...................................Lola Raine
Teddy Simpson..............................Margaret Sullavan
Sissy Carrol................................Mildred Baker
Mina Gutherie..............................Claudia Morgan
Dr. Franko................................Alfred Kappeler
Ella......................................Marcella Swanson
Act I.—Scene 1—Corner of the Card Room, Rob's Club. 2—Teddy's Bedroom. Act II.—Tweed's Camp. Act III.—Teddy's Sitting-room.
Staged by Stanley Logan.

Teddy Simpson is wild with curiosity concerning sex at 17. Being brought up by a spinster aunt who wants to marry her off as soon as possible, Teddy agrees to become engaged to Rob

Winslow, some years her senior, but flirts with a variety of men. She is most enamored of a young married man named Hazard, who is also a friend of Winslow. Hazard agrees to help teach Teddy a lesson. He arranges a rendezvous with her at a camp in the woods, permits her naïve advances and is duly surprised by the arrival of Winslow. Teddy finally agrees to marry Winslow on condition that he will leave immediately for South America, leaving her to Hazard. After marriage she decides all men are wonderful and sticks to her husband.

THE WAY OF THE WORLD

(8 performances)

A comedy in three acts by William Congreve. Revived by the Players' Club at the Guild Theatre, New York, June 1, 1931.

Cast of characters—

Fainall.......................................William S. Rainey
Mirabell.......................................Walter Hampden
Witwoud.......................................Gerald Hamer
Petulant.......................................Moffatt Johnston
Sir Wilfull Witwoud.......................................Ernest Cossart
Waitwell.......................................Eugene Lockhart
Footman.......................................Eliot Cabot
Messenger.......................................Ben Lackland
Coachman.......................................Samuel Merwin
Footman.......................................Charles McCarthy
Another Footman.......................................Alan Campbell
A Singer.......................................Paul Parks
Lady Wishfort.......................................Alice Fischer
Mrs. Millamant.......................................Fay Bainter
Mrs. Marwood.......................................Cora Witherspoon
Mrs. Fainall.......................................Selena Royle
Foible.......................................Kathleen Lockhart
Mincing.......................................Dorothy Stickney
Betty.......................................Sheelagh Hayes
Peg.......................................Erna Rowan
A Singer.......................................Mary McCoy
Staged by B. Iden Payne.

The most pretentious of the revivals made of the Congreve comedy, which is periodically brought to light by Little Theatre groups.

* THE THIRD LITTLE SHOW

(16 performances)

A revue in two acts assembled and produced by Dwight Deere Wiman in association with Tom Weatherly, at the Music Box, New York, June 1, 1931.

Principals engaged—

Ernest Truex	Beatrice Lillie
Carl Randall	Constance Carpenter
Walter O'Keefe	Sandra Gale
Jerry Norris	Dorothy Fitzgibbon
Edward Arnold	Gertrude McDonald
William M. Griffith	Dorothy Waller
Jack Riano	

Staged by Alexander Leftwich.

THE GONDOLIERS

(16 performances)

An operetta in two acts by W. S. Gilbert and Arthur Sullivan. Revived by the Civic Light Opera company at Erlanger's Theatre, New York, June 1, 1931.

Cast of characters—

The Duke of Plaza-Toro............................Frank Moulan
Luiz..Dudsworth Fraser
Don Alhambra Del Bolero...........................William Danforth
Marco Palmieri....................................Howard Marsh
Giuseppe Palmieri.................................Joseph Macaulay
Antonio...Bobby Fuller
Francesco...Sano Marco
The Duchess of Plaza-Toro.........................Vera Ross
Casilda...Ruth Altman
Gianetta..Dorothy Seegar
Tessa...Cecilia Branz
Fiametta..Frances Moore
Vittoria..Mabel Thompson
Giulia..Rosalind Shaw
Inez..Belle Flower
Gondoliers, Contadine, etc.: Misses Frances Moore, Olga Schumacher, Roslyn Shaw, Patricia Clark, Florence Little, Edith Artley, Eleanor Gilmore, Gertrude Waldon, Frances Baviello, Margaret Bickel, Mabel Thompson, Flora Bell, Helen Hosp, Isabel Norwood, Belle Flower, Rosa Rubenstein, Mary Joe Matthews, Georgina Dieter, Marie Pittman. Messrs. Charles Froom, Edward Taylor, Bert Melrose, Hobson Young, Charles Maduro, Edward Lambert, Felix Noonan, Allen Ware, Frank Murray, Martin Lilienfield, Frank Dowling and Harrison Fuller.

Act I.—The Piazetta, Venice. Act II.—Pavilion in the Palace of Barataria. Year 1750.

Staged by Milton Aborn.

"The Gondoliers" was revived in December, 1918, by the Society of American Singers, Inc., with Herbert Waterous as the Duke, William Danforth as Don Alhambra, Craig Campbell as Marco, Gladys Caldwell as Tessa, Blanche Duffield as Gianetta and Josephine Jacoby as the Duchess.

* UNEXPECTED HUSBAND

(15 performances)

A comedy in three acts by Barry Conners. Produced by Richard Herndon at the Forty-eighth Street Theatre, New York, June 2, 1931.

Cast of characters—

Jules Perot...Walter Armin
"Rusty" Rafferty...Alan Bunce
Willie Van Loan...Robert Ober
Perry Morrison...Arthur Aylesworth
Dorothy Atwater...Mary Howard
Mr. Egbert Busty...Hugh Cameron
Mrs. Egbert Busty...Josephine Hull
Bell Boy...Robert Guion
Garrity...James Kelly
Izzy Farbstein...Frank Lewis
Mr. Atwater...Henry Pemberton

Act I.—A Private Dining Room in Jules and Jacques Place, Westchester. Acts II and III.—A Room in the Hotel Mercedes, Jersey City.

Staged by Milton Siefel.

Dorothy Atwater, restless and tired of life in Texas, runs away to New York intending to elope with a Broadway playboy named Willie Van Loan. Changing her mind afterward she makes an appointment to meet Van Loan at a New Jersey road house to tell him so. To screw her courage to the sticking point she drinks several old-fashioned cocktails with Perry Morrison, a rich bachelor friend, and they both pass out. Good New Jersey samaritans, Mr. and Mrs. Egbert Busty, take them to a hotel and, believing them married, put them in the same bed. Consternation and complications when they awake to find themselves trailed by a tabloid reporter who is after the story and Dorothy's Texas father who is after Dorothy. They decide to marry to avoid further complications.

* THE BAND WAGON

(13 performances)

A revue in two acts by George S. Kaufman and Howard Dietz; music by Arthur Schwartz. Produced by Max Gordon at the New Amsterdam Theatre, New York, June 3, 1931.

Principals engaged—

Fred Astaire
Frank Morgan
Philip Loeb
John Barker

Jay Wilson
Francis Pierlot
Adele Astaire
Tillie Losch
Helen Broderick
Roberta Robinson
Helen Carrington

Staged by Hassard Short; dances by Albertina Rasch.

* A REGULAR GUY

(13 performances)

A comedy in three acts by Patrick Kearney. Revived by Jules J. Leventhal at the Hudson Theatre, New York, June 4, 1931.

Cast of characters—

Ma Tuttle....................................Gertrude Ritchie
Edie Tuttle....................................Charlotte Wynters
Hazel Williams....................................Allys Dwyer
Melville Tuttle....................................Glenn Hunter
S. Barret Blackstone....................................Lathrop Mitchell
Charlie Groff....................................Edward Pawley
Mabel Plant....................................Neville Westman
Joe Plant....................................Arthur Mack
Marjorie Tuttle....................................Jane Jonson
Herb Brown....................................Philip Van Zandt
Eddie Nelson....................................Richard Bender

Acts I, II and III.—Combination Living and Dining Room of the Tuttle Home in Harlem.
Staged by Patrick Kearney.

Under its original title of "A Man's Man" this "comedy of New York life under the L" was produced by an organization known as The Stagers at the 52d Street Theatre in New York, October 13, 1925. It continued for 120 performances. The story is of Melville and Edie Tuttle, urban innocents, who are duped by a slicker. Melville pays Charlie Groff a hundred dollars to get him into the Elks, which Charlie fails to do, and Edie gives herself to the same Charlie on his promise to make a moving picture actress of her. The Tuttles are disillusioned and battered by the adventure and are left trying to forgive each other and get a new start.

GASOLINE GYPSIES

(3 performances)

A comedy in three acts by Charles Conger Stewart. Produced by Norman Miller at the Lyric Theatre, New York, June 6, 1931.

Cast of characters—

Jean Warren....................................Gene Byron
Phillippa Jenks....................................Mabel Colcord
Ruth Warren....................................Gertrude Flynn

Peter Davis....................................Emmett Lynn
Wallace Frazer....................................Edmund Donald
Royal Murphy....................................John Hibbard
Bess Beggs....................................Dorothy Randall
Sam Beggs....................................Roy Earles
Acts I, II and III.—The Beggs Farm.
Staged by Norman Miller.

Jean Warren starts with her aunt and sister for Florida to go into the real estate business. They are traveling in an old Ford. Camping on the Beggs farm in New Jersey they are overtaken by Wallace Frazer who is in love with Jean. Farmer Beggs threatens to throw them all off the place. Jean, thinking she has discovered oil, buys the farm. The oil turns out to be a plant, but rich clay is discovered to take its place.

*EBB TIDE

(8 performances)

A drama in three acts by Harry Chapman Ford. Produced by Artmart Productions, Inc., at the New Yorker Theatre, New York, June 8, 1931.

Cast of characters—

"Ginnie" Lee....................................Adele Carpell
Jed Oliver....................................Charles Aitken
"Cove" Carrie Lee....................................Marjorie Main
Carl Blake....................................Sidney Eliot
"Dossie" Lee....................................Eleanora Barrie
Sim Carter....................................William Castle
Robert Loughran....................................Samuel Flint
"Dandy" Dan Loughran....................................Sydney Mason, Jr.
Mike Perez....................................Saul Z. Martell
Belle Steaver....................................Janice Dawe
Acts I and III.—"Cove" Carrie's Hut in the Chesapeake Basin.
Act III.—The Cove.
Staged by J. Kent Thurber.

Cove Carrie Lee has lived all her life by the shores of an out-of-the-way inlet on Chesapeake Bay. She is one of the Basin, or lowland, women who have always been considered the legitimate prey of the Hill men. She knew and loved Colonel Loughran before and after she married. Her youngest daughter, Ginnie, is really the colonel's child. Dandy Dan Loughran, the colonel's son and a black sheep, has also known Cove Carrie's oldest daughter, Dossie. Dandy Dan comes back to hire Cove Carrie to pick up a floating box of dope off the inlet and runs into trouble. Dossie still wants Dandy Dan and her Basin lover, Carl Blake, is prepared to shoot him if he don't do right by Dossie.

Cove Carrie has a hand in straightening out the mess and Ginnie, the colonel's daughter, stands a fair chance of getting a white dress and an eddication.

* PATIENCE

(8 performances)

Operetta in two acts by W. S. Gilbert; music by Arthur Sullivan. Revived by the Civic Light Opera Company, at Erlanger's Theatre, New York, June 15, 1931.

Cast of characters—

Colonel Calverley.............................William Danforth
Major Murgatroyd............................William C. Gordon
Lieut. the Duke of Dunstable.......................Howard Marsh
Reginald Bunthorne............................Frank Moulan
Archibald Grosvenor..........................Joseph Macaulay
The Lady Angela...............................Dean Dickens
The Lady Saphir..............................Frances Moore
The Lady Ella....................................Sarah Bair
The Lady Jane...................................Anne Yago
Patience.......................................Vivian Hart
Rapturous Maidens: Olga Schumacher, Roslyn Shaw, Patricia Clark, Florence Little, Edith Artley, Eleanor Gilmore, Gertrude Waldon, Frances Baviello, Margaret Bickel, Mabel Thompson, Flora Bell, Helen Hosp, Isabel Norwood, Belle Flower, Rosa Rubenstein, Mary Joe Matthews, Georgina Dieter, Marie Pittman, Marynia Apel, Julia Reid, Adele Story, Charlotte LaRose.
Dragoons: Charles Froom, Edward Taylor, Bert Melrose, Hobson Young, Charles Maduro, Edward Lambert, Felix Noonan, Allen Ware, Frank Murray, Martin Lilienfield, Frank Dowling, Harrison Fuller, Alphonso Iglesias, Francis Clark, Ramon Recalde, John Cardini, Bernard Lane and Lee Talbot.
Staged by Milton Aborn.

The two most recent revivals of "Patience" were made in the season of 1926-27, when Perke Hamberg Productions, Inc., offered the operetta with James Watts as Bunthorne, Joseph Macauley as Grosvenor and Vivian Hart in the name part, and that of 1928-29, when a semi-amateur group called the Play-Arts Guild, Inc., of Baltimore, came over to sing the operetta at the Masque Theatre with Donald Kirkly as Bunthorne, Edmund Leonard as Grosvenor and Mary Bokee as Patience.

STATISTICAL SUMMARY

(LAST SEASON PLAYS WHICH ENDED RUNS AFTER JUNE 15, 1930.)

Plays	*Number Performances*
Ada Beats the Drum	46
Apron Strings	224
Artists and Models	55
Change Your Luck	17
Fifty Million Frenchmen	254
First Mrs. Fraser, The	352
Flying High	357
Garrick Gaieties	158
Green Pastures, The	557
Hotel Universe	81
It's a Wise Child	378
Last Mile, The	289
Let and Sublet	40
Lost Sheep	96
Lysistrata	252
Michael and Mary	246
Sons o' Guns	295
Stepping Sisters	333
Strictly Dishonorable	557
Strike Up the Band	191
Three Little Girls	104
Topaze	159
(Return engagement, 56)	
Uncle Vanya	80
(Return engagement, 16)	
Young Sinners	249
(Return engagement, 40)	

LONG RUNS ON BROADWAY

To June 15, 1931

Plays	*Number Performances*	*Plays*	*Number Performances*
Abie's Irish Rose	2,532	Kiki	600
Lightnin'	1,291	Blossom Time	592
The Bat	867	Show Boat	572
The Ladder	789	The Show-off	571
The First Year	760	Sally	570
Seventh Heaven	704	The Green Pastures	557
Peg o' My Heart	692	Strictly Dishonorable	557
East Is West	680	Good News	551
Irene	670	The Music Master	540
A Trip to Chinatown	657	The Boomerang	522
Rain	648	Blackbirds	518
Is Zat So	618	Sunny	517
Student Prince	608	The Vagabond King	511
Broadway	603	The New Moon	509
Adonis	603	Shuffle Along	504
Street Scene	601	Bird in Hand	500

PULITZER PRIZE WINNERS

"For the original American play performed in New York which shall best represent the educational value and power of the stage in raising the standard of good morals, good taste and good manners."—The Will of Joseph Pulitzer, dated April 16, 1904.

In 1929 the advisory board, which, according to the terms of the will, "shall have the power in its discretion to suspend or to change any subject or subjects . . . if in the judgment of the board such suspension, changes or substitutions shall be conducive to the public good," decided to eliminate from the above paragraph relating to the prize-winning play the words "in raising the standard of good morals, good taste and good manners."

The committee awards to date have been:

1917-18—Why Marry? by Jesse Lynch Williams
1918-19—None
1919-20—Miss Lulu Bett, by Zona Gale
1920-21—Beyond the Horizon, by Eugene O'Neill
1921-22—Anna Christie, by Eugene O'Neill
1922-23—Icebound, by Owen Davis
1923-24—Hell-bent fer Heaven, by Hatcher Hughes
1924-25—They Knew What They Wanted, by Sidney Howard
1925-26—Craig's Wife, by George Kelly
1926-27—In Abraham's Bosom, by Paul Green
1927-28—Strange Interlude, by Eugene O'Neill
1928-29—Street Scene, by Elmer Rice
1929-30—The Green Pastures, by Marc Connelly
1930-31—Alison's House, by Susan Glaspell

PREVIOUS VOLUMES OF BEST PLAYS

Selections of the ten best plays of each season since 1919-1920 in preceding volumes of this Year Book of the Drama are as follows:

1919-1920

"Abraham Lincoln," by John Drinkwater. Published by Houghton Mifflin Co., Boston.

"Clarence," by Booth Tarkington.

"Beyond the Horizon," by Eugene G. O'Neill. Published by Boni & Liveright, Inc., New York.

"Déclassée," by Zoe Akins.

"The Famous Mrs. Fair," by James Forbes.

"The Jest," by Sem Benelli. (American adaptation by Edward Sheldon.)

"Jane Clegg," by St. John Ervine. Published by Henry Holt & Co., New York.

"Mamma's Affair," by Rachel Barton Butler.

"Wedding Bells," by Salisbury Field.

"Adam and Eva," by George Middleton and Guy Bolton.

1920-1921

"Deburau," by H. Granville Barker. Published by G. P. Putnam's Sons, New York.

"The First Year," by Frank Craven.

"Enter Madame," by Gilda Varesi and Dolly Byrne. Published by G. P. Putnam's Sons, New York.

"The Green Goddess," by William Archer. Published by Alfred A. Knopf, New York.

"Liliom," by Ferenc Molnar. Published by Boni & Liveright, New York.

"Mary Rose," by James M. Barrie.

"Nice People," by Rachel Crothers.

"The Bad Man," by Porter Emerson Browne. Published by G. P. Putnam's Sons, New York.

"The Emperor Jones," by Eugene G. O'Neill. Published by Boni & Liveright, New York.

"The Skin Game," by John Galsworthy. Published by Charles Scribner's Sons, New York.

1921-1922

"Anna Christie," by Eugene G. O'Neill. Published by Boni & Liveright, New York.

"A Bill of Divorcement," by Clemence Dane. Published by the Macmillan Company, New York.

"Dulcy," by George S. Kaufman and Marc Connelly. Published by G. P. Putnam's Sons, New York.

"He Who Gets Slapped," by Leonid Andreyev. Published by Brentano's.

"Six Cylinder Love," by William Anthony McGuire.

"The Hero," by Gilbert Emery.

"The Dover Road," by Alan Alexander Milne.

"Ambush," by Arthur Richman.

"The Circle," by William Somerset Maugham.

"The Nest," by Paul Geraldy and Grace George.

1922-1923

"Rain," by John Colton and Clemence Randolph.

"Loyalties," by John Galsworthy. Published by Charles Scribner's Sons, New York.

"Icebound," by Owen Davis. Published by Little, Brown & Company, Boston.

"You and I," by Philip Barry. Published by Brentano's, New York.

"The Fool," by Channing Pollock. Published by Brentano's, New York.

"Merton of the Movies," by George Kaufman and Marc Connelly, based on the novel of the same name by Harry Leon Wilson.

"Why Not?" by Jesse Lynch Williams.

"The Old Soak," by Don Marquis. Published by Doubleday, Page & Company.

"R.U.R.," by Karel Capek. Translated by Paul Selver. Published by Doubleday, Page & Company.

"Mary the 3d," by Rachel Crothers. Published by Brentano's, New York.

1923-1924

"The Swan," by Ferenc Molnar. Published by Boni & Liveright, New York.

"Outward Bound," by Sutton Vane. Published by Boni & Liveright, New York.

"The Show-off," by George Kelly. Published by Little, Brown & Company, Boston.

"The Changelings," by Lee Wilson Dodd. Published by E. P. Dutton & Company, New York.

"Chicken Feed," by Guy Bolton. Published by Samuel French, New York and London.

"Sun-Up," by Lula Vollmer. Published by Brentano's, New York.

"Beggar on Horseback," by George Kaufman and Marc Connelly. Published by Boni & Liveright, New York.

"Tarnish," by Gilbert Emery. Published by Brentano's, New York.

"The Goose Hangs High," by Lewis Beach. Published by Little, Brown & Company, Boston.

"Hell-bent fer Heaven," by Hatcher Hughes. Published by Harper Bros., New York.

1924-1925

"What Price Glory?" by Laurence Stallings and Maxwell Anderson.

"They Knew What They Wanted," by Sidney Howard. Published by Doubleday, Page & Company, New York.

"Desire Under the Elms," by Eugene G. O'Neill. Published by Boni & Liveright, New York.

"The Firebrand," by Edwin Justus Mayer. Published by Boni & Liveright, New York.

"Dancing Mothers," by Edgar Selwyn and Edmund Goulding.

"Mrs. Partridge Presents," by Mary Kennedy and Ruth Warren.

"The Fall Guy," by James Gleason and George Abbott.

"The Youngest," by Philip Barry. Published by Samuel French, New York.

"Minick," by Edna Ferber and George S. Kaufman. Published by Doubleday, Page & Company, New York.

"Wild Birds," by Dan Totheroh. Published by Doubleday, Page & Company, New York.

1925-1926

"Craig's Wife," by George Kelly. Published by Little, Brown & Company, Boston.

"The Great God Brown," by Eugene G. O'Neill. Published by Boni & Liveright, New York.

"The Green Hat," by Michael Arlen.

"The Dybbuk," by S. Ansky, Henry G. Alsberg-Winifred Katzin translation. Published by Boni & Liveright, New York.

"The Enemy," by Channing Pollock. Published by Brentano's, New York.

"The Last of Mrs. Cheyney," by Frederick Lonsdale.

"Bride of the Lamb," by William Hurlbut. Published by Boni & Liveright, New York.

"The Wisdom Tooth," by Marc Connelly. Published by George H. Doran & Company, New York.

"The Butter and Egg Man," by George Kaufman. Published by Boni & Liveright, New York.

"Young Woodley," by John Van Druten. Published by Simon and Schuster, New York.

1926-1927

"Broadway," by Philip Dunning and George Abbott. Published by George H. Doran Company, New York.

"Saturday's Children," by Maxwell Anderson. Published by Longmans, Green & Company, New York.

"Chicago," by Maurine Watkins. Published by Alfred A. Knopf, Inc., New York.

"The Constant Wife," by William Somerset Maugham. Published by George H. Doran Company, New York.

"The Play's the Thing," by Ferenc Molnar and P. G. Wodehouse. Published by Brentano's, New York.

"The Road to Rome," by Robert Emmet Sherwood. Published by Charles Scribner's Sons, New York.

"The Silver Cord," by Sidney Howard. Published by Charles Scribner's Sons, New York.

"The Cradle Song," by John Garrett Underhill. Published by E. P. Dutton & Company.

"Daisy Mayme," by George Kelly. Published by Little, Brown & Company, Boston.

"In Abraham's Bosom," by Paul Green. Published by Robert M. McBride & Company, New York.

1927-1928

"Strange Interlude," by Eugene G. O'Neill. Published by Boni & Liveright, New York.

"The Royal Family," by Edna Ferber and George Kaufman. Published by Doubleday, Doran & Company, New York.

"Burlesque," by George Manker Watters. Published by Doubleday, Doran & Company.

"Coquette," by George Abbott and Ann Bridgers. Published by Longmans, Green & Company, New York, London, Toronto.

"Behold the Bridegroom," by George Kelly. Published by Little, Brown & Company, Boston.

"Porgy," by DuBose Heyward. Published by Doubleday, Doran & Company, New York.

"Paris Bound," by Philip Barry. Published by Samuel French, New York.

"Escape," by John Galsworthy. Published by Charles Scribner's Sons, New York.

"The Racket," by Bartlett Cormack. Published by Samuel French, New York.

"The Plough and the Stars," by Sean O'Casey. Published by the Macmillan Company, New York.

1928-1929

"Street Scene," by Elmer Rice. Published by Samuel French, New York.

"Journey's End," by R. C. Sheriff. Published by Brentano's, New York.

"Wings over Europe," by Robert Nichols and Maurice Browne. Published by Covici-Friede, New York.

"Holiday," by Philip Barry. Published by Samuel French, New York.

"The Front Page," by Ben Hecht and Charles MacArthur. Published by Covici-Friede, New York.

"Let Us Be Gay," by Rachel Crothers. Published by Samuel French, New York.

"Machinal," by Sophie Treadwell.

"Little Accident," by Floyd Dell and Thomas Mitchell.

"Gypsy," by Maxwell Anderson.

"The Kingdom of God," by G. Martinez Sierra. Published by E. P. Dutton & Company, New York.

1929-1930

"The Green Pastures," by Marc Connelly (adapted from "Ol' Man Adam and His Chillun," by Roark Bradford). Published by Farrar & Rinehart, Inc., New York.

"The Criminal Code," by Martin Flavin. Published by Horace Liveright, New York.

"Berkeley Square," by John Balderstone. Published by the Macmillan Company, New York.

"Strictly Dishonorable," by Preston Sturges. Published by Horace Liveright, New York.

"The First Mrs. Fraser," by St. John Ervine. Published by the Macmillan Company, New York.

"The Last Mile," by John Wexley. Published by Samuel French, New York.

"June Moon," by Ring W. Lardner and George S. Kaufman. Published by Charles Scribner's Sons, New York.

"Michael and Mary," by A. A. Milne. Published by Chatto & Windus, London.

"Death Takes a Holiday," by Walter Ferris (adapted from the Italian of Alberto Casella). Published by Samuel French, New York.

"Rebound," by Donald Ogden Stewart. Published by Samuel French, New York.

WHERE AND WHEN THEY WERE BORN

Abbott, George ....Hamburg, N. Y. 1895
Adams, Maude ....Salt Lake City, Utah 1872
Aherne, Brian ....King's Norton, England ..1902
Alexander, Katherine ....Arkansas 1901
Allen, Viola ....Huntsville, Ala. 1869
Ames, Robert ....Hartford, Conn. 1893
Ames, Winthrop ....North Easton, Mass. 1871
Anderson, Judith ....Australia 1898
Andrews, Ann ....Los Angeles, Cal. 1895
Anglin, Margaret ....Ottawa, Canada 1876
Anson, A. E. ....London, England 1879
Arliss, George ....London, England 1868
Arthur, Julia ....Hamilton, Ont. 1869
Astaire, Adele ....Omaha, Neb. 1900
Astaire, Fred ....Omaha, Neb. 1899
Atwell, Roy ....Syracuse, N. Y. 1880
Atwill, Lionel ....London, England 1885

Bainter, Fay ....Los Angeles, Cal. 1892
Barbee, Richard ....Lafayette, Ind. 1887
Barrett, Edith ....Roxbury, Mass. 1904
Barrie, James Matthew ....Kirriemuir, N. B. 1860
Barrymore, Ethel ....Philadelphia, Pa. 1879
Barrymore, John ....Philadelphia, Pa. 1882
Barrymore, Lionel ....London, England 1878
Bates, Blanche ....Portland, Ore. 1873
Best, Edna ....England 1901
Beecher, Janet ....Chicago, Ill. 1884
Ben-Ami, Jacob ....Minsk, Russia 1890
Bennett, Richard ....Cass County, Ind. 1873
Bennett, Wilda ....Asbury Park, N. J. 1894
Berlin, Irving ....Russia 1888
Binney, Constance ....Philadelphia, Pa. 1900
Blackmer, Sidney ....Salisbury, N. C. 1896
Boland, Mary ....Detroit, Mich. 1880
Bordoni, Irene ....Paris, France 1895

Brady, Alice ....New York 1892
Brady, William A. ....San Francisco, Cal. 1863
Brian, Donald ....St. Johns, N. F. 1877
Brice, Fannie ....Brooklyn, N. Y. 1891
Broadhurst, George H. ....England 1866
Bryant, Charles ....England 1879
Buchanan, Jack ....England 1892
Buchanan, Thompson ....Louisville, Ky. 1877
Burke, Billie ....Washington, D. C. 1885
Burton, Frederick ....Indiana 1871
Byron, Arthur ....Brooklyn, N. Y. 1872

Cahill, Marie ....Brooklyn, N. Y. 1871
Calhern, Louis ....New York 1895
Cantor, Eddie ....New York 1894
Campbell, Mrs. Patrick ......England 1865
Carle, Richard ....Somerville, Mass. 1871
Carlisle, Alexandra ....Yorkshire, England 1886
Carr, Alexander ....Russia 1878
Carter, Mrs. Leslie ....Lexington, Ky. 1862
Catlett, Walter ....San Francisco, Cal. 1889
Cawthorne, Joseph ....New York 1868
Chaplin, Charles Spencer .....London 1889
Chatterton, Ruth ....New York 1893
Cherry, Charles ....England 1872
Churchill, Burton ....Toronto, Can. 1876
Claire, Ina ....Washington, D. C. 1892
Clarke, Marguerite ....Cincinnati, Ohio 1887
Cliffe, H. Cooper ....England 1862
Clifford, Kathleen ....Charlottesville, Va. 1887
Coburn, Charles ....Macon, Ga. 1877
Coghlan, Gertrude ....England 1879
Coghlan, Rose ....Petersborough, England ...1850
Cohan, George M. ....Providence, R. I. 1878
Cohan, Georgette ....Los Angeles, Cal. 1900
Colbert, Claudette ....Paris 1905
Collier, Constance ....Windsor, England 1882
Collier, William ....New York 1866
Collinge, Patricia ....Dublin, Ireland 1894
Collins, José ....London, England 1896
Connolly, Walter ....Cincinnati, Ohio 1888
Conroy, Frank ....London, England 1885
Cooper, Violet Kemble ....London, England 1890

Cornell, Katharine ....Buffalo, N. Y. 1900
Corrigan, Emmett ....Amsterdam, Holland 1871
Corthell, Herbert ....Boston, Mass. 1875
Courtenay, William ....Worcester, Mass. 1875
Courtleigh, William ....Guelph, Ont. 1869
Coward, Noel ....England 1899
Cowl, Jane ....Boston, Mass. 1887
Craven, Frank ....Boston, Mass. 1880
Crews, Laura Hope ....San Francisco, Cal. 1880
Crosman, Henrietta ....Wheeling, W. Va. 1865
Crothers, Rachel ....Bloomington, Ill. 1878
Cumberland, John ....St. John, N. B. 1880

Dale, Margaret ....Philadelphia, Pa. 1880
Dalton, Charles ....England 1864
Daniels, Frank ....Dayton, Ohio 1860
Dawn, Hazel ....Ogden, Utah 1891
Day, Edith ....Minneapolis, Minn. 1896
De Angelis, Jefferson ....San Francisco, Cal. 1859
Dean, Julia ....St. Paul, Minn. 1880
De Cordoba, Pedro ....New York 1881
Dillingham, Charles B. ....Hartford, Conn. 1868
Dinehart, Allan ....Missoula, Mont. 1889
Dixey, Henry E. ....Boston, Mass. 1859
Dodson, John E. ....London, England 1857
Doro, Marie ....Duncannon, Pa. 1882
D'Orsay, Lawrence ....England 1860
Dressler, Eric ....Brooklyn, N. Y. 1900
Dressler, Marie ....Cobourg, Canada 1869
Drew, Louise ....New York 1884
Dunn, Emma ....England 1875
Dupree, Minnie ....San Francsico, Cal. 1875

Edeson, Robert ....Baltimore, Md. 1868
Eldridge, Florence ....Brooklyn, N. Y. 1901
Ellis, Mary ....New York 1900
Elliston, Grace ....Wheeling, W. Va. 1881
Ellinger, Desirée ....Manchester, Vt. 1895
Elliott, Gertrude ....Rockland, Me. 1874
Elliott, Maxine ....Rockland, Me. 1871
Eltinge, Julian ....Boston, Mass. 1883
Emerson, John ....Sandusky, Ohio 1874
Errol, Leon ....Sydney, Australia 1881

Fairbanks, Douglas ....Denver, Colo. 1883
Farnum, William ....Boston, Mass. 1876
Farrar, Geraldine ....Melrose, Mass. 1883
Faversham, William ....Warwickshire, England ...1868
Fenwick, Irene ....Chicago, Ill. 1887
Ferguson, Elsie ....New York 1883
Field, Sylvia ....Allston, Mass. 1902
Fields, Lew ....New York 1867
Fields, W. C. ....Philadelphia, Pa. 1883
Fischer, Alice ....Indiana 1869
Fiske, Minnie Maddern ......New Orleans, La. 1867
Fontanne, Lynn ....London, England 1892
Forbes, Robertson, Sir J. .....London, England 1853
Foster, Claiborne ....Shreveport, La. 1899
Foster, Norman ....Richmond, Ind. 1907
Foster, Phœbe ....New Hampshire 1897
Foy, Eddie, Jr. ....New Rochelle, N. Y. 1906
Franklin, Irene ....St. Louis, Mo. 1878
Frederick, Pauline ....Boston, Mass. 1884
Friganza, Trixie ....Cincinnati, Ohio 1870
Frohman, Daniel ....Sandusky, Ohio 1850

Gahagan, Helen ....Boonton, N. J. 1902
Garden, Mary ....Scotland 1876
Gaythorne, Pamela ....England 1882
George, Grace ....New York 1879
Gerald, Ara ....New South Wales 1902
Gillette, William ....Hartford, Conn. 1856
Gillmore, Frank ....New York 1884
Gillmore, Margalo ....England 1901
Gleason, James ....New York 1885
Glendinning, Ernest ....Ulverston, England 1884
Gottschalk, Ferdinand ....London, England 1869
Greenstreet, Sydney ....England 1880
Grey, Katherine ....San Francisco, Cal. 1873

Haines, Robert T. ....Muncie, Ind. 1870
Hale, Louise Closser ....Chicago, Ill. 1872
Hall, Laura Nelson ....Philadelphia, Pa. 1876
Hamilton, Hale ....Topeka, Kansas 1880
Hampden, Walter ....Brooklyn, N. Y. 1879
Hanson, Gladys ....Atlanta, Ga. 1887
Harding, Lyn ....Newport, England 1867

Harris, Sam H.	New York	1872
Harrison, Richard B.	London, Ontario	1864
Hayes, Helen	Washington, D. C.	1900
Hazzard, John E.	New York	1881
Hedman, Martha	Sweden	1888
Heggie, O. P.	Australia	1879
Heming, Violet	Leeds, England	1893
Herbert, Evelyn	Brooklyn, N. Y.	1900
Herne, Chrystal	Dorchester, Mass.	1883
Hodge, William	Albion, N. Y.	1874
Hopkins, Miriam	Savannah, Ga.	1907
Hopper, DeWolf	New York	1858
Hopper, Edna Wallace	San Francisco, Cal.	1874
Holmes, Taylor	Newark, N. J.	1872
Howard, Leslie	London, England	1890
Hull, Henry	Louisville, Ky.	1893
Hunter, Glenn	Highland Mills, N. Y.	1896
Huston, Walter	Toronto	1884
Inescort, Frieda	Hitchin, Scotland	1905
Irving, Isabel	Bridgeport, Conn.	1871
Irwin, May	Whitby, Ont.	1862
Janis, Elsie	Delaware, Ohio	1889
Joel, Clara	Jersey City, N. J.	1890
Johann, Zita	Hungary	1904
Jolson, Al.	Washington, D. C.	1883
Kaufman, George S.	Pittsburgh, Pa.	1889
Keane, Doris	Michigan	1885
Kennedy, Madge	Chicago, Ill.	1890
Kerrigan, J. M.	Dublin, Ireland	1885
Kerr, Geoffrey	London, England	1895
Kershaw, Willette	Clifton Heights, Mo.	1890
Kosta, Tessa	Chicago, Ill.	1893
Kruger, Alma	Pittsburgh, Pa.	1880
Kruger, Otto	Toledo, Ohio	1895
Lackaye, Wilton	Virginia	1862
Larrimore, Francine	Russia	1898
La Rue, Grace	Kansas City, Mo.	1882
Lauder, Harry	Portobello, England	1870
Lawton, Thais	Louisville, Ky.	1881

Lawrence, Gertrude	London	1898
Lean, Cecil	Illinois	1878
Le Gallienne, Eva	London, England	1900
Leiber, Fritz	Chicago, Ill.	1884
Leontovich, Eugenie	Moscow, Russia	1894
Levey, Ethel	San Francisco, Cal.	1881
Lewis, Mabel Terry	London, England	1872
Lillie, Beatrice	Toronto, Canada	1898
Logan, Stanley	Earlsfield, England	1885
Loraine, Robert	New Brighton, England	1876
Lord, Pauline	Hanford, Cal.	1890
Lorraine, Lillian	San Francisco, Cal.	1892
Lou-Tellegen	Holland	1881
Lowell, Helen	New York	1866
Lunt, Alfred	Milwaukee, Wis.	1893
Mack, Andrew	Boston, Mass.	1863
Mack, Willard	Ontario, Canada	1873
Mackay, Elsie	London, England	1894
MacKellar, Helen	Canada	1896
Marlowe, Julia	Caldbeck, England	1870
Marshall, Herbert	London, England	1890
Matthews, A. E.	Bridlington, England	1869
Matthison, Edith Wynne	England	1875
Maude, Cyril	London, England	1862
McIntyre, Frank	Ann Arbor, Mich.	1879
Meek, Donald	Glasgow, Scotland	1880
Meighan, Thomas	Pittsburgh, Pa.	1879
Melba, Nellie	Melbourne, Australia	1866
Mercer, Beryl	Seville, Spain	1882
Merivale, Philip	Rehutia, India	1886
Miller, Marilyn	Findlay, Ohio	1898
Mitchell, Grant	Columbus, Ohio	1874
Mitchell, Thomas	Kentucky	1892
Mitzi (Hajos)	Budapest	1891
Moore, Victor	Hammonton, N. J.	1876
Moran, Lois	Pittsburgh, Pa.	1909
Morgan, Helen	Danville, Ill.	1900
Morgan, Ralph	New York City	1889
Morris, McKay	San Antonio, Texas	1890
Nash, Florence	Troy, N. Y.	1888
Nash, Mary	Troy, N. Y.	1885

Nazimova, Alla ....Crimea, Russia 1879
Nielsen, Alice ....Nashville, Tenn. 1876
Nugent, J. C. ....Miles, Ohio 1875
Nugent, Elliott ....Dover, Ohio 1900

O'Connell, Hugh ....New York 1891
Olcott, Chauncey ....Providence, R. I. 1862
O'Neill, Eugene Gladstone ....New York 1888
O'Neil, Nance ....Oakland, Cal. 1875

Painter, Eleanor ....Iowa 1890
Pawle, Lenox ....London, England 1872
Pennington, Ann ....Philadelphia, Pa. 1898
Perkins, Osgood ....Boston, Mass. 1892
Philips, Mary ....New London, Conn. 1901
Pickford, Mary ....Toronto 1893
Post, Guy Bates ....Seattle, Wash. 1875
Power, Tyrone ....London, England 1869
Powers, James T. ....New York 1862
Pryor, Roger ....New York City 1901

Quartermaine, Leon ....Richmond, England 1876

Rambeau, Marjorie ....San Francisco, Cal. 1889
Rathbone, Basil ....Johannesburg 1892
Reed, Florence ....Philadelphia, Pa. 1883
Rennie, James ....Toronto, Canada 1890
Revelle, Hamilton ....Gibraltar 1872
Richman, Charles ....Chicago, Ill. 1870
Ring, Blanche ....Boston, Mass. 1876
Ring, Frances ....New York 1882
Robson, May ....Australia 1868
Ross, Thomas W. ....Boston, Mass. 1875
Royle, Selena ....New York 1905
Ruben, José ....Belgium 1886
Russell, Annie ....Liverpool, England 1864

Sanderson, Julia ....Springfield, Mass. 1887
Sands, Dorothy ....Cambridge, Mass. 1900
Santley, Joseph ....Salt Lake City 1889
Sawyer, Ivy ....London, England 1897
Scheff, Fritzi ....Vienna, Austria 1879
Scott, Cyril ....Ireland 1866

Segal, Vivienne .... Philadelphia, Pa. 1897
Selwyn, Edgar .... Cincinnati, Ohio 1875
Serrano, Vincent .... New York 1870
Shannon, Effie .... Cambridge, Mass. 1867
Shepley, Ruth .... New York 1889
Schildkraut, Joseph .... Bucharest, Roumania 1896
Sherman, Lowell .... San Francisco, Cal. 1885
Sidney, George .... New York 1876
Sidney, Sylvia .... New York 1910
Sinclair, Arthur .... Dublin, Ireland 1883
Sitgreaves, Beverly .... Charleston, S. C. 1867
Skelly, Hal .... Allegheny, Pa. 1891
Skinner, Otis .... Cambridgeport, Mass. 1857
Smith, Ben .... Waxahachie, Texas 1905
Sothern, Edward H. .... New Orleans, La. 1859
Spong, Hilda .... Australia 1875
Stahl, Rose .... Montreal, Canada 1872
Standing, Sir Guy .... London 1873
Starr, Frances .... Oneonta, N. Y. 1886
Stone, Fred .... Denver, Colo. 1873
Stone, Dorothy .... New York 1905
Sydney, Basil .... London 1894

Taliaferro, Edith .... New York 1892
Taliaferro, Mabel .... New York 1887
Tanguay, Eva .... Middletown, Conn. 1878
Taylor, Laurette .... New York 1884
Tell, Alma .... New York 1892
Tell, Olive .... New York 1894
Thomas, Augustus .... St. Louis, Mo. 1859
Thomas, John Charles .... Baltimore, Md. 1887
Tobin, Genevieve .... New York 1901
Tobin, Vivian .... New York 1903
Toler, Sidney .... Warrensburg, Mo. 1874
Truex, Ernest .... Red Hill, Mo. 1890
Tynan, Brandon .... Dublin, Ireland 1879

Ulric, Lenore .... New Ulm, Minn. 1897

Varesi, Gilda .... Milan, Italy 1887
Victor, Josephine .... Hungary 1891

Waldron, Charles .... New York 1877
Walker, June .... New York 1904

Walker, Charlotte	Galveston, Texas	1878
Warfield, David	San Francisco, Cal.	1866
Warwick, Robert	Sacramento, Cal.	1878
Ware, Helen	San Francisco, Cal.	1877
Waterous, Herbert	Flint, Mich.	1863
Webb, Clifton	Indiana	1891
Weber, Joseph	New York	1867
Welford, Dallas	Liverpool, England	1874
Westley, Helen	Brooklyn, N. Y.	1879
Westman, Nydia	White Plains, N. Y.	1906
Whiffen, Mrs. Thomas	London, England	1845
Whiteside, Walker	Logansport, Ind.	1869
William, Warren	Aitkin, Minn.	1896
Williams, Hope	New York City	1901
Wilson, Francis	Philadelphia, Pa.	1854
Winwood, Estelle	England	1883
Witherspoon, Cora	New Orleans, La.	1891
Wood, Peggy	Brooklyn, N. Y.	1894
Wright, Haidee	London, England	1868
Wycherly, Margaret	England	1883
Wyndham, Olive	Chicago, Ill.	1886
Wynn, Ed.	Philadelphia, Pa.	1886
Yurka, Blanche	Bohemia	1893
Zabelle, Flora	Constantinople	1885
Ziegfeld, Florenz, Jr.	Chicago, Ill.	1867

NECROLOGY

June 15, 1930—June 15, 1931

Henry Jewett, actor, 68. Born in Australia. Came to America in 1892; rose to prominence as leading man for Julia Marlowe; was prominent in support of Richard Mansfield. Organized the Henry Jewett Players in Boston, Mass., and later the Repertory Theatre, which became one of the famous American stock companies. Died West Newton, Mass., June 24, 1930.

Russ Whytal, actor, 70. Prominent in many productions. Wrote "For Fair Virginia" and starred in it for many years with his wife (Mary Adelaide); had successful engagements in "The Witching Hour," "Common Clay" and "Redemption." Started with Boston Museum company. Born Boston, Mass.; died New York, June 24, 1930.

Joe Schenck, singer, 39. For many years the partner of Gus Van in the popular vaudeville team of Van and Schenck. Later a featured pair in Ziegfeld "Follies" and part owners in cabaret ventures. Born Brooklyn, N. Y.; died Detroit, Mich., June 28, 1930.

Rudolph Schildkraut, actor, 68. Achieved prominence in the New York theatre after having gained a reputation in both Europe and America as a Jewish star. Was engaged in directing motion pictures in Hollywood at the time of his death. Born Constantinople; died Los Angeles, Cal., July 15, 1930.

Oscar Figman, actor, 48. Prominent as leading comedian in many musical comedies, including "The Merry Widow" and "The Student Prince." Played with Laurette Taylor in "Peg o' My Heart" and in "The Fool." Died Neponsit, L. I., July 18, 1930.

Emma Marble, actress, 87. Granddaughter of William Warren, Sr., who came to America in 1796 with the second company of English actors; daughter of Danford and Anna Warren Marble; niece of William Warren, comedian of Boston Museum company. Acted with Edwin Booth and Lawrence

Barrett. Born Buffalo, N. Y.; died New York, July 26, 1930.

Carl Anthony, actor, 52. Played prominently in support of many stars, notably as Thomas Jefferson to George Arliss' Alexander Hamilton in "Hamilton." Was playing in "Strictly Dishonorable" at the time of his death. Died Spencertown, N. Y., July 27, 1930.

Gustave Frohman, manager, 76. Preceded his brothers, Charles and Daniel, in show business, first as manager for Callendar's Georgia Minstrels. He was the first manager of the old Madison Square Theatre, and helped the Mallory Brothers, its lessees and both ministers of the gospel, to produce "Hazel Kirke" as a sample of what a clean play should be. Born Sandusky, Ohio; died New York, Aug. 16, 1930.

Milton Sills, actor, 48. Rose to prominence on the speaking stage, after starting as an amateur in Chicago. Was a member of Donald Robertson's New Theatre company in Chicago. Played in support of many prominent stars. Went into pictures some years ago and achieved considerable success as a picture star. Was an organizer of the Academy of Motion Picture Arts and Sciences. Born Chicago; died Los Angeles, Cal., September 15, 1930.

Jack Donahue, dancer and comedian, 38. Came out of vaudeville and into Broadway prominence as a dancer with a musical comedy called "The Woman Haters." Grew in popularity and importance until he was featured with Marilyn Miller in "Sunny" and "Rosalie." Was starred in "Sons o' Guns" in 1929. Acquired many outside interests and was doing considerable writing for magazines and the stage at the time of his death. Born Charlestown, Mass.; died New York, October 1, 1930.

Dolly Nobles, actress, 67. Wife and co-star with the late Milton Nobles for many years, their joint successes including "The Phœnix," and "Love and Law." Born Cincinnati, Ohio; died Brooklyn, N. Y., October 6, 1930.

Clare Eames, actress, 34. Became an actress in 1918 and in the succeeding twelve years played a wide range of parts successfully, achieving a definite personal success both in New York and London. Was associated with the Theatre Guild in New York and prominently cast in her husband's (Sydney Howard) play, "Lucky Sam McCarver." Played in Howard's "The Silver Cord" in London and later in a revival of "Milestones." Had played notably in Drinkwater's "Mary

Stuart" and Ibsen's "Hedda Gabler." Born Hartford, Conn.; died London, November 8, 1930.

Willis Sweatnam, minstrel, 76. Was a featured singer and dancer with all the famous minstrels, starting with Frank Clark's Lilliputians and ending with Jack Haverly and in troupes of his own. Played two legitimate rôles, those of the porter in "Excuse Me" and that of Sassafras Livingston in "The County Chairman." Born Zanesville, Ohio; died New York, November 25, 1930.

Wesley Hill, Negro actor, 55. Started 40 year stage career as barker and dancer with touring medicine show. For 17 years toured vaudeville with act, Hill and Hill. Achieved unusual success as Gabriel in "Green Pastures." Played in "Uncle Tom's Cabin," "Old Kentucky," "Shuffle Along" and "Porgy." Born Baltimore; killed in automobile accident, New York, December 10, 1930.

Charles K. Harris, musical composer and publisher, 65. For 12 years director of the American Society of Composers, Authors and Publishers; made famous by popular song, "After the Ball," later a motion picture. Also wrote "Break the News to Mother," and " 'Mid the Green Hills of Virginia." Born Poughkeepsie, N. Y.; died December 22, 1930.

Flo Irwin (Campbell), vaudeville comedienne, 71. Was well known in song and dance act with her sister, May Irwin. Born Whitby, Canada; died Los Angeles, December 20, 1930.

Mary Hampton, actress, 63. Starred at 15 on Broadway; with Charles Frohman for seven years; played barge woman in original cast of "Anna Christie." Born Kentucky; died New York, February 1, 1931.

Anna Pavlova, dancer, 48. World's greatest ballerina; trained in Imperial Ballet school, Petrograd. With Theodore Kosloff danced in command performance before Czar Nicholas II; with Michael Mordkin toured Europe, South Africa, Australia and America; married M. V. Dandre. Body lay in state in London at the Russian Orthodox Church of St. Philip. Born Petrograd, Russia; died The Hague, January 23, 1931.

Louis Mann, actor and author, 65. Played as youth with Lawrence Barrett and John McCullough in San Francisco stock and with Salvini, Lewis Morrison and Marie Prescott in New York; later associated with E. H. Sothern and Cyril Maude; starred with Sam Bernard in "Friendly Enemies"; wrote

"The Cheaters" and in collaboration with others "The Laughing Girl," "The Bubble," etc.; prominent in Actors' Fidelity League and Jewish Theatrical Guild; married Clara Lipman, actress and playwright. Born New York; died New York, February 15, 1931.

Lillian Leitzel, aerial performer, 36. Died after fall from trapeze on which she had made name for herself as world's greatest feminine athlete; played vaudeville two seasons; featured in Ziegfeld's "Follies." Born Czecho-Slovakia; died Copenhagen, February 15, 1931.

Louis Wolheim, actor, 50. John and Lionel Barrymore persuaded him to join cast of "The Jest"; gave up teaching at Cornell University for stage career; won recognition in "Hairy Ape" and "What Price Glory"; later famous for hardboiled parts in pictures. Married Ethel Dane, actress and sculptor. Born New York; died Los Angeles, February 18, 1931.

Nellie Melba (Helen Porter Mitchell), soprano, 71. A child prodigy at 4; had mastered violin, organ and piano at 10; début in "Rigoletto" coached by Verdi in person; coached in acting by Bernhardt, Duse and Ellen Terry; sang with Caruso and the De Reszkes; British Empire created her Dame Commander for countless concerts she gave for the wounded soldiers. Born Melbourne, Australia; died Melbourne, February 23, 1931.

Fred G. Nixon-Nirdlinger, theatre owner, 54. Shot and killed in Nice, France, by his third wife, Charlotte Nash, who was "Miss St. Louis" during beauty pageant of 1923. Owner of the Nixon-Nirdlinger theatres in Philadelphia. Died Nice, France, March 11, 1931.

James Neill, actor, 70. First stage success in "The Senator" with William H. Crane in New York, 1883; later established stock companies in Denver, Cincinnati, St. Paul, Minneapolis and Winnipeg; member of original Lasky-Famous Players Stock company. Married Edyth Chapman, actress. Died Glendale, Cal., March 15, 1931.

Edward Hanlon, pantomimist, 72. Last of once famous "Six Hanlons"; famous for their "Superba." Died March 15, 1931.

Robert Edeson, actor, 63. For fifteen years played in Frohman stock companies in New York; starred in 1902 at Savoy Theatre in "Soldiers of Fortune" and "Strongheart"; played Rev. Gavin Dishart to Maude Adams' "Babbie" in "The

Little Minister"; left stage for screen, 1914. Born New Orleans; died Hollywood, March 24, 1931.

John J. McNally, dramatic critic and playwright, 77. Drama editor of Charlestown *Chronicle,* Boston *Times* and Boston *Herald;* wrote a series of comedies for Rogers brothers, German comedians,—"Rogers Bros. in a Reign of Terror," "In Wall St.," "In Harvard," etc. Born Charlestown, Mass.; died Brooklyn, N. Y., March 25, 1931.

Arnold Bennett, novelist and playwright, 63. Law student and magazine editor previous to writing plays; these included "The Great Adventure" dramatized from his novel "Buried Alive"; "Milestones" (with Edward Knoblock), and "What the Public Wants." Born Shelton, Staffordshire, England; died London, March 27, 1931.

Maclyn Arbuckle, actor, 68. Gave up law for stage; created famous stage characters, notably James Hackler in "The County Chairman," and Slim Hoover in "The Round-up"; was president of the San Antonio Pictures Corporation and starred in many screen dramas. Born San Antonio, Texas; died Waddington, N. Y., March 31, 1931.

Herbert Druce, actor and producer, 61. Stage début at 17 in London, 1887; appeared with Richard Mansfield in London and came to America with him; was prominent in support of many American actors; last engagement in the revival of "The Admirable Crichton." Born Twickenham, England; died New York, April 6, 1931.

Mary Moore (Lady Wyndham), actress, 70. Widow of Sir Charles Wyndham; supported her husband in all his plays, including "Cyrano," "Mrs. Dane's Defense," "The Liars," "The Mollusc," etc.; accompanied Sir Charles on his American tours; was his partner in the Criterion Theatre; with him built the New and Wyndham theatres in London; president of the Actors' Benevolent Fund. Born London; died April 7, 1931.

Mabel Fenton Ross, actress, 63. Years in vaudeville with Charles Ross (Ross and Fenton); playing burlesques of "Anthony and Cleopatra," "The Virginians" and "The Heart of Maryland"; prominent in Weber and Fields' famous music hall company; ran Ross-Fenton farm in Asbury, N. J., famous as show place for actors and sportsmen. Born Van Buren County, Michigan; died Hollywood, April 19, 1931.

Harry Conor, actor, 75. Character comedian in musical comedy; created leads in Charles H. Hoyt plays; notably "A

Black Sheep" and "A Trip to Chinatown"; with Leo Ditrickstein and Blanche Ring in "Vivian's Papas" in 1904. Died Roxbury, Mass., April, 1931.

David Belasco, producer and playwright, 76. Began theatre career in 1873 as callboy at Metropolitan Theatre, San Francisco; stage manager Baldwin and Metropolitan theatres and Grand Opera House, San Francisco, 1878; stage manager Madison Square and Lyceum theatres, New York, 1882; gained fame as a creator of stars and producer of meticulously staged dramas; wrote many famous plays in collaboration with Henry C. De Mille, Franklyn Fyles, John Luther Long and others, including "The Wife," "The Charity Ball," "The Girl I Left Behind Me," "The Heart of Maryland," "Zaza," "Du Barry," "The Darling of the Gods," "Madame Butterfly," "Girl of the Golden West" and "The Return of Peter Grimm"; first independent production "The Ugly Duckling" with Mrs. Leslie Carter. Born San Francisco; died New York, May 15, 1931.

Andrew Mack (William Andrew McAloon), actor and singer, 68. From variety artist in Boston (1876), to star in New York (1895), when he played Myles Aroon in "Ivy Leaf"; starred in Irish romances; was Irish father in "Abie's Irish Rose"; Sir Lucius O'Trigger in Mrs. Fiske's revival of "The Rivals." Born, Boston; died Bayside, L. I., May 21, 1931.

Sydney Rosenfeld, dramatist, 75. Wrote or co-authored many comedies including "The Vanderbilt Cup," "Mlle. Mischief," "The Mocking Bird" and "The Optimist"; once president of the American Dramatists' Society. Born Richmond, Va.; died New York, June 13, 1931.

THE DECADE'S TOLL

(Players of Outstanding Prominence Who Have Died in Recent Years)

	Born	*Died*
Bacon, Frank	1864	1922
Belasco, David	1856	1931
Bernhardt, Sarah	1845	1923
Crabtree, Charlotte (Lotta)	1847	1924
Crane, William H.	1845	1928
Drew, John	1853	1927
De Koven, Reginald	1861	1920
De Reszke, Jean	1850	1925
Ditrichstein, Leo	1865	1928
Duse, Eleanora	1859	1924
Goodwin, Nathaniel	1857	1920
Hawtrey, Sir Charles	1858	1923
Herbert, Victor	1859	1924
Mantell, Robert Bruce	1854	1928
Miller, Henry	1858	1926
Morris, Clara	1848	1925
O'Neill, James	1850	1920
Patti, Adelina	1843	1919
Rejane, Gabrielle	1857	1920
Russell, Lillian	1861	1922
Shaw, Mary	1860	1929
Terry, Ellen	1848	1928

INDEX OF AUTHORS

Abbott, George, 541, 542, 543
Adamson, Harold, 455
Akins, Zoe, 7, 419, 539
Alsberg, Henry G., 542
Alter, Louis, 468
Ames, Winthrop, 448
Anderson, John, 469
Anderson, Maxwell, 19, 24, 29, 392, 445, 541, 542, 543
Andreyev, Leonid, 28, 521, 540
Ansky, S., 542
Anspacher, Louis K., 7, 412
Archer, William, 539
Aristophanes, 22
Arlen, Harold, 399, 480
Arlen, Michael, 542
Armstrong, Eunice Barton, 525
Arno, Peter, 465

Backwitz, Hans, 512
Baird, Anthony, 498
Balderston, John L., 515, 544
Barnes, Carman, 459
Barrie, James Matthew, 8, 14, 501, 539
Barry, Philip, 13, 20, 27, 74, 222, 392, 479, 540, 541, 543
Bart, Jean, 497
Baum, Vicki, 355, 397, 452
Beach, Lewis, 541
Benatsky, Ralph, 476
Benelli, Sem, 539
Bennett, Ralph Culver, 28
Bernstein, Henri, 15, 517
Berr, Verneuil and Blum, 476
Berstl, Julius, 504
Berte, H., 500
Besier, Rudolf, 13, 317, 396, 487
Biancardo, Pascal, 524
Bibesco, Prince, 400
Blackmore, Madeline, 28
Blake, Eubie, 438
Bolitho, William, 286, 395, 465
Bolton, Guy, 8, 430, 502, 539, 541
Bonner, Eugene, 496
Boyd, Hutcheson, 526
Braddell, Maurice, 486
Bradford, Roark, 543
Braggiotti, Mario, 447
Brennan, J. Kiern, 413
Bridgers, Ann, 543
Brill, Leighton K., 468
Brocklebank, Katherine, 25
Browne, Maurice, 543
Browne, Porter Emerson, 539
Buchanan, Thompson, 446
Buchman, Sidney R., 438
Buckner, Robert L., 458
Burrell, James, 446
Burtis, Thompson, 436
Butler, Rachel Barton, 539
Byrne, Dolly, 539

Cæsar, Irving, 415, 507
Campbell, Lawton, 430
Cantwell, John, 400
Capek, Karel, 540
Carlo and Sanders, 399
Carr, Philip, 436
Carroll, Earl, 5, 17, 399
Carstarphen, Frank E., 519
Carvalho, Claire, 497
Casella, Alberto, 20, 492, 544
Caspary, Vera, 432
Caylor, Rose, 417
Celestin, Jack, 508
Chekov, Anton, 417
Chlumberg, Hans, 505
Clarke, Harry, 400
Cleary, Michael, 453
Cohan, George M., 5, 7, 22, 398
Cole, Kenneth, 28
Collier, Constance, 514
Colton, John, 540
Colum, Padraic, 28
Comstock, Howard Warren, 488
Congreve, William, 16, 530
Connelly, Marc, 538, 540, 541, 542, 543
Conners, Barry, 532
Cook, George Cram, 395
Cormack, Bartlett, 543
Cowan, Sara, 28
Coward, Noel, 13, 483
Coxe, Daniel, 446

Icebound, 538, 540
If Booth Had Missed, 16, 525, 526
In Abraham's Bosom, 538, 542
In the Best of Families, 486
Infinite Shoeblack, The, 27
Inheritors, The, 395
Inspector General, 469
Insult, 410
Iphigenia, 5
Irene, 27, 537
Is Zat So, 537
It's a Wise Child, 6, 23, 27, 536

Jane Clegg, 539
Jest, The, 539
Jonesy, 21
Journey's End, 543
Joy of Living, 512
Julius Cæsar, 20, 471
June Moon, 544
Junior Opera, 25

Kebec, 25
Kiki, 537
King Lear, 20, 471
Kingdom of God, The, 543
Kiss of Importance, A, 463

Ladder, The, 537
Ladies All, 6, 400
Ladies of the Jury, 22
Lady Beyond the Moon, 510
Lady from Alfaqueque, The, 427
Lady in Pawn, 21
Lady Patricia, 396
Last Enemy, The, 443
Last Mile, The, 22, 23, 355, 536, 544
Last Night, 28
Last of Mrs. Cheyney, The, 542
Lazzaro, 20
Lesson in Love, A, 396
Let and Sublet, 536
Let Us Be Gay, 186, 394, 543
Life Is Like That, 469
Life Line, The, 473
Light Wines and Beer, 450
Lightnin', 537
Liliom, 539
Little Accident, 543
Little Orchid Annie, 24
Little Show, Second, 7, 407
Little Show, Third, 16, 530
London Calling, 434
Long Play Tournament, 524
Long Road, The, 409
Lost Sheep, The, 24, 27, 536
Love Apples, 25
Love Duel, The, 11
Lower Depths, The, 25
Loyalties, 540
Luana, 12, 413
Lysistrata, 21, 22, 25, 28, 536

Macbeth, 20, 471
Machinal, 543
Made in France, 450
Male and Female, 502
Mamma's Affair, 539
Man in Possession, The, 20, 27, 444
Man Saul, The, 27
Man's Man, A, 533
Many Waters, 27
Marigold, 428
Marius, 22
Marseilles, 453
Mary Rose, 539
Mary the Third, 394, 540
Medea, 28
Meet My Sister, 12, 22, 476
Melo, 517
Menschen im Hotel, 355, 397
Merchant of Venice, The, 20, 24, 28, 464, 471
Merton of the Movies, 540
Michael and Mary, 20, 27, 536, 544
Midnight, 254, 474
Mighty Nimrod, The, 524
Mikado, The, 15, 522
Minick, 541
Miracle at Verdun, The, 14, 505
Miss Lulu Bett, 538
Modern Virgin, A, 16, 529
Month in the Country, A, 19, 22
Mountains Come to the Goldsteins, The, 28
Mr. Gilhooley, 8, 12, 424
Mr. Samuel, 448
Mrs. Bumpstead-Leigh, 27
Mrs. Moonlight, 8, 423
Mrs. Partridge Presents, 541
Music Master, The, 537
Mystery Moon, 399

Napi, 504
Napoleon Had It Too, 28
Nest, The, 540
New Moon, The, 537

New Yorkers, The, 11, 12, 465
Nice People, 394, 539
Night Lodging, 397
Nina Rosa, 7, 415
Nine Till Six, 421
Ninth Guest, The, 6, 404
No More Frontier, 27
Noble Experiment, The, 441

O. Henry in Prison, 28
Oh, Promise Me, 10, 459
Ol' Man Adam and His Chillun, 543
Old Man Murphy, 16, 527
Old Soak, The, 540
On Approval, 25
On the Spot, 9, 26, 443
Once in a Lifetime, 7, 24, 27, 110, 222, 392, 418
One, Two, Three, 422
Ostrich, The, 28
Othello, 27, 28
Outward Bound, 541
Overture, 286, 395, 396, 465

Pagan Lady, 9, 22, 435
Paging Danger, 497
Paradise, 524
Paris Bound, 392, 543
Paris in Spring, 25
Pariser Platz 13, 397
Parlor, Bedroom and Bath, 28
Patience, 535
Peg o' My Heart, 537
Perfectly Scandalous, 526
Peter Ibbetson, 15, 514
Peter Pan, 24, 27
Petticoat Influence, 12, 22, 466
Phaea, 397
Philanderer, The, 27
Philip Goes Forth, 13, 478
Pinafore, 15, 527
Play's the Thing, The, 542
Plough and the Stars, The, 543
Poor Nut, The, 28
Porgy, 15, 24, 27, 543
Precedent, 15, 515
Pressing Business, 454
Princess Charming, 8, 429
Private Lives, 483
Privilege Car, 499
Prodigals, The, 25
Prude's Fall, The, 396
Puppet Show, 442
Purity, 470

Queen at Home, 475
Quits, 25

Racket, The, 543
Rain, 9, 537, 540
Rap, The, 512
Rebound, 20, 23, 27, 544
Regular Guy, A, 533
Rhapsody, The, 7, 412
Rhapsody in Black, 16, 523
Richard III, 20, 471
Richelieu, 27
Right of Happiness, 510
Ripples, 22
Road to Rome, The, 542
Roadside, 147, 394, 421
Roar China, 9, 29, 440
Rock Me, Julie, 486
Romeo and Juliet, 426
Room of Dreams, 446
Round Heels, 28
Royal Family, 543
R. U. R., 540

Sacred Flame, The, 20
Sally, 537
Salome, 25
Saturday's Children, 392, 542
Scarlet Pages, 24
Scarlet Sister Mary, 11, 20, 460
School for Scandal, The, 25
School for Virtue, 519
Schoolgirl, 459
Sea Gull, 20
Second Little Show, 7, 407
Secrets, 396
Seventh Heaven, 537
Shanghai Gesture, The, 27
She Lived Next to the Firehouse, 489
She Means Business, 483
Show Boat, 537
Show-off, The, 537, 541
Shuffle Along, 537
Shyster, The, 25
Sideshow, 525
Siegfried, 436
Silent Witness, The, 14, 508
Silver Cord, The, 542
Simple Simon, 502
Sisters of the Chorus, 436

Sita, 5, 478
Six Characters in Search of an Author, 516
Six Cylinder Love, 540
Skin Game, The, 540
Smiles, 455
Solid South, 430
Song and Dance Man, The, 5, 398
Sons-o'-Guns, 22, 536
Spring Song, 27, 28
Stepdaughters of War, 8, 425
Stepping Sisters, 21, 536
Strange Interlude, 538, 542
Street Scene, 24, 27, 537, 538, 543
Strictly Dishonorable, 23, 536, 537, 544
Strike Up the Band, 21, 536
Student Prince, The, 485, 537
Subway Express, 22, 23
Success, 14
Sunny, 537
Sun-up, 541
Suppressed Desires, 395
Suspense, 401
Swan, The, 540
Sweet Adeline, 22
Sweet and Low, 9, 454
Sweet Chariot, 440
Sweet Stranger, 437
Symphony in Two Flats, 7, 12, 412

Taming of the Shrew, The, 24
Tarnish, 541
Tavern, The, 5, 22
Tea for Three, 28
Technique, 525, 526
That's Gratitude, 7, 21, 27, 110, 186, 410
That's the Woman, 407
They Had to See Paris, 453
They Knew What They Wanted, 538, 541
Thief, The, 15
Third Little Show, 16, 530
This Is New York, 10, 462
This One Man, 438
Thought, 28
Three Little Girls, 21, 22, 536
Three Men and a Woman, 25
Three's a Crowd, 8, 432
Through the Night, 402
Tiresias, 25
To the Ladies, 28
Tomorrow and Tomorrow, 13, 27, 74, 222, 392, 479
Tonight or Never, 6, 10, 456
Topaze, 5, 13, 20, 24, 27, 403, 491, 536
Torch Song, 6, 21, 24, 27, 404
Trifles, 394
Trip to Chinatown, A, 537
Truth Game, The, 12, 472
Twelfth Disciple, The, 25
Twelfth Night, 8, 20, 431
Two-gun Grandman, 25
Typhoon, The, 24
Tryout, The, 451

Uncle Vanya, 22, 417, 536
Under the Virginia Moon, 28
Unexpected Husband, 532
Up and Up, The, 408
Up Pops the Devil, 7, 22, 24, 27, 110, 406

Vagabond King, The, 537
Vanderbilt Revue, The, 447
Vanities, 5, 6, 17, 399
Venetian Glass Nephew, The, 496
Vinegar Tree, The, 10, 25, 457
Violet, The, 423

Watched Pot, The, 27, 28
Waterloo Bridge, 27
Way of the World, The, 16, 530
Wedding Bells, 539
Well of Romance, The, 448
What Every Woman Knows, 27
What Price Glory, 392, 541
When Father Smiles, 21
Whispering Friends, 27
Who Cares?, 6, 400
Why Marry?, 538
Why Not?, 540
Wild Birds, 541
Wings Over Europe, 25, 543
Wisdom Tooth, The, 542
Wiser They Are, The, 14, 511
With Privileges, 411
Woman Denied, A, 497
Wonder Bar, The, 14, 507

You and I, 392, 540
You Said It, 13, 480
Young Sinners, 16, 24, 518, 536
Young Woodley, 542
Youngest, The, 392, 541

DATE DUE
vhl
3.- a